The Greatest Show in the Arctic

THE AMERICAN EXPLORATION AND TRAVEL SERIES

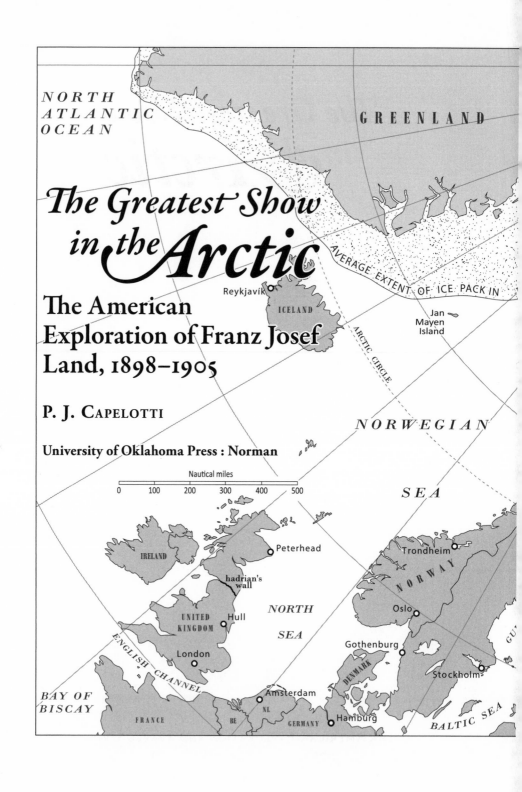

The Greatest Show in the Arctic

The American Exploration of Franz Josef Land, 1898–1905

P. J. CAPELOTTI

University of Oklahoma Press : Norman

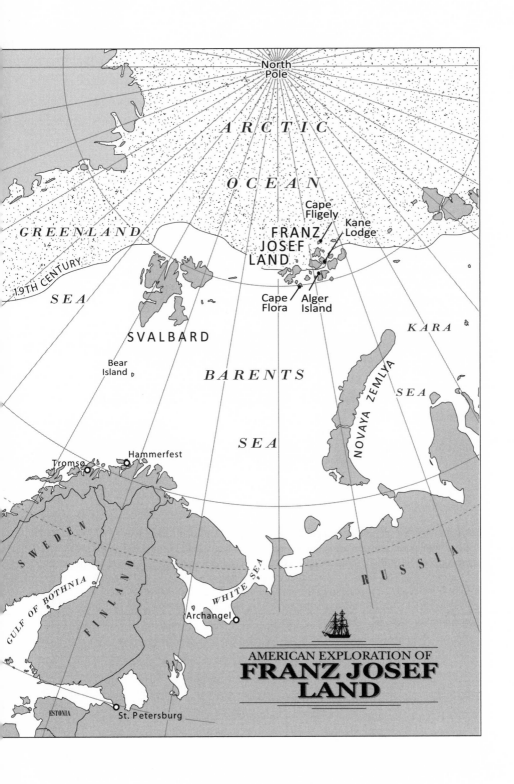

North Pole

A R C T I C

O C E A N

Cape
Fligely

Kane
Lodge

FRANZ
JOSEF
LAND

GREENLAND

19TH CENTURY

SEA

Cape
Flora

Alger
Island

SVALBARD

KARA

Bear
Island

B A R E N T S

NOVAYA ZEMLYA

SEA

SEA

SEA

Hammerfest

Tromsø

SWEDEN

FINLAND

GULF OF BOTHNIA

WHITE SEA

R U S S I A

Archangel

ESTONIA

St. Petersburg

AMERICAN EXPLORATION OF

FRANZ JOSEF LAND

Publication of this book is made possible through the generosity of Edith Kinney Gaylord.

✳

Library of Congress Cataloging-in-Publication Data
Names: Capelotti, P. J. (Peter Joseph), 1960– author.
Title: The greatest show in the Arctic : the American exploration of Franz Josef Land,
    1898–1905 / P.J. Capelotti.
Description: Norman : University of Oklahoma Press, [2016] | Series: The American
    exploration and travel series ; 82 | Includes bibliographical references and index.
Identifiers: LCCN 2015040522 | ISBN 978-0-8061-5222-6 (hardcover : alk. paper)
Subjects: LCSH: Franz Josef Land (Russia)—Discovery and exploration. | Wellman
    Polar Expedition (1898–1899) | Baldwin-Ziegler Polar Expedition (1901–1902) | Ziegler
    Polar Expedition (1903–1905) | Americans—Russia—Franz Josef Land—History.
Classification: LCC G810 .C37 2016 | DDC 919.8/504—dc23
LC record available at http://lccn.loc.gov/2015040522

The Greatest Show in the Arctic: The American Exploration of Franz Josef Land, 1898–1905
is Volume 82 in The American Exploration and Travel Series.

The paper in this book meets the guidelines for permanence and durability of the
Committee on Production Guidelines for Book Longevity of the Council on Library
Resources, Inc. ∞

1 2 3 4 5 6 7 8 9 10

To the memories of our Norwegian elkhounds,
BEOWULF (2000–2014)
and
GRENDEL (2002–2013),
who taught us so much about
love and loyalty, security and affection.
Anyone granted the privilege of sharing life with
these magnificently stubborn northern work animals gains, as
Russell Porter wrote from Franz Josef Land more than a century ago,
"a profound feeling of gratitude for my dogs."

In battles of no renown
My fellows and I fall down,
And over the dead men roar
The battles they lost before.

A. E. HOUSMAN

Contents

EXPEDITION ONE

The Great American Act of Hustling
The Wellman Polar Expedition
1898–1899

Contents

EXPEDITION TWO

Cigarette-Smoking Dudes
The Baldwin-Ziegler Polar Expedition
1901–1902

Contents

Illustrations

Illustrations

Maps

Preface

Three American expeditions tried to reach the geographic North Pole from the Arctic archipelago of Franz Josef Land. None succeeded. Many years later, the University of Chicago geophysicist Ernest Leffingwell, who served as a surveyor on the second of the three expeditions, wrote: "The real story of the Baldwin-Ziegler Polar Expedition has never been told. . . . In my opinion, the expedition was doomed before it started, and doomed all along the line."[1]

Since Leffingwell could just as easily have been writing of all three American expeditions to venture into Franz Josef Land in hopes of using the islands to reach the North Pole, *The Greatest Show in the Arctic* attempts to tell this "real story," the story of a geographically sprawling, comically epic, and massively misspent seven years of American presence in the islands. The real story of all three expeditions has never been told, for reasons that deserve exploration—beyond the primary fact that all three expeditions failed to reach the pole or come anywhere close to it and have therefore been relegated to footnotes in the history of American polar exploration.

The race to be first to the North Pole, occurring as it did alongside the expansion of American newspapers and newspaper advertising, created a geographically literate population almost as familiar with Teplitz Bay on Crown Prince Rudolf Land in Franz Josef Land as it was with Buzzards Bay off Cape Cod in Massachusetts. This geographic literacy has not survived.

Americans of the twenty-first century might be vaguely aware that Arctic Canada was the site of famous British Arctic disasters such as the Franklin expedition or that Greenland was the proving ground of Robert Peary's career. In the late nineteenth and early twentieth centuries, these remote locales appeared almost daily in America's newspapers, and during and after the Second World War tens of thousands of Americans actually experienced these places firsthand, early on as sailors on the Greenland Patrol and then as workers on the Distant Early Warning (DEW) Line.

To add to our current geographic dimness, even in an era of global positioning and Google Earth, the Arctic archipelago of Franz Josef Land—relatively well known during the early years of the century—largely vanished from the American consciousness during the twentieth century. Annexed by the Soviet Union in 1926, the islands became a critical staging area for the Soviet polar expeditions of the 1930s and 1940s, as well as for polar aviation operations during the Cold War. Between 1930 and the fall of the Soviet Union six decades later, the islands were sealed behind the Iron Curtain, an area closed and forbidden to Westerners. Not until 1990 did a joint Russian-Norwegian expedition venture into the archipelago to explore historical sites and give the modern West its first brief glimpse into what had once been a primary preserve of European and American Arctic exploration.

A third reason for the absence of Leffingwell's "real story" is that many of the primary sources from these expeditions have only recently emerged into the light. Crucial letters that passed between Walter Wellman and his brother in the fall of 1898 were archived only in 2004, the same year that Evelyn Briggs Baldwin's journal of the Wellman Polar Expedition was finally published, more than a century after it was written. The papers of the original secretary of the Baldwin-Ziegler Polar Expedition, Leon Barnard, are inexplicably split and housed in archives thousands of miles apart: the Library of Congress in Washington, D.C., and the archives of the Scott Polar Research Institute in Cambridge, United Kingdom. The descendents of Charles Seitz and Anton Vedoe made truly heroic transcriptions of their forbears' Arctic diaries, but these have been publicly available only in the last twenty years. The papers of Anthony Fiala remain private and still reside with his descendents, who kindly gave permission for their use in this volume.

Arthur Railton's articles, based on the journals written by Captain Edwin Coffin, Jr., during the terrible days at Elmwood in 1904–1905, appeared in 1999 and 2000. Russell Williams Porter's lovely and sensitive diary was

heavily bowdlerized when it was published in 1976 and requires one to have
the surviving fragments of the original—housed in the excellent Stefánsson Collections at the Rauner Library of Dartmouth College—alongside.
Some men, like Archibald Dickson, were scathing in their criticisms of their
expedition leaders while in the field, only to completely change their tune
decades later when interviewed by newspaper reporters.

The remembrances of many of the Scandinavians who worked for the
Americans in Franz Josef Land have also survived. In Norway, Eivind Klykken recently transcribed the diary of his grandfather Emil Ellefsen, written
during the difficult weeks of the Wellman expedition. This remarkable
document was then translated into English by my Swedish colleague Magnus
Forsberg. This work, along with the consistent Norwegian scholarship over
the past thirty years by Susan Barr, Kjell-G Kjær, Tom Bloch-Nakkerud,
and many others, and in Sweden by Urban Wråkberg and especially by
Anders Larsson—who has brought to light diaries of the Swedish sailors
on the Baldwin-Ziegler expedition—have enabled the story to be told from
Scandinavian points of view.

John Edwards Caswell, who in the 1950s wrote the first—and to this day,
only—synthesis of the scientific results of all American Arctic exploration,
did not even attempt to sort out the machinations and mischievousness, the
dissention and deaths, of the three expeditions to Franz Josef Land. Something approaching the real story of the American exploration of Franz Josef
Land has only become possible, then—and more than half a century after
Caswell—on account of the aforementioned emergence of private diaries
from the obscurity of family attics in both the United States and Europe,
combined with the partial—and brief—opening of Franz Josef Land itself
to Western eyes.

The author saw the islands firsthand in the summer of 2006, during two
expeditions to the North Pole on a Russian nuclear icebreaker. The ship
called at several of the sites mentioned in this account: once-famous locales
such as Cape Flora, Cape Norvegia, Cape Tegetthoff, Rubini Rock, Champ
Island, and Teplitz Bay. For a decade—beginning with the return of Fridtjof
Nansen and the *Fram* expedition—all were well known to a newspaper-
devouring American public. With the benefit of being one of the few Americans to have visited Franz Josef Land, along with a previous archaeological
survey of the site of Walter Wellman's 1906–1909 dirigible expeditions on
Danskøya in the Norwegian Arctic archipelago of Spitsbergen (which has

been called Svalbard since it came officially under Norwegian sovereignty in the summer of 1925), as well as editing Evelyn Briggs Baldwin's 1898 journal of the Wellman Polar Expedition and writing the first biography of Benjamin Leigh Smith, the British pioneering explorer of Franz Josef Land, I was finally prepared to attempt Leffingwell's "real story" of the American exploration of Franz Josef Land. For better and for worse, it heavily relies on the words of the explorers themselves, while placing the story within the loose confines of the last years of the Gilded Age. In this, it is both historical and—to the degree that we are living in a second American Gilded Age, with billionaires sending rockets into space rather than millionaires sending men to the North Pole—precisely contemporary.

THE FIRST of the three American expeditions to use Franz Josef Land as a staging area entered the field in 1898. The third retreated from Franz Josef Land in 1905, more than four years before both the maniacally driven Robert Peary and his nemesis, the genial liar Dr. Frederick Cook, made their suspect claims to priority at the North Pole. It was, in fact, Robert Peary's presumption over any route to the North Pole that originated in northern Greenland or Arctic Canada that in part drove his American competitors further east, to a group of dimly understood islands in the Russian Arctic called Franz Josef Land.

These three expeditions were led, in turn, by a *bon vivant* Chicago journalist engaged in a desperate search for greater fame than the impossibly rich and powerful men he routinely interviewed; by an addled Midwestern government meteorologist and fantasist who was offered a king's ransom to reach the North Pole and used it to stockpile Swedish conserves far and wide across Franz Josef Land; and by a naïve photographer and graphic artist from Brooklyn who viewed the polar world all but exclusively through the lens of his devout and ultimately debilitating Christianity.

Each of these expeditions received some modest levels of assistance from the United States government in the form of loans of equipment or scientific expertise, but the main source of their funding derived solely from the distended accounts of Gilded Age millionaires, for the American exploration of Franz Josef Land was both a direct product of the spectacular levels of untaxed private wealth of the Gilded Age and a monument to that age's inevitable collapse. The final retreat of the Ziegler Polar Expedition from

Franz Josef Land in August 1905 somewhat appropriately followed the death of its massively wealthy patron by just ten weeks.

William Ziegler's fatal stroke in May 1905—and the subsequent legal tussle over the tens of millions of dollars he left behind—was contemporaneous with the fraud conviction of one of the Chicago railroad and banking tycoons who had helped finance the first American expedition to Franz Josef Land in 1898. The American exploration of Franz Josef Land and the Gilded Age expired simultaneously, the former having only survived on the generous oxygen of the latter.

The islands of Franz Josef Land were formally annexed by the Soviet Union in 1926 and, while the Soviets managed to temporarily rid their landscape of so many religious and royalist place-names like St. Petersburg and Nicholas II Land, they failed in their attempt to rename the royalist Franz Josef Land as Fridtjof Nansen Land, after the Norwegian international hero of science, exploration, and diplomacy. Specifically ironic of the American retreat from Franz Josef Land in 1905, it is perhaps more astounding that the arbiters of Soviet geographic nomenclature allowed place-names derived from so many millionaires of the American Gilded Age—some, like John R. Walsh, long dead after serving prison terms for financial fraud—to remain fastened to the Franz Josef Land landscape. But they did, and now, a century after the last American explorer left the archipelago, the ironies multiply.

New Americans—many the tycoons of a second Gilded Age—return to the islands on board former Soviet nuclear icebreaking ships. These prosperous tourists—far less geographically attuned than their forbears—are more often than not unaware that this archipelago in the Russian Arctic is in many respects a geography of American capitalism. The Austro-Hungarians who first explored the islands in 1873 left behind royalist place-names—the original Kaiser Franz Josef Land derives from Emperor Franz Josef I of the Austro-Hungarian Empire—but they also attached place-names largely derived from the international fraternity of polar explorers. The English explorers who followed—Benjamin Leigh Smith in the 1880s and Frederick G. Jackson in the 1890s—used place-names culled from favored relations and a few obligatory royals, but primarily sought names from the great lights of science in nineteenth-century Britain: Sir Joseph Hooker, Henry Walter Bates, Henry Bowman Brady, Albert Günther, and Alfred Newton.

For the Americans, they primarily sought to memorialize the millionaires who made their presence in the islands possible. An argument could even be made that the American failure to advance to the North Pole from Franz Josef Land was in large part the result of a preoccupation with the location of new geographic places—bays and capes, islands and straits—to which the names of powerful, influential patrons could be attached. The Americans never advanced farther north than Crown Prince Rudolf Land (today Rudolf Island)—the ice-covered, northernmost island in the Franz Josef Land archipelago. But they did succeed in two related and enduring enterprises.

First, they would largely resolve the many geographic mysteries that remained even after the expeditions of the Austro-Hungarians, the British, and the Norwegian icon Nansen. This achievement alone was the result of dogged hard work and was both singular and unprecedented in the American exploration of the Arctic. The second achievement was to leave behind in the future Soviet islands an enduring catalog of geographic place-names that reflected the height and reach—and ultimately the collapse—of private American capital in the Gilded Age. Places like Pierpont Morgan Strait, Vanderbilt Sound, and Helen Gould Bay, all testified to the power of the American experiment in the generation of wealth. In the survival of names like Cape John R. Walsh and William Ziegler Island lies the history of the tug of war between capital and its restraints—and the downfall of those too greedy to recognize the crowded limits of money.

THE VARIOUS THREADS of the American exploration of Franz Josef Land first came together in the person of a Chicago journalist covering the stupendous World's Columbian Exposition of 1893. At the exposition, the journalist—a Washington correspondent of the *Chicago Herald* named Walter Wellman—saw a huge painting that depicted the dramatic struggles of the Austro-Hungarians as they first explored Franz Josef Land. Nearby, in the Norwegian exhibit, Wellman was equally fascinated by the stories of historic Vikings and modern Norwegian sea-hunters of the Arctic. To Wellman, the latter seemed eminently capable of reaching the North Pole—if only provided with an energetic little push by "the great American act of hustling."

When five years later he finally reached Franz Josef Land, Wellman lost little time in rearranging the place as an homage to the enterprising Midwestern capitalists he so admired. Capes with names like Leiter, after Levi Z. Leiter, the Chicago pioneer in dry goods stores who became a major philanthropist in the city, or Kohlsaat, for Herman H. Kohlsaat, the businessman and publisher who in 1898 owned Walter Wellman's newspaper, the *Chicago Times-Herald,* reflected the central powerhouse of the American Midwest just six decades after the founding of Chicago with a population of barely two hundred souls.

FRANZ JOSEF LAND was one of the last major landmasses discovered in the Arctic. The history of its subsequent exploration, as we shall see, is complex and international, involving many nations and dozens of expeditions. The American contribution to the exploration of Franz Josef Land between the years of 1898 and 1905 derived from the close relationship between the expedition leaders and the political, scientific, and especially the financial elites of turn-of-the-century Chicago, Washington, D.C., and New York City. These associations even extended to three presidents of the United States. In the years leading up to and including the American expeditions to Franz Josef Land, New Yorkers Grover Cleveland and Theodore Roosevelt and Ohioan William McKinley, as well as many of their closest associates, provided moral support, institutional backing, and direct funding to the expeditions.

The place-names attached to Franz Josef Land by the 1898–1899 Wellman Polar Expedition, the 1901–1902 Baldwin-Ziegler Polar Expedition, and the 1903–1905 Ziegler Polar Expedition, reflected these networks, and more especially the ascendant American global power promoted by McKinley and Roosevelt. That these names survive into the twenty-first century is both one of the deliberate accidents in the history of the American polar exploration and, until now, its last great untold story.

Abington, Pennsylvania
1 July 2015

The Greatest Show in the Arctic

Off the American Route

One can trace with a fair certainty the precise moment when the Arctic entered into the American consciousness. On Tuesday, June 3, 1845, this brief notice appeared on the front page of the *New York Herald*:

THE ARCTIC EXPEDITION—The *Erebus,* Capt. Sir John Franklin, and the *Terror,* Captain Crozier, discovery vessels, left Greenhithe yesterday for their destination. Each ship had been supplied with 200 tin cylinders for the purpose of holding papers which are to be thrown overboard, with the statement of the longitude, and other particulars worthy of record, written in six different languages, and the parties finding them are requested to forward the information to the Admiralty.[1]

In the days that followed, this note about the British search for a Northwest Passage through the ice to the Orient was widely syndicated in newspapers throughout the country. By the end of the summer, British naval officers Franklin and Francis Crozier—and more than 120 officers and men—had sailed their two ships into the tangle of icebound islands north of Canada and vanished. Years passed without word from the expedition. By 1849, it was clear that a catastrophe had occurred. The British Admiralty sent eight more ships in search of the original two and then offered a massive reward for the rescue of Franklin and his men.

Franklin's wife, Lady Jane, invested her entire existence in the organization of even more search expeditions. She made constant appeals to her own government, then to Russia, and then to the United States. Twice in 1849 she wrote to President Zachary Taylor long and tortured letters, which successively begged, bribed, shamed, and cajoled the United States into action.[2] It worked. Little more than three decades after the conclusion of the War of 1812—and prefiguring the "Special Relationship" by nearly a century—Taylor responded, on behalf of England's "kindred people," that the "people of the United States, who have watched with the deepest interest that hazardous enterprise, will now respond to [your] appeal, by the expression of their united wishes that every proper effort may be made by this government for the rescue of your husband and his companions."[3] In his brief sixteen months as president, Taylor twice asked Congress for funds to send a search expedition north.

It was at this point that a wealthy New York shipping merchant named Henry Grinnell offered the U.S. government two vessels for the task, whereupon Congress agreed to staff the ships with officers and men of the U.S. Navy. There was talk that the voyage would be commanded by Charles Wilkes, the martinet who led the Great U.S. Exploring Expedition to Antarctica a decade earlier and the only American naval officer with significant experience in ice navigation. But the command was eventually given to Edwin Jesse De Haven, a thirty-four-year-old lieutenant from Philadelphia who had served on the Wilkes expedition—and lost his ship, the *Peacock,* off the Oregon coast in the summer of 1840. A British surgeon serving in the Franklin search described him as "as fine a specimen of a seaman, and a rough and ready officer, as I had ever seen."[4]

In the summer of 1850, De Haven led two small sailing vessels, the 88-foot *Advance* and the 65-foot *Rescue,* into the Canadian Arctic. That late August, De Haven and his men discovered the graves of three of Franklin's men, sailors who had been buried on Beechey Island four and half year earlier. With the onset of cold weather in mid-September, De Haven tried to lead his exploring convoy east toward Baffin Bay, the body of water that separates Greenland from Ellesmere Island in Arctic Canada, but was stopped by the ice. The ships drifted north into Wellington Channel, where they sighted land that was later named Grinnell Peninsula after the expedition sponsor, and then drifted south into Lancaster Sound, where the movement of pack ice shifted them eastward a few miles each day throughout the winter and spring of 1851.

When the ships finally reached Baffin Bay and broke out of the ice in early June, De Haven found refuge in Greenland so that his men could rest and recover from scurvy. Two weeks later, they were on the move north once again. Unable to maneuver in thick ice, De Haven ordered the ships home in August. There, the job of writing the official report of the voyage was given over to another Philadelphian, the expedition's surgeon, Elisha Kent Kane. Kane's report on the first significant American foray into the Arctic quickly made him the expedition's most famous veteran.[5]

Seizing his chance, Kane quickly gathered support for another northern expedition from Grinnell, Secretary of the Navy John Pendleton Kennedy, and the international merchant and financier George Peabody. Kane used the Franklin search as cover for his real objectives: a return to northern Baffin Bay and an attempt to reach the Polar Sea thought to lie to the north of it.

As was De Haven's expedition, Kane's launched under the formal sanction of the U.S. Navy, with scientific instruments recommended by the navy's influential oceanographer, Matthew Fontaine Maury. The new expedition sailed from New York on the *Advance* on May 30, 1853, and made directly for Baffin Bay. At the northern edge of the bay, the ship sailed through Smith Sound and into a basin that Kane named for himself. At the northern end of Kane Basin, the surgeon-turned-explorer discovered a frozen waterway he named Kennedy Channel after his avid supporter in the navy department.

In his account of the voyage, Kane described how two of his men stood at 81° 22' North latitude, a point Kane later named Cape Constitution, where they heard "the novel music of dashing waves; and a surf."[6] This sound of soughing waves, Kane believed, was caused by an "open polar sea," an ocean at the top of the world that would—if one could but reach it—allow a ship to sail directly to the North Pole.

Kane was thirty when he first witnessed the Arctic with De Haven. By the time he was buried on a bluff overlooking the Schuylkill River in Philadelphia's Laurel Hill Cemetery less than seven years later, his imagination of an "open polar sea" had gained a permanent siren grasp on the nineteenth-century theory of Arctic geography. His Kennedy Channel thereafter became the "American route" to the North Pole.

Kane died in Cuba in early 1857, his body returned to Philadelphia by ship, by riverboat, and finally by train in a prolonged cortège—the final stage of which has been described as the third greatest railway mourning in American history, behind only the funerals of Abraham Lincoln and Robert F. Kennedy.

With such an example of national and international fame laid before him, it was more than enough to entice Kane's own expedition surgeon—and yet a third Pennsylvanian—Isaac Israel Hayes, to return to Baffin Bay to search for Kane's open sea. Not nearly as well connected as Kane, it took Hayes five years to raise the money required to fund an Arctic expedition. Finally, in the summer of 1860, Hayes sailed from Boston in a small refitted schooner rechristened the *United States*. The twenty-eight-year-old was bound for Kane Basin.

Ten months later, on May 18, 1861, after a winter in which local Inuit women made new fur clothes for him and his crew, Hayes reached the northern terminus of his efforts. Ascending to a cliff he reckoned was about 800 feet above the sea, Hayes looked out over a polar ocean filled with loose ice, arrayed so as to appear as a magical road leading northward. It was "like the delta of some mighty river discharging into the ocean, and under a water-sky, which hung upon the northern and eastern horizon, it was lost in the open sea."[7]

Hayes's observations appeared to support those of Kane, and were just as confounding. But Hayes was unable to capitalize on them. He returned to a nation torn apart by civil war and suddenly and entirely disinterested in Arctic exploration. To worsen matters, Hayes returned to meet a tenacious rival for the extremely limited number of dollars available to support further work in the north.

Hayes's adversary was a self-made explorer from Cincinnati, Ohio: Charles Francis Hall. Gathering support from Grinnell and a whaling company in New London, Connecticut, Hall determined to sail north to solve the mystery of Franklin by using the one source of data that had seemingly eluded all other searchers: the local knowledge of the natives of Arctic Canada.[8]

Through a fortuitous meeting with an Inuit couple named Ebierbing and Tookoolito—both had been to England and spoke English—Hall's first entry into the Arctic was remarkably productive. A true anthropological explorer, Hall began to learn the Inuit language, corrected Frobisher Strait to the bay that it is, and then, through local knowledge, uncovered both native history and the historical archaeology of the expeditions of the British explorer Martin Frobisher three hundred years earlier. Forced by ice conditions to remain in the north for a second winter, Hall took the opportunity to scout even further afield.

Like Hayes, Hall returned to the United States in 1862 and found a country at war with itself and little interested to support Arctic exploration.

It was two years before Hall was able to return to the region, hopscotching north on board several whaling ships of opportunity. It was five years more before Hall finally reached his intended destination of King William Island. There, using his layman's experience in recording both history and archaeology, he expected to learn more of Franklin's fate from native testimony and from any artifacts that might lie around the island. At Shepherd Bay, opposite King William Island on Boothia Peninsula, Hall found what he was looking for: a cache of Franklin relics that he immediately traded for. In addition to the artifacts, Hall recorded native testimony about a trail of British bodies that lay exposed across King William Island. Through these oral histories, Hall reckoned that he had accounted for nearly eighty of Franklin's lost officers and men.

Hall remained in the Arctic for five whole years, returning to the States only in the late summer of 1869. He had demonstrated that Franklin and his crew died fairly quickly—as they clung to the material anchors of their Victorian society. He had also proved that it was possible to survive for many years in the Arctic by adopting and adapting to an Inuit way of life. With the Civil War over and America again in search of new frontiers, Hall intended to exploit his knowledge of northern life in a journey to the North Pole itself.

Hall's mass of experience enabled him to secure a titanic government grant of fifty thousand dollars. Even more startling, he also secured command of a U.S.-sponsored vessel called *Polaris,* given over to him with the express mission of reaching the pole. And, at the start of his expedition, his fabulous run of luck continued. Unlike Kane and Hayes, Hall's new polar research ship breezed through Kennedy Channel into a wider basin beyond which Hall proudly named after himself. Hall and the *Polaris* eventually reached the very northern shores of Greenland, the highest point attained by any ocean vessel to that date and a remarkable feat of daring. As an experienced Arctic traveler, Hall was now poised to take to the ice and strike for the North Pole in the spring of 1872.

What happened next went unexplained for nearly a century. Hall was taken suddenly and violently ill. He complained that he was being poisoned by, among others, the Smithsonian Institution scientist on board. He died in agonizing pain that same October and was buried in a stony grave on the shores of Greenland at what is now called Polaris Harbor. The following summer, as the *Polaris* began the long and dangerous retreat to the south, the ship was quickly and fatally caught in the ice. The expedition members who survived were split when one group was marooned on an ice floe and began a long drift southward. They were finally rescued off the coast of Labrador. The crew that remained on board *Polaris* drove the ship ashore near Etah in northwest Greenland. There, unforgivably, one of them tossed Hall's archive of papers overboard. Hall's library of Arctic books, along with the logbooks of the *Polaris* and some scientific instruments, were cached on shore and never found again.

In 1968, a Dartmouth College professor of English and biographer of Hall's by the name of Chauncey Loomis received permission to exhume Hall's body from its frozen grave. Loomis snipped some small clippings of Hall's hair and fingernails and then returned them to the United States to be tested. The tests revealed that Hall had indeed been poisoned. But the arsenic found in his body may have been administered by Hall himself—at a time when arsenic served as both medicine and poison.

American newspapers seized upon the epic of Charles Francis Hall. James Gordon Bennett, publisher of the *New York Herald* and the same man who had sent reporter Henry Morton Stanley to Africa in search of the British missionary Dr. David Livingstone, was equally fascinated with the Arctic.[9] In 1873 Bennett dispatched two reporters to search for the survivors of Hall's expedition. Five years later, he assigned a reporter to yet another Franklin search expedition, this one sponsored by the American Geographic Society. Led by a U.S. Army lieutenant named Frederick Schwatka, the expedition ventured into Arctic Canada on the strength of a rumor that John Franklin's diary would be found on King William Island. No such document was ever found, but Schwatka did retrieve several relics as well as a few skeletal remains of Franklin sailors who had perished on the island.

Bennett sponsored his greatest venture in the Arctic in 1879. A U.S. Navy captain, George Washington De Long, was given orders to locate the "lost" expedition of the Swede Adolf Erik Nordenskiöld—and then attempt to reach the North Pole itself. De Long sailed from San Francisco in the *Pandora,* a former Royal Navy vessel that Bennett had purchased and renamed *Jeannette* after his sister. The navy agreed to man the ship if Bennett paid all the expenses of the expedition.[10]

Even before the *Jeannette* reached the Arctic, Nordenskiöld and his ship *Vega* broke through the ice north of Russia and emerged into the Bering Sea. With no dramatic rescue to report, De Long continued with his secondary mission and turned north toward Kane's open sea and the

North Pole beyond. The *Jeannette* was soon beset in the ice north of the New Siberian Islands. After two grueling years drifting about in the ice, the ship was finally crushed. Taking to the ship's small boats, De Long and his men made a desperate retreat to the Lena River delta on the Siberian coast. Only one of the three boats reached safety; another vanished with all hands, and De Long's own small boat made it to shore, where he and all but two of his men starved to death as they waited in vain for relief. To intensify the disaster, a newly commissioned U.S. Navy vessel sent to find De Long, the USS *Rodgers,* was itself burned to the waterline and blown to pieces.

An even greater disaster was in store for the Americans in the Arctic. In 1881, in an attempt to better understand the physical dynamics of the Arctic, several nations agreed to establish meteorological stations in the high north to record weather observations across a full year. The American contingent to this "First International Polar Year" was led by a U.S. Army officer, Adolphus Greely.[11] Greely set up his encampment on Ellesmere Island in Canada, in a bay named for Lady Jane Franklin that was just a few miles west of where Charles Francis Hall lay buried on the shore of Polaris Harbor in Greenland. The expedition descended into a national catastrophe when a promised relief ship could not reach the men. When the expedition was finally found—three excruciating years later—only Greely and six of his twenty-five men were still alive.

The public and congressional outcries over the dismal failures of Hall, De Long, and Greely would have far-reaching consequences for future American polar explorers. Not until the strategic value of the Arctic was rediscovered during World War II would any significant public money be spent on its exploration or exploitation. Until then, American explorers like Robert Peary and his many contemporaries would have to rely on their own wits to secure private donations. Along with newspaper sponsorships, advertising tie-ins, and the backing of newly formed special interest organizations like the National Geographic Society and the Arctic Club, no explorer after Greely could seriously hope to sail north before he became adept at generating publicity and raising funds in this new and bewildering commercial universe.

Peary, even though he was employed as a civil engineer for the U.S. Navy, nevertheless carried on nearly all of his northern exploration at arm's length from any official government sanction. Heavily influenced by the writings of Kane and Nordenskiöld, Peary made a brief reconnaissance of the interior of Greenland in 1886. Five years later, in an expedition that included a recent medical school graduate named Frederick Cook and a young Norwegian artist and expert skier by the name of Eivind Astrup, Peary crossed the northwestern corner the Greenland icecap and showed that Greenland was not some kind of massive peninsula hanging southward from the North Pole.[12]

An 1894 effort to expand the scope of the previous expedition's geographic research failed, but it was during this time that Peary learned of the location of a meteorite at Cape York. This massive object had fallen from space some ten thousand years earlier, fragmenting as it spread across northwestern Greenland. Peary returned to Greenland in 1896 and 1897 to remove three meteorite fragments—the largest weighed over thirty tons—from the shores of Melville Bay and Meteorite Island. These he sold to the American Museum of Natural History in New York in order to finance more exploration.

After 1897 Peary's goal became the North Pole itself. With his base in northwest Greenland, he claimed the "American route" as his own and guarded it jealously. By 1900 this massive stretch of the Arctic ran all the way from Baffin Bay and north into the series of straits and basins named for American explorers and secretaries of the navy: Kane Basin, Kennedy Channel, Hall Basin, and, at the edge of the Arctic Sea, Robeson Channel, after George Robeson.

Peary's claim of priority effectively closed Greenland and northern Canada to anyone else and forced these other explorers and their expeditions to search elsewhere for a base from which to attempt to reach the North Pole. Two such areas now became such bases: the Arctic territory north of Norway called Spitsbergen and a group of Arctic islands north of Russia called Franz Josef Land.

Norwegian sealers had operated in the waters of Franz Josef Land for years before the first confirmed sighting of the islands. They called the area East-Spitsbergen, and good waters in which to hunt for walrus, the hugely valuable and increasingly scarce prey in Spitsbergen proper. It is possible that the islands were seen as early as 1865, from the decks of the schooner *Spitsbergen,* by the Hammerfest sealing masters Nils Fredrik Rönnbäck and his companion Johan P. Aidijärvi.[13]

The formal discovery of a distinct Arctic archipelago east of Spitsbergen came two years after the death of Charles Francis Hall. In the summer of 1873, an Austro-Hungarian expedition led by a German named Karl Weyprecht

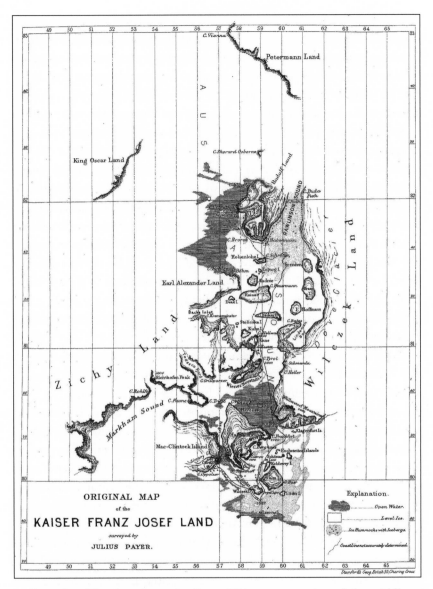

Franz Josef Land as drawn by Payer. This representation of the middle
and eastern sectors of the archipelago went largely unchanged through the
expeditions of Leigh Smith and Frederick Jackson. Nansen showed that
"Petermann Land" was a mirage. This map would have been in the Americans'
minds as they arrived in Franz Josef Land for the first time, in the summer
of 1898. From Julius Payer, *New Lands within the Arctic Circle: Narrative of
the Discoveries of the Austrian Ship Tegetthoff in the Years 1872–1874,* 2 vols.
(London: MacMillan and Co., 1876).

and a Bohemian by the name of Julius Payer, had been frozen into the ice northeast of Spitsbergen for more than a year. At midday on August 30, from the decks of their three-masted schooner *Tegetthoff,* the men saw a collection of islands off to the north. Two months later, *Tegetthoff* drifted near an island that Weyprecht and Payer named after the expedition's sponsor, a wealthy and scientifically minded member of the Austro-Hungarian nobility named Count Hans von Wilczek. The archipelago as a whole they named after their emperor, Kaiser Franz Josef.[14]

Almost from the moment of its formal discovery, the explorers viewed Franz Josef Land as a potential pathway to the North Pole. In the spring of 1874, Payer led a series of sledge expeditions northward along an ice-covered waterway he named Austria Sound. As he passed numerous new islands and other geographical features, Payer named them after the Austrian monarchy. The northernmost land that Payer reached he named for the son of Franz Josef, Crown Prince Rudolf. A bay on the western shore of Rudolf Land Payer named for his hometown of Teplitz in Bohemia, in the modern-day Czech Republic. A large land mass on the eastern side of Austria Sound was also named for the expedition patron Wilczek.

Payer led his team southward and regained the *Tegetthoff* in late April. One member of the crew, the ship's engineer, Anton Krisch, had died of tuberculosis a month earlier and been buried on "Wilczek Land." Weyprecht and Payer abandoned the still-trapped *Tegetthoff* in mid-May and led their expedition south in small boats through a chaotic jumble of ice floes, open channels of water, and slush. By mid-July, Weyprecht had to employ all of his leadership skills to keep the crew from turning around when they caught sight of *Tegetthoff* drifting in the distance. The men finally reached open water in mid-August. They sailed south to rescue by Russian schooners anchored off Novaya Zemlya on August 24, 1874.

The discoveries of Weyprecht and Payer were followed by two remarkable voyages by a wealthy British yachtsman and explorer named Benjamin Leigh Smith.[15] A shy and retiring member of the gentry, Leigh Smith sought to engage in detailed surveys of uncharted Arctic coastlines, conduct oceanographic research, and gather geological and biological specimens for natural history collections in Britain.

Leigh Smith's plans to explore Jan Mayen Island and the northeastern coast of Greenland in the summer of 1880 on board his private oceanographic research vessel *Eira* were thwarted by fog and ice, as was his attempt to pass beyond Amsterdamøya off Northwest Spitsbergen. His way blocked to the north and west, the Englishman revealed a commendable flexibility in the execution of his research cruise when he steered *Eira* toward the known parts of Franz Josef Land. The archipelago was sighted on August 14 and, from a point west of the area explored by Weyprecht and Payer, Leigh Smith began to survey the archipelago westward.

The brief expedition was a terrific success, as Leigh Smith charted the shorelines of McClintock, May, Hooker, Etheridge, Bruce, and Northbrook Islands (the latter of which Leigh Smith named after Thomas Baring, Earl of Northbrook, the late president of the Royal Geographical Society), as well as parts of George Land and Alexandra Land. A striking amphitheater-like natural anchorage discovered between Bell and Mabel islands was named Eira Harbour.

Before he returned to Spitsbergen in September and then home to England in October, Leigh Smith surveyed more than 100 nautical miles of previously unknown coast and extended the geographical knowledge of Franz Josef Land by fully nine degrees of longitude. Marine organisms dredged from Franz Josef Land waters, as well as flora and geological specimens collected on various islands, were sent to the British Museum. Two live polar bear cubs that had been captured in the archipelago were delivered to the London Zoological Gardens. The Royal Geographical Society rewarded Leigh Smith's triumph of private exploration with its gold Patron's Medal.

Leigh Smith returned to Franz Josef Land the following summer, with the same ship and a similar number of crew. This time, the Arctic conditions did not favor him. With the ice fast in all directions, Leigh Smith erected a prefabricated storehouse named Eira Lodge along the shore of its namesake harbor. He had intended to search eastward for the lost ship *Jeannette,* but ice conditions forced the ship to a halt off Cape Flora on Northbrook Island. There, on August 21, 1881, *Eira* was nipped by the ice and sunk in eleven fathoms. The crew salvaged about two months' supplies from the research vessel before it sank, so the prospect of overwintering was not as bleak as it could have been. A stone hut, "Flora Cottage," was constructed in a fortnight, and small boats were sent in September to fetch further supplies from Eira Lodge.

Leigh Smith and his men survived the winter in fine style. The following June, they set off in four small boats. After a daring and difficult voyage, they gained the beach at the strait at Matochkin Shar on Novaya Zemlya, on

August 2, 1882. The next day, dressed for the occasion in their best yachting clothes, they were rescued by relief ships sent from England to search for them. His active exploration career at an end, Leigh Smith continued to take an interest in the exploration of Polar Regions. He supported whaling expeditions to the Antarctic and promoted Eira Harbour as the ideal staging area for a British attempt on the North Pole.

The decade of the discovery and exploration of Franz Josef Land and the disasters of the De Long and Greely expeditions were also the formative years of a Norwegian biological oceanographer by the name of Fridtjof Nansen.[16] In 1884, when wreckage from the *Jeannette* washed ashore in southwestern Greenland, nearly 3,000 nautical miles from where the ship sank, the twenty-three-year-old Nansen paid keen attention. Nansen had begun his university studies in zoology at the University of Oslo in 1881 and during the summer of 1882 participated in a sealing expedition in the seas between Spitsbergen and Greenland. He had even been frozen in for a time off the latter coast, which he longed to explore.

After his return to Norway, Nansen took up a post at the Bergen Museum. There he spent the next six years, studying the origins of the nervous system even as he planned a return to Greenland. In 1888, just two days after he defended his doctoral dissertation in neuroscience, Nansen departed for an expedition that accomplished what Robert Peary had failed to do two years earlier: the first crossing of the Greenland ice cap.

It was now Nansen's turn to propose an expedition to the North Pole itself. Carl Lytzen, the Danish governor in Julianehåb, Greenland, had reported the *Jeannette* wreckage to the Danish Geographical Society in 1885. Professor Henrik Mohn, a Norwegian meteorologist, believed that the wreckage had fetched up in Greenland through the action of a transpolar ocean current flowing east to west across the polar basin and perhaps over the pole itself. Nansen used these observations to speculate to the Royal Geographical Society in 1892 that if the wreckage of a ship could be carried from one side of the Arctic to another, why not an entire ship, intact, with its crew safe and warm on board?

Nansen's scientific credibility and his expedition across Greenland enabled him to raise the funds necessary to build the *Fram,* a vessel especially constructed for Arctic exploration and a test of his polar-drift hypothesis. A year after his talk to the RGS, Nansen placed *Fram* into the ice not far from the spot where *Jeannette* had been beset fourteen years earlier. Nansen and his special ship, captained by Otto N. K. Sverdrup, then vanished into the North Polar basin, where many believed he would soon share De Long's fate.

Leigh Smith had feared Nansen's challenge to British claims in the Arctic. His own challenge for a British expedition to continue polar exploration from Franz Josef Land was taken up by Frederick G. Jackson and his Jackson-Harmsworth Expedition of 1894–97.[17] Financed by newspaper magnate Alfred C. Harmsworth, the expedition reached Franz Josef Land in late August 1894 with the ship *Windward*. There, at Cape Flora, Jackson established a field headquarters that he called Elmwood, just a few feet from the site of Leigh Smith's Flora Cottage. During the summers of 1895 and 1896, Jackson explored Franz Josef Land by sledge and by boat. He came to the conclusion that the archipelago was not a great Arctic subcontinent but rather a loose collection of islets and small- to moderate-sized islands. It certainly did not appear to be a land bridge to the North Pole.

Just as Jackson was coming to this conclusion, two grubby and grimy men wandered into his camp. These turned out to be Nansen himself and one of his companions from the *Fram*, Hjalmar Johansen. On March 14, 1895, Nansen and Johansen had left the *Fram* as it drifted across the polar ocean. At about 84° North, the two men began a dash to the North Pole with skis, sledges, and twenty-eight dogs. Within a month, they were more than 150 nautical miles closer to the North Pole than anyone before them and attained their now-famous latitude of 86° 14' North. They then began a long retreat south, and spent the winter of 1895–96 in an improvised shallow hut dug out of the shoreline of an island in Franz Josef Land that Nansen would later name for Frederick Jackson. In mid-June 1896 they strode into Jackson's camp.

Fram that same summer had drifted out of the pack and landed at Danskøya, Spitsbergen. There the ship was welcomed by the startling sight of a polar balloon expedition led by a Swedish engineer, Salomon A. Andrée.[18] Nansen and Johansen returned to Norway on board Jackson's relief ship *Windward* in the late summer of 1896 and, later, Nansen and *Fram* returned together to a spectacular welcome in the harbor at Kristiania, the capital of Norway.[19]

Frederick Jackson remained in Franz Josef Land for another year before he and his expedition retreated following a largely successful geographic reconnaissance of the western reaches of the archipelago. He left behind at Cape Flora a wealth of supplies that he intended for the use of shipwrecked expeditions. This large cache would be soon be augmented by supplies left behind by a polar expedition led by a minor Italian noble, Luigi Amadeo, the Duke of the Abruzzi,[20] and also by Swedish expeditions sent in search of Andrée, who had since disappeared over the Arctic Ocean in his balloon and was thought by some, including Walter Wellman, to be lost somewhere in Franz Josef Land. Andrée and his two companions were destined to remain lost in the Arctic until the summer of 1930, when their bodies and much of their equipment were found on an island between Spitsbergen (newly renamed Svalbard by the Norwegians) and Franz Josef Land.

Andrée died still many miles away from the mass of relief supplies left behind at Cape Flora. Instead, these supplies were used for the relief of all three of the American expeditions that would use Franz Josef Land as a base from which to attempt to reach the North Pole from 1898 to 1905. These remarkably inept expeditions, organized to reach the North Pole while staying out of Robert Peary's patch in northwestern Greenland, would fail—in increasingly spectacular ways—to get anywhere near the pole.

Like some kind of macabre gypsy caravan, the Americans would leave behind a trail of encampments to offer silent archaeological testimony to American polar ambitions at the turn of the century, and include the graves of two Norwegians employed as crew, the skeletons of ponies and dogs, small boats, broken ski, tins of potato chips, evaporated onions, malted milk tablets, hundreds of rounds of ammunition, a collection of felt hats, scientific instruments, and, on one of the most northern spots of land on the planet, a printing press, a library, the wreck of a steamship, and boxes and boxes of American flags.

For the next century, these artifacts would be found scattered around the archipelago, found by somewhat bemused Soviet geographers and polar aviators, Norwegian ethnologists, Russian entrepreneurs and historians, Swedish naturalists, and—as late as 2006—an American archaeologist. Along with the letters, diaries, and reports of these Americans and their Scandinavian compatriots, the artifacts provide a dimly lit trail into an American past that has gone without examination for more than a hundred years. This volume walks that trail. In doing so, it uses as its primary guide the words of the original explorers, words recorded by men of several different nations as they observed and experienced the greatest show in the Arctic, the American exploration of Franz Josef Land.

The Great American Act of Hustling

The Wellman Polar Expedition
1898–1899

✳

Walter Wellman.
From Walter Wellman, *The Aerial Age*
(New York: A. R. Keller, 1911).

ONE

A Useful Corps of
Newspaper Correspondents

Walter Wellman was born in Mentor, Ohio, in early November 1858. The future polar explorer arrived into the world a year and a half after the passing of Elisha Kent Kane, the first American to achieve fame in the Arctic, and within a cluster of births of men who would come to define polar exploration in the late nineteenth and early twentieth centuries, including Robert Peary (1856), Fridtjof Nansen (1861), and Frederick Cook (1865). The day of Wellman's birth, November 3, was barely a week after the arrival of Theodore Roosevelt, the paragon of American muscularity whom Wellman would profile in his newspaper more than a decade before Roosevelt became president of the United States.

Wellman's family descended from Thomas Wellman, a Puritan who fled London for Barbados in the mid-1600s before settling eventually in Massachusetts.[1] After fighting in the American Civil War, a descendent of Thomas by the name of Alonzo Wellman resettled his family from Ohio to a small town in south-central Nebraska called Sutton. There, his sixth son, Walter, established a newspaper at the age of fourteen. It was not unusual for boys to start newspapers during these years, since "manufacturers of printing presses in the United States [had begun to produce] smaller versions of their commercial offerings for use in the home [that lead to] an explosion of newspapers written, edited, and printed by teenage boys."[2] Walter Wellman would be associated with newspapers for much of the rest of his life.

In his early twenties, Wellman returned to his native Ohio. He married Laura McCann in 1879 and the five daughters subsequently born to them were all given "R" names: Ruth, Rose, Rae, Rita, and Rebecca. Along with his brother Frank, at the age of twenty-two Wellman founded another newspaper, this one in Cincinnati, Ohio, and called the *Penny Paper.* They eventually sold the paper to two other brothers destined for much greater fame in newspaper publishing, James E. and Edward W. Scripps. Renamed the *Cincinnati Post* in 1890, the paper remained in business for over a century until December 31, 2007.[3]

Wellman received his big break in February 1885, when at the age of twenty-six he arrived in Washington, D.C., as correspondent and political reporter for the *Chicago Herald* and its successors, the *Times-Herald* and the *Record-Herald.*[4] It was in the nation's capital that Wellman perfected the craft that would soon make him one of the most recognized names in American journalism. In Washington, wrote Wellman, "there is no profession so interesting as the profession of journalism."

> Here we have professional politicians, professional statesmen, professional lobbyists, professional farmers, professional everything; but of them all none form such a compact, picturesque, little understood and withal so useful a corps of workers as the newspaper correspondents. Being a member of this corps, I hope I shall not be accused of blowing my horn when I say that I am often amazed at the intelligence, the industry, the wide range of information, the acumen and the shrewdness of the men who represent here the great newspapers of the land.
>
> I would sooner take the judgment of the correspondents on the probable outcome of an attempt to pass a certain bill, on the nominations to be made by the great political parties, or anything of that sort in which information and discernment are requisite to the making of a good estimate, than the judgment of all the senators or all the members of the house, or both combined.[5]

Over the next twenty years, Wellman would travel back and forth between Washington and Chicago to chronicle the politicians and capitalists of the Gilded Age and the successive economic depressions spawned by its speculative excesses. Wellman's articles were syndicated across the Midwest, and as a result he was introduced to a vast new audience of newspaper readers. These were citizens—many newly literate thanks to Civil War–era initiatives in public education—hungry for stories of the men and machines that were creating a new world of rapid transit, rapid information, and rapid wealth.

Wellman found much to admire in this new breed of capitalist, men whose frontier ventures were generating stupendous, almost unimaginable, amounts of untaxed wealth and—very often to accompany it—singularly megalomaniacal visions of social control. One early piece by Wellman attempted to put the best face on a planned community south of Chicago. Conceived by George Pullman for Pullman sleeping-car workers, it was a place deliberately designed as a "national model for efficiency and order,"[6] described by Wellman as a place where the "health, morality and happiness enjoyed by its inhabitants could be raised to a much higher level than that usually found among communities of laborers and mechanics."[7]

Wellman visited several of the homes in Pullman, where he found that in "only one of two [were there] odors arising from negligent housewifery."[8] Even though he correctly identified the factors that eventually doomed both Pullman the man and Pullman the town—"The residents have no voice in local matters. There are no home politics, no caucuses, no town meetings. Pullman attends to all affairs of local government and consults only his own wishes"[9]—Wellman did not recognize them as such. Revealing his own developing sense of both American politicians and the people they presumably served, Wellman asked:

> what proportion of workingmen in any community really enjoy voice in local government? How much better than Pullmanism is that citizenship which gives to a clique of pot house politicians the actual control of things, and which fastens upon the public treasury a coterie of chronic leeches? . . . It may be un-American to say so, but in local affairs, except where things are going all wrong and a Tweed ring is to be broken up, the precious right of suffrage is largely a delusion and a farce. . . . The social organization of Pullman is such that the monocrat or whoever represents him must use his best skill and energy to keep all at work. All well paid, all content, all healthy, all happy. Failure to do this is his own failure and ruin.[10]

Wellman continued to develop this theme whenever he was assigned to profile another tycoon. In an article written in the summer of 1888, Wellman described all of the new millionaires he had become acquainted with in Chicago and Washington. He had a special fondness for those men who had moved from the East and then risen from "country storekeepers" to control vast fortunes in banking and railroads, such as Albert and Henry Keep, who "used to be country store keepers up in Wisconsin" but now owned a railway.[11]

In 1892 Wellman got himself onboard a yacht owned by Joseph R. De Lamar so that he could conduct an interview with the entrepreneur who had made fortune in maritime salvage operations in the Atlantic and silver mining in the West. The axial notion of Wellman's subsequent article—that the possession of millions of dollars in untaxed profits was too much of a bother—typified much of what he wrote during the Gilded Age. De Lamar, according to Wellman, was a rough and ready capitalist whose only desire was to have a few friends he could consider as something more than importuners after his cash. "I do not want to be a capitalist," Wellman decided.

> I will stick to the newspaper business, working hard for a living, racking my dull brain to please both readers and managing editor, and when I fall back done for, worked out, no longer able to satisfy public and employer—as it is said all writers fall back sooner or later—I will take up the stick and rule and set type. Anything but being a capitalist.[12]

A month later, Wellman rode in a Pullman car to Asheville, North Carolina, where he interviewed George Vanderbilt and in the process became lost in the cavernous foundations of the colossal mansion Vanderbilt was then constructing—even today still the largest home in the United States. "It is to be a stone palace of 100 rooms. . . . Vanderbilt travels in Europe, picks up new ideas and comes back here and spends millions upon them. One of his notions is an arcade or gallery running about 500 feet from the house to an astronomical observatory, and down a marble cascade from observatory hill is to run a stream of mountain water."[13] A decade later, many of these bankers and capitalists and editors, men such as dry goods pioneer Levi Z. Leiter and Wellman's own boss at the *Chicago Herald,* John R. Walsh, would have their names attached to remote bays and headlands of Franz Josef Land as a result of their patronage of Wellman's second polar expedition in 1898.[14]

Wellman would also place the names of several Washington politicians in Franz Josef Land. These, however, would be only those who offered direct financial support to his expedition, since the longer he stayed in Washington the lower sank his opinion of the nation's politicians. As an example, in a scathing piece written in 1890 in the wake of a Senate committee investigation into the public naming of journalists writing unpleasant "facts which the senators think ought not to be printed," Wellman heaped scorn on any notion of the "dignity" of the United States Senate:

> As if the dignity of a great body like this depended upon the action of a few newspaper writers, and could be maintained by locking those writers behind iron bars for performance of their duty to their employers and the public. There is nothing new in all this. Ever since it was born the United States senate has been striving to keep up its dignity. It has paid more attention to dignity than brains, and in consequence has constantly degenerated.[15]

Wellman ridiculed Washington "tea parties," where "no tea is served" but there was plenty of champagne. "A swell tea in Washington, particularly in a big house where the hostess is ambitious and the invitations numerous, is one of the most soul harrowing and provoking instruments of torture I ever had the misfortune to meet with."[16] Secretary of State James G. Blaine could only be interviewed by appearing at his front door and passing single questions written on small note cards back and forth, one at a time, via a servant.[17] And Grover Cleveland, twenty-second and twenty-fourth president of the United States, could occasionally be buttonholed for an interview if one desired to follow him "to a Turkish bathroom."[18]

As for the opposite sex, "in Washington the American woman appears to know rather more about taking care of herself than she does in other cities, develops greater facility for getting what she wants, going where she wishes and ascertaining what she desires to know."[19]

Not all residents of the capital came in for such criticism. One young man, a recent appointee to the U.S. Civil Service Commission, caught Wellman's eye as one of a handful of "literary statesmen."

> Nothing gives the young civil service reformer greater delight than to sit down and write a sharp, stinging, sizzling letter to somebody who has criticised [*sic*] the civil service board, or in some other manner

roused the combativeness of Mr. [Theodore] Roosevelt. . . . Scorning stenographers and typewriters, he sits down, pen in hand, and scratches, scratches, metaphorically tearing people's eyes out. . . . The phrases about which he is most particular are those which cut the deepest, and these he turns and re-turns, each change sharpening them, till they are like razor edges. [In spite of his writing], he is a delightful companion—vivacious, sympathetic, entertaining. He has a merry, ringing laugh. His teeth, which are perfect in form and of dazzling whiteness, he shows a dozen times a minute.[20]

Little more than a decade later, following the stunning assassination of William McKinley, Roosevelt would become, at forty-two, the youngest president in the history of the United States. In the summer of 1906, Wellman would send him the first telegram from the Arctic, delivered by wireless transmission from a base camp on the remote island of Danskøya in the Spitsbergen archipelago.

In between his profiles of the powerful and the rich of America's Gilded Age, Wellman engaged in the kinds of dogged feature-article writing that editors sew into the shirts of every journalist. A visit to Mammoth Cave in Kentucky, the longest cave system on the planet—"a weird, uncanny voyage"[21]—was followed by a visit to the U.S. Patent Office to study dozens of models of passenger elevators—"The fastest elevator in the world is the Chicago elevator. This is conceded by all authorities, and nobody denies that it is in keeping with the characteristics of the place."[22] An essay on "Advertising as Art"[23] was followed by another on "Memorable Names," wherein Wellman "collated from official sources a list of about 10,000 of the men who have held conspicuous place in the public service since the foundation of the republic."[24] A trip to Cape May, New Jersey, to report on the relaxation habits of President Benjamin Harrison on summer holiday[25] was followed by a chance encounter at the Army and Navy Club with the Civil War commander of the USS *Monitor,* Admiral John Lorimer Worden.[26]

Wellman also wrote scores of articles that attempted to predict the future of technology, with varying degrees of prescience. An insightful 1892 essay entitled "Electrical Power: It Will Soon Be Used for Railway Locomotives"[27] was followed by the slightly less omniscient 1894 article that, while correctly foreseeing the coming awesome destructiveness of aircraft, suggested that this fact would make warfare impossible: "Aerial Destroyers: Prediction that War Will Soon Be Impossible."[28]

TWO

On Watlings Island in Characteristic American Fashion

Walter Wellman's favorite journalistic subjects involved exploration, in all its forms, beginning with his obvious enthusiasm as he ventured into Mammoth Cave in the fall of 1887. So when Chicago won the right to host the 1893 World's Columbian Exposition—a massive international gathering to celebrate four hundred years of social and technological progress since Christopher Columbus—his editor at the *Chicago Herald* asked Wellman if he could pinpoint the precise landing spot of Columbus in the New World in 1492. The *Herald* paid for Wellman to lead a small expedition to the Bahamas in the summer of 1891 to search out the actual location and place a marker on the spot—all in time for the Chicago exposition. Wellman leapt at the opportunity. Here was a heaven-sent chance both to get out of Washington and to pursue his passion for exploration.[29]

At the age of thirty-two, this was to be Wellman's debut as an explorer. It also marked his first real opportunity to drop hints as to his future ambitions. When given his assignment—"find the spot where Columbus discovered America and mark it with a memorial"—Wellman wrote that his unfazed response was "'Will try.' If it had been a request to find the north pole or capture a mermaid I supposed the answer would have been the same. The newspaper correspondent is not surprised at anything."[30] He might not live to capture a mermaid, but it is clear from this offhand remark that the North Pole was very much in his thoughts as early as the spring of 1891.

Along with Charles Lederer, the *Herald*'s staff artist, and four others, Wellman left for Nassau on June 3, 1891, on board a Ward Line steamship from New York. In a bit of irony, at that very moment and directly across the East River in Brooklyn, Robert Peary prepared to depart for his first exploration of northern Greenland. It would be Peary's "claim" to the area between Greenland and northeastern Canada as his exclusive province, as well as the lure of finding the lost Swedish balloonist Andrée, that would later force Wellman's own polar ambitions to be staged further east, via Spitsbergen and Franz Josef Land.

As for Wellman, he set himself to the Columbus task with a good amount of rigor. He intensely studied previous attempts to locate the exact landing place of the Genoese explorer in the New World and recognized that they all shared the same flaw: all were hopelessly theoretical. No one had actually ventured to the islands of the Bahamas in an attempt to match the geographic descriptions in Columbus's journals with the oceanic landscape of the islands themselves.

Wellman thereafter determined to make the discovery his own way. "This was a queer task," he wrote, "but a fascinating one."[31] Wellman attacked it for what it was: an academic problem in historical geography. On his arrival in Nassau, he secured an interview with the governor, who in turn provided a letter granting the American journalist access to the islands. Wellman then set about in search of a boat charter. "The people here take real interest in the project and are doing everything to help us. I have every confidence we shall be able to erect the monument in good shape."[32]

I went at it in characteristic American fashion—that is, jumped at it. I ransacked the Congressional library and other libraries. I cabled to London for a book which was not to be found in America. I procured from the hydrographic office charts of the Bahamas made by our government and the British admiralty. . . .

Five islands had been put forward as the real San Salvador, and hundreds of books and pamphlets written in support of these theories. The correct theory must be based upon two conditions: The island itself must have certain features described by Columbus—lagoons, reefs, harbor hard by a headland through which the sea had cut its way . . .

and it must lie at certain distances and in certain directions from five other islands visited and described by Columbus. . . . Watlings [was] the only one that would fit the geometrical lines of Columbus' first voyage through the Bahamas. If it contained the physical features which Columbus had found in his San Salvador, then the mystery was solved. Oddly enough, the learned historians, geographers and cartographers who had supported the claims of rival islands had not taken the trouble to visit the region of which they discoursed.[33]

The Bahamas had been transformed throughout the nineteenth century by African-Americans escaping the slave trade. By the time of Wellman's visit, the archipelago had settled into life as a fairly sleepy outpost of the British Empire (on Andros Island, a young British entrepreneur by the name of Neville Chamberlain was then in the first months of trying to make a go of his family's sisal plantation). Wellman hired the only steamship tender in Nassau, "a crude craft with a bottom as flat as a street car, keelless [sic] and not lovely," raised an American flag, and steamed off.[34]

From Nassau, Watlings Island was 200 nautical miles away. Wellman's charter passed Cat Island and, though it had been advanced as a possible spot for the first landing, Wellman saw in it nothing to compare with Columbus's writings.

The expedition continued on to Watlings. There they dropped anchor and were approached by a small boat. "It contained all the officials of the island—the local magistrate, the port officer, the postmaster, the sheriff, the colonel of the militia and many more—all in the person of Captain Maxwell Nairn, the only white resident of the island, a veritable Pooh Bah, monarch of a coral isle."[35]

Wellman and his party went ashore to find an island twelve miles by six, with a "salt lagoon [that] appeared to echo back [Columbus's] name.

> The spirit of Columbus dominates everything in Watlings, overshadows everything, leaves nothing else to be thought of or written about.
>
> And no wonder. Here was everything that Columbus described in his journal—the "large lagoon in the middle of the island," the luxuriant verdure, the "reefs running all round that island," the hills near the shore . . . All these and many more . . . we found, and at first knew instinctively . . . that this was the birthplace of the New World.[36]

The monument Walter Wellman constructed on San Salvador in 1891 to mark the spot where he believed Christopher Columbus had landed in the New World. This photograph was taken in 1964. *Courtesy of James St. John, Ohio State University at Newark.*

Wellman narrowed his search on Watlings to a small bay, which he chose "as the very spot at which the landing was made."[37] Above this bay, native islanders, pressed into service, cleared a path upon which blocks of limestone coral and the cargo of cement could be dragged. Thirty barrels of cement, along with a marble globe and the memorial tablet all brought from New York, were now lugged to the promontory above the bay. The tablet read: *On this spot Christopher Columbus first set foot upon the soil of the New World. Erected by The Chicago Herald, June, 1891.* Several days later, Wellman wrote, the "result was beautiful. In the coral limestone are all the tints of the rainbow, all the marine forms."[37]

After his fascinating voyage to Watlings, the business of discovery must have seemed the best sort of career contrivance for a journalist bent on getting out of Washington, D.C., as often as possible. It was time for Wellman to see what other possibilities lay on the horizon.

THREE

Wellman at the
1893 Columbian Exposition

Wellman's article on the Watlings Island adventure was held over by his newspaper to be published in October 1892, on the precise four hundredth anniversary of the original landings by Columbus. In the meantime, Wellman returned to Chicago to cover the titanic groundwork necessary to prepare the city for the Columbian Exposition. Several cities had bid to host the fair, and in 1890, after intense lobbying by millionaires from both Chicago and New York, Congress chose the bid of Wellman's Chicago. Over six hundred acres were filled with two hundred temporary buildings displaying exhibits from every state and dozens of nations.

Wellman described the scene, with admirable provincial immodesty, more than a year before the official opening on May 1, 1893:

> Chicago is without question the most interesting city on the world. Imagine a square mile or more of ground which less than two years ago was for the most part a swamp. Chicago passes over it the wand of her magic energy, and now you behold a dozen palaces rearing their roofs toward the sky. The swamp is converted into a park. Lagoons and wooded islands embellish the landscape. Hundreds of miles of sewers, water mains, gas pipes, electric conduits are put in—it is like creating a city in a night.[38]

Wellman was soon back at work in Washington, to cover the presidential elections of the fall of 1892, and even gained an interview with President-elect Grover Cleveland just prior to Cleveland's inauguration in March 1893.[39] But after his expedition to the Caribbean and the innervating spectacle of the construction of the Columbian Exposition in Chicago, the attractions of conservative Washington were fading and fast.

Wellman followed President Cleveland to Chicago to witness the opening of the World's Fair on Monday, May 1, 1893, and then remained in Chicago throughout the summer, where he wrote dispatch after dispatch from the Columbian Exposition.[40] It was impossible for an ambitious young man to remain unaffected by the electric environment of the exposition, and Wellman's articles testify to his burgeoning enthusiasm for the spirit of cultural and technological progress represented in the fair's exhibits. It was also here that his ambition to explore began to coalesce around the biggest geographic prize of all: the North Pole.

The fair was filled with technology and transportation exhibits, many placed in an international context, such as the aisle of the transportation building where a "typical American railway train" was placed opposite "a train from the London and Northwestern railway of England. . . . The foreign locomotive is without that graceful and sometimes useful appendage known in this country as a 'cow-catcher.' This is not needed in England because the track—or 'permanent way,' as the English have it—is never bothered with cows. The line is protected by fences or walls which are cow-proof."[41]

The ethnological exhibits—every state and many nations sent representatives of their indigenous or pre-industrial populations—also fascinated Wellman.

> Ethnology, anthropology and archaeology are big words. To the popular mind they suggest only dull and dry scientific inquiry. But in fact they signify studies which are not only interesting but fascinating. When it was decided to have in the World's fair a department devoted to this purpose the professor naturally wanted it called by its proper scientific title. The exposition managers, however, said the words "ethnology," "anthropology" and "archaeology" would repel instead of attracting the people. Was there not some popular title that would do just as well? Possibly. The professor would see. A little later, with a sigh for professional pride cast down, he reported that a popular

interpretation of the trio of big words would be "Man and His Works." So, "Man and His Works" it is. This may not be a strictly accurate title, but it suffices; besides, it doesn't drive people away from the door.[42]

Another article appeared during the first week of the fair under the headline "Walter Wellman on Future Modes of Travel." In it Wellman was already looking forward to a Columbian Exposition on the five hundredth anniversary of the European landing in the Americas, in 1992. "I am neither an engineer nor an inventor," he wrote, "but I think I see that we are on the eve of improvements and departures in travel which will in the space of 50 or at most 100 years amount to revolution." It was here—following his comment on Watlings Island about a hypothetical newspaper assignment to find the North Pole—that Wellman revealed his thoughts about which mode of future travel would best suit his own ambitions:

Aerial navigation will come within the next century. It may not become universal or largely commercial, but it will be used for special travel, for exploration, for pleasure. It will be accomplished not by balloons, since a balloon that floats in the air cannot be steered at will, but by the aeroplane in combination with stored electric energy operating through engines of marvelous power and lightness. Within 25 years aerial navigation will solve the mystery of the north pole and the frozen ocean.[43]

In mid-June, Wellman wandered into the Fisheries Building, a sprawling complex that included displays documenting the fishermen as far afield as Alaska, Massachusetts, and, central to Wellman's future, Norway. The ornate building—actually a large central pavilion flanked by two smaller pavilions connected by curved arcades—held ten aquaria that included several saltwater tanks holding eighty thousand gallons of Atlantic seawater, "evaporated to reduce both its quantity and weight for transportation, and then, once at the fairgrounds, restored to its proper density with freshwater from Lake Michigan."[44] "Every day I saw streams of people going in and out of this structure, and finally I determined to see what it was that exercised such fascination over them within."[45]

It was in the Fisheries Building where Wellman saw the possibilities of global fame if he could repeat his relatively painless expedition to the Bahamas with a similar voyage north of Norway. The Norwegian exhibit centered on the boats and techniques used in the catch of cod fish in the Lofoten Islands, but it was the Norwegian hunt of walrus, seal, and polar bears even farther north that drew Wellman in.

> The Northmen are famous fishermen. The theater of their operations extends from Christiana in the south to the limit of the polar ice pack north of Spitzbergen. These Norwegians start early in the year for the Arctic ocean, driving their little schooners into the ice with an intrepidity which astonishes the Arctic explorers who, fitted with steam vessels and all appliances for fighting ice, are afraid to follow. Fishermen from Tromsoe [sic] and Hammerfest every year accomplish feats in the northern waters which would add to the fame of Arctic explorers, but the Norwegians are after fish, seal, walrus, eider down, whales, not glory. Almost every year some of these little craft go north of Spitzbergen and reach a latitude that is within 500 geographical miles of the north pole. Occasionally one is nipped in the ice up there, and the master and crew, unless rescued by other fishermen, must pass the long Arctic winter in improvised huts and subsist upon such game as they may be able to take before darkness sets in about the first of October. Sometimes they do this successfully, others, their bones are found in the spring where starvation and scurvy left them.[46]

In fact, the Chicago exposition took place in the middle of a half century of increasingly intensive Norwegian exploitation of the seas around northern Norway. Between 1859 and 1909, despite the general poverty and a decided lack of capital in the region, Arctic sea hunting operations increased in both number and efficiency, as Norwegian maritime hunters took aim at populations of seals and walrus, reindeer and polar bear, and cod and herring. As one species was depleted, the sea hunters of north Norway went off in search of another, and it was this constant search for exploitable species that forced these men to range far and wide across the high Arctic, from Greenland in the west to the newly discovered islands of Franz Josef Land in the east.[47]

Here, then, was the model of Wellman's first Arctic expedition, and his polar imaginings were further fired by, of all things, a visit to the fair's art building. Once again, as with the Norwegian fisheries exhibit, the long lines of visitors in the Austrian exhibit surprised Wellman. They were drawn to a painting of a famous episode in the history of polar exploration—and one painted by the explorer himself. This was the famous *"Nie zurück"* (No return), a rendering by Julius Payer of perhaps the most dramatic moment of his discovery of Franz Josef Land twenty years earlier. Wellman was not so much impressed by the skill of the artist-explorer as he was by the obvious effect of the work on the thousands of visitors who came to see it.

> It represents a moment of despair in the history of the North Pole expedition sent out by the Austrians in 1872 and led by Payer and Weyprecht. After spending two years in the waters and on the land of Franz Josef land, an Arctic region hitherto unknown, these explorers abandoned their imprisoned ship and set out across the surface of the frozen sea for Europe. [After two months of constant and futile struggle, the] men were in despair, and begged to be permitted to go back to the ship. . . . This is the scene which the artist, Payer himself, has put on canvas, modestly leaving out his own figure. From an art point of view it is not a great picture, but the manner in which it attracts the multitude is proof of the fascination which Arctic adventure has over the popular mind.[48]

The exposition laid all of Wellman's exploring ambitions right in front of his face: the increasing speed and excitement of transportation technologies, the rugged sea hunters of Arctic Norway, the magnetic heroism of Payer and Weypricht in Franz Josef Land. And the journalist could not fail to sense the urgency of history. On the very same morning that Wellman's article on the Payer painting was published, far up in the long and wide fjord tipped by the city of Kristiania, Norway, the great rounded hull of the specially designed polar vessel *Fram* slipped its anchorage and headed to sea. As cannons from the nearby Akershus fortress boomed across the forest-rimmed fjord, thirty-one-year-old Fridtjof Nansen and his crew on board the *Fram* began their three-year voyage of exploration of the North Polar Basin. Three weeks later, as *Fram* prepared to depart from the northern Norwegian port of Tromsø, a last-minute addition was made to the crew. A "qualified mate, who had sailed the Arctic for years,"[49] by the name of Bernt Bentsen, grabbed his sailor's advance pay and immediately invested it in a morning's round of drinking at saloons along the harbor. Bentsen reported back on board in time for *Fram*'s departure from Tromsø at 1 P.M. on the afternoon of July 14, 1893. In five years' time, Bentsen would sign on for another—and for him, far more fateful—Arctic expedition, one led by Walter Wellman.

FOUR

The Matchless Energy of Americans

In Chicago, in widely different exhibits at the fair, Walter Wellman had been given glimpses into his future as an explorer: the geographic stations of Spitsbergen and Franz Josef Land from which he would stage five attempts to reach the North Pole; the aeronautical technology he would employ on his final three expeditions from Spitsbergen in an attempt to defeat the polar ice cap; and, perhaps most important to him as an already well-known national journalist, the potentially overwhelming international fame that would attach to him if he were successful in reaching his goal.

By early August, Wellman's experiences at the Columbian Exposition had launched him on his way to the north. Moreover, the kinetic atmosphere of the fair, combined with the success of the Watlings Island expedition, had injected the journalist with an almost messianic belief that there was no project or place—no matter how difficult or remote—that could not be cracked by an American journalist employing the latest technology. Indeed, the fair had "demonstrated the matchless energy of Americans."[50]

From this moment forward, Wellman's attention would turn largely away from Washington politics to a much grander but vastly more straightforward mystery—the search for the North Pole. Toward this grail the journalist would direct five expeditions and over half a million dollars, in the process scattering across the high Arctic the wrecks of two airships, a steamship, an assortment of base camps and small boats, dozens of place-names, and finally the graves of two of his expedition crew members. He would not give up for over a decade and a half, not until September 1909—the dramatic month when the announcements of both Robert Peary and Frederick Cook claimed to have reached the North Pole—thoroughly blasted the worlds of exploration and geography and of journalism and popular culture.

In the fall of 1893, as he was about to turn thirty-five, Wellman made his first pilgrimage to Norway, to consult with the same kinds of sealing skippers and master fishermen he had met at the Norwegian fisheries exhibition in Chicago and "to investigate conditions and possibly to prepare for an expedition of my own."[51] Norwegian fishermen at the time possessed vast experience in Arctic sea hunting. They chased Greenland shark from the north coast of Norway to Spitsbergen and, in the latter place, operated a major cod fishery from 1874 to 1882, until the cod finally disappeared in 1883.[52] Wellman had read William Edward Parry's account[53] of hauling heavy boats north of Spitsbergen in 1827 and thought he could adopt Parry's method but go Parry one better "with lighter craft and a more modern equipment."[54]

As much as he sought knowledge of the ice conditions around Spitsbergen, what Wellman was truly after was a shortcut to the North Pole. By now, Wellman had convinced himself that there had to be a quicker passage than the kinds of archaic sledging engaged in by Parry. Such methods had gone virtually unchanged in seventy years, and one only had to look toward Robert Peary, hopelessly bogged down in his explorations of the Greenland ice cap, to chasten a newspaper reporter seeking to satisfy both his personal luxuries and his journalist's nose to stay tight to a deadline.

Even radically new methods, such as Nansen's trans-polar drift, were similarly flawed when viewed from Wellman's perspective. Early reports from Nansen's polar-basin drift were not encouraging—one report that appeared in Wellman's own newspaper in late October 1893 even held that Nansen's revolutionary ship had been lost. This false rumor did not stop with the claim that the *Fram* had vanished in the Arctic, but gratuitously added that Nansen himself had "become restless, melancholy and vacillating."[55]

It went against all of Wellman's journalistic experience and instinct to spend months in a plod behind a sledge like Peary or years marooned on a boat in pack ice like Nansen. In the years before wireless communication, Arctic expeditions such as those of Peary and Nansen were often out of contact with the civilization to the south for years at a time, something completely abhorrent to a journalist who had hustled himself up from cub reporter in Nebraska to editor of the city desk in Cincinnati to Washington correspondent for a Chicago daily. The intrepid journalist who enjoyed a front row seat to the unpredictable, frenetic events of the Gilded Age had by now become something of a name himself, to the point where he could be forgiven if he believed that he was almost as famous as those who created the headlines. For such a rising star, Wellman was only too aware that any news not immediately exploited went rapidly stale.

The innervated fall of 1893 did nothing to alter the frantic rush of events. On the day after the great Chicago fair closed, the mayor of Chicago, Carter H. Harrison, was assassinated by a disgruntled and disappointed office-seeker. A financial panic dropped the United States into an economic depression that would last five desperate years. In some states, unemployment topped 40 percent. Support for the "radical measure" of a graduated income tax and other populist policies allowed a young congressman from Nebraska by the name of William Jennings Bryan—a year and a half younger than Wellman himself—to leap into national prominence. The last decade of the nineteenth century was accelerating to light speed, fueled by advertising and exploited by mass communications. The explorer who won the race to the North Pole would take over both the front pages of the news and the back pages of a newspaper's advertising and become, at a shot, both instantly famous and fantastically rich.

Wellman returned to Washington where, seemingly quick as a flash, he used his new connections and "secured the necessary capital, organized an expedition, [and] chartered an old ice-steamer in Norway."[56] Most of the cash came from Wellman himself, and many of these connections came from his role as president of the Press Club, as Wellman saw it a much more democratic institution than its restrictive cousin the Gridiron Club. While the Gridiron limited itself to just forty Washington insiders, the Press Club allowed for hundreds of members.[57] But even from his lofty Press Club perch, Wellman's journalism, from the spring of 1894 onward, seemed less a regular profession than a way to introduce his expedition plans to potential patrons and the politicians who might in some other ways make themselves useful.

The Norwegian ice steamer Wellman chartered, called *Ragnvald Jarl* (*Earl Ragnvald*), was based out of the port of Ålesund and skippered by Captain Johannes Bottolfsen. It had been built in 1873 and was used in bottlenose whaling. The name of the ship derived from a famous Viking leader from the Norwegian west coast, Ragnvald Mørejarl.[58]

To make good on his promise to go Parry one better, Wellman had three aluminum boats specially built, along with several light-weight aluminum sledges "to facilitate travel over the polar pack in the summer."[59] These would be named after previous polar explorers, including Parry himself, as well as American polar icons Elisha Kent Kane and James B. Lockwood, the latter having set a new mark for farthest north during the Greely expedition. Fifty dogs to pull the sledges would be purchased in Belgium.

"WILL TRY TO REACH THE NORTH POLE," announced the front page of the *Philadelphia Inquirer* on February 25, 1894. "Walter Wellman, who for some years has been a prominent newspaper correspondent . . . is the projector and leader of the enterprise."[60] With this announcement, Wellman had made a full transition from reporting the news to making it. He also made clear his intention to stay out of the way of the mercurial Robert Peary.

The expedition abandons the Greenland route, which had been fol-lowed by so many previous expeditions, and goes by way of Norway and Spitzbergen, the latter a group of islands to the east of Northern Greenland. . . . Unless the season proves to be an extraordinary one the steamer will sail from Tromsoe [*sic*] to the [expedition's proposed Spitsbergen] headquarters in five days, and the party will thus be easily and quickly placed as far north as the average Arctic explorer is able to penetrate by months or years of efforts by the Greenland route. At their headquarters the Wellman party will be 700 statute miles from the Pole. The plans of this party call for a dash toward the Pole.[61]

Wellman would be accompanied by three other Americans: Charles R. Dodge, a thirty-year-old artist and photographer from the Navy Depart-ment, Owen B. French, a twenty-eight year-old surveyor from the Coast and Geodetic Survey, and Dr. Thomas B. Mohun, the forty-one-year-old expedition doctor. Set to come on board in Norway were ten more expedi-tion members, "several of them being scientific investigators connected with the university at Kristiania, and others, men of experience in the ice fields."[62] These included a thirty-seven-year-old Swedish cook and mountain guide named Hans Wästfält, along with several students from Kristiania, among them thirty-year-old geologist Peter Øyen, twenty-seven-year-old meteorolo-gist Helge Alme, twenty-five-year-old Jens Dahl, and twenty-three-year-old Trygve Heyerdahl.[63] The first officer, Emil Pedersen, had been the former master of *Ragnvald Jarl* when the ship was engaged in whaling.[64] Two parties of seven men each would work their way north for about twenty-five days, at which time one group would fall back and the main party would continue onward for perhaps fifty or sixty days.

Wellman predicted that the expedition could make upward of ten miles per day, a pace that would allow for a rapid round-trip to the North Pole from Spitsbergen of less than six months' duration. Over a ton of "the specially concentrated foods of this age"[65] would allow the men to survive on a pound and a half of food per day. Whenever a dog failed, it would be fed to the dogs that remained, and thereby save more weight. Wellman outlined his plans at a monthly meeting of the Geographical Club of Philadelphia, where he shared the stage with Dr. Frederick Cook, who was there to discuss a proposed expedition to Antarctica.[66]

Wellman and his fellow Americans sailed from New York on Wednesday, March 14, 1894. Prior to leaving for New York, Wellman's colleagues at the Press Club in Washington held a special meeting where they presented him with "a handsome silk flag of the United States, which the club desired he should nail to the top of the north pole or plant in the hole discovered,"[67] the latter a reference to a belief still held by some that the North Pole was a cavernous opening into the center of the planet.

A month later, from Bergen, Norway, Wellman wrote a letter to his parents and his brother Arthur "before leaving civilization." In the entire month from Washington, D.C., to Norway, the weather had been perfect. The journey included stopovers in both England and Belgium, where Wellman displayed his preference for publicity over planning, as well as what he called "the great American act of hustling":

> We were ten days in London, and attracted a great deal of attention there. The newspapers were full of accounts of us and our plans; we were given a farewell luncheon at one of the small clubs; in fact, the English paid us more attention than we had expected, had more confidence in us than our own Americans displayed, and treated us better. . . .
>
> We bought a great deal of stuff in London—concentrated foods, clothing, etc. We have taken everything we could find that seemed likely to do us good. Many people called on us and gave us good advice.

From London we went to Liege, Belgium, to buy our dogs. We had a great time. The people there said it would take us three weeks to get them. In three days we had our 53 dogs in stable and paid for. The next day we took them by train to Rotterdam to catch the steamer for Bergen. And how do you suppose we took them? They have no such thing as an express company over here. The freight was too slow. So we made passengers of our dogs, bought 53 3rd class tickets, and went away in triumph, greatly to the astonishment of the people, who for the first time saw the great American act of hustling.

Our dogs are pretty good beasts. . . . They pull amazing loads. We paid as high as $14 for the best, and the average price was $8. But in addition to this were many [other] expenses—agents, stables, etc. I have two tons of dog food on the way from London.

We left Rotterdam Friday morning, [April] 6th, by steamer, and arrived here Sunday evening. Our dogs, in boxes, filled the deck of the steamer. It cost $100 to get the dogs to Rotterdam, and another $100 to get them here, besides our own expenses. Last Sunday night we transferred them to another steamer and sent them on to Aalesund. Three of our men went with them, and one staid [sic] here with me. We go to Aalesund tonight. There the dogs are on an isolated island, as we are not permitted to bring them ashore. No dogs are permitted to be imported to Norway, and we had to get government permission to do even this much.

My party is practically complete. Five from America, including [Alfred] Franklin, an athlete of Norwegian birth, but a citizen of America. He is about the fastest skater in the U.S. One from Belgium, a young English engineer [named Lionel Winship], capital fellow, who has lived three years in Liège and knows how to handle the dogs. He goes without pay. Five scientific men from Kristiania, the capital of Norway. One mountain guide, cook and sportsman from Bergen [the Swede Wästfält]. An executive officer from Aalesund, former master of one ship. Three men from Tromsoe, carefully picked.[68]

The northern Norway men included two who would become central figures in Wellman's 1898–99 expedition to Franz Josef Land: twenty-two-year-old Emil Ellefsen from Hammerfest and thirty-six-year-old Paul Bjørvig from Tromsø.[69] Wellman concluded with remorseful thoughts of his lonely wife and ailing mother and with the hope that he would see them all the next winter in Nebraska. A few days later, as the *Ragnvald Jarl* made its way from Ålesund to Tromsø, Wellman reported that he was pleased with both the men he had found to accompany him and the ship itself, which, instead of "smelling badly she has been scraped and painted, and in short is as nice and clean as a newly bared babe."[70]

At the same time—and despite having yet to set foot in the Arctic—Wellman basked in his newfound international attention as a celebrity polar explorer. He showed the press in Norway a letter he had just received from Clements Markham of the Royal Geographical Society that expressed the pleasure of the president of the RGS "at seeing such gallant enterprises undertaken."[71] As Wellman boarded his chartered steamer at Ålesund, a band "played an American air and the people cheered. They waved their handkerchiefs at us as long as they could see us. We went out with salutes from the fort, and with the American colors flying from our fore-peak—the same flag that I used at the point where Columbus discovered America."[73]

FIVE

Success or Nothing

All of Wellman's newfound attention was enough to lead the journalist into a false sense of ease as he approached the moveable trap that was the north polar pack with its daunting, heavy, multiyear ice. He was, as he wrote to his family, the "absolute master" of the ship, and seems to have completely misunderstood both the role itself and why the Norwegians might be content to have it this way.

> The captain comes to me for orders. . . . The steamer is absolutely under our control. We can sail her where we like, and after we leave her they must do with her as I say. This is a tremendous advantage, and more than I hoped for, because it enables us to take advantage of every possible change of the situation. If the ice is open, we can do as we please about taking the steamer into risks.[73]

Without realizing the full implications of what he was writing, Wellman noted that the "owner will not care much if she is lost, I think, because he wants to sell her, and has her heavily insured."[74] Unlike the owner, who was protected whether the expedition succeeded or not, Wellman confessed that he had to reach the pole, for "unless I make [a] success I am financially ruined . . . so it is success or nothing."[75]

Wellman had in fact contributed $12,000 of his own money to the expedition, an amount that would equal more than $300,000 in 2013 dollars. Another $2,500 came from the rights to tell his story in U.S. newspapers. John R. Walsh, owner of the *Chicago Herald,* also offered a letter of credit for $10,000 that Wellman could draw upon. The five-month charter for *Ragnvald Jarl* had alone cost $5,300. And, scattered from Chicago to Norway, Wellman had also left nearly $1,500 in bills due, with instructions to his brother Arthur that these be paid out of his life insurance if he failed to return.

Other newspapers noted that Wellman had become the toast of the entire Norwegian coast, feted with local concerts, fjord tours, and even sitting for a local sculptor for a planned bust of the journalist-explorer. A dispatch from London, which appeared in American newspapers on May 20, was among the last words heard from the expedition for two months. When next heard from, the news surely did nothing to ease the suffering of his wife and mother, but no doubt thrilled the owner of the *Ragnvald Jarl.*

"LOST IN THE ARCTIC FLOES," reported the *New York Times* on July 25. Numerous reports from London, and based on word gathered by correspondents in Norway, claimed that the pack ice around the north coast of Spitsbergen was especially thick and that Wellman's chartered vessel had been crushed by the ice and sunk. Norwegian sealers operating along the north coast of Spitsbergen had reported extremely heavy weather, and feared for the American expedition and its Scandinavian complement.[76] The likelihood of any survivors was considered remote.

There was also a sub-plot that involved Peter Øyen, the geology student from Kristiania, who was found in early June at the headquarters of the expedition on Danskøya. Øyen was in "an almost dying condition," declaiming "bitter reproaches" against Wellman for abandoning him on the remote island in "frightful solitude."[77]

At the time, as well as nearly twenty years later when he wrote his exploring memoirs, the accusation that he had abandoned the geologist on Danskøya rankled Wellman, who nevertheless disingenuously claimed that the event was his "first taste of newspaper sensationalism and misrepresentation," hardly likely for someone who had been in journalism already for two decades.[78] "We offered to leave one man with him for comrade, but he objected to that, and preferred to remain alone [in] a good house [with] tons of provisions, a gun and a dog."[79] When a party of English sportsmen visited the island during the summer, they found the geologist *in extremis,* and Wellman claimed that "the only supplies his English visitors had given him to save him from starvation was a case of Scotch whiskey, not a drop of which was left by the time we were able to get back to the depot."[80]

The depot on Danskøya had been set up after a rapid voyage from Tromsø that had been "favored by an unusually open sea."[81] As the *Ragnvald Jarl* closed on the southern tip of Spitsbergen and then made a rapid voyage along its western coastline, Wellman had been exultant, at least up until the very moment when he saw the fastness of Spitsbergen and, almost simultaneously, felt the ship rattled by its first contact with the ice. The fantasy of a simple road to the North Pole—the easy short cut that he had imagined as he reported on the Chicago fair—was about to be replaced by a reality at once more profound, more magnificent, and vastly more dangerous. "Never before, so far as we know, did one make the voyage, as we have done, absolutely without interruption by ice," Wellman wrote in his first dispatch from the Arctic:

> But it was a wild ride. We left Tromsö on Tuesday evening, May 1. Early next morning we were out of fjords to the north and in the open sea. . . . All through the voyage north from Bear Island we have been looking for ice. . . . No one could tell where the ice had gone, but the splendid fact was that it had all disappeared and we were steaming without hindrance through the very waters where we had most expected trouble and where the whale-fishers have in the past found it necessary to wait many a weary week before finding an opening.
>
> Last evening we were enough within the lee of the land, the south coast of Spitzbergen lying due east of us, to have the advantage of a sea a little less boisterous. . . . Those of us who remained up until midnight were rewarded with a glimpse of one of the distant high peaks of Spitzbergen. . . . The spectacle was really beautiful beyond the power of my poor words to describe, and in that deep-blue back-ground, so far behind so many films of various tinted clouds, the great sun was now and then to be seen flitting, in a downward course, straight for the all-snow peaks of Spitzbergen. . . . It is not easy to realize that for four months we have bid good-bye to night, and that the sun we are to have always in the heavens. . . .
>
> This morning we rose to find a bright sun, a calm sea, and Spitzbergen but a few miles on our starboard bow. . . . Nothing colder or more

forbidding than this ice-mantled region could be imagined, but to those of us who had been talking Spitzbergen, scheming Spitzbergen, dreaming Spitzbergen for many a long month, it was a land of beauty and of promise for hard but successful work to come.

We have still to meet the ice which every one [*sic*] predicted would block our way. But stay—what is that? The *Ragnvald Jarl* strikes some obstacle and shivers in every bone of her body; it is the ice at last! All rush on deck to behold, for the first time for most of us, the sea of ice. Another crash, which makes everything in the cabin of the *Jarl* rattle and shake.[82]

The following day, as the expedition sailed along Prins Karls Forland on the western coast of Spitsbergen, *Ragnvald Jarl* was less than forty nautical miles from Danskøya, where Wellman hoped to make his base camp. The ice encountered by the ship was in small masses and less than a foot in thickness. Much thicker and denser ice lay to the north, but the rapid progress from Tromsø lulled Wellman into a false sense of what a surface ship could accomplish once it rounded the northwestern corner of the archipelago.

On Sunday, May 6, the day before the *Ragnvald Jarl* reached Danskøya, divine services were held on board: "Dr. Mohun read 'The Sermon on the Mount'; Mr. Dodge led in singing 'Nearer My God to Thee,' accompanied by Mr. Franklin on the harmonica, our only musical instrument; and Professor Oyen offered prayer in Norwegian. Thus passed our first Sunday in the Arctics."[83]

Not everyone was soothed by the relatively easy passage of the Norwegian charter from Tromsø to Spitsbergen. Henry Wemyss Feilden, an experienced military officer who had served in the Black Watch in India and China, fought as a volunteer for the Confederacy during the American Civil War, and then served as a naturalist on Sir George Nares's 1875 Arctic expedition on board HMS *Alert* and afterward became a Fellow of the Royal Geographical Society, was cruising around Spitsbergen in early 1894 on board his Royal Yacht Squadron vessel *Saide*.[84] It was Feilden who had discovered the forlorn Øyen at Danskøya and reported his apparently abject condition to the press. Feilden had also spoken with the Norwegian seal and walrus hunters who operated around Spitsbergen and came away with a less than hopeful view of both the Wellman expedition and the chartered vessel that carried it northward:

The *Ragnvald Jarl* is an old schooner, fitted up with some sort of steam power, which gives her under favourable circumstances four or five knots an hour, but that she is in no way fitted for encountering the Polar ice. I was further led to believe that amongst the whole of Wellman's expedition there was no one with any practical experience or acquaintance with Polar exploration or Spitzbergen ice. . . . Wellman or those who are guiding him have no practical acquaintance with Arctic exploration, nor with the extraordinary vicissitudes inseparable from attempting to navigate Polar waters.[85]

Feilden was convinced that the amount of supplies Wellman had cached at Danskøya were unsuited to the support of an expedition that might be forced to overwinter there. Feilden recommended that Wellman's "friends" would be well advised to quickly dispatch a ship loaded with supplies to the expedition headquarters before the late summer weather closed the route down.[86]

Wellman's charter landed at a narrow, shallow harbor on the northern shore of Danskøya on Monday, May 7, 1894. Just two summers hence, the site would see the construction of Salomon Andrée's polar balloon shed. Already there existed on the remote stony shore a single hut, ready-built in mainland Norway and then moved to the island and assembled there by an English sportsman by the name of Arnold Pike. Pike had lived in the house more than five years earlier, over the winter of 1888–89, and Wellman now appropriated the house as his expedition base camp.

"We spent three days at Danes Id. [Danskøya] arranging our headquarters," Wellman wrote to a friend in Chicago.[87] This letter, combined with Wellman's annotated chart of "Spitzbergen" shows that his expedition advanced from Sørkapp (South Cape), the southern tip of Spitsbergen, all the way to the Sjuøyane (Seven Islands), at the very northern point of the archipelago, from May 3 to 12, 1894. On Danskøya, the expedition spent three days setting up the base camp and an emergency supplies depot.

On May 10, leaving Øyen and a single dog at Pike's House, Wellman and the remainder of his expedition party sailed north and east on the *Ragnvald Jarl*. Forty-eight hours later they arrived near the Sjuøyane, the northernmost collection of islands in Spitsbergen. It was another extremely fast and extremely lucky passage. "Capt. Bottolfsen," wrote Wellman, "says we might try for forty years without doing it again."[88]

At a small crescent-shaped island named Waldenøya (Walden Island), Bottolfsen moored the *Jarl* behind a projection of fast ice and there the expedition gathered itself. It was only here that Wellman sensed—perhaps for the very first time—just what he had gotten himself into. For it was not until twelve days later, on May 24, that Wellman, along with thirteen men, forty dogs, and provisions for over one hundred days, finally screwed up the courage to leave the ship and move off across the ice.

The plan, as Wellman described it, was to "make headway over the pack toward the north with sledges and our light aluminum boats."[89] Wellman was even said to have brought with him aluminum bridges that, when connected together, formed a miniature tramway over which boats, sledges, men, and dogs could pass.

Soon after leaving the *Ragnvald Jarl* at Waldenøya, Wellman saw, for the first time, the thick multiyear pack ice that guards the North Pole. After just four days in the field, the apparent impossibility of a passage over the ice came as a shock, which only intensified as a storm sprang up from the northwest, bringing the polar pack upon Waldenøya and "heaping it mountain high."[90] At the same time, on the southeastern corner of the island, as the crew drank their afternoon coffee, pack ice crushed down upon the *Ragnvald Jarl* and punched holes in its hull. Captain Bottolfsen sent out messengers to overtake Wellman, who by this point had reached Martensøya (Martens Island), fifteen nautical miles to the northeast of Waldenøya, and deliver the news.

Wellman and three others in the polar party quickly turned about and returned to Waldenøya, where they found the ship pinned against the island and half filled with water, "held up only by the ice that had pierced her; when this was withdrawn she was sure to sink to the bottom of the sea."[91] As the ship settled lower in the water, Wellman remembered his steamer trunk with his papers in it. "A hole was cut in the deck of the vessel, and a sailor dove down and brought up the mail . . . and it was dried over the oil stove that they used."[92]

Wellman does not record the name of the lucky sailor chosen for this icy assignment and, twenty years later, he remembered the incident differently in his polar and aeronautical memoir, *The Aerial Age,* implying that he was the one to dive in: "Captain Bottolfsen and some of the sailors helped me rescue the trunk, all the time protesting that the ship was likely to go to the bottom at any moment."[93] In truth, Bottolfsen had used dynamite to blow a hole in the ship's side in order to rapidly remove coal, furniture, and wood from the ship and onto the island.[94]

The expedition used timber, sailcloth, and a galley salvaged from the ship to construct a small hut on Waldenøya. The hut was designed to accommodate the crew should they be unable to retreat to Danskøya and instead find it necessary to winter on Waldenøya. The salvaged coal provided some warmth. The chartered vessel could still be seen a month later, still pinched against the ice, after which it either went to the bottom or was broken up and scattered by the ice.

Despite this disaster, Wellman decided that his polar expedition could and would continue, "though in prudence [we had] to modify the plan in important particulars."[95] These "important particulars" included the only particular that mattered: abandoning the attempt to reach the North Pole, the reason for the expedition in the first place. As would become the case during his second polar expedition, to Franz Josef Land, Wellman now sought "discoveries," the location of previously unknown or unremarked islands and capes and other geographic features that could be named for expedition patrons, in the hope that these might deflect attention from the expedition's failure to achieve anything in the way of progress toward the pole. To this end, Wellman now began a journey across the northern edge of Spitsbergen in order to answer an age-old geographic mystery in the archipelago, the location of a mythical area called "Giles Land," thought to exist somewhere to the north and east.[96]

Wellman left Captain Bottolfsen and his marooned sailors on Waldenøya and returned to his polar party on Martensøya on May 31.[97] By this time the summer sun had warmed the pack ice into a wet mass of shifting slush. After just a few days of desultory travel across the ice, Wellman abandoned the aluminum sledges in favor of the aluminum boats. In so doing, he ordered all of the dogs killed were they stood. Wellman tried to justify this atrocity because "they could not get accustomed to their strange surroundings. They were plainly homesick. . . . It was a relief when open water and the need of taking to boats made it necessary to abandon them. Instead of leaving them to starve we mercifully shot every one of them."[98]

The men managed to reach Kapp Platen, less than twenty nautical miles to the southeast. There they made camp amid massive logs of Siberian driftwood and the occasional reindeer that wandered by. Wellman was still more than 50 nautical miles from reaching the northeastern corner of

Spitsbergen and a legitimate attempt to solve the mystery of Giles Land, but after a desultory attempt to make further progress east, he appears at this point to have given it up. Wellman claimed that from Kapp Platen the men "made a desperate effort to get out upon the polar pack and start toward the Pole," but this was special pleading.[99] There was no serious effort to continue an exploration on the polar ice cap after the loss of the *Ragnvald Jarl.* Even at top speed, Wellman's sledging never amounted to much more than four miles a day, which, had they persevered that far, would have placed his party at the North Pole, and in their graves, around November 1.

Wellman later told journalists that he had then "traversed the coast of Northeast Land [Nordaustlandet], most of which was explored. Prof. O. B. French surveyed much of the coast, adding to the map Capes Gresham, Whitney, Armour, and Scott and Walsh Island."[100] Even these minor accomplishments did not stand up to close scrutiny. Whether or not these were actual newly discovered features in Nordaustlandet, none of the names have survived in the present-day geographic nomenclature of Svalbard. Worse, the unforgiveable slaughter of the dogs was a black indictment of Wellman's leadership.

Two men of Wellman's party left him on June 17 and returned to Waldenøya, reporting Wellman's lack of progress over insurmountable ice. Ten days later, Captain Bottolfsen and four other crew members, Heyerdahl, Winship, Hovde, and Wästfält, took to one of the aluminum small boats, the *Kane,* and headed south in search of relief.[101] For almost a month, from June 28 to July 22, the men struggled with extreme hardship through and across the ice, taking the overloaded *Kane,* with bare inches of freeboard showing above the waves, across Hinlopenstretet and finally reaching the huts built at Mosselbukta (Mossel Bay) in 1872 by Adolf Erik Nordenskiöld.[102] Finally at Raudfjord (Red Bay) they were able to make contact with the sealing vessel *Malygen,* captained by her owner, Bernard Pedersen, which transported the men to Danskøya where they met Øyen. Expedition member Trygve Heyerdahl remained behind on Danskøya with Øyen, while Bottolfsen and three others were delivered to Tromsø on August 1.

Still wandering the north coast of Spitsbergen, Wellman and his remaining men were soon exhausted and freezing. With their clothes and equipment soaked by slush and falls into open leads of sub-freezing water, they staggered back to Waldenøya. One of the men, the meteorology student from the Kristiania named Helge Alme, broke a bone in his foot and, with the fate of the dogs clearly in mind, began to worry that Wellman might leave him behind.[103]

Wellman and his exploring party returned to Waldenøya on August 4. From there, he and the remaining survivors of the loss of the *Ragnvald Jarl* took to the remaining small boats, the *Lockwood* and the *Parry,* and two sealing boats from *Ragnvald Jarl,* and retreated toward Lågøya (Low Island) off the northern coast of Nordaustlandet.

The same day that Wellman and his men abandoned Waldenøya and began their final retreat, his plight attracted the attention of Nordenskiöld, an international icon of polar exploration who knew the area of Wellman's operations better than perhaps any other explorer. Nordenskiöld also knew too well the fate of those caught on the northern coast of Spitsbergen, as his own expedition had been twenty years earlier. He recommended to the Royal Geographical Society that an immediate relief expedition be sent north. *The Times* agreed, writing a scathing note that it was now "too late to express any opinion upon the foolhardiness of an expedition undertaken by men who have absolutely no experience in ice navigation. . . . No doubt Wellman's countrymen will take steps without delay to prevent the possibility of a lamentable catastrophe."[104] Henry Feilden, in a letter to the *Standard,* also thought a relief expedition should be sent without delay, to which the *Standard* agreed, writing that Wellman's original programme was "hopeless," despite his "typical American grit."[105]

When Wellman and his party reached Lågøya, they met the Norwegian seal and walrus-hunting sloop *Berntine,* captained by Nils Johnsen. Wellman paid Johnsen eight hundred dollars to leave his summer grounds and return the expedition to Norway via Danskøya, where they retrieved Heyerdahl and Øyen.[106] The expedition returned to Tromsø on the evening of August 15. Five days later, still in Tromsø, Wellman was writing to his family that he had "nothing to regret save a little loss of money—all I have in the world, and more too. I came out in debt a good many thousands of dollars."[107]

After his deceptively rapid progress from Tromsø to the northern islands of Spitsbergen, Wellman had been disappointed to find nothing but "impossible ice . . . bad ice everywhere."[108] Rather than a bold attempt to reach the North Pole, as he wrote in his memoirs, Wellman confessed to his family that "To have started north over it might have ended in all our deaths," a thought that seems to have only just then occurred to Wellman. "I was tempted—much tempted—to try it, but am glad I did not.

I do not understand why the European dispatch-makers have attacked me so viciously. To tell the plain truth, I am glad they did; but I shall have some fun with one or two of them before I get through. Especially, that Col. Fielden. Wait till I get to London, and I will look him up. You were right; poor Oyen was starving to death surrounded by seven tons of provisions—better food than he ever ate in his life before! His sickness was homesickness and the medicine left for him by Fielden was whisky![109]

By early September, Wellman and his fellow Americans were in Paris and wondering what all the fuss was all about. Despite the loss of the *Ragnvald Jarl* and the massacre of every dog he had brought north to Spitsbergen from Liège, Wellman told a newspaper correspondent that all the concern over his fate "was quite unjustified, as they were never in any serious danger during the whole journey."[110]

Wellman found fault with neither his level of experience to conduct such an expedition nor with the equipment he chose to employ. All of his difficulties stemmed solely from "a sudden change for worse in the weather."[111] Now thoroughly grabbed by polar fever, Wellman even announced that he would seek the pole again the following year. Privately, he wrote to his parents and his brother: "If I were not married, should *surely* go to the Arctics again next summer. I may go, anyway, and may not. I can't tell yet. But I like it!"[112]

SIX

The Intrepid Explorer

Wellman's first Arctic experience had been disastrous, but he was far from discouraged. To the contrary, the resultant publicity from his first voyage into the ice left Wellman extremely pleased. Newspaper reports no longer referred to him as a mere journalist but as "Professor Wellman"[113]—as if he were on a par with the legitimate doctor of science Fridtjof Nansen—or "Commander Wellman . . . the intrepid explorer"[114]—as if he were the first American Arctic explorer since Edwin De Haven to hold military rank, which he was not. Other venues more accurately described him as "the famous newspaper explorer."[115] In the United States in September 1894, Wellman's dispatches from the Spitsbergen expedition were full page news. Typical was the *New York Herald*'s September 2 banner headline: "Wellman in Arctic Seas: The Daring Explorer Describes the Opening Stages of His Brilliant Dash into the Icy Regions of the North."[116]

As for the future, Wellman's dreams were undiminished. As he speculated to newspaper reporters on his future in Arctic exploration, Wellman was convinced that he could mate his belief in the power of technological progress to the search for the North Pole. "[P]ushing and pulling the heavy sledges and boats over the rough ice on this expedition," Wellman later wrote, "the idea first came to me of using an aerial craft in Arctic exploration. Often I looked up into the air and wished we had some means of travelling that royal road where there were no ice hummocks, no leads of open water, no obstacles to rapid progress."[117]

Upon his departure from Norway, Wellman had traveled to Paris. There he conferred with the French aeronauts and balloon builders Louis Godard and Edouard Surcouf and witnessed the ascents of free balloons. Wellman wrote of a plan to construct a balloon capable of lifting fifteen thousand pounds of supplies, sledges, dogs, and men. It would ascend on a favorable wind from his base camp on Danskøya, travel as far north as possible, and, if not at the pole itself, would at least deposit the crew within striking distance of another polar dash.

The money necessary to support such an expedition—Wellman estimated the cost at more than one hundred thousand dollars—was also in Paris, though Wellman missed his chance at it. An American businessman named Herman H. Kohlsaat had just sold his newspaper, the *Chicago Inter-Ocean*, and was subsequently in Paris with thousands of dollars in cash burning a hole in his pocket. As Wellman wrote, Kohlsaat "was hunting me in Paris with the intention of offering me the capital to equip another expedition!"[118] There may have been a grain of truth in this story. When Wellman returned to the Arctic four years later, Kohlsaat did in fact donate some money to the expedition, but the sum was five hundred dollars, not two hundred times that amount.[119]

From Paris, Wellman traveled to Germany, "intending to inspect a novel balloon, now being manufactured in Hanover, with a view to using it in his next polar expedition."[120] But when the balloon was not ready to fly, Wellman continued on to London and then returned home to the States.

While expressing his distrust of free balloons, Wellman nevertheless wrote in his aeronautical memoir in 1911 that only the failure to make connections with Kohlsaat in Paris had kept him from an aeronautical attempt on the North Pole in 1895. Wellman planned to return to Pike's House on Danskøya and there set up a new base camp for the expedition. He considered the site perfect for such an aeronautical expedition because it could "be reached every summer by ship from Norway, and because it is only 600 nautical or about 700 statute miles from the Pole, being, in fact, just halfway between Tromso, the smart town in northern Norway, and the Pole."[121]

But the shoreline where Arnold Pike had erected his Arctic house was destined to be named Virgohamn (Virgo Harbor) in 1896, by the polar balloon expedition of the Swedish engineer Salomon A. Andrée, an expedition delivered to the site by the ship *Virgo*. Wellman wrote that Andrée had "[taken] up the balloon idea; had a balloon built in Paris—not as large and good a one as we had planned . . . and . . . built his balloon house and established his base at the very spot . . . I had picked out."[122]

As with the missed funding from Herman Kohlsaat, there may have been some truth to this story, but after a few weeks when he watched balloons float over Paris, the idea could not have been especially appealing for Wellman. It was a theme Wellman would repeat when later he met with compatriots of Andrée who, Wellman claimed, told him that the Swede knew that the polar balloon expedition was suicidal.[123] One thing seems certain: Wellman had little desire to renew acquaintances with the polar ice cap if a way could be found to avoid it altogether.

As much as Wellman might have wished to continue his new career as a polar explorer, caution signs were all around him as he returned to a hero's reception from his fellow newspaper correspondents in the fall of 1894. And he never seems to have sought potential backers in the United States for an attempt by balloon. It seems unlikely that a journalist who made a living through his contacts and ability to convey information rapidly had suddenly found that he was incapable of making connections with wealthy sponsors. There were other reasons for his reluctance. The Spitsbergen expedition had left him heavily in debt. Also, his growing family, and particularly his wife, could not have been enthusiastic at another dangerous polar expedition. As Wellman laconically wrote, his "enthusiasm [for using a balloon to reach the pole] had cooled with reflection."[124]

It is also likely that Wellman's enthusiasm had waned because the previous mad international rush to be the first to the North Pole had suddenly stalled. He could take some comfort in the fact that all of the supposed "professional" explorers who attempted to explore the polar regions in 1894 had failed badly. Frederick Cook, leading a small expedition that included a young architecture student from the Massachusetts Institute of Technology named Russell Porter, reached the northwestern coast of Greenland where the expedition ship *Miranda* was wrecked and the men had to be rescued. Robert Peary's attempt to return to the northeast coast of Greenland was stopped by storms and dissension in his ranks.

When a relief ship arrived at Peary's camp, the naval engineer allowed only two expedition members to remain with him. All of the rest he sent away. These included an American meteorologist named Evelyn Briggs

Baldwin and the Norwegian athlete Eivind Astrup. Fearing that the dismissed men might let slip the expedition's myriad problems that stemmed from his obtuse leadership, Peary forestalled such criticism by speeding a dispatch ahead of them. This note cast aspersions on the toughness of the men he had discarded.[125] So it was small wonder when, within two weeks of arriving in the United States, Astrup was laying plans for a polar expedition of his own.[126]

By the time he had returned to his native Norway, Astrup had gone even further, telling his side of the Peary story to the Norwegian newspaper *Morgenbladet.* Astrup reported that members of the expedition had been made sick by, among other things, being forced to eat decade-old pemmican originally cooked for the Greely expedition.[127] Such a notion might be forgiven on an extreme expedition, save that Astrup also claimed that the men were food poisoned while Peary and his wife Josephine segregated themselves from the rest of the expedition and ate all of the best stocks of supplies.[128] As Wellman looked for balm to soothe his own shortcomings, these failures demonstrated that 1894 had been an "extremely unfavorable season" for Arctic exploration.[129]

When Wellman arrived back at his home in Washington, D.C., on September 28, he was asked about the reported dissension in Peary's expedition. Wellman dismissed such notions as little more than "what we call 'kicking' incidental to such an expedition. . . . Men must expect hardships when they undertake such work."[130] A week later, Wellman accompanied his wife Laura to Canton, Ohio, where he told reporters that his Arctic experience had so invigorated him that he felt as if ten years had been added to his life. Accordingly, from Ohio he was traveling to Chicago to consult with the owners of the *Herald,* in order to "arrange for another trip."[131]

In November, Wellman even corresponded with Evelyn Briggs Baldwin, now home from his service as Peary's meteorologist in Greenland and still smarting from the humiliation inflicted on the members of the expedition after Peary had them sent away in August. Like Eivind Astrup, Baldwin was now casting about for the means to launch an expedition of his own. Wellman wrote that he was glad to hear that Baldwin "was still of the Arctic mind. So am I. But I have found it necessary to defer my next trip until 1896, as it was impossible to get ready to go next spring."[132]

Despite this demurral to Baldwin, less than a month later newspaper stories continued to suggest that Wellman would head north again in 1895.

One reporter quoted Wellman to say that once Congress had adjourned, he would travel to Norway and scout the landscape for another attempt on the North Pole. Just six months previous, his first Arctic ship had been crushed and he had massacred all of his Belgian dogs, yet now Wellman claimed that "There is scarcely any danger involved in such an expedition. A summer in the arctics [*sic*] is really a pleasant experience. There is no physical discomfort because of the temperature. Nothing comparable to the sufferings endured by those who spend the winter in the blizzard-swept prairies of the Northwest."[133]

In any event, 1895—and the dramatic presidential election year of 1896 that followed—found Wellman tied to his newspaper correspondent's desk in Washington, D.C. The newspaper business reflected the uncertain political scene, as indeed it did the nation and society at large. In early March, Wellman's newspaper, the *Chicago Herald,* merged with the *Chicago Times* to form the *Chicago Times-Herald.* As a result, Wellman was returned to writing banal political profiles in the capital. Some of these were routine piffle—U.S. representative Michael McEttrick was "the strongest man in congress."[134] But others almost seemed designed to butter up potentially useful future patrons of exploration, like Secretary of State Richard Olney, the man "who prepared practically all of the case in favor of the Monroe doctrine and against Great Britain."[135]

As for the search for the North Pole, it had assumed a temporary stasis. Nansen and *Fram* remained out of contact with the world, presumably—despite the rumors to the contrary—still adrift somewhere in the polar basin, while Peary's renewed attempt to explore northeast across northern Greenland had ended once again in failure. At the same time, with the deepening economic depression of the mid-1890s, potential sponsors for a new polar expedition had become few and far between.

Brief reminders of Wellman's polar ambitions floated in and out of the press in 1895, just enough to prick and tease an ambitious man on the make. A desultory notice appeared in October 1895 of an official U.S. Navy investigation into the aluminum small boats that had survived from Wellman's 1894 debacle. These tests "showed that the material had so deteriorated that it could be easily crumbled in one's hand."[136]

By the late summer of 1896, just as the race to the North Pole once again began to simmer, Wellman found himself pulled in several different directions. He was now at the top of the national newspaper profession and in some quarters was even described as the "greatest newspaper correspondent in America."[137] Amid the dramatic 1896 election between the firebrand Midwestern progressive William Jennings Bryan—to this day the youngest candidate for the presidency of the United States—and the eventual victor, the stolid William McKinley of Wellman's home state of Ohio—Wellman's prepossessed dispatches confidently predicted victory for McKinley.

As Wellman approached middle age, even such heady newspaper fame paled next to his polar ambitions. And those already innervated dreams received a massive jolt in the early morning of August 13, 1896, the moment when electric news coming from the north coast of Spitsbergen permanently supercharged the entire atmosphere of polar exploration. After three years, *Fram* had emerged from the polar basin—minus Fridtjof Nansen, who had left the ship a year and a half earlier in an attempt to dash across the ice and claim the North Pole for Norway.

With appropriate irony, as the expedition emerged from the ice, the first ship seen by *Fram's* Captain Otto Sverdrup was the *Søstrene,* a sealer out of Tromsø skippered by Sivert Bottolfsen, the brother of Johannes, Wellman's erstwhile captain from *Ragnvald Jarl.* Sivert Bottolfsen not only jumped from his own vessel in order to join *Fram's* triumphant return to mainland Norway, but he also alerted Sverdrup to the Swedish expedition then encamped at Virgohamn on Danskøya and about to launch three men in a hydrogen balloon toward the North Pole.

This was something Sverdrup had to see for himself. After so much time locked in the ice, the Norwegian crew of *Fram* was understandably skeptical that a Swedish balloon team proposed to cover in thirty days the distance they themselves had drifted in three and a half years. Sverdrup immediately turned *Fram* about and dropped anchor at Virgohamn both to see the balloon and to learn if its captain, a Swedish engineer by the name of Salomon August Andrée, knew anything about the whereabouts of Nansen.[138] When Andrée could offer no news of the *Fram* expedition's leader, Sverdrup hurried south to Tromsø.

SEVEN

Nansen Is Getting Rich

When an aging Benjamin Leigh Smith challenged his fellow English-men to take up the polar exploration work he himself had begun in Franz Josef Land, his call was answered by a Warwickshireman named Frederick G. Jackson, veteran of a long expedition across northwestern Siberia in 1893. The resulting Jackson-Harmsworth Expedition of 1894–97 was financed by Alfred C. Harmsworth, a pioneer in tabloid journalism who founded the *Daily Mail* in 1896 and, like several other newspaper publishers in the nineteenth century, saw polar exploration as one of many ways to lure readers and the advertisers that followed them.

Jackson reached Franz Josef Land in late August 1894, the same month Walter Wellman retreated from his inaugural expedition to Spitsbergen. Jackson set up his field headquarters at Cape Flora, hard by the site of the stone hut constructed in 1881 by Leigh Smith and his stranded crew from the wreck of the research vessel *Eira*. During the summers of 1895 through 1897, Jackson's wide explorations by sledge and boat led him to the conclusion that Franz Josef Land was not a great Arctic subcontinent but rather a loose collection of islets and small to moderate-sized islands. Along with the results of Nansen's *Fram* expedition, it was now clear that the archipelago did not reach higher than 82° North and almost certainly was not the land bridge to the North Pole that many had believed after Julius Payer reported his visit to Cape Fligely on Rudolf Land in 1874.

Jackson's expedition did much to answer many questions that remained of the geography of Franz Josef Land, but it is best remembered today for its unexpected and dramatic rendezvous with Nansen and the introduction of the use of horses in polar exploration. After *Fram* had sailed into the frozen ocean near the New Siberian Islands in 1893 and become locked in the polar ice, it began to drift across the North Polar Basin, just as Nansen had predicted it would. It eventually became clear, however, that the trajectory of the ship would not take it close to the North Pole. So Nansen and Hjalmar Johansen had left the ship on March 14, 1895, and within a month were closer to the North Pole than anyone before them.

Nansen had also lost track of his time, which in a featureless polar waste meant that he could not be certain exactly where he was. As Roland Huntford writes, Nansen "was thrown on his own resources in a way we, with instant communications and satellite navigation, are increasingly unable to comprehend. He did not have the view from space which has given us a picture of reality. His view was bounded by the horizon; exactly like that of the earliest men."[139] Nansen knew that he and Johansen were somewhere north of Payer's Kaiser Franz Josef Land, so the two began a long retreat southwestward in the general direction of that land. They reached the northern islands of what they assumed was Franz Josef Land in the late summer of 1895. On an island Nansen would later name for Frederick Jackson, the two men built a crude improvised stone hut dug out of a raised shoreline and spent the winter of 1895–96 uncomfortably tucked into it.

The following spring, in the conclusion of one of the great epics of human survival, Nansen and Johansen continued their voyage south. By mid-June, still unsure of his precise location, Nansen believed they were possibly close to Leigh Smith's old hut at Cape Flora. When Nansen made a short reconnaissance on June 17, he heard the bark of dogs in the distance. They had reached Jackson's camp. Starved for conversation with someone other than Johansen, Nansen and Jackson stayed up for forty-eight hours talking while awaiting Jackson's relief ship to return them to Norway.

Fram meanwhile had continued its drift across the polar pack, finally emerging off northern Spitsbergen on August 13. Sverdrup dropped anchor at Virgohamn on Danskøya the next day, there to be welcomed by Salomon Andrée. After Jackson's relief ship *Windward* delivered Nansen and Johansen to Vardø in northern Norway, the two men caught up with Sverdrup and *Fram* in Tromsø on August 21.

By now, Nansen had heard that Peary's latest expedition in Greenland had accomplished nothing. Three days later, Andrée arrived in Tromsø with the news that adverse winds had prevented any launch of the Swedish balloon. Even though Andrée promised to try again the following year, the practical result of the failures of both Peary and Andrée was that Fridtjof Nansen was now the undisputed dean of polar exploration. Nansen and his reunited crew on board *Fram* made their triumphant way south along the coast of Norway to a delirious national welcome in the fjord at Kristiania.

For Walter Wellman, still stuck in the United States to cover a political campaign, the news from the Arctic must have come as a fresh breeze. All of the contenders for the prize of the North Pole, Nansen included, had fallen short of the mark. This rapid succession of events—the continued futility of Peary in Greenland, the dramatic return of *Fram* in August 1896 followed soon after by the reappearance of Nansen himself, and Andrée's promise to try another launch of his polar balloon in 1897—all would come to influence Wellman's choice of a route for a renewed attempt on the North Pole.

If Wellman could breathe a bit easier in the knowledge that no one had yet reached the North Pole, there was still no time to lose if he hoped to be the first. The transcendent welcome for Nansen—and the burgeoning global fame that followed it—all but guaranteed that others would take to the field, in the hope of grabbing the pole itself and, along with it, a large slice of Nansen's glory. Peary might have returned in failure, grumbling that he was too old for another polar expedition and that the only way he would ever see the North Pole was if someone brought it to his home in Maine.[140] But Jackson's British expedition was still in Franz Josef Land and Andrée's Swedish balloon—if it could be successfully launched from Danskøya in the summer of 1897—was a wildcard that could theoretically span the distance from Virgohamn to the North Pole in mere hours instead of months or years.

To hurry Wellman's preparations, in December 1896 still more rivals appeared on the scene. A brief note from Paris announced that the French aeronauts Godard and Surcouf would organize their own balloon expedition to the North Pole. Moreover, to distance themselves from Andrée's failure to launch in 1896, the pair stated that the idea for such an expedition had been suggested to them three years earlier, by none other than the American journalist Walter Wellman.[141] Details of the proposed French aeronautical expedition arrived in the United States soon after New Year's Day 1897:

M. Andrée's unsuccessful attempt, far from frightening our aeronauts, has but served to stimulate their zeal, and two among them whose names alone are a guarantee of victory—Louis Godard and Edouard Surcouf—are preparing to go and pluck for France the palm reserved for the hardy ones who first climb the Pole.

Their project is not one of yesterday. It was conceived in 1893.

The following year the idea budded in the brain of Wellmann [*sic*], the American, an intrepid explorer who had already made two [*sic*] attempts, one by water and one by land. He, finding himself face to face with insurmountable difficulties, conceived the idea of overcoming them by means of a balloon. Wellmann wrote to MM. Godard and Surcouf asking for plans and drawings, but determined to wait until after the Andree expedition, which was started just about that time, and therefore countermanded his order.

It is this plan, carefully revised and thought out by Godard and Surcouf, which is about to be put into execution now. The balloon which they purpose to use will be called *La France*.[142]

Throughout the spring and summer of 1897, reports of the fantastic sums advanced to Nansen for his account of the *Fram* expedition only increased Wellman's ardor to head north again. His desire to put some distance between himself and Washington, D.C., was no doubt intensified by romantic troubles, entangled as he was in an affair with a young woman named "Miss Willard," an assignation that soon led to an illegitimate daughter.[143]

At the same time, by mid-summer of 1897, Wellman's journalism had begun to parallel and in fact promote the headlong American rush onto the world stage, as he proselytized for the annexation of the Republic of Hawaii[144] and sent up unmistakable trial balloons for the McKinley White House over a potential American intervention in the War of Cuban Independence:

Cuba is to be a dependency of the United States. . . .

It is a determination to annex both Hawaii and Cuba, to strengthen our strategic outposts, to go out to sea for an extension of our jurisdiction, our commerce, our empire.

This policy has not yet been disclosed. It will not be disclosed till the auspicious moment arrives. That it now exists may even be denied.

But the events of the coming six months will amply justify the statements made in this dispatch.

The United States has asserted and is prepared to maintain the Monroe doctrine. This doctrine is nothing more nor less than a declaration that the magnitude, might, position and interest of our Nation in the western world make it the standard of reference of all questions pertaining to redistribution of territory affecting the balance of power in the Americas. . . .

In administration circles I find a conviction that intervention is well nigh inevitable, that the revolution will be a peaceful one and that it can result in nothing but virtual annexation either under the territorial system—a local self-government presided over by a Governor appointed by the President—or a nominal Cuban independence under the protection of the United States. In either case the ruling power in the island will have to be American.[145]

Such breathless propaganda might seem a bit too zealous to be true, but it was not. And it goes a long way to understanding the origin of many of the names that appeared on Wellman's list of patrons of his 1898–99 expedition to Franz Josef Land. The roster is not a modest one, and includes many of the men directly responsible for the rise of the American empire: President McKinley, Vice President Garret Hobart, J. Pierpont Morgan, and William K. Vanderbilt, as well as several other Washington, D.C., Wall Street, and Chicago banking and media tycoons.[146]

With his professional stock at a career high and a personal *cherchez la femme* well hidden behind the scenes, Wellman left Washington with his wife, Laura, in the summer of 1897 for a trip to England, Norway, and Russia. With the United States broadly extending its influence around the western hemisphere, if Wellman could claim the North Pole, he would crown an era of American expansion and put himself in the front rank of explorers right alongside Nansen.

All of these fervent hopes were contingent, of course, upon Andrée failing in his balloon expedition. This remarkable Swedish enterprise had finally lifted off from Danskøya on July 11, 1897. Two brief, tantalizing messages, sent by carrier pigeon from the basket of the balloon, showed the expedition blazing north over the ice. Then, just as suddenly, the messages ceased and Andrée and his two companions vanished into the polar mist.

For Wellman, the silence from Andrée's balloon expedition was the equivalent of a green light to his own ambitions. He confided to his trusted brother Arthur on July 10, 1897, that he expected to be in Europe for upward of two months, after which he would have a big announcement to make:

> I go to make arrangements for another Arctic venture. . . . Mr. Kohlsaat is very much interested in it, and will do everything he can. He promises to help me raise the money, and I think I shall be able to raise a fund ample for my needs. . . .
>
> You will notice that I am to be out one winter. Unless Andree spoils the game with his balloon plan, or something else occurs, I think I shall be in the fight again.[147]

In England in mid-August, Wellman got into an argument with four Englishmen in a London club. The British complained about the vulgarity of American newspapers, to which Wellman responded by saying that the British newspaper currently achieving the greatest gains was Harmsworth's *Daily Mail,* whose genesis was a stay of several months in the United States, "studying our cheap newspapers. He returned to London and started *The Mail.*"[148] When the men challenged Wellman on whether the United States planned to annex the Republic of Hawaii, Wellman responded bluntly: "Of course we are." Pressed further on Cuba—and even if the United States had designs on Bermuda and the Bahamas—Wellman was equally direct:

> Never fear. We shall not walk on your toes. We do not want the Bermudas or the Bahamas. But it is a strange thing that you English prick up your ears at the first suggestion that the United States is going to annex an island. For many years you have been roaming around the world, gobbling up all the inhabited and uninhabited lands you could get your clutches on, until you make your jubilee boasts of the extent of your possessions, and just as soon as a little dot of an island down in the Pacific asks us to take her in that she may be saved from Asiatic domination you lift your hands in horror at the greediness of these Yankees.[149]

On August 23, Wellman arrived in Norway, where he sought to hitch himself directly to Nansen's brilliant star. Wellman hurried to Polhøgda (the

Polar Heights), Nansen's "beautiful home . . . overlooking that matchless sheet of water, the Kristiania fiord,"[150] where he went into a "a long conference" with Nansen "to discuss a projected polar expedition."[151]

The Norwegian press soon revealed details of Wellman's plan, one heavily influenced by Nansen's experiences. Since Nansen had returned through the islands of Franz Josef Land, Wellman conceived of a similar "polar dash" using the same islands as his starting point. Wellman would hire a Norwegian Arctic sealing vessel and, along with eleven other participants, occupy Frederick Jackson's recently abandoned base camp at Cape Flora on Northbrook Island, and then try the following spring to reach the pole from Cape Fligely on Rudolf Land.[152] This was the first public notice of Wellman's intent to start again for the North Pole, and this meeting with Nansen, combined with the return of Frederick Jackson to England from Franz Josef Land in early September, decided Wellman on his course of action.

Jackson had remained in Franz Josef Land for another year after his own dramatic meeting with Nansen, before he also retreated. Jackson had led a largely successful geographic reconnaissance of the western reaches of the archipelago but had not made any progress toward the North Pole itself. He had also left behind a wealth of supplies and the infrastructure of his base camp at Cape Flora. These he intended for the use of expeditions shipwrecked in the area—as his inspiration Benjamin Leigh Smith had been in 1881 (or "balloon-wrecked," as Andrée might now be after his disappearance in July). To Wellman, Jackson's ready cache of supplies was one he could not ignore and, with his newspaper contacts with Jackson's sponsor Lord Harmsworth, could gain immediate access to.

Wellman met Nansen again, this time in Washington, D.C., in December 1897. Nansen was in the middle of a grueling lecture tour of the United States that did nothing to improve his opinion of Americans, whom he came to see as a "blinkered and short-sighted breed."[153] The titanic energy unleashed by a burgeoning Gilded Age society had left Nansen entirely unimpressed. As Roland Huntford writes, Nansen "scorned what he saw as American materialism, commercialism and absence of culture."[154] Nansen's *fin de siècle* mood was hardly improved by the small size of the crowd that came to hear his Washington lecture.

While the interminable lecture tour further depressed a Nansen already morose from his post-expedition let-down, Wellman to the contrary saw in Fridtjof Nansen everything he wished to become: internationally famous,

newly and almost obscenely wealthy, and the very model of the modern scientific explorer and multilingual media star. The title of the article Wellman
wrote to describe Nansen's Washington, D.C. lecture said it all:

NANSEN IS GETTING RICH

"Altogether Dr. Nansen must have earned $40,000 or $50,000 in the six
or seven weeks he has been in America," Wellman wrote, with scarcely
disguised avarice over what would be well over one million dollars in 2013
money.

> Some day a lucky explorer will go nearer the pole than Nansen did,
> or even succeed in reaching that spot which for three centuries has
> been the charm of arctic venturers, and then Nansen will have to take
> a back seat.
>
> I am told on pretty good authority that since his return from the
> arctic regions, a little more than a year ago, Dr. Nansen has earned
> about $300,000. This makes him a rich man in Norway, where large
> fortunes are rarely met with, and where the tastes of the people are
> exceedingly simple. To begin with, his book brought him $50,000 in
> cash for the English language alone. Besides this the royalties have
> been large. . . . His lectures in England were enormously profitable
> [where he] made money most rapidly, doing even better there than he
> has done in the United States.[155]

To see the giant blonde Norwegian on stage and witness firsthand the
riches and fame that resulted from Nansen's Arctic triumph was too much.
Wellman made his move. On the very same day that he listened to Nansen's
lecture, press reports announced that Wellman had bought a 153-ton sealer
at Tromsø named, with appropriate irony, the *Laura,* "for the expedition
which he will lead to Franz Josef Land in June next."[156] A quick strike across
the polar pack in the spring of 1899 would put Wellman at the North Pole
and place Nansen-like fame and fortune in his pocket barely six months
after his fortieth birthday.

EIGHT

My Plan Is Very Simple

The details of Wellman's renewed attack on the North Pole, common knowledge in Norway since late summer, emerged in the United States only on New Year's Day 1898. Taking advantage of Fridtjof Nansen's new status as the arbiter of all things polar, the press reported that Wellman had "just returned from Europe, and held a long conference with Nansen concerning his plan, which Nansen approved with warm terms."[157] Wellman would establish a base camp in the summer of 1898 at Cape Flora on Northbrook Island and planned to augment his supplies with all of those left behind at the cape by Frederick Jackson. In the autumn, a small team would be sent to establish an advance encampment two or even three degrees further north.

Wellman and his men would winter over at the advance camp, only seven or eight degrees from the North Pole. As soon as enough daylight returned in February to allow the men to travel, they would start for the pole with sixty or seventy dogs pulling a few sledges. In this way, Wellman would have favorable conditions to make a "dash" of some one hundred days to the North Pole and back. There would be a small measure of ancillary scientific research, in order to adhere to the forms of a modern polar expedition. But this was mere cover for the main chance. As Wellman wrote: "My plan is very simple . . . [since] all attempts to reach the North Pole now-a-days are dashes.

Dr. Nansen made his dash from the *Fram*. Lieut. Peary proposes to make a dash from the north of Greenland. Dr. Nansen believes, if he had had a base of supplies to fall back upon and a large number of dogs, he could have reached the pole. He says it can be done in the way I propose, and I am naturally eager to have a try at it, and, if possible, to plant the American flag at the spot where there is no other direction than south.[158]

A few weeks later, press reports indicated that Wellman's expedition would be a small one, with no more than ten men who—an almost certain reflection of his "long conference" with Nansen—would be Norwegians.[159]

Two months later, a further rationale emerged for the expedition, as Wellman sent word via the U.S. State Department to the United Kingdoms of Sweden and Norway that he was willing to carry a Swedish party on board his expedition ship to enable them to search Franz Josef Land for the missing polar balloonist Salomon Andrée and his two companions. Reviewing the few messages that had been recovered from carrier pigeons that Andrée had dispatched from his balloon, Wellman was convinced that the aerial expedition had most likely been swept toward Franz Josef Land and, if that were the case, then Andrée and his companions would have made for the supply caches at Cape Flora. The Swedish government did not plan any search for their missing countrymen, "but if no news of Andrée is received by July gratitude would be felt if Mr. Wellman were to permit several persons familiar with the arctic regions to accompany his expedition for that purpose. The Government of the King has learned with deep gratitude of the courteous and generous offer made by Mr. Wellman."[160]

These foreign expressions of gratitude no doubt also reflected the nascent wisdom of governments to find themselves on the correct side of the United States of America. The accidental explosion of the armored cruiser USS *Maine* in Havana Harbor on February 15, 1898, had been used to start a drumbeat for a war against an elderly Spanish Empire. Once the war hawks in Congress and the Yellow Press persuaded President McKinley to support such a war, the U.S. Navy comprehensively destroyed Spanish squadrons in Manila Bay on May 1 and again off Santiago, Cuba, on July 3.

In less than six months, the formerly insular United States was elevated to the status of a world power.

During William McKinley's five years in the office before his assassination,

American exports doubled and the war with Spain provided new overseas territories in Puerto Rico, Guam, and the Philippines, all virtually simultaneous with the annexation of Hawaii. At the center of all of this, as Kevin Phillips writes, was McKinley, the "hinge president—the prime decision maker during America's rise to world power."[161] It was this pivotal figure in the ascendancy of the United States to global power who would soon be memorialized by Wellman's expedition to one of the remotest corners of the planet.

Wellman's long work in Washington and his profiles of the political and financial figures of the Gilded Age now paid their dividends and sent him on his way to Franz Josef Land. By May, Wellman had raised nearly $13,000 for expedition, with $1,000 contributions from financier J. Pierpont Morgan, railroad heir William K. Vanderbilt, and John Milton Hay, who was then U.S. ambassador to the United Kingdom and soon would be named secretary of state. Hay also loaned Wellman a further $740. Contributions of $500 apiece came from Wellman's Chicago newspaper contact Herman H. Kohlsaat, banker and president of the American Museum of Natural History Morris Ketchum Jesup, and Senator Marcus A. Hanna from Ohio. Smaller contributions arrived from the president and vice president of the United States themselves, as well as from a host of U.S. senators and cabinet secretaries.[162] The National Geographic Society, less than ten years into its existence as a Washington, D.C., institution where wealthy patrons could mingle with explorers, formed a scientific committee to assist Wellman's planning and one of the society's founders, James H. Gore, was tapped to accompany the expedition.

Even with such generosity on the part of his rich and famous contacts, Wellman still faced a shortfall of $6,000, money he was forced to put into the expedition himself and which he could only hope to recoup if the voyage produced significant results. He was well and truly out on a limb. His correspondence to his brother Arthur, one of the agents charged with sorting his tangled finances in the United States, indicate something of his recklessness and muddled thinking as he departed for Norway and then Franz Josef Land.

I have put in nearly $6,000. I owe Ambassador Hay $740. I want him paid out of my estate if anything happens. If Mr. Eckels [James Eckels of Commercial National Bank of Chicago, another individual acting on Wellman's behalf] got $500 from H. W. Leman, Chicago, that is

a loan & should be repaid. All the remainder are subscriptions to the
fund, save that I have promised bear-skin rugs to Messrs. Vilas, Tree,
Gorman, Hobart, Lamont, Brice, Frick, Fairbanks.

A few bills are unpaid—$60 Kalamazoo Canvas Boat Co.; $600 the
Bovril Co., London; $40 Knorr, Heilbronn, Germany; $30 A Garstin,
London, & about $75 Military Stores & Equipment Co., London, or
only $800 in all. No hurry about these. They can wait till I get back.

The outfitting has cost more money than I thought it would, &
I have just about enough to get away with, after settling my dog
account.[163]

Wellman had other, more personally distressing events on his mind. As
he wrote to his brother, when he arrived in Norway he found no letters from
his children awaiting him, and his wife Laura could barely bring herself to
write to him. "It was too bad, because this letter from Laura is the only one
save the first one of reproach she has sent me, so far as I know, & I did want
to know that she had forgiven me—if she has—before starting away for
more than a year."[164] It seems clear enough that this silent treatment from
his wife and daughters was caused not only by his looming absence. Wellman's affair had been discovered, and thereafter the relationship between
the journalist and his wife entered an area of permanent storms. One of
Wellman's companions in Franz Josef Land even wrote that Wellman was
treated by the expedition doctor for an injury to his left ear that had been
caused by a "*love tap* from Mrs. Wellman," one she had delivered some three
or four years earlier and that now flared up at the worst possible moment.[165]
It was an inauspicious way to begin an endeavor across polar ice that might
last for a year or more.

Still, with all the skill of a hustling newspaper correspondent, Wellman
kept both his personal and professional troubles largely segregated from the
men he chose to accompany him. As his second-in-command, Wellman
had picked Evelyn Briggs Baldwin, who now worked for the U.S. Weather
Service, and Baldwin dutifully embarked on a lecture tour to try to raise
further funds. Baldwin was in Sapulpa, Oklahoma, in late April, to lecture
in what was then known as Indian Territory, when a tornado struck the
town and the lecture cut short so that everyone in the hall could "betake
themselves to the cyclone cellars with which the town is well-provided,"
and there to hide for the night.[166] From Indian Territory, Baldwin headed

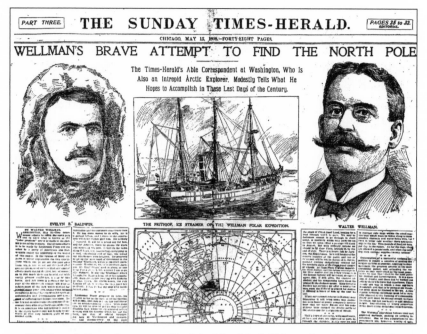

"Wellman's Brave Attempt to Find the North Pole." From the *Chicago Sunday Times-Herald*, May 15, 1898, in Evelyn B. Baldwin's scrapbooks, Western Historical Manuscript Collection, University of Missouri at Columbia.

first for Chicago, and then on May 23 to New York to catch a steamship that would take him to Norway and a rendezvous with Wellman and the remainder of the expedition team in Tromsø.

Wellman and Baldwin were accompanied by three other Americans: Quirof Harlan of the U.S. Coast and Geodetic Survey, a doctor and zoologist from Michigan named Edward Hofma, and the aforementioned professor of mathematics and geodesy at the Columbian University (now George Washington University) named James Howard Gore. Gore was not only a respected member of the faculty at Columbian University, but one of the thirty-three original founders of the National Geographic Society in 1888.

In Norway, the Americans would be joined by five Norwegians: Paul Bjørvig and Emil Ellefsen—both of whom had been with Wellman during the 1894 fiasco on the northern coast of Spitsbergen—along with Emil's brother Olaf, as well as Daniel Johansen and Bernt Bentsen. The Ellefsen brothers were from Hammerfest, while Bjørvig, Bentsen, and Johansen were Tromsø men. Bentsen possessed more Arctic experience than all the Americans combined, from three years spent on board *Fram* with Nansen, while Bjørvig had long experience as an Arctic hunter in Spitsbergen.

Wellman saved money by paying no salary to any of the other Americans. As Wellman wrote to his brother, each had signed onto the expedition in the hope to receive "a share of the *profits*. There is a contract with Dr. Hofma, too, but he gets no share of the profits, unless I choose to give him something."[167] The Norwegians were all on salary, each man to receive 100 kroner, or $27, per month (Kr 6,250 in 2013, about $1,000), with half of this amount paid directly to the men's families while they were away. The one exception was Paul Bjørvig, who received 270 kroner, or $72.90 per month (Kr 17,200 in 2013, about $2,800). Despite his claims that an Arctic expedition posed no dangers whatsoever, the Norwegians were signed on for what Wellman promised would be a "very troublesome" journey.[168]

To Wellman, the actual care of the Norwegians' families was "a small matter." He had asked Kohlsaat to turn over $25 a week to the banker Eckels for this purpose, the money finding its way to Tromsø where it could be distributed by Consul Andreas Aagaard, Wellman's agent in Norway. While describing this to his brother as "*a debt of honor* & must be met. The families of the men depend upon it for their living," Wellman was not especially anxious over it. "I hope after two or three months you will see Mr. Eckels & learn if it is being attended to. It must be in some way or other. The money I still have with Mr. Aagaard will pay it for three months & then it must come from America."[169] This casual concern for his men strikes one as both shortsighted and even cruel. The very success of the expedition rested on his Norwegian crew. To leave in the air such a critical matter as the pay of his men was another sign of Wellman's carelessness in the planning of such a complex and risky operation.

WELLMAN'S CHOICE of the European Arctic archipelagoes of Spitsbergen and Franz Josef Land as the staging points for his polar expeditions was no accident. From the contacts he had made at the Chicago fair, he knew that sites in Norway provided the kinds of rapid international communications junctions unavailable in Robert Peary's patch in Greenland. Then, too, with his sense of racial and cultural superiority, Wellman considered that Norwegians made for superior assistants when compared to the heathen Greenlanders employed by Peary. Moreover, unlike the irrepressible Frederick Cook, Wellman was not about to challenge Peary for native labor in northern Greenland.

A passage from Evelyn Briggs Baldwin's Franz Josef Land diary further illustrates the ethnocentric thinking that placed Americans at the forefront of exploration and ranked other groups according to their perceived abilities to speed the Americans on their way. "Mr. Wellman had said that Norwegians were better than Eskimos to assist in the work and therefore the Expedition had come to Franz-Josef Land. That while Peary is trying to march northward along the west coast of Greenland, [we had] five Norwegians, upon whose efforts we depended for success."[170]

There was also the very special extra offered by staging an Arctic expedition from either Spitsbergen or Franz Josef Land: the chance to make instant front-page news by discovering the whereabouts of the lost Swedish polar balloon expedition. "While taking observations [in Franz Josef Land], we shall try to hunt up Andree," Wellman told the press. "If he is alive, I believe he is near there."[171]

More than most, Wellman was acutely aware of the enormous publicity that would attach to the expedition that located the missing Swedes. With the spectacular (and globally newsworthy) meeting of Nansen and Jackson two years earlier fresh in everyone's mind, Wellman could repeat such publicity for his own benefit, and Nansen himself had shown Wellman just how rich those benefits could be. Even if every other aspect of his second polar expedition failed, if he succeeded in finding Andrée, he would enter the histories of both exploration and journalism on a par with Henry Morton Stanley and Stanley's famous 1871 trek to find and meet David Livingstone at Lake Tanganyika. "Andrée's balloon was drifting [toward Franz Josef Land] from Spitsbergen," Wellman wrote, "and as he knew of the existence at [Cape Flora] of a good house amply stocked with provisions, it was not impossible he had been able to make his way hither the previous autumn."[172]

By the time Wellman reached Tromsø, the poor state of the expedition's finances had changed the planned purchase of the sealer *Laura,* which in any case turned out to be too small, to the more economical charter of a larger ice-steamer named *Frithjof,* with Captain Johan Kjeldsen at the helm. It was an irony that reflected both the personal chasm between himself and his wife as well as his reliance on both the advice and the model of Nansen.

Wellman liked the ship, save for the fact that "she does not steam as fast as she was said to do by three knots."[173] Armed with the lessons of the disaster at Waldenøya in 1894, Wellman did not attempt to sail for Franz Josef Land from the northern Norwegian port of Tromsø until late June. *Frithjof* finally weighed anchor and departed the fjord roadstead on June 26, 1898.

From Tromsø, *Frithjof* stopped for the night "at the whale station of Consul Giaver, owner of the ship, where we had a big farewell dinner."[174] Two days later *Frithjof* arrived at the extreme northeastern Norwegian port of Vardø, where Wellman was entertained on the Arctic steam-yacht *Blencathra,* then owned by Andrew Coats, "the wealthy Scotch thread maker."[175] Even in an impossibly remote outport like Vardø, Wellman's nose for millionaires did not fail him. *Blencathra* had departed Scotland on the first of May for a summer of Arctic birding and geologizing with a small team of scientists that included William Spiers Bruce, who would go on to lead the Scottish National Antarctic Expedition. After stops in the northern Norwegian ports of Tromsø, Hammerfest, and Honningsvåg, the expedition reached the Russian island of Kolguev. After an exploration northward along the coast of Novaya Zemlya, *Blencathra* returned for a rest and refit in Vardø on June 25 and remained for a week, there to meet with Wellman's outbound expedition.

Wellman wrote to his brother that Coats was now going to try and reach Franz Josef Land with *Blencathra,* a perfectly dangerous and esoteric summer jaunt for energetic *fin de siècle* wealth.[176] The visit to *Blencathra* must have jogged another of Wellman's misplaced administrative calculations. As if he suddenly realized that he had a rather important dilemma on his hands, Wellman blithely wrote to his brother Arthur that he had "made no arrangements for a ship to come after us next year, because I do not think it necessary.

> There is almost sure to be a steamer or two or three up after walrus or for other purposes. All this I have left in the hands of Consul Aagaard, a safe & responsible man. If it is *necessary* to hire a ship he will ask my friends in America for the money, & they will simply have to raise it. But it will not be necessary, in my judgment; & if it is the amount will not be large. In October you might write to Consul Aagaard, Tromso, for information as to the outlook. I have written Eckels, Kohlsaat & others as to this feature of the situation.[177]

After telling his brother to worry, Wellman then added: "Do not worry about it, as there is no fear but it will come out all right."[178]

From Vardø, *Frithjof* made for the northwestern Russian port of Archangel, on the eastern side of the White Sea. There the expedition took on board eighty-three dogs that had been driven in a large pack from from the Ostiak tribe and delivered by Alexander I. Trontheim. Trontheim had delivered Siberian Samoyed dogs to Nansen in 1893 and a year later would deliver dogs for the Franz Josef Land expedition of the Duke of the Abruzzi.

From Archangel, Evelyn Baldwin wrote a rapturous letter to Wellman's brother Arthur. "I am highly pleased with the expedition in every way. Your brother is a success," Baldwin wrote after just two weeks exposure to his leader.

> He is a Prince of Good Nature and commands the respect of all. We four Americans are *agreed* and I am quite certain that our Norwegian allies are the best that could be wished for. All of them are intelligent fellows, strong and willing to work. I like every man in the party—and that is saying a very exceptional thing. . . . [I have] the firm belief that we shall all meet next year from October, the happiest lot of men on earth.[179]

With the howling dogs now crowded onto the decks of the steamer, the expedition sailed northward into the Barents Sea on July 4 where it met pack ice at 77° North. Unable to penetrate the ice, *Frithjof* was soon short of coal and forced to retreat back to Vardø to take on board more fuel. Still successfully hiding his true feelings from his men, Wellman was in fact disconsolate—and not mainly because of the stunted progress of the expedition. The "Prince of Good Nature" had been all but written off by his wife and, as he saw it, each of his daughters as well. As he wrote to this brother, there had been no letters at his final port of departure, not from his wife "or anybody else. Not a single letter from anybody. Not one of my girls has taken the trouble to send me a letter here, though I am sure they would do it but for their mother's interference. Well, it is a selfish world. I have been selfish in a way—now it is her turn."[180]

The expedition had taken on board some lumber with which to build a hut in Franz Josef Land and that expense, along with the cost of the dogs in Archangel, left Wellman with barely three hundred dollars to his name.

This he sent to Consul Aagaard in Tromsø in order that there would be *something* to sustain him when he returned from the north.

If Wellman's troubles were well hidden, one person who saw danger signs even at this point was the National Geographic Society's James Gore. It is unknown if the Columbian University professor had learned that no relief ship had been arranged to retrieve the men from Franz Josef Land the following summer. It hardly mattered. After he witnessed the *Frithjof* struggle in the pack ice, he promptly jumped ship in Vardø and returned posthaste to the United States. Gore's brief Arctic experience was not a total loss, however, "for he was able to make a series of important observations to determine the force of gravity by which to ascertain the curvature of the earth with the Arctic circle. The geography tells us that the earth has the shape of an orange and is flattened at the poles, but geographers are anxious to find out exactly how much, and the observations of Prof. Gore are directed to [this] end."[181]

On Friday, July 15, 1898, after Gore's defection at Vardø, Evelyn Briggs Baldwin began to keep a formal journal of the expedition. As *Frithjof* was coaled, Baldwin recorded numerous visitors to the ship. In one of the few displays of harmony that the forthcoming voyage would produce, all of the remaining members of the expedition—the five Norwegians and now four Americans—enjoyed a two-hour Russian bath in the midnight sun. "All received a good beating with birch whisk (with leaves) by Norwegian maiden," wrote the nonplussed Baldwin, "quite expert at the business."[182] For his part, Wellman took care not to mention Vardø's more hedonistic delights in his last letters home.

The following evening, Baldwin accompanied Wellman to the home of the local postmaster, Adam Egede-Nissen. There they "enjoyed a smoke and glass [while] Fru Nisson [*sic*] played three very fine selections upon the violin—Mr. Wellman's favorite instrument. Green plants and flowers rendered room still more cheerful in this happy Arctic home, while two little girls (5 and 3) and a little chap of two, made it joyful."[183]

The *Frithjof* anchor was raised later that same evening, and by 11:00 P.M. the ship departed once more for the north. For Wellman, still smarting over the lack of correspondence from his wife and children and now staring at an unhappy isolation of a year or more in Franz Josef Land, this parting view of the world in the form of a 'happy Arctic home' undoubtedly did little to lift his spirits.

NINE

A Paradise of Opportunity

On the morning of Friday, July 22, 1898, from his perch in the crow's nest, Captain Kjeldsen called out to Wellman. The captain of the *Frithjof* informed Wellman that, perhaps fifty miles distant, were "the glacier-capped mountains" of Franz Josef Land. "To our imaginations," Wellman wrote of his first view of the archipelago, "it presented itself as a paradise of opportunity."[184]

With the mid-summer breakup of the pack ice, the voyage to Franz Josef Land from Vardø had taken just five days. On July 16 Wellman had written to his brother that he hoped to be able to get far north into British Channel, a waterway that splits the western third of Franz Josef Land. If the *Frithjof* could not force its way through the channel, Wellman hoped to deploy a steam launch from Cape Flora in order to land the expedition's supplies as far north as possible. "We are out for the Pole this time [and] the only man I am afraid of is Sverdrup, who has gone to Greenland in the *Fram*. He says he is [not] up for the Pole, but I believe he is."[185]

During the cruise from Vardø, the men had begun to work each other out. Wellman thought Baldwin "fine" but the doctor and Mr. Harlan merely "good."[186] For his part, Baldwin had already begun to reveal himself as a duplicitous martinet, by turns imperious and devious toward the Norwegians and unctuously servile with Wellman. As Baldwin un-self-consciously wrote in this journal the day after *Frithjof* departed Vardø, he had taken

The map of Franz Josef Land that resulted from the Wellman expedition. "Graham Bell Land" has been discovered, as have the eastern limits of the archipelago, but "Crown Prince Rudolf Land" has not been delimited and the four islands Wellman claimed to have seen to its northeast were found by the Italians under Abruzzi to be mirages. From Walter Wellman, "The Wellman Polar Expedition," *National Geographic* 10 (12): 481–505.

"advantage of the quiet on board today and had Johannsen oil all our great sea boots."[187]

For Paul Bjørvig, an intelligent and philosophical soul who rightly would have been placed as second-in-command if not for Wellman's need to pretend that his was an American show, Baldwin's high-handedness was an ominous sign of things to come: "All had to be done with American style speed. We Norwegians were not really used to springing into action, we were used to taking time to think through the best approach. But no, here we simply had to obey orders, and that is the best. But then you could surely expect that the boss was equal to the task, though that was not for us to say of our second in command, who was to go with us northwards."[188]

To Bernt Bentsen, it soon became clear that Wellman's plan explicitly asked the Norwegians to do all of the hard manual work while the Americans reserved for themselves whatever credit might accompany those efforts. As a former member of Nansen's *Fram* crew who had experienced firsthand both the conduct of a professional scientific expedition and the reception it received when it returned home in well-earned glory, Bentsen would soon dismiss Wellman's Franz Josef Land effort as a "Norwegian Expedition, at 3 kroner and 50 øre a day."[189]

That same evening out of Vardø, Emil Ellefsen translated news reports from the Norwegian press about the Spanish-American conflict in Cuba, which at that moment was nearing its climax. Theodore Roosevelt's 1st U.S. Volunteer Cavalry, the Rough Riders, had charged San Juan Hill east of Santiago de Cuba on July 1 and the Spanish Caribbean Squadron had been destroyed by the U.S. Navy in the port of Santiago de Cuba on July 3. On almost the opposite side of the world, as *Frithjof* carried its tiny American contingent north through the Barents Sea, Baldwin exclaimed ecstatically: "What glorious news all this is!"

> Of course our first inquiries on coming into harbor were concerning the welfare of our Navy and Army. And my little Cuban flag presented me by the Women's Auxiliary Committee of the Chicago Cuban Relief Committee is now a proud emblem on board the *Frithjof*. I carry it with pride and joy in my heart—it will be the first Cuban flag to be carried Poleward and that it should be carried by the Wellman Expedition gives me greatest pleasure.[190]

After the other Americans, Harlan and Hofma, had recovered from sea-sickness, the American contingent lolled about, playing whist and checkers, while the Norwegians went about the actual preparations for the expedition, remaining largely segregated from the Americans as they constructed an odometer for the polar sledges. Wellman and Baldwin both indulged in fantasies of finding traces of the Andrée expedition and, with it, the instant fame and fortune they both craved. As Wellman "dreamed of finding message in copper cylinder from Andrée" so too did Baldwin write that he had woken from a dream "of Andrée several days ago and also dreamed last October (21st and 22nd) that I saw him and comrades make successful descent on that date, seemingly in Siberia. I have always believed, however, that he would be found in Franz-Josef Land."[191]

The following day, which happened to be Captain Kjeldsen's fifty-eighth birthday, *Frithjof* came across the *Victoria,* the yacht of the British sportsman-adventurer Arnold Pike. As Baldwin related, both vessels were engaged in feeling their way northward, until "our rapid and buoyant progress was brought to end about 6:00 P.M. upon arrival at heavy ice in about latitude 79° 61', longitude 40' E., (according to Captain Nielsen of the *Victoria*).

Progress during day amidst detached floes on every hand, smooth sea, bright sunshine, good wind, etc. Anchoring to ice, *Victoria* soon came along side and exchanged calls. Mr. Pike not aboard. Norwegians in charge of *Victoria* and hunting polar bears for Mr. Pike. Delivering some letters brought to crew of *Frithjof* (*Victoria* having left Norway after departure of *Frithjof*) the *Victoria* returned to edge of outer floes to hunt bears. Heads of two large seals showed themselves at safe distance from *Frithjof.* In course of day *Frithjof* lost one hour by some of the sailors (including Bjorvik and Bentzen) going in futile chase for polar bear, etc. The mate thoughtlessly gave permission to stop vessel unknown to Wellman or Captain.[192]

At 6:00 A.M. the following morning, Thursday, July 21, Baldwin's thoughts about going off in search of polar bears had changed completely, when Olaf Ellefsen announced that one could be seen in open water near the ship. Aware now that even the smallest movements of the ship had to be cleared by the Americans, Captain Kjeldsen sent word to Wellman and asked if the men could go off to hunt the bear. Wellman instantly agreed, aware of his promise of several polar skins to his expedition benefactors back in the United States. As Baldwin wrote, "with Olaf Ellefsen and Johannsen of our party and some of the sailors we put off in whale boat."

Good breeze stirring—bear saw us, and put off. Sea rather rough and boat bobbed up and down, now leaving bear's head in view, now concealing him. But soon we were upon him. I made ready and fired the first shot, taking effect so far as hitting the bear somewhere is concerned and causing him to rise angrily from the water and to growl lustily. Then followed a lively chase, but water rough and prevented accurate aim at head. However, after several bullets had been put into his body and neck, he bowed to the inevitable and became a prize to my "45–90." It was the "first bear" of the voyage and the first I had ever shot in open water. It proved to be a three-year-old she-bear, its stomach showed that she had just eaten a seal—hairs, claws, and all. Bear skin hung along ship to soak in seawater as we moved along.

Evening fast to ice again. Dressed in nightgown I endeavored to creep upon the seals on ice floe. But they were wary and disappeared through ice.[193]

On Friday, July 22, *Frithjof* remained moored to the ice all day. It was Baldwin's thirty-sixth birthday and, for the expedition's second-in-command, it was one of

great sadness as well as joy . . . sadness, because it marks the natal time of my dear departed brother Edwin Miles Baldwin as well as my own; joy, because the Expedition *have* made it a day long to be remembered. *First,* upon going on deck this morning, the Captain called out from the crow's nest for Wellman, who also ascended to the barrel and upon coming down put hand congratulatingly upon my right shoulder and said: "Well, we have the land in sight right ahead, 50 or 70 miles." Wellman has from the first said that we should see the land on my birthday. I then went into the crow's nest and also had a view of the land—as I thought about 50 miles ahead. The weather from the first and all day was glorious, making one feel like living forever amidst Arctic scenes, etc., etc. *Frithjof,* with banners flying and sails full set, photographed and cinematographed by Harlan—Captain and Wellman on bridge, and in crow's nest, sailors on yards, etc., etc. At 2:00 P.M., entire party assembled in cabin for dinner—first time together at meal (owing to small size of cabin and table within. Cabin decorated with Expedition flag, National Capital Press Club, Washington, D.C., Arctic Club of America (N.Y. section), Cuban flag (with emblems of Co. L., 4th Illinois National Guard, presented to me by Captain Franz Muench, Olney, Illinois), and with [Union] flag of Norway and Sweden. At conclusion Wellman "toasted" me upon 36th birthday, stated that there were or are but two officers of the Expedition—himself and myself as second-in-command, bespoke same loyalty to me as to himself, etc. Immediately after dinner I had two "sets" of dogs put upon the ice, with one of the copper sledges and one of the two very large boat-sledges and such a jolly, rollicking time as men and dogs had! Bentzen and Johannsen, each on ski, turned somersaults by teams, overtaking and running them down, etc. The test proved dogs and sledges to be first class, notwithstanding surface was very wet. Bjorvik, in his best element and Olaf Ellefsen ditto. Upon the big sledge I sat and reinitiated myself as a dog driver, noting points, picking out leaders, etc. Had harnesses of Samoyede and own pattern (much after Eskimo style) used side by side and decide that Eskimo pattern is best. Harlan took photos, also dive into sea. The dogs also took sea baths, some accidentally, some by force and one voluntarily who swam entirely round vessel. Also rolled in snow, etc. Dogs shedding old coats, etc. All this over, large bear seen on ice half mile distant, and men on ice and I with others in whale boat went in pursuit. Captain, running with men on ice fired twice first, but missed, then I fired and wounded bear, blood making crimson the water about him. Then a bullet through brain from eye to eye settled him, or rather her, for she proved to be a large three-year-old she-bear. Thus my second bear has been secured. Again, just after supper, another bear seen on ice, and half dozen men run in pursuit, finally one of harpooners securing it just as my boat arrives at point where I might have got it had I had a chance to fire. It was a two-year-old he-bear. . . . Dr. Hofma closed incidents of day by shooting two ivory gulls. Glorious weather of day turned to fog and uncertainty tonight.[194]

Still a week away from arrival at Cape Flora, Wellman was well on his way to rewarding his patrons with bearskins and making a film record of the expedition that could be produced as a motion picture when he returned to the United States. These early days seemed to promise more good results, but for the next four days, *Frithjof* made little progress northward. Together now for over a month, the other Americans had become familiar with one other—too familiar for Wellman's stratified tastes, and he "cautioned [them] regarding addressing one another in polite form."[195]

Frithjof struck open water on Wednesday, July 27, and cruised northward toward land. The rigging was coated with ice amid the persistent fog. Wellman, Captain Kjeldsen, and Baldwin all repeatedly climbed to the crow's nest throughout the day to check on their progress. By mid-afternoon, Franz Josef Land appeared once again, and just ahead. The ship had arrived off Cape Grant and, after shooting another polar bear, the expedition steamed into Nightingale Sound, toward Capes Stephens and Forbes. "Weather *glorious* and Wellman and Captain in crow's nest and I on ladder underneath when not in crow's nest proper," wrote Baldwin. "Finally steered toward Eira Harbor (between Bell and Mabel Islands)."[196]

The expedition had arrived in historic waters, the area first explored and the harbor discovered and named by Benjamin Leigh Smith eighteen years previous and where, the following year, in the summer of 1881, Leigh Smith had erected a wooden storage lodge that survives to the present day. *Frithjof* dropped anchor in the harbor and soon the members of the expedition had picked out the lodge on shore. There was every good reason for Wellman to be thrilled to have arrived at this spot, both on account of Captain Kjeldsen's excellent ice navigation and for the potential to solve the mystery of the disappearance of the Swedish expedition. A *frisson* of excitement ran through the men as they considered how close they might be to solving that mystery, and the men traded thoughts on whether Andrée and his two companions were at that moment inside the lodge. Baldwin believed that indeed they were, and fast asleep.

Once ashore, the men crept to the lodge and gently pushed open the unlocked door. "Old bottles, pictures, some provisions, etc., lying about. Finally came upon notice that informed us that the house was the winter quarters of the Leigh Smith party (1881). Notice also stated that Cape Flora was about ten miles S.E., across bay between Bell and Northbrook

Islands."[197] But there was no trace of the Swedish expedition. Wellman took the opportunity to raise the American flag above the British hut, and then the expedition quickly continued on its way.

Ten nautical miles to the southeast, they had arrived at Cape Flora and the remains not only of Leigh Smith's stone hut from his forced 1881–82 overwintering after the shipwreck of the *Eira,* but all of the materials left behind from the three-year occupation of the site by Frederick Jackson, the main building of which Jackson had named Elmwood. Baldwin wrote that he came ashore at 5:00 A.M. on the morning of Thursday, July 28, where he quickly picked the lock of the front door of Elmwood and let the men in.

> Placed English flag on pole and American beneath as act of courtesy, etc. By permission of Mr. Harmsworth took some of the stores left there—of which *very* great quantity still remains. Andrée not there— as I had fully believed he would be. Stores left there for Andrée still in good shape—but we took two boxes of same thinking that perhaps we might meet him farther north. As so many supplies left there by Jackson still remain and Andrée may use same, we were fully justified in doing this. Indeed I believe it was our duty to take this precaution of assisting Andrée should we meet him. Am glad so many provisions still remain at Cape Flora. A year hence we may return there from our journey northward and will need them.[198]

For Wellman, the failure to find any trace of Andrée or his two companions, Knut Fraenkel and Nils Strindberg, was the first serious blow of the expedition. There was to be no dramatic meeting *à la* Nansen-Jackson or Stanley-Livingstone. "When last heard from, Andree's balloon was drifting in this direction from Spitzbergen," wrote Wellman later, "and as he knew of the existence at this point of a good house amply stocked with provisions, it was not impossible he had been able to make his way hither the previous autumn. Great was our disappointment when we saw the doors and windows of Jackson's house all boarded and barred, for we realized that thus ended all reasonable expectation that the brave Swedes were to be seen again among the living."[199]

At the moment when Wellman stepped ashore at Cape Flora, he was a thirty-nine-year-old active explorer. Without any way to know it, he was only about a day's sail from the island roughly 175 nautical miles northwest

Jackson's huts at Cape Flora, as Wellman and his men found them in the summer of 1898. *Courtesy National Air and Space Museum (NASM 9A10647), Smithsonian Institution.*

of Eira Harbour where Andrée had died the previous fall. It would be another thirty-two years—and Wellman would be 4,000 miles away in New York City and a long-retired seventy-two-year-old—before Wellman finally learned what became of the Swedish balloonist and his crew.

The expedition remained only about twelve hours at Cape Flora, just time enough to gather up supplies along with one of the small eight-sided wooden supply huts left behind by Jackson. As Paul Bjørvig later wrote, they took away not only the hut with its sailcloth roof, but "a little stove, a few tins, a canvas boat and a sextant. From Andrée's expedition depot we took a theodolite."[200]

From Cape Flora, Kjeldsen attempted to steam further north through both the British and Austrian Channels that led to the northern islands of the archipelago, but each time the way was blocked by ice. As Bjørvig recalled, along the southern coast the waters were largely clear, "but all the bays, the sounds and the fjords were under fast ice."[201]

Baldwin stayed up late, climbing into the crow's nest to make sketches of the shorelines they passed. As *Frithjof* approached Cape Tegetthoff on Hall Island, he had his first opportunity to hunt walrus:

Approaching the Cape in a glass-like sea, there flitted about an occasional gull or guillemot. All at once the Captain called up from the bridge: "See there, Mr. Baldwin, the walruses sleeping in the water!" Sure enough, there lay two large brown masses of flesh with a smaller black one lazily drifting with the current.

Quickly descending from the crow's nest I was soon in a whaleboat with Olaf (harpooner) and two of the sailors. Making ready the line and harpoon, all in the boat crouched low save a single oarsman who bent low in the stern of the boat and quietly rowed toward the sleeping creatures. Suddenly Olaf stood erect and with unerring aim thrust the sharp steel deep into the flesh of the largest of the walruses. With a bellow the wounded mammal thrust her head high in the air, her tusks of ivory contrasting savagely with the dark blue of the sea and her own coarse dark hide. Thus alarmed the two old walruses and the calf tumbled over one another making the sea appear as though a submarine spring had suddenly burst through the otherwise calm sunrise. At an opportune moment I fired—one of the large walruses sank for a moment, but her head soon again appeared reeking with blood. She had been hit, but not in a fatal spot. Quickly firing, Olaf put a bullet through the tough folds of skin on the back of the neck, the missile penetrating into the brain and putting an end to the strain upon the walrus line. Olaf's opportunity for making this shot was an act of affection between mother and offspring. After my shot wounded the creature, she turned toward the calf opening wide her mouth at the same time. Thereupon the young one swam directly toward its mother and affectionately placed its lips to those of its maternal protector. A second time Olaf's rifle spoke and the other large walrus also hung fast to the second harpoon line. At the same time I fired and the calf, weighing about three hundred pounds, also lay dead upon the water. We then towed all to a floating pan of ice and brought them up—the fat and hides for the owner of the *Frithjof* to be thrown into the commerce of the world, the flesh for our dogs.[202]

Once he stepped foot upon Cape Tegetthoff, named after the Austro-Hungarian ship that had discovered Franz Josef Land in the summer of 1873, Baldwin again thought he had located evidence of the missing Swedes. Coming across a series of old boot tracks, he exclaimed, "Andrée!"

> Could these be the tracks of a sole survivor—of Andrée or Strindberg or Fraenkel seeking aid or endeavoring to reach Cape Flora? Observing Wellman and Captain putting off in boat for *Frithjof* I called to Wellman and he and party came forward and also examined tracks, whereupon Wellman decided to send out two parties for further search, I, with Harlan, Olaf Ellefsen and Bjorvik pursued a northerly course—Bjorvik, Olaf Ellefsen and I going well toward Nordenskjold Fjord. The other party went along the shore westward for a short distance. Neither party were able to see other tracks than those in the immediate vicinity of the Cape, as, had there been any, they must have disappeared with the melting of the snow. And so the matter rested and we went aboard at 5:00 A.M.[203]

The mystery of Andrée continued to preoccupy the men as *Frithjof* attempted to get northward by steaming around the southeastern islands of the archipelago, in the area where the *Tegetthoff* had been abandoned in the pack ice in 1874.

Passing south of Wilczek Land, Baldwin wrote that they came across four small previously unknown islands, two of which Wellman named after benefactors of the expedition, Lambert Tree and Charles G. Dawes. Judge Lambert Tree was a former ambassador and arts patron who had presided over corruption trials of city officials in Chicago. Dawes, who like Wellman was born in Ohio and lived part of his early life in Nebraska, later became famous as chair of the committee that authored the Dawes Plan for reparations following the First World War. Dawes received the Nobel Peace Prize in 1925 for this work, and he served as the thirtieth vice president of the United States under Calvin Coolidge.[204]

They were now in an extremely remote corner of this remote archipelago and so were further startled to come across another ship. Again their imaginations could conceive only one explanation: that a Swedish rescue expedition had come in search of Andrée. But instead it was a lone Norwegian sea-hunting *jakt* out of the port of Sandefjord, cruising Franz Josef Land waters in search of a summer's catch.

> [B]y this our good Captain knew that one of his own countrymen had beaten him in the race for the first catch of walruses. Sure enough, it was the *Hekla* from the south of Norway, which, baffled off the east coast of Spitzbergen, had followed the edge of the ice to Nova Zembla [Novaya Zemlya] and then into open water northward to the south of Salm Island.
>
> The mate of the *Hekla* coming aboard, informed us that his vessel had secured 212 walruses up to date, that *perhaps* some of his men had gone ashore at Cape Tegetthoff and made the tracks which we had observed—but he thought not. Moreover, none of his men wore Lapp shoes, and some of the tracks appeared to have been made by parties wearing such gear. And again, the mystery of the cause or causes of the strange boot prints became deeper than ever.[205]

Frithjof's final attempt to find a way northward was soon brought to a halt by a solid front of ice. With access denied to a more suitable northern island on which to base the expedition and the example of the successful walrus hunters before him, Captain Kjeldsen was increasingly anxious to discharge his passengers and their kit and be on his way. Accordingly, *Frithjof* retreated back to the southern shoreline of Hall Island where it arrived at Cape Tegetthoff on Saturday night, July 30. On Sunday, Wellman and his men spent a leisurely day ashore in search of the right spot to locate a base camp—and add the first American hut to the remnants of Austro-Hungarian, British, and Norwegian expeditions in the islands.

With the plum of solving the Andrée mystery now seemingly beyond his grasp, Wellman moved on with his primary mission, a rapid expedition to the North Pole. Despite his later claims that the expedition was only a local geographic survey of the islands, there is no question as to Wellman's main objective. If there was any doubt, his own newspaper, the *Chicago Times-Herald,* had published an extended front-page article in May 1898, the text framed by sketches of Wellman, Baldwin, and *Frithjof,* and headlined "Wellman's Brave Attempt to Find the North Pole."

On Monday, August 1, 1898, Wellman exerted his executive authority and placed Baldwin in charge of building the camp on shore. Wellman

Paul Bjørvig. The redoubtable and philosophical Norwegian, resting with some the expedition's dogs on the ice near the expedition ship *Frithjof. Courtesy National Air and Space Museum (NASM 9A10649), Smithsonian Institution.*

then retreated to his cabin on board *Frithjof* to write his final articles for his newspaper and letters to his family before the ship departed and left the expedition to its own devices for a year or more. Baldwin wrote: "Wellman put me in charge of work on shore and I had Doctor Hofma, Bentzen, Johannesen, Bjorvik and Olaf Ellefsen busy all day.

> End of day's work found lodge in place, dogs enjoying themselves on mossy bed beneath great basaltic cathedral resonant with ceaseless screams of hundreds and hundreds of birds and the howling of the dogs. Much of equipment, etc., etc., in place. Of course I did my share of the heavy work along with the rest. Wellman busy all day planning, writing, etc. Harlan and Emil Ellefesen superintended sending of stuff ashore as discharged by the sailors.[206]

For Wellman's part, he was still trying, even from the cabin of a ship anchored off a stony shoreline at 80° North latitude, to patch things up back home in Washington, D.C. He had still managed to conceal from his men any hint of either the poor state of his relations with his wife and family or the expedition's frail finances. He sent a few photographs and a copy of his journal to his wife, and to his brother he anxiously wrote on August 2 that the expedition had "made a rather lucky voyage so far.

> I did have hopes we could get the ship farther north, but we are at 80:06, & directly south of Cape Fligely, which is much better than Cape Flora, at least 50 or 60 miles nearer. Besides, we all believe the traveling is better here than from the vicinity of Cape Flora.
>
> We are all well. The party is in good shape. We have a good house on shore & lots of provisions; coal also for fire; & though we are going to try our best to travel up to Fligely to winter, according to my original plan, it is comforting to know we have a good home [indistinct], good, at least—to fall back upon in case of trouble.
>
> I am very anxious to reach Fligely this fall, that we may have one try for the Pole & make sure of getting back next year. I would sooner lose an arm than stay up here two years—& yet we must have a success before returning.
>
> If I *do* stay two years—which is unlikely—borrow money on life insurance; finance the thing some way; beg money from everybody.

You can get it. I did. People who have money can be worked if you go at them in the right way. Promise to pay in my name, & I will make it good. I rely on you to see that my dear wife & girls are protected—& I know I do not hope in vain. This is my *last* Arctic trip. Fail or win I promise this upon my honor.[207]

That Wellman would go on to lead *three* more Arctic expeditions is an indication of the low state of his morale as he began his North Pole expedition in Franz Josef Land. Contrary to the mask he presented to the members of his expedition, he bluntly confessed to his brother that only "up here in the lonely, cheerless Arctic would I have had incentive to look into my heart, to analyze myself. I now know that Laura is the only woman in the world I really love.

I know because when my heart is heavy, when I think of myself as ill or hurt or old, it is with her I would be, to her I look instinctively for comfort & companionship. That is the true test, & noble, patient girl that she is, she has forgiven me, & written me sweetly, & if the fates spare me to get back to her I will make full amends for all my wrong-doing.[208]

As if his troubles on the home front were not enough, Wellman also continued to blithely pass over the need to arrange for a ship to retrieve the men the following year, telling his brother Arthur that "several ships have come to F.J. Land this year, & doubtless several will come next year. With one of them we can get home."[209] While Baldwin and the men worked to get the hut constructed and compose their final communications home before the departure of *Frithjof,* Wellman desultorily climbed alone into the hills behind the shore at Cape Tegetthoff to gather Arctic poppies to enclose in his letters to his family.

At Cape Tegetthoff, Wellman and his men would soon be the sole human inhabitants of an archipelago spanning some 6,000 square miles. As he wrote to his five daughters, his new base camp was at 80° 05' North and 58' East, approximately 600 nautical miles or 850 kilometers from the North Pole. "That is a good ways from Washington, isn't it, girls? As I write it is 9 o'clock in the evening. With you in Washington it is noon. So we are just 3/8 of the way around the world."[210] After asking his daughters to read his journal to get a better sense of the expedition, Wellman remembered that there were some details about the human incursion into the Arctic that might need explanation—or that perhaps he had unwittingly provided something of a metaphor for the current state of his family relations:

> Girls, it made me feel queer to see [my crew] shoot that poor little baby walrus. It was crying for its dead mother, and if I could have stopped the men without making myself ridiculous I would have done so. But he tasted very good. . . . [W]hen a mother walrus scents [*sic*] danger she takes her calf between her flippers and dives as deep as she can in the water & does not come up till she is a long ways off. These queer animals have great love one for another, as well as for their children.
>
> A few days ago two walrus came along side the ship. They were apparently a married pair. They were very happy, & very curious to see what manner of thing this was that had come into their domain, and their eyes sparkled with delight as they came swimming along with their heads just out of the water & side by side. Capt. Kjeldsen seized his gun & shot one of them, and as the blood gushed forth the other put his flippers under his wounded mate as if to help her away. Both went down, down, and we saw them no more. Man is a cruel animal, isn't he, girls?[211]

With the materials they had brought on board *Frithjof* along with the small stores hut and the other materials taken from Cape Flora with the permission of Alfred Harmsworth, Wellman's crew constructed "Harmsworth House," the expedition's headquarters. As the men worked on the hut and the dogs scrambled over the shore, Harlan took cinematograph footage of all of the activity for a planned motion picture.

Two significant events interrupted the work. The first was a meeting called by Wellman to outline his plan, such as it was, for the expedition. Once the hut was finished, but no later than August 5, Baldwin would be ordered to lead an advance team charged with reaching Cape Fligely, the northernmost point on "Crown Prince Rudolf Land," as it was called during Wellman's expedition, and the last bit of solid ground between Franz Josef Land and the North Pole.

Beyond this spare outline, there were few details. After his letter to his brother written from Vardø on July 16, there had been no further mention in Wellman's letters of any steam launch attached to the expedition. It does not appear, then, as if a steam launch was ever procured while the expedition was still in Norway or that one was ever carried northward on board *Frithjof.* Given the state of the expedition's finances, this was no surprise. Yet without such a steam launch—absolutely required if the men were to tow boat-loads of supplies northward through the archipelago when ice-filled channels briefly cracked opened during the summer—Wellman's men would be forced to carry every ounce of supplies on sledges, kayaks, and their own backs. It all but guaranteed that the transport of the necessary supplies needed to build an advance base at Cape Fligely before winter was impossible. It also made something of a mockery of Wellman's decade-long fascination with balloons and other forms of advanced technological transport—to say nothing of the "American ability to hustle"—when, at this crucial moment, he had not even been able to hustle up so much as a small steam launch.

The second event involved Baldwin and the dogs and almost ended the expedition right then and there at Cape Tegetthoff. On Monday evening, as Baldwin visited the dogs, patting them on their snouts, one of the dogs leapt at him and bit into his left wrist and then snapped at his right wrist, "holding me fast like a savage wolf," as he later wrote:

Finally kicking myself loose, I started toward the lodge but wrists benumbed so that I could not use them. Seeing that I was badly hurt, Olaf Ellefsen and Johannesen came to me—but I had received such a sudden shock that I soon collapsed. When I "came to" I felt as though I had been in some fairy land, as though awakened from a pleasant dream. But I soon realized that cold water was in my face, in my boots, all over me, with Olaf Ellefsen and Johannesen doing their bravest and best for me. Next I was jolting up and down on a ladder with Olaf Ellefesen and Johannesen carrying me to a boat. Bjorvik and Bentzen, at work upon a sledge, were also called and I was soon put aboard where the Doctor's good treatment and Wellman's kindness soon made me feel more like a living being. In fact I was quite able to dispose of two plates of hot cornmeal mush, and two or three cups of tea. However, my wrists, especially the right one, pained me much, as the wolf-dog's teeth must have "touched" one or more of the sensory nerves. It was at once decided that not only the "Criminal" but also another of the dogs with biting proclivities must be shot.[212]

Olaf Ellefsen was given the task to shoot the dogs, after which Baldwin ordered him to skin them as well. The skins of the offending dogs were then hung on the wall of the hut.[213] For days afterward, Baldwin tried to get some sensation back into his hands while he also limped back and forth between the ship and the shoreline, having injured his foot in his attempts to kick the dog off of him.

Remarkably, these injuries did not cause Wellman to reconsider Baldwin as leader of the advance party to Cape Fligely. While Baldwin convalesced, Wellman sat with him and planned the fall march to Rudolf Land. As Baldwin wrote in his journal, "Wellman and I have been planning some for my advance party.

> I want, if possible, to leave here Friday, August 5th. Expect to take thirty-five (35) dogs, four sledges, one Lapp (wooden) boat, one canvas boat, with equipment, etc.
>
> Route: Austria Sound to Crown Prince Rudolf Land (Cape Fligely, if possible). Object: Hunt walruses, polar bears, build winter hut for party, etc., and then return to assist other party (main party) under Wellman, etc.
>
> Well, I shall rejoice when once under way. (No one can imagine what a shock it was for me when I was bitten last evening, for I feared that I was hurt much worse—in fact that I might not be able to drive a team, etc., but when I found that a few days will soon make all right again, the pain seemed to lessen.)[214]

The night before *Frithjof* steamed away, as the Norwegians rushed to complete the work of the base camp, the Americans stayed on board the ship in a rush to finish their last letters and journal entries and engage in one last game of whist around the galley table. The expedition photographer, Quirof Harlan, was proving to be difficult, and had refused Wellman's request to develop a batch of photographs prior to the departure of *Frithjof*. Harlan eventually complied, but his insolence, along with the problems with Baldwin and the dogs, the failure to procure a steam launch, the greater failure to arrange for a proper relief ship the following year, and the general lack of any real plan for the expedition, did not bode well for success.

His own pains evident, Baldwin wrote that the other Americans were having difficulties as they adjusted to the life of the polar adventurer. Wellman's left ear was still ringing, and Dr. Hofma's wrists were also "much swollen and quite painful owing to the severe exercise given them yesterday while he and I were carrying boxes to the house.

Harmsworth House we named it today in honor of Young Harmsworth of London, Mr. Harmsworth, the partner of the Jackson-Harmsworth Expedition, having given Wellman permission to use of the material left at Cape Flora, we brought to this point not only the provisions before mentioned, but also one of the small double canvas-roofed lodges at Cape Flora.[215]

On Wednesday, August 3, *Frithjof* steamed away, with Captain Kjeldsen intent on a last look around for Andrée and to hunt a few more walrus to pay for the Franz Josef Land voyage before he returned to Norway. Wellman and his men were now "the only human inhabitants in that vast region, and our nearest neighbors were Russians and Samoyedes in Nova Zembla [Novaya Zemlya], five hundred miles to the southward."[216] As Baldwin wrote, "Captain Kjeldsen, the mates and seamen all bidding us *heartfelt* goodbyes. Captain came ashore and one could see that he felt deeply the farewell performance.

Ashore our party *at once* set about making preparation for my advance party. Bjorvik and Bentzen, putting German silver on runners of two remaining sledges. Time might have been saved by having had this done while on board. But one never knows just what *is best* at all times. No one stood about in a reflective mood as *Frithjof* disappeared in the West. All were too busy, to give way to *feelings* that might have been encouraged but for the necessity of repressing them.[217]

"It is not a happy night," Wellman wrote to his brother the night before the ship sailed. "The heart is full. To add to the gloom Mr. Baldwin was badly bitten by a dog tonight & fainted away from nervous shock."[218] Wellman later wrote that it was "Anything but a joyful moment was it that morning when we stood upon the wind-swept plateau of Cape Tegetthoff, and watched the *Frithjof* steam away . . . yet not one of us wished to be upon the ship"—unconvincing words when placed alongside his private letters.[219]

As the Norwegians completed much of the expedition preparation work on shore, Wellman unsuccessfully struggled to match his words to the magnificent Arctic surroundings of the Franz Josef Land archipelago. Wellman's public writings tended to incline toward a form of cloying nonchalant bonhomie, as if written for a boy's own magazine, or a strained attempt to recreate the transcendent mysticism of Elisha Kent Kane. "Already we were under the influence of the Arctic spell. Its glamour was in our eyes, its fever in our blood. We were in the mood to appreciate the beauties which nature had lavishly strewn about our future home. . . .

> The cliffs of Cape Tegetthoff, showing black where the snow and frost had fallen from their precipitate sides; and the glaciers debouching into the little valleys, melting in the heat of this mid-summer sun, and pouring musically-gurgling streams down to the sea.[221]

Privately, to his daughters, Wellman wrote that he already looked like a tramp, "with my big cow-hide boots, dirty silk handkerchief for a cravat, and awful, awful whiskers."[222] He promised to bring home pets in the form of one of the dogs—this despite his graphic description of how one of them had just maimed Baldwin—as well as an Arctic fox and a polar bear cub. Seeing to the more immediate priority to satisfy his patrons, Wellman sent four bear skins on board *Frithjof* to Consul Aagaard in Tromsø, there to be fixed up as rugs. From his lonely outpost, he signed his last letter to his daughters in the most remote and inaccessible way: "Walter Wellman."

TEN

To Advance as Rapidly as Possible, and as Far as Possible

The night after the *Frithjof* sailed off westward, the walrus hunter from Sandefjord appeared during the night and a few of its men came ashore to see the Norwegian creation that nonetheless flew the American flag. Baldwin failed to see the visitors, as he was under the expedition's canvas boat fast asleep, alongside Bjørvig, Bentsen, and Emil Ellefsen. Baldwin had decided that it was time "to sleep out of doors from the very beginning. So it may be some time, if ever, that I shall sleep in Harmsworth House."[223]

According to Wellman, the prefabricated segments of Harmsworth House went up on the shore at Cape Tegetthoff in just a few hours, after which assembly the men ate the first "meal in the most northerly inhabited house in the world, and, in fact, the most northerly of all habitable dwellings, excepting only two—the Greely house in Grinnell Land, and the hut which the Wellman expedition of 1894 erected out of the timbers of the ice-crushed steamer the *Ragnvald Jarl* at Walden Island, Spitzbergen."[224]

> This was about the queerest sort of house that human beings ever passed an Arctic winter in. It was made in England, in sections all ready to be fitted together. For three years it had stood at Cape Flora, where the Jackson-Harmsworth expedition had used it as a storehouse,

and Mr. Jackson had said it was not fit for human occupation [as its] walls were very thin, merely three-quarter-inch boards. There were ten sections of these boards, all fitting together with bolts, and they also matched the floor, which was likewise in ten pieces. Over this structure of decagonal shape were stretched two thicknesses of oil canvas.[225]

To Jackson's original prefabricated structure the Norwegians added a third surrounding wall and then drew over the whole lot a sail found at Cape Flora that had been discarded from the Jackson-Harmsworth ship *Windward*. A space for stores was attached to the ten-sided hut, as well as a small vestibule. "When the storms came later in the fall, the whole camp, living-room, store-shed, vestibule and all, was buried under a snow drift."[226] The interior of the hut was heated by a small iron stove—fifteen inches in diameter and burning upward of fifty pounds of coal per day—that was dropped through a hole cut in the center of the flooring so that its heat radiated to every corner of the hut.[227]

The next day, Thursday, August 4, 1898, the men worked all day to prepare for the departure of the advance party on August 5 and paused, as Baldwin wrote, only for a supper of "one of Cousin Louisa's fruit cakes and all enjoyed it."

Just before going to our sleeping bags, Wellman had all assemble and the "success" of my party was drunk. Wellman felt sincerely the *meaning* of departure of this party. He and I have talked over the matter and the work in hand, and I have written "instructions" from him, a copy of which he keeps that there may be no misunderstanding. My first objective point will be Cape Frankfurt, about eighteen (18) miles N.E. of Cape Tegetthoff.[228]

Wellman's orders to Baldwin required him to establish an outpost as far north as possible, one that would serve as the spot where Wellman's planned "dash" for the North Pole would jump off in the spring of 1899. Baldwin was to build a hut as far as 82° North on Rudolf Land and then stock it with a ton and a half of polar bear and walrus killed and dried en route, along with other provisions and supplies carried from Harmsworth House. All this was to be accomplished in five weeks. As Wellman wrote to Baldwin on the eve of departure of the advance party:

Cape Tegetthoff, August 4, 1898
Mr. E. B. Baldwin, Second in Command

Dear Sir:

With your advance party, composed of yourself, Bjorvik, Bentzen and Emil Ellefsen, you will set out tomorrow morning for the north.

Your business is to advance as rapidly as possible, and as far as possible this fall, before stopping to establish a winter station.

You should stop not later than September 10th, and probably some days earlier. You will make careful selection of site for this station, having in view of first importance plenty of game—bear, walrus and seal—second, proximity to drift-wood, if any there is, and third, a comfortable, dry place to build a hut. Before actually beginning work at the station you should cause the coast to be well searched for the most advantageous spot.

A large supply of game should be taken and carefully preserved from bear, for our own use and feeding the dogs through the long winter.

It is well to keep in mind that the game may move with approach of winter or change of ice conditions, and you should, therefore, make your catch as soon as possible after arrival.

Also, house building is easier before cold weather comes, and you should lose no time in preparing some sort of a habitation for the men. The details of this hut building I leave to your excellent judgment, according to the circumstances which you find, but suggest a half-cellar should be dug, and the roof be put over that high enough to enable us to stand erect within. Also, that there should be a vestibule, with an inner and outer door of skins, this vestibule to be large enough for a cook house, that we may avoid scent in the living apartment as much as possible.

Unless you find good reason for another course you should pass up the west side of Rudolf Land. At both Capes Brorck [Brorok] and Habermann cairns with records should be left in case you take the east side, and at Cape Brorck if you take the west side. In the absence of cairns or records, we will assume that you have taken the west side.

On your northern journey, if conditions permit, you will try to pass Capes Frankfort, Tyrol, Easter and Hellwald, Becker Island or Staliczka [Stoliczka] Island, Rainier [Rainer] Island and Karl Alexander

Land, Coburg Island and Hohenlohe Island to Cape Brorok. Upon all these points, or those which lie near your course, you will erect marks and leave records of your course, that we may follow in your course and get all possible benefit from your discoveries as to ice conditions, etc.

If you take the east side of Austria Sound you will erect cairns and leave records at all conspicuous points.

You will avoid glacier-crossing if possible, and if compelled to ascend a glacier will do so with great caution.

You will continually impress upon your men the importance of *caution* in all the work, caution as to their health and physical condition, avoidance of accidents, care of equipment, etc. Be especially cautious in the use of fire-arms, and do not waste cartridges. Do not take risks by attempting to sail far from land in case of open water.

On your journey you are not confined to a ration but may use what you please and as much, your own idea of economy being the best criterion as to the quantities you shall use.

The second party, under my command, will leave here about August 10th, and proceed northward at a rate of about three miles a day, our loads being very heavy.

There are two critical points to which I call your attention. One is that at the southern point of Rudolf Land we must *know* which route you have taken here and there. The second is that if you stop this side of Rudolf, as you may be compelled to do, we must be apprised of that fact, by record or otherwise, so we do not pass the winter station.

I do not anticipate that you will find it necessary to stop this side of Karl Alexander Land, and I will make it a special point to search for records under cairns on that land and Coburg Island, also Hohenlohe Island. Near your stopping place, wherever it is, you should erect a number of cairns for our information, each containing written notes.

Probably my party will reach Karl Alexander Land about September 10, but we may be there earlier, or later; and the importance of cairns is the greater because of the probability of much stormy, thick weather at that season.

It is highly desirable that the winter station be as far north as 82°, if that be possible; and you are authorized to leave a part of your load in a safe cache on Rudolf Land, or even farther south, if in your judgment it is best to do so, and by sending back a party later in the autumn all the supplies can be assembled at the winter station before the first of November.

In every detail of the work I trust implicitly in your judgment and zeal, and hope our party shall be reunited at Cape Fligely or beyond, sixty days hence.

Sincerely yours,
Walter Wellman
Harmsworth House,
Cape Tegetthoff,
Franz Josef Land[229]

This maze of instructions for a five-week flying expedition offered Baldwin no fewer than fifty-one directions, orders, requests, and authorizations, many of them contradictory, some of them—to keep the aroma in the hut tolerable, for example—bordering on the bizarre. They were also, in the end, a complete fantasy, as Baldwin would not gain so much as half the distance that Wellman required. As for Wellman, in a landscape of glaciers and large ice-corrupted bays, he had ordered Baldwin to pass no fewer than eleven capes, but to do so by "avoid[ing] glacier-crossing . . . [or] . . . attempting to sail far from land in case of open water."

The very next day, Wellman handed Baldwin an additional dozen orders.

August 5, 1898
Mr. Evelyn B. Baldwin, Second in Command

Dear Sir:

To avoid any possibility of misunderstanding I have put in writing, supplemental to the instructions given you yesterday, the following:

In case through any mischance I should fail to reach your winter camp this autumn, you will, according to your judgment, endeavor to ascertain where we are and if in need of assistance. But you will in no wise endanger your own party on our account.

If I do not join you this fall or early next spring you will not attempt to make the Pole in 1899, but will, after trying to ascertain what has become of us, push out caches as far north as the land extends, preliminary to an attempt to reach the Pole in the spring of 1900. And you

Harmsworth House at Cape Tegetthoff on Hall Island. This sketch appeared in Wellman's articles about his first weeks in Franz Josef Land in 1898.

are authorized to make that attempt in 1900 if I have not previously joined you or changed these instructions.

In case messengers are sent either way, they should follow the course marked out in my letter of yesterday, as nearly as possible, leaving records at all conspicuous points.

Sincerely yours,
Walter Wellman[230]

After giving this order, Wellman retired to Harmsworth House, where he spent much of the fall writing more fantastical orders to Baldwin in the field. These orders not only bound his second-in-command to a conflicting series of unworkable plans, with more than enough contradictions to sap any field commander's self-assurance, but laid the groundwork for Wellman to disclaim responsibility should a debacle occur on the ice. It was Wellman's show, but he could hold Baldwin responsible if something went wrong. And go wrong it quickly did.

Paul Bjørvig wrote that the advance party set out with three Norwegians and just one American, Baldwin. Bjørvig was less than optimistic. The party took with them about four-dozen dogs and two small boats lashed to sledges. One of the boats was a so-called "Lapp boat," a wooden, doubled-ended affair built by Sami Lapps. It looked roughly like a twenty-foot-long Viking boat, a craft also known as a Nordlandsbåt.[231] The Lapp boat was filled with supplies, just about everything except, unbelievably, a tent, "as our leader [Baldwin] thought it was unnecessary."[232]

The other boat, made of canvas, was large enough to seat nearly all of the dogs in one go. With one man to keep the peace amongst the mass of dogs in the canvas boat, the other men and the remainder of the dogs rode in the Lapp boat, which then towed the canvas boat behind. When ice hemmed them in, the boats would be removed from the water, placed on the sledges, and pulled forward. It would prove to be a back-breaking and futile method to advance supplies northward, and the crude system very quickly led to hard feelings all around.

From the good offices of Willis L. Moore, chief of the U.S. Weather Bureau, Baldwin had been supplied with a set of meteorological recording instruments to include "standard wet and dry thermometers, self-registering maximum and minimum thermometers, aneroid barometers, a barograph, a thermograph, an anemometer, and a water thermometer."[233] With these Baldwin would keep up a nearly continuous series of weather observations during the advance march and during the winter at Cape Tegetthoff that followed. The anemometer, to measure wind speed, was mounted on the top of a seven-foot-long pole made of hickory. The self-registering instruments were placed atop an inflated rubber pillow inside a large basket. This basket was secured in the middle of a sledge given the name "Uncle Sam" since it was doing the work of the Weather Bureau in Washington, D.C.

On Friday, August 5, Baldwin and the Norwegians set out to establish the advance hut. Their first objective, Cape Frankfurt, was less the twenty miles away at the eastern end of Hall Island. With a steam launch, they could have waited for open water along the shore and raced to Cape Frankfurt in a few hours. Instead, the fast ice along shore was smooth and level, and it lured the men away from Harmsworth House with a promise of smooth running northward. But very quickly the character of the ice degenerated so that the silver runners on the sledges could make little progress over it. It was then, as Bjørvig remembered, that gaps in the fast ice began to appear: "When we got to a large opening in the ice we had to take our stuff over in the canvas boat and row to the nearest ice edge where we loaded the sledges and began to drive over the ice until we came to a new lead. This was how it was for several days. We had to take the dogs the long way around the edge of the leads."[234]

Mr. Harlan rallied himself down to the shoreline in order to take photographs of the departure of the men. He only remained long enough for one exposure, however, much to Baldwin's annoyance.

> *Took one shot*—time exposure 16 seconds. My party then returned for our dogs, and with this group stretched in long line I led the way with "leader dog," Bjorvik, Bentzen, and Emil Ellefsen "hanging on" to great rope as tightly as possible. This was a "lively time" indeed, with the forty howling creatures at our heels and tumbling over one another as occasion permitted. "Ace" and dog that had been badly bitten followed.
>
> As I anticipated, floes from near edge of ice field began to move off during our absence, notwithstanding had placed equipment a safe distance from the edge. Doctor Hofma moved copper sledges and part of equipment from one floe that floated away. Upon our arrival entire

party kept busy moving everything from one floe to another and had to work quickly. In midst of all this excitement I sent Doctor Hofma to headquarters to report the danger, etc. I began to send written communication to Wellman, but danger of losing sledges, etc., demanded my *muscular* assistance at once and, therefore, I simply sent verbal communication by the Doctor. After an hour's hard work, supplies were removed to place of safety—where the floes were stronger—and then we began to advance at from three hundred to five hundred (300 to 500) paces before "trebling back" at each advance. This sort of work continued till about midnight, when we went into camp.[235]

Far from advancing "as rapidly as possible," Baldwin now began an excruciatingly slow crawl along the southern shore of Hall Island. One of the expedition's novelties was a series of copper tubes that had been transformed into sledges through the expedient of soldering runners to the tubes. These tubes contained the bulk of the expedition's preserved food, and they were designed on the theory that one dog could be assigned to pull one of sledges. In the event, rather than pull in teams, the dogs, individually harnessed to individual tubes, began to behave like cats as they scattered the make-shift sledges in all directions.

This became apparent on the second day's march, when the advance team left its camp at 8:00 A.M. and ran directly into a day of wandering through fog and over heavy wet snow. The dogs had not been broken in to the unique work they were now asked to do and, during the first days at Cape Tegetthoff, while Wellman combed the hills above the site in search of Arctic poppies, no work had been done to train them. As Baldwin wrote, the dogs were not "accustomed to one another in the harness, to their new style of gear and to our manners of driving (to English, Norwegian, and German tongues), little wonder that they were unruly, as we thought. Moreover, very few would do anything at all pulling the copper sledges (tubes) singly and it became necessary to tie the sledges (copper) dogs and all behind the larger ones. Even then several dogs expressed a desire to choke to death rather than be compelled to pull in the rear. Almost invariably, however, each of these behaved well when in the team. (It is indeed hard to teach an old dog new tricks)."[236]

In this way the men were obliged to advance a few hundred yards, then double back for more supplies, and in the process cover every distance made good at least three times—to "treble" the route, as Baldwin called it. By Saturday evening, August 6, the advance party had made good only about six miles from Cape Tegetthoff when it halted for its second camp. Even at this very early stage, after just two days on the march, the physical differences between an American desk-jockey meteorologist and Norwegians with several years of the hardest kinds of outdoor manual labor—walrus and polar bear hunting and sealing—under their belts, had become painfully obvious, even to Baldwin himself. "I promised the men a long sleep if they would willingly work late in order to get off the floe that night," Baldwin wrote on the evening of August 6.

> They had not grumbled, however, and I think would never do so when they see that *I* am as willing to work as *they are.* They're such strong, strapping fellows—and I so small and weak, physically, when compared with them. But then I can eat and drink about as much food and coffee as any one of them. However, I am certain I can not sleep—neither can I snore—as do they, for at the end of the day's march every muscle in my legs aches! Last night we went into camp with feet sopping wet—I wrung the water from my socks as though they had been soaking in clear water all day, and of course, my muscles in the limbs will protest. Making a sudden bend in my lower limbs last night sent the "cramps"—just the same old fellows who called upon Entrikin and myself when on the sledge journey with Peary in 1894—through the muscles of my legs. But no one save myself knew it—for I did not cry out, but immediately straightened my limbs and all went well.[237]

By the following morning, as he rose stiff and wet even before setting out for his third day on the march, Baldwin composed and sent the first of what would become a series of plaintive dispatches back to Wellman at Harmsworth House. "Had hard fight in getting over the ice floe during the last two days. Surface smooth but *very wet* and was obliged to 'treble' the route. Leave this A.M., first rounding low point to north of this signal—then going east and northeast following snow on low land north of ice foot. North wind prevents use of boats."[238]

Coming only two days into the march, this was the first of many messages to Wellman that should have caused some serious reflection over the failure to bring at least one if not two or three steam launches into the archipelago. It was also the first indication that Evelyn Briggs Baldwin had very quickly gotten in over his head. If Baldwin was the hardest American in the group, then the expedition had little hope to advance very far. It was a fact that the Norwegians had already begun to notice. Emil Ellefsen wrote in his diary on this day that "Baldwin is away and has already fired 8 shots at three loons."[239]

Sunday evening found the men a few more miles along the shore, near a raised beach to which Baldwin gave the name Loon Lake Camp. The spot appealed to him, as a "bare gravel waste on summit of which is a small lake.

> Here further progress came to an end, notwithstanding I searched carefully for a way round and across it, going personally, entirely round the gravelly place about two miles in circumference. On east side of beach, found skeleton of stranded whale—vertebrae, "hip" bones, and one large rib. Also several pieces of driftwood—probably spruce. Finally I decided to move along south beach to end of passable or traversable ice-foot, to S.E. corner of lakelet and go into camp. Barometer falling and bad weather on, with steady north wind.
>
> Farther progress, save by boat in good weather, out of the question.[240]

Baldwin ordered the men to pitch a camp near a small outlet leading from the "lakelet," to the sea, before he then invested more time in digging a "temporary lair [and] gathering in few pieces of driftwood—for use later in the season if necessary."[241] Before long, all this effort seemed wasted when the fog lifted to reveal open water to the north. Leaving Bjørvig to watch the camp, Baldwin had Bentsen and Emil Ellefsen row him in the Lapp boat across the open water for two hours until they gained some fast ice extending about two miles outward from Cape Berghaus. At the edge of the ice, "about twenty white whales arched very gracefully and for about twenty minutes in the sea near the boat while quite as many small seals quickly popped their shy heads continually up and down."[242]

Unable to land near Cape Berghaus—the last major obstacle on the march to Cape Frankfurt—the men deposited their load of supplies on the ice and then the Norwegians rowed Baldwin back to Loon Lake Camp. There Baldwin found Bjørvig fast asleep in his bag and promptly berated him for leaving his camp chores undone before he rested: "I immediately sent him with Bentzen and Emil Ellefsen to transport two more boat loads (Lapp and canvas boats) to place on the floe where we left the first one. Just before starting them off, we had supper—strong coffee, hot oatmeal, etc., and a half of Cousin Louisa's fruit cake (the second one) which the men seemed to relish very much. I decided to remain on watch in camp and to do my journalizing, etc., till the return of the men."[243]

While the Norwegians made for the ice floe near Cape Berghaus, Baldwin puttered around Loon Lake Camp, writing in his journal and wondering if the march should be conducted at "night," when presumably the snow would not be quite as soft and slushy as it was during the fogbound "days." Perhaps glad to be rid of Baldwin for a few hours, the Norwegians did not return to Loon Lake Camp until well after midnight. All of the men finally crashed into their sleeping bags and slept until 4:00 P.M. on Monday afternoon, when Baldwin roused them in order to load the boats on an incoming tide. While the men drank coffee and ate oatmeal, another boat appeared from Cape Tegetthoff that carried the two remaining Norwegians, Olaf Ellefsen and Daniel Johannesen, who were ferrying more supplies. Baldwin sent the entire flotilla away to the ice floe near Cape Berghaus, while he sat in a reverie atop a "granite boulder near Loon lake, preserving peace among the dogs, and more especially guarding their precious lives against the attacks of wayfaring bears.

> The sea is as smooth as glass as far as Koldewey and Salm Islands, but overhead a blanketing of dark stratus clouds prevents only now and then a glimpse of the sun. The sentinel rocks of Cape Tegetthoff are veiled in thin mist. But for the occasional requiem-like howling of the dogs, all nature would be at rest. A long line of gulls, tired of wing, rests upon the summit of a stranded berg just opposite the camp, while a mother walrus near at hand upon a floe three hundred paces distant, gives suck to her newly born babe. Innocent-looking little fellow, he rubs his nose like a fat pig against the great black belly of his fond parent as she raises herself aloft on fore-flippers and appears very cute in the entire performance.[244]

Baldwin hoped to advance beyond Cape Berghaus and make his next camp at Cape Frankfurt, where the expedition would jump off on the road north through Austria Sound, but by Tuesday, August 9, at the conclusion of five straight days of desultory advances, Cape Frankfurt was still several miles off and the men were encamped on the same ice floe about two miles south of Cape Berghaus. Several trips had been required to move all of the gear and dogs from Loon Lake Camp to the camp on the ice floe. In each of them, the Norwegians had rowed the Lapp boat while Baldwin and many of the dogs were towed in the canvas boat behind. In this way it took three hours of hard pulling to get to the ice floe, a journey that a steam launch would have accomplished in minutes.

With the rest of the Americans burning fifty pounds of coal a day to snug Harmsworth House, Baldwin sidestepping the majority of the physical labor, and the dogs fairly useless on the soft slush of the rotten ice floes, the Norwegians were left to move everything by hand. There were soon exhausted by the effort—and the expedition was less than a week old.

On the ice lay our impedimenta without order and besides this, the sledge and boat brought by Olaf and Johannesen. Johannesen was up and ready to catch our line, but Olaf lay in sleeping bag. Poor fellow, he had fallen through the ice and was wet to the armpits. He and Johannesen, with five of their copper sledges, had been unable to get ashore and had left the sledges near open lane of water near land and returned to our "station." Upon my arrival, I at once sent them to same place with their five other sledges letting them use several of my dogs for the purpose—two to each sledge.[245]

When Baldwin took Emil Ellefsen and the canvas boat to assist Olaf and Daniel, they found that Daniel, too, had fallen through the rotten ice. Daniel stripped immediately and tried to wring out his clothes. Baldwin sent him back to the camp on the ice and ordered the Ellefsen brothers ashore with the supplies while Baldwin went to scout a way ahead to Cape Frankfurt. When all the men had returned to the camp on the ice floe to rest over lunch, the sea underneath them began to undulate and the floe began to break up. As Baldwin wrote, he "decided to move everything farther in.

Accordingly, all hands were called and for an hour we worked hard and were none too soon, for what *had* been at 1:00 P.M. our "camping ground," immediately put to sea. All then turned in, but *I* could scarcely sleep, for an hour and a half later I again called *all hands out!* The sea was fairly upon us and we had barely time enough to get things to a place of safety. One after another of the ice pack quickly went adrift. Olaf and Johannesen, too, concluded to get their boat once more afloat and return to Harmsworth House. So quickly did the ice separate that before he could spring into the boat with Olaf he was cut off. My party continued to advance before the separating floes and have worked incessantly till now (11:00 P.M.) to get on a more stable foundation. All are tired and sleepy and we *must* have rest. I would not stop now were it not that probably we shall have to put forth great efforts in passing over about a mile of *very* rotten ice and then in boats another mile to the shore.

Storm clouds are in the sky, the wind is blowing briskly, and I fear that we will have trouble before we shall have slept long.[246]

As August 9 turned to the 10th, the men were still several miles short of Cape Frankfurt. Wellman's original plans had called for Baldwin's advance party to be approaching Rudolf Land by now. But Rudolf Land was still 150 miles away at the northern end of Austria Sound, a waterway Baldwin still had not seen. It was not long before Baldwin began to blame the poor progress on the Norwegians, Bernt Bentsen in particular. As Ellefsen watched on August 12, Baldwin took Bentsen aside for a sermon (*straffepreik*), "as he thought he was not obeying his orders and pointed out to all of us to remember this."[247]

Baldwin's physical limitations were increasingly obvious to the Norwegians. Added to this, with no native English speakers to talk to or to help work through his problems, Baldwin's spirit as well as his body was already on the verge of being played out. To fully complicate matters, Baldwin seemed aware of only one style of leadership, that of the martinet—a martinet further handicapped by incompetence.

In Camp on Ice Floe
Tuesday, 5 P.M., August 9, 1898
Walter Wellman, Esq.,
Leader Expedition.

Dear Sir:
Olaf Ellefsen and Johannsen are just on the point of returning to Harmsworth House after an experience which I do not think they

would gladly repeat. Had it not been that they overtook my party it is likely that they would have lost all the sledges sent by them or else have been compelled to return with them. I do not believe it *safe* for two men to be thus *alone* at this season. The ice is in much worse condition than you suppose, I fear. We are having a *hard fight* of it trying to reach Cape Frankfurt—just now an exceedingly trying time in endeavoring to reach the land at Cape Berghaus, faster than the ice a few rods back of us break away. We have worked at least thirty-six out of every forty-eight hours since leaving Cape Tegetthoff. I shall *rejoice* if I can get everything once more safely on *land*—*I shall take no more risks* if I can avoid it, but will do all I can to accomplish the ends of the party if it is possible to do so. However, if conditions continue the same as they have been since the advance party left you, it will be utterly impossible to make the journey to Cape Fligely until either more open water exists or the sea shall have frozen over. I am sorry that I cannot *talk* with you and that you cannot see for yourself just what this rotten ice is like and the real danger of working in it.

I have had just two hours sleep during the past forty-eight hours and had I not kept one eye open while all hands got a little sleep this afternoon, the entire impedimenta, etc., would have been adrift on a dozen floes. I called *all hands out just in the nick of time.* As it was the small boat used by Olaf and Johansen went adrift, Olaf in it—but Johansen cut off before he could spring in.

In order to save the tube sledges brought by Olaf and Johansen, Emil and I were obliged to go with them with dog teams and get them across water along shore. For this purpose we used the canvas boat. Olaf and Daniel both fell into the water and got thoroughly wet, etc.

If I do not find conditions different by the time we reach Cape Frankfurt I think it will be best not to tempt *sure fate* beyond that point till later. I deeply regret this but it will be the best course to pursue. I will then endeavor to get game for the dogs as well as for our party and remain *in the field if possible.* I will not return to Harmsworth House till *fate* compels me to or unless I receive a message from you calling me back. I have seen but one bear or even bear tracks since leaving the House—and that was on the floe just off the House itself. We have seen but few walruses thus far—still I think they are to be found in this water. There are many white whales here—and small seals.

It was a great mistake to put the sledges with German silver runners into the water, for the water froze and sprung the tacks loose. The silver runners are useless in wet snow unless *securely* fastened and *perfectly* soldered—both of which were lacking in two of my sledges (the large ones). Bring all the sledges possible and *all* the German silver; also hard wood for uprights to sledges.

Faithfully yours,
Evelyn B. Baldwin,
Observer, U.S. Weather Bureau
Second in Command[248]

With the sledge runners already breaking down, with the constant shifting of supplies from sea to shore to ice floe and the men falling through rotten ice, Baldwin ascended the cliff above the beach at Cape Berghaus and spied little on the horizon save for more areas of rotten ice. In exchange for five days of the heaviest donkey work, the men had been exhausted and the expedition had advanced little more than ten miles.

All of Wellman's cavalier planning and lack of competent administration were now revealed. For Paul Bjørvig, the expedition even at this early point was already a comedy. The Norwegians with Baldwin "thought well enough that it was all too soon to be having a tough time, but perhaps it was best for us that right from the start we were getting a taste of what lay ahead of us."[249]

ELEVEN

To Storm Bay and a Change of Plans

To reach 82° North, build a winter hut, and then dash back to Harmsworth House before the onset of winter, Baldwin's party would be required to move northward at least four miles each day. On the few days when weather and ice conditions actually allowed travel, the party crawled ahead less than two. As they struggled to cross dangerously broken floes and shorelines strewn with the debris of glaciers, the team moved north for fully a month.

The adverse conditions, the pressure to set the advance camp as far north as possible, his lack of Norwegian language and personal leadership skills: all quickly demoralized Baldwin. Two days out, the advance team walked into the teeth of a north wind. "Had hard fight in getting over the ice floe during the last two days," Baldwin wrote to Wellman, as the two men began to exchange correspondence via Norwegian couriers. "Surface smooth but *very wet*."[250] The north wind made the party's unpowered boats near to useless; they were obliged to place the boats atop the sledges and drag the heavily burdened sledges through the slush.

Encamped on an ice floe in the evening of August 9, after another day of pitiful progress, Baldwin finally began to realize that Wellman's lack of foresight with regard to the necessity of a motorized maritime craft had all but doomed the expedition. By August 17, when Baldwin gazed north from Cape Hansa on Wilczek Land, the full impact of the chance that had been lost struck home. He saw open water "northward as far as eye could reach.

Small steam launch would probably have placed our entire party near Carl Alexander Land or Rudolf Land by this time."[251]

A steam-launch expedition to either island would have placed the expedition, at a minimum, a whole degree and more likely two whole degrees closer to the pole. This theme now came to dominate Baldwin's thoughts, and he would return to it throughout the march of the advance party: the back-breaking toil that the Norwegians undertook could have been avoided completely by a small, nimble expedition of just two or three steam launches. Instead, an American polar expedition mounted during the hyper-technological Gilded Age and led by a journalist who celebrated speed had adopted instead the exact same method of man-hauling boats over the ice that had been used by the British expedition of Sir William Parry more than seventy years earlier.

On the afternoon of August 10, the men moved their equipment and dogs "over some of the rottenest ice I ever saw," as Baldwin wrote.[252] For every mile forward, the men now had to travel five miles, as they were forced to go back and forth over the ice to bring up first the equipment, then the dogs. Often, one or more of the dog teams would run off, usually back toward Cape Tegetthoff, and would then have to be tracked down and dragged back to the head of the advance column. When the boats were launched along the edge of the fast ice toward Cape Berghaus, the men encountered yet another challenge. Because they were trying to advance along an Arctic shoreline where groups of walrus hauled up out of the water and onto the beach, the walrus viewed the boats as the foreign intruders that they were and began to attack them as they passed.

By evening, the men had at last reached the sandy beach at Cape Berghaus, where Baldwin found "great boulders lining shore as far as can be seen.

To west and north, I walked for fifteen hundred paces and found open water along shore till north side of the Cape—a bold stratified cone-shaped summit surmounted by precipitous basaltic wall, on which nest innumerable gulls. During this walk or series of walks on both sides of encampment, I found and brought to camp a generous supply of driftwood. I therefore determined to build a fire and cook the three loons which I had shot at Loon Lake, knowing that the fire and feast of fowl would encourage the men as well as myself. Driftwood found from ten to fifty feet elevation above seawater. Also found tusk of walrus partly buried in dirt at about forty feet above sea. It was inches long, reckoning curvature. Later found part of skeleton of walrus one hundred feet elevation. Tusks had been broken from skull—probably by human agency and probably by members of *Tegetthoff* Expedition.[253]

A fierce snowfall began that stopped five minutes after it began, to be followed by bright sunshine. After the exertion of reaching Cape Berghaus, the men sprawled out on the beach and immediately fell asleep. Their rest was short-lived as a line of walrus approached the beach and set the dogs into a frenzy. As Baldwin wrote, the walrus had "doubtless come to inquire why strangers had taken possession of their basking beach. Creeping out, I sent two or three shots after the visitors and in the retreat which followed I saw one of them turn white hind flippers into the air and go to the bottom."[254] Rather than let his tired men get some rest, Baldwin ordered them to pursue the retreating beasts:

Up jumped Emil and Bjorvik, followed with sleep still on countenance, by Bentzen. Indeed, could see on faces of all that sleep was preferable to chasing walruses. And then Emil explained that it would be unsafe to follow in Lapp boat, as all Norwegians thought. But I insisted that if Lapp boat were not to be used in getting walruses, then I wished to find it out now and not later. Therefore, with Bjorvik and Emil, I gave chase and approached two large ones on floe. Firing, I wounded one, but both tumbled into water and moved to attack boat. I again fired and killed one, whereupon Bjorvik harpooned it. Other one came madly out. Again I fired, killing it instantly but as we had no harpoon for it, it went to the bottom. Then began pull for shore. Had not gone far before herd of five or six, led by huge bull, rushed to attack. Rising majestically from water and plunging forward our little boat seemed doomed. "*Bursa! Bursa!*" ("Fire! Fire!") shouted Bjorvik. Bang! My rifle had spoken. A surprised splash in the water and a more surprised walrus bull would be hard to imagine. He was not dead, but his blood colored the sea as he and his followers made the sea boil. Then they beat a retreat for the time being. We at once made fast our prize and pulled toward shore against current, wind, and dead weight of walrus, which we were obliged to tow side-wise, owing to position of harpoon point. Suddenly three or four walrus heads emerged from water and again showed fight. "*Bursa!*" shouted Bjorvik. "Snap!" went rifle trigger. I had miscalculated the number of cartridges in magazine to rifle and had failed to reload. Seizing an oar, Bjorvik prepared to defend boat from attack, thinking rifle out of order. But it was not, for I at once reloaded and just at a very opportune moment got in a telling shot at the leader of attack. Every head disappeared and we rowed forward, Bjorvik and Emil redoubling efforts at oars and it was not till we had neared shore that we were again molested. For third time the herd moved toward the boat and I prepared to receive the leader, holding fire till the last. But when about two rods distant and just as I had about decided to let go a bullet, leader checked his progress and I spared the cartridge. We were now so near the shore that the herd ventured not nearer, but lingered about in state of great excitement. A few moments later and boat and dead walrus were on the beach. All at once heads of two walruses appeared near at hand and I decided to give chase. The boat was off. They were off, in the direction of a single large head with gleaming tusks. About it, we soon observed, blood coloring the water. We were again face to face with the wonderful bull and while the two in pursuit of which we were, continued to flee, this one prepared to attack. But great loss of blood rendered all his movements clumsy and another cartridge and the harpoon made him ours, and he, too, was soon upon the beach.[255]

The fresh exertion further exhausted the men, who dragged themselves back to camp to find they had no fresh water. Now thirsty as well as tired, Baldwin led the men to a small pool of water he had seen in his wander around Cape Berghaus the previous evening. As they reached the shallow pool, Bjørvig stepped across several stones to the center of the pool, where he dipped his cup in the water and recoiled in disgust. The water was tainted with alum. Bjørvig hurried from the pool, but not before he slipped into the water and lost one of his boots in the mud below. Another step and his stocking foot plunged even deeper into the mud. Bentsen pulled Bjørvig from the muck, and Baldwin then added to the insult as the men returned to camp when he immediately sent Bjørvig out to a stranded iceberg to gather snow and ice.

The men were then set to work to skin and cut up the walrus, while Baldwin wandered off for three hours in search of driftwood. In the process, Baldwin made one of the first significant discoveries of the expedition, that Cape Berghaus was not the end of a peninsula attached to Hall Island but rather the southern corner of a small island in its own right.

During this time I found quite a number of pieces of timber, one of them a trunk of a tree twenty feet long and more than two feet in diameter, on east side of mountain, the slopes of which were dotted here and there with bright yellow poppies. When nearly opposite east side of the mountain, two walruses seen on floe stranded near shore. But I passed on without disturbing them. Continuing, I observed drift at usual elevation of from ten to fifty feet. I began now to cross small streams fed by snow melting from east and north side of mountain, the water from which was invariably of strong alum taste. When on southeast face of mountain on fourth terrace and one hundred feet elevation, found rib, long, flat board-like bone, and vertebrae of whale. Still advancing I soon discovered that the north slope of the mountain is separated from the mainland by a channel about a mile in width. Along the north shore were open water spaces and at several places along the beach were large sticks of driftwood. Across the channel lay the face of the great glacier extending as an unbroken wall from Cape Littrow nearly to Cape Frankfurt. I still walked on, passing tracks of foxes and bears, until I arrived on west slope of mountain to place opposite where I was yesterday. Thus I had demonstrated that we were encamped on an island, the south projection of which is Cape Berghaus. On the west slope, I came upon and brought to camp three or four small pieces of driftwood which, when first picked up, lay at an elevation of one hundred feet above sea level.[256]

The dimensions of this new island Baldwin estimated to be "about three or three and one half miles north and south by two or two and one half miles east and west, and elevation two thousand feet."[257] Curiously, given his later obsession with the location of islands, capes, and bays to which the expedition could attach "good American names," this first discovery of a new island does not appear to have immediately impressed Wellman, perhaps because of his severe disappointment at the advance party's lack of progress or because his eyes were, at this stage, still focused upon a much larger goal.[258]

Friday morning, August 12, 1898, dawned with "beautiful, sunshiny" weather, according to Baldwin. He left the Norwegians to repair the battered sledges and boats prior to a planned move to Cape Frankfurt and, flush with discovery, took the chance to ascend to the summit of his new island and gain a view of the way ahead. Along the way, Baldwin took in the nests of birds and noted the fine fossil shells eroding out of the mountain's flanks. As he reached the summit, his barometer gave an elevation of 1,262 feet. "Formed small circle of stones, one *large boulder,* at extreme north or northeast point of summit. Fine view to north and northeast and could *overlook* promontory of Cape Frankfurt and see much open water with floating ice pans in Austria Sound," Baldwin wrote and, once again, the open water beckoned an expedition with the foresight to bring a steam launch into the islands.[259]

Thoughts of motorized transport must have been at the forefront of the minds of the Norwegians as well, as they rowed toward Cape Frankfurt with two boatloads of supplies. They were not happy to be forced to make the attempt amid a large sea swell. Their unhappiness must have only increased as they rowed and paddled against the current for three and a half hours, only to arrive at Cape Frankfurt to find a heavy swell running against a long line of boulders on shore and no possibility to make a landing. The men were forced to pass around the southern tip of Cape Frankfurt until they spied a small shelf along the ice foot that formed a small harbor where they managed to get the canvas boat onto the ice. From this exposed spot, and despite the swell that heaved the water and ice around them, they got themselves onto the land. They returned to Cape Berghaus three hours later, where they found Paul Bjørvig hastily moving the remaining supplies further up the beach, as the heavy swell tossed thick chunks of ice onto the bank and drowned the site of the dinner campfire. The swell prevented any further work toward Cape Frankfurt so the men turned in after midnight.

It was not until 2:00 P.M. on Saturday, August 13, before the men were ready for another pull around Cape Frankfurt. Baldwin sent the men off in the two small boats while he remained behind in camp, "looking after the dogs, doing meteorological work, getting things ready for final departure tonight, as I intend our next sleep will be on Austria Sound.

> While on the mountain yesterday I could see a continuous black line of open water from southeast side of Salm Island, thence to southeast coast of Wilczek Land. What a pity the *Frithjof* is not here or that we have not a steam launch to take everything at once to the west coast of Wilczek Land![260]

The Norwegians, who now subsisted almost exclusively on a diet of walrus meat and coffee, suspected that Baldwin also dispatched them away from camp so that he could dig into the tins of preserved food that they hauled northward. The men, as the equanimous Bjørvig wrote, "had already realised our leader would use us to the full. Fair enough he had enough to do on several occasions, but that had no significance as to what he wanted us to perform.

> Now there is one thing, that on a sledge expedition in the Arctic a man must be careful with food supplies from the start, and this is only sensible, as no one can know how long a trip might last. But it is important that everyone plays their part. But our leader took care quite calmly to fill himself with food when he could without us noticing.
>
> However we suffered no hunger as we shot more walrus and polar bear than we and the dogs needed. It was more difficult to get cooked meat, as the primus stove could only be operated for a few minutes to save oil, and so the meat was never cooked, but we never got ill. Luckily we had had plenty of water until . . . we first had to melt ice. And here on Franz Josef Land there is very little drift wood.[261]

When the men returned, Baldwin had a dinner of boiled walrus meat and hot chocolate waiting for them, after which Bjørvig and Bentsen rowed the final two boatloads of supplies around Cape Frankfurt. Before Baldwin and Emil Ellefsen drove the dogs overland to the other side of the cape, Baldwin wrote out a brief note to Wellman:

> Just leaving with last of equipment by boat for Cape Frankfort [*sic*], on shore about three-quarters of a mile north or northeast of that point.
>
> I leave here greater part of two walruses in pit about three hundred paces west or southwest of ten copper sledges. . . .
>
> Considerable driftwood is to be found among boulders east and northeast of here at from ten to fifty feet above sea-level and for distance of a mile or more.
>
> Made first trip to Cape Frankfurt last night and was caught in sea swell, but got clear without damage. Our first encampment here was partially submerged—but removed everything before any damage was done.
>
> If possible bring *large size* shot and some powder—I have about one hundred capped shells, but no powder and shot. Had chance of

getting some geese here, but small shot not effective. Bring all string, cord, rope and sledges possible.

Cape Berghaus south point of an island as I ascertained yesterday. Elevation of mountain is 1,252 feet by aneroid. Have been eating walrus meat two days. It is excellent.[262]

Baldwin and Emil Ellefsen then led the dogs up and over the cliff above Cape Frankfurt, to cross a snow field and then a succession of streams and boggy areas interspersed with strips of frozen ground. They crossed over a slope of ice, and then descended to rendezvous with Bjørvig and Bentsen as they rowed from the new camp at Cape Frankfurt. Once again, the men in the boats were attacked by herds of walrus, which lead to another bloody fight as Baldwin attempted to shoot the walrus from the Lapp boat as it pitched in the roiled waters: "Firing, I wounded severely one of the walruses who then retreated only to repeat the attack led by one of the bulls. Again firing I made him withdraw to ice-foot and being so severely hurt he could not escape, and Bjorvik and I managed to so maneuver the boat and ourselves that I got in another shot at the great brute as he struggled in the water. This time the shot was fatal and he was soon in tow of our boat. But it was a hard pull against the current for two of us to reach camp, a quarter of a mile distant."[263]

It was 6:00 A.M., on Sunday, August 14, 1898, and the advance party had, after ten horrendous days, finally made it into camp at Cape Frankfurt and the southern end of Austria Sound. The men slept until the afternoon and then cut up the walrus that had been killed the previous evening. As he gazed northward over the open water of Austria Sound, Baldwin could only wonder where the advance party could have been had they been properly outfitted.

Once again, he sent the Norwegians away in the boats while he puttered about the camp. Only this time, the Norwegians were ordered to take the two small unpowered boats all the way across Austria Sound and make a landing at Cape Hansa, on the southwestern tip of Wilczek Land: "A good breeze from the southwest this evening and I therefore decided to send the men with two boat loads to point north of Cape Hansa, not daring to venture toward the Hayes Islands, the distance there being too great to run such risk in our small boats. Open water is visible as far as eye can reach both north and south and I find myself hourly regretting that we have not a steam launch."[264]

As the Norwegians towed the first loads of supplies across Austria Sound, Baldwin remained behind in camp, shifting the dogs from place to place and worrying over the fate of the men as he felt the wind rise and Austria Sound begin to boil. "But I felt certain that the men made a successful landing upon Wilczek Land, before it became so bad."[265]

Paul Bjørvig estimated the crossing of Austria Sound to be about five Norwegian miles. Given that the Scandinavian "land mile" was more than six times the English mile, this meant that the men would have to row or sail the small boats some thirty nautical miles across a turbulent Arctic strait filled with broken ice. Modern charts put the straight line distance between capes Frankfurt and Hansa at ten kilometers, about six nautical miles, while the straight line distance from Cape Frankfurt to Storm Bay is about double that. But Bjørvig can be forgiven a bit of exaggeration here. He, Bernt Bentsen, and Emil Ellefsen were forced to row ill-suited boats deeply laden with all of their supplies—not to mention cumbersome sledges and more than three-dozen unruly dogs—across an ice-filled strait and often against winds and currents.

Their troubles soon worsened. "In the middle of the bay a storm rose from the south west," Bjørvig later wrote.

We had to run for shelter behind an ice berg. When the wind dropped we rowed over the sound and got to [a place we called] Storm Bay. Here there is no bay, but a long lowland and shallow shelving, so the boat had to stay off shore and we had to wade in the water up to the waist to get our gear to shore. We got everything ashore and were about to row back. Then the storm from the south west blew up again. To row back was impossible. We tried three times but had to turn back. We were once again soaked to the skin and had no change of clothes, no tobacco, matches or primus. These were all with our leader on the other side of the bay. . . .

We turned the boat over on the beach and crept under it, but because we were so soaked it got so cold that we had to jump about a bit to get some warmth into our bodies.[266]

On the western side of Austria Sound, a melancholy Baldwin tended a fire and kept up hot coffee and meat all night as he lamented the missed birthdays of his sister and niece. It would be twenty-three hours before the Norwegians returned, cold, hungry, and exhausted, by which time Baldwin had let the fire go out and had to hustle to get hot food for the men. "Of course, they had biscuits and butter, etc., for lunch, and had not gone hungry while on the trip," Baldwin wrote. "On the outward voyage they were obliged to take in the sail after rounding glacier point just north of this camp and thence to row seven hours to gain place above Cape Hansa, which point I had indicated as probable landing place—a low, swampy coast—but nevertheless a safe one near end of bay above the Cape. But before crossing and just after rounding glacier point they were obliged to unload and take boats ashore on account of sea swell."[267]

Bjørvig's remembrances, written many years later, were a bit off, as he recalled crossing Austria Sound with only one boat and remaining at Storm Bay for nearly two days, when in fact the men had crossed in both boats and remained on the other side about twelve hours. But these are trifles, and completely understandable given the exhaustion and exposure the men now experienced as a routine. The advance party had no tents and, as they crossed Austria Sound, not even sleeping bags. The canvas boat that the men occasionally doubled up as a sleeping cover was by now soaked inside and out and gave little shelter. Baldwin, brought on the expedition by Wellman on account of his previous experience in the north, now wrote obtusely: "I now promise myself that I will never be again caught on another Arctic trip without a good tent, for use when emergency demands at any rate."[268]

As the Norwegians returned to Cape Frankfurt, Bjørvig recorded that the men "were not a little surprised that our leader had made hot coffee and cooked walrus meat for us. We ate until we were full and drank strong black coffee, and then lay down for a sleep between the rocks. Now we had our sleeping bags and the snow lay smooth and soft, we could not have had it any better and we fell asleep straight away and forgot all the troubles of the world."[269] The strenuous and dangerous passage across Austria Sound had done them all in, and the men slept nearly twenty hours.

Back at Harmsworth House, Wellman had read Baldwin's dispatches with a growing sense that the expedition was going nowhere fast. By August 15, as he saw that Baldwin had not been able to advance off the very same island that Wellman himself was encamped upon, Wellman realized that the whole conception of the expedition had to change if anything meaningful was to be salvaged from it. He therefore composed a long memorandum that restructured the entire plan of the work for the fall, a note that in fact tore up the optimistic plan that Wellman had conceived of a year earlier, after his "long conference" with Fridtjof Nansen in the crenellated tower at Polhøgda. Olaf Ellefsen was ordered to catch up with Baldwin and deliver the dispatch, and then deliver himself and his boat to Baldwin's advance party as well:

> On account of weather and conditions of travel I do not believe it well for us to adhere to the original plan of the expedition in a strict sense. Probably your party will not be able to get far enough for a winter station to make the outpost of much avail as a starting point in the spring; and if you are able to do so, it will still be impossible for me to bring up the remainder of the impedimenta and enough provisions to insure passing the winter with all hands in health and strength. It is now clear to me that some of us who are to go north in the spring must winter here at Harmsworth House, and in that case all, or nearly all of us, should do so. The more men wintering here the smaller the quantity of stuff that must be taken north for winter consumption, and therefore, the more can be advanced for establishment of depot for consumption by the dash-for-the-Pole party next spring. The value of the plan to winter all hands north depends largely upon the degree of northing thus obtained for a starting point in the spring. Latitude 82° or even 81° 30' would give a distinct advantage over the plan to winter all, or nearly all of the party here; but I do not believe it possible to get all hands and the necessary equipment and provisions beyond 81° and that is scarcely worth doing. Indeed, the per cent of advantage, in this case, in my opinion, lies upon the side of wintering here and throwing out an advance post or depots to be picked up in the spring.
>
> I have, therefore, upon careful reflection, decided upon the following plan of campaign, which in some respects modifies that described in my former letter of instructions to you.
>
> The party by whom this is sent will, if it overtakes you (and it is instructed to do so at all hazards, unless an impossibility presents itself) upon arrival fall under your control.
>
> This will give you the best men in the expedition, the available boats, and a good equipment.
>
> With this party at your command your business will be *to advance the tube sledges as far northward as possible this fall,* together with such weights of other provisions as may be available and suitable for depots. Every pound taken northward now will facilitate our work next spring.

During the next three or four weeks you are likely to have more or less open water, and with three good and handy boats, and a man to each, you should be able to do a good deal. There will be much stormy weather, but by using the best days some progress may be made. From now on the surface for sledging is likely to be better and better, with falling temperature and diminution of snow.

At a point to be selected by yourself, but which I hope will not be this side of 81°, you may find it practicable to build a hut of some sort and to accumulate there game for the use of dogs during the winter. At this station, wherever it is, two men should be left to winter and take care of the dogs, while the others return to Harmsworth House. If it is not practicable to establish this depot as far north as 81°, let it be farther south, *but beyond 81° if possible;* and the farther the better.[270]

Wellman gave Baldwin all of September and the early part of October to reach his new objective north of 81°, after which he was to bring himself back to Harmsworth House for the winter. If this could be accomplished, then Wellman could "make an early—an exceptionally early—start northward next spring for a rapid push with light loads to the outposts, there, getting the benefit of more dogs and more men to push on northward again and be able to make our dash for the Pole under favorable auspices.

It is highly important as you have so often said to me, that we have dog food enough to winter our pack in good condition. In my opinion this can be done only by *dividing the pack into two lots*—one at the post which you are to establish and the other here.

With the feed which we have here, and the game which I think we shall get later in the fall, I believe we can get through the winter with the pack which is now here. The dogs you have *must* be wintered farther north, and probably you will decide to leave Bjorvik and Bentzen in charge of them.

I am extremely anxious, as I know you are, that we get affairs in such shape this fall that we may make our dash next spring and get home next summer. Whether or not we shall be able to do this depends upon the success met with by you and your party this fall. Please say to your men that I shall warmly appreciate and *liberally reward* their very best efforts.[271]

Wellman insisted that he had always intended to join Baldwin on the trail and had even gone so far—two or three times—as to make preparations to set out from Harmsworth House, "but weather or something else stopped us.

> Upon reflection, however, I have decided that it is my duty to remain here, for in case of a messenger from you, or any accident in the field, I should be here to take action accordingly. It is strongly against my inclination to remain here, but I see no way of avoiding it at present.[272]

Wellman told Baldwin that he could request all the men come forward and winter at the advance hut, but Wellman considered this "as extremely unlikely."[273] In a private note appended to his dispatch, Wellman finally admitted that the three boats the expedition had at its disposal were unsuited to the task at hand. They had entered an archipelago that afforded them several weeks of summer travel by water without even modest technological capabilities to take advantage of the conditions. Even at this, Wellman was still oblivious to the potential of a motorized boat, as he bemoaned only that he had not bought another rowing craft:

We are handicapped by lack of boats.

Now I know I should have bought a whale-boat. I came near doing so at Vardo—within an ace of it. Have lain awake nights cursing myself and chewing the bitter rag because I didn't. A big boat would have helped me north instead of tying us up here. That is, we could have gotten twice as much stuff up, even if not the whale outfit. We have had bad weather down here, drifting winds and ice that knock all our plans in the head and suppose you have had the same experience.

My dear fellow, you see I have really placed the success of the expedition in your hands. Unless you succeed this fall we shall either fail or have to stay two years—and I think you agree with me that must be avoided if possible. I feel in my bones you will do the best mortal man could do, and that the work could not be in better hands. Stick to it as long as you can, and *make your men hustle*. They will have all winter to rest. Establish your little hut, take it easy yourself, and send the rest out to make things hum. . . .

Before you leave the outpost be sure to inform the men you leave that they must not open the copper sledges unless *necessary*. Show them which are "winter tubes"—those which may be opened—and which are for the northern journey. The winter tubes are numbered—and some of them have oil in them—you have three of the oil tubes—Nos. 41, 42 and 45. But I want to keep all the copper sledges we can for next spring work.

One reason why I do not go north with Olaf and Johansen is that I know you will do better work and get better work out of the men if you are alone than you will if I am with you. Next spring I shall probably turn the whole thing over to you and simply go as a passenger. If you make a success of this your honors will be great. And you may depend upon it that there will be no Peary business this time.

Too bad how things work. You dragged two good boats over ice, and when we were ready to forward stuff through water, we didn't have the boats to do it with.[274]

This extraordinary private note, in which Wellman treated the Norwegians as disposable labor even while he teased the unstable Baldwin with the possibility of commanding the polar party itself, was little short of a disaster. Since he was not with the advance party, he could not know how much the Norwegians had turned against Baldwin. But he had a sense of how they viewed the Americans generally. When he "offered the services of Mr. Harlan to the men on this trip, thinking he might be company for you . . . I could see by the looks on their faces they didn't want him. Then I told them they could go with or without him just as they pleased, and they said they would go without.

Since last Monday night . . . I have been worried lest you should come back here or at least stop at Cape Frankfort or thereabouts. If you were not to get farther, and we were to leave here with everything, then it would be necessary to bring everything back again. This did not stop me from making preparations to go north as originally planned, but it set me thinking. Your fear, as expressed in your letter, that the conditions were unfavorable, gave me disquiet, and after several days of hard thinking—and nights, too—I have concluded to winter here unless *you* say the road is clear for the original plan.[275]

As the fate of the expedition teetered on the edge of a cliff, Wellman then gave it a final shove. By his decision to remain in the comfort of Harmsworth

House throughout the fall and winter, Wellman had consigned the Norwegians to months of backbreaking labor under a lone and lonely American who knew nothing of command in the field. To the contrary, Baldwin gratuitously insulted and offended his men at every turn. Wellman also lost any opportunity to push the expedition to a point further north—a point that would be required before any serious attempt on the North Pole could be made in the spring of 1899.

Even Wellman's demoralized dispatch required three days to send, as the Norwegians could not launch the remaining boat from the shore at Cape Tegetthoff because the seas were too rough. By the time they were able to get away, Wellman had had time to add two more windy postscripts. The first was, in part, a further reflection on the expedition's lack of proper watercraft: "The boat we have is a very poor one, and I believe the Lapp boat better suited to this work. If you get a chance to send men back after tube sledges, use the Lapp boat as first choice, and then the wooden boats, saving the canvas canoe as much as possible."[276] Astoundingly, Wellman then sought to change the plan of the fall advance yet again, as he remarked that it "occurs to me that from Kane Island, Kuhn Island, or the Stalizcka Islands it is only some twenty-five miles to the Nansen winter hut, probably through fiords.

> There must be fiord ice running through there, and the bear and walrus Nansen saw in such great numbers must be still in the neighborhood. If we have a winter outpost somewhere there the game question should be solved—I mean an outpost on Kane, Kuhn, the Stalizcka [*sic*] Islands or in that vicinity.
>
> With such a half-way house, and the greater part of us wintering here, our copper sledges advanced to the outpost this fall, plenty of dried meat at the outpost ready by spring, the two packs of dogs and all the men in good condition, I believe we shall have a show next spring, notwithstanding we shall start farther south than we had counted upon.
>
> I call to your attention that when you and your party return to Harmsworth House there will be an advantage in leaving at the outpost all the boats not absolutely needed for your return journey. If you could leave there the Lapp boat and the canvas canoe I think it would be well to do so.[277]

As for the Norwegians, Wellman once again stressed that they were to eat as little as possible of the expedition's supplies and, as far as possible, to be made to eat off the land. His final postscript was only one line: "I regard the establishment of an outpost beyond 81, with two men left in charge of it as *vital* to the success of the expedition."[278]

To Wellman's armchair calculations, Baldwin responded on August 17 that he was just then ready for another crossing of Austria Sound, and almost taunted Wellman with the fact that the waterway was now free of ice all the way to the northern horizon. "Two trips with both boats have already been made and still another must follow. . . .

Much driftwood to be found along beach on other side. No game of any kind seen here. Open water seen from bay north of Cape Hansa northward as far as eye could reach. *Small steam launch would probably have placed our entire party near Carl Alexander Land or Rudolf Land by this time.* Boats so small that men cannot take large loads and row to any advantage. Wind generally and current *always* against us and progress necessarily slow. But we are working and not sleeping and will get there if *possible.* This is all that I can now promise.[279]

Baldwin asked Wellman to send him more coffee, as well as sugar, rope, leather for dog harnesses, sledges, and also, "if possible, something *for tent:* Bags and clothing get wet while canvas boat is out on trips."[280] This brief note from Baldwin was one of the few clearly worded communications to pass between Wellman and Baldwin throughout the entire voyage. It was, all things considered, a staggering indictment of an expedition that had been in the field for less than two weeks. After they were joined by the rest of the Norwegians from Cape Tegetthoff, they had become an advance party, as Paul Bjørvig wrote, "of five Norwegians under an American leader. . . . Now the storms of autumn began to show themselves."[281]

TWELVE

The Dark Side of Things

On Tuesday, August 16, 1898, the four men at Cape Frankfurt lay in their sleeping bags as a snowstorm blew up out of the northwest. As Baldwin had written to Wellman, without any tents, their sleeping bags— along with every article of reserve clothing—would soon be soaked through. The canvas boat that doubled as a shelter when overturned on a beach was also thoroughly wet and, in any case, had been left a half mile away from camp when the men returned from Storm Bay. As Baldwin lamented, "what cannot be cured *must be endured*."[282]

The men remained in their uncomfortably exposed beds until early evening, when they ate a dinner of fishmeal, coffee, and biscuits. Baldwin had boiled up a stew the evening previous, but the dogs had gotten into it and destroyed his planned breakfast for the men. To add to Baldwin's nervous disposition, the violent storm had triggered a rock slide from the cliff above the men, with "great boulders flying to pieces down the rocky precipice."[283]

After the fishmeal, Baldwin sent Paul Bjørvig and Bernt Bentsen north to drag a large stranded tree trunk back to camp. By 9:00 P.M., the weather finally moderated and, despite a heavy sea swell, Baldwin sent the men with two boatloads of supplies and gear back across Austria Sound to Storm Bay. Once again, the advance team leader decided to remain behind in camp while he sent the men on the dangerous crossing. "At first I thought I would accompany them, taking the dogs, sleeping, cooking and meteorological equipments, but finally decided that it would be better and safer to wait for smoother sea," wrote Baldwin, a notion that did not sit well with Bjørvig.

> Bjorvik said something in Norwegian when I decided to send the men on this trip, and upon asking Emil to interpret what he said, Emil replied: "He says that he knows we cannot make it against the current and the wind." Bjorvik, however, expressed an *opinion,* and not displeasure at my decision, in this remark, and willingly set to work making preparations. Then I said "we'll all take a look at the sea from a higher position," and this done, Emil said, "Well, Sir, you've only to say the word and we'll do it." Thereupon I said: "Go!" and at once there was activity among all of us.[284]

After the men had rowed off into the sound, Baldwin remained behind to busy himself "picking up things about camp, knocking out the snow from sleeping bags, fur, and woolen suits, untangling dogs, etc. I have just now crawled into my sleeping bag to write the foregoing and to watch for the return of the men."[285] While Baldwin was tucked up in his bag, he drifted off to enjoy a dream that he "had found Nansen's and Johanssen's hut—a great underground room in white sand."[286] Four years later, unlikely though it seemed at the moment, this heroic dream would move from fantasy to premonition.

The Norwegians reached Storm Bay and returned exhausted to Cape Frankfurt twelve hours later. Baldwin let the men get some rest before he woke them late in the afternoon to prepare to ferry the dogs across Austria Sound.

The whole advance party left Cape Frankfurt at 10:00 P.M. on the 17th, with two boats and twenty-nine dogs. When several dogs could not be rounded into the boats amid the rough surf, they were simply left behind. Baldwin also left behind the party's three-man sleeping bag, the men's personal gear, and his meteorological recording equipment. Propelled by a strong breeze, the overburdened boats crossed the sound in four hours. The miniature flotilla then rowed to the south end of Storm Bay—little more than an indentation north of Cape Hansa on the Wilczek Land coast—four hours later still.

Storm Bay is located at 80° 30' N. In other words, two weeks of intense labor had placed the advance party just 25 miles further north than the expedition's base camp at Cape Tegetthoff—and still 570 nautical miles from the North Pole. If the expedition continued to advance at this rate, it would take nearly two *years* to reach the North Pole and return to Franz

Josef Land. Conditions at Storm Bay were hardly ideal for the establishment of even a temporary encampment, with near-constant winds blowing from the south that brought with them rain, sleet and snow. "Low beach and very bad landing: ice floes crowding the shore," wrote Baldwin.

> Had to carry everything from boats, wading in water nearly to boot tops. Ashore, I went mile northwest to where other supplies had been left, for biscuits and butter. Return found Bjorvik sick—suffering pain in stomach and could scarcely breathe. Had no medicine, being left at Cape Frankfurt with meteorological outfit. I then at once returned to the other supply station for bottle of Russian rum or other concoction. Gave Bjorvik two big drinks and pain relieved. Also hot coffee helped him out. Had intended sending men back to Cape Frankfurt for balance of impedimenta but Bjorvik's illness caused me to change plan, although I said that I would let Bjorvik remain here and go in his place. But Bjorvig then said that he was able to go and wished that I would not do so.[287]

Bjørvig's sudden recovery indicates just how little time the men wished to spend in Baldwin's company. But even when they tried to get away, several leaks were found in the battered canvas boat, and so the four men were stuck at Storm Bay until the boat could be repaired. Baldwin set out alone, to walk around to the northern end of the bay and have a look ahead. Once again, open water lay to the north as far as the eye could see. Across Austria Sound, Baldwin could plainly make out the islands of Hayes and Wiener-Neustad.

When he returned to the Storm Bay camp several hours later, Baldwin sent the men in the Lapp boat to advance their supplies up the western coast of Wilczek Land as far as possible. The first landmark north of Storm Bay was Cape Heller, at 80° 46' North. It was only sixteen miles away, but was separated from Storm Bay by a continuous ice front that allowed nowhere for the men to land if winds and currents pushed them toward shore. The men returned in due course, unable to row into a northwest wind or to push beyond the large ice front. A second try a few hours later ended just as quickly. "Nothing remains but to *wait*," lamented Baldwin.[288]

The next day the storm moderated enough for Baldwin to walk along shore toward the middle of the Storm Bay shoreline, while the Norwegians followed, rowing the Lapp boat. After they deposited their supplies, Baldwin then sent the men back to repair the canvas boat and to cross over to Cape Frankfurt to retrieve the rest of the supplies there. With the Norwegians off across the sound, Baldwin ascended the glacier above the northern shore of the bay for a look around, but by the time he reached the summit the weather had closed in and there was no view to be had. He returned to camp "wet, tired, thirsty, and hungry. No dry place save under piece of canvas and fur coats. Had two cups of ice cold coffee and biscuits."[289]

Soon after, Baldwin heard the sound of Norwegian voices and saw Olaf Ellefsen and Daniel Johansen rowing toward the camp. They had left Harmsworth House at noon the day previous and spent the night at the Loon Lake Camp. Leaving at 9:00 A.M., they rowed via the camps at Capes Berghaus and Frankfurt before arriving at Storm Bay thirteen hours later "after heavy row," as Baldwin noted.[290] Having gathered up the three-man sleeping bag at Cape Frankfurt, they spied Bjørvig, Bentsen, and Emil Ellefsen as they rowed across Austria Sound, but were too far away to make contact. They delivered both Wellman's new instructions to Baldwin as well as themselves to the advance party. They also carried a small boat cover that Wellman had sent for the men to use as a tent. Baldwin thought it might be large enough for two men to sleep under.

At 4:00 A.M. on Saturday, August 20, the men with the canvas boat arrived from Cape Frankfurt with the remaining supplies and the dogs that had been left behind. As ice crowded the shoreline and the wind steadied at 20–25 knots, it was again impossible to discharge the cargo without a good soak in the icy surf. Baldwin allowed Daniel Johansen to sleep with him under the new "tent," while the rest of the Norwegians once again flipped over the canvas boat and crawled underneath it to try to sleep.

At 8:00 P.M. Baldwin roused the men and imparted Wellman's new instructions, namely that they had to hustle north as quickly as possible and with as little sleep as practical. He sent them all away in the boats with orders to move all the supplies across to the northern edge of Storm Bay. "They are not to return till all supplies are on other side of Storm Bay, if weather permits. Told them Wellman is a big-hearted fellow and we must stand by him and the expedition and do all in our power to succeed. But, of course, the men know our success is doubtful with our very small boats and especially unless we can soon find walruses for the dogs."[291] The men also knew that their venture was increasingly unlikely with their present field leader.

By now, with the obvious lack of progress, none of the men retained much hope for the expedition's success. At 11:00 P.M. on Sunday, August 21, as the Norwegians rowed away, Baldwin remained behind to putter around camp, "looking after dogs, digging things from snow drift, meteorological and medical outfit, guns, etc."[292] As Emil Ellefesen caustically recorded, "we all four started to push on with the two wooden boats as Baldwin stayed alone in his sleeping bag of course."[293]

When the Norwegians had gone, Baldwin again climbed a few hundred feet to the top of a "peak" on the northern edge of the camp, and the weather cleared enough for a view back across Austria Sound. When the men had not returned twelve hours later, Baldwin again gave in to his native nervousness:

How I wish I could get some word to Mr. Wellman. I know the poor man is almost worried to death. He knows not of Olaf's and Daniel's arrival nor of our whereabouts. But I *must* make use of every man and every hour. We *must* get where we can find game for man and dogs. The success of the entire expedition depends upon it. And only two small boats to move everything! One man must remain in or near camp to guard against the attack of bears, etc. I wish that two or three of them would visit the camp now, for I have two rifles in readiness for them. I hope that my nerves will, should such an event occur while I am alone, be equal to the emergency.[294]

The Norwegians returned late in the afternoon, after successfully moving the expedition supplies to the northern end of Storm Bay. With the wind and snow again against them, Baldwin let the men sleep for eight hours before he called them out again to move the balance of the gear and the dogs to the new camp. "They have had a good sleep—I not a wink of it—for planning," Baldwin wrote, and again the lack of boats returned to vex him: "I never cease regretting that we have not larger and stronger boats. And, too, I cannot rest easy till we shall have secured plenty of walrus meat. Captain Kjeldsen should have left a store of it at Harmsworth House before the *Frithjof* steamed away. I often requested that it be done. Now, an infinite amount of *uncertainty* and hard, trying days lie before us and useful time is thus wasted in getting equipment northward."[295]

At 3:00 A.M. on Sunday, August 22, Baldwin and Olaf Ellefsen left the camp with the dogs while the rest of the Norwegians rowed the four nautical miles across Storm Bay with the balance of the advance party's gear. Before long, the dogs were running wild and Olaf's shoes had split apart, exposing his heels to the stony shoreline. Two and a half hours later, the dogs caught the scent of the new encampment and broke into the run, dragging Baldwin behind them. The boats came in at 8:00 A.M. and Baldwin was faced with his first real crisis: a dwindling supply of food for the dogs. They were down to just 120 pounds of dog food; it was essential that more polar bear and walrus be brought in, or they could advance no further.

Wellman's admonition to get the Norwegians to hustle preyed on Baldwin's mind, so as soon as the boats arrived he "ordered 'big feed' of frozen beans, cold water, lime juice tablets, and biscuits."[296] The men put up the makeshift tent, whereupon Baldwin told Daniel Johansen that he would remain behind at the camp with the dogs while the rest of the men—for the first time to include Baldwin himself—would set out with all the gear loaded into the three boats and make for Kane Island and a hunt for game. Baldwin ordered Paul Bjørvig and Bernt Bentsen to take all of their personal gear, as they would be placed in charge of the advance hut that the men would build once they found enough game to lay in winter stocks for the dogs.

That Baldwin thought he could row to Kane Island—some thirty-five nautical miles north and on the opposite side of Austria Sound—when they had as yet been unable to reach even halfway up the coast of Wilczek Land, and then make the same round trip once again with the dogs, sounds like desperation, but that was now his plan. Delayed an hour by a polar bear that wandered into the camp and was eventually shot for food for the dogs, the men did not set off until 1:00 P.M. on August 22. Their first objective was the north end of Wiener Neustadt Island, more than twenty nautical miles to the northwest and across Austria Sound.

The start was promising, as Baldwin wrote that the "sea was smooth and the sun shone brightly," but the men soon rowed into trouble:

> For two hours our course was among a fleet of icebergs borne southward by the strong current, ceaselessly endeavoring to escape from the icy North through Austria Sound. Then for another two hours arm and boat carried us nearly parallel with the great glacial wall which, uninterruptedly from the north side of Storm Bay to Cape Heller, sweeps into the Sound. . . . But soon the busy ant dream of conquest was over. There was ice ahead—a long white line, extending seemingly

clear across the Sound. But we pushed on. Cape Heller stood boldly forth and seemed to double the distance between the line of sea ice stretching westward and the north side of Storm Bay. How quickly even hope fled. We met the ice and could go no farther northward.[297]

The men rowed west and then southwest, with a thought to landing on Wiener Neustadt Island. But Bjørvig warned them off, seeing that they would never get the boats through the fast ice along the island's shore. To make matters worse, the wind sprang up from the west, hemming the boats in the pack ice. With the men exhausted, Baldwin insisted on shooting at some nearby seals. He killed several but failed to secure them before the dead animals sank into the depths, as the boats continued to be pushed southward.

After nine hours of useless exertion, the boats were virtually back to where they had started, and just a bit north of the Storm Bay camp. There the men deposited their cargo: "ten copper sledges, five crates of biscuits, large tin of kerosene, two sealed tins of matches, five small tins of 'spiritus' for 'primus' stove, twelve tins of roast beef, and about one hundred fifty pounds of Bovril stuffs. This deposit was made here thinking that perhaps I might later cross glacier to either Cape Heller or Cape Schmarda."[298] The group was reunited with Daniel Johansen at midnight, after an exhausting day that accomplished nothing.

At mid-morning on Tuesday, August 23, Baldwin ordered all the Norwegians away in the boats to retrieve all of the remaining copper sledges from both the Loon Lake and Cape Berghaus camps, and for Olaf and Daniel to continue on to deliver a message to Wellman once they reached Loon Lake. But as Baldwin prepared for an extended stay as the only human inhabitant of Wilczek Land, a ferocious storm blew up and kept the entire advance party pinned down for the next two days. Baldwin remained alone in the tent while the Norwegians sheltered under the overturned canvas boat while the winds howled up to fifty knots and the camp was buried in snow.

It was not until 5:00 P.M. on Thursday, August 25, that Baldwin could send all the men save Olaf away to Harmsworth House. As Emil Ellefsen wrote, Baldwin was keeping Olaf in camp so Baldwin could stay in his sleeping bag while Olaf went "outside to make the readings of the wind speed and temperature."[299] The Norwegians who left camp carried a long letter from Baldwin to Wellman updating the progress of the advance party. It was not a happy dispatch.

(No. 5.)
In Camp, 5:00 A.M., August 25, 1898
(Storm Bay, Wilczek Land)
Walter Wellman Esq.,
Leader Expedition

My dear sir:

We have met the weather and we are his—for the present at any rate. Your several communications, 15th, 16th and 17th, were delivered to me in Camp on Bay just north of Cape Hansa by Olaf and Daniel, at 10:00 P.M., 19th. Since then they have been read and re-read that I might not err in either word or act. I am perplexed, yes worried, beyond imagination. Stormy weather, heavy sea-swells, bad ice along shore and on sea, besides too small boats, as you now see, have harassed us ever since our first start on 5th inst. As an example, it required four trips with both the Lapp and canvas boats to make the shift from Cape Frankfurt to Camp on Bay (a bad place for landing, but unavoidable owing to thick weather) north of Cape Hansa. On one of these trips the men were out twenty-three hours. Altogether the shift required from 9:00 p. m., August 14th to 4:00 A.M. 20th.[300]

Baldwin went on to describe the failed attempt to either reach Kane Island or land on Wiener Neustadt, plus the fact that since leaving Cape Frankfurt, they had not seen a single walrus. As supplies ran low, Baldwin warned Wellman in a private note that "no coal other than that for making coffee and cooking be used during September, October and November—leaving every other pound of it, together with spare wood, etc., for use during December, January, February and March. We shall need it most during the bitter cold. . . . I'm bitterly disappointed at the little progress made."[301]

The problems with the substandard or even non-existent gear were ever present. The sleeping bags could not be kept dry, and the absence of a tent was leading to exposure. And Baldwin returned again to the boats: "To attempt to cross the glacier to Cape Heller or to Cape Schmarda I deem too hazardous and to try to cross upon sea ice at this season even more so. Besides, one large and one small sledge are quite out of repairs although Bjorvik has done the best he could to fix them up again. The canvas boat leaks badly (the iron ribbings on the bottom, etc., causing the canvas to wear too much on those particular parts) and it requires much bailing to keep the boat afloat."[302]

Frustrated by the failure of the expedition's gear, Baldwin now suggested that the advance party would not be able to make progress further north until later that fall, when Austria Sound froze over and the men could travel by sledge. Baldwin also shocked Wellman when he suggested that the poor progress made thus far required the entire team, along with all the dogs, to return to Harmsworth House to spend the winter there. The dogs required food and soon, as to feed them with walrus meat and blubber was not exactly the simplest procedure:

> It's extravagant sport this attacking walruses in small boats as you will see. I have already learned, but I am willing to do it provided we can find the victims for attack. Were we on the British Channel in the vicinity of Nansen-Johannsen's hut, I do not doubt that we could get them. But how are we to get them *now*? If you think best I am willing to attempt to cross the glacier north of here to see if any of them are to be obtained near Capes Heller or Schmarda—but I do not regard such an attempt advisable.[303]

Worse, the food depot already laid by the advance party could not be secured from bears. It wasn't all bad news for Wellman: Baldwin had also sent back several polar bear skins, so that Wellman now had enough Arctic presents to satisfy his patrons. Baldwin also praised his Norwegian companions, remarking on their "very pleasant courteous and loyal conduct."[304]

Privately, however, Baldwin again lambasted Wellman for the failure to equip the expedition with adequate watercraft, on which he pinned the failure of the advance party. "A hundred times I have wished that I could have made you feel what I *knew absolutely* with regard to use of whale-boat, steam launch, and supplies of walrus meat and coal at Harmsworth House, before the *Frithjof* left us. But I'm certain that you now have the same *feeling* and so my misery has company. . . . Of course I'm bitterly disappointed at the little progress made—but have done the very best that I could do. You shall have the perusal of my journal at the earliest possible moment and then you may judge for yourself as to what have been our efforts."[305]

Addressing Wellman as "my dear fellow" and "my friend," Baldwin now claimed to know Wellman's "mind and heart as I know my own."[306] Wellman's response, which began—pointedly and formally—with "Dear Sir," showed just how little Baldwin understood of Walter Wellman's inner thoughts. "I am by no means discouraged as to the general outlook," replied the expedition leader. "To the contrary, I feel confident that all things are working out well. . . .

> Frankly, dear Baldwin, you have as much courage and nerve as any man I ever knew, but you are too prone to look on the dark side of things. You *act* like a hero, but talk like a man who is nervous, something always wrong or going wrong; if this had been so, or that the other way, all would be well; and so on. I am not scolding or lecturing, but I wish you would write more cheerfully.[307]

Unwilling to allow the well-founded criticism of the boats to stand for one minute more than necessary, Wellman showed his natural hustler's ability to take a crippling negative and turn it to advantage. "As to the whale boat I know I made a mistake," Wellman admitted, but this honest admission was quickly followed by Wellman's deliberately obtuse telescoping of events: "and yet—see how things work out—if we had had a whale boat we should have made the greater mistake of pushing northward with all our stuff and being now in a pretty pickle. You see, unlike you, I am the genuine optimist who tries to make even his own mistakes—for the whale boat business was wholly my blunder—turn to good account."[308]

Worse for Baldwin than Wellman's "genuine optimism," the expedition leader now took the opportunity to add thirty-one more vague requests-*cum*-orders to his earlier missives, and including four absolute imperatives:

> I have noted and carefully considered your suggestion that *all* of the party winter here. But I must adhere to the plan outlined in my last letter to you. I see my way, or at least believe I do—to a successful dash northward next spring and a return home next summer if only certain things are now achieved by your party in the field.
>
> It is *vital* to the success of the plan which we are to work upon:
>
> That at least twenty-six (26) copper sledges be advanced to 81° or beyond, this fall.
>
> That at 81° or beyond, an outpost—a hut—be established.
>
> That two men—possibly three—pass the winter there, with all the dogs you now have with you.
>
> That enough game be taken this fall not only to winter the dogs

and in part the men, but to enable the men at the outpost to dry by February 1st not less than 2,500 pounds of meat for the dogs—this 2,500 pounds of dog meat to be taken northward by the Polar Dash party when it reaches the Outpost early in February.[309]

But even Wellman's sunny attitude could not change the fact that his plan to establish the advance winter hut near 82° North was in a shambles. He implored Baldwin to use the month of September and the first half of October to relentlessly push the Norwegians forward. Wellman begged for just thirty or forty more miles north and a winter outpost on or near Kane Island. If Baldwin could do that, Wellman wrote, he would be content.

There you will be near the fiords which run into the mainland— through it, in all probability, water which Dr. Nansen found teeming with walrus, and lands about which he found alive with bears. It is impossible that there should be plenty of game twenty or thirty miles west of there in 1895 and none in the neighborhood in 1898. Dr. Nansen and Lieut. Johansen found September and the first part of October their *best season for game,* and so, in my opinion, will you.

If you can reach your winter station about September 10th, you will have three or four weeks in which to put up a hut—it should be large enough for nine men to squeeze in for a few days—and to shoot bear and walrus. For wintering your forty dogs and providing the 2,500 or more pounds of partly dried meat which the Polar party will want in February, you will have a total of ten or twelve thousand pounds of meat, perhaps rather more. Ten or fifteen bears, and half a dozen walrus will come very near pulling you through.

On no account short of imperative necessity—total failure of game—should you bring your dogs back here. With the fish and tongue we have and the few bears we are likely to get, we can worry through the winter. But in my opinion the region you are entering has much more game than this coast, which is practically open sea, and it is, therefore, necessary your dogs should be wintered north.

It is my opinion, further, that you will find more game on the *west* coast of Austria Sound than on the east coast, and I advise you to seek the first opportunity to cross the Sound to Wiener Neustadt Island and then work along the coast.

As to the method of doing so, I leave that to you but you have tried the glacier and know whether or not it is a thoroughfare. According to Payer it is only twelve miles or so wide, and if water and sea ice fail you I would try the glacier, were I you, unless, of course, your examination of it shows to be too dangerous. But please bear in mind that every day counts with you now.[310]

In fact, Baldwin had neglected to tell Wellman that he had *not* tried to cross the glacier north of Storm Bay, to learn whether the men could use it as a rapid road to Cape Heller. It was something that should have been done the moment that all of the supplies had been ferried from Cape Frankfurt. Wellman again implored Baldwin to build the hut "at 81° or beyond," and that "two—possibly three—pass the winter there. . . . The Polar party will expect to get at the outpost next spring. . . . Under no circumstances, short of absolute necessity, will you permit any deviation from these instructions"— and then, later, to the contrary: "As in my former letter of instructions, you are given authority to vary the programme laid down herein according to circumstances and your own judgment."[311]

This was the Wellman expedition in a nutshell. While Baldwin's Norwegians worked eighteen hours each day to advance little more than a mile per day, Wellman sat by the fire at Harmsworth House and planned his polar dash for the following spring. "I am convinced," he wrote Baldwin, "that it is only by *cavalry* speed after leaving the land at 82° 30' or thereabouts, that we can [reach the Pole] . . . perhaps an average of twelve miles per day."[312] No dent was made in Wellman's warm calculations by the fact that in twenty days of marching Baldwin's advance party had averaged just a mile and a half a day. Wellman gave himself twenty days in the spring to advance from the forward hut at 81° North to the far northern edge of Franz Josef Land. Since Cape Fligely lay at 81° 51' North, Wellman would need to top Baldwin's daily averages by at least a mile a day.

What Wellman feared more than anything else was the "dreadful thought" of having to remain in Franz Josef Land for two full years.[313] What he did not share with Baldwin—and, since they never truly became friends on any level, never would—was that he was heavily in debt, had a deteriorating marital situation on his home front, and was under no circumstances prepared to dally around the glaciated islands of Austria Sound for two more years in an aimless search for a few walrus.

THIRTEEN

Norwegians

After nearly a month in the field, the one issue that seemed to trouble
Baldwin the most—other than the imperative to locate food for the
dogs—was the impending moment when he had to leave two Norwegians
behind for a winter at the advance hut. Wellman refused to give Baldwin
his definite feelings on the subject, even as he favored the return of certain
expedition members, and even as Baldwin had formed his own evaluations
of his Norwegian crew. Two in particular, Paul Bjørvig and Bernt Bentsen,
seemed continuously at odds with Baldwin.

Prior to the expedition, Wellman had written of his Norwegian companions almost as one might describe a dog: "There is nothing about ice, bear,
seal, walrus, boating, sledging that these Norwegians do not know, and they
are faithful men in all emergencies. . . . Lieutenant Peary believes in the
use of Eskimaux, but I prefer Norwegians. The latter have all the technical
skill of the Greenlanders, possess greater endurance and are infinitely more
intelligent and loyal."[314]

As the expedition had sailed from Vardø, Baldwin had felt precisely
the same. Before the expedition was a month old, however, these initial
feelings toward the Norwegians had become quite the opposite. Baldwin's
journal is filled with notes that slight or denigrate the Norwegians, even as
they performed most of the logistical work, and combined with murmurs
of approval when he felt the Norwegians had paid him what he considered

his due respect. In all this, Baldwin reserved the bulk of his ill feeling for Bjørvig and Bentsen. This becomes evident as one reads Baldwin's journal: a strange pattern begins to emerge. Baldwin habitually refers to Bjørvig and Bentsen by their surnames, all the while he called the other Norwegians by their Christian names. This would be an insignificant trifle, save that "Bjørvig and Bentsen," as they became linked, also seem to have come in for much of the heavy lifting, while as often as not the other Norwegians received camp duties. "[S]ent Bjorvik and Bentzen one-half mile north for large tree trunk, while Emil made coffee," runs a typical entry.[315]

When Paul Bjørvig and Bernt Bentsen, along with Emil Ellefsen and Daniel Johansen, rowed away from Storm Bay on the 25th of August, Baldwin was left at Storm Bay with Olaf Ellefsen. The other four Norwegians would not return from their trip back to Harmsworth House for more than four days, during which time Baldwin wrote that the camp at Storm Bay was "exceedingly quiet," with at first but little to do save for "eat, sleep and care for the dogs.

> We have not yet seen either a walrus or a seal in the waters of this bay. There are, however, great numbers of shrimps, or "sea life." Very few birds are also to be noticed—only now and then an "ice gull," a robber gull, or an Arctic tern, visits the camp. Olaf and I have been wishing that another bear might make us a call. We are prepared to give him or her a warm reception.[316]

On Saturday, August 28, Olaf left camp to check on the cache that the men had laid upon the shore some two miles further north. He found that it had been knocked about by bears, confirming Baldwin's fears expressed in his letter to Wellman that the caches could not be protected. Baldwin himself then went to visit the depot to see the damage for himself. As he approached, he came across "a box of 'Vril'" about four hundred paces south of the depot: "The bear had endeavored to open it, but the 'key' or opener having evidently become fast between the bear's teeth, he had precipitately retreated from the depot in his endeavors to escape from the can. His tracks indicated that after the can had become disengaged he had returned to the depot wreaking vengeance upon another of the same sort of tins, chewing it and 'Vril' into a shapeless mass. The snow, however, was covered with the bear's blood, showing the effects of the sharp edges of the tins upon the bear's mouth. The copper 'tube sledges' being quite heavy had not been much disturbed."[317]

As he returned to camp, Baldwin came across the first walrus he had seen since his arrival on the shores of Austria Sound. Only this specimen consisted of the bleached skull and tusks of a walrus long dead, resting four hundred feet from shore and twenty feet above sea level. "Nearby was also a great quantity of broken clam shells, which in decades long past, had probably rested upon a favorite feeding ground of the walrus."[318] Thus did Baldwin wander the shoreline of Storm Bay like Prince Hamlet.

The Norwegians who had crossed Austria Sound returned to Storm Bay at midnight on Monday, August 29. They had reached Cape Berghaus at 9:00 A.M. on the 26th and found a lone starved dog there, still muzzled and surviving on scraps of walrus the men had cached on the site. It refused to be caught and ran off. The men spent the day at the spot, to attack and skin more walrus before proceeding to Harmsworth House, where they arrived early on the morning of the 27th. They remained at the expedition's base camp only long enough to exchange the correspondence between Wellman and Baldwin before they returned along the Hall Island shore to collect more tube sledges at the Loon Lake Camp. They encamped back at Cape Berghaus that same night and made Storm Bay the following day.

Baldwin let the men sleep for a few hours before he sent them away at 8:00 A.M. on Tuesday, August 30. "The men were directed to proceed to north end of Neustadt Island, if necessary and possible, *via* Cape Heller."[319] Observing that two of the oars had been broken, Baldwin gave "them another talk about exercising great care in such matters," but by now the Norwegians had had enough of Baldwin. As politely as possible given the circumstances, "they explained that so much rowing with such light material must soon render others useless."[320] Baldwin himself once again bowed out of any logistical work. "It was only that I feared for the safety of the canvas canoe that prevented me from accompanying them with *it* fully loaded or as fully burdened as its leaky condition would permit."[321]

Reinforced with the Lapp boat and a second smaller wooden boat from Cape Tegetthoff, Baldwin now ordered the Norwegians to make a second attempt to reach Cape Tyrol, the northern tip of Wiener-Neustadt Island and more than 20 nautical miles to the northwest across Austria Sound. The

Norwegians soon rowed directly into a line of pack ice through which they could not proceed. Instead, rather than return to Storm Bay and Baldwin, they landed at a small island in the middle of the sound, one that was south of Wiener-Neustadt and distinct from Hayes Island further west. Baldwin later wrote that he had seen this island—he accurately described it as in fact two small islands—from a perch on the glacier above Storm Bay:

> My vision was aided by means of a good pair of binoculars (the same used by my father during his army life). Not seeing the boats I judged that they must have been quite close under the face of the glacier, creeping toward Cape Heller. To the southwest lay a very low island seemingly about half way between the glacier and the Hayes Island. Whether it is really one of this group, or not, I am unable to say, but I believe it to be one not noted by Payer on his sledge-journey up the Sound in March and April a quarter of a century ago. So low is that island, that at that season of the year, it would undoubtedly be covered with snow and appear as a portion of the frozen surface of the Sound. The sun at times shone very brightly upon it and it had the appearance of a newly raised seabottom, or like the beach land on this side of the Sound.[322]

Surprisingly, neither Wellman in 1898 nor Baldwin during his own expedition in 1901–1902 left a place-name (or two) on these islands, bits of land that lay smack in the middle of Austria Sound.[323] Paul Bjørvig described how the men had been caught almost immediately in a storm that blew up out of the northeast. They landed on one of the small islands, where they emptied the boats and turned them over to create shelters. For once, the Norwegians had been allowed to carry one of the two primus stoves with them, so they soon had a hot meal of polar bear meat stewing in a pot. As Bjørvig wrote, they had soon "sorted ourselves out cozily under" the boats.

> We lay here for two days. Then we got good weather and began to row north east. Further north we met brash ice. It was pretty thin to begin with so we thought we could get through it. The further we got, the thicker it became. We eventually came to a dead stop. Now we realised we had been really stupid. But we had to do whatever we could to get ourselves out of it, for it would mean certain death if we could not free ourselves. The brash ice was too thick to row through,

but too thin to walk on. If we could not get out we would freeze to death in the boats before the ice got thick enough for us to walk on.[324]

One man was placed astride the bow of the boats to try to punch through the ice while the other crewman poled the boat forward with the hook designed to capture seals. As they attempted to reach Wiener-Neustadt Island, the ice continued to hold them offshore, and the channel they were breaking eventually led them northeast, toward Cape Heller on Wilczek Land. The men eventually broke through to open water but, once again exhausted by the exertion, they made for Cape Heller, on the northwest corner of Wilczek Land, where the fast ice along shore was cracked in enough places to allow the men to land in a small bay just south of the cape. For Bjørvig, it was the finest day of weather they had experienced to that point, "autumn still and mild with fine sunshine."[325]

After they dragged the boats ashore, they flipped one over and arranged their sleeping bags underneath. They stripped off their wet clothing and socks and laid them across the boat to dry in the sun. They promptly fell into a deep sleep, to awaken many hours later to find Cape Heller enveloped in fog and their clothes still sodden and even frozen, "like lumps of ice, but we had to put them on because we did not have any others."[326] Ice had also moved in to the shore and temporarily locked the men where they were.

While the men were away, back at Storm Bay, Baldwin continued to putter around the camp and the glacier to the north of it. He tried his hand at digging an igloo, "but soon struck frozen earth and stone and next made another attempt higher up and in deeper snow. The snow, however, being a part of the glacier had become ice and I was obliged to abandon the effort."[327] He climbed the glacier and for the first time had a clear view of Austria Sound and witnessed the apparently undiscovered islands that the Norwegians had just landed upon—a significant geographic discovery if Baldwin had reported it as such. Once again he noted open water as far as Cape Tyrol, seas "smooth as glass the entire distance" that could have been exploited if only the men possessed a steam launch.[328]

As he wandered down from the glacier, Baldwin came across the remains of a reindeer antler "near the bed of a summer rivulet," and was immediately off into another Hamlet-like reverie of past worlds and "the strange contrast between the times, the pleasant long ago and the weird now, when large herds of the graceful reindeer fed in peace upon these same fields covered with an abundant verdure and beautiful flowers but now the wild wastes of gravel where only the hungry bear wanders treading savagely upon an occasional poppy and vainly endeavors to appease his appetite by devouring here and there a tuft of stunted grass or other Arctic plant."[329]

At Storm Bay, the days continued like this. A "long and refreshing slumber" was followed by an order to Olaf to dig driftwood out of the snow and ice, while Baldwin "lay thinking of this thing and that" and interspersed with "stew of evaporated potatoes and Armour's tinned roast beef."[330] After castigating the Norwegians for their excessive use of cartridges, Baldwin emerged from his "warm, cosy nest" on Thursday, September 1, 1898, to expend nearly ten shots in killing a polar bear mother and her two cubs. "The snow and wind being exceedingly disagreeable to work in on the outside I have had Olaf extend the tent opening over a pair of ski so that he can skin the bears with considerable comfort, practically within the tent, for he now sits quite at the foot of my sleeping bag working away as happy as a king. There is room for but one to work and so I do the writing while my young Norse comrade does the rest."[331]

Olaf Ellefsen was to have been a crewmember on board *Fram* as Otto Sverdrup explored west of Ellesmere Island from 1899 until 1902—and in the process discovered the Sverdrup Islands. Now, as Ellefsen dressed the three bears killed by Baldwin, he found that one of the cubs had been torn apart by five bullets with "once in shoulder, once in neck, once in head, tearing away the lower jaw, once in chest and once in fore part of back, the ball passing through the body just under the spinal column."[332] He turned to Baldwin and pointedly remarked: "Had you hit her a few more times, you'd have made sconce (chopped meat) of her."

"Poor bears," wrote Baldwin, "I realize that it was cruel to have wounded them so frightfully before succeeding in killing them, but it would have been still more cruel to have now on my hands a pack of faithful, trusting dogs howling with hunger."[334] The contents of the cub's stomach also carried their own irony, consisting of "several pieces of paper forming one of the boxes which had contained some of our Chicago 'Quaker Oatmeal.'"[335]

September 2 found Baldwin again tucked into his sleeping bag, where he wrote that he could only "wait, wait, wait, for hours to pass and ask myself time and again: 'Will we be able to make our "Northing" even at 81° this fall?'"[336] He did rouse himself to take a few photographs of the camp and give an order to Olaf to haul in some more driftwood before turning in for the night.

Baldwin did not sleep long, for early on September 3 the men returned from Cape Heller. They had rowed for thirteen hours, proceeding slowly south along the glacier front that separated Cape Heller from Storm Bay. The last six hours of their efforts had been accomplished against an opposing tide that "ran like a river" against the boats.[337] Hearing their tale of the fight against the brash ice of Austria Sound, Baldwin now decided that the progress—or lack of it—of the advance party necessitated that the winter hut be constructed at Cape Heller. Less than a month after he left Cape Tegetthoff, Baldwin now abandoned any progress that might be made during the remainder of the fall. If indeed Cape Heller was the best he could do—and in the end it was—then Baldwin had burned out his men in exchange for an "advance" hut only 41 nautical miles north of Harmsworth House at Cape Tegetthoff. This was far short of Wellman's original goal of an advance post at Cape Fligely on the northern tip of Rudolf Land, which from Cape Heller still lay 65 miles north and in any event was best approached from the west side of Austria Sound and not from Cape Heller.

The decision made, Baldwin now claimed that he was not troubled by the lack of progress, as he had tried repeatedly to force a way north along the west side of Austria Sound, only to watch as the men were pushed to the east side of the channel each time.

I believe after these *repeated* attempts to get into the other side of the Sound that my reasons for establishing winter quarters near Cape Heller will be held good. From that point I believe that later in the season and during the winter I can advance the tube sledges and other supplies to Becker Island at least, and perhaps to Rainier [sic] Island. We will thereby lose no time in traveling westward and will be in line to proceed northward early next spring or late in the winter along the *east* coast of Rudolf Land, on unexplored territory, and where we are likely to have the advantage of getting driftwood occasionally.

I have always believed and am now more than ever of that opinion that but little if any "open water" ever exists in the vicinity of either Kane, Kuhn, or Stolicza islands—that the ice about them as it is or may be broken up and forced out through the various channels, etc., between them, is immediately replaced by ice driven in from the northeast. Once west of the main channel of Austria Sound beyond Cape Heller I do not believe that walruses abound this side of the east side of the British Channel, as in the vicinity of Nansen and Johansen's hut. To attempt to go there would, of course, mean expeditionary suicide.[338]

Baldwin cut a small hole in the wall of his "tent," so that he did not have to leave his sleeping bag but could still press his eye to the opening and gaze "upon this sterile waste so thinly clad with snow, there rises from it in trembling undulations as from a prairie after an autumn fire, the so-called 'heat waves' marking, I suppose, the rapid radiation of the golden sunshine which lay upon this cold beach for a few hours."[339] The spy hole also allowed him to observe the line of the dogs as well as the Norwegians as they lay asleep under the canvas boat.

Less than twenty-four hours after they had arrived back at Storm Bay, the men were sent off in the boats again, this time with Olaf replacing Daniel Johansen. Once again Baldwin struggled with his conscience, wanting to accompany the men but "upon reflection concluded that I would not, *should* not do so, as thereby I might defeat the prime object of the expedition—the securing of meat for the dogs at Cape Heller before I dare venture to leave this camp."[340] The Norwegians were ordered north to Cape Heller, there to secure "*at least* six or eight walruses (and a dozen if possible) as a "starter" for work" at the site.[341] Only when this was accomplished would Baldwin move the Storm Bay camp north the sixteen miles to Cape Heller.

Once again, with the men gone, Baldwin entered into several days of "delightful inactivity," to enjoy long rests, to poke around the few patches of reindeer moss where he uncovered fleas in the sand ("I poured some warm water upon a granite rock, some of the water soaked into the frozen gravel and sand around the edges of the rock and there immediately appeared a swarm of very small black insects"[342]), to order Daniel to fetch more driftwood, and in general to do "[n]othing much of importance."[343] By Friday, September 9, Baldwin began to lament the "continuance of 'dull times'" as he gazed out on a clear Austria Sound and, forgetting his canvas canoe, declaimed "how much I wish that we had another boat that Daniel and I might employ our time more fully!"[344]

By Friday, September 16, just as he grew increasingly anxious over the fate of the men, they arrived back in camp, but without the boats. Stymied in their attempts to get away from the shores of the bay on the north side of Cape Heller, the men abandoned the boats and left Cape Heller at 11:00 A.M. on the morning of September 15 and simply hiked across the glacier that separated them from Storm Bay. They arrived in the Storm Bay camp after a continuous walk of nearly fourteen hours.

Paul Bjørvig wrote that the men had been able to kill and process almost three-dozen walrus, as well as a few polar bears, during their time at Cape Heller. The increasing cold as they slept under the boats caused the men to gather stones from the surrounding hills and begin the construction of a proper hut: "The hut was a metre high in the walls but a little higher at the roof ridge. That was big enough for us, five or six metres long, but it was set on a base of ice and stone. For the roof we used walrus hides, and a stone slab for a fireplace. For a chimney pipe we had a tin can, that was the extent of the building. We took scarcely a day to build the hut."[345]

Frozen in at Cape Heller, the men left their rifles behind—praying that they would encounter no bears up on the glacier—slung their sleeping bags over a harpoon pole and, provisioned with a can of beans, ascended the glacier. "The glacier turned out to be fine to walk on. We did not come across a single crevasse. . . . [The glacier was] still as smooth as a floor."[346] When the Norwegians regained Storm Bay, they found that their "leader had sorted himself out well. He had taken the tarpaulin from the canvas boat and made himself a tent."[347]

The Norwegians took the sleeping bag they had with them and settled underneath the overturned canvas boat. According to Bjørvig, the men arrived back at Storm Bay exhausted and hungry, but Baldwin had no food ready for them, and he would not allow them to prepare food on their own. "Our leader would not turn out to let us get something to eat, and there was nowhere else to find food.

We fell asleep quickly—when we awoke we were completely covered in snow. It was absolutely impossible to get ourselves out of the sleeping bag. We heard the roar of the storm, which was raging at its full strength. It was not so pleasant in our sleeping bag, but if the storm had hit a few hours earlier while we were still on the glacier, it would never have gone well. As day dawned our companion came and got the snow off the bag. He had got himself into the leader's tent. He had got orders to cook us some bear meat but it was impossible to get the primus going in this storm.

We could maybe have been given a tin of something or other. But no, this chap was all for looking after himself.[348]

The report from Bjørvig, on the rapid route across the glacier, must have cut Baldwin to the quick. This was, after all, the same path that Wellman had assumed Baldwin had already tried and found impassable. Baldwin told the men that as soon as they had gotten some sleep the entire party would move *en masse* across the glacier to Cape Heller. The Norwegian discovery of the glacier route meant that Baldwin had squandered *four full weeks* at Storm Bay and effectively doomed the entire expedition. The same glacier, upon which he had dallied each day as he dreamt of geographic conquest and snapped a few photographs, uncovered sand flies and postulated on the origins of driftwood, all the while had offered a rapid sledge route directly to Cape Heller. This route could have been exploited in a matter of hours during the good weather of mid-August. Now, when he finally rallied the men to cross the glacier, in mid-September, he drove the advance party directly into a blinding snowstorm.

FOURTEEN

A Better Hut Than This

Despite Baldwin's sudden urgency to move, a fresh storm at Storm Bay kept the advance party pinned down until Sunday, September 18. It was now a full thirty days since Baldwin had first arrived at Storm Bay, and thirty-six days since the Norwegians had crossed from Cape Frankfurt and deposited the first boatloads of supplies there. Far from "advancing as rapidly as possible," Baldwin had wasted more than a month in shifting supplies less than thirteen miles from Cape Frankfurt across Austria Sound to Storm Bay. It was an exercise in pitiful field leadership by the American—and worse was to come.

By the time Baldwin was finally ready to move the advance camp across the glacier from Storm Bay to Cape Heller, just sixteen miles north, the wind and snow had increased to the point where it "now lies in heaps upon sleeping-bag, boots, gun, provisions" and to cross a glacier in such conditions would have been considered madness.[349] But winter was clearly on its way and Baldwin, having squandered the best month of the year for small boat travel in the archipelago, was now in a position of extreme embarrassment. Therefore, even in horrendous weather on Friday and Saturday, September 16 and 17, Baldwin ordered the Norwegians to drag the bulk of the party's gear to the base of the glacier preparatory to a crossing. On the morning of the 18th, as the snow continued to fall and the winds held steady at twenty knots, Baldwin reluctantly roused the men out of their cold, wet sleeping bags and ordered them to break camp. Pulling on clothes that were also soaked and frozen, the Norwegians finally cleared the Storm Bay camp at 1:30 P.M., and the painful progress to move the men and dogs up and over the glacier began:

> With six or eight dogs hitched to the larger of the sledges ("Uncle Sam" sledge—because it carries the Weather Bureau complements, etc.) and with Bjorvik and Emil now tugging at same, now pulling with the dogs, now balancing the sledge, with myself in the lead followed immediately by Yellow Kid, the best *leader* in the pack, we made our way cautiously and fatiguingly along the slippery and narrow rims of shore ice, for everywhere else on land, the high winds had completely removed the snow. Following the sledge came Bentzen, Olaf, and Daniel with the dogs. When about half way to the glacier, we were obliged to take to the remnant of the sea worn ice-foot, which in several places was so narrow that there was not room enough to admit of passage of sledge without first cutting away projecting points and then holding the sledge from slipping into the sea by means of a long line.[350]

After crawling along the shoreline, the men finally reached the glacier front at 5:00 P.M. Despite an increased wind, Baldwin ordered the party on, but they had not gained more than 100 feet of elevation onto the glacier when the driving snow forced the men into camp. Baldwin ordered the men to place the large "Uncle Sam" sledge parallel to a snow bank and then dig his "*grave*—just large enough to admit sleeping-bag.

> This rested upon bamboo poles, ski, and dog-harnesses. Over all was placed as a "roof" the spare boat covering or "tent." Meanwhile, some of the men were at work making snow igloo in another snow bank close by and were not long in getting into comfortable quarters (after the Eskimo fashion).[351]

Tucked up in his sleeping bag and under his tent, Baldwin sent the men up the glacier to retrieve some wood they had cached there the previous day. This they were allowed to use to make a cooking fire "in order to save our precious petroleum."[352] The men finally ate their meal at 9:00 P.M. and turned into their igloo on the glacier just as the snow turned to sleet. Bjørvig wrote that he and his fellow Norwegians climbed into their snow cave and lit the primus stove to make coffee in deliberate disobedience to Baldwin's instructions. It was a clear signal that the Norwegians had had enough of Baldwin's food and supply rations and the continued lack of leadership, and that they had begun to look after themselves. "We thought we had it pretty good," Bjørvig added, "as the storm howled over us."[353]

The next morning, Monday, September 19, the men could see the sun as it glinted off the glacier above them. Baldwin ordered Olaf to prepare breakfast while the other three Norwegians dragged the sledges further up the glacier. Baldwin occupied himself with meteorological readings that showed the temperature at 28°F with a gentle wind out of the west. And he worried, feeling "anxiety as to what might be our fate or fortune in crossing the glacier and *especially* from the occasional efforts of one of the dogs to get into my snow pit, not, I apprehend, from a desire to keep me company, but to secure some of the dried fish—the very last of our dog food—which I had stowed away along side my sleeping-bag. This I cut into a half-ration for each before getting out of my sleeping-bag and then the men fed it to our faithful howlers as a last meal till we should get across the glacier."[354] Neither man nor dog had enjoyed access to even a morsel of food without Baldwin's express permission.

It was 1:00 P.M. before the entire party was underway, and they dragged the cumbersome driftwood to an elevation of 500 feet only to discard it there when Baldwin deemed it too heavy to drag any further across the glacier. After they had climbed northeast to 1,100 feet, Baldwin then led the party due north for several hours. The winds freshened to a manageable 20 knots out of the west. "The surface was smooth and sledges ran well and dogs behaved nicely," wrote Baldwin.[355] By late evening, they had been on the march for nearly twelve hours without food or water. Baldwin passed out lime juice tablets to each of the men to try and keep them on the march.

By 1:00 A.M. on Tuesday, September 20, Cape Tyrol came into view across Austria Sound and the men began their descent toward Cape Heller. It was now thirty-seven days since the Norwegians had first landed at Storm Bay, thirty-seven days for the advance party to move just sixteen miles. For Bjørvig, the glacier crossing, after the first uncomfortable night, had been fairly simple. "Over the glacier we made good speed. The dogs pulled well so we sat on the sledges most of the way. Getting down was difficult. We had to let the sledges down on ropes."[356]

But they had done it: they had moved the entire Storm Bay camp across the glacier to Cape Heller in less than twenty-four hours. For their reward, the men had to wait to receive a hot meal until well after noon, as Baldwin first set up the meteorological instruments in a small weather observation post on the ridge above the stone hut. These showed that temperature at Cape Heller was 30°F and the wind gusting to 29 knots. With this knowledge in hand, the dogs were fed and then the men finally allowed to enter the stone hut and bundle themselves together in a small corner of it.

As Bjørvig wrote, when the men "had got everything into the shelter, Baldwin took the inner area of the shelter for his own space. We five Norwegians had to lie near the entrance where the snow was always drifting in as soon as there was any wind."[357] It was only now—as it became clear that Baldwin had no intention to proceed farther than Cape Heller—that Bjørvig finally ventilated his feelings about his American leader:

> Baldwin was the last type of man you could want, and the fact that we did not thump him was a little strange. He was not so big that any one of us could not have given him a thump.
>
> Since we had contracts to say we would carry out whatever we were ordered to do, either on land or at sea, and would be supplied with food, which would be the same for everybody. Now that rascal was lying there and eating away in the dark, we did not see him but he could not hide the empty cans.[358]

It was also about this time that Emil Ellefsen began in his diary to replace the name "Baldwin" with the epithet "*Susæg,*" as in his September 28 entry, "*Susæg* is in his sleeping bag the whole day."[359] The precise meaning of this northern Norwegian colloquialism is unknown in modern context. It is without doubt a Norwegian surname, and it may have been attached to Baldwin because the Norwegians with him associated Baldwin with a particularly hated personage back home, perhaps a tax collector or other notorious personality. According to Per Sparboe, a Norwegian lawyer who translates old Norwegian, Lapp and Finn documents, "*Susæg* is a word of abuse worth taking good care of."[360]

If the exact meaning of this shorthand curse has been lost, there is little to mistake in the other terms that the Norwegians also began to apply to Baldwin, such as "*agurka,*" the cucumber. As Magnus Forsberg explains:

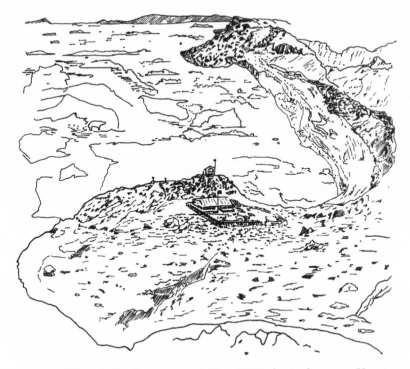

A view of Cape Heller from the south. Fort McKinley in the center. Kersting Bay (later Bentsen Bay) is to the north of the cape. Redrawn by C. L. Devlin from a sketch by Baldwin that was published in the New Orleans *Times-Picayune*, January 31, 1900.

"In Sweden we have the expression '*han är en riktig surgurka,*' meaning: 'He is a real sour cucumber.'"[361]

After a long night's rest, the sour cucumber had the Norwegians back at work on the morning of Wednesday, September 21, "breaking stones loose from the ridge and laying the walls of the east wing of the hut."[362] When this basic work was completed, Baldwin took it upon himself to christen the outpost Fort McKinley,[363] after the man perhaps singularly responsible for the American ascent into empire. As he later wrote in his report to the U.S. Weather Bureau, the outpost "I named out of respect to the President of the United States."[364] The elevation above the hut where Baldwin had set up the U.S. Weather Bureau instruments he named Observatory Ridge.

Fort McKinley was located at the base of the south-facing slope of Observatory Ridge. The ridge itself formed the majority of Cape Heller, a small hook that projected from the west coast of Wilczek Land into Austria Sound. The cape split the waters around it into two small bays, the one on the south Baldwin named Operti and the northern bay called Kersting. Here Baldwin had used names associated with the Arctic expeditions of Robert Peary and Frederick Cook.[365]

As for Fort McKinley's "West Wing," as Baldwin called it, the American now appropriated that as his own private space. Here he now composed a bizarre message that he meant to be secreted under the southeast corner of the structure. The message announced to anyone who found it that the hut lay roughly east to west on low land extending westward from Cape Heller, a point that would be obvious to anyone retrieving the note from the selfsame hut. "I arrived at this point yesterday forenoon with the above named members of the expedition, forty dogs, sledges and balance of equipment for winter use after having crossed the glacier extending between this and Storm Bay. All well. Evelyn B. Baldwin, Second-in-Command Expedition."[366] It was this particularly cloying form of play-acting at exploration that had long ceased to amuse the Norwegians.

Working twelve hours a day to finish the winter shelter, the men took breaks only to chase the occasional walrus unfortunate enough to venture into Operti Bay. In the inadequate boats, the men were often subjected to counterattacks by enraged walrus that thrashed about and came close on numerous occasions to sinking the boats and the men with them.

The day after the party reached Cape Heller, Baldwin sent four of the Norwegians south to retrieve the canvas boat and the driftwood that still lay about the base of the glacier near the Storm Bay camp. Emil remained behind to cut up the two walrus shot in Operti Bay the day before, while Baldwin "put in considerable time writing."[367] He castigated the men for the loss of the party's only shovel before Baldwin found it the next day next to the hut. He then complained when a walrus could not be secured because of a dull harpoon blade, even though the expedition had provided the men with nothing upon which to sharpen their blades and knives. On Saturday, September 24, with the balance of the men still at Storm Bay, Emil broke the party's only pickaxe as he tried to loosen the frozen ground for material needed to bulk the walls of the hut. All of the men now walked in boots and shoes with large rents in them from the hard labor of the previous two months.

On the evening of September 24, Baldwin and Emil watched as the boats returned through the ice of Operti Bay. Baldwin ascended Observatory Ridge, "that the men might catch sight of me outlined against the glacial background northward, and thence walked westward to the ridge point.

> Fortunately, my maneuvers were observed and an hour later the boats were opposite the end of the ridge. It was growing dark rapidly, but I could see that both boats were being driven rapidly northward under sail and oar with the canvas boat in tow. A half hour later all were safely through a long stream of loose ice that was drifting to the northwest, and making toward the point upon which I stood signaling in token of a good land place. As the boats were swept somewhat round into Kersting Bay, by wind and current, I could see that all were loaded with our precious driftwood, and there was an indescribable joy in my heart for with the supply of walrus and bear flesh already on hand and the driftwood, we are reasonably certain of the safe wintering of my party and the forty dogs now already here.[368]

The winter hut was completed over the next several days. Gravel and earth dug from the frozen ground was used to fill in the spaces in the larger stones of the walls, and a large flat stone became the hearth. The chimney was formed from an empty biscuit tin, "on each side of which is the manufacturer's label printed in large letters *First Cabin*."[369] Driftwood paddled from Storm Bay in the south and dragged from Cape Schmarda to the north formed ridge poles, while a few ski and bamboo poles and some smaller pieces of driftwood formed rafters. Over these, the men draped a growing collection of walrus hides, a dozen or more, to finish the roof, exactly as Nansen and Johansen had done to create their winter hut on Frederick Jackson Island in 1895.

With Olaf now sick and the other Norwegians needed to finish the hut, Paul Bjørvig was put to work to construct a pen for the dogs that would also enclose the walrus blubber, the dog food, and the driftwood. As Bjørvig wrote, he did this through the expedient of building a wall of snow. "It was about 20 metres in each direction and 2 metres high. The shelter stood in the middle. The idea was the dogs could be loose inside the wall, at the same time being a protection against bears."[370]

On the afternoon of September 27, a fierce wind blew up from the southwest and carried the leaky canvas boat clear from the shore of Operti Bay and over Observatory Ridge, and then straight out onto the ice of Kersting Bay to the north. There it lay on thin ice, shattered and just out of the men's reach. When the men were finally able to retrieve it four days later, it was dragged ashore with two ribs missing and a three-inch hole sliced through the bottom.

The wind continued to howl on the 28th, as the men began in earnest to cut the frozen walrus carcasses into uniform blocks that would form the food for the dogs for the winter as well as for the sledge party that would go north the following spring. That night, Baldwin rigged a lamp for the hut that consisted of an empty roast-beef tin filled with walrus blubber oil and a piece of flannel for a wick. "Olaf entertained us with his mouth-harp and several of the boys sang (in Norwegian, of course)."[371] When Baldwin found that moss made a better wick, he had the men scour the frozen surroundings and collect basketfuls of it.

On the last day of September 1898, with the canvas boat all but useless, Baldwin lectured the men on the necessity of caring for the two wooden boats that were now their only lifeline to Harmsworth House. Baldwin then "placed them specially in care of Bjorvik and Bentzen, these two men to be responsible for their safety, etc., except when in actual use by other members of the party. This special charge they by reason of their age and experience as seamen, I informed all of them is to be considered as a compliment to each of them.

> I also talked to them concerning the next boat trip to Harmsworth House to communicate with Mr. Wellman and to get the remaining copper sledges—ten at Cape Berghaus and six or eight at Loon Lake. I also informed all where I had observed pieces of driftwood between Storm Bay and encampment north of Cape Hansa and also on island, this side of Cape Berghaus. The talk concerning care of boats, etc., was by no means the first time that I have cautioned them. The smaller wood boat leaks badly and must be repaired before another trip can be made in it.[372]

Baldwin's reward for this new charge was to inform the Norwegians that the advance party was nearly out of both coffee and tobacco. Baldwin broke into one of the tube sledges to provide a new supply of coffee, but he began to ration the tobacco, handing out a small tin to each man that had to last for ten days. "Emil, Olaf and myself can do very well on our allowance, but Bjorvik, Bentzen, and Daniel (each of whom also *chew*) seem to have much difficulty in limiting themselves—especially Bjorvik and Bentzen, as I have observed."[373] When Bjørvig failed to reel in several walrus that same day, Baldwin complained that, "in my opinion, the majority of these men are careless and need constant watching—someone to see that they do just so and so, or else everything will soon go to ruin."[374] This treatment of the Norwegians as overgrown children can be traced, at least in part, to Baldwin's feelings of insecurity and inferiority toward men who were not only physically bigger and stronger than he but vastly more experienced in Arctic conditions, men who had sailed with the Norwegian merchant fleet, to say nothing of their superior linguistic capabilities, as virtually all of them were fluent in both English and German as well as Norwegian.

After all of their exertions of the past two months, the news that they would now be placed on even tighter rations infuriated the Norwegians, who began to grumble openly. As September turned to October, relations between Baldwin and the Norwegians fell to their lowest level yet. On October 3, using their code word for the field leader, Emil Ellefsen noted with surprise in his diary that "*Susæg* has also worked today."[375]

Olaf's illness had given Baldwin some pause ("these men, although they may be 'hardy Norsemen' are after all 'human flesh and blood' "[376]), yet he continued to drive the men to exhaustion. The men now voiced their complaints in full, starting with the poor footgear and then the failure to provide adequate supplies of food and tobacco. When Baldwin's extreme economy of fuel led to a potful of partially cooked bear stew, he tried to shame the men into eating it, claiming that "certainly it was more than cooked enough for 'explorers' and I tried to make them believe that it would be good for them to eat even raw meat now and then, and also told them that it was expected we might be obliged to eat much raw meat in order to accomplish the work of the expedition. Still, upon going out of the hut, I found one man's meat allowance partly cooked lying in front of one of the muzzled dogs. Upon inquiry, I found that Daniel is the only one of all the men who has ever eaten raw meat, while Olaf could only say that he had 'tasted it.' "[377]

Two days later, Baldwin castigated the men for not smiling more. Emil Ellefsen noted that it was not out of any indifference on the Norwegian side. "Yes, we are now totally fed up with this cucumber and we speak behind his back almost the whole day. The funny thing is, I think he understands everything and knows just what we think of him."[378] "*Susæg*," of course, had no idea what the men were saying, but he was paranoid enough to see treachery in anything but the most reverential obeisance to his authority.

The Norwegians were now largely segregated from Baldwin throughout the day. As they cut and stacked the blocks of frozen walrus and tried to gather moss through the drifts of snow, Baldwin removed himself to Observation Ridge and the meteorological station. When he did sit with the men on October 3, it was to inform them that, in order to save blubber for the dogs, only two men would be allowed to spend the winter at Fort McKinley. Once again, Baldwin could not help but be disingenuous and "stated to them that I *hope* to be one of the two,"[379] all the while knowing full well that this issue had been decided by Wellman two months earlier. Bjørvig and Bentsen were to remain at the hut—but they simply would not be informed of the fact until the last possible moment.

On Tuesday, October 4, Baldwin completed work on the meteorological station on Observation Ridge. "It is built entirely of stones loosely laid so as to admit of the free circulation of the air about the thermograph and thermometers. Even the roof consists of stones—large, flat ones laid overlapping, Eskimo igloo fashion."[380] From this point until the bulk of the advance party returned to Harmsworth House, the Norwegians were ordered to cut and stow the frozen chunks of walrus into the copper tube sledges and when not occupied in this task they were to scour the area around the cape for more moss. Baldwin spent his time "sorting and arranging equipment."[381]

When Bjørvig asked if the expedition would have a tent for the expedition in search of the North Pole the following spring, Baldwin answered that that was what the canvas boat was for. Bjørvig muttered some words in Norwegian "which from his manner of expressing it, I judged to be in criticism of the idea of trying to get along without a tent."[382] Baldwin said that perhaps they could make a tent of the sail that had been removed from Jackson's camp at Cape Flora, even though this had already been used as part of the roof of Harmsworth House.

On Friday, October 7, as the men put together a small celebration in honor of Bernt Bentsen's first wedding anniversary and as a curtain of the aurora shimmered to the east of Cape Heller, Baldwin continued to sort equipment while the Norwegians cut dozens of basketfuls of frozen walrus meat. The weather continued to be horrendous, yet Baldwin informed the men that, if the weather cleared in the morning, that three of them would attempt to reach Harmsworth House in the boats. Privately, Baldwin expressed doubts that such a journey could be made successfully, because "the 'open water' space is so full of thick, mush-like young ice floes that I do not believe the trip can be made. Still, I have resolved that the attempt shall be made. Upon calling for volunteers to make the attempt, all were willing to do so 'if I said so, but did not believe it could be done.' I then told Bjorvik, Olaf and Daniel to hold themselves in readiness to start by daylight and therefore all turned in immediately after supper."[383]

Baldwin's urgency to get a boat to Harmsworth House was triggered by little more than his lack of communications with Wellman. It had been six weeks since he had last written to the expedition leader—and small wonder. Those six weeks had seen the advance party move north only the sixteen miles from Storm Bay and, even at that, they had failed to advance nearly twenty of the copper tube sledges north from Loon Lake and Cape Berghaus to Fort McKinley. For Baldwin, it finally was time to offer Wellman an explanation for his utter failure to place the winter quarters at or near Wellman's target of Cape Fligely on Rudolf Land:

Owing to the very treacherous character of the ice in the Sound—drifting ice floes and the "young" ice of this season, I could not effect a landing on the west side of the Sound, notwithstanding repeated attempts were made to do so. As a matter of sheer necessity I was obliged to go into winter quarters at this point, where I arrived in person September 21st, after having crossed the glacier intervening between here and Storm Bay. The last of the equipment arrived from Storm Bay at 8:00 P.M. September 24th, and since then it has been utterly impossible to use a boat in the Sound save for a short distance from headquarters. The ice (young and old) has constantly shifted itself to and fro in the Sound since that date and not until this afternoon have conditions for boating been in the least safe and even now I despatch the boat with but faint hope of the men being able to reach you. The young ice is very treacherous at this late date and the men have been cautioned as to their own safety and that of the boat and they are to return if after a fair trial either themselves or the boat would be endangered by attempting to proceed the whole way, unless they can reach Cape Frankfurt and proceed there afoot, following the coast to Cape Tegetthoff.[384]

As he had repeatedly done with the Norwegians, Baldwin told Wellman that he had earnestly wished to come south himself, but the camp required his complete concentration. In parting, Baldwin again obliquely blamed Wellman for the lack of adequate watercraft, the poor construction of the sledges, and for underestimating the number walrus and bear required to feed the dogs and men. Baldwin then lied about the health of the party and his provision of "well-cooked game"[385] for the men. He concluded with a virtual taunt to Wellman to come north himself if he wished to visit the new fort "and if you desire I will return with you to Harmsworth House although as a matter of course I would prefer to remain here with my party, especially as I have here established a Weather Bureau meteorological station after having succeeded in keeping all my instruments in good order and constantly (almost) at work, over ice-floes, tossing waters and a great ice glacier."[386] As with all of Baldwin's communications, it was difficult to know how much of this was outright brass, or naïveté, or self-delusion, or some combination of all three, and its particular tone all but guaranteed problems with Wellman. In the event, it would be more than four months before Wellman bothered to write to Baldwin again.

Baldwin tried to launch the men on their way on Saturday, October 8, but the new ice in Operti Bay held them off. By dinner time, the men had cut and stored nearly a hundred baskets of dog food in the form of walrus blubber. Emil Ellefsen noted that it was "really sour to be outside cutting up meat. *Susæg* was outside for a walk but returned inside to his sleeping bag.

> At 12 o'clock I sang out to him from the outside because we could barely keep our eyes open but never received any reply. At 13.30 we all went inside and started up with our private issues. As we were about to get to sleep for the night, we found the whole sleeping area iced in, even inside the sleeping bag. It will be nice in the winter. I requested *Susæg* to come over to see the glory and he at least had the good sense to admit that something needed to be done. . . . It will very soon just be only meat to survive on. Salt has been forbidden fruit for a long time.[387]

Baldwin rewarded the men's labor with a supper of "fish meal, a good and wholesome food,"[388] and asked how the men liked it. When all of the Norwegians expressed their disgust, Baldwin then suggested that perhaps they were all eating too much! This gave Baldwin an excuse to cut the men's biscuit ration down to two a day, as the advance party was now down to just four crates of biscuits.

When the men—who at this point must have been completely flabbergasted by this strange American—protested this decision, as well as the short rations of sugar, they got nowhere. It was not an "extreme hardship," shrugged Baldwin. Privately, Baldwin wrote that "Emil and Olaf have been much about the world and have acquired quite a taste for 'nice things.'"[389] When Bentsen complained, Baldwin wrote that "Life on board the *Fram* seems to have spoiled him."[390]

By the morning of October 10, the Norwegians were in open revolt. "The first thing this morning was an insult from Bentzen and much ado from Emil.

> Bentzen began by addressing me in German and said: "Mr. Baldwin, you say we are not school boys any longer, but I say any school boy could build a better hut than this . . ." The occasion of the remarks was the accumulation of snow on the sleeping bag [even inside the hut]. . . . To Bentzen's remark I paid little attention, thinking best to let the matter rest till temper were over. Emil also remarked that the men all thought that the work of the Expedition should be more evenly distributed. I took it to mean that the men thought that Mr. Harlan and the Doctor ought also to be in the field and I replied that the men (Norwegians) were the only ones receiving pay for their services—and then, in a calm way told all (Emil translating) that all should remember that no one had been promised anything but *hardship* on this Expedition (referring to the meeting in the cabin of the *Frithjof,* at which all were present). I also stated that Mr. Wellman had sent us forward to build a winter hut but with the understanding that life in the hut *might* involve as much privation as that endured by Nansen and Johansen in their hut, and that a comparison of the two huts and all the equipment, etc., within and about each, would, I thought, put any man to shame who would complain of life within *this* hut. I also stated that I came upon this trip with the understanding above mentioned, and also stated that if we did any sledging we must expect to get snow upon our sleeping-bags.[391]

But the men were not sledging. They were sleeping in what Baldwin had described in his journal as "superior accommodations"[392] with "a floor of dry gravel and a carpet and interior lining of bearskins . . . *cozy* quarters."[393] The gratuitous comparison to Nansen and Johansen was a stunning admission of poor expedition planning and, predictably, did nothing to calm the Norwegians. They knew as well as anyone that Nansen and Johansen had survived a winter in Franz Josef Land *at the end* of a brilliantly conceived and executed three-year expedition. Baldwin demanded that the Norwegians of the Wellman expedition endure extreme levels of privation and exposure *at the very start* of what they had been led to believe was a well-funded and -supplied American expedition.

Worse, the advance party's problems went much deeper than the snow in the hut, short rations, and poor equipment. The men now suspected—and Baldwin in his castigation of the men now proved—that the expedition had little real intent to achieve its objective. Wrote Baldwin, "I told them that although we might not reach the Pole, or even the farthest north, yet the Expedition was certain of success, for we were at the very threshold of more unexplored coast than had been traversed for many years."[394]

So that was it. It was now clear that the Norwegians had been ordered to make absurd sacrifices so that the Americans, most of whom were enjoying a leisurely Arctic holiday at Cape Tegetthoff, could add place-names to some islands and capes and waterways in Franz Josef Land. The Norwegians would carry the Americans and all of their kit to these places, while the Americans reserved to themselves the right to name these newly discovered spots after Chicago bankers and politicians from Washington, D.C. If any of them didn't like it, Baldwin informed them, they could put their complaints in writing. He then ascended to Observatory Point to check his meteorological recordings and collect some moss, but not before Baldwin "counseled all to endeavor to avoid getting the blues and to try to be more cheerful."[395]

For the Norwegians, the meager rations and continued exposure to the cold had transformed the expedition from a desultory forced march into a potentially lethal folly. When Bernt Bentsen commented that they "had to lie there like dogs," Emil Ellefsen went him one further. The Norwegians, he said, "might as well go out on the ice-cap and lie down to die."[396]

FIFTEEN

Norwegians Are Better Than Eskimos

The sun burst through the clouds and storms on the morning of Tuesday, October 11, 1898, but the tension between Baldwin and the Norwegians was not eased. Baldwin again absented himself from all of the work that he assigned the men, yet then proceeded to skulk nearby, noting that the Norwegians "waste good time in talking, but I dislike to say anything to them about it."[397]

When the Norwegians began chatting amiably amongst themselves over dinner, Baldwin took the opportunity to insert himself and chastise them once again. Only now did he seem to realize that his own position was becoming untenable and, if relations did not improve, he faced a potential mutiny. As Emil translated his words, Baldwin told the men what they already knew: that Wellman sent them forward to build an advance hut. Baldwin also told the Norwegians—as if it were not clear already—that they would very likely have to eat much raw meat. Only one of the five ever had—a distinction between Norwegians and Eskimos that Baldwin now used to castigate them further: "[I reminded them] that Mr. Wellman had said that Norwegians were better than Eskimos to assist in the work and therefore the Expedition had come to Franz-Josef Land."

That while Peary is trying to march northward along the west coast of Greenland, I had been put in charge of leading this party, five

Norwegians, upon whose efforts we depended for success. That I had received explicit instructions from which I was *not to deviate except in case of absolute necessity.* That I had been instructed to build a winter hut at the northernmost point to be attained by this party, and that I was *allowed* four weeks in which to build it, etc. That I was to leave there two or three men for the winter, who should care for the dogs, equipment, etc. That I had arrived here September 21st and the hut was now completed and that therefore the men had offered a criticism which not only reflected upon me, but also upon the organizers of the Expedition.[398]

It is a testament to Baldwin's obtuseness that he believed this speech had been highly effective. He wrote in his journal that "soon all had turned in, *wiser,* and I believe, better men."[399]

On Friday, October 14, one day after Baldwin told himself that his talk to the men "seems to have been effective," morale instead sank further. As the men turned into their cold and wet hut for another long day of cutting up walrus and following Baldwin on fruitless pursuits of polar bears on the thin ice of Operti Bay, Bentsen growled that they were engaged in a "Norwegian Expedition, at 3 *kroner* and 50 *ore* a day."[400] Baldwin also heard him mutter something he believed "referred to Mr. Wellman and companions at Harmsworth House. All others kept perfect silence. In cutting meat this afternoon Bentzen cut about one-third (1/3) what Bjorvig did, the two working side by side."[401]

By mid-October, as Baldwin and Daniel Johansen "went in search of a few geographical points as a farewell remembrance of sunshine for the present year,"[402] the Norwegians had cut and stored 150 baskets of walrus meat. Baldwin occupied himself in determining the elevation of the highest point at Cape Heller (320 feet). Baldwin then walked about 6 nautical miles northeast to Cape Schmarda, which he fixed at 350 feet. He then ascended to an outcrop of rock on a glacier to the northeast. From here, at an elevation of about 700 feet, Baldwin spied a large bay northeast of Cape Schmarda. In the bay was a small island that Wellman would later name Lyman Gage Island after the man who at that moment was the secretary of the Treasury of the United States. Beyond this, Baldwin saw another, more substantial island, before a gathering snowstorm forced him to quickly return to Cape Heller.

Enticed by the potential of more discoveries, Baldwin returned with Emil Ellefsen to near the same spot the following day, Sunday, October 16, and believed that the larger of the islands he had seen the previous day was rather a peninsula connected to Wilczek Land. In this Baldwin made the same mistake as had Julius Payer twenty-five years earlier, when Payer named the area La Ronciere Peninsula. In fact, Baldwin's first observation was correct. La Ronciere Peninsula was in fact La Ronciere Island, and the large bay Baldwin had scouted was in fact a strait that separated Wilczek Land from La Ronciere Island. Wellman would later give names to all of the capes Baldwin identified along the north coast of Wilczek Land, and the newly discovered strait he would name after one of his major benefactors, William K. Vanderbilt.[403]

When Baldwin returned to Fort McKinley that evening, he announced that two men would remain behind in the hut over the winter, something that Wellman had already written to him two months earlier. At that time, Wellman had "suggested" to Baldwin that he "first explain the circumstances and then ask for volunteers; afterward make your own detail. Whether the number shall be two or three I leave to your judgment and that of the men who are to stay—for their wishes should perhaps be consulted—but two is my preference." He had then held out a bribe: "The men who remain will be specially rewarded," Wellman wrote.[404] The expedition leader would live to regret these words.

As for Baldwin, after he was pinned down by a storm for several days, he sent several of the men away on the morning of Thursday, October 20, to test the condition of the ice in Austria Sound. When the men returned with a favorable report, Baldwin called the Norwegians together that evening and informed them that he had chosen Paul Bjørvig and Bernt Bentsen to remain at Fort McKinley over the winter, along with all of the dogs. Baldwin himself and the remainder of the Norwegians would return to Harmsworth House on October 22.

In his exploring memoir, *The Aerial Age,* Wellman wrote: "Late in October . . . [Baldwin] called for two volunteers to remain at the outpost during the winter. . . . All the men offered themselves."[405] But it is clear in his letter to Baldwin of August 27, two months earlier, that Wellman had already made the decision. "In case you do not want to take responsibility of deciding who is to stay at the Outpost I say Bjorvik and Bentzen, and a third if necessary, Emil. But I want you to fix this matter in your own way, for by this time you know the men better than I do. I did say something to Olaf and Daniel

Evelyn Briggs Baldwin at age twenty-five. *Courtesy of the Scott Polar Research Institute Archives.*

about their wintering [at Harmsworth House], but it was not a promise and you are free to dispose of them."[406] This was another unfortunate choice of words and, in any case, Wellman's description of this winter "volunteering" in his memoir is somewhat different. "Paul Bjoervig and Bernt Bentzen were chosen," wrote Wellman in *The Aerial Age,* "whereat Emil and Olaf Ellefsen and Daniel Johansen were grievously disappointed."[407]

Instead, as Baldwin's journal makes plain, after their experience on the ice, Olaf Ellefsen and Daniel Johansen had gone so far as to ask Wellman to be allowed to winter at Harmsworth House. Yet Wellman wrote in his memoir: "As for Bjoervig and Bentzen, they were delighted. . . . This chance of spending an Arctic winter in a snug little hut, with plenty to eat and smoke, was to them the realization of a dream."[408]

Just after noon on the 22nd, Baldwin ordered Emil, Olaf, and Daniel to pull the sledge southward while Baldwin skied ahead of them. Even this scene was soon reduced to farce, as the men could not move the sledge over the soft ice. Accordingly, seven dogs were hitched to the sledge along with the men. A mile from the fort, even this was inadequate, so Baldwin sent Emil Ellefsen back to the fort for two more dogs. Now, fully one quarter of the dogs—dogs that Baldwin had spent nearly three months to move some forty miles north—would return to Cape Tegetthoff from where they had started on August 5.

Baldwin at Cape Tegetthoff after the disastrous fall of 1898.
Courtesy National Air and Space Museum (NASM 9A10656),
Smithsonian Institution.

Baldwin thought they could cover the distance to Cape Tegetthoff in four days. In actuality, as the dogs and men crawled southward across thin, cracking sheets of ice, they could not gain Harmsworth House in less than eight. It took the men five full days just to make their way down the coast of Wilczek Land to Cape Hansa and the jump-off point to cross Austria Sound to Cape Frankfurt.[409]

During this time the Norwegians repeatedly implored Baldwin to turn the sledge around and return to Cape Heller. As darkness gathered around them and with the ice not yet solid enough to support the combined weight of the men, the dogs, and the sledge, the conditions were too dangerous to force a passage across Austria Sound.

To add to his increasing indecisiveness as the Arctic night closed in, Baldwin was also troubled by disturbing dreams. On the morning of October 25, he awoke to grave disappointment as he realized that he had not in fact returned to being a boy with all of his brothers, especially the youngest, Edwin, who was long since deceased. He was still stuck on a moveable sheet of ice on the eastern edge of Austria Sound in Franz Josef Land. "But I at once said to myself, 'No, I will not give way to feeling for I am now a man in command of men. Today I will go forth with courage and make a desperate effort to pass beyond Storm Bay.' "[410]

The party passed Storm Bay on October 26 and, just after 10:00 A.M. on Thursday, October 27, the men were abreast of Cape Hansa and made the turn southwest toward Cape Frankfurt. They crossed Austria Sound in four hours and gratefully made camp at Cape Frankfurt that night. As darkness fell on Sunday, October 30, the small party arrived back at Harmsworth House after three months of prodigiously pointless exertions.

SIXTEEN

Born Again Up Here

As he returned to Harmsworth House, Baldwin wrote that he was "warmly received by Mr. Wellman and Mr. Harlan and Dr. Hofma. I never before realized what a difference there is in the companionship of those of one's own mother tongue till I again heard the voices of my own countrymen."[411] However, Wellman's feelings toward his second-in-command did not remain sunny for very long.

The first hints that Baldwin was not fit to lead others came immediately, as the returning Norwegians had to be issued fur suits to sleep in when their sleeping bags were found to have "become the refuge of vermin and the men were obliged to take a wash and change their clothing immediately after supper."[412] Baldwin disavowed any knowledge of the condition of the men's sleeping bags, especially since "very fortunately none of the objectionable creatures had found their way to my sleeping bag and clothing."[413]

Far worse for Wellman than the ruined gear of the Norwegians was the utter failure of Baldwin to lead the advance party anywhere near to the goal Wellman had assigned to it. As the crow flies, Harmsworth House was separated from the northernmost point of land in Franz Josef Land at Cape Fligely by 106 nautical miles. Baldwin had advanced less than 40 percent of this distance and, in the process, utterly poisoned relations between the Norwegians and the Americans.

It was a tremendous fall for Baldwin, who can be seen as the personification of the Middle American striver of the Gilded Age, with equal parts assumed haughtiness, Christian patriotism, and blundering hayseed. At the beginning of their efforts in Franz Josef Land, just as Baldwin and his Norwegians started northward, Wellman had written to Baldwin with the fascinating submission that Wellman was considering giving up his leadership of the "Polar Dash." "Next spring I shall probably turn the whole thing over to you and simply go as a passenger. If you make a success of this your honors will be great."[414]

Less than two weeks later, as he observed the weakness of Baldwin's efforts, Wellman had already changed his mind, and wrote to Baldwin that "the Polar Dash calls for six men—three Americans and three Norwegians,"[415] but specifying neither which three Americans nor again offering to "turn the whole thing over to" Baldwin.

As for Wellman, he had problems of his own, some at Cape Tegetthoff and several others brewing further south. Wellman later wrote that the three Americans left behind at Cape Tegetthoff had "plenty to do" but, in truth, during the three months that the advance party was away, almost nothing of substance was accomplished at Harmsworth House.[416] As Wellman himself described it, he and Dr. Edward Hofma and the querulous Quirof Harlan "wrote letters, sewed at our clothing, played cards, read books, [took] regular baths"[417] and ate "plenty of fresh bear meat, and American oatmeal, bacon, and flapjacks."[418]

During the late fall and into the winter, Baldwin carried out some dogged scientific work, making regular recordings of temperature, pressure, and wind speed. With the onset of winter, he added to these a study of the aurora borealis.[419] These latter tended to be almost poetical rather than strictly scientific, as in his description for the evening of March 3, 1899, when he observed "an intense display of coronal type, covering the heavens from the belt of Orion, in the south southwest, to the lower limbs of Hercules, in the north, and from Virgo, in the east, to Pegasus and Pisces, in the west. Rapid movement of streamers and curtains from west to east and from south to north. Delicate tinting of the display in all its parts, but particularly striking along the edges of the enveloping or outer curtains."[420]

As for Dr. Hofma and Mr. Harlan, the entire expedition seemed to involve little beyond eating and playing cards at Harmsworth House. Wellman later wrote that Harlan had also dabbled in a study of the aurora, "particularly from the point of view of its effect upon the magnetic needle . . . as well as his general study of the physical conditions of Franz Josef Land."[421] Wellman intended to publish the report "in proper form and place as soon as possible," but he never did. Likewise, the doctor "had a most interesting report concerning the fauna and flora" of Franz Josef Land, one that, like Harlan's work, never saw the light of day.[422] Given their self-imposed confinement on Hall Island, the reports of Harlan and Hofma would in any case have been limited in scope and in the end neither work was ever published.

On New Year's Eve 1898, Wellman composed a long letter to his brother Arthur and sister-in-law Emma. In it, he announced that he would start on the North Pole dash in forty days. "All our energies & equipment are to be thrown into the effort to attain the highest north, & I believe we shall do it. Eighty-seven [degrees north, which would best Nansen's record by forty-five nautical miles] would satisfy me, but if we should happen to have good instead of bad luck—there might be such a thing—& the Pole were attainable, you may be sure we shall go for it. I have my heart set upon beating the record, and will *do it* unless the most extraordinary & unexpected disasters interpose."[423]

Wellman wrote about the advance hut, Fort McKinley, being "just under the 81st parallel," though Wellman knew it to be well short of that mark. Wellman expected to reach the fort no later than February 16. He expected five of the seven men at Harmsworth House to make the trip—again, Mr. Harlan and Dr. Hofma were to be left behind—and they would join the two at the fort. There the new party of seven men and approximately fifty-five dogs would gather thirty-five hundred pounds of supplies and start for the North Pole on February 20. Three of the Norwegians would form a supporting party that would travel north for twenty days and then pass their supplies to the men headed to the pole before they retreated south. There, presumably at about 83° North, the remaining four—in this letter Wellman listed himself along with Baldwin and two picked Norwegians—would form the "Polar Dash Party": "We shall start with about 40 dogs—the best of the pack—three sledges & 10 copper tubes—a total load of about 2400 lbs—600 to the man & 60 to the dogs. These are lighter loads than Dr. Nansen had at the start—his total being 1600 lbs for 2 men. Our loads will lighten so rapidly that when we shall have been out 20 days the total will be only 1600, with 4 men & 36 dogs, & lightening still more every day."[424]

Wellman planned to travel for forty day after he reached 83° North, forty days to travel the 420 nautical miles to the pole, an average of 10.5 nautical miles each day. But Wellman had before him the example of Baldwin's fall work, which in the end could not average even one mile per day. And with that Wellman revealed his true purpose: "If we can travel 35 (of forty days) at the same rate Dr. Nansen made—about *7½ miles per day, we shall reach 87° 20"*, or more than a degree nearer the Pole than Dr. N."[425] Wellman knew that the shifting nature of the polar ice cap would force any polar dash team to average closer to 12 nautical miles of more if they hoped to reach the North Pole itself. As he wrote to his brother and sister-in-law, "perhaps this is too much to hope for."[426] Beating "Dr. N" and then racing home to cash in, as he believed Nansen had done: this was now Wellman's clear object, if ever there had been another.

While the dash party was thus engaged, the men who remained at Cape Tegetthoff would engage in "very important geographical work in exploring unknown lands in this archipelago. If we fail & they succeed the expedition will still have accomplished something worthy."[427]

Beyond his immediate expedition headaches, Wellman was also tormented by his fractured relations back home. He insisted that he must return home in 1899 and not be caught for a second winter in Franz Josef Land. "Life is too short to spend much of it apart from a wife as dear & children as sweet as mine. . . ."

> I also wish you to know how carefully I have analyzed myself up here, & how clearly I now see where my ambitions and affections lie. They are *wholly* centered in my home at Washington, without any mental reservation or the slightest trace of the old spirit of adventurous wandering. You know what I mean, & you may know I write with dull deliberation & conviction. . . . Never before have I appreciated wife & children and brother & sister as I do now—and my little talents, too, & I only want a chance to get back & be a more useful, wholesome, man. I feel that I have been "born again" up here.[428]

For a man burrowed inside a snow-covered hut on a wind-swept cape in Franz Josef Land to write that he was done with his "old spirit of adventurous wandering" was a bit of a stretch. But that is not what Wellman meant, as he made clear to his brother in his next letter. This Wellman wrote from Harmsworth House on February 16, 1899, the same day that he had previously planned to be already at Fort McKinley and ready for the dash to the pole.

As he prepared what could be thought of as a will, Wellman was still troubled over the state of his marriage. If he were to die on the ice, Wellman instructed his brother to immediately collect his life insurance and he wanted *"all debts in Tromso or Norway paid. . . .*

> The wages of [the] men R debts of honor & must be paid. I do not care about anything else. If I lose my life other people can afford to lose the little they have put in. My wife & children should have every dollar they can get hold of. And you should have your money back, every penny of it, for you have a family & cannot afford to lose it.
>
> There may be some other obligations that come to the surface—I can't think of all those things now—& you may deal with them on their merits.[429]

One obligation that Wellman clearly foresaw rising to the surface was Miss Willard, the mother of his illegitimate child. Wellman believed she was at that moment living in Hanover, Germany, and it was an indication of his priorities that he gave his brother considerably more instructions on how to deal with her than he had in the procurement of a relief ship for his entire expedition. "She shall be treated . . . generously. I left an arrangement of $3,500 life insurance for her, for the child's benefit, & I want her to have it without any questioning or caviling.

> If I return I shall provide for the child, & help her to get settled in life, treating her as a man of justice would treat a divorced wife, but I should *never* go to her, or be with her, or even see her if I could avoid it. I respect her, & admire her, & have no word of complaint of her to utter. She is a magnificent, noble girl, & I wish her happiness & contentment. But my *love* henceforth is all for my wife. . . . If I get back I shall attend to Miss W's future, so far as I have anything to do with it, & that is wholly financial & helpful. If I do not return I ask you to see to it, & without hurting her by revealing what I have here written. If I die that settles everything.[430]

"What a lot of trouble I am & have been to you!" Wellman wrote to his brother and no lie, before he added a postscript: "I borrowed $725 from Ambassador [John Milton] Hay, London, & he should be repaid. I regard that as a debt of honor."[431]

Wellman at Cape Tegethoff on Christmas 1898, during the long and lonely winter at Harmsworth House. *Courtesy National Air and Space Museum (NASM 9A10648), Smithsonian Institution.*

Debts to Wellman's mistress and ambassadorial patrons aside, both Arthur Wellman in the U.S. and the expedition's agent Andreas Aagaard in Tromsø already had their hands full to try to secure a ship to retrieve the expedition in the summer of 1899. Arthur Wellman had sent funds to Aagaard to cover what the expedition owed to the Norwegians up to the first of January 1899, but that cash had run out. More money soon arrived to cover these expenses through mid-March, but by the middle of January

1899, Aagaard was writing to Wellman's banker in Chicago that he had been given no money to charter a vessel to bring Wellman and his men back to Norway. As with so many of his arrangements, Wellman had tasked first his brother, and then Aagaard, with the chore, and then left neither of them the required funds to carry it out.

Understandably, Aagaard was unwilling to make a move to engage a relief ship without them. "Nobody can blame me for not taking the risk of guaranteeing the freight without being protected by funds from America."[432] Wellman wanted to purchase this freight as cheaply as possible, by the expedient of hitching a ride on one of the Norwegian walrus-hunting vessels he blithely assumed would cruise to Franz Josef Land in 1899. But after the huge catch of walrus in the summer of 1898, Aagaard explained that the price of walrus hides had fallen dramatically, and no one seemed inclined to risk a journey to the high Arctic to pursue more of them in 1899.

In 1898 *Frithjof* had been chartered out of Kristiania for 25,000 Kroner. To bring the Wellman expedition out of Franz Josef Land, the owner, Magnus Giæver, now demanded much more, plus insurance and wages, and then tacked on an additional 25,000 Kroner if the ship was frozen in anywhere in the islands. "You must understand," Aagaard wrote, "that there are very few ships to choose from. Only strong wooden steamers built expressly for forcing ice can be used."[433] Aagaard went on:

> Besides the *Frithjof,* there are some such ones in the south ports of Norway. Before chartering the *Laura* (afterwards exchanged with the *Frithjof*), Mr. Wellman's commissioner, Capt. Bonnevie, had applied to the owners of these other ships, but their demands were considerably higher than that of *Laura*'s owner. I am awaiting a decisive answer from the owner of the *Balaena* in February, but if the *Balaena* is not going to Franz Josef Land on catch of walrus, there must be chartered a ship expressly for fetching Mr. Wellman's party back and consequently I must ask you as soon as possible to open me a confirmed credit in a bank in Europe for kr. 30,000.[434]

Aagaard wrote to Arthur Wellman that if Wellman's banker did not come through, then Arthur needed to get in touch with Herman Kohlsaat at the *Chicago Times-Herald* and, failing that, to Alexander Graham Bell of the National Geographic Society and explain to them "the state of things."[435]

The "state of things," the utter failure to plan for—much less finance—a ship to bring the expedition back, was a dog's breakfast that soon drew wider attention. As early as January 2, 1899, no less than Fridtjof Nansen himself wrote a scathingly formal note to Aagaard saying that "I don't know how Wellman was equipped and how much provision he had [or] if sufficient for several years. Neither I know if he and his men are clever enough to provide the wanted food by shooting, if the provisions should not be sufficient, but I should consider it inexcusable if there be not made a definite agreement with a ship about going in search of the expedition."[436] The superintendent of the U.S. Coast and Geodetic Survey, Henry S. Pritchett, which had seconded Quirof Harlan to the expedition, wrote to Arthur Wellman and demanded to be informed of just what arrangements had been made to bring the men home.[437]

Arthur Wellman responded to Aagaard's letter as best as circumstances allowed. All he could do was to repeat his brother's obtuse notion that some ship or other would show itself in Franz Josef Land in the summer of 1899 and that Walter would make sure that they "would be suitably rewarded should they find him" and return the expedition to Norway.[438] Arthur suggested that Aagaard send all appropriate vessels a copy of Wellman's last instructions to see if any of them were interested to earn the charter that summer. Otherwise, he suggested that they put off the question until May or June.

This would simply not do for the competent and reliable Aagaard, and by late February he had secured a contract with the *Capella,* a steamer based in Sandefjord, Norway, and owned by Ishafvet AB of Göteborg, Sweden. The vessel planned to hunt seal at Jan Mayen and Greenland that summer and would, probably in late July, take on coal at Vardø and detour to Franz Josef Land in search of walrus and, incidentally, the Wellman expedition.[439] If *Capella* did find Wellman and his expedition at Cape Tegetthoff, the charter would be paid the bargain price of £400, about 7,500 Norwegian kroner—and a quarter of what Aagaard thought it might cost in January.

As if these far-off troubles weren't enough for a man about to lead a team of men and dogs onto the polar ice pack, Wellman's polar-dash party was shrinking by the day. On February 15, 1899, Wellman wrote to his brother that he would be off in three days, more than a week behind his planned schedule. This meant that if Wellman hoped to copy Nansen's movements of about 7½ nautical miles per day, he was already sixty miles—one full degree of latitude—behind.

Worse for Wellman's "American expedition," he had by now discarded from the North Pole attempt every single one of the other Americans. By early February, Baldwin's problematic character had thoroughly poisoned the atmosphere within Harmsworth House. He had accused the Norwegians of stealing blankets in order to repair their torn and worn pants and continued to treat them as servants who never showed him proper levels of respect. By early February, Wellman and Baldwin could barely speak to one another, and were reduced to writing formal memoranda to each other to sort out trivialities around the base camp that had blown up into mini-crises.

Wellman wrote to his brother Arthur that the polar dash would now consist of Wellman himself and the Norwegians. All of the other three Americans would remain at Harmsworth House, including Baldwin, who had taken ill. "Besides," Wellman wrote, "he has not behaved very well, and is a very timid, gloomy, despairing, apprehensive man."

> He writes down the spirits of his associates—an undesirable thing when the battle is severe enough at best. He has apologized in public . . . & I have forgiven him, & that should be the end of it, & will be if he behaves well. I don't want a single word of this breathed to any one unless it should be necessary to defend me.[440]

Wellman made it clear to Arthur that he wanted Baldwin expressly forbidden from any role in publishing a book about the expedition. Further, he reminded Arthur that Baldwin, along with all the members of the expedition, were under contract not to write or publish or lecture for two years without Wellman's consent.

Wellman hinted that Baldwin had threatened to reveal the poor planning and equipment of the expedition, especially that the men "were not properly supplied with warm clothing."[441] Wellman went on to list more than a dozen separate items of clothing and gear that the men had been supplied with, including "one heavy sleeping bag of best rein[deer] skin," "always . . . enough to eat," and "good boats & sledges & skis and all that."[442]

The dogs were another problem. Disease and in-fighting had reduced their numbers from the eighty-three the expedition brought to Franz Josef Land to not more than forty by mid-February. Whatever Baldwin's faults—and they were numerous—if Wellman did not know by this point that his expedition's plan and gear were uniformly sub-standard, he was either blindingly incompetent or willfully obtuse. One leans toward the latter, as Wellman possessed an irrepressible optimism in his personality that the "gloomy" Baldwin would never own. Baldwin was an almost congenitally insecure résumé padder. Wellman probably never wrote a résumé in his life and seemed to bounce buoyantly from one chance to another. He was a natural improviser. As he wrote to his ever-tolerant brother, "I glory in meeting & overcoming difficulties."[443] That Wellman himself created each and every one of these difficulties never seems to have intruded on his fundamental good humor and ability to look on the bright side of every situation.

On February 16, the day after he described the parlous state of the expedition to his brother, Wellman wrote to Baldwin to formally notify the second-in-command that he would not be a member of the polar party. He then further reduced Baldwin's status to that of a co-equal if not a subordinate to Dr. Hofma. In the event Wellman failed to return from his polar dash, he now entrusted to Hofma all papers and photographs generated by the expedition, and specifically ordered Baldwin to turn his personal journal over to Hofma before the surviving expedition members reached Norway on the voyage home.

When Wellman returned alive but wounded from his polar attempt, he either forgot to demand Baldwin's journal or did not believe it any longer important. The critical journal was found amongst Baldwin's papers more than a century after the expedition's unsuccessful conclusion.

SEVENTEEN

The Death of Bernt Bentsen

When Baldwin and the remainder of the Norwegians in the advance party departed Fort McKinley at Cape Heller on Saturday, October 22, 1898, they left behind Paul Bjørvig and Bernt Bentsen. Wellman later wrote that this assignment was the "realization of [a] dream for the two men . . . to pass a winter in the Arctics in a little hut well stocked with food and tobacco." Wellman, who must have known the truth by the time he wrote these words, insisted that both Bjørvig and Bentsen "were happy and well when their comrades left them."[444]

To the contrary, Baldwin's incompetence had thoroughly destroyed the men's morale and, carrying Wellman's instructions to extreme limits, he ordered Bjørvig and Bentsen to survive the winter on the frozen meat of ten walrus and two polar bear carcasses and to do so with as little fuel as possible. "Warming up the shelter is not even to be considered."[445] The two Norwegians obliged by cooking the meat and blubber only twice a day. They then settled in to a routine that included reading and re-reading the solitary newspaper they'd been left with. When that had been gone over, they started on the printed labels of the canned goods that were stored in the fort.

The two men entered into a period of uttermost isolation and privation. They had been subject to hard physical labor on short rations for three straight months, all while enduring daily exposure to cold, wind, rain, sleet, and snow. Their sleeping bags had been soaked through ever since leaving

Cape Tegetthoff in early August, and as late October turned to November, the bags froze solid. Bjørvig was not slow to lay the blame for their plight upon Baldwin, "who has treated us like animals. While we spent the nights out in snow and fog, he took the best and driest places. There he lay, eating chocolate and anything else nice, while we ate walrus meat."[446]

On the last day of October, ten days after the rest of the advance team had gone south, Bjørvig was confronted with a new problem when Bernt Bentsen took ill with a persistent sore throat. A week later Bentsen's condition worsened. He could not keep any food down, and Bjørvig wrote that his "bowel movements consist of almost nothing but blood."[447] With no medicines left at the fort, there was little Bjørvig could do to ease Bentsen's pain. Soon, Bentsen could not move enough even to leave the hut, which only increased the cold he felt. When he was thirsty, Bentsen had to wait for Bjørvig to start a fire in order to melt some ice.

To add to the miserable scene, the men would lie in the low-walled hut and listen as polar bears climbed onto the walrus hide roof and scratched away at it. Afraid that a bear might fall through the roof and crash down upon them, Bjørvig would track the movements of the giant paws as they silently depressed the walrus hides. When directly overhead, Bjørvig aimed the rifle and blasted a shot through the hides to drive the bears off.

As the winter came on and the Arctic settled down to several months of perpetual darkness, Bjørvig's lone consolation was the moon, which he wrote "shines clearer here than in Norway."[448] The moonlight bathed the landscape in an almost luminescent glow, often accompanied by curtains of the aurora shimmering on the horizon.

For Bentsen, there was no such relief. He began to hallucinate and to speak with numerous invented personalities, in particular to a friend named Hans, all the while wondering why Bjørvig could not see them or talk to them also. At night when Bjørvig settled down in the sleeping bag, Bentsen asked him to move over and make room for Hans. He spoke of a return to Tromsø, and assured Bjørvig they could be there quickly. He repeatedly called out whenever Bjørvig ventured from the hut, and feared that if a bear killed Bjørvig then Bentsen would not be far behind. For Bjørvig, who had his hands full to maintain his own sanity, it was a sad and transformational trial.

Whenever a bear approached the fort, the dogs would send up a howl, and many would break their leashes to confront the bear. On one occasion,

Bjørvig wounded a bear that then retreated to Operti Bay with five dogs chasing it. When the wounded bear sat down at the edge of the water, one of the dogs came too close and a single swipe of the bear's paw killed it instantly. Undeterred, the remaining four dogs chased the bear over the ice. Two dogs returned the following morning and another came back two days later, so frightened it would not leave Bjørvig's side. The fourth dog he never saw again. "Baldwin said we should feed the dogs only once every other day," Bjørvig wrote, "but I give them food every day. Maybe Baldwin thought there would not be enough food, [but] I shall see to it that they get enough food all the time we are up here."[449]

On December 22, Bentsen called out to Bjørvig to thank him for all he had done for him. According to Bjørvig, Bentsen now said that "it is all up with me now. When I am dead you must get yourself back to Cap [*sic*] Tegetthoff, or else you will end up like me." "I didn't know what to say," wrote Bjørvig, "as the tears were pouring down my face. I asked him if there was anything he wanted me to say to those at home if I got back. 'Tell them what it was like for us here, that is all.'"[450]

By Christmas Eve, "the most monotonous and miserable Christmas Eve anyone could experience,"[451] Bentsen no longer had any feeling in his body below his waist. His body had turned as white as snow. It was only at this fatal juncture that Bjørvig finally broke down and raided Baldwin's precious food supplies and found a tin of milk and some lumps of chocolate. As he shared these with Bentsen, the men talked and imagined how their families and friends back in Norway were passing the day and somehow managed to enjoy a few moments of cheer.

> We did not have the permission of Baldwin to do it, but this time I was disobeying orders. We shall celebrate Christmas. Now I realised that Baldwin had a cake in his box which was still here. He once told me the cake was from his grandmother in America. He said that his grandmother said the cake was for Christmas. As Baldwin had not come back to fulfill her wishes, I thought it was best to help him enjoy the cake. But his grandmother must have made the cake when she was young, as the cake was rock hard, and we could not eat it.[452]

As 1898 dwindled to its miserable conclusion, Bentsen began to sing "Beautiful is the earth" and ask delirious questions such as what his brother

Simon was reading. At this, Bjørvig knew the end was near. The end came early on Monday morning, January 2, 1899. In the natural irony of things, it was the same day that Fridtjof Nansen wrote the vehement letter to Andreas Aagaard that excoriated Wellman's "inexcusable" lack of planning. As the reflective Bjørvig laconically noted: "Much is hidden that we just do not understand."[453]

Bjørvig lay next to Bentsen's body for a long while, as he wondered what he should do. In the end, he decided that he had only one option: to try to survive as best he could until the men from Cape Tegetthoff came north, which he expected in early February. In the meantime, Bjørvig honored Bentsen's request to leave his body in the hut in order to protect it from predation by bears and dogs. Accordingly, he melted some ice, washed Bentsen's face and hands, and left him in the sleeping bag where he died. "It is pretty miserable to lie together with a dead man," wrote the calmly reflective stoic. "It was cold enough while he was alive to lie in the sleeping bag, and it feels a lot worse now he lies there dead. I have to take it as it comes. Perhaps it will get better."[454]

The situation did in fact get better, if only in predictable starts and strange fits. By mid-January a faint light appeared on the southern horizon. The northern archipelago was tilting slowly back toward the sun. But the rotation carried with it no heat. To stay warm, Bjørvig took five of the dogs into the hut to sleep with him. "It is not exactly better, as they do all their business on the bear skin."[455] In the mornings, Bjørvig would chase the dogs off and wait half an hour. By then, both the bear skin and the dog leavings had frozen solid and he could simply shake the blanket and ready it for the next evening. "I often think that my dead companion has it better than I do," Bjørvig wrote, "because he escaped the feel of the cold."[456]

As the supply of blubber dwindled, Bjørvig began to eat the uncooked bear meat that had lain frozen at the hut for six months. He wasn't worried that he would starve, but more than anything else he feared the loss of coffee, the one specific that had sustained him over the winter. A rummage through a basket left behind by Baldwin produced an assortment of random items as arcane as they were useless: barber's knives, old photographs, even a stocking "holding almost 70 *kroner* in silver coins from 25 *øre* pieces to crowns. What he had thought to do with this up here in the north, heaven alone knows."[457]

By February 22, long after he expected the men from Harmsworth House to have arrived, Bjørvig walked outside to see the sun shining on the clouds and "revealing so many and such fine colours that I can barely describe them, and an artist could scarcely reproduce them. . . . And here stands a black, ragged soul to stare at the view. . . . If an artist had painted it with a ragged, filthy figure in the foreground it would have been a weird picture."[458]

EIGHTEEN

The Polar Dash

The winter at Harmsworth House was scarcely less tense than that endured by Paul Bjørvig 41 nautical miles north at Cape Heller, despite Wellman's later claim that "not a word of discord between Yankees and Norsemen marred the novel experience."[459] To distract himself from his troubles, Wellman continued to fantasize over his projected daily mileage totals, "like organizing an army corps for campaigns in an enemy's country."[460]

When Wellman finally posed for a farewell flash-powder photograph and headed north from Cape Tegetthoff on February 18, 1899, his "army corps" contained not a single American. Baldwin had fallen completely out of favor, and there is scant record that Dr. Hofma or Mr. Harlan accomplished anything during the entire expedition. Instead, Wellman was accompanied by the three Norwegians—the brothers from Hammerfest Olaf and Emil Ellefsen, along with Daniel Johansen—all of whom had returned with Baldwin from Cape Heller the previous October.

Wellman's plan consisted of little more than walking northward as far as he and the men could, until his calculations told him that they had to turn around. He later wrote that, in order to succeed, he and his men had to "get up right early in the Arctic morning,"[461] but their eventual departure date from Harmsworth House was already two days later than Wellman had originally expected to be at Fort McKinley.

The start was unpromising, "stumbling along like drunken men in a gloom. . . . Each of the three Norwegians had a sledge and team of dogs in charge. A snow storm was raging, but we were ready to start and could not stop for a little storm. I led the way, 'tracking' for the dogs as best I could in the darkness and snow-laden air. The sun had not yet risen, but in the middle of the day was near enough to the horizon to give us a gray, hazy dawn light. The snow was soft, and we sank into it to the ankles and often to the knees. Underneath there were frequent ridges and protuberances of rough ice to trip the weary feet."[462]

It required twice as long as Wellman planned in order for the men to reach Cape Heller. When the cape was finally in sight, on the afternoon of February 27, 1898, the three Norwegians stood back to allow Wellman to make his triumphal entry into the "fort." "But aside from an overturned boat, half buried in the snow, a collection of empty biscuit and provision tins, and a group of dogs chained to the top of a bank of ice, I could see nothing at all indicating a human habitation."[463] It was Emil Ellefsen who pointed Wellman in the right direction. "The hut is just before you, Sir, right behind the dogs."[464]

That same morning, Paul Bjørvig had just endured his fifty-sixth night sharing a sleeping bag with a frozen corpse. He woke, brushed the snow off himself, shook the dog feces from the blankets, and then got up to feed the dogs. In the afternoon, he crawled back into the hut and again lay down on the sleeping bag he shared with the body of Bernt Bentsen. Soon afterward, the dogs began a tremendous racket. Bjørvig thought a bear had entered the camp again, so he got his rifle and crawled through the entrance tunnel, pushing the rifle in front of him. As he neared the entrance, he realized that the bear was standing only a few feet away, at the opening to the hut. He lay on his back and prepared to shoot when he saw that he was aiming not at a polar bear but a human. As he wrote: "I was not at all surprised, immediately thinking it was a man who had been shipwrecked. Now for more than a month I had been watching out for them from Cap [sic] Tegetthoff, but at this instant my thoughts were far from there."[465]

"Hello, Paul," said Wellman, and grasped the Norwegian tightly—both to express his thanks to see the man alive and to prevent the gun in his hands from an unwelcome discharge in his direction. They retreated out of the falling snow and crawled into the hut. There Bjørvig quickly got water on for coffee, since "now I didn't need to be thrifty any more."[466] When Wellman asked after Bentsen, Bjørvig pointed to the sleeping bag at Wellman's feet. Wellman said nothing, as he tried to process the implications of the macabre scene before him. Bjørvig and Bentsen were both experienced Arctic hands, but clearly something had gone very wrong. When Wellman did speak, it was to ask if Bjørvig wished to greet his comrades outside. Bjørvig wrote: "It was the first time it dawned on me that he couldn't have come north alone. My thinking had certainly packed in for a while. "I crawled out again. Down below the snow drifts on the ice stood all my Norwegian friends, who had journeyed south last autumn. Only one person was missing, that was Baldwin—and I was glad about that."[467]

As for Wellman, he stared at the sleeping bag and the body inside, both "frozen as hard as a rock" and "marveled that Paul Bjørvig was still sane."[468] Wellman later invented a whole series of conversations he claimed Bentsen had uttered in his delirium, including stories of "his home and his wife in Norway, of the green hills there, of Dr. Nansen and Captain Sverdrup, and the cruise of the *Fram*; at times he was once more in the ward-room of that famous ship; again he was after bear or walrus with Bjoervig and the boys in our little Lapp-boat; now he was on a sledge trip to the Pole 'with Mr. Wellman.' "[469]

There was of course no mention of the imaginary "Hans," or Bentsen's very real hatred of Baldwin, or of the substandard gear and criminal lack of food and warmth that contributed to Bentsen's premature death at the age of thirty-eight. Instead, Wellman used his natural talent to turn every bad event to good account and described the incident, with almost loving over-statement, as "one of the most remarkable tragedies known to the history of Arctic exploration."[470] When the remainder of the party settled into the hut that night, Bjørvig could not sleep, so Wellman gave him a dose of morphine, narcotic pain relief that would have gone far to relieve Bentsen's suffering if Baldwin had thought to carry it to Fort McKinley the previous fall.

The following day, the last of February 1898, Bentsen's bodied was rolled in sailcloth and buried under a tomb of rocks near the fort. According to Wellman, Bjørvig spent an entire day in temperatures well below zero in a collection of smaller stones and "patiently chinking up all the little interstices between the rocks which covered the grave."[471] Making a cross from two boat thwarts, the Norwegian carved the inscription "B. Bentzen Död 2-1, '99" and placed it over the grave.

It was a terribly inauspicious way to begin an arduous trek onto the polar ice cap. Worse, the polar-dash party had only half of the dogs that the expedition had brought to Franz Josef Land. Of the fifty-eight dogs that wintered at Cape Tegetthoff, only twenty survived to reach Fort McKinley;

The Norwegians with Wellman. This image was apparently taken during the "polar dash" with Wellman in the late winter of 1899. According to his grandson, Emil Ellefsen is the figure seated on the sledge, while Paul Bjørvig leans against the sledge. *Courtesy National Air and Space Museum (NASM 9A10653), Smithsonian Institution.*

of the twenty-seven dogs left at the fort the previous autumn, only eighteen remained. With only forty-two dogs left to help pull the men toward the North Pole, the efforts of the polar-dash party predictably did not last long.

Paul Bjørvig wrote that the polar party started from Fort McKinley on March 7, while Wellman wrote that it was March 17. The dates in Bjørvig's diary do seem off in many cases; still, it is difficult to imagine Wellman and the Norwegians hanging around the fort for nearly three weeks before moving northward. Whichever the case, the men found good smooth ice in Austria Sound, and by March 21 they had traveled nearly a full degree north and approached the east coast of Rudolf Land, at latitude 81° 40' North. If Wellman's departure date of March 17 is to be believed, then he and the Norwegians traveled farther north in three days than Baldwin had *in three months.*[472]

Bjørvig wrote that they had excellent weather as well as ice conditions until they reached a cape on the eastern side of Rudolf Land that Wellman named for his loyal brother Arthur. There, off Cape Arthur Wellman on March 21, the "ice was now beginning to be rafted up quite severely; further north the ice was so thin that the sledge was almost going through."[473] Worse, the sledges were beginning to stick so badly—Bjørvig thought that the salt in the ice was the cause—that the dogs were increasingly unable to effectively pull them. "The ice was no more than 4 inches thick and free of snow."[474]

All things considered, however, Bjørvig was happy with their progress and with Wellman. The Norwegians enjoyed oatmeal, coffee and biscuits for breakfast, chocolate for lunch, and for dinner canned food and coffee. "It is food that a man can get strength from, when you have been manhauling all day."[475] Even better for morale, all of the men, Wellman included, shared the exact same rations. Gone were the extreme food rations, the forced diet of frozen walrus meat and blubber, and the secretive consumption of goodies that the Norwegians had experienced with their erstwhile leader Baldwin.

Unfortunately, the apparent bonhomie was all for naught. The "polar dash" was already finished. The day previous and just three days after leaving Fort McKinley, Wellman's sledge had become stuck and in the process of urging his dogs onward Wellman had slipped on the ice. His right leg went into a crack in the ice, his shin bearing the brunt of the impact. The pain was crippling, but Wellman thought he had only suffered a bad bruise. In fact, he had fractured his leg and, when he tried to move the following day, the pain only increased.

At this point, Wellman placed their position at about 140 nautical miles north of Cape Tegetthoff. In fact, they were only 100 nautical miles north of Harmsworth House and now, stuck in their tent with the North Pole still nearly 500 nautical miles away, Wellman's injury finished their prospects. As if to reinforce the point, a fierce storm blew up out of the north the next day, March 22, and ripped the pack ice apart. Leaving the tent to do his business during the storm, one of the Norwegians just as quickly ducked his head back in and told Bjørvig to come outside. When he did, Bjørvig was horrified. The piece of ice on which they were camped had fractured and there was open water as far as the eye could see.

Bjørvig called the rest of the party to action. They scurried from the tent just as the wind knocked it down and the ice began to crack around them. With the dogs howling, the men dragged the tent onto a bigger floe and then went back for the tent's ground sheet, which was littered with the primus stove, the rifles, and the sleeping bags. The whole lot was dragged to the new pan of ice. Sledges began to tip into the sea. In the confusion, Wellman slipped again and his foot was caught between two converging ice floes and nearly crushed. The Norwegians tried to get the tent back up but in the end took shelter in the lee of a grounded berg in order to wait out the wind.

For Wellman, the painful ordeal was just the stuff a born storyteller lived for. The crack in the ice had not formed in the distance, but "opened directly under our sleeping-bags, and in its black depths we could hear the waters rushing and seething." No sooner had Wellman pulled his foot from the water than the two pieces of ice snapped closed "like a vice, and with such force that the edges of the blocks were ground to fragments and the débris was pushed up into a quivering ridge.

> Ten feet away lay a dog with his head cut clean off by a similar opening and closing of the ice upon which he had been sleeping. How the animal had managed to get caught in the trap we could not imagine; but there he was, as neatly beheaded as if an executioner had done the job. . . . Some of our sledges, with their precious stores, were already toppling into the waters. . . . Under our feet and all around us the ice was shaking and breaking—here pushing up, there sinking down—and the violently agitated sea was spouting through the openings. . . . The spot where our camp had stood . . . was in a volcanic state of eruption. Masses of ice were gushing up into the air like flames. The brittle blocks were crushing, grinding, snarling, biting at one another. The sea was rushing wildly through and over the débris.[476]

By morning, the wind had died down and the men could make coffee and take stock. Unlike Wellman, Paul Bjørvig was characteristically blunt: "Nearly all our food was gone. The instruments, the dog food and any clothes we were not actually wearing were gone. We were just about out of everything."[477] They had also lost fourteen more dogs, and the ice was red with blood where those dogs had been squeezed to death by the ice quake.

The party still had three rifles and a few cartridges, but Wellman was now a cripple and could not walk. He sat amid the destruction of his expedition and began to weep. As Bjørvig wrote, "the whole journey was wasted."[478] There was little to do now but to beat a hasty retreat. The Norwegians were particularly anxious to transport Wellman as rapidly as possible back to Harmsworth House. Not only did his injuries require whatever assistance Dr. Hofma could provide, but they knew it would not look good if they returned minus the only American in the group. Moreover, Wellman was the only American they trusted, and to return to the inevitable hostility and trouble that they would face from Baldwin and perhaps the other two Americans, it didn't bear thinking about.

Accordingly, on March 24, 1899, the polar-dash party began a new dash, this one south to Cape Tegetthoff. The next day they were able to shoot a bear, so the food situation was immediately improved. In the chaos of the loss of their gear, the scavenge for food, and the care of Wellman, it took twelve days for the men to retrace their steps to Fort McKinley, where Bjørvig found that bears had entered the hut but that Bentsen's grave had not been disturbed.

Wellman later wrote that he "attempted to go ahead and pick the road in the rough ice . . . little caring what happened to me," but Paul Bjørvig's notes make it clear that the Norwegians dragged Wellman all the way south on one of the sledges that had survived the ice quake.[479] Bjørvig knew they had to move as quickly as possible and, soon enough, Wellman did also. His injured leg "was filled with inflammatory product from toes to trunk, and was swollen much beyond its natural size."[480] In the end, Wellman was fortunate to survive without amputation.

From Fort McKinley, the party raced back to Harmsworth House, and arrived on April 9, 1899. There, at Cape Tegetthoff, Bjørvig saw the mountainside alive with ivory gulls and little auks. "It was the first night in 9 months that I knew what it was to be warm at night," he wrote, "and just as long since I had experienced artificial heating. Even if it is the poorest sort of overwintering hut they have there, it is still a palace compared to [Fort McKinley]."[481]

Wellman was laid out on the floor, but in truth there was not much Dr. Hofma could do for him. For the next three and a half months, Wellman would remain prone on the floor of Harmsworth House, "tormented with the most agonizing itching, weak, feverish, despondent, sleepless."[482]

Eventually, Wellman's agonies were partially relieved from a completely unexpected quarter. Evelyn Briggs Baldwin, disgraced and demoted, had spent the preceding six months mechanically recording the weather at Cape Tegetthoff for the U.S. Weather Bureau. Now, in April 1899, just as the first American expedition to Franz Josef Land was about to slink home with nothing to show for its catastrophic costs, the expedition's erstwhile second-in-command, of all people, stepped forward to save the reputation of the Wellman Polar Expedition.

NINETEEN

The Discovery of Graham Bell Land

With the "polar dash" a failure and Wellman unable to leave his bed, he now attempted to salvage some good result from the expedition. He asked his erstwhile second-in-command to follow up on his earlier sightings of islands and capes along the northern edge of Wilczek Land. Baldwin thought he had seen new features in that direction during the desultory advance of the previous fall, and Wellman was now desperate to confirm these observations. Hopelessly in debt and with one man lost, any new geographic features that the expedition could locate would likely be Wellman's last chance to salvage some tangible result from his costly voyage to Franz Josef Land.

For Baldwin, the unexpected side trip offered an opportunity for redemption. To lead a spring sledge expedition "upon the unexplored east coast of this famous archipelago" was not only the chance to redeem an otherwise failed expedition. In his unpublished journal, he wrote that it would be "at least a partial compensation for my bitter disappointment at not having been able to accompany the Polar dash party."[483]

At some point prior to Baldwin's death in October 1933, a granite obelisk was placed in Oswego Cemetery in Oswego, Kansas. It identified Baldwin and his brothers as the sons of Elias B. and Julia C. Baldwin, gave the birth dates of the brothers, and then awaited their respective deaths so that these ending dates of their lives could be rendered *intaglio* in the stone. Below the spot where his eventual death date would be placed, Baldwin had two dramatic words incised. These were: "Arctic Explorer." If he has any such reputation, it rests on two achievements from his time in Franz Josef Land: the unlocking of the islands of "Zichy Land" in 1902 and his exploration of the eastern limits of the archipelago and his discovery of "Graham Bell Land" in April and May 1899.

On April 26, Baldwin set out with the four surviving Norwegians: Daniel Johansen, Emil Ellefsen, Olaf Ellefsen, and Paul Bjørvig. Baldwin's field notes from this spring sledge expedition, along with the notes of the redoubtable Bjørvig, reveal the first glimpses of Graham Bell Land, the easternmost island in the Franz Josef Land archipelago and the largest land mass that remained to be discovered in the islands.

For much of the first three days, the party was snowbound on familiar ground: five miles from Cape Frankfurt, near the eastern tip of Hall Island and the place where they would cross Austria Sound to Wilczek Land. The spring temperatures hovered between –5°F and –13°F. On Saturday, April 29, they reached Cape Frankfurt and crossed an ice-filled Austria Sound to Cape Hansa on the southwest corner of Wilczek Land. After covering fourteen miles, they made camp that evening north of a group of islets that the *Tegetthoff* expedition had named the Klagenfurt Islands.[484] Beyond this point, no one had yet ventured. Baldwin was appropriately excited, and felt himself "upon verge of discoveries."[485]

On Sunday, April 30, the march continued along the southern coast of Wilczek Land, in weather Paul Bjørvig described as "really fine . . . with sun and no wind."[486] It was good territory for the sledges, with the land flat and covered with snow. The men sledged past two basaltic cliffs, with views of the interior mountains of Wilczek Land, all separated by glaciers, until the team reached Cape Höfer. There, on the southeast corner of Wilczek Land, Baldwin spotted three islands to the southeast.[487] With Emil Ellefesen, Baldwin ascended the heights above the cape to take a round of bearings, shattering the thermometer in the process. As they slid back down the snow-covered slope, Baldwin recorded that he nearly broke his right arm and Ellefsen his back.

In camp, the Norwegians shot a bear and the following morning breakfasted on its kidneys and heart. Bjørvig wrote that the bear had walked with a limp, and when the men skinned it they found a round lead bullet surrounded by a thick layer of blubber. The Norwegians agreed that the bullet had likely sat there for many years. "It is about 25 years since Norwegian hunters used muzzle loaders," wrote Bjørvig, "but it is also possible that Samoyeds have shot at it."[488]

Once the sledges were re-stowed, the party continued on for 2.3 miles and then, after lunch, north for another 5.4 miles, along a broad lowland spit east of Cape Höfer. They set up camp near a large berg "in a large bay never before seen by man."[489] Following his instructions from Wellman, Baldwin gave this a placeholder name: "Bay A." This became Helen Gould Bay, after the multimillionaire heiress daughter (1868–1938) of the notorious robber baron Jay Gould. Baldwin later wrote that it was "one of the most picturesque localities in these regions. In it I counted nearly sixty large icebergs, forming now a great white ice-locked fleet, the majority of which had perhaps been launched from the precipitous glacial wall forming the southern, western and northwestern sides of the bay, the northern boundary of which is formed by a basaltic cape."[490]

On May 2, the team crossed 5.3 miles of twisted ice in Helen Gould Bay toward what Baldwin temporarily named "Cape C" (later Cape Lamont, after Daniel S. Lamont, another of Wellman's benefactors), where they camped. Despite his glacier glasses, Baldwin now began to suffer painfully from snow blindness. The following day, Baldwin and Olaf Ellefsen ascended the northern slope of the cape to an altitude of 1,040 feet. The very steep terrain made getting to the top—which they estimated at 1,700 feet—impossible, but they saw what appeared to be a large fjord or sound that extended further northward.

Once again on the march, Baldwin observed a rocky cape about ten miles north of Cape Lamont, one that Wellman later named Cape Elkins. At the same time, he noted a glacial slope on the eastern side of the sound. For the first time, Baldwin began to believe that what he now crossed was not a sound but a strait. Paul Bjørvig thought it looked like the end of Hornsund, the southernmost major fjord on the western side of Spitsbergen.

Baldwin was correct. Indeed this proved to be a waterway that separated Wilczek Land from what Baldwin now realized was a large and previously unknown island. To the strait, Wellman would give the name of John Pierpont Morgan (1837–1913), one of the wealthiest bankers in the world. As for the new island, which Bjørvig wrote was "not on the map we brought with us," it proved to be the last major geographic discovery ever made in Franz Josef Land.[491] Befitting its size and significance, Wellman later gave it the name of Alexander Graham Bell, after the famous inventor and then-president of the National Geographic Society.

The Norwegians shot a polar bear that wandered too close to the party. The bear had two cubs. "We put a cord round the necks of the young ones and brought them back to the sledge where we killed them," wrote Bjør-vig. "It occurs to me that men are more like a beast of prey than the bear, because it makes use of all it kills, while we do not always need what we kill."[492] The men skinned the cubs carefully, hoping to save the skins, but Baldwin ordered them to leave the skins behind. Bjørvig kept up his running commentary about Baldwin when the party came across four walrus on the ice. They did not need the meat or blubber, but Baldwin took a few shots at them anyway, and "showed his worth as a hunter by shooting one and wound[ing] two of the walrus."[493]

Baldwin and his men reached the cape on the opposite shore of Pierpont Morgan Strait on the evening of May 4. This Wellman later named Cape Leiter after still another patron, a Midwestern dry-goods pioneer by the name of Levi Z. Leiter. The cape turned out to be the southernmost point of Graham Bell Land. While the Norwegians set up camp for the night, Baldwin walked toward the east, to try and find a passage northward along the coast of this new shore. "But I had never before seen such a chaos of broken-up ice—the vast floes and pans being screwed together in a most frightful manner, as far as the eye could see in either an eastern or north-easterly direction."[494]

On Friday, May 5, 1899, Olaf Ellefsen called all hands for breakfast at 8:00 A.M. Baldwin wrote in his field notes: "9:40 start with Emil and Daniel, ascend the new land and is as I surmise island, 900 ft. . . . Bright sunshine and islands Nos. 1, 2 and 3 to se."[495] But he almost certainly means "sw" here, as the newly discovered islands off the southeast coast of Wilczek Land would now appear in the southwest from his vantage point, from where he could also see Cape Höfer. A mile northeast from the camp, they encountered a granite knob, from which they could see the coast of Graham Bell Land trending off to the northeast "a succession of small bights and intervening ice and snow-covered tongues of land."[496] A noontime observation put their position at 80° 38' 23" North, 62° 38' 30" East.

Baldwin traveled about six miles along the coast, watching as two or three guillemots flew overhead from the east. The eastern side of the new island was impassable, with rough ice at the bottom of a steep, 900-foot cliff. With his way hopelessly blocked in that direction, Baldwin turned the party west, and began a 6.4-mile trip over smooth ice back toward the strait. They camped on the night of May 5 on the southwestern bend of Graham Bell Land, across from "Cape D" on Wilczek Land, which later became Cape Vilas.

Baldwin estimated "Cape D" to be six or seven miles away and thought he might have seen this point the previous October during while he wandered north and east from Fort McKinley. As they turned the corner of the island, the party now headed northeast, toward a low point on the western side of Graham Bell Land that became Cape John R. Walsh, after the Chicago banker and owner of Wellman's newspaper. Baldwin made camp soon after, intending to travel eastward across the island the next day.

On May 7, they started due east, ascending for four miles to an altitude of 500 feet. They then descended for a mile and half, before a steep ascent to 1,080 feet about six and a half miles from the morning camp. The runners on the big sledge gave way and were repaired with skis. The men could see a rocky ledge all along the northeast coast of the island, but Bjørvig wrote that for much of the time, all they could see was snow and ice. After a march of another two miles, the party made camp just as a heavy storm began that would drop snow on them for the next thirty-six hours. They rode out the storm on the strength of several meals of polar-bear-cub stew. Baldwin, as if he wished to remind the men why they despised him so, again assumed his unfortunate pattern of ordering the Norwegians about whenever domestic chores were required. "Called Olaf and we ate our breakfast-dinner. . . . Called Daniel to make a cup of coffee for each man."[497]

On the morning of May 9, as the wind still flapped the sides of the tent and his attempt to take photographs was thwarted by a frozen camera, Baldwin broke camp and continued northeast for four miles, into the bottom of a valley that extended north and south. The party then bore east-southeast, until Baldwin wrote that they had, at 3:45 P.M., reached the "extreme eastern point and summit of this island . . . , [a] windswept ice knob and evidently glacier faced on east side. Valley to n. and low flat ice-point extending a little further east. . . . To east, no land, but great extent screw ice and much open water and heavy dark clouds overhead. Elevation of ice knob probably from 900 to 1,000 ft."[498]

They had reached both the extreme eastern edge and the highest point on Graham Bell Land. They also stood on the easternmost point of the Franz Josef Land archipelago itself. Wellman later named the spot after Richard

Olney, who had just completed a term as secretary of State of the United States as the Wellman Polar Expedition departed for Franz Josef Land.

From this icy land's end—which even today would be considered all but impossible to reach—the men turned north to attempt to define the northern reaches of the island. Baldwin described it as "rolling ice country."[499] Surrounded by ice and snow yet without proper stops to melt these into water, the men suffered from extreme thirst. Baldwin wrote that they soon all paused in an attempt to refresh themselves with lime juice tablets. Then, as soon as they were in camp, as the primus was started to melt drinking water, a storm blew up that pinned them down for more than forty hours. When the storm cleared on the afternoon of May 11, Baldwin reluctantly ordered a march northward, anxious to locate the northern point of the island. Sarcastically, one of the Norwegians remarked that he "felt like going fifty or sixty miles today."[500]

They walked for what Baldwin estimated to be about eight miles—the odometer had long since become disabled on the march—before a storm stopped them again. They disposed of dinner quickly and in good cheer, "notwithstanding that Olaf chanced to spill a part of the coffee, that Bjorvik's stockings were found to be frozen to his feet upon getting into the bag, that Emil was compelled patiently to wait nearly an hour for his muffler to thaw loose from his whiskers, that Daniel had the odometer to repair, or that I have this journal to write!"[501]

Late in the day of May 12, the team moved northward and steadily downward for another four miles, "when lo! dark lines, as of open water lanes or streaks of land lay just ahead. The downgrade, too, suddenly became steeper and I awaited the arrival of the sledges and ordered a halt pending a reconnaissance. With alpine rope about the body I pushed carefully forward the odometer another half mile."[502]

Baldwin suddenly found himself standing upon land. The following morning, when the weather cleared, the men beheld "a panorama of snow-clad peaks and ridges that lay stretched before and below our feet," one that trended away to the south on both sides.[503] It was now certain. They had reached the northernmost projection of the island. No other islands could be seen to the north. Bjørvig wrote that the men could see piles of sand and stone stretching northward for a couple of miles. He walked toward the east to find a cape, one that Wellman later named after his inveterate patron Herman Kohlsaat. Curiously, the northernmost point of Graham Bell Land was left without a place-name, but Baldwin did not forget the spot and took the opportunity during his own later expedition to Franz Josef Land to pencil in the name of his father and call the spot Cape Elias Baldwin.[504]

After he took a series of bearings, Baldwin decided that this was a prudent moment to begin to retreat. Accordingly, on Sunday morning, May 14, the team began to move southward, covering fifteen miles across a fogbound series of ice domes. The next day saw more than fourteen miles put behind them. Before they turned in, the team discussed whether another island existed to the west, one not marked on Payer's chart. From his experiences the previous fall, Baldwin thought, correctly, that this was Payer's "La Ronciere Peninsula," the peninsula that was actually an island.

After a further 15 nautical miles on May 16, the men had reached the northwestern coast of Wilczek Land and familiar territory from the sledge expedition of the previous fall. By the following day, they had made a complete circuit and had returned to Fort McKinley. For Paul Bjørvig, the area that had been a house of horrors the previous winter "now . . . looked even more miserable. A bear had ripped the roof off the shelter. Now I could see the space in which I had survived an arctic winter."[505] Nor did his return to the scene of Bernt Bentsen's agonies do anything to mollify Bjørvig's view of Baldwin: "Baldwin had been snow-blind for a couple of days. He had a man to lead him. Luckily I escaped being his travelling escort. That was certainly the best thing for Baldwin, for if I had had to lead him, I doubt that I would have led him along the best route, even if it cost me trouble and difficulty."[506]

After a three-day stay at the Cape Heller, Baldwin and the Norwegians began their return to Harmsworth House. Baldwin briefly entertained visions to travel westward, to visit the overwintering hut of Fridtjof Nansen and Hjalmar Johansen, "but owing to scarcity of dog food, the limited amount of petroleum now on hand and the necessity of getting both wooden boats to Harmsworth House while we have dogs and sledges, that anticipated pleasure must be abandoned."[507] Baldwin would come to regret his failure to reach the Nansen hut in 1899. His dalliance there in 1902 would become one of the main reasons for his eventual dismissal as leader of the Ziegler polar expeditions.

Nine days later, at 11:00 A.M. on Monday, May 29, 1899, the successful exploring party arrived back at Cape Tegetthoff. Wellman was still bedridden, but heartened to have dozens of new places to which he could attach the names of his patrons.

For his part, Baldwin seems to have quietly returned to his daily recordings of weather. And at least one of the other Americans troubled to bestir himself. In mid-June, perhaps ashamed at his manifest inactivity during the expedition, Quirof Harlan ventured from Harmsworth House along with Paul Bjørvig and two other Norwegians. They traveled west to McClintock Island, across the intervening Negri Fjord. Bjørvig was excited in the belief that the men had discovered that the fjord was actually a strait that separated the two islands, but this fact had been known since the explorations of Benjamin Leigh Smith nearly twenty years earlier.

This brief excursion lasted eight days, after which there was little to do but watch and wait for a relief ship, the same relief ship Wellman prayed that his brother had arranged to come and save him.

TWENTY

The Cooperation of Nations
in Arctic Exploration

During the first days of July 1898, the men scanned the southern horizon for a relief ship. The Norwegians took one of the boats to nearby Lamont Island to erect a signal beacon, and then did the same atop the cliff plateau that rose up behind Harmsworth House at Cape Tegetthoff. Paul Bjørvig wrote that while engaged in this task, the men discovered several huge logs of petrified wood, some nearly twenty feet long. "If you had bad eyesight, you might take them for timber, but they were as hard as a rock. We could also see tree rings in each end."[508]

With some time to finally appreciate their surroundings, the Norwegians found other fossils, as well as multicolored rock crystals, and located a walrus jaw and set of tusks nearly a mile from the edge of the sea. Bjørvig also uncovered a thick seam of a metal he thought looked like lead. He broke off a piece and later gave it to "Conservator Scheider at Tromsø Museum."[509]

Before Wellman slipped on the ice to the east of Rudolf Land and the polar-dash party was forced to retreat, he imagined that he had seen four islands to the northeast. These he now named for "well-known American scientific and public men who had befriended the expedition,"[510] including Secretary of State John Milton Hay (1838–1905) and the president of the American Museum of Natural History, Morris Ketchum Jesup (1830–1908).

None of the islands existed; all were mirages. In his memoirs, Wellman reduced his error by half, to only two islands, named after "two most valued friends, Ben T. Cable and Tom Johnson," and then added the further admission that the Duke of the Abruzzi's subsequent expedition to Franz Josef Land "found that what I had taken for two islands must have been only ice hummocks."[511]

After Wellman had been carried back to Harmsworth House by his Norwegians—"as brave as lions and as tender as women"—he soon exhausted the new locations he had found or thought he had found.[512] The discoveries of several new geographic features by Baldwin's party allowed Wellman from his bed another chance to honor his patrons. So it is that much of the geographic nomenclature of the northeastern sector of Franz Josef Land remains, to this day, Walter Wellman's personal tribute to the wealthy and powerful of the American Gilded Age.

The cost of the privilege to attach these rarified names to a remote Arctic archipelago had been steep. Bernt Bentsen was dead, Wellman was left with a permanent limp and, just as in 1894, nearly all of the dogs that Wellman had brought north were dead. In addition, hundreds of wild animals throughout the eastern half of the archipelago—including no less than forty-seven polar bears—had been killed. Many others had been grievously wounded and left to drown or bleed to death.

Was it worth the cost? Beyond some desultory geologizing and Baldwin's meteorological recordings and his nearly 150 records of auroras, the expedition's primary results were in its corrections and additions to the map of the eastern third of Franz Josef Land. The discovery of Graham Bell Land completed the geographic picture of the eastern limits of the islands. As Wellman wrote, Julius Payer had located "an enormous glacier [Dove Glacier], capping a land of continental dimensions, extending northward from Wilczek Land."[513] Nansen had taken the first slice out of this continent in 1896, and then Baldwin had finished it off in 1899. Baldwin had also shown that Payer's "La Ronciere Peninsula," north of Cape Heller, was in fact an island. Wellman tried to name it Whitney Island—for another Gilded Age financier, William Collins Whitney (1841–1904), and a former secretary of the navy from 1885 to 1889—but Payer's name ultimately won out, and this island just north of Wilczek Land and west of Graham Bell Land became La Ronciere Island, so even this successful geographic work failed to be marked by a lasting tribute.

As for Evelyn Briggs Baldwin, the Wellman Polar Expedition of 1898–99 can be seen as the final brick in the creation of his heroic self-image. The successful sledge expedition to Graham Bell Land marked the high point of Baldwin's polar career and allowed him with some justice to claim the title of "Arctic Explorer" and even have it carved for all eternity onto his gravestone in a dusty cemetery in Kansas. But any lessons about leadership and command that Baldwin might have learned during the expedition were left behind in the snow. Ahead lay the fiasco of the 1901–1902 Baldwin-Ziegler Polar Expedition, when Baldwin would return to Franz Josef Land with more money and more supplies than even he could have imagined. Indeed, it would be arguably the best-equipped and -financed American polar expedition to that moment, one that Baldwin would fritter away in a remarkably pointless series of cache-laying exercises—and a sad repetition and even intensification of his worst martinet behavior during the advance to Cape Heller in the fall of 1898.

It is very likely that his apparent bitterness at discovering so many islands and capes, bays, and glaciers in the spring of 1899—only to watch Wellman reserve the right to name them—led Baldwin to make a series of disastrous decisions during the Baldwin-Ziegler Expedition. Rather than make the dash to the pole that William Ziegler had paid for, Baldwin obsessed over the location of still more new islands within Franz Josef Land, along with a few special extras: primary among them the recovery of the message left by Nansen at his winter hut on Jackson Island, as well as Baldwin's long-held personal quest to follow Salomon Andrée north in a balloon.

From his base on Alger Island, Baldwin would organize a massive effort to fill several hydrogen balloons and send them aloft to carry pleas for relief in June 1902. By one account he even carried an observation balloon with the capability to carry an observer/photographer aloft which he apparently intended to launch from his ship.[514] But after the expedition returned to Tromsø in the summer of 1902, Baldwin, as we shall see, was bitterly denounced by members of the expedition and quickly relieved of further command by William Ziegler.

ON JULY 27, 1899, from the ridge behind Harmsworth House, one of the Norwegians spied a ship out in the ice. Bjørvig and two other Norwegians tried to row out to it, but the ice prevented an approach. Fortunately, the ship had seen their efforts, and immediately hoisted a Swedish flag and approached Cape Tegetthoff. It was indeed the *Capella* from Göteborg, Sweden. Based in Sandefjord, Norway, and crewed by Norwegians, it already had on board six thousand slaughtered seals from a summer's work in the north. When the ship dropped anchor at Cape Tegetthoff, the men of the Wellman Polar Expedition rushed on board. By that same evening, they had left Harmsworth House behind.

As the ship entered De Bruyne Sound the following morning, *Capella* doubled back toward Markham Sound in search of walrus and polar bear. In the process, the vessel discovered a new channel on the northwest corner of McClintock Island. Here there were also several small undefined islands, so Wellman took this unexpected and welcome opportunity to attach several more place-names to the archipelago: Alger Island, the Simon Newcomb Islands, the Willis L. Moore Islands.

Capella remained in this area for a week. Bjørvig wrote that in this period they shot and killed 25 polar bears and an astounding 225 walrus to go with the seals already on board. When they emerged into the British Channel on the morning of August 4, 1899, they sighted another ship. This was none other than the *Stella Polare,* the polar expedition ship of the Luigi Amadeo, the Duke of the Abruzzi, a minor Italian noble and major figure in mountaineering circles, now the leader of an Italian expedition in search of the North Pole. Wellman was roused from his bed and rowed over to greet the Duke. "Rather a strange meeting, this," he later wrote, "between a son of kings and the son of a western farmer who had been a private soldier."[515]

Abruzzi's expedition would fare far better than Wellman's. *Stella Polare* was able to slice through clear waters all the way to Teplitz Bay. There, on the west coast of Rudolf Land, the Duke and his expedition were able to start on their polar attempt at a point further north than Wellman had finished his. In the summer of 1900, four members of the expedition, led by a Italian Royal Navy captain, Umberto Cagni, bested Fridtjof Nansen's farthest north by twenty nautical miles.

Paul Bjørvig wrote that, while the two ships were rafted together, one of *Stella Polare*'s crew members died of cerebro-spinal meningitis. The Norwegians made a coffin for the man and carried him to the *Capella* to be transported back to Tromsø for burial. *Capella* finally cleared Franz Josef Land on August 10. The ship touched land at Ingøy in far northern Norway on August 18, and two days later was in Tromsø. Bjørvig wrote that he was "quite healthy," but that "this overwintering is something I will never forget, no matter how old I become."[516]

As for Wellman, the man who had once been described as "a plucky young American leaving his editorial chair in Washington and, without any practical acquaintance with ice navigation . . . [starting] off helter-skelter to make a rush for the North Pole"[517] now found himself once again in the headlines, and for all the wrong reasons.

"WELLMAN BACK, A CRIPPLE" was the headline in the *New York Times* the day after the *Capella* docked in Tromsø. The expedition had been out of touch with the outside world since the *Frithjof* had carried its last letters and dispatches from Franz Josef Land nearly a year earlier. Wellman's crew had not returned as heroes who had conquered the North Pole but rather as "survivors of the polar expedition led by him." While the discovery of new islands was duly noted—even those that eventually turned out to be mirages—the main focus was on the "grim story of arctic tragedy," the death of Bernt Bentsen. This was compounded by Wellman's severe injuries, as he was "still unable to walk, and will probably be permanently crippled."[518]

Ten days later, the Americans were in Hull, England, where Wellman, his "right leg . . . drawn up a foot from the ground," was hurried to London to consult a specialist. Wellman explained to a reporter that his polar-dash party had turned back "twenty-five miles northwest of Freeden Islands, where Dr. Nansen landed in 1895. North of these islands we photographed three islands and some large land, unseen either by Payer or Nansen."[519] Of course, neither Payer or Nansen had seen these places because they did not exist.

On September 12, in London, Wellman underwent what was expected to be the first of several operations to straighten his right leg. This did not prevent him, just one week later, from delivering an address on his adventures to the British Association.[520] Wellman also met his wife Laura in London, and together they returned to New York on the steamship *Umbria,* arriving on October 8. As he emerged on deck, Wellman walked with the aid of crutches and had to be helped from the ship by his estranged wife.

The couple immediately continued on to Washington, D.C. There, despite Wellman's lonely pledge to his brother from Franz Josef Land that he was finished with polar voyaging, he lectured to the National Geographic Society on November 17 and suggested that the U.S. Congress should make an appropriation of $150,000 for an American *Antarctic* expedition.[521]

Within a year, Wellman had successfully hidden his Franz Josef Land travails behind a blizzard of purple prose. He was once again "the famous arctic explorer," back in the midst of the rich and well connected, to pass the late August days of 1900 with his wife at the Porcupine Hotel in Bar Harbor, Maine.[522]

The Wellman Polar Expedition, Wellman explained to a reporter soon after he arrived in the United States, had been organized "to explore the unknown portions of Franz Josef Land; and to reach a more northern point than [anyone before]." Wellman could be forgiven this obvious attempt to salvage something from what was in all regards a failure to reach the North Pole. What was unforgiveable was his transparent snub of the Norwegians who had carried both his supplies north and then an incapacitated Wellman south. "We are giving the islands, straights, and points good American names," Wellman blithely told the press. It was as if the Norwegians on his team had never existed, as Wellman cruelly announced that "I don't favor the cooperation of nations in Arctic exploration."[523]

In contrast to the loud headlines from May 1898 proclaiming that the expedition would make a heroic dash for the North Pole, Wellman sought on his return to the United States in the autumn of 1899 to mute his original ambitions. The end of the first American expedition to Franz Josef Land was therefore marked by Wellman's convenient revision of his original goal of reaching the North Pole, by his ethnocentric pronouncements and attachment of geographic place-names that ignored those most responsible for whatever success Wellman had achieved, and by Wellman's skillful avoidance of responsibility for Bentsen's death by obscuring it in the heroic light of Paul Bjørvig's survival. Norwegians might have been "better than Eskimos to assist in the work" of American polar exploration, but not so much as to receive fair dues for their efforts.

In the end, there was a kind of belated recognition of the awful suffering of Bernt Bentsen. The names that Baldwin gave to the bays south and north of Cape Heller—Operti and Kersting—do not survive on the Soviet charts of Franz Josef Land that were drawn up from the 1930s to the 1970s. However, the northern bay, where the Norwegians once chased across the ice after their woefully inadequate canvas canoe, has since 1933 carried the words бухта Бентсен, Bentsen Bay. The man the bay is named for still lies nearby, just across Observatory Ridge, in the grave Paul Bjørvig dug for him in that bitter cold February in 1899.

Cigarette-Smoking Dudes
The Baldwin-Ziegler Polar Expedition
1901–1902

✳

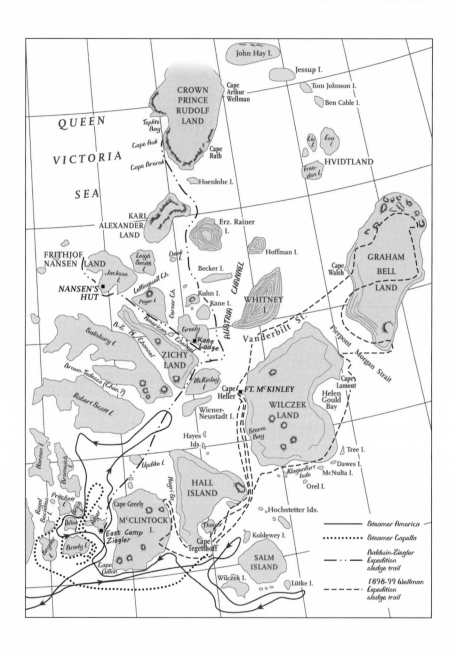

John Hay I.

Jessup I.

Tom Johnson I.

Cape
Arthur
Wellman

Ben Cable I.

CROWN
PRINCE
RUDOLF
LAND

QUEEN

Teplitz
Bay

Cape Auk

Cape Rath

Lia
I.

Eva
I.

VICTORIA

Cape Brorok

HVIDTLAND

Free-
den I.

SEA

Hoenlohe I.

KARL
ALEXANDER
LAND

Erz. Rainer
I.

GRAHAM
BELL
LAND

FRITHJOF
NANSEN LAND

Leigh
Smith
I.

Deak
I.

Hoffman I.

Cape
Walsh

Jackson
I.

Becker I.

NANSEN'S
HUT

Leffingwell Ch.

AUSTRIA CHANNEL

Cerner Ck.

Kuhn I.

Payer I.

Kane I.

WHITNEY
I.

Pierpont

Morgan Strait

Salisbury I.

American

B.-Z. N. Channel

Greely
Channel

Vanderbilt St.

Kane
Lodge

ZICHY
LAND

Brown-Tedesco (Chan.?)

McKinley

Cape
Heller

FT. McKINLEY

Cape
Lamont

Robert Scott I.

Wiener-
Neustadt I.

WILCZEK
LAND

Helen
Gould
Bay

Nansen I.

Hayes
Ids.

Storm
Bay

Bromwich

Tree I.

Updike I.

Dawes I.

Klagenfurt
Isds

McNulta I.

Negri Br.

HALL
ISLAND

Orel I.

Royal
Societies
I.

Pritchett

Hochstetter Ids.

Bliss

Bay

Alger I.

Cape Greely

McCLINTOCK
I.

Thayer

Snyder
I.

Brady I.

East Camp
Ziegler

Cape
Tegetthoff

Koldewey I.

Cape
Dillon

SALM
ISLAND

Wilczek I.

Lütke I.

Steamer *America*

Steamer *Capella*

Baldwin-Ziegler
Expedition
sledge trail

1898-99 Wellman
Expedition
sledge trail

TWENTY-ONE

Pluck

Evelyn Briggs Baldwin was born in the American Midwest in midsummer 1862, on the same day that President Abraham Lincoln presented the Emancipation Proclamation to his cabinet. Baldwin was the first son of an itinerant teacher who served as an infantry officer in the Illinois volunteers and later as a cavalry officer in the Missouri cavalry volunteers. The family moved to Iowa after the American Civil War, and Baldwin's mother died soon after, in 1866. His father remarried, to "a woman of superior affection, culture and ability."[1] Baldwin's father eventually settled the family—several boys and a girl—on a Kansas farm, so that his three "mischievous boys might escape the evil influences of town life."[2]

In a "Short Autobiographical Sketch" Baldwin wrote for William

---

Opposite: Redrawn version of Baldwin's 1902 revision of Wellman's 1898 chart. On Baldwin's original chart, he erased Wellman's phantom islands northeast of Rudolf Island and completed the disassembly of "Zichy Land" into several smaller islands, including Ziegler Island (which survives), and Robert Scott and William McKinley Islands (which do not). McKinley Island became Greely Island and home to Kane Lodge, while Robert Scott Island was broken into two islands, Luigi Island in the west after the Duke of the Abruzzi and Champ Island in the east after William Ziegler's personal secretary. Numerous other errors exist on the original chart, most of which were cleared away by the incomparable Russell Porter during the Fiala expedition.

Ziegler—a stunningly self-serving catalogue that ran to seven pages—Baldwin wrote that he had been fascinated by geography since attending grade school in Illinois. "It was the sight of unexplored coast-lines as indicated in my little 'Cornell's Geography,' especially the unknown Northern coasts of Greenland, that seemed to create within me an intense desire to explore. I can't explain it," Baldwin wrote (after doing just so).[3] Near the end of his life, he tried to explain the motives for his career in exploration to a lecture audience:

> [During] my boyhood days . . . on a western farm I chanced to find a three line advertisement which read "*10,000 miles in a balloon* for 10 cents, address such and such a company." I entrusted my little 10 cent piece to the mail and sure enough in the next few days I received "*10,000 miles in a balloon.*"
> *10,000 miles in a balloon* was an appeal to the imagination. . . .
> This happened about the same time that people were talking about Simm's [*sic*] Hole. Simm's hole was the possible location of a point where the waters of the Arctic Ocean flowed into the earth, or the North Pole.
> Therefore, my interest in life became two-fold. Aviation and Polar investigation.[4]

If one assumed that Baldwin read this pamphlet as a ten-year-old boy, then the year would have been 1872. By this time, the ideas of the Ohio theorist John Cleve Symmes—that the Earth was hollow and made up of concentric spheres that could be explored through holes at both poles—had been thoroughly discredited for more than half a century. If the idea was discussed at all, it was with the derisive nickname "Symmes's Hole,"[5] which is how Baldwin would have heard it referred.

This was also the same time period when Baldwin's cousin Thomas Scott Baldwin made his first ascents in balloons on the county-fair circuit across the Midwest. Thomas Scott Baldwin went on to become an internationally recognized balloonist, parachutist, dirigible pilot, and heavier-than-air pilot.[6] In 1901, it was to his cousin and his cousin's two brothers that Evelyn Briggs Baldwin would turn for the messenger balloons he would use in the Arctic—and for his first ascent in a passenger-carrying balloon.

Baldwin went on to enroll in North-Western College in Naperville, Illinois, west of Chicago, in 1881.[7] It was at North-Western where Baldwin met the brothers Theodore and Alfred Snyder. According to Baldwin, all three men "taught school and engaged in various laudable enterprises to assist ourselves through the college."[8] It was the Snyder brothers who would, fifteen years after graduation, provide Baldwin with an introduction to the fantastically wealthy chemist and armchair geographer William Ziegler.

Baldwin and the Snyders went their separate ways after graduation, the brothers to make their fortunes and Baldwin to travel in Europe for a year, a tour he financed by selling subscriptions to a monthly magazine he called "Europe Afoot." Beginning as a pedestrian in Ireland, he learned to ride a bicycle in Glasgow and then proceeded "on the wheel" through Scotland, Wales, England, Belgium, France, Switzerland, Germany, and Holland. Baldwin had worked up a subscription list of two thousand to follow his adventures. He sent copy to another former North-Western College classmate in Chicago, who published it and acted as Baldwin's business manager. The proceeds paid for his year in Europe.

Baldwin returned to Illinois and taught for a year before moving to Oswego, Kansas, where he quickly worked his way up to principal of the local high school and then superintendent of schools. His vacations consisted of more bicycle tours, including one through the American West, where he claimed to be the first to ride a bicycle through Yellowstone National Park, "compelled often to follow mere trails through the pine forests, and to wade streams, carrying the wheel on my back."[9]

After five years of teaching and school administration, Baldwin abruptly resigned, "having decided to devote more time to scientific research and travel." He went to work for the U.S. government as an assistant observer for the U.S. Weather Bureau stationed in Nashville, Tennessee. It was while in Nashville in the early 1890s that Baldwin began to seriously study Arctic literature and, as he wrote, "to lay plans for work within the Arctic circle."[10]

Baldwin's plans matured rapidly when in 1893 he used his experience as a meteorologist and his newfound knowledge of the literature of Arctic exploration to gain membership in Robert Peary's second expedition to North Greenland. Peary's first visit to Greenland, at the age of thirty, was just that: a brief penetration of the ice cap in 1886 that was financed with five hundred dollars of his mother's money and enabled by a grant of six months' leave from his duties as a civil engineer with the U.S. Navy.

It was five years before Peary reached the ice again, this time on a legitimate expeditionary attempt in 1891 to investigate whether Greenland was an island or a vast peninsula reaching to the North Pole. Peary was joined by his new wife Josephine, his servant and constant companion Matthew Henson, and a small and *au fait* assortment of expedition members that included the young Norwegian ski expert Eivind Astrup and surgeon and ethnologist Frederick Cook. Peary broke his leg just as he reached north-west Greenland, but went ahead with the expedition anyway. With Astrup, he reached the northeast corner of Greenland the following summer and claimed that he had proven Greenland to be an island. Even more rashly—and against Astrup's wise cautions—Peary decided that even more land lay to the north of Greenland, possibly including an icy road reaching all the way to the North Pole.

Tasting real fame for the first time after his announcement of the insularity of Greenland, Peary convinced the navy to grant three whole years of leave for a new expedition. He intended to follow the small-scale 1891–92 expedition with a much larger effort to Greenland that would include his now-pregnant wife as well more than a dozen others, eight of whom Peary planned to lead across the Greenland ice cap to try for the North Pole.

Peary needed a new man to handle weather recordings, since John Verhoeff, the meteorologist from the 1891–92 expedition, had disappeared without a trace in Greenland.[11] Evelyn Briggs Baldwin, dutifully recording the weather in Nashville, Tennessee, while he studied Arctic literature, became Verhoeff's replacement.

Frederick Cook had temporarily left Peary's orbit, but Eivind Astrup and Matthew Henson were both back and, on June 26, 1893, the new expedition left Philadelphia and reached Inglefield Gulf in northwest Greenland in early August. There, on the shores of Bowdoin Bay, Peary's men constructed their winter quarters: Anniversary Lodge. It was here that Baldwin set up his self-registering meteorological instruments and kept notes on weather and aurora phenomena for an entire year, from August 3, 1893, to August 1, 1894.

The expedition was not a happy one. The large ice cap party, including Baldwin, left Anniversary Lodge on March 6, 1894, and ran directly into bone-rattling cold and skin-carving winds that stopped both men and dogs in their tracks. Many of the dogs went into a kind of Arctic mania called *piblockto* and were shot. As Baldwin later wrote: "So intense was the suffering of the poor dog which first fell victim to the scourge, that he almost gnawed off his legs."[12] Astrup contracted food poisoning from tainted pemmican and along with another expedition member had to be escorted back to the base camp. Two more men were forced back soon thereafter. Only four men remained on the ice cap with Peary, and these included Matthew Henson and Evelyn Briggs Baldwin. These men promptly trudged into a brutal spring storm, one that brought the expedition to a full stop.

> Baldwin's anemometer, barograph and thermograph, which, as a result of his ingenuity and perseverance, had kept on recording throughout the storm, showed that for thirty-four hours the average wind velocity had been over forty-eight miles per hour, and the average temperature about −50° Fahr., with a minimum of over −60° Fahr. When these figures are considered in connection with our elevation of some 5,000 feet, the unobstructed sweep of the wind, and the well-known fact that ice-cap temperatures accompanied by wind are much more trying to animal life than the same temperatures at sea level, it is believed that the judgment will be that this storm beat the record as the most severe ever experienced by any Arctic party.[13]

To go on with so few men and with more dogs suffering from *piblockto* and dying of exposure was pointless, so Peary turned the party around on April 10, 1894, just 128 miles from Bowdoin Bay. The men descended to the base camp suffering from various degrees of exposure and snow blindness and covered in body lice.[14] Of ninety-two dogs that started the journey, only a shocking twenty-five remained and, of those, less than half were still able to do any work.

The quote above, purportedly from Peary, appears in Baldwin's fund-raising tract *The Search for the North Pole*. It continues on with fulsome praise for Baldwin's "superior qualifications [and] depth of his character" as well as his "perserverance [*sic*], ingenuity, courage and skill, [and] power of endurance."[15]

In his curriculum vitae–cum–autobiography produced for William Ziegler, Baldwin aimed a few passive-aggressive barbs at Peary for turning back after the great storm on the ice cap, and even hinted that things would have been different had he been in charge. Baldwin wrote of his disappointment at being ordered to retreat, calling it "the most bitter moment of my life. However, as Mr. Peary was in command, I do not wish this to be considered as criticism—only stated to show that we returned through no inability personally considered to proceed on the journey."[16] According to Robert Bryce, Peary thereafter retreated with his wife to their segregated living quarters at Anniversary Lodge, there to dine on a specially secreted cache of foods while the men in their freezing quarters subsisted on seal and walrus meat.[17] It was a perverse lesson in expedition leadership that Baldwin would never forget and, almost from the moment he was given the chance to lead his own parties in the Arctic, he would imitate many of the same selfish and malevolent traits he had learned from his first Arctic mentor.

When Peary's relief ship *Falcon* arrived in early August, Peary sent most of his expedition home, including Baldwin and Eivind Astrup. Since 1894 had been such a disappointment, Peary and two others, including Matthew Henson, would stay on for another year. Baldwin concluded his yearlong effort to record the weather at Bowdoin Bay and, along with Mrs. Peary, joined the remainder of the expedition sailing south. Back in Philadelphia, the men were shocked to learn that Peary had sent a letter ahead of the *Falcon* to announce that he was carrying on in Greenland despite being abandoned by his men. It was another painful lesson in duplicity that Baldwin never forgot.

To Eivind Astrup, Baldwin wrote in October 1894 to ask if the Norwegian had seen Peary's defamatory letter. "You bet I did," the Norwegian responded. "Wonder if he will use the word 'desert' about us, when he gets home next year. It probably would not pay him. Particularly if the most of us are out again next season, [thus] proving that we are just as good as him. . . . My dear Baldwin, I hope you will show up your colors on the icefields next season, and I promise you that I shall show mine, the 'dog drivers,' and if we should not be successful next year, we are bound to be so one of the following 25 seasons."[18]

From Philadelphia, Baldwin traveled south to seek out Walter Wellman in Washington, D.C. He thought that the journalist might have a spot for him on a new polar expedition, but Wellman was still smarting from the loss of the *Ragnvald Jarl* in Spitsbergen.[19] This was apparently the first contact between the two and, though Wellman replied that he was "glad to hear that you are still of the Arctic mind," he explained that a planned expedition for 1895 had to be put over to 1896 and, as we have seen, it was not finally organized until 1898.[20]

Astrup in the meantime had written up the results of his survey of northeast Greenland, the only real result of Peary's expedition and one that sharply contradicted Peary's claim of discovering the insularity of Greenland. For his part, Baldwin went to work on his own book, *The Search for the North*

Pole. In it he described Peary's efforts as a "partial failure . . . clearly owing to inadequate provisions and equipment."[21] It was axiomatic that no one ever got away with double-crossing a double-crosser like Peary, and Baldwin's words led to a permanent rift with the volcanic naval engineer.

In December, Astrup oversaw the transport of five "beautiful full-blooded Eskimo dogs" that he had brought from Greenland, from their temporary shelter at the Zoological Gardens in Philadelphia to his home in Norway. As he prepared to leave for Norway himself, Astrup wrote to Baldwin to remind him not to "forget to keep me posted in your future plans and movements, my dear old friend, and I promise you to do the same in return."[22]

Together, the two men carried their feud with Robert Peary into 1895. A letter from Baldwin to Astrup in July 1895 notes the imminent return of Peary from Greenland, as well as the expeditions of Frederick Jackson and Fridtjof Nansen, and adds the optimistic thought that there "will be more to do—for us?—than we can possibly accomplish when they shall have done all they can."[23]

But it was Peary's ill will that continued to preoccupy Baldwin. "Yes, Astrup, I expect to lecture some during the coming year, and if Peary talks, I shall talk back." Baldwin also approvingly noted that Astrup had taken up ballooning, as during the long winter in Greenland, "we used to talk about that plan so much."[24] Astrup had also been in touch with Salomon Andrée about the possibilities of ballooning in the Arctic. Among Astrup's papers are all of Andrée's published writings on the subject, all with personal inscriptions from Andrée to Astrup.[25]

By late summer, as Peary's relief expedition readied to return him from another unsatisfactory exploration of northeastern Greenland, Baldwin and several other members of the expedition feared that Peary's arrival from the north would occasion more slanders against them. Seeking to proactively armor themselves against any such eventuality, they swore out a resolution against Peary and his wife for, among many other things, "misrepresenting the facts concerning the return of the 'North Greenland Expedition of 1893–4'" and breaking "not only the written but also the moral and verbal contracts existing between the said Peary" and the members of the expedition.[26] Besides Baldwin, who appears to have written the document, it was signed by surgeon Edward Vincent, naturalist George Clark, and the expedition's second-in-command, Samuel Entrikin. A space for the signature of expedition artist Frederick Stokes was blank.

Nor was Astrup's signature to be found—in fact Astrup may have quashed the effort, since the only surviving copy of the resolution was found in Astrup's papers. By early September, Baldwin's growing paranoia over Peary was intensified by an article published in the *Brooklyn Standard-Union*. The article quoted from a private letter praising Peary and was purportedly sent from Kristiania by Astrup himself. While honestly claiming not to know what to expect from Peary's latest efforts, the letter writer described Peary as deserving of "full success on account of his pluck. It is pluck, after all, that pushes the world forward . . . and if you Americans fully understood the pluck that Lieut. Peary has shown under the Stars and Stripes, there would be no more room for criticism."[27]

This was a little too plucky for Baldwin's liking. He wrote to Astrup to ask if the quotes were true, as they rang so false from Astrup's earlier communications. Just four days later, Baldwin feverishly wrote Astrup again, begging to know whether Astrup had written the letter. "You certainly did not write it," Baldwin prodded his former comrade. "We are all expecting to receive a statement from you concerning Peary's treatment of us so that if he makes any further misrepresentations concerning us—or even if his wife or friends do—we mean to fight him and stand up for the right and our privileges as free Americans. We are not cowards!"[28]

In the event, Peary had more than enough to worry about when he arrived in St. John's, Newfoundland, on September 21, 1895, without continuing his machinations against former expedition members. The first newspaper accounts of his 1895 effort in Greenland were not kind. While Peary would have been pleased with such headlines as "the Most Remarkable Journey in Arctic History," his pluck would have been sorely tried as he read further. "Peary tried to cross Greenland last year, but failed on account of the weather. He tried again this year and succeeded, but, beyond that bare fact he accomplished nothing."[29] In fact, Peary, along with Henson and one other remaining expedition member, Hugh Lee, were extremely fortunate to be alive after a desperate sledge journey to Independence Bay and back. The slender results from the summer of 1895 did not allow Peary the luxury of renewing the back and forth over who was responsible for what during the winter and spring of 1893–94.

Following this minor dust-up that eventually came to naught, Baldwin does not seem to have ever heard from Eivind Astrup again. By now, the young Norwegian was firmly lodged back in Kristiania and deep into a study of ballooning along with the pioneer aeronaut Francesco Cetti and Norwegian businessman Christian Helgesen. In fact, in mid-September, just as Baldwin was growing increasingly frantic in his anticipation of what slanders Peary might return with from Greenland, Astrup was in a balloon, drifting over Drammenfjord. It was on this ascent when Astrup took one of the earliest aerial photographs in Norway—ironically using a camera given to him by Peary.[30] A transcript of a letter, written by Helgesen a few years later and found in Baldwin's papers—the letter fragment does not make clear if the letter was sent to Baldwin—offers clear evidence that the last months of Astrup's life were full of adventure and daring:

> The Meteorological Institute here had requested me among other things to measure the temperature at different heights, and Mr. Eivind Astrup was of course an excellent assistant. He was, moreover, greatly desirous of making aeronautical trips. On one of these we descended in central Sweden during a very strong gale, making the descent of no small danger, that for a moment reminded me of the official responsibility of the precious cargo carried by the gondola.
>
> We rushed along at railway speed through a long valley, the gondola and anchor sweeping away fences, well-sweeps, the roof of a barn, and similar things, but we managed to get down all right.
>
> During our descent from a height of 1400 metres we met three different strong winds, and made, moreover, several quite interesting observations.
>
> This was, alas!, Eivind's second and last aeronautical trip.[31]

On his way home to Norway, riding in a freezing, unheated rail car, Astrup caught a chill. He had not entirely recovered when, at Christmastime, he began a journey on ski toward Dovrefjell north of Kristiania. His body was found several weeks later in the snow, three thousand feet above sea level, near an ancient ski hut at Hjerkinn. The tragic news finally reached the United States on January 21, 1896, and stunned Baldwin—but not so much that he failed to use the opportunity to advance his own associations. "His death is a profound shock to me. He purposed [sic] coming to Chicago to study geology with me. We were to fit ourselves for further Arctic explorations. He was only 25 years old and would certainly have gained distinction in the field of scientific exploration."[32]

Crazy rumors soon followed on the news of Astrup's death, including the fantastic notion that Astrup had been killed in a duel with Peary, one fought over Peary's wife. Given Astrup's status as the one man who could (and did) contradict Peary's claim to the discovery of the insularity of Greenland, even this newspaper silliness had to be faced with the full and "intense indignation by members of the Geographical Society."[33] Along with the unexplained disappearance of Verhoeff, the death either by accident or, as some reports soon had it, suicide of Astrup, made it increasingly evident that a prudent man might wish to remain well clear of the path of Robert Peary.

For Baldwin, the death of his lone *au fait* Scandinavian colleague left him in desperate need of another. With Nansen's fate still a mystery, Baldwin was briefly mentioned in March 1896 as the leader of a notional American expedition to the Arctic shores of Russia to search for the Norwegian.[34] The effort was to be backed by an unnamed Chicago "syndicate," a euphemism for the likely fact that Baldwin had no money but was putting himself in front of the public as the man to search for a "lost" Nansen.

When Nansen reemerged from the Arctic in the summer of 1896, any such rescue by Baldwin was off the table. Baldwin instead set about to raise money for his own polar expedition. Later in 1896, he published *The Search for the North Pole,* a long derivative fundraising tract woven into a treatise on Arctic exploration. Baldwin's purpose was to show how private and corporate sponsorship—most especially from fellow "members of the great and noble Order of Free and Accepted Masons"[35]—had led to geographic and natural resource discoveries all redounding to the eternal fame of the sponsor.

Soon represented by a lecture agent in Chicago, Baldwin took his new gospel of polar exploration as Masonic imperative on the road. Flyers advertising his appearances promised talks based on his now "famous" book, "ALL ABOUT ICE BERGS, GLACIERS, THE AURORA BOREALIS, ETC., ETC.," that were "THRILLING, PATHETIC, ENTERTAINING [and] INSTRUCTIVE." At least in public, the rift with Peary was temporarily placed on the back burner, as among Baldwin's associations was "meteorologist to the Peary North Greenland Expedition, 1893–94."[36] Baldwin certainly resented his treatment by Peary, but not so much as to fail to recognize that the easily distracted mind of the American public saw Peary as the most famous American polar explorer since Elisha Kent Kane.

More central to Baldwin's pressing need for a new Scandinavian connection, the next to last chapter of his new book described the just-announced polar balloon expedition of the Swedish engineer Salomon A. Andrée. What especially impressed Baldwin in this remarkably daring aeronautical assault on the North Pole was Andrée's apparent skill to wheedle eight thousand dollars from Oscar II, the King of Sweden himself. In Salomon Andrée, Evelyn Baldwin began to imagine he had found his next Eivind Astrup. As in so much else in Baldwin's life, his sudden compulsion to associate himself with the Swede soon mutated into an obsession. And this new obsession would come to dominate the rest of his life.

TWENTY-TWO

No Place in the Basket

If Evelyn Briggs Baldwin was something a bit more than an odd duck, then Salomon August Andrée was a whole flock of wild geese. Books continue to be churned out in an attempt to define the innervated psychology of this first polar aeronaut. A disciple of both biological and social Darwinism, Andrée liked the out of doors less than he looked forward to the subjugation of Nature through scientific laws. Andrée's scientific search for the North Pole made a rapid and apparently deliberate progression from purposeful balloon flights across the Swedish countryside to a full-on Promethean obsession worthy of Victor Frankenstein.

At age twenty-two, Andrée visited the United States, where he begged for and received a janitor's job in the Swedish section of Philadelphia's Centennial Exposition. He swept the floors and studied the exhibits and, on a day off, tracked down and introduced himself to American balloonist John Wise. Andrée had developed an interest in aeronautics and Wise gave him a notebook full of technique from the practice of four hundred ascents. After reading the Swedish meteorologist C. F. E. Björling's 1875 tract on the regularity of trade winds, *On the Laws of the Winds (Om vindarnas lagar och försöken till väderleksförutsägelser)*, Andrée decided that such winds could push both cargo and passenger balloons along predictable air routes. Wise invited Andrée on a flight, but the balloon they were to use suddenly burst while being inflated, and Andrée lost the chance.

After six months in America, Andrée returned to Sweden and a succession of mechanical jobs: assistant to a mechanical engineer, co-owner of a machine shop. Then a professor with whom he'd studied in college offered him an assistantship. His faith in science ("everything is subject to law") solidified.[37]

In 1882, while the Americans James Lockwood and David Brainard of the Greely expedition were reaching their Farthest North, eleven nations established twelve meteorological stations in the Arctic and two more in the Antarctic as part of the first International Polar Year. Sweden anchored its effort in Spitsbergen. Nils Ekholm of the Meteorological Institute of Stockholm led the Swedish expedition. Andrée found his way into the position of procurer of technical equipment and would also take atmospheric and electrical observations at the Swedish base camp at Cape Thordsen.

With characteristic thoroughness, Andrée found a way to keep water in a measuring device fluid, even at −22°F, and took fifteen thousand observations when most of the other international expeditions came to a halt as temperatures dropped far below freezing. For a month, he shut himself away in the expedition's main building, to discover if the yellow-green color that came to skin during polar darkness was just a visual reaction after the long polar night. He emerged into the sunlight after a month in darkness to discover that it wasn't. With all the frustrations of the applied scientist, he wrote of the Spitsbergen experiments: "As usual, much work and little result."[38]

Back in Stockholm, Andrée passed his thirtieth birthday as chief engineer of the Swedish Patent Office. As with Evelyn Briggs Baldwin, the idea of a lifetime commitment to a woman seemed never to have seriously entered into Andrée's well-ordered universe. He carried on an extended affair with a married woman named Gurli Linder, a convenient arrangement for a man who had placed a marriage of his own out of the question. With a woman, Andrée wrote, "one has to deal with factors which cannot be arranged according to a plan."[39]

In February 1895, before the Royal Swedish Academy of Sciences, Andrée proposed to use drag lines and sails attached to an otherwise free-floating hydrogen balloon in order to "guide-rope" the aerial craft from a balloon shed constructed in Spitsbergen all the way to the North Pole. He possessed a small amount of actual ballooning experience upon which to base his ideas, beginning as a passenger when Francesco Cetti made balloon ascents during a visit to Stockholm in 1892. Andrée soon found an enthusiastic group of financial patrons in Sweden, including Alfred Nobel, Oscar Dickson, and Oscar II, the king of Sweden and Norway. His ideas on polar aeronautics also fascinated ambitious young explorers like the American Baldwin and the Norwegian Astrup, and Andrée's largely ascetic personality in particular would have appealed to the very strange and tightly wound Baldwin.

Elsewhere, however, Andrée was met by a less fulsome reception. As Jennifer Tucker points out in her analysis of the career of the British balloonist James Glaisher, attempts to transform the balloon into a kind of flying scientific laboratory during the half century after 1840 were fraught with dangers that were by turns theoretical, practical, cultural, and even spiritual. "Many who commented on the 'balloon craze' in Regency and Victorian England expressed tremendous moral ambivalence about balloon ascensions, symbols not just of discovery, innovation, and exotic travel, but of excited crowds, riots, humbuggery, French decadence, reckless endangerment of passengers and spectators, and the loss of reason and moral propriety."[40] If a crowd was not sufficiently pleased with a balloon ascent, they often as not would attack and destroy the balloon and threaten the balloonist.

Andrée felt much of this same scorn for his project. "This Mr. Andrée," wrote an Austrian paper, "who wishes to go to the North Pole and back by means of an air balloon, is simply a fool or a swindler."[41] Such comments, along with the obviously fantastical aspects of a scientific balloon expedition, especially in the Arctic, had the effect of making any such proposed expeditions seem eccentric if not outright insane.

In the case of Andrée, they also obscured for more than a century the real and dramatic transformation in polar technology he had wrought. In Urban Wråkberg's minutely detailed analysis of Andrée's flight,[42] he writes that previous polar expeditions had struggled over the ice at a rate of barely a single nautical mile per day, whereas Andrée's balloon—in the first hours after it was launched on July 11, 1897—had covered this same distance every five minutes and thirty seconds. Such unheard-of progress was the equivalent, during the Heroic Age of Polar Exploration, of travel at light speed.

In the summer of 1896, Andrée built an elaborate base camp on Danskøya in northwest Spitsbergen, on the same shoreline where Wellman's forlorn Professor Øyen had passed the desultory and, according to Wellman, whisky-soaked summer of 1894. The site was complete with an apparatus for making hydrogen gas on a large scale. When the required southern winds did not materialize, Andrée postponed the expedition to the summer of 1897.

It was at this point, in the fall of 1896—as he cast about for a new polar ally after the death of Astrup—that Baldwin entered into a one-sided correspondence with the Swedish engineer as Andrée prepared to return to Spitsbergen the following year. Andrée's two brief responses to Baldwin—bluntly stating that there was no place for him in the expedition—did not dissuade Baldwin in the summer of 1897 from an attempt to reach Andrée's base camp on Danskøya. As he later and repeatedly claimed, he apparently intended to talk his way into the car of Andrée's balloon *Örnen,* offering for qualifications his skills as a meteorologist.

When Andrée's balloon disappeared into the Arctic in July 1897, its whereabouts became an enduring international mystery. Andrée had on board the balloon several carrier pigeons as well as buoys made from cork that could be tossed from the gondola and mark the expedition's progress over the ice. Within hours of the launch, the birds began to relay brief but optimistic messages from the balloon. Over the next months and years, the buoys began to wash up around the Arctic, including the buoy Andrée had designed especially to drop at the North Pole.

For Baldwin, each of these messages spurred his fantasist's imagination. Taken together—his brief summer 1897 journey to Spitsbergen along with the eerie messages trickling from the ice—these marked the beginning a life-long attempt by Baldwin to tie himself to the fate of the doomed expedition. They also intensified his desires to take up the mantle of Arctic ballooning from the departed Astrup and the now-missing Andrée.

Baldwin arrived at Andrée's launch point on board a tourist steamer more than two weeks after the expedition lifted off, and it was on the shoreline at Virgohamn that Max Wiskott, a passenger on the cruise, noted that as everyone gathered up tiny souvenirs, "our lone American [Baldwin] was looking for all possible and impossible memories—he would have preferred the whole balloon house packed up and taken away to the United States!!"[43] As late as August 1897, while traveling through Sweden, Baldwin wrote a letter to Andrée—one the balloonist would never receive—expressing Baldwin's hopes for a safe return.[44] Soon after, Baldwin began to claim that had he arrived in time, he would have been in the basket of the balloon with Andrée and therefore shared his fate.

This story, which claimed a close relationship to the expedition that never existed, became, along with his service with Peary, the core element of Baldwin's résumé as an Arctic explorer. Despite Andrée's curt responses to his attempts to join the balloon—the kind of routine dismissals familiar to all organizers of geographic expeditions—Baldwin to the end of his life insisted that only his late arrival at Danskøya prevented his participation in the expedition.

In the years that followed, Baldwin would tell numerous public versions of his attempt to reach Andrée's base camp and secure a place in the gondola of Andrée's balloon *Örnen,* but his private papers make it clear that Andrée had no use for the American on what was always a purely Swedish expedition. These various versions are nevertheless invaluable for evaluating both Baldwin's character and the problematic expedition leader he eventually became.

In the *Los Angeles Times* of March 24, 1912, Baldwin told a reporter that "in 1897 [Baldwin] volunteered to accompany Andre [*sic*] in his balloon but arrived at the starting point two days after Andre and his two companions had departed for the North Pole never to be heard of again."[45] The *San Francisco Examiner* of March 10, 1911, was much more direct: "[Baldwin] was with the Spitzbergen balloon expedition in 1897."[46] In the organization journal *Masonic Standard* of March 3, 1906, Baldwin dramatically arrived just after lift-off: "In 1897 [Baldwin] made the voyage to the Andree balloon station, as a volunteer to join Andree, in case his services could be utilized, but arrived too late, the balloon having sailed with the first southerly breeze."[47] In the boy's newspaper *Grit* of July 7, 1901, Baldwin arrived before liftoff, but found the balloon too small: "[I]n 1897 [Baldwin] barely escaped sharing the fate of Andree. Baldwin went to Spitzbergen, Norway, with the full intention of accompanying Andree, but when he arrived he found that the balloon was too small to carry a third passenger, so he was forced to abandon the trip which in all probability proved fatal to Andree and his companion[s] in aeronautic Arctic exploration."[48]

In a newspaper interview in the *New Orleans Daily Picayune* of January 31, 1900, where he was stationed by the Weather Service in the aftermath of the Wellman expedition, Baldwin chose the "no room in the basket" version:

My second trip to the arctics, in 1897, was for the purpose of accompanying Mr. Andree, if possible. . . . I was disappointed in not having been able to accompany Mr. Andree, as there was not room enough in the basket for me. . . . I enjoyed the personal acquaintance of Captain [Ernst] Andree (the explorer's brother), who was an ex-officer in the Swedish navy, and whom I had met in Sweden. With Mr. Andree I frequently corresponded during his preparation of the balloon, and I had volunteered to go with him. . . . Although before reaching

Spitzbergen I had been informed that there would be no room in the basket for one more person, yet I kept on my journey, hoping that at the last moment, through some fortuitous occurrence, there might be room for a substitute.[49]

The reality was something entirely different. Baldwin's "frequent" correspondence with Andrée amounted to just two terse replies from the Swedish engineer. When he finally responded to Baldwin's pleadings, Andrée wrote that he was glad to have Baldwin's confidence in the balloon idea, "but as all the places in the basket are occupied I can on no account give you one."[50] Undeterred, Baldwin wrote again in the spring of 1897 and again Andrée abruptly dismissed him, this time in one line: "Dear Sir! I am sorry to say that there is no place for you in the basket. Yours truly, S. A. Andrée."[51]

Even this was not enough to dissuade Baldwin. As noted, he made his second journey to the Arctic in the summer of 1897, this time to Spitsbergen. Baldwin traveled not as an explorer but as a tourist on board the steamer *Lofoten,* captained, as luck would have it, by Otto N. K. Sverdrup, the captain of the *Fram* during Nansen's three-year polar drift from 1893 to 1896. In one of his many versions of this trip, Baldwin had the *Lofoten* arriving at Danskøya two days after the departure of Andrée in his balloon.

This dramatic account is contradicted by Baldwin's own papers, as well as accounts of visits to Spitsbergen that same summer by the British mountaineer Sir Martin Conway and a German tourist, Max Wiskott.[52] Among the receipts that survive in Baldwin's personal papers are several showing that Baldwin was still in Kristiania in mid-July. Among other things, he was purchasing photographs of Nansen's 1896 homecoming for use in his freelance articles.[53] When *Örnen* came down on the ice on July 14, 1897, three days after its launch, Baldwin was paying his bill of seven kroner, six øre at Kristiania's Grand Hotel.[54]

It is clear enough that Baldwin did make a very brief journey to Spitsbergen later that July, not only because both Martin Conway and Max Wiskott saw him there, but because he was later able to recoup part of his expenses by selling some botanical specimens to his alma mater in Illinois. He was likewise not shy about trying to earn a living from the efforts of his imagined Swedish polar colleague, whether alive or dead. In a macabre incident in the winter of 1897, Baldwin brazenly attempted to sell the rights to an American lecture tour by Salomon Andrée for one thousand dollars. Aside from the fact that he did not own such rights, Baldwin was unwittingly arranging a speaking tour for someone who at that moment had been dead for about four months. The lecture promoter seemed well aware of this possibility: "I can make as big a fortune for Andree as any man ever made in this world, at this business, *if he turns up.*"[55]

Baldwin's failure to join the Andrée balloon expedition, combined with the continued harsh American economy of 1896–97 that curtailed both his travel and his fundraising, led Baldwin to attach himself to Wellman's 1898–99 expedition to Franz Josef Land. After Wellman and Baldwin first went ashore at Cape Tegetthoff and noted footprints along the shore, Baldwin hurried off a letter about the discovery to Andrée's brother Ernst in Sweden. The report of these footprints in Franz Josef Land—almost certainly left behind by walrus hunters operating in the area—was one of dozens of similar reports to raise false hopes that Andrée and his crew might still be alive.

As Wellman's expedition retreated from Franz Josef Land in the summer of 1899, the Italian noble Luigi Amadeo was just arriving in the archipelago. The two expeditions met and Wellman and his team rowed over to Amadeo's ship, the *Stella Polare.* It was likely here that Baldwin had a chance to learn of the Duke's plans to use hydrogen balloons on his way to the pole,[56] which had already aroused much discussion, with articles noting that "[g]reat interest is being taken in the possible results to be arrived at by the use of the two balloons, which the party is taking with them."[57] Added to his existing fascination with Andrée's expedition and his earlier correspondence with Eivind Astrup on the subject, such intelligence would have only inflamed Baldwin's desire to return north with an "aeronautic outfit" of his own.

Back in the United States in the fall of 1899, Baldwin was determined to continue his pursuit of the North Pole. But he was broke and needed cash—lots of it. When Ernst Andrée revealed that several expeditions were on their way north in search of his brother's lost balloon expedition, Baldwin saw his chance to both the return to the Arctic and fulfill his ambitions to follow Salomon Andrée in a balloon over the ice.[58]

On April 25, 1900, the Italian expedition under Luigi Amadeo bested Fridtjof Nansen's farthest north of 86° 14' North by twenty nautical miles, and established a new farthest north of 86° 34' North.[59] As the Italians made their way back to mainland Europe in mid-summer 1900, Baldwin announced that he had again been in contact with Ernst Andrée in Göteborg, Sweden.

Using the Wellman expedition's brief search for Andrée in the summer of 1898 as his qualifications, Baldwin was more than eager to join in the search for the missing Swede. As had Wellman, Baldwin knew the worldwide fame that would attach to anyone who could find the lost balloonists or answer the lingering questions over their fate. Even more than the gathering international race for the North Pole, the drama of a search for Andrée promised to be more interesting, less dangerous, and perhaps even more lucrative than another "dash" to the pole. And, in the summer of 1900, as Baldwin dramatically told reporters, time was of the essence.

"At this very hour, several of [Andrée's] buoys may be lying on the shores of the Atlantic or floating on its waves or be within the course followed by the *Fram,* Dr. Nansen's famous ship, buried in the sea or sands awaiting liberation. I firmly believe that discovery will reach us this summer, and that we will have news of the lost explorer, living or dead, and of the missing balloon."[60] But Baldwin did not want to stop there. He not only wanted to solve the mystery of the Andrée expedition but at the same time add his own chapter to the early history of aeronautics in the Arctic.

Baldwin returned briefly to service with the U.S. Weather Bureau in Washington, D.C. He was then posted to New Orleans on special duty to write up the meteorological results of the year in Franz Josef Land, to include "his observations of the magnificent auroral displays of that region [and] the first tracings of barograph and thermograph curves obtained in the arctics, that have ever been published."[61] These ran to some ninety published pages and were printed as part of the annual report of the operations of the Weather Bureau for the fiscal year of 1900.[62]

Unfortunately for Baldwin, he had left Wellman's expedition on no better terms than he had left Peary's and accordingly had few references he could leverage for support of a new expedition. Perhaps because of this, Baldwin continued his attempts to grab onto the guide ropes of Salomon Andrée's balloon. Interviewed by a reporter in New Orleans in January 1900, Baldwin offered his estimation of where the lost balloonist might be found and then, as that was not enough, added that the Swede, whom Baldwin had never personally met, was "one of the most cultured and courageous men that I ever knew."[63]

Such gilded lilies made clear that Baldwin, like many other would-be polar explorers of the turn of the century, was desperate for a patron, and if reeling one in required Baldwin to invent and re-invent both his qualifications and his associations, then so be it. As he told the New Orleans paper, the search for Andrée, along with the search for the pole itself, offered "a good chance for some one to be generous-hearted and public-spirited as well, to contribute a sufficient sum to fit out an expedition for the purpose of endeavoring either to rescue Andree . . . or to complete the exploration of those regions."[64]

By the time Baldwin completed his report for the Weather Bureau in the summer of 1900, he had finally tied together all of his personal fascinations into one great romantic quest. At the age of thirty-eight, all he required was an open-handed millionaire to make his dream come true. But the economic depression of the 1890s had made such personalities considerably tighter with their Gilded Age purses.

As the century turned and Robert Peary doggedly continued his attempts to reach the North Pole from Greenland, the Norwegian Otto Sverdrup commenced his explorations of the Canadian Arctic. At the same time, much of the rest of the polar world had turned its attention southward, toward the much more promising void of Antarctica. It seemed a hopeless environment in which to gain support for yet another Arctic expedition. Evelyn Briggs Baldwin, lugging around a mound of baggage from the Peary expedition and with Bernt Bentsen's demise during the Wellman expedition on his conscience, would seem to have had no chance. He had blatantly concocted a supposititious association with the missing Swedish balloon expedition. He was—or should have been—radioactive to any potential patron.

That Baldwin now managed to attract the modern equivalent of several millions of dollars for a second American polar expedition that would stage from Franz Josef Land was little short of miraculous.

TWENTY-THREE

Purely American in Character

In a stunning reversal of fortune, within a year of returning from what otherwise was a catastrophe in Franz Josef Land, Evelyn Briggs Baldwin had found his millionaire. Early in 1900, Baldwin made a long trip to visit his college friend Theodore Snyder. Snyder lived in Mobile, Alabama, but owned a banana plantation in Colombia, South America, and Baldwin now sought him out there. The trip proved a success on several levels. Not only was Theodore now in a position to financially assist Baldwin, but so was his brother Alfred, another friend from Baldwin's college days in Illinois who lived in New Orleans. Both now promised Baldwin financial support for any expedition he cared to propose. Much more important, the Snyder brothers had a cousin who might be interested as well. This cousin was a German-American chemist and businessman by the name of William Ziegler.

Born in 1843 in western Pennsylvania, William Ziegler was a full generation older than Baldwin and the Snyder brothers. He also possessed vastly more money. The same year Baldwin was born, Ziegler enrolled in the Eastman Business School in upstate New York; after graduation he worked for chemical and drug companies in New York. In 1870, he founded the Royal Baking Powder Company. When he sold out to his two partners in 1888, he pocketed more than three million dollars (nearly eighty million in 2013 dollars).[65] At the age of forty-five, Ziegler had become one of the many Gilded Age multimillionaires that Walter Wellman so loved to rhapsodize about.

When he was introduced to Baldwin by the Snyders, Ziegler had immediately fastened onto the idea of a polar expedition, a goal Ziegler had also apparently carried because of his "deep interest in arctic matters since Dr. Kane's time."[66] The first announcement that Baldwin would lead a new American effort in search of the North Pole and funded by Ziegler came before a Philadelphia meeting of the Geographical Club of the Academy of Natural Sciences on October 14, 1900: "Baldwin is to be backed in his expedition by William Ziegler, a New York city millionaire, who has a hobby for chases of this nature."[67]

In this case, the nature of the chase was "to uphold the glory of the Stars and Stripes in an international race for the North Pole,"[68] an Arctic allegory to the lightning-speed American occupations, in the wake of the Spanish-American War, of the Philippines, Puerto Rico, Guam, and Cuba, as well as the annexation of Hawaii. Ziegler announced his intention to spare no expense "to make this the best-equipped expedition that ever started out, and when he leaves Mr. Baldwin will receive from his patron these instructions: 'Find the Pole, and don't come back until you do.' "[69] The announcement added that the newly christened "Ziegler-Baldwin expedition will be purely American in character."[70]

Just what appealed to William Ziegler about Evelyn Briggs Baldwin—enough to offer him more money than any other American polar explorer of the Heroic Age of Polar Exploration—can be seen in the seven-page "Short Autobiographical Sketch" that Baldwin provided to Ziegler, as well as in numerous interviews Baldwin provided to newspaper reporters once the expedition had been announced. There was also a slender Midwestern connection, as Ziegler as a young man had worked as a druggist in Iowa.

Once again, Baldwin's résumé was inflated, this time his membership in "*several* of the earlier Peary expeditions."[71] After hinting to Ziegler that, if he had been in charge of Peary's expedition the American flag would very likely already be waving from the pole, Baldwin described his valiant attempt to accompany the Swedes:

Therefore, when Andree whom I knew to be a thorough scholar and physicist, and meteorologist, as well as a navigator of balloons, was starting, I made application to accompany him on his aerial voyage. I was willing to take the risk, as I believed him to be entirely

William Ziegler.
From Anthony Fiala, *Fighting the Polar Ice*
(New York: Doubleday, Page & Company, 1906).

trustworthy. However, Mr. Andree informed me that he was only sorry that he had not room enough in the basket of the balloon for me. . . . I knew that Andree had not had experience as a traveler on the ice-fields. That he knew nothing from experience as regards sledging over the ice of the North, and thought that if he as a young man could secure sufficient funds for an expedition, that I would likewise be successful.[72]

Baldwin put down his inability to finance an expedition after his experiences with Peary to the "hard times of 1896 and 1897 and the unsettled political condition of the country." He therefore accepted "an interest" in the Wellman expedition, where he was "at once put in charge of an advance party to establish an outpost, and after having been absent from headquarters for three months I returned having successfully accomplished the object for which I had been sent out. This outpost I named 'Ft. McKinley.' "[73]

This, of course, was another considerable exaggeration. Not only had Baldwin not "successfully accomplished the object for which I had been sent out," he had left the expedition nearly a full degree south of where Wellman had ordered him to set up the advance hut. In addition to the failure to establish a northern depot on Rudolf Land, Baldwin's manifest lack of leadership skills had thoroughly poisoned his relationships with his Norwegian comrades and led directly to the death of Bernt Bentsen.

When Baldwin related his successful sledge journey in the spring of 1899 that discovered Graham Bell Land, he made sure to point out that he returned with everyone alive, a claim he at least did not try to make from the work of the previous fall. He then went on to compare himself favorably to each and every one of his contemporaries:

Now, if Peary who made his most successful trip in 1891, with but very little previous experience, if Nansen who made his great voyage after a short journey across the Southern point of Greenland, almost entirely this side of the Arctic Circle, if Andree, who only a few years previous had paid his expenses while visiting America by sweeping floors, and if the Italian Duke with no previous record . . . if these men could be relied upon to lead expeditions, I think that my friends can see no reason why I should not now, with my previous experience, be capable of also leading one beneath the Stars and Stripes.[74]

Baldwin met with Ziegler for the first time at the latter's offices in New York City. He carried a letter of introduction from another citizen of Mobile, Alabama, a Colonel Edward L. Russell, a Confederate veteran of the Civil War and now vice president of the Mobile and Ohio Railroad, as well as a letter from a former federal judge by the name of John F. Dillon, then in private practice in the city.[75] Both of these connections were almost certainly provided through the good offices of Theodore Snyder.

At this meeting, Baldwin shared his "secret" plan to reach the North Pole, a plan so strange and complicated it almost seemed deliberately designed as a confidence game. "For several years I have gradually evolved, as a result of experience and observation, the scheme which is now known to you. This plan for Polar Research I kept secret until I could retain it no longer, and therefore, confidentially outlined it to my bosom friends Alfred and Theodore Snyder."[76]

It is difficult to understand why Ziegler would throw so much of his financial weight behind Baldwin—save for the obvious gratification of egocentric and nationalistic desires to attach his name to a polar enterprise entirely in keeping with the expansionist spirit of the age. Ziegler was himself too old to contemplate accompanying such an expedition himself, but at the same time he was nobody's fool. He was a savvy and extremely successful businessman. In his chosen field he was referred to as the "Baking Powder King." All of which makes it very odd that he does not appear to have closely vetted Baldwin's assertions either about his qualifications or his previous experiences when placed in a leadership role on an Arctic expedition.

What Ziegler did possess—and this all but blinded him to Baldwin's obvious flaws—was a firm belief that there was no problem, from baking soda to polar exploration, which could not be solved by American capital. He proceeded to offer Baldwin whatever he needed to organize and lead a new American attempt on the North Pole. It was a disastrous miscalculation. Ziegler would learn too late that the same qualities that led to dissension in Wellman's ranks in 1898 resurfaced quickly when Baldwin was placed in command of Ziegler's effort in Franz Josef Land.

It was soon reported that Ziegler had attached one million dollars of his personal fortune to the expedition in hopes of attaching his name to an island in the Arctic.[77] In his papers, Baldwin himself recorded the sum as $142,000, not the fantastic sum of a million dollars but nevertheless close to three and a half million dollars in 2011 buying power. Even the lesser sum was eight

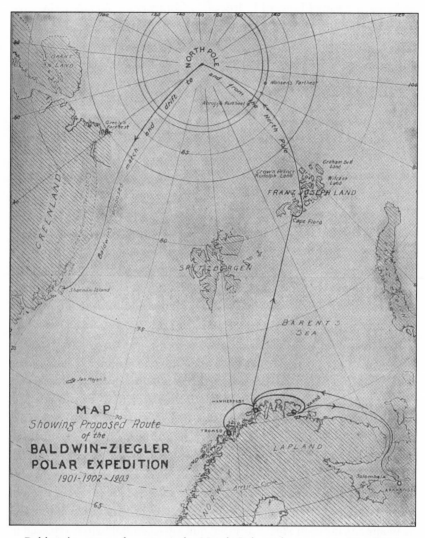

Baldwin's proposed route to the North Pole and retreat via Northeast Greenland. From Evelyn Briggs Baldwin, "How I Hope to Reach the North Pole," *Windsor Magazine* 15 (1): 59–69, 1901.

times the amount Wellman had raised for the 1898–99 expedition to Franz Josef Land, and when Wellman learned of it he must have shaken his head in utter disbelief. Baldwin himself wrote that Ziegler had offered him "unlimited means to carry out my plans."[78] Yet for all this, in the end he would advance no closer to the pole than had the modestly funded Wellman in 1899.

A British newspaper took up this theme when it opined that "if unbounded confidence and unlimited cash can do the trick it looks as if, in the fulness [*sic*] of time, the Stars and Stripes will flutter in that fascinating region. . . .

> Britishers will probably regret that Mr. William Ziegler, the millionaire who is to finance this latest Polar expedition, is not of their nationality, and that the prospective glory of the enterprise will not belong to the Union Jack. There are so few big goals left to the explorers of to-day that a Britisher may be pardoned for feeling a wee bit sorry that a Yankee man of millions should have outdistanced the monarchs of Park Lane in the patriotic endeavour to secure for their country the biggest "plum"—geographically speaking—of all yelept [named] the North Pole. . . . Well, if the enterprise is successful, mankind will forgive Mr. Ziegler the accumulation—the unholy accumulation, as some think—of so many millions.[79]

In news interviews after his arrangement with Ziegler, Baldwin was reluctant to offer many details of the expedition—beyond its near-limitless financial resources, his imagined alliance with Salomon Andrée, and his own sterling character. "He is a rugged, hardy and courageous traveler, inured to the privations and alive to the dangers which attend all attempts at reaching the pole" went a typical notice after the announcement of the expedition. "The new aspirant for arctic honors is a native of Illinois and is an expert meteorologist, thus uniting in his person all the physical qualifications and scientific knowledge which make up the ideal traveler in quest of the unconquered north."[80] Just why being a native of Illinois might particularly endow one with "physical qualifications" went unexplained, and in any case Baldwin was a native of next-door Missouri.

Baldwin himself, taking the natural-born explorer theme a step further, told a reporter that "the north pole fever was born in me. I can't remember when I didn't have it." And he then took even his imaginary relationship with Andrée a notch too far. "I had planned to go with Andree in the balloon expedition, and *went with him* to Spitzbergen for that purpose. It was found that the car would not accommodate more than three, and, much to my regret, I was left behind. Yes, I still regret it."[81]

The reporter did not challenge the absurd idea that the meticulous engineer Andrée—who analyzed and planned to the minutest degree—would not have known, months if not years in advance, that his balloon car, to say nothing of the expedition's food and equipment, were designed for three Swedes—and certainly not three Swedes and one besotted American.

While describing his new expedition as "purely an American enterprise," Baldwin nevertheless mentioned that he was on his way to Europe to see to the expedition's preparations. Baldwin also teased a rumor that he had an aerial operation of his own. "I don't care to say anything about my experience as a balloonist or whether balloons will be employed in conjunction with the steamers."[82] Of course, he could not speak to his experience as a balloonist, because as of November 1900, he had none.

This was too much for reporters, especially at a time when the plans of polar explorers made regular appearances on the front pages of major newspapers, where "the public could be intoxicated by exciting reports about heroic struggles to master nature, particularly in what were perceived as her most dangerous environments, Africa and the Arctic."[83] Predictably, such reticence led reporters to draw their own conclusions. "The impression created by this secrecy is that Mr. Baldwin will resort to some radically new method."[84]

In 1900 there were only two such potentially "radically new methods" available to polar explorers. The first was under the ice, with a submarine, as had been proposed as early as 1891 by the Swedish polar researcher Axel Hamberg, and renewed a decade later by the German engineer and inventor of the gyro compass Hermann Anschütz-Kaempfe.[85]

It was a scheme that even Walter Wellman, who as a rule latched onto any technological means he could find to advance his polar ambitions, found too daunting. "Yes, I have heard of it," he told a reporter when asked about a North Pole submarine adventure. "All I can say is if the explorer has faith that his boat can travel 2,000 miles under water, or rather under ice, and is prepared to take chances on finding open water when he wishes to come up for additional air, he might succeed. I would not wish to try it myself."[86]

The other radically new method was through the air, in a balloon. Andrée had pioneered the aerial path to the North Pole, and the specter of the daring Swedish balloon expedition hung over all of Baldwin's preparations. As one report noted, "what if, when they get [to the pole], they find a dismantled balloon and, maybe, a corpse or two—to show that Professor Andrée has been before them? Stranger things have happened."[87]

Baldwin arrived in London on December 10, 1900, "to consult with scientists and inspect ships,"[88] and set about to liberally employ William Ziegler's very deep bank account to secure supplies and ships for the expedition. London buzzed with news of North Pole expeditions. Besides the Americans under Peary and Baldwin and the Norwegians with Sverdrup, the Russian icebreaker *Ermak* under the command of Admiral Stepan Makarov was being readied at a Newcastle shipyard for an expedition in the European Arctic, while in London itself a Canadian explorer by the name of Joseph Bernier was trying to drum up support for a similar effort in the Canadian Arctic. Nansen himself was reported to be working with the Duke of the Abruzzi on a new expedition in the north.

No less than nine different expeditions were on the move in the polar regions in 1901 and these included Otto Nordenskjöld's Swedish Antarctic Expedition and the British National Antarctic Expedition, the latter as the first official U.K. expedition to explore the southern continent in sixty years. "With these expeditions and the German expedition the year 1901 promises to be eventful in the history of searches for the north pole."[89]

In this accelerating international race for priority at the poles, Evelyn Briggs Baldwin would lead by far the largest and most well-funded expedition aimed at the north—and certainly the most well-heeled private American Arctic expedition ever to take the field. Baldwin's continuous, and disingenuous, self-promotion since 1895 had paid off in spectacular ways. In the spring of 1901 he was being mentioned in the same company as Nansen, Scott, Peary, Borchgrevink, and the Duke of the Abruzzi.

There was no question of Baldwin trying for the pole from Greenland. With Peary still encamped in northwestern Greenland and Otto Sverdrup exploring northeastern Arctic Canada, there was even less room along the "American route" for Baldwin than there had been in the basket of Andrée's balloon—and the reception he would have received would have been even frostier. It was at this point that Baldwin, like Wellman before him, sought to avoid any unpleasant encounters with the prickly Peary. Baldwin soon confirmed that he intended to return to Franz Josef Land and use those remote islands as a base from which to seek the pole.

TWENTY-FOUR

Hit Him Squarely between the Eyes

The "eventful" year of 1901 in polar exploration opened with Evelyn Briggs Baldwin in Sweden, where he met with Ernst Andrée to discuss "the researches of the forthcoming expedition."[90] These "researches" included a continuation of the search for Andrée's lost brother, which by now was almost as much of an obsession for Baldwin as it was for members of Andrée's own family. It was soon reported that Baldwin's "purely American" "crew will include a number of Swedish sailors who have at various times served on expeditions sent out for [Andrée's] relief."[91]

Through this connection, Ernst Andrée was used to engage many of the Swedish crew (whose numbers grew despite the "American" pledge). It would prove a fateful decision and affect the entire course of the expedition once the Swedish-crewed expedition ship finally reached Franz Josef Land. Though still reticent to discuss his own aeronautical plans, Baldwin's attempt to link himself directly to the search for the lost Swedish expedition was a decision that would eventually and ironically lead to his own destruction as an expedition leader.

Anxious to avoid any pre-expedition scrutiny of his plans, with their inevitable (and negative) comparisons with Andrée's experience, Baldwin also sought to avoid similar comparisons with Andrée's apparent fate and, with it, the label of "balloonatic": "I will say, however, that the expedition will be practical in every way and the work will be done on practical lines only."[92] This approach put Baldwin in a double bind. Balloons in the Arctic were his obvious fascination, yet he could not talk about his foremost obsession if he was to avoid both scientific scrutiny of his research plans as well as potential editorial scorn of his lack of aeronautical experience.

Baldwin returned to the United States in early February, having purchased thousands of dollars in gear and supplies while in Europe. These orders included the charter of "two of the best boats to be had for arctic exploration," a steam whaling barkentine called *Esquimaux* that Baldwin renamed *America,* and the same Norwegian vessel, *Frithjof,* that had helped the Wellman expedition on its way to Franz Josef Land and which Baldwin planned to employ as a supply vessel. "In securing the *America* I had to compete with two firms who are endeavoring to monopolize the seal trade," Baldwin told the *New York Times,* "and also [Robert Falcon Scott's] British Antarctic expedition which wanted her in case the boat now building for that expedition at Dundee was found to be deficient."[93]

There were also echoes of his many failures to take proper care of the Norwegians who served under him during the advance work in Franz Josef Land in the fall of 1898. Baldwin had purchased new sledges, furs, skis, and, revealingly, more and better tents and sleeping bags. "Some of my tents are of canvas and others of raw silk. *There will be no more sleeping out.*"[94] The *New York Times* reporter did not pursue what cold experiences lay behind this seemingly curious statement, but it was an indication that the ghost of Bernt Bentsen still haunted Baldwin.

Baldwin also responded to accusations that he had also cornered the market for dogs, as he had ordered more than four hundred Siberian and Eskimo dogs to go with fifteen Siberian ponies: "Yes, I have the dogs. I have more polar dogs now than have ever been taken before on an Arctic expedition." He then added, bizarrely, "And I could sell them to-day at a very good profit."[95] It was another indication that the Baldwin-Ziegler Polar Expedition was to be of a size and scale completely unimaginable by Walter Wellman in 1898.

To the Norwegians of the 1898 advance party, who bestowed upon him the obloquious epithet "*Susæg*" and unfavorably compared him to a cucumber, Baldwin was mad as a March hare. If one can read anything into a photograph of a twenty-five-year-old Baldwin taken in Illinois in 1887—to say nothing of the even more unscrewed look in his eye in a photograph taken eleven years later on Christmas Day at Cape Tegetthoff—the future Arctic explorer does nothing to dispel an impression of a kind of mental derangement. It was therefore inevitable that William Ziegler's grant of unlimited means to such a man was all but guaranteed to lead to the erratic, almost unhinged oddities it soon produced. The Ziegler-Baldwin Polar Expedition soon transposed to become the Baldwin-Ziegler Polar Expedition. But this forgivable bit of ego would barely scratch the surface of what would become one of the strangest and most tangled episodes in the history of American polar exploration.

Newspapers reported that Baldwin would venture north at the head of "the largest transport train in the history of Arctic exploration."[96] By mid-April an elephantine mass of supplies, "a huge mountain of hermetically sealed tins,"[97] carried atop dozens upon dozens of cart-loads—each hauled by four horses—began to arrive at the docks of New York for transshipment from the States toward Norway. The precise tonnage of these supplies is uncertain, but there is no question that it was both massive and unprecedented. Newspaper sources guessed that it amounted to anywhere from 170 to 300 tons and included hundreds of pounds of tobacco, twenty tons of cornmeal, and ten tons of bread. A receipt for nearly five tons of supplies shipped on the Hamburg-American Line steamship *Phoenicia* on April 19, 1901, includes three cases of "Books & Drugs," weighing 172 lbs., along with a quarter ton of bacon, three hundred pounds of eggs, fifty cases of emergency rations, and twenty-four cases of pemmican, along with a ton of canned meat from Armour and Company.[98] The cost—only the shipping cost, and for this one shipment alone—was nearly five thousand dollars, or nearly a third of the cost of Walter Wellman's entire 1898–99 expedition.

The new American attempt on the pole was to be the very opposite of the methods of successful explorers, such as Roald Amundsen, who at the same moment were beginning the perfection of small, agile, lightly equipped polar exploring expeditions, methods pioneered by earlier American explorers of the Arctic such as Charles Francis Hall. Worse, the effort would be led by a man with—in the best of times—a borderline grip on reality. Evelyn Briggs Baldwin, the *Susæg* who tormented the five Norwegians in his charge in 1898 and—*res ipsa loquitur*—killed one of them through sheer negligence, was about to return to Franz Josef Land with a vengeance, at the head of a crew of more than forty men.

All in all, Baldwin's staggering mound of supplies was meant to last his party of forty-two men for more than two years. In the middle of this prodigious buying spree, however, and perhaps because of it, Baldwin found little time for practical testing and technical preparation and orientation of the machinery he proposed to bring to Franz Josef Land. The prime example was the steam launch. Determined to correct the fatal flaw in Wellman's expedition, Baldwin ordered a small gasoline-powered motor launch, the one vehicle—as Baldwin constantly lamented in 1898—that could swiftly move men and supplies in the narrow channels of Franz Josef Land during the few summer weeks when the ice loosened its grip.

But even as he made preparations to purchase more than 425 dogs and 15 ponies, Baldwin only ordered one motor launch and, worse, did not allow for the necessary time required to learn how to operate it. The launch was built by Wolverine Motor Works, a marine and auto engine manufacturer only recently incorporated in Grand Rapids, Michigan, by a friend of Baldwin's named Claude Sintz. Sintz begged Baldwin to visit the company so he could "spend a few hours in showing him how to run the launch to the best advantage possible."[99] This appeal was written on June 3, 1901, less than a month before the expedition sailed for Europe.

In the end, the small vessel was never tested before the expedition departed the United States and then never even used once the expedition reached the Arctic. It was perhaps Baldwin's refusal to share the burden of moving supplies with the Norwegians in the fall of 1898—day after day of backbreaking rowing through horrendous sea conditions—that led to a failure of his brain to register the importance of bringing half a dozen such small launches to Franz Josef Land. These could have been used for innumerable and essential tasks, from advance reconnaissance, geographical survey, search and rescue, to the movement of the expedition's mass of supplies. All this would now have to be accomplished, just as in 1898, by men and dogs.

By late spring 1901 the expedition personnel also began to take shape. As with so much else in Baldwin's frantic preparations, there were too many people added with no clear plan on how to use them all. The men were selected not so much for their particular skill set in polar exploration but rather for their "willingness to bear hardship without grumbling."[100] This was a clear reference to Bentsen, whose defiant attitude Baldwin blamed for the majority of his troubles in the fall of 1898.

Besides Baldwin himself, the expedition included fifteen Americans.[101] The senior member was Francis Long, a German-born American who, at nearly fifty years old, was one of the few surviving members of the Lady Franklin Bay expedition under Adolphus Greely twenty years earlier.

At the request of Baldwin, Long and all other members and crew had to report any personal "habits"—did they smoke or drink alcohol? Long's perfectly crafted one-word answer: "Normal." Henry P. Hartt, the other old-timer besides Long, was forty-one, a chief engineer on board ocean steamers, a heavy drinker and an inveterate pipe smoker who, when he wasn't smoking and drinking, was talking a blue streak. The only American amongst the Swedish officers of the expedition ship, he "has made a reputation as the most profane and expressive curser aboard, he having the most abrupt and clear-cut adjectives and manners."[102] Archibald Dickson, an army veteran from Pennsylvania who had served in campaigns against the Sioux in North Dakota, was thirty-four and another smoker. He was the manager of a business college when he was chosen for the expedition.

Most of Baldwin's other Americans were young Midwesterners eager for experience in the Arctic. Ernest de Koven Leffingwell, a talented twenty-five-year-old physicist from the University of Chicago, had served as an able-bodied seaman on board the USS *Oregon* during the Spanish-American War. Charles Rilliet, from St. Louis, Missouri, was an outspoken twenty-three-year-old familiar with the operation of stationary balloons. He was chosen to run Baldwin's imagined "Aeronautical Division." Twenty-year-olds Joseph Hare, Jr., of New Jersey and Herman Andree of Ohio had been chosen for some limited photographic skills, while the latter's name had the fortunate advantage of being the same as Baldwin's Arctic hero. Neither was remotely cut out for a year or two of Arctic isolation.

Medical doctor William Verner, a twenty-five-year-old Pennsylvanian, had a year under his belt of breaking trails in Alaska. Two other Philadelphia doctors, both twenty-three years old, were Charles Seitz and James DeBruler. Seitz and DeBruler were longtime friends and both smoked, but only DeBruler admitted to an occasional drink. Both signed on to the expedition in mid-June, at the very last moment, in what appears to have been a kind of spur-of-the-moment lark for each man.

Leon Barnard, the expedition secretary from Naperville, Illinois, was also twenty-three. He was also concealing the fact that he was Baldwin's cousin, in hopes that he would not suffer from accusations of favoritism. One of Barnard's uncles—who was not on good terms with the expedition leader himself—had already warned Barnard about the hazards of the trip and, prophetically, about Baldwin himself. He reassured his nephew that he was correct to get Baldwin to sign a contract that guaranteed Barnard's services and pay. It was a precaution that would go for naught when, one year later, Baldwin in the wake of the failed expedition willfully refused to honor the side contracts he himself had signed. Still, the uncle sent Barnard off on a hopeful note: "You I hope will come back all covered with *Glory* & the *Pole* you will have a chance to see & learn & with your *contract* . . . you will be all right. . . . Evelyn goes with the best equipped of any party that ever started for the north."[103]

Beginning on July 1, 1901, Barnard's thirty-month contract paid him twenty-five dollars per month, to be paid upon the return of the expedition. To this and all other contracts Baldwin had added a rider, one that should have given pause to every member of the expedition: "For inefficient, disrespectful or disloyal service, the said Barnard agrees to forfeit all claims against the said Baldwin or the Baldwin-Ziegler Expedition."[104]

Besides the scientist Leffingwell, there were two others who would become critically important with regards to the documentation and history of the expedition. These were the surveyor and artist Russell Williams Porter, a thirty-year-old architect and surveyor from Vermont who had studied at the Massachusetts Institute of Technology and had the experience of trips to Greenland, Baffin Island, Labrador, and the Yukon already behind him, and Anthony Fiala, a deeply devout and sweetly naïf thirty-two-year-old from New Jersey who wrote for the *Brooklyn Eagle* and had served in the U.S. Army during the Spanish-American War. Porter would conduct some of the only meaningful surveying work during the expedition and added a series of excellent sketches and watercolors to illustrate the work of the men, while Fiala would record the expedition in still images and motion-picture footage. He went on to be named Baldwin's successor when William Ziegler fired Baldwin in the fall of 1902.

The American members of the expedition were generally slight and short in stature, as was Baldwin himself. Leffingwell and Porter were solidly built men, but DeBruler, Andree, the Kansan Robert Vinyard—these men were typical of the crew in that none of them were over 5 feet 7 inches and none weighed more than 150 lbs. Barnard was tall at 5 feet 10 inches, but weighed only 145 lbs. Fiala was 5 feet 9 inches and barely 150 lbs. A profile of him during the Spanish-American War—written by his own newspaper, no less—described him as a "quiet soldier, gentle as a girl in manner, yet dashing and efficient in the field."[105]

One man who could have helped the expedition immeasurably, both with his genial disposition and polar experience, was Dr. Frederick Cook. There

The crew of the *America* at Dundee. Baldwin is at center left. To his left is the indeterminate Swedish captain/sailing master, Carl Johanson, who seems already to be leaning away from Baldwin. Unresolved disagreements between the two would go a long way to destroying the expedition. From Evelyn Briggs Baldwin, "How I Hope to Reach the North Pole," *The Windsor Magazine* 15 (1): 59–69.

were hints in late May 1901 that Cook might join the expedition, but in the end he elected to stay in Brooklyn and write up the results of the *Belgica* expedition to Antarctica.[106]

The Americans on this "entirely American" expedition were outnumbered 2 to 1 by foreigners, including, with fitting irony, the crew of the *America*. The expedition ship included seventeen Swedes led by thirty-three-year-old sailing master Carl Johanson, who, before he met Baldwin, had worked for publisher Gordon Bennett on board two of the newspaper tycoon's yachts (and therefore indirectly connected Baldwin back to the Bennett-sponsored *Jeannette* disaster). Unlike most of the Americans, a majority of the Swedes were six-footers and averaged nearly 180 pounds. Most of these crew members,

The officers of the *America* pose in front of an American flag. *Front row, left to right:* the American chief engineer, Henry Hartt, and two Swedes, the captain/ sailing master, Carl Johanson, and the second mate, Ralph Bergendahl. The two men behind are unidentified. From Evelyn Briggs Baldwin, "How I Hope to Reach the North Pole," *The Windsor Magazine* 15 (1): 59–69.

including Chief Officer Johan Menander, were smokers and "alcoholists," a term apparently meant to describe an occasional drinker who was not an alcoholic, and most of them lived in and around Göteborg, Sweden. Menander had sailed on board the *Antarctic* with Swedish explorer Alfred G. Nathorst during an 1898 voyage to northeast Greenland in search of the Andrée expedition. A Swedish-American, Carl Sandin, acted as translator.

Two other Scandinavian members of the land party, the young brothers Anton and John Sverdrup Vedoe, had been born in Stockholm to Norwegian parents, but they had lived for several years in Boston. When asked to describe his "weak points," Anton Vedoe replied: "I don't know of any." His "strong points" were "ambition for knowledge."[107]

A boatswain, John Jacobsen, was from Tromsø, Norway, and a young cartographer with some previous Arctic experience and a world of polar ambition was Ejnar Mikkelsen of Denmark. Like Baldwin, Mikkelsen had tried to talk himself into the basket of Andreé's balloon and been rebuffed. With admirable persistence, he had then tried to attach himself to the expeditions of Otto Nordenskjöld, Otto Sverdrup, Carsten Borchgrevink, Adrien de Gerlache, and Eduard von Toll.[108] Mikkelsen and Ernest de Koven Leffingwell soon became fast friends and would later join forces to lead the 1907 Anglo-American Polar Expedition to Alaska's North Slope.[109]

Baldwin was in Europe for much of the month of April, calling at Hamburg, Kiel, Göteborg, Kristiania, Dundee, and London, at "all of which points his presence was required to complete arrangements for the expedition."[110] He again consulted with Ernst Andrée and again promised the Swede a renewed search for his missing brother.

Baldwin was back in New York in mid-May, where he formally announced to the *New York Times* that he would in fact search for Salomon Andrée, as he casually employed what had by now become an accepted part of his *curriculum vitae*: "You know, I suppose, of the narrow escape I had from sharing his fate. Only lack of room prevented me from accompanying him, as I had journeyed to Spitzenberg [*sic*] for that express purpose. Our crew will include a number of Swedish sailors who have at various times served on expeditions sent out for his relief."[111]

It was as if Baldwin had pioneered an alternate pathway to the American Dream, one without the need to prepare for a desired life as an explorer through hard physical work, intellectual thoroughness, or moral integrity. Instead, he merely substituted the persistent publicity of a personal mythology and—*verba non acta*—his Gatsby-like private fantasy of a close association with Salomon Andrée had now become his public reality and opened the door to the north.

This accomplished, Baldwin set out on a round of farewell dinners. Brimming with confidence, he found time to pose for a ridiculous studio photograph. In this, Baldwin was draped in Arctic furs and surrounded by stuffed dogs and holding what was apparently supposed to be a dog whip but was instead a bandmaster's baton. The preposterous image—which Baldwin would with unselfconscious pride employ to illustrate articles for years to come—gave him the unfortunate look of an orchestra leader atop a glacial podium and conducting an invisible orchestra in front of an audience of precisely no one.

More seriously, Baldwin also brimmed with paranoia. He had sworn Ziegler to secrecy with regards to his proposed crew and their intended destination. Ziegler had then compounded this caution with an unfortunate statement in the *Brooklyn Eagle* that was aimed squarely at Walter Wellman. Hoping to keep his exploring persona before the public at a moment when multiple Arctic expeditions were heading into the field—on the odd chance that some Ziegler-like millionaire felt compelled to drop a few thousand dollars in his direction—Wellman had announced in late April that he had purchased another Norwegian vessel and hoped to make another trip to Franz Josef Land.[112]

It was clear that such a voyage was little more than a hope and hardly a serious proposition, not least because Wellman was still recovering from the battering he had endured on the ice east of Rudolf Land in 1899. Yet this mild bit of publicity all too quickly mutated into a bizarre and fantastic rumor—one that could only have been invented and then fueled by Baldwin's growing paranoia—that Wellman not only intended to make another polar attempt from Franz Josef Land, but would do so by following in the wake of the Baldwin-Ziegler expedition and scavenging the supplies that Baldwin would cache there. Such a rumor was guaranteed to incense the proprietary Ziegler, who replied: "we do not wish to place any information of value in the hands of those who are our competitors in the race to the pole. . . .

This Arctic exploration is like playing a game or conducting a campaign. There are lots of other fellows watching every move we make. We cannot afford to give them any advantage in knowing who our party will be.

If a man dares you to knock a chip off his shoulder, don't touch the chip. Hit him squarely between the eyes. That is what we are doing. Mr. Baldwin has to do the work, and I do not feel like telling anything that he does not want told. I have reason to believe that another exploring party is planning to trail us and to live from our supply.

We have a crew of sharpshooters and the first man who lays a hand on anything of ours will be a dead man. I have given Mr. Baldwin emphatic orders on that point. . . .

I do not intend to have any other expedition live from our supplies. I have been credibly informed that there is another polar expedition which will start over the route which we have mapped out at about the same time we are to start, in the hope of using our supplies.[113]

As one might expect, this direct threat to either punch his lights out or shoot him did not go over well with Wellman, and he let Ziegler know it. For his part, Ziegler was completely unfazed. He proudly stood by his threats, like the impervious and untouchable Gilded Age millionaire he assuredly was: "Anyone whom the shoe fits . . . may put it on. It doesn't fit many."[114]

Baldwin, having almost certainly fed Ziegler the idea of Wellman as an Arctic pirate, proceeded to feign any knowledge of the miniature tempest, even as he made an astounding claim of priority to the polar staging grounds of Franz Josef Land. "I have no quarrel with anybody," he told a reporter after the Arctic Club presented him with an American flag at a farewell dinner at the Marlborough Hotel in New York in mid-May. "But I would like to say that it is well known that I selected Franz Josef Land as a starting point at least four years ago."[115]

This comment, from someone who was given his first glimpse of Franz Josef Land by Walter Wellman, was as ungenerous as it was disingenuous. It also served to conceal the real story behind the dust-up: Baldwin was hiding his plans from public view not because he feared they would be stolen, but rather because he had no real plan to reach the North Pole. Baldwin led William Ziegler to believe that the secrecy and obfuscation were necessary to shield their polar plans from greedy importuners, but in fact there were no plans. Ziegler, the shrewd multimillionaire, had bought a pig in a poke, though it would be a year before he realized it.

As for any possible aeronautical element to his plans, Baldwin still offered only vague hints, as he continued to conceal the scope of his aeronautical ambitions in the Arctic along with his own obvious lack of training to carry out any such plan. He continued to fend off questions over whether balloons would be used, and his reluctance to address his experience as a balloonist was understandable, since on the eve of his departure for Franz Josef Land he still had none. In this he was very much unlike his hero Salomon Andrée, who had several cross-country balloon flights to his credit before attempting his North Pole flight from Danskøya. Baldwin's first (and only) flight in a balloon would come the following month, when he made an ascent near St. Louis with his famous aeronaut cousin Thomas S. Baldwin.

Baldwin's last-minute visit to say good-bye to relatives in the Midwest in early June allowed the local newspapers to breathlessly exclaim that "the eyes of two hemispheres, it can be said without exaggeration, are centered upon this Kansas man, who will sail next month on his perilous expedition to the North Pole.

Seen in a crowd of men, Mr. Baldwin would hardly be apt to attract attention. He is a small man physically and unassuming to the point of diffidence. However, there is a world of purpose in the piercing steel gray eyes and the rather English set to the clean-shaven chin is a mark of resolution that is not to be mistaken.[116]

Given his erratic behavior—a tincture of paranoia laced with delusions of grandeur—the "piercing steel gray eyes" can now be seen for what they were, a physical manifest of the increasingly unbalanced mind that the Norwegians had seen in *Susæg* in 1898. It was only at this moment that Baldwin and his clean-shaven chin finally called upon his cousins, the aeronautical experts who ran Baldwin Brothers Balloon Company in Quincy, Illinois. The brothers had made balloons for the World's Columbian Exposition in Chicago, and Baldwin had placed a large order for small message-carrying balloons with them.[117] On June 6, 1901, after posing for a photograph with Thomas S., Samuel Yates Baldwin, and Ivy Baldwin, near their giant balloon *Mars*, Evelyn Briggs Baldwin made his very first (and apparently the only) balloon ascent of his life.

Baldwin's order for and shipment of forty balloons—along with two hydrogen generators and dozens of tiny message-carrying buoys that would be carried by them—did not include the participation in the expedition of any of his aeronautically experienced cousins. As with his hurried purchase of a single motor launch, Baldwin's procurement of so many message-carrying balloons has the feel of a half-formed thought, a sudden inspiration that, given the rushed preparations for the expedition, had not been properly thought through.

Baldwin had also ordered a series of larger buoys, modeled on the message buoys used by Andrée. These had been produced for Baldwin at the Wiklunds Mekaniska Verkstad (Wiklund's Engineering Firm) in Stockholm.[118] It is likely that Baldwin had placed his order for these larger buoys during his trip to Sweden earlier in the year, possibly before he even knew quite what he would do with them. Such seemingly random purchases—enabled by the luxury of Ziegler's unlimited budget but made in haste without much thought given to their purpose—were the rule for Baldwin during the frenetic spring of 1901, and seemed designed to do little more than satisfy Baldwin's need to link himself to the Swedish balloon expedition.

Emboldened by his first taste of aerial exploration, Baldwin finally let slip some of his plans to the Chicago newspapers. This was the first public notice that Baldwin planned to combine balloons with message buoys into a single balloon-buoy system. In keeping with his strange variant on the American Dream, this system, the articles made clear, would not be used to carry the expedition northward but to deliver expedition publicity southward.[119] The unmanned balloons would "mark the path of the expedition," though Baldwin failed to explain how he intended to set up new hydrogen-generating stations at each stopping point in the islands of Franz Josef Land, much less while the expedition was on the move over the ice.

> To each will be attached ten [large, Swedish] buoys, ten feet apart, hanging one below the other, weighing ten pounds each and arranged with a liberator for detaching the buoys one at a time as they strike the earth.
>
> Each buoy will contain a message, showing the latitude whence the balloon was sent up, and such other word as the explorers care to leave behind.
>
> The buoys are made of copper and cord and are shaped like a top. In the center is a hollow space which will contain the messages. When a certain amount of gas has escaped the balloon will descend. As soon as it gets near enough to the earth for the buoys to strike, the lower one is detached and, liberated from its weight, the balloon at once begins another ascent. This operation is repeated automatically until all the buoys have been dropped.[120]

While the logistics of inflating balloons at more than one location would render the whole project impossible, the basic notion of using balloons to carry messages in the Arctic was not as preposterous as it sounds today. Guglielmo Marconi's first transatlantic wireless transmission was still six months away—it would in fact take place when Baldwin was in winter quarters in Franz Josef Land. Until then, Baldwin was left with a system of message transmission that would leave hundreds of cork buoys scattered across the Arctic, to await random and quite unpredictable retrievals. Many would not be discovered for decades.

For Baldwin, the balloons were a critical component of what he now described as his life's work. As he told a reporter, "I will never return until the North pole ghost is laid forever. It is my life work, and unless the expedition is a success civilization will have seen me for the last time."[121] These were strong words and, in less than four months, Baldwin would be forced to eat them.

TWENTY-FIVE

The Dogs Are Becoming Uncomfortable

Baldwin and the other Americans of the expedition began arriving in Dundee, Scotland, in late June 1901. While waiting for others to show, Dr. Verner and artist-surveyor Russell Porter took the opportunity to rent bicycles and enjoy "a glorious week" touring from Aberdeen to Balmoral.[122] Expedition secretary Barnard, along with DeBruler and Vinyard, arrived in Dundee via London, where they had enjoyed a five-day holiday before Baldwin arrived to retrieve them. It was enough time for Barnard to take in *Faust*, *Othello*, and a play in which Henry Irving portrayed King Charles I. While he failed "to find anything agreeable to eat," Barnard nevertheless "enjoyed every moment of the time, however, and completely changed my whole attitude toward the British people and would not have any other as parent of Uncle Sam."[123]

In Dundee, the Americans met for the first time with the Swedes in charge of sailing the *America* to Franz Josef Land. It was also where Baldwin created the first of the innumerable fissures that would soon fracture the expedition. Once the whole combined crew had been assembled, Baldwin suddenly placed new and separate personal services contracts before them. These new contracts bound the men to Baldwin himself, not William Ziegler or the Baldwin-Ziegler Polar Expedition. They forbade any expedition member to bring on board or use any photographic apparatus, or to write or lecture on any aspect of the expedition. They further specified that permission to do so "shall only be granted by the Commander of the Expedition, Evelyn B. Baldwin. . . . This we fully understand and agree is embraced in the terms of our several contracts and agreements, whether written or verbal, in connection with said expedition."[124] Three thousand miles from home, with little or no money to return if they disagreed with the new terms, the men were obliged to sign the new documents.

At twelve minutes before midnight on Friday, June 28, 1901, the *America* left her dock in Dundee bound for the Norwegian Arctic port of Tromsø. Captained and crewed by Swedes, the *America* flew the Stars and Stripes and the emblem of the New York Yacht Club. Leon Barnard, for one, was almost overcome, and moved to quote Oliver Wendell Holmes.

> Never have I taken part in or seen a more calmly beautiful, deeply significant, solemnly sad-and-yet tremendously enthusiastic scene than was here presented. . . . The night had drawn its garment of darkness, it had indeed "buttoned it with stars" and they shown with a luster and brilliancy to be found only in the depths of the black canopy of heaven itself on a clear night. The full moon, high in the sky and directly opposite the dock, flooded everything with a light all its own—softening and mellowing into itself every slight ruffle on the quiet bay. The gentlest of zephyrs came in from the sea, and this, together with the momentum of the ship, caused the flags to stand out in relief against the starry background of unbroken space. Under these conditions the destinies of another polar expedition rode out upon the tender mercies of the future.[125]

While the *America* departed for Tromsø, Baldwin himself left the expedition and went to Kristiania. There, on July 6, he issued orders to Johan Bryde, the captain of a third chartered vessel, *Belgica,* to land caches of supplies on the coast of northeast Greenland, in the event that Baldwin returned in that direction after reaching the North Pole. In addition to the supplies, *Belgica* would carry prefabricated houses made by the firm of F. O. Peterson in Göteborg, the same company that built the prefabricated balloon house erected by the Andrée expedition at Virgohamn—and yet another chance for Baldwin to link himself to Salomon Andrée.

In directing where and how many of the expedition's supplies should be cached in Greenland, Baldwin ordered that two separate depot of provisions be landed on Koldewey and Shannon Islands. At the first chosen site, Bryde was to erect the first two of the F. O. Peterson huts. These would store the expedition's perishable goods. A third hut would be placed at the second site.

The lists of the supplies carried by the *Belgica* reveal the scope of Baldwin's fantastic itinerary from the previous winter and spring, when he made repeated journeys around the United States and to Europe to make contacts and contracts with William Ziegler's money: dozens of boxes of Swedish conserves from Sveriges förenade konservfabriker AB in Lysekil—said to be the largest order a Swedish cannery had ever received—the Peterson expedition huts, and over a hundred boxes of other sundries ordered from shipping agent Borlind, Bersén and Co in Göteborg, medicines from the United Kingdom, army rations from Armour in Kansas City, Kansas, four boxes of flags from Astrup and Smith in Kristiania—all of this to go along with thirty tons of coal.[126]

At the northernmost depot, Bryde was to leave behind two kayaks and a case of Kabo coffee; at the southernmost, two whaleboats and a packet of charts and some personal packages for Baldwin. Notices were to be left up and down the coast in both Norwegian and English.[127]

To top all this off, Bryde was to deposit at the Greenland stations several more hermetically sealed balloons from the Baldwin Brothers, along with the vats of acid and iron filings shipped from Dundee that were required to create hydrogen gas for them. The acid and metal for the prospective balloon inflation operations in Greenland and Franz Josef Land had only been ordered in late June, along with instructions given to Baldwin on how to use the correct ratios to create the greatest amount of hydrogen gas. It was another example of an extremely complex operation being left to the very last minute.[128]

By mid-July, the combined American and Swedish crew on board the *America* had arrived in Tromsø for a rendezvous with *Belgica*. There were several tourist steamers in port, so in between loading the mass of supplies on board the *America,* the men enjoyed the rounds of the port as well as invited dinners on board the tourist ships.

On the evening of July 16, *America* and *Belgica* weighed anchor and, with one flying the Star and Stripes and the other the Norwegian flag, steamed off toward the north. *America* sailed for its rendezvous with the expedition's other supply vessel, Walter Wellman's old expedition ship *Frithjof,* while *Belgica* shaped a course toward the islands of northeast Greenland. The other vessels in the Tromsø roadstead gave the small fleet a parting cheer.

Flush with cash, men, ships, and supplies, Baldwin was in jubilant spirits. He had just picked up an experienced Norwegian ice pilot by the name of Magnus Arnesen and, just two years after his ignominious retreat from Franz Josef Land, he was leading a massive American polar expedition back toward an Arctic staging area he knew well. His ships groaned under their burdens of food, supplies, and equipment, including the shipment of hermetically sealed balloons and the vats of acid and crates of iron filings that would create the hydrogen required to send them aloft and fulfill Baldwin's Arctic aeronautical fantasies.

At Honningsvaag, in the extreme northeast corner of Norway's Arctic coast, the *America* met with the *Frithjof,* which would accompany the main expedition ship to Franz Josef Land. This small convoy proceeded to Archangel in northern Russia, where Baldwin marked his thirty-ninth birthday on July 22.

In Russia, the expedition procured 428 dogs and 15 ponies, as well as 6 Siberian Russians who would attend to them. All were loaded upon the already overloaded vessels. The local British proconsul then gave the crew a dinner with vodka toasts and several varieties of wine and cigars. *Frithjof,* with Long and DeBruler seconded to it, left the mainland and proceeded to Franz Josef Land ahead of the main expedition ship.

By the end of July, the expedition, totaling an unwieldy forty-two members speaking a dozen dialects of at least four different languages, was back on the coast of northern Norway, from where it took its final departure from the port of Vardø on July 27. The rough and dirty conditions on board *America* had already led to the death of one of the dogs, as the decks were not washed down nearly often enough to account for the urine and feces produced by so many tightly packed, highly strung, exercise-deprived work dogs and ponies. One of the doctors, Charles Seitz, immediately realized that the dogs were in for a very tough turn: "[The expedition's dogs] are too crowded—the decks are filthy & are not cleaned enough; & they do not get enough water to drink. Several dogs are sick—weak & trembling. One is nearly dead this evening having convulsions like the others that died."[129]

Two more of the dogs went mad and died soon after, at the same time that several others began to convulse and show other signs of general distress. Baldwin himself was under the weather, but not on account of the sea state. Engineer Hartt visited the bridge at midnight on July 31 and, finding Baldwin staggering under the influence of liquor, was forced to carry the expedition leader down to his cabin.[130] Combined with the general seasickness of the Americans as the overburdened ship rolled northward, it was an inauspicious departure from civilization.

In mid-August the *America* arrived at Cape Flora at the western end of Northbrook Island. There the men toured the ruins of structures left by the previous British explorations led by Benjamin Leigh Smith and Frederick Jackson. Barnard looked upon the site "as tho on holy ground" with a mixture of wonder and dread, the "few, little storm-beaten huts huddled together a short distance up from the beach and there swept over us a sense of the desolation and isolation of this seemingly God-forsaken spot and the whole archipelago."[131]

Arriving in the archipelago well ahead of the *America,* the *Frithjof* had already been at Cape Flora for two weeks. The Norwegians of *Frithjof* had already stashed three and a half tons of meat at Cape Flora from the slaughter of thirty-two walrus and several bears, and then left two days before the slower *America* turned up. Within two days of the *America*'s arrival, the men of the two vessels would kill another two-dozen walrus and several more bears. Archibald Dickson, interviewed about the expedition thirty years later by the *San Francisco Chronicle,* claimed that the Russian icebreaker *Ermak* even showed up at Cape Flora to greet the *Frithjof,* "having been ordered by the Czar of Russia at St. Petersburg to contact with the expedition."[132] Seven dogs were now dead, with more becoming sick every day.

From Cape Flora, Baldwin directed the ships into the maze of channels that separated the islands of south central Franz Josef Land, where Walter Wellman, aboard *Capella* in 1899, had picked out numerous islands to name after the patrons of his expedition. It was also here, in August 1901, where Baldwin's plan, such as it was, ran aground, and more completely than Baldwin ever realized then or, in fact, for the rest of his life. The whole point of bringing so many men and such a large tonnage of supplies into the islands was to have a ship deliver them to the highest latitude possible, in particular to try and imitate the Duke of the Abruzzi's expedition in reaching Rudolf Land by ship, to take advantage of the northernmost point of land in Franz Josef Land for the anticipated dash for the pole.

Instead, Baldwin found the many channels between the islands frustratingly blocked by ice. On August 18, the expedition arrived at the western edge of a small island, six miles by two. Barnard wrote in his diary that the island was as yet unnamed, which he could have only heard from Baldwin, who in turn had to have known that Walter Wellman in 1899 had already named it after Secretary of War Russell A. Alger as Wellman's retreating expedition steamed around it in the *Capella*.

With his progress northward blocked, Baldwin ordered one of the medical doctors on board to grab a pencil and notebook and accompany him ashore on Alger Island in search of a suitable spot to establish a supply station. A whale boat was lowered from *America* and Baldwin, along with the doctor, as well as Fiala, Barnard, Arnesen, and several Swedish sailors, rowed to a shoreline that no recorded human had ever set foot upon. The spot was "covered with moss with clusters of yellow flowers (the Arctic poppy) scattered here and there in little clusters, gave both life and cheerfulness to the place, which otherwise was void of all signs of vegetation.

> Coming directly from warmer climes this floral life of the Arctics is truly astonishing. Here on this narrow slope grow these beautiful little yellow flowers giving life and summer to the scene, while five hundred yards above a creeping glacier of ice and snow is forcing its way into the sea.

Mr. Baldwin was evidently pleased with the spot. The only shadow reflected upon his face from his mind, after a glance around, was that no pools of fresh water were in sight. A suitable location for the station must of necessity have fresh water, and after a short consultation with Pilot Arnesen, Mr. Baldwin decided to be rowed back to the *America,* by way of the *Frithjof,* which was afloat near, to give the captains of both steamers instructions to follow if signaled, as he intended to row farther up the coast in search of a place where water could be found.[133]

Baldwin had the two ships follow the coast of the island a bit further, but when he found no other suitable spot, he ordered a return to their first landing, "with the intention of establishing a station there, digging a small artificial pond, or reservoir, which would soon fill with rain and snow water."[134] This place had been in Baldwin's mind for weeks, as he made clear in a letter to William S. Champ on July 16. But, in a list of preferred places to establish a winter camp, Alger Island was no more than Baldwin's *sixth* choice.[135] A minuscule islet, found just offshore from the site of the new camp, Baldwin named Matilda Island.[136]

The off-loading began the next day at what Baldwin would soon name Camp Ziegler. Anton Vedoe, who like several other expedition members had been discouraged by Baldwin from keeping a diary, kept one anyway. His Scandinavian language entries, written on tissue paper, were bound up with rivets or string. His notes relate that—just as it had been for Wellman's crew in the fall of 1898—the exercise of moving a pack of dogs from ship to boat to shore and then securing them once ashore, proved almost too much for the men:

> The dogs are becoming uncomfortable aboard, were taken today ashore. There was a dragging and hauling of the poor animals, who seemed quite happy once they found themselves freed from the unpleasant captivity. We had some difficulties in getting the first boats ashore. It was not easy to control the dogs, and more than one got a bath in the cold water. As soon as they saw the possibility of reaching land, they jumped into the water and swam one after another. Well ashore, they ran towards the snow for a deserved bath. Some, whose joints were not too stiff, sped toward the highest mountain top where they curled up and rolled like balls down the steep snow-covered slope to again be captured and tied to wires which we placed at the foot of the mountain.[137]

The following day, August 19, the unloading at Camp Ziegler continued as a storm hit the island. As Vedoe and others watched from shore, several boats began to be swept away by the increasing winds. It was the first of many indications that, in only bringing one steam yacht, Baldwin had repeated Wellman's mistake of relying on rowing craft. As with Wellman, this reliance almost ended in an early disaster. It was also the first time that Barnard, on board one of the small boats with Baldwin, could not fail to note the terror in his expedition leader's eyes as the boats began to drift away. As Vedoe recorded the scene:

> We had [just] got four boatloads ashore, and the last two were just on their way when the storm became so violent that they were powerless with the oars and just drifted farther away. Watching from land it seemed quite dangerous. When they started to wave their caps asking for help, two of us jumped in a boat and started to row toward the one in distress. Another boat left from our ship and, going in the same direction as the wind, it soon arrived there. After some tough

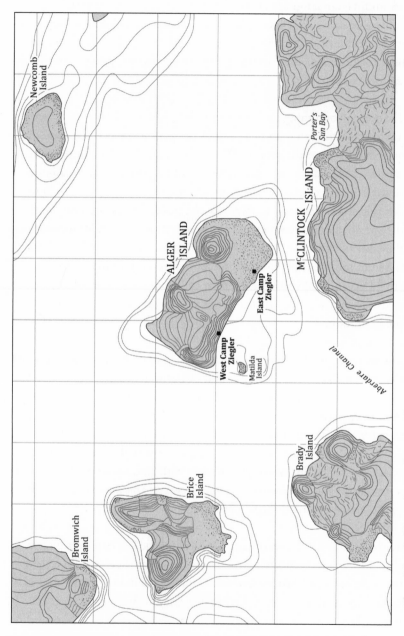

Alger Island. Chart drawn from modern Russian cartography, to show the locations of West and East Camp Ziegler, as well as the proximity of Aberdare Channel, Porter's "Sun Bay," and McClintock Island, where both Baldwin's and Fiala's men would seek and find rescue. *Copyright © 2016 The University of Oklahoma Press. All rights reserved.*

rowing, we also reached the boys fighting for their lives. The two boats carried a heavy load, and after we had fastened a rope from our boat and with united efforts tried to move toward land, we found it was to no avail. We just drifted farther and farther away. When we had worked for about an hour, soaking wet from the waves and with no progress, we noticed that *Frithjof* started to move. She had lifted anchor and now came to our rescue. *Frithjof* took us back to *America* where we were delighted to exchange the wet cold clothes for clean and dry ones. After dinner we tried again to reach land in order to raise the houses, but in vain.[138]

The weather moderated and the men were soon able to get ashore again and raise one of the expedition's huts. After this, since *Frithjof* was soon to return to Norway, the men were engaged in the dirty work of creeping through bunkers on hands and knees to retrieve the supplies of coal in the depths of the supply vessel. In a severe blow to the expedition's crew, Francis Long, forty-nine years old and the only member of the expedition besides Baldwin with the experience of overwintering in the high Arctic, took this moment to return on board the *Frithjof.* A member of the *Frithjof* crew, a Hungarian named Lukas Wirth, exchanged places with Long and remained behind in Franz Josef Land.

Baldwin had now unloaded the bulk of his supplies at the camp on the southwestern corner of Alger Island. Yet, even with the construction of Camp Ziegler, he was acutely aware that a failure to move the supplies farther north would be fatal to any attempt on the pole the following spring. It would be 1898 all over again, when he failed to push out Wellman's advance hut even half as far as Wellman had ordered. Accordingly, Baldwin took every opportunity to climb the hills of Alger Island to check the ice conditions further afield. It wasn't long before he was rewarded.

On August 22 Baldwin ascended the heights behind Camp Ziegler and saw only a thin belt of rotten ice around Alger Island. Beyond this, he saw open water as far as the eye could see. Given the time of the year, this was to be expected, even anticipated, and constituted the perfect conditions for a breakout by the ship. Baldwin returned to the camp and ordered all the men and supplies back on board the ship. He told them that the *America* would be put into winter quarters much farther north. With the *Frithjof* departing the next day, there was no time to lose.

The small camp on the southwest corner of Alger Island would remain as a small emergency supply depot. There the men had already rigged up a fireplace and barrel for melting ice. As Vedoe wrote, "the boys will be fairly comfortable, although lonely. Dr. [*sic*] S. Winyard [Vinyard] and the Hungarian machinist from *Frithjof,* [Lukas], who will stay with us, and three of the Russians are chosen to be left at the Camp. For how long, no one knows."[139] One of the Swedish officers, Svante Rudolf (Ralph) Bergendahl, also volunteered to remain behind at the camp.[140]

When its supplies were finally off-loaded the next day, August 23, the *Frithjof* circled offshore a few times and then swung by the port side of the *America* to say goodbye. The Norwegians were apparently happy to make their escape, as just before departure Ejnar Mikkelsen overheard a blazing row between Baldwin and Johan Kjeldsen, the formidable captain of the *Frithjof.*[141]

William S. Champ, Ziegler's major-domo who had accompanied the expedition as far as Franz Josef Land to keep an eye on things, was on board the *Frithjof* as it began its long return south. He carried with him six tins of motion-picture film to be delivered to the Warwick Trading Company in London for development.

Champ also carried with him another venomous denunciation of Walter Wellman, one that would make the rounds of American newspapers that fall. After describing his journey to Franz Josef Land, Champ told reporters that the Ziegler expedition had found the conditions in the islands "more favorable for the dash to the pole than Mr. Baldwin had dared expect," a dubious suggestion with little evidence on the ground to support it. Champ then "intimated that there might be some misunderstandings with Walter Wellman, who is conducting a polar expedition over practically the same route."[142] Even after seeing Baldwin all the way to Franz Josef Land, Champ and, presumably, Ziegler, were still looking over their shoulders at the nonexistent threat from Baldwin's former commander.

Baldwin rarely let such moments as the departure of *Frithjof* pass without an ostentatious demonstration of his knowledge of the forms of the explorer, and this was no exception. Barnard, who had no experience with which to judge the moment and who still believed he was taking down the critical early moments of the first expedition that would reach the North Pole, recorded it dutifully:

As [*Frithjof*] came abreast, B., standing on our bridge, called out in a voice full of feeling and of meaning, "Gentlemen of both the *Frithjof* and of the *America,* three cheers for William Ziegler of New York!" I do not need here to note that the hills of Alger Island and the lone, barren rock composing Matilda re-echoed to our hearty response!—it came from the bottom of every heart, not only for, and on behalf of the man on the bridge, but also for our country and ourselves. The *Frithjof* made a wide circle round us, as we lay at anchor, and again passed as before. As she did so, Champ, Mr. Ziegler's private secretary, who had been with the *Frithjof* many weeks—at Tromsoe and afterward—shouted from her bridge, "Gentlemen of the *Frithjof,* three cheers for Mr. Baldwin"; and after they were given, B. responded, "Gentlemen of the *America*," three cheers for Champ.[143]

With this, the Norwegian vessel disappeared and the sound of its engine gradually died away, as Long remained on her stern, "waving the Stars and Stripes in encouragement and God-speed."[144] Without the experienced Long or the tightly connected Champ, Baldwin was now left to his own devices with no one else who possessed either the experience or the gravitas to challenge his authority. It was now that the first of the strange incidents took place that was to begin the sea change in the men's perception of Baldwin and lead to what can only be described as the strangest American polar expedition ever.

Having been handed more men and supplies than any Arctic explorer since Sir John Franklin, Baldwin now began to exhibit an increasingly disturbing inability to do anything with them. Baldwin told the men that the *America* would start its breakout northward the day after *Frithjof*'s departure. The next morning, as the crew waited expectantly, Baldwin failed to emerge from his cabin. While the crew looked for things to do, "Baldwin remained in his cabin all that day and the next, and the next and the next."[145] It was five full days, on August 28, before the expedition leader reappeared on deck, claiming a severe cold.

The loss of these precious days, filled with constant daylight hours when the expedition's vast tonnage of supplies could potentially have been moved all the way to the very northern edge of the archipelago at Rudolf Land, was fatal. By the time the ship was finally put to sea on August 28, Baldwin ordered it proceed not northward, but *southeast,* and toward Wellman's old base camp at Cape Tegetthoff. So began a series of such maddening side trips that the increasingly bewildered crew labeled "the mail route."[146]

The second mate Bergendahl recorded that the men went ashore on the southwest corner of McClintock Island on September 1, where Baldwin left behind an American flag and a bottle stuffed with letters and gave the spot the name of Cape Dillon.[147] Unbeknownst to the men, who thought they had signed up for an expedition to the North Pole, they were in fact at the opening stages of Baldwin's yearlong effort to drop favored place-names wherever he could find a previously unclaimed bit of geography.

When not steaming aimlessly back and forth to Cape Tegetthoff, the men were put to work to load, and then unload, and then load again, supplies from the holds of *America*. They responded by initiating a derisive expedition newspaper, the *Midnight Sun,* edited by a "Petty Officer Larbear," a play on "POlar Bear." Baldwin soon forbade any further publication.[148]

By the time Baldwin finally made a tentative move north, the ice was again so thick the *America* could not force a way through it. So began thirty days during which the vessel "vainly endeavoured to find a way farther north.

> The British Channel—which two years previous was open early in August and permitted the Italian Expedition, under the Duke of the Abruzzi, to steam even beyond the eighty-second parallel—remained heavily blocked this year with ice throughout the whole of the month of August. This was equally true of Markham Sound; while the ice in that portion of Austria Sound between Hall Island and Wilczek Land remained as impregnable as in the dead of winter.[149]

During all this steaming back and forth, Baldwin did nothing to improve his standing with the men when he placed rations first on butter, then on sugar and, finally and most painfully, on tobacco. Frantic betting with these commodities soon commenced in earnest. Only Hartt, with his access to the scarce supply of washing water in the boiler room, could name his own price and therefore got his daily bread buttered and sweetened. Through late August, through all of September, and even into early October, Baldwin tried to force the ship through the ice that surrounded Alger Island. Fourteen separate attempts were made to cross to the opposite side of Markham Sound. This was especially frustrating as the men could walk across the hummocks of ice eastward toward Austria Sound and see open channels of water leading northward. As one of the medical doctors, most likely DeBruler, wrote on September 9:

> In the morning it snowed a little so that we had to remain in our safe harbor. But in the afternoon it cleared and the sun shone on the most beautiful landscape imaginable. There lay the snow-covered ice floes and glittered like diamond-fields in the sunshine, and in the horizon rose high snow-covered ridges and icebergs alternating with silvery belts of open water, all tinted with varying hues of all kinds. Again we went out into the open sea and made unsuccessful attempts to break the ice-belt that separates us from Austria Sound where we have discovered open water as far as the eye can reach to the north. However, we had to turn around.[150]

If ever there were an opportune moment for a small flying expedition using the gasoline-powered launch, this was it. But despite the best efforts and curses of Chief Engineer Hartt, the machine could not be made to work.

With the failure to break out to the north, Baldwin ordered several attempts to round the southeastern corner of the archipelago in the *America*. He had a close knowledge of this area from the discovery and exploration of Graham Bell Land in 1899 and should have known that any such effort was doomed from the start. Indeed, in the area of Salm Island, the *America* went aground and was only extricated with great difficulty when the crew shifted the vessel's cargo and waited on an incoming tide.

There cannot be any doubt that Baldwin wanted to establish an advance camp on Rudolf Land, after having failed to do so in 1898 and witnessing the disastrous results firsthand. Any expedition that left its advance work undone in the fall was doomed in the spring. But Baldwin never let on to his men that the failure to do so would not only kill any hopes the expedition had of making a serious attempt at the North Pole in the spring of 1902. Worse, such failure would also require the men to do the work of the ship. The *America* could have easily carried the men and dogs and ponies and the tonnage of supplies the 100 nautical miles from Alger Island to Rudolf Land. Now, on account of Baldwin's mysterious five-day absence during the high days of August, every last pound of those supplies would have to be carried across ice and snow and scree slopes by the men, the ponies, and the dogs.

Baldwin never did tell his men this fact directly. But his seemingly bizarre announcement in mid-September—that he would return to Norway for the winter with the *America* and leave Leffingwell and Verner in charge of Camp Ziegler, along with any volunteers who wished to remain behind—should have given them a clue. The North Pole was off, certainly in 1902. No serious attempt could be launched until 1903 at the earliest. The year 1902 would be given over to a back-breaking struggle to move supplies over snow drifts and ice hummocks atop sledges pulled by a sick and dwindling pack of dogs.

Far worse even than this, the men were soon and steadily losing their faith that Baldwin even knew what he was doing. Their leader had begun to exhibit the bizarre, almost comedic quirks of behavior that had doomed Bernt Bentsen in 1898 and now began to lead his men right up the edges of catastrophe. As described by Anton Vedoe, Baldwin took a rifle and led a small party up the hill behind Camp Ziegler, where they were "hindered by a vertical mountain wall which was a few meters high and ended in a plateau.

> When Mr. B. got his head over the top, he saw two playing bears. He immediately asked the others to crouch and to keep quiet. Then he gave each bear a bullet and shot a third one. Both bears were injured and furious. He had emptied his magazine and had only cartridges left. The others hurried toward him, but Mr. B. asked them to rush to the boat. They ran and tumbled over each other. Fiala today had visible marks after the somersault, and Barnard feels sore all over.[151]

In the chaos, Fiala had slipped and fallen headlong among the rocks and received cuts to this forehead and left temple. Barnard wrote that "B's excitement was a great surprise to us below him."[152] They had all assumed that the self-advertised Arctic expert would be able to handle a routine encounter with a polar bear with a bit more assurance. As if this *opera bouffe* weren't enough for one day, Baldwin took a pot shot at a bear on the ice but, again, did not kill it, so the men were sent across rotten ice in an attempt to corral the bear. Just as they reached the animal, Baldwin sent another bullet through it and the mortally wounded animal fell and crashed through the ice, nearly taking the men with it. For Vedoe, the episode ended as it now seemed all such episodes were ending on the expedition, with a staged photograph of the men astride the dead animal.

Similar scenes from the almost continuous hunt for game had already become commonplace for the men who had never experienced the Arctic before this moment. As soon as the ships had arrived in Franz Josef Land, the slaughter of the local wildlife had commenced in earnest. One of the medical doctors, most likely DeBruler on board *Frithjof,* recorded the scene when the ship encountered a group of walrus in late July.

At about noon three walruses were sighted a short ways from the boat asleep on an ice floe. Again we crept close up to them and fire was opened at about 100 yards. Although every shot struck all three beasts got into the water. The captain now ordered out the boats. Two boats put out from the ship 4 men in each and working their way between the broken ice towards the point where the walrus had come up to blow out clouds of blood, prepared to harpoon them. . . . Shot after shot was fired into [one of the walrus'] head on the ice & still he lived & tried to escape, belching out great streams of blood. When he finally fell over we found his skull literally broken into fragments so the pieces grated together upon moving the tusks. I never saw anything live so persistently as he.[153]

For Barnard, who thus far had successfully concealed the fact that he was Baldwin's relation, the idea that his previously idolized and famous cousin might not be as advertised had struck hard at his tough but young and impressionable psyche. "B. has been a conundrum to me during the last few weeks (in one way or another ever since New York)," he wrote in his diary on September 11, 1901:

For years I have been firmly convinced that he is the man of all others to discover the North Pole; that the name he bears is entitled to just that. In my way I have believed that his ambition to do this lay heavily on his heart, almost warping it at times; in fact, even to my own intense nature, he has seemed extreme in this, as I knew him in other relations. But in the actual working out of the thing, one is able to see but few evidences of such a deep feeling. If his heart bleeds in this daily postponement, he shows so little of it that it is surprising really. . . . It may be that his taking so complete control of everything all along, even to the minutest detail, is explained by his wanting thereby to drown anxiety by over-occupying himself—I hope the cure don't prove worse than the disease.[154]

As expedition secretary, Barnard was a faithful aide to Baldwin, but he was no toady. He worked hard, prudently kept a low profile, and wisely kept his ear to the ground. He already knew that the more experienced expedition members like Leffingwell and Porter thought too much time was being wasted going after walrus and seals and far too little trying to force the ship further north. With the late summer state of the ice changing rapidly, the ship needed to be positioned to take advantage of every lead north, since such leads could close just as rapidly as they appeared. What the crew did not—and could not as yet—realize, was that for all his previous Arctic experience, Baldwin knew nothing about ships or the even more specialized skill of ice navigation. The Swedes, especially the experienced Chief Officer Menander, as well as the Norwegian ice pilot Arnesen, should have been able to help, but they were at the mercy of Baldwin's conflicting operational orders as well as Baldwin's nascent power struggle with the *America*'s captain, Johanson. "But I dare say," Barnard wrote, "B. knows why he is getting so much fresh meat for the dogs at this time." Even as these words appeared, Barnard continued, teasing out a thought that most of the men now harbored: "I want to say somewhere here, however, that into the mind of every American with us, has slowly, but surely, stolen the realization, and there are many to whom it did not occur before, that even the Baldwin-Ziegler Polar Expedition *may fail.*"[155]

TWENTY-SIX

The Naked Future Is Nude Indeed

On the evening of September 11, a few hours after Barnard had written down his first forebodings, the *America* rounded Cape Frankfurt and open water was seen a far way north in Austria Sound. Baldwin once again ordered the ship turned around and returned to Alger Island, where almost everyone and everything was once again loaded on board for another attempt north. The effect was instantaneous: "Joy unbounded!" was Barnard's comment. It took the better part of twenty-four hours, but by 7 P.M. on September 12, the ship was again loaded with men, dogs, ponies, and supplies; messages written to "Finder" were scattered everywhere.

The ship rounded Cape Tegetthoff, probing its way north. But once again, no sooner had the attempt began than the ice moved in and a thick belt of it, nearly a mile wide, blocked any progress. Frustrated, Baldwin ordered the ship back to Alger Island, where on September 17 the anchor was dropped once again. The sudden spike in the men's hopes just one week earlier was now just as quickly dashed and the expedition again lapsed into demoralization.

It had been a month since the departure of *Frithjof,* and with no progress to show for the men's efforts, ill feelings began to surface. Barnard recorded that the overbearing manner of the Swedish captain, Johanson, made him "heartily disliked by all the sailors. Allied to all this, there somehow sprang up in his mind a misconceived notion of his position in the Expedition— relative to the Americans and to all in general."[156] As he would so often in the expedition, Barnard had placed his finger directly onto a major problem. This "misconceived notion," one that Baldwin unforgivably allowed to fester for six months, was to cause untold grief both in Franz Josef Land and as soon as the expedition returned to Norway. There was no question, even to a Midwestern buckwheater like Barnard, that Johanson should never have been hired and that either the ice pilot Arnesen or, to a lesser degree, the chief officer Menander, would have been a better choice for the command of the *America*.

Events soon reached a head. For days, Baldwin had hinted that he might leave a few men at Camp Ziegler and return to Norway. Barnard was appalled. Such talk of retreat "sound[s] queerly to my ears. I wonder what the newspapers—what our friends—would say if they could look in upon us here now in almost the same spot where the *Frithjof* bade us farewell and from whose decks everything looked so promising."[157]

What Barnard could not know at that moment was that no one back home in the United States could be bothered to give a moment's thought to the fate of the Baldwin-Ziegler Expedition. They were directly obsessed with the fate the nation itself, after the seemingly inexplicable assassination on September 6 of the popular President William McKinley—the very progenitor of the American empire, a bulwark of big business, and the eponymous inspiration for a low-walled stone fort on a remote cape in Franz Josef Land.[158]

Another sudden view of open water on the September 18 had the men temporarily excited. But by now they were getting used to their surroundings and took it in stride. When both gunpowder and explosive guncotton failed to break a way through the ice, the *America* once again returned to Alger Island.

Other failures also weighed on the men. The steam launch—the lack of which had been so keenly felt and so often noted during the Wellman expedition—was found to be useless, despite the best and most profane efforts of Hartt to coax it to life. The expedition was again paying the price for Baldwin's insistence on carrying a piece of unproven technology into an unforgiving environment, without coherent plans of either how to employ it or to fix it when it broke down. "This steam launch has a history," lamented Barnard, "it won't work.

> Mr. Hartt, the engineer, worked hard and long at it but failed to make
> a favorable impression upon it. For a long time it was a risky thing to
> even pass him while at work there. Every few minutes he would cuss
> the atmosphere into a foamy sea and throw out a look that would give

us an idea of what the approaching night might be like. . . . With our appearance at Tromsoe, Master Ralph Shainwald came to the front and proceeded to show the engineer of the *America* a thing or two—among others, when the time was ripe, how to fix up a half-cocked steam launch, with nothing, in the Arctic. Hartt may be an engineer but he is not a mechanic; Shainwald may be an inventor, but he don't know everything. Under the circumstances it was the funniest thing I ever saw.[159]

Hartt finally spat at the machine and gave up. On September 9, as Bergendahl recorded in his diary, the motor was removed from the launch and thereafter the empty hull was used for salting hides in.[160]

By now it was clear not only that the expedition had failed in its primary purpose of placing its base camp on Rudolf Land, but that the expedition leader intended to desert the men for the winter. Even today, no one really knows why Baldwin chose to leave several of his men behind on Alger Island and make a run for it back to Norway and New York. Baldwin was a natural-born fantasist, if not worse, so any analysis of his behavior has to be approached sideways, since for all his eventual special pleading he himself never did write his planned narrative of the expedition. And it was that "narrative" that now led to the final severance of Baldwin from the esteem of his men.

Baldwin began by asking a half a dozen of the men if they would stay in Franz Josef Land for the winter, ostensibly to guard the supplies and dogs and ponies while he returned to organize a new effort the following summer. Several agreed, so Baldwin went to Barnard and told him he could either stay with the men who remained or sail back to Norway with the ship and remain on board in Tromsø over the winter, all while Baldwin went home to New York. Once again, Barnard was floored: "All this was so new, so unexpected, and so pregnant with far more than I shall state here, that I refrained from giving an immediate answer." When Baldwin told Barnard that this was his chance "to get into the history of the Expedition," Barnard reacted almost violently. "This does not appeal to me at all!

I am not seeking free advertisement [and] for a person who will in all probability live the rest of his days in comparative obscurity to have some one chapter of his life thrown flaringly out before the world like a red feather on a sailor hat and the rest of it bound up in coverless, letterless silence of the plain, unknown and unheralded, would be most disagreeable, indeed. . . . I had no occasion to fear either freezing or starvation, but during these few days it seemed that the core of my life was laid bare and that the naked future was nude indeed.[161]

Barnard carefully considered the whole situation and came to the realization that he could never, in good conscience, leave his mates behind and not share their fate. He informed Baldwin that he would stay on Alger Island. Once again, time was very short, so the remaining prefabricated huts carried on board the *America* were hastily brought ashore and assembled at a new site near the eastern end of Alger Island. This new camp was also given the name Camp Ziegler, intended primarily as a place where the ponies and dogs could be cared for ashore. The first camp, about six miles west of the new camp, was now renamed West Camp Ziegler.

There was no obvious need for this second, or "East Camp Ziegler," on Alger Island, and throughout the fall and the winter that followed, a series of pointless shuttles of supplies took place between the two camps, drudgery that would serve only to remind the men that this work should have been accomplished before the *America* was eventually frozen in for the winter. Before these movements commenced, however, there was the odd incident of the abandonment and the reunion.

The ship departed with great ceremony on the afternoon of Friday, September 27. Before it did, Baldwin himself hammered what would become the final nail in his own coffin. He found eight men—Drs. Verner and Seitz, along with Barnard, Mikkelsen, Leffingwell, Rilliet, Vinyard, and Lukas—willing to remain behind, and he now placed a whole new contract in front of them. This contract separated the men from the Baldwin-Ziegler expedition and re-engaged the men under personal service contracts to Baldwin himself. These irresponsible documents included the usual secretive amendments, with the men swearing that they would not lecture, write, "or reveal any of the plans or accomplishments resulting from" their service to Baldwin, "to turn over to the said Evelyn B. Baldwin . . . all collections and written material pertaining to such service." They further agreed to partake of the supplies at the camps Ziegler in a Spartan manner, to accept no transport out of Franz Josef Land without authorization from Baldwin himself, and to "perform all duties in a cheerful, loyal and efficient manner, in failure of which he hereby agrees to forfeit all claims against the said Baldwin, his heirs or representatives."[162]

Ferrying ponies and dogs ashore from the *America*, a treacherous and laborious process in the best of conditions. From Evelyn Briggs Baldwin, "The Baldwin-Ziegler Polar Expedition, Part III," *Wide World Magazine* 10 (60): 587–93.

For all this, the men would receive the munificent sum of five dollars per month. Why Barnard ever signed this infamous document is a mystery, especially as he already had a contract that paid him five times as much. The same could be said for the other men, especially the doctors and Leffingwell. These were professionals who could have been expected to gain, if anything, more favorable terms than their original contracts. But they had quite earnestly come for experience in the Arctic and were bound to have it, and not return ignominiously to the mainland without the accomplishment of a single thing of significance.

As for Baldwin, on some level he must have known that such a document—one that severed the contractual connection between Ziegler and the very expedition the millionaire had financed—would explode in his face. As with so much of Baldwin's erratic behavior in Franz Josef Land, it is impossible today to fully comprehend his motives. Perhaps he possessed a hope that somehow, by the time he returned to New York, the infirm Ziegler might have died and the massive tonnage of supplies carried to Franz Josef Land would then be Baldwin's to do with as he wished.

However one figured it, Baldwin had crossed his personal Rubicon and certainly seemed aware of the fact. As the *America,* unburdened of its dogs and ponies and supplies and eight of its men, departed Alger Island on the evening of September 27, 1901, Barnard stood on shore and recorded "Baldwin's lone, dejected figure, standing in his cabin door apart from the rest."[163] An hour later, the expedition ship was lost to sight beyond the fast ice along shore.

When Engineer Hartt came on deck to see what progress the *America* was making through the ice, he again, as he had when the ship left Norway, encountered Baldwin under the influence. According to Hartt, he found Baldwin coming down from the bridge "with a crying drunk on. He tried to get to the bridge again, but could not make it, and went to his room, where there was a keg of whisky."[164] Hartt did not see Baldwin again until the following day, after Baldwin had suddenly ordered the ship turned around and returned to Alger Island. According to Hartt, Baldwin had emptied the entire keg of whisky and gone to work on the second of two kegs on board the ship.

In the meantime, the men who had remained on Alger Island got on well and, without Baldwin's hovering presence, enjoyed their first real rest since the arrival of the expedition in the islands. They also ate well, with Vinyard frying up all the pancakes they could eat. Barnard, like all the men, had been starving on the same kinds of short rations Baldwin imposed on the Norwegians of Wellman's expedition, and Barnard regretted only that he did not have a bigger stomach. "When I get back, I am going to buy and eat pan-cakes and syrup until my stomach aches twenty-five hours every day and eight days a week."[165]

The day after the departure of the ship, five of the men rode ponies the six miles to West Camp Ziegler in order to complete the roof of the hut there. They were stopped by high winds that started at the midpoint between the two camps, a place of basaltic spires the men called the "Cathedral," so that by the time they reached the southwest corner of the island, any work on a roof was out of the question. They returned to East Camp Ziegler, which itself had been built on an open, flat stretch of sand, one also buffeted by the winds that whistled down upon it from the hills behind the site.

On Wednesday, October 2, the men woke to a depressing thought: if the *America* had stayed on schedule, she would be docking back in Tromsø that very morning. Perhaps at that very moment some of their comrades were tucking into a well-deserved steak or pulling on a bottle of beer. It was also a stormy morning, and Dr. Seitz, whatever his medical talents, was cook for the day, depressing the men even further. But the biggest shock came when Seitz stepped out of the hut into the storm, then ducked his head back in to announce that the *America* was just offshore. It was a truly bad joke, until, one by one, the men went to the door and looked for themselves. Barnard went last. "There, a few rods out in the bay, and indistinct in the thickly falling snow, lay the ship."[166]

An expedition that had been merely a farce was now transformed into a tragedy, and the men who had remained behind knew it. As Barnard wrote: "B. said before he left that it would be impossible to make the pole from this latitude, and his return here now, therefore, means that we are to accomplish nothing but a more or less complete charting of this archipelago. This day is ten times more dark than the one on which we were turned back before the ice. B. soon came ashore and before leaving dramatically announced that 'We are working for our lives now,' but the spirit is gone out of everybody."[167]

Baldwin, fearing a backlash from Ziegler over his duplicitous contracts, requested that each man return them and all did—except for Leon Barnard. He kept his hidden away for the rainy day he seemed to know was coming. The following day, the mood in the camp sank even lower. The men were called out to heave the *America*'s anchor and try and drag the ship a quarter mile closer to shore. Barnard recorded the scene: "Everybody 'sore' at management; spirit utterly crushed, disgusted at the emptiness of it all. B., I must say, I don't understand. . . . It may be the way a North Pole Expedition Commander should act; I don't know; my inexperience refuses to judge."[168]

The temperatures dropped to zero and the winds increased. Winter was still a month or more away. Word soon spread among the men who had remained that the ship really could have returned to Norway, but Baldwin wavered drunkenly for two days and then ordered Johanson to turn the ship back to Franz Josef Land. Baldwin made one last half-hearted attempt to find a northern base camp, but it was far too late in the season. The dogs, too, were literally frozen in, with the colder temperatures freezing many to the ground overnight, whereupon the men had to chop free those who survived to the next morning.

By October 12, 1901, as the Northern Lights made their first appearance and after a further few desultory wanderings in the ship, it was clear to all the men that no advance camp would be built that fall on Rudolf Land or anywhere else. The *America* was returned to Alger Island, along with a now completely bewildered Evelyn Briggs Baldwin in the bargain, and run aground just offshore, to be "moored to the remnant of a stranded iceberg on her port bow, while her stern was within three or four rods of the land itself. The keel of the vessel astern rested upon a sand bottom formed at this point by the discharge of a small stream."[169] As Baldwin himself laconically confessed, this "winter berth of the *America*, resting as she was upon land, water, and ice, could not, upon general principles, be said to have been ideal."[170]

In the fall of 1898, Baldwin had wasted week after week sledging supplies across the same ground, "trebling the route," a method that quickly exhausted the men under him. Exactly three years later, just as his men could reasonably have expected a rapid autumn dash over the ice to Rudolf Land to set the stage for the polar dash in the spring of 1902, Baldwin had instead squandered more than two months in a pointless shuttle of the *America* back and forth to Cape Tegetthoff, all while he established not one but two supply stations on Alger Island. His erratic attempts to force the *America* north were the work of a nautical amateur with no ability to competently issue orders to either the captain or the ice pilot. His abrupt retreat toward Norway and almost instantaneous about-face and return to Alger Island were the work of a deeply unstable individual who was increasingly out of control. These combined operations were fatal to any hope of achieving the North Pole. The neophyte crew sensed it; Baldwin knew it. The North Pole—certainly any attempt in 1902—was now beyond him. Baldwin therefore announced what may very well have been his plan all along. He now intended to chart the central islands of Franz Josef Land and name each and every new bit of geography he could find.[171]

Even if Baldwin had wished to make a quick autumn dash for Rudolf Land before winter set in, another crippling problem now held him back. An internal parasite was attacking the dogs and rapidly killing them off. Even before the *America* was set into her treacherous winter berth, fully 60 of the 428 dogs brought from Siberia—nearly 15 percent of the total pack—were dead. Bergendahl wrote in his diary that parasitic worms several feet long (*flera meter*) hung grotesquely from the dogs' anuses. On one occasion he tried to roll one up with a stick but the parasite broke off after he had gathered in nearly ten feet.[172]

The doctors were kept busy—in addition to all the other menial camp duties Baldwin assigned them—conducting a running series of autopsies on the dogs as they expired or were killed by other dogs. These tests revealed that the dogs suffered immeasurably before death, experiencing a kind of "paralysis . . . [and] convulsive contractions of the muscles, the legs being stretched out, then doubled up, as if the dog were suffering severe abdominal pain."[173]

One of the ponies had already been shot when it was injured on the voyage from Norway. Another was shot at the end of October when Baldwin thought the expedition was short of fodder to keep all the ponies alive during the winter. In ordinary conditions, these could have been seen as ill omens. In fact, they were merely confirmations that the expedition was over before it ever really began.

TWENTY-SEVEN

The Men Were "Put on the Mat"

By October 17 the *America* was completely frozen in, just offshore from Alger Island, with the exception of the area around the propeller blades, which several sailors spent hours each day to keep ice free in case the fast ice along shore began to shift. Archibald Dickson remembered these first nights of darkness as a time when the men were finally able to gain the acquaintance of the dogs assigned to them:

> On October 17 the sun had disappeared for the beginning of the Arctic night, which was now upon us, confining men to their various duties mostly within the ship or after the selection by each member of the scientific staff of his fourteen dogs, twelve for driving and two supernumeraries, from the big pack to segregate them and get practice in the hitching and driving of the sledges, repair of the harness and the training of the dogs to respond to English, instead of Russian commands to which they had been accustomed.
>
> There is nothing on earth more trying to the patience of an ordinary individual than the stubborn, mischievous antics of these Russian wolf dogs until an acquaintance and thorough understanding has been arrived at. The first real signs and recognition of obedience of these at first fierce, but after acquaintance most companionable dogs of the frozen north, were seen in response to those members of the expedition trying

to train the dogs who cussed them most. The dogs really seemed to quickly understand and like that part of the game, and soon every man who had a dog team could be heard on all sides, cussing them roundly in words profane and more terrible than they had ever used before."[174]

The men did their best to settle into winter routines, with the doctors looking after the health of the men—the Russians had carried head lice onto the ship and the infestation quickly spread throughout the vessel, especially after Baldwin ordered the scientists to bunk in with the Russians. The doctors, as best they could, also looked to the health of the dogs and ponies. A few of the Russians—along with Lukas, who had become their nominal supervisor—lived ashore in order to tend to the animals, but most lived on board the ship itself. Fiala continued with his photographic record of the expedition. Russell Porter sketched and painted. The other men cooked cornmeal mush for the dogs, sledged ice from nearby icebergs to melt for freshwater on board the ship, made and repaired sledges, and took meteorological and astronomical observations.

While shopping for balloons, balloon buoys, and vats of sulphuric acid to make hydrogen to lift his balloons and balloon buoys, along with dozens of boxes of his favorite Swedish conserves, Baldwin had failed to properly equip the expedition with enough sledges, ropes, dog and pony harnesses, dog whips, sleeping bags, tents, or even underwear. All of these had to be made by hand during the winter. It was another monstrous lapse in preparation, as Barnard bitterly documented: "All understood that everything in the way of Arctic clothing was [to be] provided by the Expedition, and we were told not to bring anything, some not even underwear."[175]

There were also the beginnings of an attempt to research the biological oceanography of the surrounding waters. As Dickson recalled, "there was [a] search for deep sea and marine vegetation and life at the bottom of the sea. . . . Winged grappling hooks attached to piano wires were let down through the propeller hole in the ice, the swift Arctic ocean currents carrying these grappling hooks or claws to great depths. They would be drawn up by the 'winch,' bringing up with them strange submarine creations of vines and green rubber-like palm trees from the lower summer gardens of a heavily ice-blanketed Arctic sea."[176]

The power went out on board the *America* on November 26, 1901. Engineer Hartt had found a dynamo on board the ship when he reported in

Dundee, but there was no suitable engine to power the generator. (He had also found boxes of required supplies missing and was told by Baldwin "not to say anything about it or cause any trouble."[177]) Hartt had asked for the engine from *Frithjof*'s launch to power the dynamo, but when the expedition arrived in Franz Josef Land, Baldwin told him he had ordered *Frithjof* to leave its launch in Norway and instead bring an extra hut. Hartt then improvised an engine that ran as long as the ship had steam from the main boiler. The electric lights went out when petroleum for the engine ran low. After November 26, Hartt later wrote, it became "necessary for us to burn blubber for light, causing considerable coughing aboard ship among the men. Captain Arnesen being a particular sufferer. If I had the boiler I could have heated the ship by steam, saving considerable coal."[178]

As for Baldwin himself, he now took up where he left off during his previous stay in Franz Josef Land, daydreaming and wandering along the shoreline of Alger Island in search of reindeer antlers and other assorted bits of natural history detritus. His religious impulses led him to disdain work on Sundays, at least at the start of the expedition, so the men were forced to cram seven days' work into every six, and even this was invariably cut down by storms, an inefficient use of time at a latitude where constant summer daylight required constant effort.

With unchallenged authority, Baldwin repeated the mistakes in leadership he had sworn in 1899 that he would avoid on any future expedition. As Russell Porter wrote, in order to harden the men for the sledge work that would be required of them the following spring, Baldwin instituted a series of sledge relays to West Camp Ziegler and back, with the men ordered to drive the dogs to the western camp, pick up supplies landed there at the start of the expedition, and bring them to East Camp Ziegler at the other end of the island. It was work for the sake of work and, by the end of 1901, it made Baldwin thoroughly unpopular with the men, who came to see his appearance at the mess tables as an oppressive shroud.

The low-key and equanimous Porter was slow to recognize the deterioration of the morale of the men around him, but eventually even he could not fail to see it. "It was during these trips that the first dissatisfaction with the commander arose among some of the men. The distance to the cache was not far—perhaps eight miles—but the trips were made in darkness, and it wasn't long before two parties were lost, and relief parties brought them back in rather bad shape, with feet and fingers frostbitten."[179]

Barnard wrote up a memo for Baldwin on February 5, 1902, evidently in response to Baldwin's demand for an explanation as to why a roll of wire netting had been left on the ice. Barnard described the utter pointlessness of these supply shuttles between the west and east camps, in total winter darkness, with overloaded sledges, men and dogs exhausted, all to shift supplies that should rightly have been delivered directly to East Camp Ziegler by ship the previous fall:

> In accordance with your instructions yesterday's sledge party left the vicinity of the ship about nine o'clock and arrived at West Camp Ziegler, placed the sledges in position to be loaded conveniently and picketed the dogs by eleven. . . . For some time I held Mr. Vedoe's sledge at "half speed," taking occasion, also, to cut out two of his poorest dogs and put in their places two of the ten or twelve loose ones that were following. . . .
>
> Vedoe's team getting into trouble and the third sledge only just beginning to assume a darker hue, I slackened my pace until the latter came up. The sledge carried Vaceliev, the second Russian; I had supposed it was in charge of either Dr. Verner or Lukas. . . .
>
> The loading of the pemmican and of two rolls of wire netting, one on each of the Russians' sledges, was readily effected, and the loads were guided down the slope onto the ice in convenient places for hitching up the teams. By half past twelve we had eaten a lunch of ship's biscuit, chipped beef, and jelly and by one were off. Realizing that the Russians had unusually heavy loads, we had installed every loose dog that would add strength to any of the teams, cutting out the weakest ones. . . .
>
> Somewhere near the halfway mark I exchanged places with Vedoe, and taking advantage of some "clear sailing," pushing on ahead. On approaching [a] berg, a fierce fight among the loose dogs attracted my attention. After watching them two or three minutes intently, I concluded that the white form moving frantically about in their midst was a bear cub. Calling to Vedoe, who was behind with Vaciliev, to take my team I began unclinging the rifle from the sledge and had nearly done so when the "white form" came bounding toward us for protection—a mere dog, but thoroughly whipped. . . . We had gotten about half a mile this side of the scene of the dog fight when Lukas,

as it proved to be, came up from the rear with a sledge and four dogs. He said he had waited till ten o'clock for Dr. Verner, as directed, and that after going on had lost his way and in consequence had wandered all over the bay. . . .

Soon . . . we over-hauled Vaceliev who, with his tired dogs, afforded all the real trouble from then on. . . . It soon became very evident that Vaceliev, his dogs and I could not make it unless the load were lightened, and at last I reluctantly took off the roll of wire netting. For some minutes before this a great sleeplessness had been taking possession of Vaceliev and even after the removal of the aforementioned part of our load, we did not make a very appreciable increase in our speed. We had not gone a quarter of a mile farther when this depreciated to a few feet at a time—Vaceliev dropping on to the snow at each stop, as did every dog of which we now had but five, one having gotten away. Under these circumstances, and with the ship but three quarters of a mile away I finally called to the indistinct forms of our companions in advance, and all the dogs were hitched together on the van sledge—Vacelievs being left where it was, on top of a hummock.[180]

This risk of frostbite and disaster was compounded by Baldwin's failure to provide proper Arctic clothing. As one of the doctor's noted: "We have been furnished with hoods of camel's hair—that is, we have been given the material, and shall have to sew them ourselves as best we can."[181] Historian Susan Barr writes that Baldwin "refused the men sleeping bags, needed to prevent frostbite when they inevitably had trouble with the route in the winter dark, as that would mean cutting down on the amount of supplies they could haul. Any trips for scientific investigations off the hauling route were forbidden, so that the scientific profit from the expedition was inevitably minimal."[182] Leon Barnard's evaluation was both pointed and spot on: "I cannot understand why in thunder some of this stuff was not made up in civilization."[183]

In particular, the talents of chief scientific officer Leffingwell, as well as Porter, the artist and surveyor, were largely wasted by their continual employment hauling supplies back and forth from the western camp. As Porter remembered, they were surrounded by unknown lands that beckoned men of natural curiosity. "With virgin land all about us, no one was allowed there. It was forbidden ground. As a result, Leffingwell produced on a meager traverse of the region bordering the freight trail."[184]

Leffingwell in particular was appalled at the waste and soon became Baldwin's implacable foe. He found a compatriot in Mikkelsen, as the two shared a cabin on board *America*. Together, before the spring sledge trips, they led a near-mutiny over the lack of sleeping bags and tents on the trail. Both men had only joined the expedition on the grounds that Leffingwell, with Mikkelsen acting as his chief assistant, would lead a thorough scientific program. Instead, they found themselves constantly diverted by trivialities, with Baldwin further micro-managing even these. Mikkelsen later wrote of these "many disagreeable hours" but said that they only strengthened the bond between him and Leffingwell, so much so that they soon became "determined to take up any Arctic project which promised sufficient results, scientific and otherwise, to justify the work, the money and the time that we should be forced to expend upon it."[185] The 1906–1907 Anglo-American Polar Expedition, led jointly, cooperatively, and companionably by Leffingwell and Mikkelsen, was the direct result of their horrid experiences with Baldwin in 1901 and 1902.

Baldwin compounded his cruelty toward the men and his mystifying degradation of the expedition's scientific work by retreating to the martinet posture he had assumed in the fall of 1898. As Porter wrote, when the men complained, they were "put on the mat" and reminded of their signed agreement to obey their commander under any and all conditions."[186] This attitude was compounded by Baldwin's maddening combination of incompetence and secrecy, which created a kind of negative feedback loop for the entire crew. He told the men nothing, and this silence left them to guess and gossip as to the expedition's future movements. This in turn only led to more whispers behind Baldwin's back that further isolated the expedition leader and intensified his paranoid behavior. As Barnard wrote on December 18: "Anything suspected but not told is promptly labeled 'expedition secret' in sarcasm and insinuation. B. is far from a popular leader and his methods have long been openly ridiculed. He does not like our talking together and his presence acts like a pall on everybody."[187]

Barnard wrote that the expedition was fortunate to have lucked into the companionship of Lukas, who could work with the Russians and treated them like human beings, something Baldwin refused to do. Relations with the Swedish crew of the *America* had likewise taken a turn for the worse. On December 1 Porter wrote that the Swedes were briefly in a celebratory mood: "Today it is Oscar's Day. We have celebrated it by singing patriotic songs and '*Ur Svenska hjärtans djup*' has sounded here more than once today."[188]

Within weeks, however, the deterioration in relations between Baldwin and Carl Johanson, the commander of the *America,* could be kept a secret no longer. It had begun during the mishandled ice navigation in August and flashed again after a seemingly minor dispute in early November. The Swedish-American translator, Carl Sandin, who had been forced into the position of ship steward, got into an argument with Johanson over a dead dog left on board the ship that Johanson thought Sandin should have promptly removed. The heated discussion soon involved Baldwin, always quick to smell any threat to his authority. It quickly escalated to a direct challenge to Johanson, whose role as either captain or sailing master of the *America* had never been clearly defined prior to the departure of the expedition from Dundee. This again was a direct result of Baldwin's failure to clearly define the roles of the Swedish crew of *America.*

By mid-December, as the conflict escalated, Baldwin took to arguing openly with Johanson. This inevitably led to questions of where the ultimate authority lay on board the vessel and even within the expedition itself. Johanson was thirty-three and a lieutenant in the Royal Swedish Navy Reserve, a lifetime sailor who listed the home of his wife Anna as the Sjomanshuset (Sailor's Home) in Göteborg. Leon Barnard, who for all his criticism of Baldwin thought that Johanson was "a fool [with] altogether too much lip," overheard and recorded a blazing row between Johanson and Baldwin a few days before Christmas 1901.[189] His transcription is quoted in full here, as it both illustrates the degree to which Baldwin had lost control of the expedition and because the issue of Johanson's status was to become, eight months hence, one of the main pieces of evidence against Baldwin when the expedition returned ignominiously to Tromsø and William Ziegler relieved Baldwin of his command.

S[ailing] M[aster] Johanson: "and I don't intend to be talked to by Sandine [*sic*] as he talked to me this morning or by anyone else.

Com. Baldwin: "And I don't intend one of my countrymen to be told that he knows no more about taking care of a lamp than a dog!"

J: "See here, Mr. Baldwin, I am captain of this ship, and I want you to understand, first as last, that I shall deal with the crew and with matters of this kind as I think best."

B: "NO, you are sailing master."

J: "I am Captain of this ship. And, first time as last time, Mr. Baldwin, if you are not satisfied with me, I want you to relieve me and send me home as soon as possible, Mr. Baldwin, that's all I have to say."

B: "Well—But you are engaged as sailing master and—"

J: "No sir, I am not. As captain."

B: "You are drawing your salary as sailing master, and your wife is receiving money now as from the sailing master."

J: "Yes, but I signed at Dundee as Master. But it makes no difference to me whether I am master or sailing master."

B: "My cablegram to Andree from Chicago was to engage a *Sailing Master.*

J: "I have the papers where I signed as master and I will get them." (Leaves office and returns.)

J: "Never have I been on a ship, and I have been at sea for twenty years, where the aft mess room is as dirty as that place down there. Sandine is supposed to take care of it and the lamp but he does not. I told him he did not and he told me to 'Shut up' and then I told him, Mr. Baldwin, that he knew no more about taking care of a lamp than a dog."

B: "When you have matters of that kind coming up I prefer that you come to me."

J: "No sir! I will not be running to you with everything; others may do it, but I will not."

B: "Sandine's deafness makes it hard—"

J: "That makes no difference, and you know, Mr. Baldwin, I have once before asked to have one of the crew do that work, and I ask again now."

B: "We must try to get along without friction and talk like this. The winter is now nearly half over, and it will not be long before the sun begins to return. Sandine's present position is a disagreeable one to him and difficult. There's no reason why he should wait on table more than any of the rest of those aft, but his deafness makes other work still more difficult for him. So, for the present, we must get along the best we can."[190]

By the end of 1901 and the turn of 1902, Baldwin's unfitness to lead the expedition had become evident to everyone. As late as mid-December he was still dropping hints about a "polar dash" in the spring but refused to be pinned down on exactly what his plan was. Barnard picked up on the rumor of a polar dash and thought that expedition might yet redeem its poor showing. Because of his longtime admiration for his famous cousin, he had long been certain that Baldwin must be carrying in his pocket a well-thought-out plan to reach the North Pole, and Barnard, along with the rest of the crew, expected it to be finally revealed over the holidays. At Christmas dinner, all of the men waited expectantly to hear the plan they were certain would finally tell them precisely how the expedition intended to claim the North Pole. In due course, Baldwin rose to give a celebratory talk that began and ended with platitudes about how the men needed to continue to soldier on and work hard. No plan was forthcoming.

Again, on New Year's Day, Baldwin rose to give a speech. Porter in particular believed that this was the moment when their leader would finally announce a specific plan for reaching the goal they had all come for: the attainment of the North Pole. As the men sat in astonished silence, they were treated to more dissembling. "This evening Mr. Baldwin made a speech, and in a few short words gave a short summary of what we had accomplished during the past months of the old year, and what was to come, without mentioning any special plan for attaining our goal."[191]

Anthony Fiala, like the rest of the crew, was listening intently to the speech and took it down as close to word-for-word as he could. At the very moment when the men were hungry for direct, forceful, optimistic leadership, the speech instead was a triumph of bluster:

I believe that every one of you believes that we can make a record. Just how that can be done depends, in a large manner, depends upon a great many conditions. I have been on two previous expeditions, and it makes me count results, and causes me to hesitate once, twice, three and more times before announcing any plans, for the simple reason that if it were frustrated, perhaps it would have a discouraging effect upon all in one way or another. The plans therefore, are to do the very best we can, and to do it with a will, meanwhile, keeping in mind that actions speak louder than word, steadily persevering at machine work, making sledges and all the other work before us to do. There is much more I would I like to say if I were guaranteed would come out in accordance with the plans which have all long since been matured and laid down.[192]

Baldwin then repeated the speech, with extra four-flushing, to the assembled crew of the *America*. He stood before a large chart of the polar basin, making special gestures toward the Swedish sailors, many of whom, because of the language barrier, likely could not begin to follow his convoluted English. It hardly would have mattered if they could.

Barnard, who attended both talks, was stupefied by the expedition leader's "over-minute reference to a map of the regions within the Arctic Circle and a sort of superior reference to various nautical matters which really served to advertise to his audience his unfamiliarity, for some time suspected by them, with the navigation of the sea, and which, too, seemed to amount to an attempt to bewilder them with his self-sufficiency and to belittle whatever they might know about it. Both speeches were painful in the picture of a landsman addressing seafaring men [and] utterly without apparent object, crisis, or conclusion."[193]

The brief rush of enthusiasm that the men had felt at the end of December, when they genuinely believed some great plan was about to be revealed before their eyes, was gone. As Barnard listened with growing incredulity, he very reluctantly—this was, after all, his own blood relation—put his reliable finger almost directly on the issue: "It was the strangest thing I ever heard. I would have thot [*sic*] him crazy if he had not guarded his secret so well. What he spoke at all for, does not appear."[194]

Barnard, along with all the rest of the men, could have been forgiven if they now chose to call William Ziegler's judgment into question. In fact, Ziegler's role in all this went completely unexamined, then or later. But in the end that was the central question: how could one of the richest, shrewdest men in the United States have allowed them all to be led into the high Arctic by a madman?

TWENTY-EIGHT

Good Luck Is a Big Factor

In the aftermath of the New Year's Day fiasco, rumors continued unabated over the size and scope of the spring work. Would they make a dash for the North Pole after all? Or merely push a cache of supplies north to Rudolf Land, their original destination the previous summer? On January 5, 1902, Anthony Fiala had a long talk with Henry Hartt, during which the engineer gave his opinion that Fiala would not be "a member of the final dash party so much talked of." The most irrepressibly guileless of all the men, Fiala took the rumor in his usual optimistic stride. "Whatever is done as long as it is honorable and for the best I am satisfied. For though I would like to be in the advance, if my staying behind with the ship will help toward the success of the expedition I am satisfied.

> It is the first Sunday of the New Year and communion Sunday. I would like to go up the old familiar aisle in the beautiful Temple and be present at the solemn service. The music of the great organ almost reaches my ears, and I can almost distinguish faces by the subdued light of the afternoon streaming through the stained glass windows. The air filled with harmony; my soul with spiritual rest and gladness.[195]

But Fiala then forced himself back to the gelid Earth: "But no, here we are a ship-load of mortals from six different nations and countries out in a solitude of ice and snow. Destitute of the light of day for the sun has hid his face from us. And even the moon is showing her shining countenance in other skies on other lands."[196]

Fiala was to all appearances a genuine and gentle soul wholly defined by faith: in God, humanity, and Nature. It did not take much for him to make the leap from the imprisoned ship to another, altogether higher place: "But we have still the stars, and at times they twinkle in their far off homes, and when clouds do not obscure their luminous spheres shine with brilliancy. And sometimes the sacred fire of Aurora, like an elusive spirit of light, throws her net of gleaming rays over the heavens. Like wild Valkyries in the charge of battle the spears of light travel across the Zenith then they are gone. Like the life of man; a flash of glory!"[197]

Two days later, Fiala gave the men a tour of his more earthly polar projects: an ice car that could lay down a track and then pick it up in transit, a flying machine, and a coal-carrying submarine "large enough to venture in any sea—with many new improvements that would be of value in such a craft. The boys laughed at me when I stated I was in earnest and intended to canvass for capital to build it on my return."[198] The laughter directed at Fiala was done with a playful indulgence for someone whom the more hardened men considered to be a babe in the Arctic. When Baldwin left on January 21 to make a preliminary trip to West Camp Ziegler, leaving Fiala in charge for the day, Hartt and several others promptly clapped Fiala in irons for the duration of Baldwin's absence. To Barnard, this was simply a piece of "frivolity and fun" and in no way malicious.[199] There was, in fact, a general and genuine fondness for Fiala.

The same could not be said of the men's attitude to Baldwin. Just as Paul Bjørvig once wondered why the towering Norwegians of Wellman's expedition didn't just haul off and punch the diminutive *Susæg* on the nose, so the Swedes and the Russians and, in the end, even the Americans of the Baldwin-Ziegler Polar Expedition, came to feel the same way over their addled leader. Most of the men shared some variation of Hartt's description: "Mr. Baldwin's word can not be trusted. He lied to me in New York, in Dundee, in Tromsoe, and when we were leaving Vardo and at various times when we were in the Arctic."[200]

Leffingwell's version of Baldwin untrustworthiness revolved around the incident with the pony. When one of the lame ponies had to be shot, Baldwin ordered the cook to serve it to the men for dinner. According to Leffingwell, everyone knew exactly what they were eating, but day after day Baldwin insisted they were eating beefsteak. "A few days after he said to us, 'You had a great joke played upon you.' That was all done for a good story in his book, and is the best illustration I can give to show what a fool he was."[201]

Baldwin created a permanent rift with both Porter and Vinyard on January 26, when he made the unforgiveable accusation that he thought both of them were drunk while on duty, when in fact they were suffering from exhaustion brought on from overwork.[202] It was also an absurd charge, as well, since Baldwin himself personally controlled the ship's alcohol stores and, according to Hartt and several of the Swedes including Captain Johanson, drank nearly the entire stock himself.[203]

In a similar fashion, Baldwin burned his bridge with Mikkelsen when he allowed himself to be overheard calling the Dane his private body servant. Mikkelsen never forgave this calumny, and Baldwin's subsequent half-hearted apology only served to inflame Mikkelsen even further.

For his part, Fiala attempted to lighten the mood with regular "chalk talks" on spiritual subjects, followed by a session where he drew caricatures of the men. For Barnard, these were some of the only moments when all of the men—sailors and landsmen, Swedes and Russians and Americans—actually came together as one. With all of the bad feelings within the expedition and between certain men or groups of men, Fiala stood out as the single individual equally trusted by all, Americans and men of other nations alike. "Fiala is as good a Christian as I know and he certainly deserves credit for these repeated efforts to take our thots [sic] to more pleasant climes and to the House of God.

> At the close he generally draws a more or less faithful representation of one or another of the seamen, and that pleases them exceedingly. The sailors not infrequently get a very striking and abrupt introduction to themselves when they look round after the sitting and behold their long hair and whiskers and square chin, big nose and high cheek bones on the canvas. Fiala is very good at it. And we usually get a good deal of fun out of it at the victim's expense.[204]

These were rare moments of fun on the entire expedition. More typical was yet another talk Baldwin gave to the men on January 31. Once again, as the Swede Bergendahl wrote in his diary, Baldwin demanded the fulfillment of the contract on "every single point [*till punkt och pricka*]" and that Fiala was now to be his second-in-command. According to Bergendahl, Baldwin became so agitated during his speech that he burst into tears.[205]

As the winter ended and the first faint signs of light returned to the archipelago, Baldwin made plans to take the ponies and several of the Russians and haul tons of supplies from East Camp Ziegler to a major new proposed camp about 50 nautical miles north. This was one of "eighteen or nineteen other camps and relay depôts" that would eventually leave an astounding tonnage of supplies strewn along a wavering line from West Camp Ziegler on Alger Island to the northernmost cache of supplies just south of Teplitz Bay on Rudolf Land.[206]

Such an operation would require the men to remove the supplies that had been left at West Camp Ziegler to East Camp Ziegler, and then from the latter camp in a series of maneuvers all the way to Teplitz Bay, more than 100 nautical miles north. The whole operation could take months, and Barnard wondered where the supplies would come from to feed so many men and dogs and ponies and repair the sledges, all to land a few tons of supplies that should have been carried by sea six months earlier. "There are lots of questions and there are none among us who knows anything about them," Barnard wrote on January 22. "B. holds his own counsel, gives no definite information, and is not approachable."[207]

Baldwin's Masonic affiliations led him to call the planned new camp on Greely Island "Kane Lodge," apparently in the hope that his Masonic brothers would take advantage of its "commodious structure [which] considering its location in the very heart of the Franz Josef Land Archipelago, is destined beyond a doubt to become more historic as the work of exploration progresses."[208] At 80° 56' North, Kane Lodge was just across Austria Sound and only 10 nautical miles further north than Fort McKinley at Cape Heller, where Baldwin had dithered away the fall of 1898 and where the body of Bernt Bentsen lay buried under a pile of stones.

The men received a taste of what Baldwin was up to as the sun returned in early March. The long and largely counterproductive winter gave rise to new hopes that, despite Baldwin's obduracy, the object of the expedition might at last be at hand. Dickson recalled "the thrill of those moments when our eyes and lungs drank in the first warm, life-giving rays of our planets' great radiator—the sun."[209] Barnard, who was close to quitting the whole enterprise, thought that even now they could have still made a dash for the

North Pole "if the party had more years and had had experience."[210] But the expedition, as Barnard now realized, was filled with men who never should have been selected. Painfully honest almost to a fault, Barnard included himself in this general condemnation:

> As to myself, I have no business to be here. First, because I have not a good enough personal and private equipment, which I own myself, and second, because I am not built for this kind of work and do not know enough about the mathematical and scientific part of it to make my presence here excusable and also creditable to me and mine. Of course hard hand labor is to be done but a mental man is not necessarily unfitted for physical work and one needs some tangible and justifiable reason for so evidently deserving the distinction of being called a fool. . . .
>
> Sometimes I don't know what to think of Baldwin. Sometimes he seems bewildered, sometimes resigned to what he evidently thinks will occur: that we shall not go beyond Rudolf Land at least. Sometimes he seems determined to make a real poleward attempt. Unless there occurs what now seems to me a miracle, and he gets to Rudolf Land in proper shape and time, such an attempt would be madness.[211]

At the top of Barnard's list of men who should not have been chosen to go to Franz Josef Land, he now added the most personally painful one of all—his own cousin, the very leader of the expedition. In an incident on February 23, the men's anger at their substandard clothing caused Baldwin to lash out at them, except that—in a bizarrely passive-aggressive manner—he did so from behind the closed door of his cabin. Barnard had had enough of the complaints over the clothing outfit and had finally gone to see Baldwin about it personally. Baldwin never allowed his cousin to say a word. Instead, without referring to anyone by name, Baldwin loudly decried the "guilty one or ones [that] had been 'spotted long before we got up here'" and said, with emphasis, that *I* should not forget it. . . ."

> He said there was a smooth talker aboard and was remarking so loudly that I cautioned him that he would be heard outside, but he replied louder than ever that he would tell them to their face . . . but he spoiled its effect on me by covering his face with his hand and smiling. . . . I

cannot fathom him and wish I could be sure that he was (perfectly) rational. There are those who believe he is not and Fiala openly said so soon after the ship returned after trying to go back last September. If he is not o.k. there is going to be some hell around here.[212]

As Baldwin's intent to push a cache of supplies to Rudolf Land became clear, the crew's spirits—briefly raised in late December and then again in mid-February over the possibility of a real dash to the North Pole—were demoralized once again. In addition to the realization that Baldwin would now grind up the men and ponies and dogs in a pointless round of donkey work better left to the ship, it also became clear that he was about to engage in a wide and tiring search for new geographic naming opportunities. Worse, the men now came to believe that Baldwin was deliberately trying to place them in artificially created situations that were not only dangerous but potentially even lethal, situations that Baldwin could exploit for his "expedition narrative." Predictably, the men were not enthused. Barnard recorded the general feeling amongst the men that they should simply wait until the breakup of the ice later in the spring and let the ship do the work of carrying the supplies to Rudolf Land.

One gains a perfect sense of the dual nature of this frustrating, almost bemusing challenge for the men, in a lovely letter written by the partially deaf artist and surveyor Russell Porter on March 2, 1902. Porter was sent by Baldwin not north but south (!) to survey the northern coast of McClintock Island and locate and mark as yet unknown places to which Baldwin could attach names. Admitting his mild but pleasant surprise that the incompetent micro-manager Baldwin had "left me to my own devices,"[213] Porter dutifully fulfilled his charge with an air of professional wonderment:

It was rather startling on nearing this cape [on the north coast of the island] which I have indicated in my notebook as C' to observe a large bay open up to the south which had little appearance of existing from the vicinity of our winter quarters: and you can imagine my surprise and pleasure is seeing glacier after glacier coming into view as I walked eastwards, each ice stream holding with its neighbor a nunatak. I counted and plotted three such icecap islands and four glaciers, the latter uniting around the head of the bay into one solid stream. From the center of this aggregation of glaciers, a wreath of vapor was ascending, I suppose from some sub-glacial stream of water. It looked exactly like smoke ascending from a chimney at home on a quiet winter's morning. This phenomenon continued throughout my stay at the bay. This noble bay is flanked on the east by the talus slopes of cape C'; has a width at its entrance of two miles and is flanked on the south west by another imposing cliff, D'. . . .

I had the delightful sensation of walking into sunlight as I crossed this bay, and saw the edge of the sun shining over one of the nunataks at its head. Whatever name this body of water finally receives, the spot will always be associated, to me, with the return of the sun and I will always remember it as Sun Bay. For, on reaching Cape C' I picked out a sheltered spot amongst the detritus along the shore, and while the life giving rays were warming my soul, I took in the beauties of this spot.[214]

Before the sledge work northward began in earnest, it was time for Baldwin to make another speech. This event was forced upon a reluctant Baldwin by Charles Rilliet who, like the other men, had grown tired of the obsessive secrecy and complete lack of any announced plans. Unlike all the other men, he was more than willing to have his say about it. Barnard wrote that everyone in the expedition was afraid to confront Baldwin—so great and imbued was the *fin de siècle,* pre–World War I respect for authority. The lone exception was Rilliet, "as he has always talked with the boys, and with Baldwin as well, in his candid straight-to-the-point way, [so] he is tolerated and listened to because he has to be." At the end of February, Rilliet let Baldwin have it with both barrels: "He told Baldwin tonight that he had no position too high or too low that he wouldn't willingly try to fill. That he had thus far done his best and would so continue. That he had come up here to help put the flag of his country farther north than that of any other and was even now perfectly willing to give his life for such but that he did not come up here to make a book of reading matter and to make an ass of himself."[215]

Backed into a corner, Baldwin gathered the men in the galley of the *America* on the evening of March 5, 1902. Before he addressed them, Baldwin made an inexplicable administrative about-face when he drew up yet another separate contract that promised the Swedish crew more money if they toed the line. Barnard described the terms "as infamous as are those which we are now serving under and it looked as though the men would not sign them but they finally did, but I feel sure they themselves did not fully understand things. The scene was pathetic. Menander translated and no one is to tell anything to anyone, as usual. They gain a little money by signing *if* Baldwin sees fit to give it to them when we return from the sledge journey."[216]

Baldwin had been shaken into action, both by Rilliet's outburst but also by a small tremor in the ice around Alger Island on March 2 that had briefly jostled the ship. Leaping from his cabin and finding Barnard, Baldwin "made much ado about telling me not to be alarmed and showed surprising concern himself in a matter which would obviously not amount to much at this time of year, and which no one else showed."[217] It was another indication that Baldwin had never spent time on board a vessel beset in the ice in the Arctic. All of his experience—both with Peary and with Wellman—had been as a member of a shore party landed from a ship in largely ice-free summer waters.

Baldwin's speech briefly recounted their desultory "progress." In all the days from August 23, 1901—the moment the ship had deposited their supplies at West Camp Ziegler—to this moment, the expedition had advanced but 6 nautical miles. Baldwin was therefore ready to announce the expedition's new goal: to drag a cache of supplies, as much as twenty tons, north from Alger Island, through the ice-clogged channels of Franz Josef Land, to Rudolf Land. As Barnard wrote, the men had guessed as much for months, but even this definite word left unspoken their supposed true goal of the North Pole, and "some of us would like to have known what he hoped to do [about the pole] inasmuch as we are taking our lives in our hands."[218]

But beyond Rudolf Land, either in word or action, Baldwin was not prepared to go. He had at the moment no goal beyond an attempt to lay in a cache of supplies near Teplitz Bay, and told the assembled men that "it is impossible to announce plans with any degree of certainty, and I will let it go with that." Fiala was also on hand and recorded the part of the speech that especially galled the men:

Now those of you who are to undertake this work, as I have stated it, must also hold in mind that neither I nor the expedition will be in any manner held responsible for loss of life or limb. This I want clear and distinctly understood that no one in the future may have any complaint to make whatever. It would be unpleasant and sad enough to me were a disaster, which I do not expect, to occur on this trip and which may occur, but it is not necessary to make anyone feel more unpleasant than that. I am also well aware of the fact that three years ago a man lost his life in connection with an expedition upon which I served. The man was like the rest of us ready and willing for the sledge work. There was no one to blame so far as I know. I want to speak of this now [in the event of] any unforeseen accident.[219]

This was the last straw for many of the men. It seemed clear to them now that Baldwin was playing with their lives. The refusal to allow the men sleeping bags and tents during the many winter forays to West Camp Ziegler struck them now as a deliberate attempt to get one or more of them killed for no reason other than to create drama for his planned book. The direct reference to the death of Bernt Bentsen—*"There was no one to blame so far as I know"*—was as close as Baldwin would ever come to an acknowledgment of his personal responsibility in the affair. Clearly, Bentsen's death continued to haunt Baldwin to an almost Hamlet-like distraction.

If the feeling of the men is to be given any weight, then it also suggests that Baldwin was well aware that Wellman had used the death of Bentsen to great dramatic effect in his published articles after the 1898–99 expedition (as he would do again in his 1911 memoir). As Rilliet had all but accused him of a week earlier, Baldwin needed similar such "incidents" to write about, especially as he so far had nothing to report but failure.

The physical condition of the Americans was also on Baldwin's mind. In what was supposed to be a wholly American affair, he and his countrymen had not acquitted themselves well in relation to the larger, stronger Swedes and the stockier, tougher Russians. Barnard thought that Baldwin "now thinks we are inferior," a feeling that was supported by the Dane Mikkelsen, who considered the Americans "young, weak and inexperienced."[220] For Barnard, raised at a time of high national temper and growing American power and influence in the world, such a new and unfamiliar awareness came as a profound shock. Like so many of his countrymen, he had never confronted the possibility that anything American might be inferior to anything European. "In the face of so much I do not know how to begin. I am almost at the end of my rope. . . . Tonight my American spirit is wounded keenly."[221]

The contrast of the growing dissent and demoralization of the Americans in Franz Josef Land with the contemporary newspaper headlines back in the United States could not have been sharper. In Baldwin's native Midwest, newspapers had geared their readers to a fever pitch by the anticipated race to the North Pole in 1902 between Baldwin, operating from his base in

Franz Josef Land, and Robert Peary, still slogging his way around northern Greenland.

"BALDWIN-PEARY POLAR RACE STARTS APRIL 1," blared the St. Louis *Post-Dispatch* on Sunday morning, March 23, 1902. Superimposed on a crudely drawn chart of the north polar basin were strikingly contrasting photographs of the rough, jauntily jut-jawed, supremely self-confident Peary while, opposite, there appeared a buttoned-down and bow-tied Baldwin who looked more accountant than explorer. The paper intensified its headline by highlighting the natural tension between the two men: "these one-time associates will now oppose each other in the most thrilling North Pole race the world has ever seen." It then went far too far and placed Baldwin ahead of Peary in every category: geography, financing, even—with particularly outlandish irony—morale:

> Emerging from his winter quarters at Cape Sabine, Robert E. Peary will rush northward as fast as his dogs can run. Eight hundred miles east of him Evelyn B. Baldwin, who has spent the winter in the vicinity of Prince Rudolf Land, will simultaneously start. It will be a race between men who previously served together. . . .
>
> None but the most pitiable comparison could be made of these racing polar expeditions. Upon the west is Peary, six times defeated and his spirit now far more willing than his flesh is strong. He has made discovery of the Pole his life's single aim. He has suffered terribly. His wife has his promise that, if he fails this time, he will never try again. . . . Everything is against him. . . .
>
> On the east is Baldwin. He is young. He has been once with Peary and once with Wellman up in the North. . . . Where Peary has a party of three, Baldwin has forty-two; where Peary has seventy dogs, Baldwin has 400 dogs and fifteen Siberian ponies. . . . Not even a king could have entered the race with a more complete equipment than Baldwin's, nor a king's humble subject with less of these things and more need of them than Peary. And so they will race the forty-two against the three, the one backed by a cool million.[222]

Even with all these advantages, the newspaper also noted that "Good luck is a big factor."[223] Unbeknownst to the readers in St. Louis that Sunday morning in late March, the extreme form of luck that had drawn Evelyn

Briggs Baldwin to William Ziegler's generosity had long since utterly run out. Baldwin was not at Rudolf Land or anywhere near it. The failure to get any supplies to that northern terminus—either by ship in the summer of 1901 or over the ice by sledge that same fall—meant that every bit of that proposed plan would now have to be accomplished by tired men and exhausted dogs and ponies in March, April, and May 1902, at the very moment when Baldwin should have been well into his "dash" for the North Pole against Peary.

This monotonous haulage was eventually accomplished, but it took its inevitable toll on the spirits of the men and the health of the animals. Besides the depot on Greely Island, Baldwin's spring sledging parties eventually coalesced large caches of supplies at two other locations: Coburg Island, an islet at 81° 32' North, where five thousand pounds of food was stashed and then, finally, at Cape Auk on the southwestern coast of Rudolf Land, where more than seventeen tons of pemmican was left on the rocky shoreline beneath the island's ice dome.

Porter, Mikkelsen, Rilliet, and the Vedoe brothers trekked to West Camp Ziegler on March 7 to tear down the hut there so that it could be reassembled as "Kane Lodge" on Greely Island. Soon after, the sight of the sprawling caravan as it left East Camp Ziegler impressed Archibald Dickson, who thirty years later recalled how he watched in awe as "a caravan of approximately 28 men, 350 dogs, 60 sledges loaded with pemmican (canned meat) food supplies, tents, boats for crossing open water channels, etc., all ready and raring to go the limit were now on the way after bidding farewell and good luck to those left on the ship.

> After weeks of sledging through storm and blizzard, digging our way through fields of hummock ice looking like cities torn by cyclones and imbedded in ice and snow, at last Crown Prince Rudolf Land, ice covered and barren was reached, where we discovered the remnants of the camp of the Duke of Abruzzi . . . and near his camp, now practically buried in the heavy ice, we made our 30,000 pounds "farthest north" cache within 360 miles of the North Pole.[224]

Dickson could be forgiven for inflating the numbers of men and dogs on this initial foray. After three decades, the details of day-to-day operations had jumbled together. The supply train that did finally start north toward Rudolf

Land on Thursday, March 27, 1902, intent on reaching Baldwin's new "half-way" station at Kane Lodge on Greely Island, was nevertheless still impressive: fourteen sledges, all loaded to capacity, and drawn by seventy dogs.

Leffingwell led the party of eight and the start was anything but auspicious. As usual, Baldwin made certain that Fiala had the motion-picture camera running, though he might have wished otherwise, as the camera recorded "the various haps and mis-haps, such as falling into numerous cracks in the ice, which invariably accompany almost every unusual event in a party of this description."[225]

A storm hit Alger Island the next day, keeping Baldwin in camp preparing for the departure of his own party. By Saturday, March 29, the sun had come out and Baldwin led his party away to the north, but only "after securing motion-pictures of the 'take-off' with the good ship *America* solidly embedded in the ice in the background."[226] Even here, as he set off in charge of his first major exploring party since the discovery and exploration of Graham Bell Land three years earlier, Baldwin could not delegate responsibility for even the smallest tasks—all while not forgetting to poke Captain Johanson in the eye one more time. "After advancing some distance I returned to the ship to caution the party remaining behind relating to certain duties to be performed during our absence, I having placed the Chief Engineer H. P. Hartt in charge of the ship and camp during such period."[227] Baldwin does not explain why these instructions could not just as easily been given at any point during the day on Friday when the weather had pinned him to the island.

As Baldwin's party went into camp that first night, his erratic behavior again got the better of him, and he returned to spend one more night on board the *America,* taking with him all the ponies. Baldwin departed the ship, once again, early on Sunday morning, March 30, and no doubt to the relief of the men who remained behind, who now thought they had seen the back of him three separate times. Even this third departure did not get away smoothly, as a rifle fell from one of the sledges, causing Baldwin to stop and turn the whole party around until it was found.

At the first depot beyond East Camp Ziegler, when the sun made a brief appearance, the sledges were reloaded and Fiala ordered to take more motion footage. Two of the sledges broke down and had to be repaired, causing further delays. "The weather continued good and the long train of men, ponies, dogs, and sledges presented an animating picture as it stretched itself like a huge serpent gliding northward upon the glistening field of ice."[228]

On the final day of March 1902, Baldwin woke to find the weather bad and learned that the team of Russians he had assigned to reach a cache of supplies the previous night were still in camp because the cook had fed them last rather than first. Baldwin finally got his men on the trail at mid-day, leaving Porter behind "to cook, sketch, and work up observations."[229] The ponies, after just two days in the field, were already lame, so the men had to ease off their burdens. Late in the afternoon, Baldwin even spied Leffingwell's party, with two day's advance, just abreast of his own. The oversized sledging parties continued in this way, "trebling" every route—in the same laborious manner as had been done in 1898—by reaching a cache, hauling some of its supplies north, and then returning to complete the retrieval.

As his sledge parties meandered toward Kane Lodge, Baldwin himself had had enough after just three days in the field. After ordering his men north on Tuesday, April 1, he remained behind in camp "to write up notes [and] pick-up about camp,"[230] behavior that would have been all too familiar to the Norwegian companions of Susæg in 1898. Baldwin's tendency to shirk was not lost on his men and, as Leffingwell wrote, would "queer him with any one who has read of the heroic men doing double work as leaders of other expeditions."[231] Porter remained behind with Baldwin, to sketch and work up his observations of latitude, since Baldwin could not make these calculations himself—something Johanson had observed when he later told a reporter that Baldwin was "incompetent, the sextant he never learned and he did not know how to use the compass as we sailed north."[232] Porter's data showed the men to be standing at 80° 38' North and less than halfway to Kane Lodge.

When Fiala returned to camp on the afternoon of April 1, he had with him Leffingwell and his entire party, which itself had not yet reached Kane Lodge. The two parties now joined together in one huge party of dozens of men, sledges, dogs, and the surviving ponies. As he had done in 1898, Baldwin now decided that he liked the location of this first camp, so beginning on April 2 he sent the men off to different cache sites to shuttle more supplies to this new spot, "as I have decided to establish this as a 'permanent' camp till all equipment remaining in the advance depots have been collected here, before advancing in a direct line to the south entrance of Collinson channel enroute to Kane Lodge."[233]

The scattershot nature of this continuous back and forth, and the restrictive nature of Baldwin's leadership, is revealed in a note Baldwin wrote in the evening of April 3:

Dr. DeBruler complaining of lameness is left in charge of the camp, while Porter is left free to sketch, and having requested to be permitted to go to the "new fjord" to westward of our present camp and having stated his willingness to comply with all requirements and orders relative thereto, is granted permission to go, and upon returning therefrom reports having seen some "little auks." Meanwhile I made a record trip to Depot No. 3, starting at 12:15 P.M. arrived at the Depot at 3:00 P.M. and returned to camp [after] covering the ten miles in about two hours "on a trot." At 5:00 P.M. Leffingwell and party returned from "North" Island whither they went yesterday, and at midnight Lucas and the Russians reach camp from Kane Lodge, where they went on the 1st.[234]

Baldwin called his new depot "Iceberg Camp." On Friday, April 4, Baldwin rose for breakfast at 4:00 A.M., but it was another five hours before he was ready to get the main supply train, "seventeen teams and sledges all heavily burdened," on the trail.[235] A separate team made up of the Russians was sent to "Depot No. 3" to retrieve the remaining supplies there and bring them to the newly created Iceberg Camp. Before the supply train itself went very far, a storm blew up, causing DeBruler and Second Mate Bergendahl to become lost. They turned up a few hours later, but the main party remained pinned at Iceberg Camp.

The Russian party was somewhere in the storm, having been given orders by Baldwin to shelter in their tent if they were overcome by severe weather. He finally went in search of them on Sunday morning, by which point they had been missing for more than forty-eight hours. They were soon found, wandering in the fog. Baldwin returned with them to Iceberg Camp, where he "ordered hot coffee and food to be made ready for them upon their arrival, which coming to pass, they presented a grotesque and comical sight, their faces streaked and begrimed with soot: they had been unable to make the primus lamp function properly in the cooking of food, and, resorting to cooking-pans, and tin cups filled with fats and coal-oil, they had endeavored to adopt the Eskimo method of preparing their meals with the result that more smoke and soot was produced than heat, as was clearly evident from the blackened appearance of their faces as well as of the utensils."[236]

The appearance of the men was hardly the only grotesque and comical sight on the march north. Porter later recalled endless days of stopping and starting, of laying down one cache of supplies only to have to move it a few days later. "There would be something almost humorous in this vagary of fate were it not for the heartbreaking drudgery expended on dragging that stuff over hundreds of miles of ice."[237]

As they advanced, so did the spring, signs of which began to appear all around them. Clouds of little auks could be seen above the thinning fog, while the ice itself was now in motion, making loud cracking sounds in the straits and channels over which the expedition traveled. Since it was now Sunday, April 6, Baldwin held the expedition back, to rest, remove snow from the sledges and, in one of Baldwin's favorite activities, tidy up around camp. "Rilliet afforded us some diversion by the rendition of some of his favorite songs while Fiala directed our thoughts towards 'the Land beyond' by the reading of the 12th Chapter of Corinthians."[238]

By this time, the men would have been forgiven for not taking pleasure "in infirmities, in reproaches, in necessities, in persecutions, in distresses for Christ's sake," much less for the sake of Evelyn Briggs Baldwin, but their contracts bound them to a man seemingly determined to grind them into dust whether they liked it or not. The men had now been away from Camp Ziegler for ten days and had advanced barely 10 nautical miles. It was a pitiable performance, now continuing for day after interminable day. The main party "trebled" toward Kane Lodge while small ancillary parties shuttled back and forth to side caches and even back to the ship itself, retrieving a kayak here, some dog food there, and then fetching heavy rolls of tarred paper northward on the off chance Baldwin might want to build a hut and required some roofing and siding materials for it.

At times, it seemed to the men that Baldwin was forming depots for the sake of forming depots, and this constant repetitive effort required trips all the way back to the ship for stores of fish with which to sustain the dogs. It was as if Baldwin was play-acting at how he thought a polar explorer should behave, at the cost of the men's health as well as that of the dogs and ponies. Baldwin's diary entries are filled with fairly pointless minutiae, as on Thursday, April 10, when all of the teams were on the trail. They hauled supplies "to new Depot No. 1, in forty minutes, and to new Depot No. 2, in 35 minutes, the dogs pulling well notwithstanding soft snow had fallen during the night, some of the teams drawing loads of 600 pounds.

By 10 A.M. we were again at Iceberg camp, and after reloading sledges and partaking of coffee and biscuits again "hit the trail" at 11:00

A.M., arriving at Depot No. 1, at noon, and at Depot No. 2, at 2:00 P.M. By 3:00 P.M. we were again at Iceberg camp, towards which the teams made "quick time," Andree's team with such speed as to upset him under his sledge and to drag him some distance before he could finally extricate himself. As for myself rode the bay colored pony back to camp, thereby demonstrating the further utility of this modern species of the sea-horse.[239]

All of this crossing and re-crossing of thinning ice was bound to lead to accidents or worse. On Friday, April 11, one of the ponies fell through the ice and was just saved from drowning when it was cut loose from the traces that held the animal fast to the sledge. The sledge itself and its heavy load of cornmeal sank and were lost in a swift-running current. The suffering animal was rubbed down, covered in sailcloth, and immediately put back to work. If the incident was not a reminder of the growing danger to the entire party, they received the message directly later in the day, when the men noticed water vapor rising into the air ahead of them and halted the sledges just short of a widening hole of open water. His party exhausted, Baldwin had no choice but to make camp for the night on the unstable ice, even though he could see land about 2 nautical miles off.

The whole party was threatened with destruction that night when a storm sprang up, which fortunately moderated the following morning. Rather than see this as a sign to get the men off the ice, Baldwin inexplicably called for Fiala to take advantage of the sunshine "to secure some fine photographic exposures and after briefly addressing the members of the expedition as to probability of meeting open-water, and my plans for continuing the march, we again get underway at 12 noon, in bright sunshine." He then led his expedition into what could have been an overwhelming catastrophe, with Fiala filming every step of the way: "So thin was the ice now plastic with salt that it bent beneath our feet in great rubber-like rolls and I gave [an] order for the teams to follow my lead at considerable distances apart. Picking out the way as conditions seemed best, they followed in one long, but winding line, often through snow knee-deep to the ponies in whose trail the dogs followed, we at length gained the shore forming the south coast of Wiener Neustadt Island and made camp."[240]

As they reached the south shore of Wiener Neustadt Island, the party was about 20 nautical miles from Kane Lodge and the halfway point to

Baldwin's goal at Rudolf Land. But the progress was negated in the days that followed by repeated trips backward to previous cache sites as well as another flying trip for the Russians all the way back to the ship to retrieve one of the small boats. When the party began to advance northward once again, Baldwin let his pony take the lead. "On this march we made our way cautiously over the broken ice-cakes forming the ice-foot and rim of ice at the base of a glacier which fall abruptly into this part of the sea.

> Taking the lead with "Dun," one of the Siberian ponies whom I allowed to take his own course, that is, to pull his sledge without guidance of rein, or halter, the other ponies followed in good order. In the performance of his duty as "guide" it was indeed interesting to note the intelligence with which "Dun" went about his business, as, noting the cracks separating the ice-pans he frequently "tested" the ice-pan next following each crack by stepping cautiously upon it before advancing bodily upon it. . . . Having noted the unusual intelligence of this particular animal in following an almost entirely obliterated trail on hard ice I became much attached to him and invariably selected him as guide animal for the trail. He had evidently been trained for such duty in the wilds of Siberia, whence we had brought him with fourteen others of his kind.[241]

When the party reached Collinson Channel, the strait that separates Wiener Neustadt Island from what would eventually be named Ziegler Island, the dogs made a frantic break-in to the supplies of butter and sausage and had to be clubbed into submission. On Monday, April 14, Baldwin sent four of the Russians north to Kane Lodge and then sent Fiala south to bring up seventeen sledges at various depot to the south, while he himself stayed in camp busying himself "in various ways."[242] Tuesday was likewise spent in retrieving items from various caches, Leffingwell being dispatched for this work. It was not until Wednesday, April 16, that Baldwin himself returned to the trail, and arrived at Kane Lodge in the afternoon, dropping off some supplies and then immediately sledging south again. The Russians were left at Kane Lodge with all the ponies in order to give both men and animals some much needed rest.

The following morning, the Russians led the ponies south to meet up with the main party, and then the entire party got underway for Kane Lodge. On this leg of the advance from Alger Island, Baldwin finally allowed Porter the freedom to move ahead of the party to sketch and make topographical observations. Fiala as usual was kept busy photographing the pack train while recording Baldwin's thoughts in a notebook, as the expedition "flew our glorious colors in the breeze from the advance sledge as we passed the lofty heights of Cape Washington, and arrived at Kane Lodge at 5:00 P.M."[243] While the exhausted men and ponies and dogs slept, Baldwin and Porter stayed up to melt ice for drinking water at a stove and a pile of coal that had been delivered to the site during Baldwin's first visit to Greely Island several weeks previous.

After Porter turned in, Baldwin hiked to the northern end of Greely Island, where he noted both a small islet not marked on previous charts and a waterway that he promptly named the American Channel. Despite the tortuous progress of the previous three weeks that had seen his massive expedition advance barely farther north than he had with the Norwegians of Wellman's expedition in the fall of 1898, Baldwin was in high spirits: "Returning from my stroll I could not repress a feeling of much pride as I looked upon a large accumulation of pemmican and other supplies which had already been safely deposited at the Lodge by the concerted efforts of twenty-seven loyal men, and the bright prospects ahead."[244]

TWENTY-NINE

From Kane Lodge to Cape Auk

The following day, Baldwin kept the men in camp, for Porter and Fiala to sketch and photograph and the rest of the men to sort goods, mend harnesses, "and arrange loads for our march northward from the Lodge."[245] A hint of a reason for Baldwin's dithering at this point came when he finally took Leffingwell aside and gave him "my plans and purposes relating to his work as Geodetest [*sic*] to the Expedition," and then took another long walk away from Kane Lodge, this time westward along the newly named American Channel, stopping only when bad weather forced him back.[246]

Baldwin knew that he stood less than 30 nautical miles from the site where Nansen and Johansen had spent the winter of 1895–96. As part of his ongoing homage to previous Scandinavian polar explorers, he was determined to find the site and bring Porter and Fiala with him in order to sketch and photograph the area. Even as he knew that he needed to rapidly shift thousands of tons of supplies over the ice to Rudolf Land, his heart was pulling him toward Cape Norvegia and the message Nansen had left behind there after his epic of survival in 1895–96.

As Baldwin's mind drifted toward the dramatic retrieval of famous messages frozen in the ice, back at Kane Lodge the scene bordered on utter chaos. The extended time in camp led to the dogs running wild, and the men now had to round them up and sort them into teams while chewed and mangled harnesses were repaired or replaced. Two of the dogs were now shot, as Baldwin wrote, "one as a 'deserter' for refusing to be caught, and the other by reason of 'chronic halt,' which rendered him useless."[247]

The reason for the shooting of the halting dog was likely not lost on the men, who continued to be placed into either dangerous or banal situations they had not signed up for. The skilled expedition members found themselves baling hay for the advance of the ponies northward. When men such as Porter and Fiala were given time to do the work they *had* signed on for—to sketch and paint, survey and film—it was because Baldwin was keen to gather illustrations for his "expedition narrative." The remainder of the men, who had themselves been sorted into teams, were now split up and reassigned to sleep in odd numbers in the 'lodge' so that the tents were not so crowded while the party was in camp on Greely Island.

Unlike the fall of 1898, when Baldwin forced his Norwegians to subsist on a diet of walrus, the 1902 sledge party lived almost exclusively on preserved and dried foods and instant beverages. A typical supper at Kane Lodge consisted of tea, hardtack, bean biscuits, oatmeal, dried apricots, and an extra allowance of sugar, the latter commodity the one the men particularly craved. The effect of the meager calories on men asked to perform the hardest possible physical labor was to further exhaust all of them.

Baldwin took Leffingwell to the tallest point of Greely Island in order to secure a series of bearings for the way north to Rudolf Land. They set out at midnight on April 20 and reached the highest point on the cliffs on the western side of Greely Island at 3:30 A.M. But Baldwin's eyes were now drawn inexorably westward, not to the north where one would have assumed his single-minded focus:

To the northward of the island on which we stood the topography appeared to consist of a series of rolling snow-ridges terminating in level surfaces, with three basaltic cliffs visible along the east shore of the island. Concluding the taking of numerous bearings at 4:45 A.M. we get out on the return trip following our outward tracks, at length arriving at the cliff where we had left rifle and ax. But as the wind was now blowing furiously we found it more difficult to get over and down the perpendicular cliff than it had been to get up and over it. This, however, we effected by first letting down the instruments by means of a long line on which Leffngwell first descended although he generously insisted that I should go first, and then I followed. To the westward of this location there was visible a large space of open water in the channel between the newly discovered island in American channel, and further westward lofty cliffs came into view.[248]

Baldwin clearly wanted to work his way westward beyond those lofty cliffs to the historic site that lay just beyond them, but his duty to William Ziegler drew him back, at least for the moment. Some of the men thought he was determined to see whether his "American Channel" was indeed a route through the middle of the archipelago that would link the Austrian Channel in the east with the British Channel in the west. Baldwin and Leffingwell returned to Kane Lodge by 7:00 a.m., where the remainder of Sunday was given over to more picture taking, and Fiala thereafter spent the day standing under a woolen blanket dyed red as a stand-in for a darkroom.

The same situation prevailed on Monday morning, as thick weather kept everyone in their sleeping bags with a mug of coffee while Fiala took more motion-picture footage. Only late in the day did the men set off, after the sledges were dug from the snow that had been allowed to cover them. They crossed the eighty-first parallel and reached the northeast corner of Greely Island just before midnight.

The following morning, Tuesday, April 22, the dogs raised the entire party when they cornered a large female walrus, which Baldwin shot dead. He and Leffingwell then tracked the walrus' movements back to a ledge above the seafront where a walrus pup, presumably the offspring of the female just killed, was also shot. Together, the carcasses were fed to the 160 dogs that remained in fit condition to work. Baldwin and Leffingwell took another series of bearings and then pushed out yet another cache to the north, between the islands of Becker and Stoliczka, while teams were sent back to Kane Lodge to relay yet more supplies to the new encampment. With Leffingwell's new bearings, Baldwin now announced his intention to shuttle supplies northward via the west coast of Greely Island, a very strange tack since the bulk of his men and supplies were already encamped on the northeast corner of Greely and ready to jump off from there.

The men were so exhausted by this point that, when the ponies broke free of the ropes and ate most of the *sennegress* the men used as insulation and absorbent in their footgear, no one roused to stop them. The ponies had become so desperate for the fodder that had long since been eaten that they were striking out anywhere they could for proper food, rather than continue to feed on the cornmeal and dried fish Baldwin had provided for them.

As the ponies tired, they were shot and fed to the dogs. One of the Swedish sailors, Birger Börjesson, watched on in disgust as one pony "was led aside and got a bullet in the forehead, and after half an hour the only remains of it were the bones. One after another the ponies were taken to feed the dogs and their intestinal parasites."[249]

The whole party advanced their tents and sledges to the camp on the ice between Becker and Stoliczka islands on the evening of April 23. Baldwin left a few men to guard the supply cache, mounted the pony Dun, and led the rest of the supply train further north to the establishment of their farthest-north encampment yet. It was an auspicious moment for Baldwin, who was now north of the northernmost point he had reached in 1899—the northern edge of Graham Bell Land. With every step from this point onward, he would establish a new personal "farthest north."

Such satisfaction was short lived, however, since Baldwin drove the ponies too fast on the return to the depot on the ice. The ponies soon ran amok through the dog teams, flipping Baldwin and Dickson from their sledges and entangling Baldwin in his own sledge's lines. The expedition leader was helplessly dragged feet first along the ice, in the process running over one of the Swedish sailors. There was no mention of Fiala being rushed to record this particular scene, though the other members of the expedition no doubt would have paid good money to watch such footage.

Resuming the advance, Baldwin led the party to the west coast of Rainer Island by midnight on Thursday, April 24. For the first time, Baldwin offered the men a choice between tea and coffee: every man but Baldwin chose coffee. From this spot, Baldwin and Fiala went north to spy a channel that separated Karl Alexander Island, the next island on their march, from an island to its south. Baldwin would eventually realize that he was looking at the north side of the same Jackson Island he so desperately wanted to explore in search of Nansen's hut. To the north, Baldwin saw half a dozen islets separating his party from his intended destination on Rudolf Land, all of them surrounded by smooth sea ice. The weather and sea ice being perfect, it was long past time to get his men on the move and finish the job of establishing the Rudolf Land cache.

Accordingly, at 9:20 P.M. on Friday, April 25, Baldwin left Fiala and Vinyard to guard the cache on Rainer Island and led the remainder of his men and their fourteen sledges toward Rudolf Land. As if he sensed that his ambitions and his realities were rapidly converging in a kind of career apogee, Baldwin's writings at this point suddenly became much more expansive. It was as if he realized that these next days in his life story would one day be heavily scrutinized and was therefore determined to document them to the smallest detail.

The men and dogs raced north for two hours before stopping for a short rest. Here, at last, Baldwin was finally on the threshold on the northernmost point Walter Wellman had achieved in 1899, and an ace away from entering the domain of Fridtjof Nansen himself. He was just a few short nautical miles away from establishing a new farthest north for the Americans in Franz Josef Land and truly blazing his own trail as a polar explorer, and the feelings of accomplishment that began to flood through him were as profound as they were premature.

> From this point at midnight with the sun resting above Rudolf Land the cliffs which I had observed during the forenoon as forming part of the west coast of Rudolf Land were replaced with snow-covered caps, while the Rocks and Islets which I had sighted from the western glacier slope of Rainer Island in the direction of Rudolf Land were again visible, and perhaps form part of the eastern shore of Payer's "Rawlinson" channel, or, as that channel does not exist they may be merely Tidal Rocks, visible only with the recurrence of low water, which may leave them bare of ice.[250] Moreover, from this point, the Hvidtland Islands, discovered by Nansen, are also clearly visible, as is the entire east coast of Rudolf Land. All these observations have been made by use of a strong pair of binoculars during excellent weather and clear visibility. No other land in a northerly direction was discerned.[251]

By now it was late April 1902, and though he was not yet forty years of age, Baldwin's career as a field explorer had barely two more months left to it. The weather continued to be fine, the air calm and the silence almost absolute. There were few polar bears or walrus to be seen, and the birds seemed to have abandoned the air. Baldwin's remark about not finding any more indications of land to the north was a needling dig at Wellman, who claimed to have found several new islands east of Rudolf Land in 1899, islands subsequently shown to be mirages by the Duke of the Abruzzi. On the evening of Saturday, April 26, Baldwin and Leffingwell lugged their survey instruments to the summit of Rainer Island. From this elevation, Baldwin not only looked ahead but also engaged in some autobiographical polish:

> Arriving at the summit at 9:30 P.M. we enjoyed a clear view of the entire horizon, the south and east coasts of Rudolf Land standing out in sharp relief against the sea-ice below, with no other land visible on the northern horizon till Hvidtland came into view, and then the northern termination of Graham Bell Land upon which three years previous I had stood after my discovery and exploration of the island while in charge of an exploring party, with the rocky coast lines of Whitney Island [La Ronciere Island] intervening, till the headlands on the north and northwest coasts of Wilczek Land swung into view, followed by what appeared to be the three peaks constituting the Wuellersdorf mountains of Payer appearing just above the distant ice-cap covering the southern part of Wilczek Land. . . . It was an exceptionally fine opportunity of securing an excellent set of bearings and we made the best possible use of it, and then and there Leffingwell made record of all data which was set down in my presence and with my assistance in a book supplied me by the Office of the United States Coast and Geodetic Survey. . . . Upon concluding our observations we erected there a cairn or beacon mark consisting of two dog-cake tins filled with ice and hard snow, a pole several feet in length, and other articles.[252]

Leffingwell, upon whom Baldwin now completely relied for all of the expedition's surveying and positioning, walked back down from the summit while Baldwin rode on the sledge carrying the survey instruments. They could see Fiala's pack train moving southward to bring up a cache of three tons of pemmican sealed in 450 tins, "now stringing out like a train of ants, and then 'bunching' as though gathering for conference every now and then, most likely to settle some point at issue between rival dog-teams."[253] The Russians arrived at Rainer Island soon after, with the ponies pulling sledges loaded with "38 tins of dog-cakes, 39 tins of pemmican, walrus meat, two canoes, baled hay, senne grass, and some other articles."[254] One of the ponies, "Billy," was exhausted by the labor and died during the night. The dead animal was quickly cut into pieces and fed to the dogs.

Breaking camp on Sunday, April 27, Baldwin reversed his sometimes stricture on Sabbath labor and sent the Russians and the surviving ponies back to Kane Lodge for more supplies, and then took twelve sledges and went to the new cache north of Rainer Island. Arriving at 10:00 P.M., Baldwin loaded the sledges and pushed on toward tiny Coburg Island, where the men arrived just after midnight and began to assemble the northernmost cache yet. The whole party was now constantly weary, and as they returned to the Rainer Island camp early on Monday morning, April 28, they promptly fell asleep, sleeping all that day and well into the next. Breakfast was not cooked and eaten until mid-afternoon on Tuesday, April 29, at which time the men again worked northward to the Coburg Island cache.

Once the men had arrived at Coburg Island, Baldwin dispatched the entire party—save for himself, Leffingwell, and Fiala—north to a spot called Cape Brorok on the southwest corner of Rudolf Land itself. Fiala was held back as cook and watchman at the camp, while Baldwin and Leffingwell ascended to the highest spot on Coburg Island to take another round of angles of the surrounding territory. To the northwest the view was both barren and bleak. To the northeast, the two men spied the nearby Lesgaft Reefs and, further to the northeast, the islands of Nansen's "Hvidtland," which "lent relief to the scene of icy desolation."[255]

On Wednesday, April 30, the last day of the month, Baldwin gathered the entire party and together they moved toward Cape Auk on Rudolf Land. Baldwin hoped to reach the cape over the ice and avoid crossing the glacier front that separated Cape Auk from Cape Brorok to the south. Another of the ponies was failing, so it was given a load of "only" 250 pounds and placed at the rear of the train. After moving across smooth ice for 2 nautical miles, the men sledged into a broken ice field where the sledges began to break down. Baldwin had no choice but to create still another temporary cache on the ice, while the men and animals continued on with lightened loads and those whose sledges were beyond repair returned to Coburg Island.

Maneuvering through the fields of broken ice, Baldwin deposited the sledge loads just short of Cape Auk, before he and the men raced back to the Coburg Island camp for hot soup and for another load of supplies. With the loads now reduced to six hundred pounds per sledge, the men made another round trip to the cache near Cape Auk.

The men returned from both the southern and northern caches after midnight and slept in until mid-morning. Leffingwell's observations placed them at 81° 33' North. The expedition was close to where Baldwin wanted it to be the previous summer, but it was now Thursday, May 1, 1902, and the window to safely sledge across the ice was rapidly drawing to a close. Accordingly, the men loaded everything from Coburg Island camp and at 5:00 P.M. made off for the north. By now, the men could see the reflection of water in the skies to the southwest and northwest—it was past time for all of the supplies to be cached on dry land.

The men and animals were worn out. Returning from the cache near Cape Auk, Baldwin came upon one of his exhausted men, asleep on a sledge behind a pony that had wandered off course until stopped by a large block of ice. If not for the sudden barrier, the man and pony and sledge would presumably have continued to wander westward and, eventually, into the sea.

On Saturday, May 3, Baldwin got underway with high hopes of reaching Teplitz Bay, a slight indentation on the western coastline of Rudolf Land where the Duke of the Abruzzi had made his camp in 1899. But he had been on the march for only a short time when, just south of the bay, Baldwin was brought up short by a large expanse of open water. The pack train had to get to shore and quickly, or the entire expedition was at risk of losing its supplies—dragged at such monumental effort from Alger Island—into the sea.

Baldwin stared at the demoralizing scene, one that meant an end to his supply train fantasy. He wrote with straightforward understatement that "I did not announce [the obvious predicament] to the party, but permitted them to observe for themselves, who in turn said nothing. It was nevertheless evident from their faces that our further advance for any great distance was under thoughtful consideration."[256]

In truth, no consideration was remotely required. Baldwin's entire pack train of several tons was advancing across thinning ice that was rapidly melting into open water. Without proper boats or the lamented motor launch, there was only one direction left to them: due east. The men quickly moved toward a landing on the southwest coast of Rudolf Land, and south of the site of the camp of the Italian polar expedition.

The risky maneuver was a near catastrophe. The ice had changed character so much that the ponies began to slide across it. They could not stay on their feet until they reached better footing along a moderately level stretch of pebble and rocky earth. There, "by the side of a huge boulder or mass of rock which had fallen from a beetling cliff began the formation of our northernmost depot."[257] Although Baldwin denied it, he had desperately wished to reach the ready-made site of the Duke of the Abruzzi's camp. It would remain then and forever just beyond his reach. With a false sense of nationalism, he pretended that he had never needed it:

> Across the open water of Teplitz Bay and the glacier this side could be seen the site of the encampment of the former Italian expedition. But as this could not be reached except by crossing the intervening glacier I deemed it inexpedient as well as not within my plan for next year's work to undertake it, as by doing so the journey from Rudolf Land to the Pole would thereby have to begin from a point farther west than I contemplate, it being my intention to make the journey via the east coast of Rudolf Land so as to profit by the westward drift of the ice-pack intervening between the north coast of Rudolf Land and the Pole, and by so doing escape being carried too far to the westward as were members of the Italian expedition upon its returned journey from its "farthest north" to Teplitz Bay. Besides, at the site of our "Boulder depot" or in the vicinity of it I discerned an enviable location for a new Headquarters entirely independent of anything which the Italian expedition may have left at Teplitz Bay.[258]

This was special pleading, and Baldwin knew it. Franz Josef Land was a place where the ice conditions in general were a living nightmare for humans, dogs and ponies, but some areas were clearly worse than others. The polar ice pack, circulating clockwise around the North Pole, ground into the east coast of Rudolf Land—into in fact all of the islands of eastern Franz Josef Land—like a slow-moving freight train, as Walter Wellman had learned to his permanent injury. On the west coast of Rudolf Land, even though Teplitz Bay was hardly a bay at all and the whole area exposed to both swirling ice and the ferocious winds streaming down from the ice dome that crowned the island, an expedition would at least have some minor shelter from the westward-setting pack ice.

The greatest irony, by far, was Baldwin's insistence that at Cape Auk—a spot that was nothing short of an extremely dangerous cliff overhang beneath the Rudolf Land ice dome—he could build "a new Headquarters entirely independent of anything which the Italian expedition may have left at Teplitz Bay." Not only would this have been a foolish duplication of effort with the Duke of the Abruzzi's camp just a few nautical miles north and readily available, but the following year, when William Ziegler placed Anthony Fiala in charge of a new Ziegler polar expedition, Fiala's ship steamed right into Teplitz Bay and dropped anchor a few hundred yards from the site of the former Italian camp. As Russell Porter put it so eloquently when he remembered these days years later: "As a result of the season's sledding, several tons of food and equipment were landed on Rudolf Land, the most northerly of the group, only to be picked up by Fiala in 1903 and carried to his winter quarters a few nautical miles farther on. There would be something almost humorous in this vagary of fate were it not for the heartbreaking drudgery expended on dragging that stuff over hundreds of miles of ice."[259]

For his part, and since he had no other choice, Baldwin still clung to the magical thinking that he was on the verge of achieving the North Pole. He believed he had "discerned a most advantageous means of shelter for an enlarged train of ponies for the final 'dash for the Pole' not far from the site of the boulder cache, and ample space for a large number of dogs—and the safety of the party being further insured by ready accessibility to Kane Lodge and the mid-section of the Franz-Josef Land Archipelago, with little if any danger of being cut off on the return journey of either the main expedition or its supporting parties, from the Pole itself."[260]

How an exposed cache of pemmican at Cape Auk enhanced his prospects for a safe return from the North Pole, only Baldwin himself knew. For a year, with the lottery prize of William Ziegler's money, Baldwin had acted like a polar exploration fantasist, to the point where his crew had begun to openly question his grip on reality. Leffingwell later felt that Baldwin "showed at times a mental condition bordering upon insanity."[261] The expedition leader's "mental condition" now took a turn for the worse. With his northernmost cache laid at Cape Auk, Baldwin's Arctic fantasies began to intensify.

THIRTY

Dr. Nansen Slept Here

Baldwin and the men hastily unloaded the sledges at what was now called the "Boulder Depot" site at Cape Auk before hurrying south to their last camp on the ice. Maneuvering along the narrow snow-covered ice-foot at the southwestern edge of Rudolf Land, they reached the cache on the ice and had coffee. During their break, they were nearly overrun by Dr. DeBruler's dogs. DeBruler was leading his dogs from the south when he saw one of the expedition's tents from the distance and mistook it for a polar bear. Without a gun, DeBruler was trying to figure the best way to deploy his dogs to defend himself when he heard the men at the coffee pot.

Following the coffee break, the ponies were used to drag 448 large tins of pemmican to Boulder Depot. The shuttle of supplies off the ice and to the new depot continued on Sunday, May 4. The open water that the men had seen near Teplitz Bay was rapidly encroaching on them. The men and animals raced to finish the cache and retreat back to Alger Island before the straits and bays of Franz Josef Land became passable only by a waterborne ferrying operation Baldwin was not equipped to mount. Baldwin made up a parcel of special goods for himself to be stashed at Boulder Depot, and then he and Leffingwell walked north from the new cache with a survey transit. Baldwin went "to the edge of the open water and having a clear view of Teplitz Bay and the glacier come to the conclusion that it would be quite impossible to cross the glacier to the site of the former Italian expedition headquarters without slipping over the face of the glacier into the water."[262]

The Italian camp was tantalizingly just out of reach. "By means of our binoculars we were able to make out clearly the 'tent-house' of that expedition and to note that nothing there appeared to be in disorder."[263] This brief glimpse of the remains of the Italian camp at Teplitz Bay was the northernmost latitude achieved in the exploring career of Evelyn Briggs Baldwin, though at the moment he still seemed to believe that it was only a matter of time before he and his dogs and ponies were bounding over the ice to the North Pole.

While Baldwin stared in his polar reverie, his men deposited another 338 tins of pemmican at Boulder Depot. The final sledge loads were shifted by 11:00 P.M. on Sunday, May 4, at which point it was time to take a round of commemorating photographs "and then, following an address of congratulations extended to the leader of the expedition by Dickson, the party gave 'Three Cheers for Old Glory' while thousands of little auks circled back and forth over the open water and under the beetling cliffs above us, thus bringing to an end our northward journey for the season."[264]

The mundane sledging of several tons of pemmican to Cape Auk was certainly not the triumph for Baldwin that the discovery and exploration of Graham Bell Land had been in 1899. At the same time, it had not been an easy feat, and Baldwin's evident pride in it seems to have blinded him to any consideration of the likely feelings of William Ziegler. The failure to move "the best equipped polar expedition of all time" even to the site of the base camp of the former Italian polar expedition—much less begin to challenge the farthest north the Italians had achieved—was guaranteed to enrage the Gilded Age multimillionaire, for whom money was all and solved all.

At 2:00 A.M. on Monday, May 5, 1902, Baldwin left his own personal farthest north at Boulder Depot and, along with his mates, began the trek south. At the tent camp on the ice, they fed the ponies and dogs and then grabbed some sleep before packing up the temporary camp and, in bright sunshine, moving south. One group of men was dispatched back to Cape Auk to retrieve a soldering kit that had been left there, while Baldwin, along with the remainder of the dogs and men, worked their way south. The eleven surviving ponies were soon ten, as one of the animals was soon declared unfit and shot to feed the dogs.

The large supply train, now largely empty of its heavy loads, quickly reached the Coburg Island cache, while Baldwin and Leffingwell made a rapid side trip to the west coast of Hohenlohe Island to take a round of angles. It had taken Baldwin forty-five days to hopscotch his supplies from Alger Island to Cape Auk. In their retreat, his men regained Kane Lodge in as many hours, returning to Greely Island early in the morning of Wednesday, May 7. Baldwin built a fire in the stove of his "lodge" while the men erected their tents.

Russell Porter had remained behind at Kane Lodge with the indisposed Andree, and Porter had used the time well, sketching scenes around Greely Island while on forays to hunt for walrus. Baldwin sent men off to secure these kills and return the carcasses to Kane Lodge, whereupon he announced that, on account of the unexpected supplies of meat, the expedition could now undertake additional sledge work, using the lodge as a base, before they returned to the ship. Here at last was Baldwin's chance to chase down the written record left behind at Cape Norvegia by Fridtjof Nansen. "Lucas and the Russians are to be dispatched with supplies for a final trip to 'Boulder cache' at Cape Auk, Dr. Verner and party to South Coburg Island, Leffingwell and party to the eastward as far as Wilczek Land if possible, while I go to the westward through the American channel."[265]

The bone-weary men tried to get some sleep in and around the "lodge," an effort made the more difficult by the ceaseless barking of the dogs, sounds amplified as the animals now took to barking at their own echoes reflected from the surrounding cliffs. The men set to work to clean up the camp and retrieve items like small boats that had been randomly cached around the area during the spring sledging work. The lodge received repairs "in order that it may be made more comfortable for future occupancy."[266] A small shed or stable next to the lodge was begun to support the anticipated work of the 1903 field season. Baldwin forbade anyone from returning to the ship until after the various side trips were complete and all men had re-assembled at Kane Lodge.

On Saturday, May 10, Baldwin called Leffingwell and Porter into his tent to give them his plans for work. Leffingwell was to explore eastward as far as Wilczek Land, "to secure observations which I hope will tie up with my survey work in that part of the Franz-Josef Land in the Spring of 1899, and Porter and Fiala to accompany me westward through the American channel for survey and photographic work."[267] Leffingwell knew that he was being further shunted away from any new discoveries and instead being used merely to confirm the ground Baldwin had already covered during the spring sledge trip of 1899. Leffingwell also knew why Porter and Fiala were now Baldwin's constant companions: they were the two men who could provide the manuscript illustrations Baldwin so desperately wanted.

In the afternoon, Baldwin, Porter, and Fiala duly set out to the west, along with eighteen dogs pulling two sledges piled high with a tent, sleeping bag, cooking gear, cameras, and walrus meat for the dogs. The men and dogs worked their way westward along the northern coast of what would eventually be recognized as an island and named for William Ziegler. One of the sledges soon broke down and the men abandoned it as they pushed on northwest toward Payer Island. The channel that separated Payer Island from Greely Island Baldwin named for Dr. Verner, who was "the first to pass through it on his trip to Coburg Island."[268]

The men continued westward on May 11 until they went into camp beneath "perpendicular cliffs of basalt rising above us like the walls of a great cathedral."[269] Perhaps reminding him of the skyscrapers of home, Baldwin gave the feature the name "New York Cliffs." The American labeling of the area continued as Baldwin named the cape formed by the cliffs after Theodore Roosevelt—without any way to know that the man who was vice president upon their departure from Vardø was now president of the United States as a result of the assassination of William McKinley.

When a mother bear and cub wandered into their camp that night, Baldwin panicked, rising in his socks and slashing a rent in the tent to get at the rifles locked in a case on the sledge. He emerged from the tent to find the mother bear fighting with one of the dog teams. Several cartridges later, the bears were dead, Fiala was put to work sewing the tent back together, and Baldwin and Porter were chasing the other dog team a mile down the channel where they finally found them entangled in their own traces and unable to run any farther. Baldwin in this chaos stumbled upon another channel, one that separated Payer Island from Jackson Island.[270]

Eagerly anticipating that they were close to the overwintering site of Nansen and Johansen, Baldwin began to imagine things that were not there. Spying a black object at the head of an unknown bay, Baldwin thought it might be a signal beacon constructed by Nansen, or even Andrée, or perhaps one of the missing members of the Italian expedition. When on closer inspection it turned out to be merely the rock-summit of an islet, "beyond which came into view the face of a steep glacier covering that section of Jackson Island," Baldwin took the opportunity to make perhaps his lone expression of unselfconscious generosity during the entire expedition: "To the bay thus traversed is given the name Querini and to the headland at its southeastern entrance the name Ollier of the Italian expedition and to the headland at its southwestern entrance the name of Stokken the young Norwegian member of the same expedition and who was son of Captain Stokken who had brought back to civilization the Wellman expedition of 1898–99. To the little island at the head of this bay is given the name of Hope with the prayer that future years may bring to light further word as to the fate of these heroes of these ice-bound shores."[271]

From the newly named Cape Stokken, Baldwin and his two companions made their way along the stony, boulder-strewn shore of Jackson Island for a few hours before stopping at a spot Porter calculated as 55° 41' East longitude. With the expedition near an end of its work for 1902, Baldwin broke into the specialties he had loaded up on in the spring of 1901, and the men tucked into coffee and crackers, butter and strawberry jam, all on top of a polar bear stew.

Before the men could get any real sleep, though, three more bears—a mother and two cubs—wandered into the camp, attracted by the smell of the meat. Baldwin, who by now was nearly snow-blind, had the presence of mind to open the tent flap rather than slice it open with a knife, but "the glaring sun-light so blinded me that I was unable to catch sight of them among the boulders till they had beaten a safe retreat high among the rocks on the snow-covered slope and where they eluded my long-range shots at them."[272]

At 3:00 A.M. on Tuesday, May 13, the men and dogs continued to pick their way along the rough shore ice and boulders of Jackson Island, closing in on the spot where they expected to find Nansen's hut. The journey came to an abrupt halt when Baldwin fell through the shore ice and was soaked to his thighs. After changing into a new set of footgear, Baldwin led the men into camp along the shore for a breakfast of coffee and bear stew. From the tenor of his writings at this moment, Baldwin was fairly beside himself with anticipation: "At this point we had expected to find the winter lair of Nansen and Johansen—but it was not to be seen. Nevertheless from the appearance of two bright spots on the slope above us and a black spot in the snow covering a flat space I conjectured that this particular spot might be the roof of the 'hut' itself."[273]

After the effort to sledge the men and dogs to the exposed spot of Nansen's overwintering hut, Baldwin then curiously passed on by it. He made another of his day-dreaming explores along the beach, leaving Porter in camp to "afford him an opportunity of adding to his collections as Artist to the Expedition."[274]

Dictating his scientific thoughts to the faithful Fiala, who dutifully followed him with a notebook and camera at the ready, Baldwin "noted deposits of mud, gray sandstones and shells" as they approached Cape Mill. Baldwin stepped carefully across the ground, like a forensic investigator at the scene of a crime. At length they "came upon a log or piece of driftwood eight feet in length upon the beach and bearing the marks made by the claws of a bear as well as by fire.

> This was evidence that we had passed the location of Nansen's hut, otherwise Nansen would have made use of this valuable asset in the construction of the lair or otherwise utilized it in the course of his sojourn here. As to the fire-marks (?) upon it they had doubtless resulted from a forest-fire somewhere in Siberia before being cast adrift at the mouth of some river in that distant land many years ago.[275]

The two men walked for a few more hours and reached Cape Mill, where they found great masses of ice pressed against the basalt cliffs. When they came to a glacier spilling into the sea from the west coast of Jackson Island, they stopped and turned back, but not before noting a small islet offshore that might present another naming opportunity. Baldwin's footgear was again soaked through and his painful snow blindness had not improved, so when they regained the tent in mid-afternoon he fell into eight hours of sleep.

"Breakfast" was served just after midnight on Wednesday, May 14. After feeding themselves and the dogs, the men finally got underway at 5:45 A.M. Returning to the area where he expected to find Nansen's hut, Baldwin caught sight of some piled up stones "which had the appearance of forming a wall, investigation proved such to be the case—the wall forming the rear end on the foundation of the stone hut which our hardy Norwegian predecessors had commenced but later abandoned for their final winter-quarters in a more favorable spot. The foundation walls for this hut enclosed a space about six feet square and were still chinked with moss just as the explorers had left them."[276]

Baldwin continued along the raised shoreline until he caught sight of a piece of walrus-hide rope protruding about six inches above the level of

Baldwin at Nansen's hut at Cape Norvegia. What Baldwin considered his singular discovery would soon prove to be his undoing. From Evelyn Briggs Baldwin, "The Baldwin-Ziegler Polar Expedition, Part III," *Wide World Magazine* 10 (60): 587–93.

the snow. "Surely the winter-lair was near at hand and calling out to my companions I announced the 'discovery.'"[277] He stood on a gravel terrace well above the level of the frozen sea and, thumping his staff on the walrus hide as if on a drum-head, heard the hollow sound of empty space. Soon he had found the ruins of the stone chimney, small and blubber-stained. "Hard bye [*sic*] was also a pile of bones with not a vestige of flesh upon them—all that was left of many a 'cave-man feast' enjoyed by the erstwhile inhabitants of the hut."[278]

Baldwin was ecstatic. He told the men that they would themselves make camp on the spot, in order to "clean house."[279] Once they had set up the tent and fed the dogs, the three men set to work clearing the snow that blanketed the famous site. Baldwin then ordered Porter and Fiala to record the hut in pen and ink and watercolors (Porter) and photography (Fiala), while Baldwin used empty tin cans as shovels to burrow down through three feet of accumulated snow.

When he found the entrance to the hut, Baldwin continued to tunnel downward, to discover that the interior was completely filled with snow. Once Porter and Fiala had finished their work of recording the hut, they joined Baldwin and soon had the interior cleared, "our efforts being rewarded through the discovery of the message which Dr. Nansen had left at his departure from the hut in a small copper cylinder attached to the ridge-pole of the hut, and also a small blubber lamp formed from the shoulder-blade of a polar bear."[280] The cylinder, with its stopper of wood, held a brief message in Norwegian and was dated on the day that Nansen and Johansen finally took their departure from the hut: May 19, 1896. Like a talisman, Baldwin would hold onto the message for much of the rest of his life, before he finally handed it to the Norwegian Legation in Washington nearly thirty years later, in December 1930.[281]

Porter took the opportunity to compose a watercolor sketch of the interior. It was a work of fine art that Baldwin would soon come to regret. But at the time, he was cock-a-hoop. With the detailed work of Baldwin's homage to the great Nansen accomplished, the men ate supper and turned in. As Baldwin later wrote: "For two days Photographer Fiala, Artist Porter, and myself were steadily employed securing photographs, colour sketches, and making notes of the memorable spot."[282]

The following morning, Thursday, May 15, final photographs were taken, including one "of "Old Glory" unfurled to the breeze at the southern end of the roof of the lair."[283] Baldwin then substituted his own message for the one he recovered of Nansen. This final mark of obeisance complete, the men left the site of Nansen and Johansen's epic survival struggle and crossed the channel that separated Jackson Island from what Baldwin soon realized was a new island.

Flush with the excitement of the discovery of the site of Nansen's overwintering, Baldwin was now moved to recognize the reason he was able to live out his Franz Josef Land fantasy. He named the new island "Ziegler," "in recognition of the financial support extended to me by Mr. William Ziegler of New York City, and in the name and behalf of the Baldwin-Ziegler Polar Expedition."[284]

They were in the very center of the Franz Josef Land archipelago, in an area filled with polar bears, walrus, and seals, and they paused to try and capture all this wildlife on camera—before shooting as much of it as they possibly could in order to feed the dogs. But the barking of the same dogs frightened away any chance of getting close to the wild animals. The men passed a small islet, but Baldwin's eyes were now all on the large new Ziegler Island that he was anxious to explore.

The small party reached the northwestern corner of the island at 3:00 P.M. and Baldwin immediately left Porter and Fiala in camp while he set off along the shoreline southward. He found a pathway to the highest point of this sector of the island and began his ascent. He soon reached a point where he "had a clear view of an unobstructed channel separating Ziegler Island on the north from Salisbury Island on the south."[285] This waterway had already been dubbed Cecil Rhodes Fjord during the Jackson-Harmsworth expedition, but Baldwin was feeling his oats now and so he renamed it "Baldwin-Ziegler Polar Expedition Channel" "in testimony of the loyalty of the members of the expedition during all the trying months of work in the field."[286] "From the summit where I stood the scenery on both shores of the channel was indeed picturesque, with much plant life at my feet, the perspective swept southward through a wide range of alternating rugged cliffs and imposing glaciers. Bright sunshine prevailing the beauty of the scene was enhanced by the presence of bands of heavy stratus and cumulo-stratus clouds casting their shadows on the snowy whiteness below and in the lonely silence about me created a feeling of inexpressible awe."[287]

Thus did Baldwin descend from this height a new man, full in the feeling that he had managed not only a successful field season but was now poised to claim the North Pole itself in the spring of 1903.

THIRTY-ONE

Downward into a Yawning Crevasse

On Friday morning, May 16, Baldwin could not resist one more exploration of his new island. He left Porter in camp to work on his sketches and took the trusty Fiala with his camera on an overland excursion across Ziegler Island. The weather, as Baldwin so often described it, was "thick," but the men could still make out the headlands on both sides of Baldwin's "American Channel." As they made their way to the summit of the island, the two men reached a high basalt cliff from which they could look down to see a bear as it ambled across the ice of a bay far beneath them.

Baldwin took out a small pocket compass and made a quick sketch of the coastline. With this final confirmation of his discovery, he retreated back to camp, where the men had coffee. They then packed and began the return sledge trip back down American Channel toward Kane Lodge. They stopped for the evening about two-thirds of the way down the north coast of Ziegler Island. With no more meat for the dogs, the animals went hungry.

On Saturday morning, Baldwin took the chance to make his fourth exploration of the island. It was a short excursion that nearly killed him: "Ascending the glacial slope from near the camp we were soon some hundreds of feet above sea-level when suddenly the snow beneath my feet gave way and I started downward into a yawning crevasse with such force and rapidity that had the opening been a little wider I must have gone to the bottom—somewhere. But luckily my Alpine stock was of sufficient length and strength to support the weight of my body as it struck the edges of the crevasse and Fiala coming to the rescue I was soon on my feet again, but not until the photographer had snapped me in an uncomfortable position."[288]

It was just the sort of incident that Baldwin desperately needed to round out his thus far rather slim "expedition narrative." That he remained posed in this awkward position—dramatically holding up his ice axe as if in mid-swing into the ice—while Fiala took his picture, is as clear an indication as any of his state of mind. After this close call, the two men traveled tied together by a long length of line made from walrus hide until they reached the southern edge of the ridge they were exploring, then returned to camp.

After coffee, Baldwin seemed to realize that he had tested his luck one too many times on Ziegler Island, so he led the men without a halt toward Kane Lodge. They soon reached the eastern end of Ziegler Island, from where they could see across Collinson Channel to Kane Lodge. They were soon seen by the men who had remained at the lodge. Once the dogs at the lodge saw the returning party, they raced across the ice to greet them.

Back at the lodge, Baldwin learned that Verner's party had returned safely after stashing a ton and a half of pemmican at the Coburg Island cache, as did the party that had brought up more supplies for the Boulder Depot at Cape Auk. The only disappointment was that Leffingwell had taken sick and was unable to make the survey to the east toward Wilczek Land, a minor setback as Leffingwell would have only been able to cover ground Baldwin had already explored in 1898–99.

Otherwise, the camp was in a bit of a mess, as the surviving dogs and ponies had been allowed the run of the island. As Baldwin's team arrived, the dogs at Kane Lodge set upon one of the returning dogs and tore it to pieces. The howling dogs and loose ponies kept Baldwin awake all night, so in the morning he ordered the men to button up the camp: they were all heading back to the ship. "First, the Lodge was more firmly fastened together and covered with an additional coating of ruberoid and an inventory taken of the stores to be left therein. Next, the black pony was shot and fed to the now ravenous dogs who, in one mad rush, soon disposed of everything except the bones."[289]

The men loaded the sledges with provisions for five days, along with two canvas canoes, but Baldwin kept the men at Kane Lodge until Monday, May 19, when the hut was made fast and readied for whatever visitors might arrive next. The men "gathered up every stray article of use about

The chaos at Kane Lodge, May 1902.
Courtesy of the Scott Polar Research Institute Archives.

the ground, placed kindling and other fuel in the stove with the Lodge and safety matches conveniently at hand in readiness for immediate use by anyone who might next arrive there, and then depositing a brief message, made fast the door, and took final leave of Kane Lodge, about 2:00 P.M."[290] Indeed it was the last time Baldwin would ever see his obviously beloved "Masonic lodge," surely the most remote such structure that any free and accepted Mason had ever placed anywhere.

Only five of the Siberian ponies now survived and, with the remaining dogs pulling lightly loaded sledges, the party made off to the south. The following day, Tuesday, May 20, Baldwin continued with his personal links to polar-exploration history, noting that it was the anniversary of his departure from Fort McKinley in 1899 after the discovery and exploration of Graham Bell Land, just as the previous day's departure from Kane Lodge had been effected on the anniversary of Nansen and Johansen's departure from the winter hut at Cape Norvegia in 1896.

The trip southward was important for more than historical reasons. Baldwin discovered another channel, this one splitting the former Salisbury Island even further. Baldwin had already found that the northern side of Salisbury Island was actually a separate island, the one he had just named after William Ziegler. He now found that the southern projections of Salisbury Island were actually two separate islands as well. To the easternmost island Baldwin gave the name Robert Scott Island, "in memory of one of the world's greatest hero-explorers and my friend," though there is no more evidence that Baldwin was a friend of Captain Scott than he was a close associate of Salomon Andrée.[291] In any case, the name does not survive, and the island was eventually named for William Ziegler's major domo, William S. Champ.

The island further to the west Baldwin named "Abruzzi Island," after Luigi Amadeo, the Duke of the Abruzzi, "in recognition of the services to science of our Italian fellow-explorer, a pleasant meeting with whom in these inhospitable regions in 1899 is still fresh in memory."[292] The channel that Baldwin found to separate Abruzzi from Scott/Champ islands he named Cook Channel after Frederick Cook.

Two names were conspicuously missing from these generous tributes to the fraternity of polar explorers—those of Walter Wellman and Robert Peary. It was a measure of the deep fissures with his former expedition commanders that Baldwin clearly did not feel any need to recognize the men who had provided him with his only meaningful Arctic experiences.

Such pettiness aside, Baldwin had cracked the geography of Zichy Land, the unknown interior of the Franz Josef Land that had remained a mysterious blank ever since the days of Payer. It was a not inconsiderable feat for a man whose self-identification as an "Arctic explorer" would forever rest on two things: the unlocking of the islands of Zichy Land in 1902 and the discovery and exploration of Graham Bell Land in 1899. The opportunities to redraw the maps of Franz Josef Land had been afforded to Baldwin by William Ziegler, whom Baldwin recognized with the naming of a large island, and Walter Wellman, whom Baldwin then and forever refused to acknowledge.

The party arrived back at "North Island" at 8:00 P.M. on the evening of the 20th. There they pitched tents for a final time but realized quickly that they were not entirely safe. They had landed on the northwest coast of North Island and fretted at the thin ice and patches of open water that separated them from Alger Island and the ship, both still fifteen nautical miles away. The men and animals had already covered forty nautical miles in one day, so Baldwin put to a vote the question of whether they should risk an immediate crossing in the gathering dusk. The thought of sleeping in their bunks aboard the *America* for the first time in two months was too much, so all voted in favor of racing to Camp Ziegler and the cache of bacon and jam the men knew was awaited them there.

Baldwin accordingly took a compass bearing to the easternmost extremity of Alger Island and led the men out onto the ice. For the first five nautical miles, level ice made for easy going, but as the darkness overtook them, the loose dogs darted in and out of the line of sledges, forcing Baldwin to stop repeatedly to check his bearings. The surface became more difficult, with enormous snow ridges appearing out of the dark. "Finally, about mid-night, a black object appearing from amidst the darkness to the southward I knew that we were pursuing the right course, for the black mass swung high above the surface could be nothing else than the lofty cliffs on the north coast of Alger Island . . . [and I soon] knew instantly that I had come into my old trail made earlier in the season when I had gone to establish the 'half-way station' at Kane Lodge."[293]

About a week before the Baldwin party returned to Alger Island, the ice around the island had begun to break up. The crew of the *America* had been forced to fire the steam boilers and get underway to save the ship from being crushed by the icebergs that now drifted into the shallow water hole where it had been anchored. As Dickson remembered, "the men aboard the *America* had been sending small parties to the tops of all the surrounding glaciers with signal flags, while those remaining on board were sending rockets every few hours in the hope of attracting [Baldwin's party] to the location of the ship at the time."[294]

As the break of day opened before them, the men caught sight of the mast of the ship and broke into a sustained cheer. Racing ahead of the men for the comfort of the ship, Baldwin, as if to reward his tired party for their back-breaking labor over two months, promptly fell through the salt ice near the shore and was thoroughly soaked. He staggered shoreward and was soon drying himself on board the ship. Dickson repaired to the cabin he shared with Fiala and looked into the mirror. "I looked for a number of seconds before I realized that it was not the picture of an Eskimo (and a rather ugly one too), hanging on the wall instead of the image of myself after being on the ice away from the ship in sunshine and storm, blizzards and cold for fifty-four days, unwashed and happy."[295]

It had been a brutal exercise to move the expedition's supplies 100 nautical miles north over a chaos of ice. It was work that should have and—as the men knew as early as the previous autumn—could have been accomplished much more easily by the simple expedient of waiting for the ice to loosen around the islands and using the *America* to transport the supplies northward. But Baldwin had chosen to bring nearly four-dozen men into the Arctic, and when the channels of Franz Josef Land had proved impassable in August 1901 he had to find something for them all to do. He also required stories for his "expedition narrative" and, in this, he was perhaps cursed for having spent his first winter in Franz Josef Land in service to a real journalist in Walter Wellman.

Yet even before this strange advance work was begun, Baldwin had known that it was far too late to make a serious attempt to strike out across the ice toward the North Pole in 1902. If he had been at the ready at his Boulder Depot at Cape Auk on Rudolf Land in late February, the huge cache of supplies that was eventually laid down there—along with the large quantities of relief supplies *Belgica* had delivered to Shannon Island and Bass Rock in northeast Greenland—would have created the ideal conditions for a polar dash in the spring of 1902.

If ever there had been a perfect moment to take a small group of picked men and dogs and strike out from Rudolf Land on a rapid dash to the North Pole, it was the months of March and April 1902. Just ten months earlier, Baldwin had sworn to a Midwestern reporter that he would never return to civilization without the achievement of the North Pole. Instead, Baldwin had misspent his time, men, animals, and energy almost since the moment he landed in Franz Josef Land. No man in history had been offered as certain a road to Arctic immortality as he, and yet at the very hour that that road had been paved for him with dollars and men and dogs, Baldwin's bizarre character had guaranteed it would not be used.

With his initial plans stymied by the ice conditions in Franz Josef Land in the summer and fall of 1901, Baldwin possessed no contingency plan to reach the North Pole. Beyond the hard labor of placing supply caches the length and breadth of the Franz Josef Land archipelago—where they became easy prey for hungry polar bears—Baldwin's program, such as it was, included back-breaking sledging exercises in search of new sites to which he might attach place-names, a side expedition to the site of Nansen's hut on Jackson Island, and a search for places and situations where he could be photographed as the doughty polar explorer he conceived himself to be.

Some of these photographs were merely the kinds of phony and juvenile offerings common to polar exploration of the time, as when Fiala had posed him "falling through a snow-bridge" on Ziegler Island (which, if it had happened that way, would have required the photographer both to ignore the mortally imperiled Baldwin and, at risk to his own life, to set up his camera on the thin, unstable snow-covering over a bottomless crevasse). Other photographs exhibited a cruelty that went beyond even the systematic slaughter of wildlife that marked the entire American experience in the islands, as when Baldwin shot and killed the large female walrus on the northeast corner of Greely Island and then went after its offspring, "teasing the young walrus, in order to note the attitudes the animal might assume under ill-treatment."[296] "By thrusting my rifle suddenly at him he as quickly responded by rising on his flippers and striking forward lizard-fashion with his head."[297] Satisfied at his scientific "research," Baldwin then shot the walrus pup and fed it to the dogs. That Baldwin himself not only wrote these words but had Fiala photograph him in the act, "as a study in zoology," speaks volumes to the self-serving fantasist's mindset that his Norwegian companions so often noted in *Susæg* in 1898.

Baldwin, still living his Arctic fantasy, felt completely to the contrary. As he regained the *America* on May 21, 1902, he felt he was in a supremely favorable position for a renewed attempt on the North Pole in 1903. So it must have come as an extreme shock when he now experienced the first of what would be dozens of defections from his camp of associates. That this first defection was a blood relation—his very own cousin, Leon Barnard—must have particularly stung.

Barnard's diary ended in mid-March, so the exact nature of his formal resignation from the expedition on May 23, 1902, is unknown, but his deeply conflicted feelings had been obvious for months, going all the way back to the near-disaster with the small boats just as the expedition arrived at Alger Island. Barnard delivered his letter to Baldwin just two days after the expedition returned to Camp Ziegler.

Barnard's uncle had warned him, albeit obliquely, about Baldwin's erratic temperament, to the point where Barnard had asked for and received contractual assurances of his compensation for signing on as secretary to the expedition. That Barnard chose this moment to resign, when he was stranded on an Arctic island, speaks to the utter hopelessness that this otherwise staunch young man finally experienced as the pointless cache-laying expedition concluded. He had written in his diary as early as mid-February that he had "made up my mind to get out of it as soon as possible."[298]

Now, to Baldwin, he wrote:

A statement of my reasons for this action is unnecessary, at least at this time—the mere fact of its existence being sufficient to warrant your prompt acceptance. I do this now at a time when it can have no effect on the thinking or actions of any other member, and I hope that it may not mar our old friendship nor cause any ill feelings anywhere.

Inasmuch as I cannot obtain other food and shelter than that afforded by the expedition, I undertake to see to it that I do enough of the useful and effective work that the membership will be called upon to perform between now and when the expedition returns to civilization next fall to properly compensate the management for my maintenance during the same period.[299]

Many of the subsequent defections from Baldwin's leadership, like this first, would be handled privately. But many others—bitter denunciations that continued steadily throughout the remainder of 1902—would eventually be conducted in the full glare of national and international publicity.

Two days after Barnard's resignation, Baldwin formally relieved Johanson of his position on board the *America* and replaced him with Johan Menander as sailing master and the Norwegian Magnus Arnesen as ice pilot and navigator. Ralph Bergendahl was elevated to first officer, though Baldwin made sure to add that the promotion included nothing in the way of higher salary.[300]

As for Johanson, neither he nor Baldwin ever agreed on exactly what job the Swede was being fired from. Was Johanson in fact the would-be maritime autocrat that Baldwin portrayed him to be—a portrait Barnard, for one, agreed with—or was he merely at long last fed up with Baldwin's peculiar brand of non-existent leadership? These questions—questions that crippled the expedition throughout the winter—would soon become immaterial when the expedition returned to Norway. Baldwin had created and then cultivated an implacable enemy. That he allowed Johanson to jump ship at the first port of call in Norway and beat Baldwin to a telegraph station is only one more indication of Baldwin's thoroughgoing incompetence.

Johanson's cables from Honningsvaag quickly led to Baldwin's comprehensive doom, the fact of which he was quickly aware. His subsequent travails in August, September, and October 1902 would leave Baldwin a shell of the confident explorer who had strode across Ziegler Island in May as the discoverer of multiple new islands in the Franz Josef Land archipelago. Before his inevitable exposure, however, Baldwin had just enough time left to mount one of strangest episodes in the history of polar exploration.

THIRTY-TWO

Louisiana Cypress on Alger Island

With Baldwin's dunking in the ocean as the supply train returned to the shores of Alger Island, the 1902 field season was officially over. A series of conferences held on board *America* now resolved, as Dickson remembered, "that the only wise thing to do would be to attempt to reach civilization if at all possible in 1902 while the chance was open before another night season, near at hand, set in and the whole Arctic world would again be frozen up as tight as the middle of an iceberg and of greater surface scope than the moon."[301]

But Baldwin was not by any means finished with the oddities that marked virtually the entire history of this remarkable episode in the triptych of the American exploration of Franz Josef Land. The commander of the expedition now decided that it was time to deploy the dozens of hydrogen balloons he had purchased from his famous ballooning cousins. Baldwin's rationale for this experiment in Arctic aeronautical operations was the early breakup of the ice around Alger Island, which had reduced the amount of coal on board *America* to a level that had begun to be a concern. Appropriately, Baldwin's poor planning and bad luck with ice conditions around Franz Josef Land caused him to use his balloon buoys not to reach northward to the pole but to send relief messages southward toward civilization.

At East Camp Ziegler, Baldwin ordered the hydrogen-generating apparatus removed from the ship and assembled on shore. The gas would be generated in the apparatus by combining sulphuric acid with iron or zinc filings. It would allow the expedition to inflate fifteen balloons, each balloon requiring slightly less than nine hours to inflate. The balloons could lift an average of one hundred pounds, in message buoys, copper floats, Royal Baking Powder tins, or any other receptacle the men could find to hand. These messages would carry "an urgent request for coal" as Baldwin wrote.[302]

The history of lighter-than-air operations in Arctic exploration between 1896 and 1930 has fixed almost exclusively upon four expeditions. Besides the balloon voyage of Salomon Andrée, there were the fascinating early dirigible expeditions of Walter Wellman in Spitsbergen between 1906 and 1909, as well as the much more well-known expeditions of Roald Amundsen, Lincoln Ellsworth, and Umberto Nobile on *Norge* in 1926 and Nobile again in 1928 in the *Italia*. Largely unknown in this history are the aeronautical operations of the Baldwin-Ziegler Polar Expedition on Alger Island in June 1902.

Of all three American polar expeditions to the Franz Josef Land archipelago, Baldwin-Ziegler stands out as both the greatest opportunity for Americans to reach the pole and as a bizarre and—as Leffingwell would write sixty years later—largely unexamined failure. And nowhere was it stranger than in the operations of Baldwin's "Aeronautical Section" in June 1902. Unlike John Cleve Symmes and all the many other theorists who speculated on the nature of the North Pole and how to explore it, Baldwin had been afforded the means to carry his ideas of Arctic communications into the field. While the system failed in its objective to summon relief to the expedition, it seeded the Arctic with hundreds of message buoys and thus ensured that Baldwin would return to the columns of newspapers each time one of the buoys was discovered. And such finds would continue for thirty years, almost to the day of Baldwin's death.

The release of small unmanned balloons for the purpose of carrying messages is not nearly as strange as it sounds when one considers that the Baldwin-Ziegler Polar Expedition took place simultaneous to the invention of wireless radio transmissions. Other explorers had considered similar schemes before Baldwin. Fridtjof Nansen himself considered the use of captive balloons flown from the deck of *Fram* prior to his 1893–96 expedition but rejected the idea on account of the cost and weight of the required cylinders of hydrogen.[303] With such cylinders prohibitively expensive, Andrée's expedition had produced its hydrogen in the Arctic, using a process that had remained essentially unchanged for more than a century.[304] This method,

The balloon launch site at East Camp Ziegler on Alger Island.
Courtesy of the Scott Polar Research Institute Archives.

known as the *vitriol,* or *acid-metal,* process, was used almost exclusively for the generation of hydrogen until the First World War, when cheaper and more direct electrolytic and steam-contact processes became the norm. Andrée arranged for delivery to Virgohamn of such an apparatus that would combine iron filings and sulphuric acid to produce hydrogen gas. The process had to be fairly simple, as there were few workers skilled in producing hydrogen that could or would join an expedition to the Arctic.[305]

Andrée filled his balloon using this method in 1897, and then disappeared over the polar ice pack. The Swedish expedition took place at the start of a technological transformation in Arctic exploration. Urban Wråkberg has even argued that the Andrée expedition was the vanguard of this transformation.[306] Whereas Fridtjof Nansen could report progress of his 1893–96 expedition across the Arctic basin on the research vessel *Fram* only after he returned home, Andrée sought to communicate news of his expedition while it was underway, a revolutionary concept that could only be accomplished in 1897 with relatively primitive methods.

Andrée had chosen two such methods: carrier pigeons and cork buoys. Both could be fitted with messages and released from the car of the balloon, with the birds flying back to Sweden and the buoys dropped onto the ice, where they could drift out of the Arctic to be picked up by the Norwegian sealing fleet. Thirty-two carrier pigeons were placed in baskets under the balloon's carrying-ring and several buoys were carried in the car. The relative speed of these methods was dramatically illustrated just four days after launch when one of the carrier pigeons was shot by the captain of a Norwegian vessel. The pigeon carried a note from Andrée reporting that at 12.30 P.M. on July 13, 1897, the balloon *Örnen* had passed 82° 02' North latitude.

No other word from the expedition appeared for two full years, when the skipper of another Norwegian vessel found Andrée's "polar buoy" on the coast of Kong Karls Land, an island in the southeast of the Spitsbergen group and about one hundred miles from Andrée's launch point. Like the other buoys designed for the flight, it was a large hollow cork bulb enclosed in copper mesh, painted in Swedish blue and yellow.

In a variation of Andrée's balloon operations that could be considered even stranger than Baldwin's "Aeronautical Section," the Duke of the Abruzzi's Italian expedition proposed in 1899 to use small balloons to lift the polar party's sledges off the ground so that they would not be quite so heavy for the dogs to pull. More than 5 percent of the expedition's budget had been spent in developing this "aeronautic outfit" at the Duke's base camp on the shores of Teplitz Bay on Rudolf Land.[307]

By such standards, Baldwin's planned system of pre-wireless balloon communications sounds positively rational. With a total of forty balloons, four hundred large buoys could be set adrift carrying messages of progress from the expedition. These messages were hooked onto a long line attached to the balloon by means of a "liberator," an ellipse of steel with a slot in the top through which slid a disc. This disc in turn had a hole in it large enough to fit a small steel ball cut with a slot to fit into the ellipse. When a certain amount of gas had escaped from the balloon, the weight of the buoys would pull it down. Once the first buoy touched down, the steel ball holding the disc in place would be released and the buoy detached from the trail of buoys. Freed from this weight, the balloon would regain its buoyancy and begin another ascent.[308]

In this way, message buoys would drift with the winds to be deposited across the Arctic, to be found by sealing or whaling vessels or even passenger liners in the North Atlantic, and their contents delivered to civilization.

For all of the elaborate care Baldwin took with these balloons and with the buoys and the liberator system, he does not seem to have thought very deeply on the operational barriers to producing hydrogen in the Arctic. The hydrogen generator he ordered from Baldwin Brothers was made of "one and one-half inch Louisiana Cypress wood bound with five one-half inch, round iron clamps or hoops. Its dimensions inside were three feet eleven inches by four feet nine inches diameter holding five hundred and nineteen gallons."[309]

Though this was nothing like the steel generators made for both the Andrée and the Duke of the Abruzzi expeditions, the size and weight of such an apparatus, not to mention the balloons and buoys, rendered it useless for sending messages from an expedition on the move across the polar ice. It could only have been used at a fixed base camp or on board a ship, and only then if Baldwin planned to send back relay teams to his base camp with updates on the expedition's progress, as Luigi Amadeo had done in 1900.[310]

As with the hydrogen generating apparatus of Andrée on Danskøya, the steel generator of the Italian polar expedition was left behind on Rudolf Land. When Anthony Fiala took over as commander of the Ziegler expedition in 1903, he returned to Franz Josef Land and quickly found the Italian gas generator. Engineer Henry Hartt cleverly made use of it as a steam boiler when Fiala's expedition ship sank in Teplitz Bay in January 1904.[311]

As we have seen, Baldwin hoped to establish his camp near the site of the Italian base camp at Teplitz Bay, the northernmost such feature in Franz Josef Land. (Cape Fligely, the nearby northern point of Rudolf Land, where the Italians kept watch for their returning sledge teams, would eventually be revealed as the northernmost point of land in the European Arctic.) With Nansen having demonstrated the westward drift of polar ice, Baldwin planned to take advantage of this drift by starting his attempt on the pole from the east coast of Rudolf Land, then retreating south from the pole in a southwestward direction, thereby taking advantage of the ice drift to end his expedition somewhere on the eastern coast of Greenland. This is essentially the same route that would later be used by the Soviet Union's *NP-1* expedition, which drifted on a large ice island from near to the pole to Greenland in 1937. Baldwin's original plan was to establish his "Aeronautical Section" on this far northern land, not 100 nautical miles to the south on Alger Island.

When Baldwin chartered *Belgica,* it was with the express purpose of establishing relief depot stations on Shannon Island and on Bass Rock in Northeast Greenland.[312] These stations would also be equipped with their own "Aeronautical Section." Baldwin ordered that the stations in Greenland be supplied not just with food and shelter, but also dozens of balloons, message-carrying buoys to be attached to these balloons, and hydrogen generators.[313]

Besides this message-carrying operation, Baldwin had also purchased two larger balloons from Baldwin Brothers, balloons large enough that they could carry one observer/photographer aloft.[314] These observation balloons Baldwin envisioned as flying from the deck of *America,* or perhaps even from Cape Fligely, in order to get a better look at the Arctic Ocean ice terrain northward. Such a system had been proposed by Arthur Berson several years earlier in *Geographical Journal.* He wrote that a relatively small captive balloon "can raise a car containing one or two persons, and enable them, from a height of say 1,600 feet, to survey many square miles of country."[315] Berson thought such an operation, mounted from a ship in the polar regions, could be particularly effective.

Interestingly, Berson's idea had only recently been tested at the opposite end of the Earth. During the *Discovery* expedition to Antarctica in 1901–1904, British explorer Robert Falcon Scott used a small observation balloon in a brief attempt to try to see over the Great Ice Barrier and into the heart of Antarctica. The idea had been suggested to Scott by Sir Joseph Hooker, youngest member of the British expedition to the southern continent six decades earlier. On February 4, 1902, first Scott and then expedition member Ernest Shackleton clung to a small basket attached to the tethered balloon as it lifted off. For Scott, who insisted that he be the first aeronaut in Antarctic history, the experience was terrifying. He wrote that as he "swayed about in what appeared a very inadequate basket and gazed down on the rapidly diminishing figures below I felt some doubt as to whether I had been wise in my choice."[316] The method of inflation was gas stored in dozens of bulky cylinders and carried on board the *Discovery.* Shackleton's ascent reached 800 feet in elevation, from which he even took aerial photographs, but thick fog combined with serious technical faults with the balloon and its valves caused Scott to pack the whole rig away as a useless death trap and a waste of space on board the ship.

However, if one could ascend several hundred feet in a tethered balloon on a clear and calm day at Cape Fligely—a dicey proposition on this windy, misty cliff overlooking the vast Arctic Ocean—one could gain a superior view of the sea ice conditions ahead. It would provide a decided advantage to any expedition hoping to voyage north across the ice. If the men trekking across the ice were equipped with flares, then a captive balloon at Cape Fligely could perhaps even allow for the progress of the ice parties to be followed for several days if not weeks.

It was not until the fall of 1901, when Baldwin was in the middle of a Franz Josef Land winter and out of contact with the outside world, that the "only announcement [was made] to the public of the plans and purposes of the Baldwin-Ziegler Polar Expedition."[317] Baldwin's choice of popular magazines— *McClure's* in the United States and *Windsor Magazine* in Britain—to detail his plans, rather than the more formal setting of the *Geographical Journal,* is perhaps another indication that Baldwin did not believe the concept could hold up under professional scrutiny. A key component of the expedition was to be the ability to relay news of its progress via message balloons. "No previous expedition to the North has ever made such complete arrangements for the transmission of news back to civilization," Baldwin wrote.[318]

Baldwin's balloon plans had also been detailed in October, in an illustrated article written for *Metropolitan Magazine* in New York by writer-photographer Waldon Fawcett.[319] The Fawcett article—entitled, with hope, "By Balloon to the North Pole"—contains several photographs of the balloons under construction and testing, as well as the only known photograph of the passenger-carrying balloon observation car. The car weighed all of thirteen pounds and was made of "Italian rope and wood."[320] The obvious flimsiness of the observation car led "many of his intimate friends, who had supposed themselves conversant with most of the details of the project [to believe] that the plan to include the balloons among the paraphernalia must have been an eleventh-hour decision."[321] The clear implication is that Baldwin also kept these plans from his expedition sponsor Ziegler, perhaps out of fear that he might be seen as just a little too frivolous with the funds supplied by the hard-headed capitalist.

The reasons given by Fawcett for the use of balloons were also different from those given by Baldwin. Fawcett wrote that they could be used for aerial photography as well as scouting the ice conditions ahead, and claimed that Baldwin would use all forty balloons "for observations," the clear implication being that these would be passenger-carrying observation balloons. But as we have noted, only two of the Baldwin Brothers balloons were large enough to attach to an observation car. The rest were only large enough to lift the balloon buoys constructed in Stockholm and at the Baldwin Brothers factory in Illinois.

The smaller balloons, Fawcett wrote, would be of value "in determining the direction and velocity of air currents," the first suggestion that the aeronautical project was as much for science as for publicity.[322] In a profound understatement amongst his otherwise evident enthusiasm for the new technology, Fawcett noted that the "character of the locality will place some limitations upon the use of balloons in the Arctic."[323]

Baldwin's article in *Windsor Magazine* was almost the reverse of that of Fawcett, which suggests that the two articles were not coordinated. Baldwin includes no mention of using the balloons for passenger-carrying observation operations, and instead focuses on the use of the balloons as unmanned, message-carrying devices. The article is notable for its chart showing Baldwin's proposed route from Franz Josef Land to the pole and return via the *Belgica* depot at Shannon Island in Greenland, as well as its photographs of the buoys and schematics of the liberator system, in addition to photographs of the balloons under construction and in their packing crates.

These crated balloons were addressed to the *Belgica*'s port in Sandefjord, and the rendezvous point for the crew with the *America* in Tromsø. "It is intended that some of these balloons will be released at intervals during the Arctic night, and each will be freighted with a number of the news-buoys, containing messages inscribed upon parchment. The buoys will be fastened to a pendant line, one beneath the other."[324]

Baldwin was as clear as he could be as to the messages that would be contained in these buoys. The expedition "was organized *to reach the Pole.* Neither scientific research, nor even a record of 'Farthest North,' will suffice; only the attainment of that much-sought-for spot where one can point only to the south can satisfy our purpose."[325] The unfortunate ice conditions of 1901 and the long struggle to drag supplies to Cape Auk precluded any use of the observation balloons and their small passenger-carrying basket to scout conditions ahead, either from the ship or from Rudolf Land. The expedition had not made it far enough to even consider such a possibility.

The scientific rationale for the large balloons was therefore rendered moot long before the expedition returned to Alger Island. With the North Pole now gone—at least for 1902—Baldwin nevertheless set his elaborate plan in motion, determined to bring his vision of lighter-than-air communications into the Arctic. By late May, with no ice-free escape channel yet open to the south, and fearing that the expedition might be entrapped for a second winter, Baldwin turned to his "Aeronautical Section." With *America* running short of coal and the remaining dogs and ponies in need of food, he ordered his aeronautical team to use the hydrogen balloons, not to send news, but to call for help.

THIRTY-THREE

The Launch of the Balloons

O n Saturday, May 24, 1902, the day after the resignation of his expedition secretary, with his polar dreams fraying and the *America* still trapped by fast ice around Alger Island, Baldwin ordered Charles Rilliet, the head of his "Aeronautical Section," to begin the construction of an area from which the message balloons could be launched.[326] This was the first time during the expedition that the balloons and the buoy-message system had been unpacked from crates on board *America*. The hydrogen generator and the containers of acid were already ashore, having been moved off the ship while Baldwin and his sledge teams were away during the spring.

On Monday, May 26, while Rilliet and Anton Vedoe began to assemble the hydrogen-purification tank, three other crewmembers—including Leon Barnard, whose help Rilliet had asked for—picked a spot to the west of the base camp huts and began to dig a large pit in the snow. The next day, Rilliet asked the ship's captain for spare masts to set up a wind screen behind the balloon pit. By May 29, to speed the work, three Russian crewmembers were given over to assist in digging the balloon pit. Other crewmembers came ashore to dig holes for the spare masts.[327]

The launch area was completed the next day. The balloon pit finished, the hydrogen generator was placed into it, and the masts were anchored into the ground with guy ropes. Spare sails and canvas from *America* were spread between the masts to create the wind screen. It had taken more than a dozen men five days to finish the job, an indication of the impossibility of deploying the system while the expedition was on the move. As this work neared completion, Rilliet and Anton Vedoe tested the buoy-liberator system and found that the release mechanism worked well.

On Saturday, May 31, Rilliet's tests to generate hydrogen were initially unsuccessful. The lead cases holding the acid had been used on shore during the winter to anchor rope lines holding the dogs, and Rilliet feared that the very low temperatures might have somehow spoiled the acid. He finally decided that the acid had been corrupted with lead from the cases. The water in the water bath—water that would be used to wash the emerging gas— froze solid. The generator finally began to produce gas when Rilliet mixed one part sulphuric acid to four parts seawater and poured the combination over the iron filings.[328]

On Monday, June 2, one of the balloons was brought ashore from the ship and the generator "charged" with seawater and acid. With a red coloring called Ruberine, "No. 1, June 3, 1902, Baldwin-Ziegler Polar Expedition" was stenciled across the fabric of the balloon in four-inch-high characters.[329] At 9 A.M., Baldwin gave Rilliet the order to inflate the balloon. The top joints of the generator leaked so badly that it was nearly noon before gas finally started to enter the envelope. When the balloon was half-full, at 4 P.M., the pressure of gas dropped sharply. Over the next three hours, Rilliet recharged the generator with 200 pounds of iron and 119 pounds of zinc.

Inflation continued into the early hours of June 4, when Rilliet disconnected the gas hose and, attaching the balloon to a spring balance, found that it had an ascension force of 123 pounds.[330] The envelope weighed approximately 35 pounds and the netting another 3, so this first balloon could carry an effective payload of 85 pounds of buoys and messages.[331] The wind had picked up, so two ropes were attached to the load ring of the balloon, one directly underneath the balloon in the pit and the other on the north side of the pit to keep the balloon away from the guy ropes as it ascended.

As the balloon rose out of the pit, the buoys were attached at intervals of six feet. Each buoy held a small note, identically worded, modified only for the date, the number of the balloon, the number of the buoy attached to that balloon, and the fact that Baldwin now claimed a position as a member of the U.S. Army Signal Corps.

The notes read:

80° 21' N   56° 40' E
Camp Ziegler, Franz Josef Land
Field Headquarters
Of the
Baldwin-Ziegler Polar Expedition
June—, 1902

To the nearest American Consulate—

Cargo coal required quickly. Yacht "America" in open water (Aberdare Channel) since June—. This year's work successful—enormous depot placed on Rudolf Land by sledge, March April and May; collection for National Museum, record from and paintings from Nansen's hut, excellent photographs and moving pictures, etc., etc., secured. Five ponies and one hundred fifty dogs remaining. Desire hay, fish, and thirty sledges. Must return early August, baffled, not beaten. Northeasterly winds prevailing. Northwesterly winds 25th, 26th and 27th. All in health.

\# Balloon   Buoy No.—
[signed] Baldwin, Signal Corps, USA[332]

When the first balloon reached the top of the windscreen, the sudden exposure to the wind caused it to jerk up and down, shaking all the buoys loose. The balloon was brought back into the pit and men stationed around, each holding a buoy and being instructed when to let it go. This method was tried twice but again, when the balloon lifted above the windscreen, it began each time to jerk its buoys loose. One buoy barely missed a sailor's head as it fell back to earth.[333]

On the fourth attempt, the men holding the north rope inexplicably gave the line a jerk as the balloon lifted above the windscreen and again all the large Swedish buoys fell back to the ground. As five crew members attempted to reel in the balloon, the wind had increased even more. The netting surrounding the gasbag began to tear until at last the balloon, with no buoys attached to it, broke free, causing three sailors still holding onto the rope to fall back into the balloon pit. The only messages carried aloft were ten small copper floats bundled into an empty sandbag labeled "MANUFACTURED BY BALDWIN BROS., QUINCY, ILL., U.S.A." Rilliet watched the balloon ascend to 2,500 feet before it "passed out of sight a mere speck to the S.S.W."[334]

After this first experience, Rilliet and Baldwin modified the launch operations. Balloon No. 2 was wrapped in two nets, and the liberator connections were wrapped in paper to hold the steel balls in position during lift-off. Rilliet thought that when the balloons finally descended in the ocean, the paper would dissolve and the buoys would be released. But Rilliet's biggest concern was the time it was taking to inflate the gasbag, which he put down to the "great amount of leakage through the wooden joints of the generator."[335] It was another example of the hurried purchases Baldwin had made in the spring of 1901. For an expedition that could purchase anything it required, Baldwin was again paying the price of bringing a substandard piece of equipment into the Arctic.

The generator was charged once more, and inflation of the second balloon began just after midnight on June 5. Inserting acid into the generator at longer intervals led to hydrogen entering the balloon that was both moist and hot. The moisture condensed as it cooled and formed a pool of water at the bottom of the balloon. Rilliet added ice to both the generator and the gas purifier to lower the temperature of the resulting gas, and inflation proceeded until it was completed at 5 A.M.[336]

In addition to the paper wrappings around the liberators, the large buoys were strung around the balloon in various configurations. Ten of them were attached to a length of oceanographic sounding wire at five foot intervals, while four others were attached by separate wires of various lengths. Ten small copper floats were put in a tin can that was punctured in several places so water would flow into it.[337]

Rilliet attached a heavier rope to the balloon and stationed several sailors about sixty feet to the leeward of the balloon's upward path, hoping to avoid the kind of sudden jerks that wrecked the first ascent. The result, however, was similar to the first attempt. The balloon swayed in the wind, tangling the various sounding wires in the retaining rope and dropping the buoys to the ground. At Baldwin's suggestion, the retaining rope was removed. Now, as soon as the balloon was cut free of its mooring cord, it would ascend without any chance to bring it back.

Rilliet asked Baldwin to do the honors and then took a position well away from the pit so that he could study the ascent. Baldwin slashed the mooring cord and the balloon leapt free, carrying all but one of the large buoys and all of the small buoys with it. "When clear of the ground," wrote Rilliet, "and a realization came to us that success was indeed ours, cheer after cheer rose

Charles Rilliet in front of a hydrogen balloon about to be released from the launch site at East Camp Ziegler on Alger Island. From Evelyn Briggs Baldwin, "The Baldwin-Ziegler Polar Expedition, Part III," *Wide World Magazine* 10 (60): 587–93.

from the crowd."[338] Like the first balloon, the second drifted away rapidly to the south-southwest, in the direction of the coast of northern Norway.

As the ice around Alger Island loosened further and the expedition ship prepared to move away from her anchorage on Thursday, June 5, all the remaining balloons except one were taken ashore. An attempted inflation on June 6 had to be aborted when the generator was found to be leaking water. It took all day to empty the generator of its "charge" of zinc, iron, tin, and water; repair the generator; and dig the balloon pit deeper.

On Saturday, June 7, a third balloon was inflated and readied with buoys. By mid-afternoon the kites employed to indicate the direction of the wind had fallen to the ground in the calm air. When the gas flow from the generator fell in the evening, Rilliet detached the hose and decided to "let the balloon go with what gas it had."[339] Again Baldwin cut the mooring cord connecting the balloon to the sand bags, and the balloon rose slowly and steadily.

In the calm conditions, Fiala was able to take a series of photographs of the ascent. "The night was beautiful," wrote Rilliet, as nearly three-dozen men stood and gazed at the balloon as it carried sixteen buoys away. "I have never witnessed a more beautiful and more perfect ascension than was this, whether passenger, dispatch or meteorological."[340] Rilliet continued to watch the balloon through field glasses as it slowly made its way westward across Alger Island. Before it disappeared from view, the balloon turned slightly toward the north, a course Rilliet thought might carry it toward Spitsbergen, where it might be seen and retrieved by a sealing vessel.

Rilliet had further reasons to be happy with the third ascent when he cleaned out the hydrogen generator in preparation for recharging it on Sunday, June 8. Unlike the first two inflations, he discovered that all of the metal had been acted upon by the acid. During the first two efforts to produce hydrogen—when he had laid pieces of sheet zinc on top of iron turnings—the acid had worked on the zinc, but underneath was left a black mass of iron, largely untouched by the acid.[341]

To obtain more complete action of the acid on metal, for the third inflation Rilliet had gathered up empty tin cans from the base camp's rubbish tip. These he used to create alternating layers of metal—zinc, iron, tin cans, zinc, etc.—in order to hold the metals apart and allow the acid to get at them.[342] Rilliet complained that none of these improvisations would have been necessary had he been supplied with the kind of wrought iron turnings used by Andrée, instead of the corrupted material supplied to Baldwin. The iron consisted mostly of soft machine-shop turnings, and Rilliet found large amounts of steel turnings and dust in it, along with "small pieces of belt lacings, wood, leather . . . evidently the sweepings from the floor under and about the machines in the machine room."[343]

The tests to determine the most effective proportions of iron and/or zinc to acid had not been done until June 2, 1902, the day before Rilliet commenced inflation of the first balloon.[344] Furthermore, Rilliet was rebuffed when he asked Baldwin to provide him with a thermograph and some other scientific instruments from the ship. Baldwin "seemed to think we were not equipped for scientific balloon research."[345]

Rilliet's improvements to the gas process and the release mechanisms led to a problem-free launch on June 9, as eighteen more large buoys were carried southward. A snowstorm that interrupted the inflation process, followed by problems with too much pressure in the generator—which at one point was enough to blow a pressure valve off the top of the generator—caused the fifth balloon to lift off with no large buoys on June 13. Without a full load of gas, it disappeared toward the west, looking to Rilliet "like a strawberry, rolling about in the distant sky."[346]

Thereafter, until the fifteenth and last balloon ascended on June 30, each balloon carried a full load of between ten and twenty large buoys, depending on the lifting force of the gas bag. Rilliet endured constant struggles with the gas-production process, from the loose wooden generator that required him to seek out and plug holes while accepting the low level of gas flow, to finding fresh water for the purifier. At one point, his assistants had to be warned not to use the water that stood in a large pool in front of the pony stable since it was "strongly adulterated" with horse urine.[347]

The effectiveness of the balloons grew along with Rilliet's experience in generating hydrogen. Only one of the first 218 messages was later found, meaning that only one of the first nine balloons managed to successfully deliver its cargo of large Swedish buoys and small copper floats. On the other hand, five of the balloons numbered ten through fifteen delivered buoys that were later found.[348]

As the expedition ship returned to camp on June 29 from its maneuvers in the loosening ice, Rilliet received a rather extraordinary real-time progress report from the fourteenth balloon. It had been seen near Negri Channel (between Hall and McClintock Islands, near Porter's "Sun Bay," and about 15 nautical miles from the launch site) about an hour after lift-off. "It came down to within fifty feet of the water, moved toward the glacier on McClintock Island, moved slowly up the side of the glacier, disappeared over its top, came back in about an hour, then came down the side of the same glacier and finally rising, disappeared again moving down Negri Fjord."[349]

After the fifteenth and last balloon was away, the "Aeronautical Section" packed away the remaining nine balloons and stowed them in the west hut at East Camp Ziegler. The unused metals were placed in the balloon pit, and the acid was left in containers to the west of the pit. The generator and purifier were cleaned of their last charge and left in place in the pit, and then the wind break and the masts were taken down.[350]

At last, Rilliet had some time to contemplate the "many difficult circumstances" he had encountered in attempting to deliver messages attached to balloons sent from a shoreline in the Arctic. His operational report, delivered to Baldwin on board the *America* on July 1, 1902, as the ship began a two-week-long effort to break out of the ice around Alger Island, should have struck Baldwin as more than slightly ironic. Unlike his hero Salomon A. Andrée, Baldwin in his balloon operations had left nearly everything to chance, and Rilliet knew it.

Rilliet identified the prime cause of the difficulties faced throughout the month of June as the lack of a generator similar to that used by Andrée. "We had no such an outfit as did Mr. Andrée, the ardent apostle of the aerial conquest of the North Pole, whom physicists say had most everything that Chemistry and Physical Science has invented for the scientific observation of gases. . . . [Had] we a similar apparatus and the instruments that the Andrée Expedition had, with our numerous inflations extending over a period of twenty-seven days with various conditions of weather, the results that could have been obtained would have been invaluable to the Science of Aeronautics."[351]

This was a considerable indictment of an expedition that, unlike Andrée's, had virtually limitless funds at its disposal. Based on an intensive month of experience, Rilliet rated the Swedish buoys and the acid and zinc from England as "excellent"; the balloons and generator and small copper floats supplied by Baldwin Brothers as "good"; and the iron filings from England and the gas purifier from Baldwin Brothers as "poor."[352]

How Baldwin reacted to this report is not known. But he evidently believed he had accomplished something of merit with his balloon buoy system. Before he left Franz Josef Land for the last time, Baldwin left behind a message at the base camp. It read in part:

> To-day we dispatch Balloon No. 15, all together more than three hundred (300) messages [by Rilliet's count, it was 422 messages] having been carried from this point by this means. Northwest winds prevailed until the 25th of June when for three days we had a gale from the northwest to west-northwest followed by a strong wind from the south on the 28th and 29th. . . .
>
> Look for signals carefully wherever possible, as also the buoys carried by the balloons. Should any be found including the balloons themselves, carefully note the locality as well as date, time of day, atmospheric conditions; also whether in water or upon the ice. Please also instruct any ships which you may meet to keep a sharp lookout for us, as also for the messages by balloon already sent.[353]

For Baldwin, the balloon operations of June 1902 were the end of his polar road. The buoys, like time-release capsules, would be found adrift around the Arctic for decades, and allow Baldwin to reappear in the press each time. But the rapid development of technological systems after the turn of the century soon rendered obsolete such a primitive system as the sending of messages by balloon buoys. In 1906 his estranged and erstwhile expedition companion Walter Wellman deployed the first wireless transmitter in the Arctic, to send dispatches from Spitsbergen to Norway and thence on to his newspaper in Chicago. The strange, archaic polar fantasy world of Evelyn Briggs Baldwin was rapidly coming to a close, and no one was more surprised than Baldwin himself.

THIRTY-FOUR

Sensational Rumors

On July 1, 1902, the entire personnel of Camp Ziegler, along with the 5 ponies and 150 dogs that had somehow survived the winter, embarked on the *America* and staggered southward in an attempt to break out of the Franz Josef Land ice before the ship's remaining coal ran out. A few days earlier, on June 25, Ralph Bergendahl noted that at 2:00 A.M. the crew was called out when the ice started to fracture and the ship began to drift away. As the *America* got up steam and established a new anchorage at the edge of the ice, Baldwin panicked, believing the *America* was about to be crushed. He personally awakened all the Americans and ordered them to be ready to abandon the ship. Bergendahl wrote only what most of the others had long come to believe: "I am beginning to have doubts about the mental health of our honored commander" (*"Jag börjar snart tvivla på vår ärade 'commanders' förstånd"*).[354]

The *America* entered Aberdare Channel south of Alger Island, where heavy drift ice closed in around the ship, and began a long struggle down the west coast of McClintock Island. For two weeks the vessel tried to make some headway through the ice. On most days, the men were on the ice alongside the ship, trying to either manually cut a pathway or set off dynamite and blast a channel through which the expedition could escape. Fiala recorded the scene on the morning of Tuesday, July 15, as the ship was caught and almost crushed in Aberdare Channel:

Awakened at 6 A.M. with the sound of grinding ice and hurrying footsteps on deck. Dressed hastily and went up on deck, a strong east wind was blowing and the great ice floe on our port side had started from land some miles east and bearing down upon the *America* had closed the lead behind, and with enormous pressure was piling up on our port side and pushing the vessel slowly toward the glacier west of us, the ice on our starboard side breaking and cracking. It seemed that the fearful pressure would take off our already damaged rudder, and at this writing—noon time—the propeller is jammed and the glacier face seems dangerously near. Truly nothing but providence can turn this gloomy picture into sunshine. The boats are being made ready for leaving in case of necessity and I am arranging in my mind methods of saving the photographic results of the past 12 months. The rain is pouring down and everything has a grey aspect.[355]

By the following day the situation looked so bleak that few of the men were in the mood to listen to Fiala's calming Biblical references. "The sarcastic arrows fired at me by some of the members every time there was an occasion where courageous trust should have been the Keynote of the hour, have penetrated deeply and made me feel very much alone."[356] Fiala may have received a few barbs during this struggle to leave the archipelago, but he was not the men's real target. The men had begun to despair that the *America* would ever leave Aberdare Channel, much less Franz Josef Land itself. A well-founded fear spread throughout the crew, one that no one wanted to contemplate—the onset of another grueling winter with the unstable Baldwin as their leader.

America finally broke out of Aberdare Channel on July 18. Much to the consternation of the crew, which itself was on the verge of going stark raving mad, Baldwin ordered the ship west toward Cape Flora, rather than south toward deliverance. The men were close to open revolt against Baldwin, whom they now saw as trying to keep them in Franz Josef Land against their wishes. Baldwin replied that he merely wanted to go to Cape Flora to see if a supply ship might be there, even though his own ship had just emerged from the ice. But the pretense fooled no one. It was as if Baldwin suddenly realized that he had been sent north with nearly three years' worth of supplies to become the discoverer of the North Pole. He was returning to Norway less than a year later as a local island geographer—without having reached as far north, even with William Ziegler's millions, as Walter Wellman had managed on a bare shoestring of a budget in 1899.

It is also possible that the realization was only now dawning on Baldwin that these might be his last days in command of an Arctic expedition, a reality he was simply not prepared to admit. The men were having none of it. They had had enough of Evelyn Briggs Baldwin and were now desperate to regain the mainland and a trip home. In this combustible atmosphere, a fantastic rumor rumbled through the ship that Baldwin was searching for a way to destroy the *America* at Cape Flora and live ashore until another ship arrived to rescue the expedition. At this, Engineer Hartt had maritime regulations read out to Baldwin to the effect that any ship owner who loses his ship through connivance or fraud with a resulting loss of the crew was guilty of manslaughter.[357]

On the afternoon of Monday, July 21, 1902, the ice pilot Magnus Arnesen refused an order from Baldwin to direct the ship toward Cape Flora. Along with Hartt, Arnesen turned the *America* south toward Norway. As if beckoning them, a wide lead opened in the ice, and the ship limped along as Hartt struggled to fix a leak in the boiler. The next day was Baldwin's fortieth birthday. In a perverse if not entirely inappropriate celebration, Baldwin meekly offered the men slices of a cake they themselves had carried all the way to Rudolf Land and back. It was a strange and bitter contrast to the warm birthday celebration Baldwin had enjoyed with Walter Wellman as they journeyed toward Franz Josef Land on board *Frithjof* in 1898.

The stops and starts in the fields of ice south of Franz Josef Land alternately thrilled and depressed the men, as the progress was by turns rapid and then non-existent. As the coal supplies dwindled, Fiala, for one, called on every reserve of his considerable faith to encourage the men that they would get home that summer. By Saturday, July 26, the leads were getting wider and the sky ahead blacker.

With the sure signs of open water to the south, the men's fears began to lessen that the ship would be lost or deliberately wrecked by Baldwin or that they would be forced to spend another winter under his command. The leads finally opened for good on Monday morning, July 28, and with them the hopes of the crew that deliverance was at hand. The sails were run up and the wind was used to propel the ship to save the dwindling coal supply.

If the crew finally experienced some relief, the expedition commander did not. The closer the ship came to land, the more Baldwin worked himself into a panic. He seemed at long last to understand that his personal judgment day was drawing nigh and that he would be found badly wanting. Any explorer worth his compass knew that an expedition's fortunes were determined as much by the initial report from the nearest telegraph station as from the actual work in the field, and Baldwin now proceeded to shape that narrative to his own advantage.

On Wednesday, July 30, as the *America* neared the Norwegian coast, Baldwin finally took action. Reverting to the only method he knew, this involved one of his posed, theatrical speeches. He addressed himself to the scientific staff of the expedition and to the officers of the ship as they approached the northern coast of Norway. Fiala recorded his words: "We are almost at Tromsoe where there will be numerous inquiries concerning the expedition, and I must be careful what I say, and I must be careful what others say, and it is to give you warning and give you this information that I have called you together at this moment, I now say to the crew of this vessel and the officers of the ship you cannot go until I give the word. You haven't my permission and I expect every man to do his duty until I know what is expected of us."[358]

The officers and men were not slow to realize the import of these words. They were to be held prisoner until Baldwin could make a favorable report to William Ziegler. Baldwin then offered the men the first of what would become dozens of risible justifications for his failure as an expedition leader, even though he had been sent north with more support than any previous American polar expedition:

This is a critical moment in the history of this expedition, and I gave my consent to make the effort to regain civilization when we left Camp Ziegler with the distinct understanding I want to say from all, but I thought it was from all, that I would be upheld in the course which I took. It was a mistake. I have already stated several times that it was a mistake. I also stated at the time that there were two horns of a dilemma, and I was resting upon those horns—One to return, and the other to remain there fully expecting a supply steamer, and the matter was so galling, if I may use that expression, that I was upon the point of remaining there and simply allowing the members of the expedition to take the ship home, because you have no idea, boys, you have no idea how sharply this comes to me.[359]

Unfortunately for Baldwin, it was the very first version of the demise of the expedition that stuck in people's minds, and that version would now be told by one of the fiercest enemies he had created over the preceding year. When Baldwin ordered the *America* sailed into the nearest coaling port, he again decreed that no one be allowed off (or on) the ship without his personal permission. Land was sighted just two days later, on August 1, and soon after the *America* entered the far northern port of Honningsvaag, from which the ship had departed for Archangel some fifty-three weeks earlier. There were barely two tons of coal left in the bunkers.

It was from this tiny outport in northern Norway that Baldwin now lost all control of his expedition, his expedition's narrative, and his career as an explorer. As the ship dropped anchor, Baldwin made the mistake of retreating to his cabin. As he did so, a small boat came out to greet the ship. Anticipating this moment for months, Baldwin's erstwhile master/sailing master/captain Carl Johanson jumped ship, bound for the nearest telegraph station. He went ashore briefly, just long enough to fire off a cable. A short time later, Baldwin chased him down. Too late. Fiala, who, unlike almost the whole crew, had no real desire to race ashore to the nearest drinking hole or fleshpot, recorded the scene:

> Capt. Johanson went ashore and made for the telegraph station. Very soon afterwards Mr. B went ashore bound for the same place. A mail steamer had steamed into the harbor shortly after we did and while she was preparing to leave, Capt. Johanson left shore in a small boat and went aboard the steamer and in a few minutes she left, the men aboard the *America* cheering him as the steamer left us for Tromsoe. Mr. B came aboard *America* after lunch feeling quite happy having sampled seemingly the coal merchant's store of "that which maketh glad the inward man." He spoke to Capt. Menander telling him that he met Capt. Johanson ashore and that Capt. Johanson called him a G—D—S—of a B——.[360]

By now, even the affable Russell Porter had had his fill of Baldwin. As he wrote with barely disguised irony, the *America* when it arrived at Honningsvaag "was in a filthy condition, fairly alive with human parasites, so the rest of us felt justified in following the captain."[361] Most of the men followed Baldwin's example by racing ashore for a snootful. Leffingwell, who would soon pen a long and detailed indictment of Baldwin, wrote that the men wouldn't have resented Baldwin nearly so much if he had shared around his supply of grog once in a while. In such a case, "I do not think we would have objected to his trying to cheer up a bit. No man ever needed something to give a few moments of happiness more than B. did. He did not have a single friend on board, and almost forty-two who hated him like poison."[362]

Baldwin's dispatch from Honningsvaag appeared in the *New York Times* on a slow news Saturday. It was a fairly straightforward account of the expedition's work, the establishment of the depots, the launch of the balloons, Fiala's motion pictures, and especially Baldwin's prized discovery of Nansen's hut and recovery of the message within. Ziegler initially responded favorably, even cabling his congratulations. The headlines, however, soon made reference to the one indisputable fact of the voyage:

BALDWIN-ZIEGLER EXPEDITION FAILS[363]

A few hours later, the coastal steamer chugged out of Honningsvaag, bound for Tromsø and its waiting reporters, telegraph station, and, in due course, a maritime tribunal for Johanson. Gathering his tipsy crew, Baldwin ordered *America* refueled and out of Honningsvaag that same night, to trail the coastal steamer to Tromsø. Now sober, Baldwin knew he would have to fight for his reputation from that Arctic port. The ship dropped anchor in Tromsø at 4:00 P.M. on Saturday, August 2, and Baldwin prepared both to defend his reputation and to begin, so he thought, to reap the financial rewards of his new status as a discoverer of Arctic islands and the message of the great Nansen.

But the game was already over. By the time *America* reached the roadstead at Tromsø, Captain Johanson's cables were already on their way to the printing presses. They appeared in the Kristiania newspapers the following morning and were front-page news in the *New York Times* at the start of William Ziegler's business week on Monday morning, August 4, 1902. The story, with a predictable admixture of facts and white-hot fantasy, would have been more than enough to make Ziegler spit his coffee:

SENSATIONAL RUMORS ABOUT E. B. BALDWIN'S EXPEDITION
A dispatch to the *Morgen Bladet* from Tromsö says that Capt. Johanson of the *America,* which arrived at Honningsvaag, Norway, on Aug. 1,

with Evelyn B. Baldwin, the arctic explorer, on board, has asked to be examined before a maritime court concerning incidents which occurred on board the *America* in the course of the voyage of the Baldwin-Ziegler arctic expedition.

To this dispatch the *Morgen Bladet* adds that there are sensational reports in circulation, one being to the effect that Capt. Johanson was deprived of his command while the voyage was in progress.

Another dispatch received here from Tromsoe says that the pilot of the *America* has demanded an inquiry into several mysterious deaths among those on board the vessel which occurred during the voyage.[364]

Just where the "several mysterious deaths" rumor got started is impossible to say. It is doubtful that it was the work of Johanson, who merely wanted to resolve the question of his command status before a maritime tribunal. It sounds more like the work of a mischievous stringer aiming for a scoop than a serious report from Tromsø. There is no question that many others in the Swedish crew of *America* also took the first opportunity to assail Baldwin's character and leadership.[365] At the moment, however, it hardly mattered. The damage had been done.

Baldwin realized that any further leaks would be fatal. On August 1, he demanded the men's diaries. Rilliet and Barnard responded by swearing out a statement to the effect that they had never been forbidden either from keeping a personal diary or "to the unlimited possession of said diaries for all time."[366]

Baldwin then threatened the men with being left off the following year's sledge work. Now afraid for their own reputations, nine of the men then swore out another statement, on August 3, to say that they felt compelled to either surrender or destroy their personal diaries, having been placed "in a conspicuous position before the entire world."[367] It was signed by Andree, the Vedoe brothers, the doctors Verner and Seitz, Rilliet, Vinyard, Mikkelsen, and Fiala. Barnard did not sign, possibly because he had already secreted his diary away.[368]

Baldwin compounded the hatred of his crew by going ahead and seizing their private diaries and even reading the telegrams that awaited them in Tromsø. The furious Americans confronted Baldwin on August 7, and Fiala was there to record the scene:

Leffingwell: Mr. Baldwin the trouble that has come up here is because the men think that because you thought you had a right to our private diaries that you wanted the private letters.

Comdr. Baldwin: I don't want anything that pertains strictly to your own private affairs. Why I am surprised that you should think that these telegrams would be opened by me.

Rilliet: There is no surprise in the expedition. I would not be surprised that there was a censorship put on our mail.

Comdr. Baldwin: I want nothing except what belongs to the expedition.

Leffingwell: Our contracts give you the right to the letters on the expedition.

Comdr. Baldwin: I don't want that at all. There is nothing of that nature. The telegraph office will have particular instructions in regard to your telegrams and cablegrams. It has always been the custom of the Arctic expeditions to have the written matter letters, etc. given into the hands of the commander of the expedition.

Leffingwell: Aren't we under the civil law and have a right to our private diaries?

Comdr. Baldwin: I don't want your private matters.

Leffingwell: You have them.

Comdr. Baldwin: I don't want anything that you have written but what belongs to the expedition.

Leffingwell: My private diary was labeled private.

Comdr. Baldwin: If it is a strictly private diary it is different.

Rilliet: I told you that my diary belonged to me and not to the expedition, and I promised it to my mother and it only had little personal things on board the ship and nothing else.

Comdr. Baldwin: That is what I asked for from each one in regard to the things they worked at, and I did not consider that private property.

Rilliet: It would have gone to my mother. It would not have gotten outside of my mother. I promised my private diary to her.

Leffingwell: Does the contract not say all literary matter?

Comdr. Baldwin: I know that General Greely gives special credit.

(Leffingwell, breaking in loudly: "That was a government affair")

Vinyard: Then you certainly ought to have our mail and telegrams yourself.

Comdr. Baldwin: I don't want them.

Vinyard: I think myself that we have a good deal of nerve to ask for them.

Comdr. Baldwin: I should like very much indeed to have had it understood that any work referring to the expedition which is an account of your doing such work should be given into my hands to judge what has been done.[369]

The contracts the men had signed had forbidden them to write or lecture on the expedition, but none had ever considered this a stricture against keeping a personal diary, much less receiving their personal mail. For some, like Russell Porter, this was literally a matter of life and death, as he received a telegram in Tromsø informing him of the passing of his mother.

Unknown to Baldwin, William Ziegler had earlier dispatched *Frithjof* from Norway, on July 7, 1902, to find Baldwin and learn of his progress. Under the pretext that the *America* might have to rescue the *Frithjof* if it were trapped in Franz Josef Land while it searched for them, Baldwin now used *Frithjof*'s absence to keep the men tethered to the *America* in Tromsø until the supply vessel returned.

The maritime court against Johanson was held on August 22, and in which he was accused of leaving the ship without authorization. The hearing was held in the office of the British vice consul, Johannes Giæver, who acted as an agent for the expedition at the request of the American Consul.[370] Fiala recorded the questioning of Menander, whom Baldwin had placed in command of *America* after the removal of Johanson:

Capt. Menander: I will tell you my view; it is this way. The written orders I got from Mr. Baldwin I can only fulfill to those who in one way or another are under my command as sailing master of the steam yacht, and when Capt. Johanson was relieved from duty, I cannot see that he was under my command at all in one way or another.

Comdr. Baldwin: Here is the point right here. The same orders were given to all the other members of the expedition, and they like gentlemen remained on board, and did not send their messages. Mr. Johanson left the ship and he repaired at once to the telegraph office where he dispatched messages.

Capt. Menander: Yes. I want you to understand the way I see the matter. Well, he, as far as I know, he asked to be relieved of duty, if his service was not satisfactory and sent home as soon as possible, and the answer you wrote to him the 26th of May this year was just corresponding to his request. I don't remember the words you stated in that letter that he asked this request but it was something like this. I just had a glance through it, but as I understand it at the time that was the meaning of the letter. I may be mistaken about it. His request was to be sent home as soon as possible.

Baldwin then tried to do what he had done so many times in Franz Josef Land and claim superior expertise in all matters Arctic. Menander was having none of it.

Capt. Menander: I have been up in the Arctic. I have been before the mast in the Arctic, but no one ever told us that we were not allowed to communicate with our friends. Of course I don't say anything against you. That is a private matter and expedition, and I understood at the time you wanted to send your words home and had arrangements with the publishers, and if any rumours or anything was stated before your letters or cablegrams had reached your publishers, it would have been in some way or another a damage to you, and I don't say anything about that.

Consul Giæver: That is quite another thing. The fact is that by this expedition every man has bound himself not to communicate anything to the public. I only mean you have been discussing the position of Capt. Johanson's leaving the ship without asking, and I feel pretty sure there is not one man aboard any ship who is allowed to do that, particularly when written orders have been issued against it by the commander.

Capt. Menander: I would like to be passenger on board a ship, and the Captain try to stop me from going ashore seeing as I hadn't done anything wrong.[371]

In the end, Baldwin won a small victory when Johanson was found to have exceeded his authority when he claimed to be captain of the *America*. But it was too late to redeem Baldwin's reputation, now in shreds and never to recover. He would soon publish a brief trilogy of articles giving his strange version of events, but the big "expedition narrative" was never written. The Swedish crew was paid off and sent home. There, Ralph Bergendahl, for one, immediately tried to sell his version of the expedition, but no one wanted to read it.[372]

When the *Frithjof,* with William Champ on board, returned from its fruitless visit to Franz Josef Land in search of Baldwin, the Americans were finally released from their nominal confinement within the port of Tromsø and sent home as well. Porter and Dr. Verner left Tromsø and enjoyed, as Porter wrote, a well-deserved "leisurely month journeying down through Norway and Sweden to Stockholm, crossing to Göteborg by canal. A week in Copenhagen, where I revisited an old Greenland acquaintance in Jutland, a day in Edinburgh to see the astronomer Royal Copeland, who had once visited Franz Josef Land, and then New York."[373]

For Baldwin, no such enjoyment would follow. All that remained for him was a fateful meeting with William Ziegler in New York. For his part, Baldwin was apparently still confident that his actions merited his continued leadership of the expedition. He had seized—or thought he had—all of the incriminating diaries and journals, and had gathered up each of the separate contracts he had forced on the men who had been selected to stay behind at East Camp Ziegler when Baldwin sought to escape to Norway in September 1901. What he did not know was that his expedition secretary—his own cousin, Leon Barnard—had kept not only his private diary, but also a carbon copy of one of those damning contracts. It was soon in William Ziegler's hands.

THIRTY-FIVE

It Won't Be a Lot of Cigarette-Smoking Dudes This Time

When newspapers in New York learned that Baldwin had not only recovered the Nansen message but spent several hours at the site to give Porter time to paint and Fiala time to photograph the scene, they had a field day. The *Brooklyn Standard-Union*—whose editor was perhaps Robert Peary's closest ally—needled William Ziegler mercilessly. In an editorial entitled "Mr. Ziegler's Expensive Picture," the paper all but called Baldwin a swindler while casting Ziegler as Baldwin's fool:

> Nansen himself would have been able to have furnished a painting of his Franz-Josef hut for a good deal less than the million which Mr. Ziegler generously paid for it. More than that, the Nansen work would have been an original from the hand of the master, a painter and artist of no mean ability, while Mr. Ziegler's acquisition must at best be but a second-hand expression of an observer. . . . Provision packers, coal dealers, ship brokers, dog drivers, balloon makers, in fact, almost every sort and condition of man throughout the northern portion of the civilized or half-civilized world, have shared in Mr. Ziegler's generous bounty.[374]

The *New York Times,* in a blistering editorial, wrote that the expedition, "certainly unsuccessful so far as the accomplishment of any useful results are concerned and possibly with grave scandals to be investigated by the courts, will tend to confirm the already settled opinion of the average citizen that polar exploration is about the least satisfactory employment of men and money which could be found. It remains to be shown that any knowledge of value to the human race is to be gained in the arctic seas."[375] Whether or not the "average citizen" had any "settled opinion" on the matter of Arctic exploration, William Ziegler had been comprehensively humiliated.

As the members of the expedition scattered south from Tromsø, they were finally free to denounce Baldwin as an incompetent martinet. With his large expenditure gone for naught, William Ziegler had to decide whether to continue to throw in his lot with Baldwin for another try at the pole in 1903. "All I want is to reach the north pole," Ziegler exclaimed to a reporter. "I don't care how much money it costs. If I can plant the Stars and Stripes there I'll be the happiest man in the United States. I'm not after scientific research, although I know we will get as much as anyone. It doesn't matter if one expedition has failed. I'll send another. It won't be a lot of cigarette smoking dudes this time. . . . I sent [Baldwin] to discover the north pole, not to eat pie or smoke cigarettes. The bone and sinew of this nation is not in its pie eaters or its cigarette smokers."[376]

These last comments—somewhat odd from a man who made his money in baking soda—show how expedition patrons at the turn of the century obsessed over the morality, or at least the public perception of morality, of the explorers they financed. Such thoughts would figure prominently in Ziegler's mind as he cast about for Baldwin's eventual replacement.

It did nothing to help Baldwin's case that several old Arctic hands—even those who had themselves been a party to major disasters in the north—now began to weigh in. One such was Rear Admiral George Melville, chief engineer of the U.S. Navy and a veteran of the *Jeannette* expedition. Melville remarked that the Baldwin-Ziegler expedition "was the best equipped that ever went to the arctic regions. Perhaps it was *overoutfitted.* The expedition may have been overburdened by the amount of things carried."[377]

Baldwin left Norway for the last time in late August. He was soon in London, where he told reporters that the "public has been deceived by false reports" and, in a comment that could not have sat well with Ziegler, claimed that he could have broken the record for furthest north "but it would have exhausted our supplies and destroyed the hope of finally reaching the pole."[378]

This was the last straw for Ziegler, who now demanded that Baldwin return to New York at once and explain himself. Previously, Ziegler had taken the stance that he had no desire to see Baldwin until he returned from the Arctic with the prize of the North Pole. Now, however, Ziegler had begun to gather reports from the men as they returned to the United States, and he had followed the maritime hearing against Johanson.

Johanson further raked over Baldwin in early October, telling a reporter in Sweden that Baldwin had been "a suspicious man, cowardly, inept, a liar, reckless, and quarrelsome," and that the expedition had been "a mish-mash without any planning" ("*allt var på hafs och utan beräkning*").[379] Asked his opinion of Baldwin as a leader, Johanson replied: "Everything about him seems to culminate in the saying: 'the ends justify the means.' His remarkable opinion is also characterized in his estimation of the crew: 'In the Arctic regions, I value a dog's life more than a human's.' Asked about the scientific results of the expedition, Johanson summarized them in two words: 'HUMBUG, Sir!'"[380]

Robert Vinyard and Joseph Hare, Jr., had also gone public with their complaints against Baldwin, claiming that the expedition had never possessed enough food to properly feed the men.

Not surprisingly, the headlines that greeted Baldwin's eventual arrival in New York in early October were hardly designed to further his cause:

BALDWIN DENIES HE LED A FIASCO[381]

Even at this late juncture, Baldwin still believed his accomplishments in laying the cache at Rudolf Land and finding the Nansen note were enough to justify his continued role as leader of the expedition. In New York, he even had the temerity to claim that he had accomplished more in one year than Nansen had in four. The whole uproar in the press, he told reporters, was nothing more than a disagreement between the Swede Johanson and the Norwegian ice pilot Arnesen. Asked what lessons he had learned, Baldwin jauntily remarked: "never take a Swede and a Norwegian together along with you if you want to avoid trouble."[382]

Baldwin was therefore unprepared for the sharp shock that awaited him at Ziegler's office. The multimillionaire was in no mood to accept anything less than the North Pole. "Arriving in New York," Baldwin later wrote, "imagine my humiliation to find Mr. Ziegler in an exceedingly belligerent mood and declaring the work to be a 'Failure, failure, failure!' "[383] Ziegler also confronted Baldwin with a copy of the secret contract he had forced on the eight men who remained behind at Camp Ziegler the previous fall, a copy personally handed to him by Leon Barnard.

Asked by Ziegler to explain himself, Baldwin painted what was later described as an "elaborate word picture" that showed "the explorer in a rather odd light."[384] It appears that this was the very first moment that Ziegler realized what the men of the Baldwin-Ziegler Polar Expedition had known for nearly a year: Evelyn Briggs Baldwin was mad.

Within two weeks, after taking an appropriate amount of time to think over the whole entire mess, Ziegler relieved Baldwin of command. The secret contract was apparently the deciding factor. So, too, Ziegler must have realized the price that had been paid—one far beyond the actual dollars spent—for Baldwin's frantic haste and secrecy in assembling the expedition and all its supplies in such a brief time in the spring of 1902. Some reports had Baldwin being paid off with a generous sum and told to quietly go away.

With Baldwin's character in ruins, Ziegler would eventually turn to the expedition's photographer, the pious and earnest Anthony Fiala, to lead the next American attempt to the North Pole from Franz Josef Land. Later that same October, Fiala wrote to Leon Barnard:

Mr. Ziegler has been very fair and it will be to Mr. B's interest to settle soon so I do not fear a long drawn out affair. I do not think much will appear in the papers as it has been faithfully kept out of them as far as we are considered . . . and the less said the better. . . .

Without the testimony of any man Mr. Ziegler states he has evidence in a certain contract that proves Mr. B's disloyalty as a traitor—and sufficient grounds for a complete severance of relations. Mr. B is probably not aware of the exact nature of the charges against him or he would settle on the generous terms of Mr. Ziegler at once. . . . Mr. B's own signature kills him, not what his men have revealed. In regard to photos I have not started on them yet and of course cannot until Mr. B settles and matters are all readjusted.[385]

Just as Leffingwell had predicted he would, Baldwin had seized both Fiala's photographs and films, as well as Porter's artwork, in an attempt to provide illustrative matter for his "expedition narrative." Ziegler saw to it that both men had their work returned to them. Porter wrote to Barnard in early November, still apparently unaware that Barnard was Baldwin's cousin:

> I can say truthfully we got along royally together with never a cross word between us and isn't that saying a great deal for an arctic winter. And I shall not forget the hero, or the hero-ine, or the villain or how you tantalized me with their fates as I hung over my bunk winter nights and watched you write-write-write away. I hope you still have your diary if so it will be valuable. . . . Let's go up again, old fellow, under the right leader. I was on to New York week before last and secured the sketches I had given Baldwin. I was very lucky. I was with Fiala and Dr Cook most of the time.[386]

In fact, for a time it looked as if Ziegler might settle on Frederick Cook to lead the next Ziegler Polar Expedition. Cook had been in the running for a spot with Baldwin, but he bowed out at the last minute to stay in Brooklyn and write up the results of the *Belgica* expedition to Antarctica. In the end Ziegler chose Fiala, and one is left to wonder on the course that American polar exploration history might have taken if the mysterious and magical Dr. Cook had been offered the kind of unconditional funds that Evelyn Briggs Baldwin had been granted in the fall of 1900. Hare wrote to Barnard a few days later, remarking that "I felt it would be a toss up between [Fiala] and Dr. Cook and I am extremely glad [Fiala] has won the day. I think he is well fit for the position."

> About Mr. Baldwin know nothing, except rumors to effect he will take the matter to law, which I feel will make things unpleasant all around. Met him a week ago at an Arctic Club dinner. It was amusing I suppose to insiders but cannot say I enjoyed the contretemps. Was standing by door talking with two lady friends of Fiala's when B. appeared. He greeted F. affectionately, was introduced to others, then warmly grasped my hand and told me how glad he was for the opportunity of meeting me again! A day or so before he had spoken to Sandine (who was also there) about certain ones stabbing him in the back—and made other disagreeable references. He did not seem at all perturbed—quite smiling and jovial as though he were still absolute dictator of the situation.[387]

As both Fiala and Hare noted, Ziegler wanted nothing so much as for the Baldwin-Ziegler Polar Expedition to be buried and forgotten. And so it was, until yet another strange and seemingly unrelated episode brought it all back to the surface a year later. As head of a lucrative baking-powder trust, William Ziegler held a monopoly on a commodity called "cream of tartar" (potassium bitartrate), a major ingredient of baking powder. When a cheaper substitute called alum (potassium alum) was introduced in the late nineteenth century, it was a direct threat to Ziegler's massive profits. Through the use of lobbyists, he launched a campaign to ban alum as unsafe. Such a law was passed in Missouri in 1899.[388]

In 1903, during an attempt to repeal the law, rumors of bribery in the state legislature surfaced and were linked to Ziegler's lobbying. Baldwin saw his chance for vengeance and testified against his former patron in a lawsuit that charged Ziegler with anti-trust violations in his attempt to corner the market for baking soda. It was only then, on December 27, 1903, more than a year after the return of the expedition, that Ziegler publicly struck back at Baldwin, devoting a whole issue of his *Brooklyn Eagle* to an exposé of Baldwin's leadership in Franz Josef Land. The result was a total demolition of whatever reputation Baldwin had left.

All of the firsthand reports gathered by Ziegler and his secretary William Champ in the fall of 1902 were now thrown at Baldwin.[389] Dickson contributed a long, bitter letter to Ziegler, saying that his "teeth unconsciously grit every time I think of what he lost for all of us who undertook the voyage." Hartt, along with a group of the Swedish sailors, detailed Baldwin's drunkenness. Barnard told the story of how he had asked Baldwin if he could have one of the many pair of walrus tusks lying about the camp on Alger Island. Baldwin refused, stating that "I have friends of my own."[390]

Leffingwell, who cuttingly described his erstwhile leader as "too small, mentally, morally and physically, for his position," went on to minutely itemize his disgust with Baldwin:

(1) He could neither command the respect nor fear of his men,
(2) He cared more for his publication than for scientific results,
(3) He did not keep faith with us nor with Mr. Ziegler,
(4) He went north unprepared in several important respects,
(5) His treatment of us, especially the Americans, was arbitrary and unkind,

(6) He showed at times a mental condition bordering upon insanity,

(7) He used spirits more than a man in his position should do,

(8) He lied publicly and privately and no one could trust his word,

(9) Instead of setting the example by working the hardest in the field he often was the first one in the sleeping bag, and last out,

(10–100) Etc., etc., etc.[391]

Baldwin had expended an enormous effort to place a cache of supplies upon the exposed southwest corner of Rudolf Land. As Porter ruefully noted, Fiala would steam right up to Boulder Depot in 1904 and have the *America* do what it should have done in the summer of 1901: easily deliver those supplies directly onto the shores of Teplitz Bay.

Baldwin had likewise orchestrated the launch of 422 balloon-borne messages southward, pleas for help that, in the end, he did not require. None of the messages preceded *America*'s arrival in northern Norway. With his attempt to emulate Andrée in a great Arctic aeronautical operation not the breakthrough he had envisioned, Baldwin would now spend the rest of his life receiving reminders of it. The balloon buoys would turn up every few years and at times find their way into the press, which in turn would give Baldwin another chance to tell his side of the expedition's story.

These incidents would also afford Baldwin the chance to agitate on behalf of various schemes meant to give him another chance to explore the Arctic. In the three decades that remained of his life, he repeatedly proposed polar-drift voyages that would make use of balloons and airships. He continued to suggest—as he had since his first trip to the Arctic—that the electricity of the aurora borealis could be harnessed to light the world. He even managed to secure an audience for his ideas with the president of the United States, William Howard Taft, in 1911. But no more patrons rallied to his side. He finished his days as a government clerk in Washington, D.C.

Many years after the expedition, Porter discovered that he and Leffingwell lived in the same town of Pasadena, California. "Little time was lost . . . in getting together and talking over old times. On such occasions Mr. Baldwin's ears must have burned."[392]

The last word on Baldwin and his disastrous misadventure, then, should probably be left, in reality as well as metaphor, to Leffingwell, though not his 1903 detailing of his many charges against Baldwin. Instead, we can refer to October 1961, when an eighty-five-year-old Leffingwell—then one of the last living members of the expedition—published an article in *Explorers Journal* entitled "My Polar Explorations, 1901–14." Even sixty years after Baldwin's crew had set up their winter quarters in Franz Josef Land, the experience still rankled. "The real story of the Baldwin-Ziegler Polar Expedition has never been told. . . . In my opinion, the expedition was doomed before it started, and doomed all along the line."[393]

Onward, Christian Soldier
The Ziegler Polar Expedition
1903–1905

✳

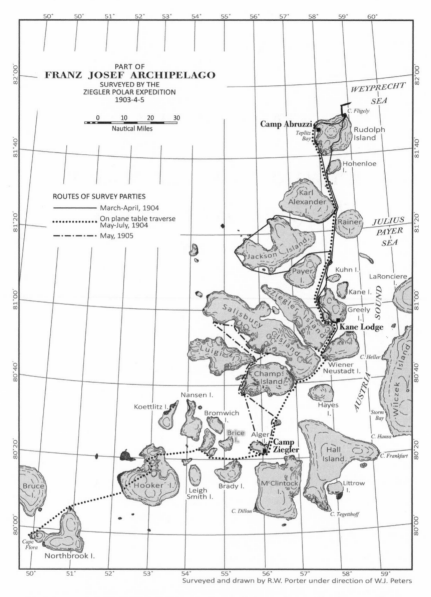

Redrawn version of Russell Porter's chart of the entire archipelago, perhaps
the greatest result of the American exploration of Franz Josef Land. *Copyright*
© *2016 The University of Oklahoma Press. All rights reserved.*

THIRTY-SIX

Money Is Success! Money Is Victory!

By December 1902, William Ziegler had managed—at least temporarily—to bury the corpse of the Baldwin-Ziegler Polar Expedition. His secretary, William Champ, would later write that "no explorer had ever sailed under more favourable or promising conditions [yet] the following summer the expedition returned unsuccessful."[1] Even a "greatly disappointed at this failure" as he was, Ziegler was undeterred in his desire to finance an American expedition that would reach the North Pole.[2] In Champ's words, the only thing standing between Ziegler and the pole was "a competent leader."[3]

Like the impatient capitalist he was, Ziegler quickly moved to salvage his polar ambitions when he rapidly decided on both a new attempt to reach the North Pole and a new leader to lead it. The choices for commander were few. Walter Wellman, whom Ziegler in 1901 had threatened to punch, was out of the question. For a brief time there were hints that Ziegler might back Robert Peary, but such rumors could as easily have been planted by Peary or his coterie of supporters, since the likelihood of Peary sharing the banner of a "Peary-Ziegler" polar expedition was nil.

Then there was the fascinating possibility of Frederick Cook. Cook, three years younger than Evelyn Briggs Baldwin, was "*Susæg's*" opposite in every conceivable way. From expeditions to both Greenland and Antarctica, Cook possessed more polar exploring experience, and his almost otherworldly equanimity—the quiet calm that so endeared him to similar personalities like Russell Porter—was the exact reverse of Baldwin's nervous, unpredictable behavior. Roald Amundsen, who shared an extremely difficult winter in Antarctica with Cook on board the *Belgica,* described him as "calm and imperturbable never losing his temper; and in addition, there are the many small things one can learn in the society of such a thoroughly practical Polar explorer like Cook. . . . He has advice on everything. He gives it in a likeable and tactful manner; not with fuss and noise."[4]

In 1902 Cook was in between his 1897–99 participation with Amundsen in the Antarctic expedition of Adrien de Gerlache and the beginning of his explorations of the Alaska Range, which in 1906 would culminate in his claim to the first ascent of Mount McKinley. Just why William Ziegler chose the relative newcomer Anthony Fiala over the much more qualified, level-headed Dr. Cook, will never be known with certainty. But after what Ziegler viewed as the moral collapse of Baldwin, Fiala was a logical candidate if one was in search of a near-saintly individual of unquestioned character.

Fiala also knew the lay of the land in Franz Josef Land and had the goodwill of the men who went with Baldwin, both distinct advantages when one was in a rush to get a new expedition into the field. Amid all the dissension and discord under Baldwin, Fiala—the "quiet soldier, gentle as a girl"—was perhaps the only member to finish the expedition with the affection of all of the other men. Fiala was also in his prime, having turned thirty-three years old on September 19, 1902, which made him four years younger than Cook and seven years younger than Baldwin. After the Baldwin-Ziegler Polar Expedition, he had returned to his job as an artist and photo engraver for the *Brooklyn Daily Eagle,* a popular afternoon newspaper whose overseers included William Ziegler.

A few days before Christmas 1902, Ziegler made a public announcement of Fiala as his chosen leader. Just as he had done with Baldwin, Ziegler placed unlimited cash before Fiala even as he placed the expedition on a very tight timeline. Fiala had bare months to prepare before the new expedition departed for Franz Josef Land, and there were dozens of corrections Fiala had to make to Baldwin's faulty equipment outfit and dubious crew selections. As the *Eagle* opined, "Fiala has Baldwin's unfortunate experience to work on, and, after thinking things over carefully, has decided to abandon a good many of the frills which went to make the Baldwin expedition so picturesque before he started out."[5]

Fiala wasted little time in separating himself from Baldwin's fiasco. No doubt the most "picturesque" aspect of the expedition—the one that, save for

Anthony Fiala.
From Anthony Fiala, *Fighting the Polar Ice*
(New York: Doubleday, Page & Company, 1906).

the painting of the Nansen site, caused Ziegler the most embarrassment—was the rather inscrutable launch of the balloon buoys. Fiala was reported to say that enough time had been wasted in order to make hydrogen, write messages, and launch balloons, that the entire expedition could have raced to the pole and back again. Fiala, Ziegler's announcement made clear, "will do none of these things, but will simply go as far north as he can and keep trying to reach 90 degrees north until something gives way and he has to come back."[6]

With so little time to prepare for such a monumental effort, Fiala none-theless rallied himself and many of the veterans of the Baldwin-Ziegler fiasco. Porter would return, as would Porter's friend Dr. Seitz. Another medi-cal doctor, Dr. George Shorkley from Maine, had served in a similar capacity on board *Frithjof* during the Baldwin expedition and would accompany the main expedition this time around. Also returning was Charles Rilliet, even though his "Aeronautical Section" would not. Rilliet was immediately put to work in New York assembling the equipment for the expedition. The Vedoe brothers signed on again, as did the prodigiously profane Chief Engineer Henry Hartt. Francis Long—the experienced Arctic hand who had been forced to leave Franz Josef Land when *Frithjof* left Alger Island in August 1901—was back again, this time as "weather observer."

"Everybody liked Fiala," wrote Porter. "Nearly all the old men wanted to go with Fiala. . . . I was told to try and improve on the cookers which had proved unsatisfactory. It must have puzzled the neighbors on Beacon Hill [in Boston] to see the iceman in the dead of winter continually leaving large quantities of ice at West Cedar Street, where I was experimenting."[7]

To avoid the international antagonisms of Baldwin's expedition—and, at Ziegler's insistence, to try to finally field a "purely American" expedi-tion—the *America* would have a nearly all-American crew. It would be led by an experienced whaling captain out of Edgartown, Massachusetts, named Edwin Coffin, and a first officer from Lynn, Massachusetts, named Edward Haven. The exceptions to the all-Americans were an outdoorsman named Pierre LeRoyer, a Canadian from Quebec who had worked as a guide for Ziegler in the north Canadian woods, and two Norwegian crew members from Trondheim, a carpenter named Peter Tessem and a fireman by the name of Sigurd Myhre. LeRoyer had been with Champ on board the *Frithjof* during the search for Baldwin in the summer of 1902, and then had been left on board the *America* as a watchman as the ship was berthed in Tromsø over the winter of 1902–1903.

Without the further participation of Leffingwell and Mikkelsen, the expedition—also at Ziegler's direction—fortified its scientific aspect by the inclusion of a topographer and geodesist from the National Geographic Society, William J. Peters. Peters was named chief scientist and, even though he possessed vastly more field experience than Fiala, second-in-command of the expedition. Peters was one of the most experienced topographers in the U.S. Geological Survey, with twenty years spent in charge of government geodetic survey expeditions in the Far West and in Alaska.

While he was charged to direct the collection of all geographic data, magnetic observations, and natural history collections, Peters's main task in Ziegler's eyes was to offer his "authoritative endorsement to any determinations which may be made of latitude."[8] Ziegler had no doubt been apprised, likely by Leffingwell, that Baldwin had had no ability to figure positions of latitude, and so he was anxious to employ a professional with long expertise in precisely such measurements. In addition to a definite determination that the expedition had reached the pole, there was another reason why positions of latitude would be so important. Fiala later told a Russian delegation that the expedition would be run on strict capitalist lines, with every degree of latitude attained translating directly into higher pay for the men.

Such a scheme was too crass for inclusion in Fiala's eventual expedition narrative. Instead, he wrote that the lesson he took away from his desultory experience with Baldwin was that money, while important, meant little if the qualities of the men of the expedition were found wanting. To Fiala, such aspects, boiled down to their essentials, meant one thing: "the highest qualities of Christian character."[9] The search for the North Pole, while it offered opportunities for science and the satisfaction of "popular curiosity," was for Fiala something of a Biblical commandment: "The Spirit of the Age will never be satisfied until the command given to Adam in the beginning—the command to subdue the earth—has been obeyed."[10] The *New York Times* described Fiala as a "Christian fatalist on account of his intensely religious thought and principles."[11]

Whether or not the North Pole possessed any religious significance, it was most assuredly a problem of logistics and administration:

From Rudolf Island, the northernmost land in the Franz Josef Archipelago, to the Pole is about five hundred nautical miles, over fields of rugged, moving ice that drift continually.

Allowing for pressure ridges and open water lanes, the distance of five hundred miles would be augmented instead of diminished by the general twist and zig-zag direction of the line of march. Of course the return distance of five hundred miles must be considered, for there would be little value in reaching the Pole unless the explorer returned. The rough character of the ice and the fact that it is moving and continually changing its form make it impossible to station auxiliary depots of supplies on the ice itself. Even if the ice were stationary it would be almost impossible to find a cache after a few days, for the wind sometimes obliterates a well marked trail in a few minutes, the flying drift covering everything with a solid hard blanket of packed snow.[12]

To lead a party of men and dogs and ponies over a thousand nautical miles of this shifting polar ice required a further series of calculations regarding food and supplies and sledges, all weighing hundreds of pounds. Fiala reckoned that the dogs could survive on one pound of food per day; a man, three. Nine dogs pulling one man and a sledge therefore required a dozen pounds of food per day. "If ten miles a day could be averaged—though it has never been done—in one hundred days the journey to and from the Pole could be accomplished [with] twelve hundred pounds."[13]

As Fiala knew, no sledge had been built that could withstand the punishment of being hauled over rough ice while carrying a load of more than six hundred pounds. And that was just the food. There was other weight to be considered: a tent, sleeping bag, cooking apparatus, firearms and ammunition, a small boat for open water, and so forth. It was a seemingly insoluble problem and, in the spring of 1903, no one had come close to cracking it.

Fiala began his expedition with some obvious advantages beyond William Ziegler's money. He had traveled the length of the Franz Josef Land archipelago and knew that nearly twenty tons of dog food was waiting in the Boulder Depot at Cape Auk. If the *America* was favored by ice conditions, it could steam right up to the Boulder Depot and take it on board. Just four nautical miles north of Cape Auk was Teplitz Bay, where the expedition could make use of the remains of Abruzzi's Italian camp. As for work animals, when the *America* had returned from Franz Josef Land in 1902, more than 180 dogs and 5 surviving Siberian ponies had been placed for the winter on the island of Tromsøya, so these would not need to be gathered afresh from Russia.

Before any of these favorable conditions could be put to use, the *America* itself had to be dry-docked for much needed repairs from the battering the ship had taken during her year in Franz Josef Land. Fiala hoped to make these repairs and refits at an American shipyard, but there was not enough time to get the ship from Tromsø to New York and back, so he sent Henry Hartt to Tromsø in January 1903 to oversee the necessary repairs and modifications. In Tromsø, Hartt met LeRoyer, who had made good use of his time over the winter to transform all of the heavy furs Baldwin had left unused on board the *America* into one-man sleeping bags, the kind of essential preparatory work Baldwin had simply ignored.

The dependable Anton Vedoe arrived in Tromsø soon afterward, on February 8. He had signed on as second assistant engineer and, when he reached the north Norwegian port, he encountered the first of the many reasons why the expedition would eventually fail. He found that the ship was in no better condition than when he had left it the previous September. Worse, his chief, Hartt, was *hors de combat* for several days with an illness followed by a prodigious bender. LeRoyer was likewise not immune from extended bouts with the bottle.

At Hartt's request, Vedoe stayed with him the whole time, out "of fear that he would go and do something wrong":

He kept the hotel awake all night going round kicking the doors like a little horse. He used the bell so frequently that they had to cut the connection in order to keep him quiet. He was down on the commercial travelers because they had kept him awake some night and now he had got into his head that he was going to tear down the whole hotel and it was a hard job to keep him from doing it. He got asleep at 5 o'clock in the morning and at that time I was so tired and sick that I sneaked down in my room and got a few hours sleep. At 8 o'clock he came down and woke me up and gave me a call down and says, "that's the way you take care of me, ey? You'd better be careful young man . . ." He is making me so tired that I wish that I had never come on the expedition.[14]

On Friday the 13th, appropriately enough, a dagger wind from the east nearly capsized the ship with LeRoyer on board. The following Monday, the formidable Johan Kjeldsen came on board to inspect the ship, a procedure that was required before the *America* could be released from the seal it had been placed under the previous fall. Kjeldsen, who by now had no doubt had more than his fill of American polar expeditions, told Vedoe that "he was sick of the whole affair and wanted to throw up his work as soon as possible."[15]

Vedoe tried to move his personal effects on board but, between Kjeldsen's inspection, the continued efforts to scrape the ship clean, and the persistent inebriation of both Hartt and LeRoyer, he continued to live ashore. When Vedoe finally got LeRoyer to help him get his things on board, LeRoyer was so drunk that he fell overboard and spent several minutes "swimming like a wild beast and shouting in the cold water."[16] When he got back on board the ship, LeRoyer took to crawling naked on the deck and pretending to shoot imaginary moose. The following day, February 19, was Hartt's birthday and of course a perfect excuse to extend his binge for a few more days.

By early March, Kjeldsen had grown weary of the continued drunkenness of both Hartt and LeRoyer and appointed a Norwegian engineer in Hartt's place to take over the repairs to the engine room. When Hartt began to receive telegrams from Fiala that contained work orders, he started to sober up, at which point it was Kjeldsen's turn to tie one on and become abusive toward the Americans. By the time both Kjeldsen and Hartt were simultaneously sober, it was already March 12 and the men had the ship nearly scraped clean and the engine fired into working order. A week later, Hartt asked Kjeldsen for the money owed him for his work to that point and, as Vedoe recorded, once the chief engineer was paid, he promptly announced that he had to leave the ship "to go to a party he was giving for the young ladies Ebeltoft at Pettersons Restaurant."[17]

Fiala reached Tromsø on the morning of March 31, 1903. The American captain and crew for the *America* had arrived two days earlier. The ship itself was anchored in the fjord, where much of the repair work was still undone. Fiala came on board the ship amid a snowstorm at 11:00 A.M., where Vedoe shook hands with him "and found him the same good old friend as of old."[18] Fiala wrote later that the "only cheerful place" on the *America* was in Hartt's engine room, but the reality behind the good cheer required Fiala's immediate attention.[19]

Vedoe had tried to limit Hartt to only a few pulls from a whiskey bottle before Fiala arrived, so that the engineer could be reasonably sober for the expedition leader. But Fiala had eyes. Fiala called Vedoe to his hotel later that evening, where he told him to get Hartt "straightened up. . . . He asked me to go up and see Mr. Hartt and tell him that he had liked to have a talk with him tomorrow and tell him that he was feeling bad about the way he found things topsy-turvy and tell him that he would not have any monkey business and there was plenty engineers besides him and that if he would not straighten up he would have to go back to N.Y. I saw Mr. Hartt and after helping him to something to eat I finally got him to take his clothes off and go to bed promising to be sober tomorrow."[20]

The caution went for naught. The next morning, Hartt went on a bender that lasted several more days. By May 6, by which time he still hadn't sobered, Hartt received a telegram from William Champ. If he couldn't pull himself together he would be fired. Hartt took this to mean that Vedoe had grassed him and proceeded to lay a stream of expletives on the twenty-two-year-old's head.

As for the rest of the ship, Fiala found the decks covered with snow, presenting "a dismal, desolate air, her ice-worn planking, paint denuded sides, and ragged rigging."[21] Tromsø did not have a dry-dock large enough to handle the ship, so the Americans, with Captain Kjeldsen acting as pilot, took the *America* to Trondheim, where the vessel could undergo repairs and be loaded for the expedition.

In Trondheim, once Fiala was satisfied with the pace of repairs, he returned to New York, to arrange for the assembly of his "Field Department." In an attempt to avoid the conflicts over job descriptions that Baldwin had created and then allowed to fester, Fiala had divided the expedition into thirds. The Deck Department, led by Coffin, and the Engine Department, led by Hartt, would be responsible for the navigation, operation, and maintenance of the ship. The Field Department would be comprised of the scientific staff and other expedition members who were not signed on the ship's articles. Fiala and Peters were in overall command of the expedition, with Porter as the lead member of the Field Department.

Once the men of the Field Department had been gathered in New York, they met with William Ziegler. As Charles Seitz recalled the scene in a letter to his father, the field team saw "Mr. Ziegler in his office and listened to a few earnest words from him in which he emphasized the fact, as with the last Expedition, that the object of this Expedition is the Pole and not just to beat the record. He said, "I speak feelingly because last time we made such d_____ fools of ourselves."[22]

Seitz was hopeful. He had sized up his fellow mates and found them a good bunch: "In my opinion we have an extremely fine set of men and with our careful equipment this time and the large cache on Rudolf Island in Franz Joseph Land, our chances for success are the best that have ever existed—leaving out the ice conditions, of course. But if we get up to Franz Joseph Land it all depends on the ice north of Rudolf Island. If this is moderately good—the Pole will be reached without any doubt."[23]

The men left New York on board the steamship *Hellig Olav.* According to Seitz, beyond the tragic burial at sea of a six-year-old child who died in steerage, the main focus of the passage was a certain Miss English. When he wasn't gambling, drinking, or reading *On the Polar Star,* the Duke of the Abruzzi's recently released account of his Franz Josef Land expedition, Seitz and all the other men were keeping close tabs on the young woman: "Just before lunch had a chat with the dashing and fast Miss English. It is the funniest thing imaginable to see the whole crowd running after her. The funniest thing is that this P.M. she has given 3 or 4 other admirers the shake & is rushing Mr. Peters."[24]

Along with Fiala, the men were in Trondheim by mid-June. The repairs to the ship were nearly complete, and the difference from its derelict condition in January was obvious. "With rigging taut, spars cleaned and painted, and a new smokestack, I hardly recognized the old ship," wrote Fiala.[25]

By Thursday, June 18, the fully assembled crew was busy stowing the mass of supplies that would be taken to Franz Josef Land, as well as sorting themselves out. As Vedoe observed: "Every day brings the old *AMERICA* nearer the bottom."

Mr. Champ is here and he seems to be quite busy. John [Anton Vedoe's brother] arrived here last Sunday night. Mr. Peters got here today from Hamburg where he has been looking after some instruments for the expedition. Last night Mr. Hartt was ordered to move up to the Britannic Hotel in order to get away from bad company and liquor. Mr. Varney, the first ass. eng., together with the cook, Mr. Smith, was sent home to America today, both having spoiled themselves by drinking.[26]

The modifications to the ship included a stable for the ponies. The structure was subdivided into individual stalls, with a raised floor to keep the animals both protected and dry on the voyage to Franz Josef Land. On the roof of the stable, a dog pen was erected to accomplish the same purpose for the dogs. In this Fiala was determined to improve on the miserable experience of the animals during Baldwin's expedition.

While the *America* was coaled, Fiala left Trondheim by train bound for
Stockholm and St. Petersburg, to inspect a further shipment of furs for
the expedition. He returned to find the newly arrived Field Department
assisting the men of the Deck Department in loading the mass of supplies
and equipment that had been ordered from half a dozen countries. Like
the Baldwin-Ziegler Polar Expedition, the amount of these supplies was
staggering. With so little time for preparation, Fiala had to quickly jettison
and then replace the small amount of human food that remained from the
Baldwin expedition. Fiala estimated that, the meat supplies notwithstanding, the *America* would haul nearly one hundred tons of food stores alone.
These included over forty tons of tallow and food for the dogs and another
similar supply for the ponies, the latter including a special supply of com-
pressed hay bales shipped all the way from the United States. "In addition
to the commissary stores for men and animals coal had to be provided and
a large equipment of sledges, harness, clothing, furs, footwear, cooking
apparatus, boats, explosives, tentage, lumber for a house, and the thousand
little things necessary for the protracted stay of a large party of men and
animals far from the shops and supply stations of civilization."[27]

Fiala had experienced the frustration of the men of Baldwin's expedition
in sorting through its stores, so from his time in the U.S. Army he adapted
a system of markings—for example, "a red star signified that the case contained pemmican; a red maltese cross meant preserved or canned meat"—so
that the men could immediately put their finger on the necessary supplies.[28]
Dr. Seitz was impressed and thought the whole expedition was immeasurably
better equipped and prepared than the expedition under Baldwin:

There is . . . a good variety of tobacco—Durham, Seal of North Carolina, etc. All the boxes for the ship are marked on all sides with some
special emblem similar to those used in the army so that it is possible
to simply walk through the warehouse and see what is in each box
without wasting a lot of time. All the sledges were made at South Bend,
Ind. out of hickory—but they are not lashed together yet. They are all
much larger than our sledges on the previous expedition. The 2 boats
are made in sections so as to be easily carried and not so easily broken
or punctured as the kayaks which have required days or weeks to repair.

The hay for the ponies is peculiar. It is of very good quality and
comes in rolls which occupy about half the space of an ordinary bale

Fiala *(right)*, on the bridge of the *America* before the ship departed Trondheim, Norway. Captain Edwin Coffin is next to Fiala and Chief Scientist and Second-in-Command William J. Peters is next to Coffin. In the rear is First Officer Edward Haven and in front is the irrepressible chief engineer, Henry P. Hartt. From Anthony Fiala, *Fighting the Polar Ice* (New York: Doubleday, Page & Company, 1906).

of hay, each roll weighing about 200 lbs. Thus, each roll is packed about 4 times tighter, and in fact is so tight that it is impossible to burn. Almost everything has been prepared before we start—dog harnesses, sledges, cookers (also a fine library and a printing press with papers from the *Brooklyn Eagle,* a sewing machine, and a very large music box).[29]

The printing press, a notion borrowed from Fiala's experience as a journalist, would produce a local newspaper for the men throughout two Arctic winters. Along with the musical instruments, these were further efforts by Fiala to avoid the problems with low morale that plagued the men under Baldwin.

The loading of the ship in Trondheim was finished at noon on June 23, 1903, when the ship departed for Tromsø. William Champ, still overseeing Ziegler's polar ambitions, was on board, to accompany the expedition through to Archangel. As the ship crossed the Arctic Circle, the neophytes on board were thrown overboard on the end of a long line and then hauled back on board to be indoctrinated as Arctic veterans.

Three days later, the ship anchored off Tromsøya, where the men took on board the dogs, which included twenty-five puppies, and five ponies. Assistant surgeon J. Colin Vaughan, who along with Le Royer was in charge of the dogs for the expedition, found them to be "very disappointing in appearance being greatly inferior to the Yucon malamoot [sic] or the McKenzie River or Hudson Bay husky in size and disposition. A good half of the dogs were cowed by previous bad training or abuse while young, and about twenty-five were too small or were bitches, which rendered them useless to the Expedition."[30] "We then steamed for the famous little town of Tromso on the northern coast of Norway in whose harbor many an expedition ship had anchored before."[31] Stopping briefly at Tromsø and then Vardø, the *America* arrived at Archangel on the afternoon of July 2.

At Archangel, Alexander Trontheim, supplier of work animals to several expeditions bound for Franz Josef Land, had brought twenty-five more ponies and two-dozen more dogs on an eight-hundred-mile journey from Siberia. Taking up where he left off with Baldwin, Fiala took motion footage of the animals as they were loaded in the new stables on board. The dogs, on the roof of the pony stable, had a canvas roof thrown over them. Besides the animals, an additional sixteen tons of oats and corn, the shipment of more furs, and a new supply of coal were all taken on board in Archangel.

Afterward, as the men retreated into town, Vedoe found the Russians acting "as if they were afraid of something unknown and dangerous. A lot of crippled beggars drag themselves around in the gutter in the most disgusting way. A taxi would come roaring by from time to time with a drunken passenger tumbling from side to side, ready to fall out at any moment."[32]

A few of the men gathered with Champ to give Trontheim a proper send-off. As Seitz wrote, "About 11 P.M. Champ, Tronthjeim, Smith & Herr Glass appeared in the lower cabin, and we proceeded to do a little celebrating. Several bottles of cherry aquavit—whiskey, etc. were opened & we had just enough to feel fine. Talked German to Tronthjeim & gave him a box of tobacco."[33]

Another young man with polar ambitions of his own happened to be in Archangel at the same moment as the visit of the *America*. Georgiy Yakovlevich Sedov—who a decade later would die and be interred at Cape Auk during his own attempt on the North Pole—was in the summer of 1903 a lieutenant with the Chief Hydrographic Administration, a branch of the Russian navy. His ship, the *Pakhtusov,* was engaged in survey and sounding work along the mainland coast of the Barents Sea, the coasts of Ostrov Vaygach, and the southern coast of Novaya Zemlya. As Sedov was returning to his ship from a visit to the port, he encountered the *America* and joined a group of Russian hydrographers as they went on board. Sedov's biographer described the strange scene as Anthony Fiala rushed to meet the Russian delegation:

[Fiala] welcomed them with strong handshakes. He began talking in condensed English sentences as if he might betray inefficiency by an uneconomical expenditure of words.

"Anthony Fiala, expedition leader. Glad to see you. Flattered by the visit of you scientists and sailors. Your servant. I beg you. . . . First I'll show you our superb ship."

After greetings in response the hydrographers cursorily inspected the deck, the superb boats, a brand-new whaleboat and a steam launch. Fiala showed them his polar horse-sledges, canvas boats or kayaks, and light Norwegian skis with patent bindings.

"The latest patent. The first examples were made for me," he boasted. He took them to the open hold. The hold turned out to be crammed almost to the top with a variety of cases. Branded on each one were the words "Ziegler Polar Expedition," and a printed symbol; a horseshoe was stenciled on some boxes, on others a red cross, a toothed wheel, a small flag, a fork, or a theodolite.

"My system," explained the American. "Pay attention to the symbols. They indicate the department to which the items in the case belong."

He called a seaman and ordered him to open one of the cases, with a flag symbol. On top of everything in the case was a list of the contents, printed on a form marked with the same symbol as on the lid. Under the list, packed in luxurious oil-paper lay voluminous coveralls with hoods, made of closely-woven silk and matching pants. On the back of each set of coveralls was printed a morbid emblem in red paint—a skull and cross-bone and a message in red: "*In hoc signo vinces* [In this sign you will conquer]."

"Special clothing for the polar party. My crest. In this clothing we will conquer the Pole."[34]

From the holds, Fiala led the Russian visitors to the saloon, where he offered them wine and pineapples and gave a remarkable account of how he had appealed to William Ziegler after the failure of the Baldwin-Ziegler Polar Expedition:

"I was very convincing," Fiala recounted animatedly, pouring out the wine and handing the steward an empty bottle. "Mr. Ziegler agreed with me. Even before I'd left the office the old gentleman gave me this little book with his own hands." Fiala pulled a long booklet in stiff covers from his pocket. "This is Mr. Ziegler's check book. Ziegler's account with this bank amounts to tens of millions of dollars. Mr. Ziegler set no limit on my expenditures. I could write out a check for each of you for any amount . . . naturally, as long as I was convinced that the expenditure would contribute towards the success of the expedition."

The young man started to laugh and, with a movement of his finger, riffled through the check stubs. Numbers in two and three figures flashed past.

"The total expenditure on the expedition has turned out to be more than half a million dollars. Yes, yes, more than 1 million rubles in your money. And there will be even more expenses. But the Pole will be ours!" continued Fiala, having perceptibly livened up after two glasses. "The Pole will be ours!" . . .

His cheeks were flushed and his eyes flashed. "Real money has been spent on this expedition. But money is success! Money is victory! I maintain that the whole of modern civilization moves on money. Money is civilization; money is everything. That's what I told Mr. Ziegler then. My exact words were: 'Give me enough money and I'll conquer the Pole and bring immortality to your name.' Mr. Ziegler is very clever and cautious but he agreed with me. Now can you understand my confidence in success? My motto is: organization and money. In that little cabin you saw the expedition's headquarters, its brain. Here," Fiala slapped his palm on the little book, "here is its

The *America* at Vardø, July 10, 1903.
From Anthony Fiala, *Fighting the Polar Ice*
(New York: Doubleday, Page & Company, 1906).

heart! No, I'm not afraid of failure. Everything has been anticipated and thought out. A special pay-scale has been foreseen for the Pole party. Every degree of latitude will double the pay scale. While at the 82nd parallel each of my companions will receive a $3 bonus daily; then at the 85th parallel he will receive $24, and at the 90th parallel $384 per day. Every one of my companions will become a rich man. Is that clear? I can see that you are convinced. Yes gentleman, money and organization; that's the way to victory."[35]

This extraordinary scene was only made even more mystifying for the Russians as they left the ship and encountered Captain Coffin.

It was clear that the captain was at odds with the expedition leader. Coffin was far from confident of reaching the pole. He said that there were many men on the expedition who had not even seen snow, let alone polar ice. Fiala himself was a cavalryman who could handle a camera well. That was all. His entire polar experience was a minor sledge trip on the previous Ziegler expedition. Nobody knew how to handle sledge dogs. They had hired some Russian, Vasily, from Kamchatka, to look after them. Coffin said that the last Ziegler expedition had been equipped almost as richly, but had returned unsuccessfully.

Balakshin, a friend of Sedov, who was easily amused, suddenly burst out laughing: "One's a braggart, the other's a grumbler. What did you say the captain's name is? Coffin? That means *'grob'* in Russian! Never in my life would I sail on board a ship with a captain whose name was Coffin! You could load me with money, Mr. Ziegler, but I wouldn't go.' "[36]

On July 4, the *America* ended its slightly surrealistic visit to Archangel and departed, but not before an elderly English stowaway was found under one of the boats, decrying that his ship had left before him and he had to somehow get back to England but would not mind going with the American expedition. When the pilot boat left the *America,* he was sent back ashore.

Fiala now took up with one of this other favorite pastimes from the Baldwin expedition, an almost ecclesiastical celebration of nature, "with the glowing orb of the sun cut on our northern horizon. As we steamed toward it the great, burning, red-and-golden luminary rose, flooding us with light and giving us a radiant pathway toward the Great White Sea."[37]

The *America* stopped for a few hours at Vardø, where Champ reviewed with Fiala the plans for sending a relief ship to Cape Flora the following summer. Fiala would detach a small group from the main expedition to go to Cape Flora. There they would meet the relief ship and provide a briefing on the progress of the expedition, "[and] Mr. Champ would learn of our whereabouts and of the success or failure of the expedition."[38]

THIRTY-SEVEN

"Knocking" against the Captain

Fiala's initial goal was clear: Rudolf Island—which, as a result of the continuous exploration of the area since Nansen, was now recognized to be an island and not the southern tip of some great "Crown Prince Rudolf Land." Fiala needed to succeed in the first place where Baldwin had failed in the end—to bring the expedition ship to Franz Josef Land's northernmost island and establish a forward base there to support a dash for the North Pole in the spring of 1904. Porter had designed a two-story expedition hut that would be taken ashore at or near Teplitz Bay and assembled there. The "Field Department" would then live in the hut on Rudolf Island over the winter, gathering up the various caches of food left behind by Baldwin, especially the large stash of pemmican just south of Teplitz Bay at the Boulder Depot at Cape Auk.

If Fiala could somehow get the *America* to discharge its enormous cargo at Teplitz Bay, the ship would then be removed slightly south, to the supply cache at Coburg Island. There it would be anchored in a place where the possibility to survive a Franz Josef Land winter would be better than on the exposed west-facing indentation that was Teplitz Bay. "From that point, in the spring of 1904, a march north with a large column of men, dogs, ponies, and sledges, would be made, the ponies to serve as dog food as the loads on their sledges were reduced. The sledge party was to be composed of a number of supporting parties that were to be detached as the main column advanced and sent back to the base camp, the final advance party to consist of four or five men, who would strike for Cape Flora on their return should they be carried toward the west by the drift."[39]

Fiala told Champ that the ship would raise anchor and make for Cape Flora as soon as the ice loosened during the summer of 1904, whether or not the polar party had returned. Champ left the *America* at midnight on July 9, accompanied by a similar if not entirely over-the-top ceremony that had attended his departure from Alger Island two years earlier. Before the *America* departed from Vardø the following day, the ship received fresh water and another fifty tons of coal. Then, with a fresh breeze from the southwest, the steam was shut down to save coal, the canvas set, and the expedition took its leave from Norway and set a course for the north and the third, and final, American attempt to reach the North Pole from Franz Josef Land.

The *America* reached the fields of ice south of Franz Josef Land three days later and was forced east, toward Novaya Zemlya. The expedition eventually encountered a Norwegian sealing sloop and, with the Norwegian carpenter Peter Tessem as translator, Fiala learned that the ice conditions were not promising. For several days, the *America* steamed back and forth along the ice edge, while "the impatient American spirit chafed under the delay, and many a young member of the expedition received his first lesson in Arctic exploration—the lesson of patience."[40]

With thirty-nine men on board and loaded down with 218 Siberian dogs, 30 ponies, and 200 tons of coal and expedition supplies, the *America* wallowed through the month of July 1903, making little headway north. As Seitz recorded, "Nearly everybody on board is impatient about our slow progress and wish the engines would be started."[41]

Fiala, who spent hours each day in the crow's nest with Captain Coffin searching for a way forward, understood the growing impatience of his men. He unveiled the first of his methods designed to improve morale on Saturday, July 25, with the publication of the first issue of the *Arctic Eagle,* Fiala's planned Franz Josef Land counterpart to the newspaper he worked for in Brooklyn. In addition to this carrot, Fiala also brought a stick, as Seitz recorded that the commander "gave us a talk in the evening about 'knocking' against the Capt. & his methods."[42]

The admonition did not work, and the men's grumbling soon increased. The expedition was filled not only with Arctic neophytes, but with men who, by now, as a result of the Baldwin expedition, possessed considerable experience in the ice. They all feared a repeat of the summer and fall of 1901, when Baldwin—as he had done in the fall of 1898—dawdled away the best weeks of the year in pointless maneuvers around Franz Josef Land. As Seitz noted: "Everybody dissatisfied with the Capt.'s methods and are sure we could have gotten past the last barrier of ice which separated us from easy going. Several expressed themselves forcibly to Fiala and there was some hot talk before dinner."[43]

What was much worse for the fate of the expedition, as it had been for the Baldwin-Ziegler Polar Expedition, was the nebulous position of the captain of the expedition ship. An experienced whaler with several seasons in Alaskan waters, Coffin had been born more than half a century earlier on Martha's Vineyard, an island off the coast of Massachusetts. Almost twice Fiala's age, Coffin had found little to recommend in the young journalist from Brooklyn. Coffin insisted that he be appointed master of the *America,* as well as sole authority to sign up the ship's crew. As Coffin told a reporter in New Bedford, Massachusetts: "One thing I shall insist on, and that is that I shall pick my men. I shall have every man on board a Yankee and I shall pick them from among the most experienced ice sailors of this area. I . . . want men who have experience in the ice. . . . It will be an experienced crew I take with me for Norway when I start for the ship."[44]

To many of the Field Department, Coffin's experience failed to override their view of the captain as an alcoholic bore with far too much of a fondness for hearing himself speak. Shorkley, who as the nominal leader of the medical staff was already at odds with both Coffin and his first mate Edward Haven for their refusal to submit to physical screenings, wrote of his disgust with Coffin's prodigious alcohol consumption. From the start of the expedition, Shorkley had kept a close eye on the health of the members of the expedition, and in his mind this included recording whatever personal quirks he happened to find objectionable. He had, for example, very quickly diagnosed Fiala with a severe nervous condition that caused the expedition leader to suffer from occasional fits of disorientation that bordered on the hysterical.[45]

One particular aspect of Fiala's personality—his uncontrolled need to spout profundities that were either absurdly pretentious or hopelessly inappropriate—so irked the doctor that he began to keep a venomous little collection of what he called "Fialaisms":[46]

"Ambition is fallacious unless backed up by true Christian manhood."

[At New Year's]: "Gee! We're having a h— of a time!"

"Why this was given me as the very first molasses for use on the table—by a Mr. Adams, a millionaire molasses merchant. He said it was the very best that could be procured & that he used [it] exclusively on his own table."

[Anticipating a sledge trip]: (Shivering): "Ugh! I wonder what makes me feel so funny! Let's see; tomorrow is Friday. I'll give the boys a bear meat dinner & we'll be all ready to start Monday." (This after postponing the sledge trip so many times that we had begun to wonder whether he intended to start at all.)

[After being told that a large mass of dog feces was in the water barrel]: "Let it go! It is too much blamed much trouble to have it cleaned!"

[After fainting]: "Why, this is strange! Just before coming away, I wore out four strong men, one after the other, at fencing."

"I haven't a man in the party who is fit to be trusted with a bottle of whisky—they all chase after whisky like dogs after a slut!"

"I am the only male member of the 'Ladies Aid Society.'"

"And at the banquet the General said that the only man in Troop 'C' whom he would be afraid to meet in personal combat, was Anthony Fiala."

It took Shorkley only moments in the company of Captain Coffin to pronounce a diagnosis of extreme alcoholism.[47] Seitz, another member of the medical staff, believed that both Coffin and Haven were hopelessly drunk at the most critical moments. Even Porter, a thoughtful, considerate man who exhibited more patience during his years of effort in Franz Josef Land that he should have, wrote that the captain "did a good deal of his thinking aloud."[48] Being partially deaf, Porter was spared most of the captain's continuous stream of "stage asides." But he could not manage to avoid those that were directed straight at him:

Gun? Rifles? Mr. Porter, how many rifles do you think I have bought and sold in my lifetime? I might say thousands. And as for walrus, I've seen them so thick you could not see anything else, thousands on thousands of 'em. But we never fool with 'em on our side. Only Norwegians go walrusing, and they can live on almost anything. Why, these walrus here are nothing. I've seen, I suppose, tusks three feet long without any exaggeration, and yet there is someone thinks they can tell me something about walrus and how to shoot 'em.[49]

In the few times when he could not avoid a mention of him in his published account, Fiala referred to Coffin not by name but as the "navigator." Anton Vedoe, who besides Porter was perhaps the most even-tempered man in the entire expedition, was as sharp as could be in a brief doggerel found in his papers and entitled, "To Eddie Coffin":

> The Roses red,
> The violets blue
> Cod fish stinks
> And so do you.[50]

In his "Rules and Regulations, Ziegler Polar Expedition," a list of no less than ninety-six separate directives formally published in Trondheim and distributed to the men there, Fiala wrote that the expedition would be organized as closely as possible along the lines most familiar to Fiala, namely the "methods of administration of the U.S. Army transport service."[51] Within this framework, Fiala was both Ziegler's "authorized representative" and also in "general charge of the ship and general supervision of the efficiency and conduct of the ship's officers and members of the expedition of all grades and in all departments."[52] In terms reminiscent of Walter Wellman's endless directives to Evelyn Briggs Baldwin in the fall of 1898, Fiala then went on to list dozens of often mutually contradictory orders to the officers and crew of the ship and the men of the Field Department. Coffin was given "full and paramount control of the navigation of the ship." Officers, crew, and men "of whatever grade of status, must be careful to respect his authority and to avoid all interference with him in the discharge of his duties," a charge that put Coffin on a collision course with Fiala's responsibilities as the man in "general charge of the ship."[53]

Such murky and poorly defined authorities made it impossible to sort the inevitable clash of roles—Coffin, the ship's master who began every sentence with a first-person pronoun, and Fiala, the expedition commander with the extreme piety and childlike faith in his fellow's better angels—before the expedition left Trondheim. By the time the expedition left Norway, it was too late. It was an unforgiveable lapse, not least given Fiala's firsthand experience with the poisonous relations between Baldwin and Captain Johanson that exploded the Baldwin-Ziegler expedition.

As the ship worked its way in toward land, the fog lifted and the lonely landscape of the Franz Josef Land archipelago rose up across the field of ice. Porter "recognized one after the other, Capes Flora, Gertrude, Stephen, Grant and the conspicuous profile of Bell Isle. All this land and ice hung over the distant pack like a vision, in deep blue and light pink, as it is would disappear should you turn the eyes away for an instant.

> I cannot describe the feeling that comes over me when I see the arctic lands emerge from an obscure distance. It seems as though one was looking on forbidden sights, from which the curtain has been drawn. How long it had slumbered in its icy stillness when discovered thirty odd years ago. How unfit for habitation it still is. How unwillingly it gives up its secrets.[54]

Even the seasoned Coffin was overwhelmed by the spectacle of the area: "Never has been my fortune to see a more desolate scenery in my experience of 28 years in Arctic oceans."[55] He continued to push back against any suggestion that he did not know what he was doing, and blamed Fiala for not stamping out the chatter from the men of the Field Department.

Worse, Coffin resented what he saw as Fiala's continual attempts to steer the ship himself: "Fiala continually saying, 'Can't we go here?' and, 'It looks as if she could work through here,' until I was tired. . . . [One day] to show him, I threw away a ton or two of coal . . . to get in a small narrow hole leading out into a field of ice . . . too thick for the *America* to buck through. . . . After this episode I never paid much attention to anything Fiala said."[56]

By early August, with Cape Flora still more than 100 nautical miles away, the men could be forgiven if they saw premonitions all around them. On August 8 a pony named Circus was found to be infected with glanders and had to be shot. As Seitz watched, the animal was "thrown overboard together with his blankets, nose-bags, bucket, halter-chain, etc."[57] The other animals, cooped up on deck for over a month, were feeling the effects as well, with the dogs howling all day long and the surviving ponies chewing away at the woodwork of their stalls when they weren't biting each other.

The following day, when a promising lead opened in the ice, the ship ran over the carcass of the dead Circus, and the lead promptly closed again. Even Fiala, who rarely if ever revealed any negative feelings of his own, recorded that the men were feeling the strain. "Gloom settled over the company and here and there an impatient or thoughtless one gave vent to his dissatisfaction in regrettable terms."[58]

With Cape Flora maddeningly in sight for several days, Fiala had even taken to the ice with gun cotton in an attempt to split it apart, with little result. Finally, at 9 A.M. on August 12 the ship reached the historic spot and a cache of emergency supplies was rowed ashore to be stowed amidst the ruins on the site. In addition to losing Circus, the expedition had also lost eleven dogs to the overcrowded conditions on board.

Seitz was one of the first to go ashore. He "looked around & inside the various houses, monument, L. Smith's hut, Monatt's [sic] grave,[59] fox tracks, snow buntings, etc. An inch or two of snow on the ground. Relics—vertebra (bears), sail-cloth, bear skull, cartridges, piece of metal, etc."[60]

Porter walked to the eastern side of the cape, to a monument that had been erected by Captain Støkken of the *Capella*—the same vessel that rescued Walter Wellman in 1899—to the three men who had been lost during the Duke of the Abruzzi's expedition. "A very plain shaft of dark rough-hewn marble resembling granite, on the north face of which bore simply the names of the heroes and 'Stella Polare,' 1901. It was erected some hundred yards to the eastwards of the huts of Jackson and at the foot of the talus. . . . On the south side a hole had been bored and a cork inserted. Evidently a record lay on the other side of that cork; a piece of brass wire four inches long stuck out from the under side of the cork."[61]

From the monument, Porter made his way along the raised shore to the ruins of the hut constructed by Benjamin Leigh Smith and his men after the sinking of the research vessel *Eira* in August 1881. He found that the foundations still remained, a rectangle of stones twelve by twenty feet and about two feet high. "The entrance opened south, facing the shore, opposite which was the fireplace. In the fireplace I found a souvenir—an old rusted knife."[62]

At Jackson's camp, the men found that the storage huts, the stable, and the house that Jackson called Elmwood were all intact, save for being damp and full of accumulated ice. It would be these huts, built by Jackson, and these stores, left behind by the Italians in case Abruzzi's lost men should wander out of the ice, that would save Fiala's men when they were forced

The *America* stopped by ice in British Channel.
From Anthony Fiala, *Fighting the Polar Ice*
(New York: Doubleday, Page & Company, 1906).

to winter at Cape Flora a year later. It was a possibility that was clearly in Porter's mind as he made a rapid survey of the camp.

> The northern octagonal building was unroofed and the walls on the north, east and west sides were down. The stores inside were ruined. The other octagonal house, repaired by the Italian relief expedition in 1901 for receiving the stores for the lost men, was in fair condition. A place in the roof over the door, three feet square, was gone. The supplies inside nearly filled the house. Coal in sacks occupied the center, and on this were cases of (probably) canned goods. One tin, which had been punctured, I noticed, contained rice that appeared to be alright. Outside, against the west side, I counted twenty-five sacks of

coal. There is plenty of wood about the place for fuel, and, with the coal, there is ample fuel for any party for a winter.[63]

The men did not remain long. Fiala knew from bitter experience that time was of the essence. Accordingly, he quickly ordered the ship away from "Cape Flora with its relics of former expeditions in an attempt to make a higher northern base for winter quarters."[64] The *America* entered the British Channel and within twelve hours was again stopped by the ice. They retreated to the area near Eaton Island, but not before the ship had reached the same latitude that Baldwin had ultimately made his winter camp on Alger Island in 1901.

Fiala briefly explored eastward in the area of the Alger Island and a possible route north through Austria Sound but soon abandoned the effort. They could not get close enough to Alger Island to go on shore and check to see if the massive cache of supplies left by Baldwin had survived.

Fiala wisely decided that he would fight his way up British Channel "if it took the rest of the season."[65] The ship retreated toward Bell Island, where Seitz could make out Benjamin Leigh Smith's Eira Lodge on shore early on the morning of August 15. The men went ashore at Cape Barents at 11 A.M. and found the record left by Baldwin, but bears had long since done for the six hundred pounds of meat that had been cached there. The ship was back at Eaton Island by 4 P.M., where the men again went ashore to build a cairn and Peters to set up a magnetic observatory tent. Porter thought that they were first humans to ever set foot upon Eaton Island, though both Jackson and Nansen had passed it during their expeditions.

Coffin engaged in station-keeping with the ship, to await a break in the ice in the British Channel. By August 20 the ship had drifted north in the channel but was still nearly 100 nautical miles from Teplitz Bay, the very distance that had defeated Baldwin so completely in 1901. As Seitz wrote: "We have drifted a considerable distance N. & quite close to Reginald Koettlitz I. There is very little water now around the ship and we are almost surrounded by ice which has closed in around us."[66]

If the ship did not get to Teplitz Bay soon, the expedition was as good as lost. Using his army days as a guide, Fiala issued a stream of "regular" and "general" orders to the men, not only to occupy their idle time on board to prepare for the polar dash, but to stop the men from further grousing about Captain Coffin's ice navigation. Seitz recorded that "Regular Orders

No. 10" directed that he and Shorkley "assist in grooming the horses & making harness."[67]

The military-style orders did interrupt the regular games of whist that Seitz and Peters played against Shorkley and Hartt, but did nothing to quiet the now habitual complaints against Coffin. As Seitz wrote on August 23: "The ice has changed a great deal & this A.M. there was a good lead in the W. extending N. as far as could be seen. Strip of water along the whole northern horizon. About a mile of loose ice separated us from the lead—but the Capt. would not try it. By now the leads had closed up & we let a good opportunity pass—a damned shame."[68]

The following day, Seitz recorded that the men's impatience had turned not only against Captain Coffin but against Fiala himself. The veterinarian, H. H. Newcomb, and assistant surgeon, J. Colin Vaughan, were both "cussing out the Capt. to Fiala. Very much ill feeling against the Capt. & Fiala."[69]

On Tuesday, August 25, a strong southeast wind pushed the *America* further north along British Channel until the ship was just off Luigi Island. Seitz watched as the broken ice drifted noticeably north and carried the ship with it. In addition to his running critique of Captain Coffin, Dr. Seitz paid close attention to the existing charts of the area: "We see (W.) C. John Murry, St. Chad's Head, Albert Armitage I., Arthur I; (N.) Mary Elizabeth I.; (E.) Cape Fisher, Cape Alice Armitage, Richtofen, Bruce Fjord, Markham Sound—toward which the ice is broken up."[70]

Some of the men might have been put off by Coffin's caution, but the Vineyarder was actually slowly and surely making the progress north that had eluded Evelyn Briggs Baldwin and Carl Johanson during the same weeks of 1901. The more affable and level-headed Porter, who never sought to command anything other than himself, watched the ship carried north "in huge delight." Given the contrast with how the men had had to drag every pound of supplies north to Rudolf Island for Baldwin, this "forging ahead sometimes ten miles to the day, we could not help but think what an admirable way it was to journey to the Pole, saving coal, saving wear and tear of outfit at a cost of food only. It was really ideal."[71]

On the 26th of August, the *America* drifted north 6 more nautical miles, after making twice that distance overnight. Coffin had brought the ship north of the 81st parallel. Given the dramatic shipwrecks of previous explorers of Franz Josef Land such as Weyprecht and Payer and Benjamin Leigh Smith, this was remarkable. So it was somewhat odd for veterans of

Baldwin's fiasco to complain now since, as Porter fully understood, they of all people had to know that every mile north by ship was one mile less they would have to drag their own supplies.

The favorable winds from the southeast continued for several days. On August 27 open water could be seen ahead through a thin belt of ice. To the relief of the crew, the engines were fired and the ship lurched forward. On the morning of August 29, the ship passed Mary Elizabeth Island and was only a few nautical miles from the scene of Baldwin's brief triumph at Cape Norvegia on Jackson Island. Seitz wrote that the men went ashore near Nansen's hut at Cape Norvegia later that morning, putting down an emergency cache of pemmican and other supplies but, mindful of the stigma attached to Baldwin's extended visit to the historic spot, they soon passed on.

Porter was exhausted from staying up in the perpetual daylight, but he wisely recognized that any and all familiarity with the local geography could save his life later. The islands and bays through which they passed, he shrewdly noted, "I may be retreating down some unlucky time when the ship has been lost," and he wanted to memorize all the details he could. As soon as he tried to sleep, Anton Vedoe knocked on his cabin door to let him know that a party was on.

> There has been an interruption here, due to the doctor declaring the embargo off a certain keg of New England rum and several tall bottles of Rhine wine used, I was told, as a chaser. So I will discreetly end this entry as the writing is swimming before my eyes and loud, free conversation comes over the partition from the living room where some of the men have decided on a game of poker.
>
> Thus is seen the effect of alcoholic liquor in these high latitudes, to men who long ago tasted it and who have since then been in the open air and labored unceasingly in low temperatures.[72]

The *America* rounded the western cape of Jackson Island and settled in a small bay at what Fiala called "a little uncharted island north of Cape Hugh Mill on Jackson Island."[73] The captain was so taken with the potential for a sheltering bay that he named it "Safety Harbor" and thought the expedition could pass the winter there comfortably:

> Went in to Safety harbor about 3 P.M. and tied up to the bay ice which is unbroken, looks as if it never broke up. 'Tis a fine harbor and a safe

one. Also an excellent spot for erecting houses and a fine exercising ground. . . . [The harbor has] plenty of water and muddy bottom for anchorage (small harbor). . . . After supper went on shore. On the south side is a gradual slope to the summit about 250 feet high . . . a fine location for a house and plenty of room to exercise dog teams or ponies clear of stones. . . . I could see this was an ideal harbor for these islands. Having seen none at any other place far as I had been with the ship and I always had my eyes open for such a place in the event of not being able to reach [Rudolf Island].[74]

Fiala ascended to the 250-foot summit, where Peters and Porter had set up a transit to take a series of angles, and from here the expedition leader could plainly see his object in sight: Rudolf Island was less than 40 nautical miles to the northeast. Coffin exhorted Fiala to give up on Rudolf Island, and Fiala even had Porter scout a camp site on shore. But then Vaughan and others assailed him over reaching Rudolf Island. According to Seitz: "Fiala would not directly say he intended to camp there, but there is no doubt he fully intended to—but he was worried to death over it & was groggy. He said it would take only a day or two to march with the ponies to Rudolf I."[75]

By now, Fiala was exhausted and at his wits' end as he retreated to the ship to sleep. He was awakened just a half hour later by Porter, who informed him that the ice had opened in the direction of Rudolf Island. Fiala returned to the heights above "Safety Harbor" with Coffin. The captain took one look and immediately returned to the ship and ordered the engine started. The *America* steamed along the northwest coast of Karl Alexander Island, "the beautiful clear, atmosphere and glorious sunshine revealing the fact that Leigh Smith Island did not exist, but that what was supposed to be that island was really the northeast end of Jackson Island, and that instead of the channel marked as De Long Fjord, there was really a deep bay."[76]

Eight nautical miles further on, a wide strip of ice stopped the ship at Cape Helland on the opposite side of De Long Bay, so Coffin moored the ship to the ice to await better conditions. They were less than 30 nautical miles from Teplitz Bay. Fiala took a few men with him to sound a small bay on the northern side of Cape Helland and then ascended a glacier on shore that rose up to 800 feet. From this vantage point, Fiala "beheld the welcome sight of open sea as far as Crown Prince Rudolf Island."[77] The following morning, Coffin crashed the ship into the ice separating it from open water, the *America* finally punching through. At 10 P.M. on Sunday, August 30, 1903, the *America* reached Cape Auk, where Fiala could clearly see the Boulder Depot, the immense tonnage of supplies dragged to the spot with such titanic effort a year earlier by the men of Baldwin's expedition.

At midnight on August 31, Coffin steamed the *America* past Teplitz Bay, where the men could see the remains of Abruzzi's headquarters on shore. As Seitz wrote, the conditions were perfect. It was a "fine warm day."[78] Coffin told Fiala that he would just have to wait to unload the ship. There was clear water to the north, as far as the eye could see, and Coffin was going to lay on all steam and try to beat the farthest north for a steamship.

THIRTY-EIGHT

The *America* Goes Farthest North

Fiala wrote that the *America* passed by Teplitz Bay in the sunlight at midnight, "the skeleton-like remains of the framework of the tent where in the past had lived the brave Abruzzi and his companions standing out in plain view."[79] Whether Fiala wished it or not, Captain Coffin let him know that he intended to steam as far north as he could, as fast as he could, in an attempt to establish a new record for the farthest north in a steamship under its own power. Given the time, with most of the men asleep, it would be hours before they could be roused to land the stores on shore at Teplitz Bay, so the stage was set for the highest latitude achieved by any of the three American expeditions to Franz Josef Land.

Teplitz Bay is located at 81° 47' 40" North latitude and almost directly on the longitude line of 58° East. Coffin aligned his course virtually parallel to the line of 58° East longitude and ordered all steam from the engine room. The ship soon passed the northern corner of the bay and continued along the shore of Rudolf Island in open water. When the *America* passed the northwest corner of the island—the highest point of land in the European Arctic—the open water continued to the northern horizon.

For five hours the ship raced north at a top speed of five knots, straining under the weight of its enormous cargo. Just before 3 A.M., the *America* passed the 82nd degree of latitude, 480 nautical miles from the North Pole. At 5 A.M., as the ship approached the thick ice of the polar pack, it was finally stopped at 82° 13' 50" North latitude. Coffin had brought the expedition 25 nautical miles farther north than Walter Wellman had managed in 1899 and more than 30 nautical miles farther north than the point at Cape Auk where Evelyn Briggs Baldwin was stopped in 1902.

It was an immense achievement by the captain, even if it was still 20 nautical miles shy of the latitude achieved by the Duke of the Abruzzi's ship *Stella Polare* in 1900 with slightly more favorable ice conditions in the same waters. Even Anthony Fiala, given such a generous starting point on Rudolf Island, would not in the end manage to reach more than a few miles north of his base camp and still well short of Coffin's latitude in the *America*.

The very nature of the expedition was to do just what Coffin had now done, achieve the farthest northern point possible. Coffin himself was convinced that he could have made as much as 50 nautical miles farther had he taken a slightly more easterly course, a result that would have put the ship beyond 83° North latitude and little more than 200 nautical miles from the existing record for farthest north across the ice. But he contented himself with his still-significant accomplishment and made a quick retreat before he endangered the unloading of the men and animals and supplies at Teplitz Bay.

What was perhaps more remarkable was Fiala's complete unpreparedness to take advantage of this sudden shift in fortunes from those experienced during Baldwin's expedition. With a small team of men, with perhaps two dog teams and a few of his Siberian ponies to lead an initial supply train before being shot for food for the dogs, Fiala could have landed at the northern latitude provided by the *America* and made a rapid strike toward the pole.

With the ship laying at 82° 13' North on the morning of August 31, 1903, Fiala was just 241 nautical miles from Nansen's farthest north, and 261 nautical miles from the new record of 86° 34' North established by Umberto Cagni of Abruzzi's expedition in April 1900. Had he been so prepared, Fiala could have made a sixty-day dash for a high northern latitude before he was forced to turn and return to Teplitz Bay—or to the supply caches laid down in 1901 by *Belgica* in northeast Greenland—before the first of November. To reach a latitude worthy of a new record, Fiala would likely need to show that he had reached at least 87° North, some 286 nautical miles away. Doubling that number for their return, and adding the 26 additional nautical miles to the base camp at Teplitz Bay, Fiala would be looking at a round-trip journey over the ice of approximately 600 nautical miles. If Coffin was correct and he could have steamed the America beyond 83° North latitude, then the round trip would have been more than 100 nautical miles shorter still.

With six weeks before the winter's dark and cold made travel all but impossible, Fiala would need to average more than 14 nautical miles per day. If the *America* could have reached 83° North, then the daily mileage would have required less than a dozen nautical miles per day. The North Pole would be beyond them but, in favorable ice conditions, 87° North would have been just within reach. Cagni on his record march had covered more than 750 nautical miles in 104 days and on some days had seen progress of more than 25 nautical miles. Such a journey by Fiala would have been audacious and extremely difficult, but not impossible, and it would have given the Americans the new record for farthest north even before the expedition settled in for the winter of 1903–1904.

Instead, the *America's* farthest north of 82° 13' 50" North latitude would remain the high mark in the American experience in Franz Josef Land. Coffin turned the ship at the ice edge and raced back to the relative shelter of Teplitz Bay, "the last 6 miles through three-inch young ice."[80] In the bay, the *America* was moored to the fast ice along shore. As Coffin recorded, the engine room was "pretty warm as we were under a strong Jingle from the start and never rung off until I shoved over the indicator to slow at the ice."[81]

Another critical issue, one that would effectively end the expedition, entered at this point. During the whole of the challenging voyage to and beyond Rudolf Island, Coffin had been on the lookout for a place where he could anchor the ship over the winter. Studying the charts of the area before leaving the United States, he had selected the area near the cache of supplies on Coburg Island as a place where he might find both shelter for the ship and sustenance for the crew. As the ship passed Jackson Island, Coffin had selected a spot at Geelmuyden Island, near the opening of the newly delineated De Long Bay and, as we have seen, even named it his "Safety Harbor."

In his published account, Fiala makes an odd comment on the historic morning of August 31 when Coffin achieved the American record of farthest north in Franz Josef Land. "On passing Teplitz Bay, Captain Coffin told me the good news that as far as he could see Teplitz Bay would be safe as winter quarters for the ship."[82] Arthur Railton, who studied Coffin's personal writings, completely disagrees with this statement. "There is nothing in Coffin's voluminous writings . . . to support that diary entry by Fiala. Coffin never favored Teplitz Bay."[83]

In fact, the same morning that the *America* returned from its farthest north and moored to the fast ice at Teplitz Bay, Coffin wrote that he "found this no place to winter any vessel, it lying entirely open an exposed from the south to WNW."[84] Fiala's comment, then, appears to be special pleading after the fact of the destruction of the *America* that occurred later that fall. On September 3 Coffin recorded his "surprise" when "Mr. Fiala handed me a communication that read that the safety of the ship was to be sacrificed for the benefit of the expidition [*sic*] by holding her at the edge of the ice where there is no shelter from the pack ice. . . . This is an entire change from the understanding at New York before leaving for Norway. I told him . . . that there was not shelter for the ship here. . . . Fiala notified me in this missive that he would hold me responsible for the Expidition [*sic*] if I moved the ship away."[85]

On September 4 Coffin responded to Fiala with his own formal memorandum, explaining why Teplitz Bay was an unsuitable location to winter the ship. There was absolutely no protection from ice moving into the bay from any point from south-southwest around to the north-northwest. Coffin recommended again that the ship be taken south to Coburg Island, only about eight nautical miles away. "Wintering off Teplitz Bay," Coffin wrote, "I will accept no responsibility as regards the safety of the ship or any cargo that remains in her."[86]

Again, the ill-defined roles and authorities of the expedition personnel had led to an inevitable clash; the "Rules and Regulations" for the expedition had all but guaranteed it. In his Rule No. 54, Fiala had written: "The placing of the ship in winter quarters is subject to the approval of the commanding officer as to position and time and the master is to confer with the commanding officer before making preparations for winter quarters."[87] Given that Rule No. 5 gave the master "full and paramount control of the navigation of the ship, and [responsibility] for the safety of the vessel," it is little wonder that Coffin found himself a bit bewildered over the precise chain of command on this issue.[88]

In the event, Fiala ignored Coffin's warnings and, on September 6 issued a formal "general order" announcing that the expedition would winter at Teplitz Bay. He further argued that the ship would not leave Teplitz Bay: "To send the *America* away with her crew, I would have been obliged to equip the entire ship's company with sleeping bags, dogs, and sledges—for there was the possibility of the ship's loss no matter where she might be taken in the

Archipelago. Then there were the added disadvantages of a divided party, the loss to the expedition of the services of the crew, and also the sacrifice of such facilities as were afforded by the work-shop aboard the *America*."[89]

Fiala believed that the only alternative was to take the entire party and shift the location of the winter quarters off Coburg Island, a step he was not prepared to take. Here Fiala was engaging in more special pleading after the fact, since he had already gained a decided advantage in the race to the North Pole through Coffin's efforts in August 1903. He was 100 nautical miles further north than Baldwin's base camp on Alger Island.

There was little danger in allowing Coffin to take the ship into a more protected location. Coffin's preferred location at Coburg Island was less than ten nautical miles south of Teplitz Bay and even a retreat back to "Safety Harbor" would only place the ship about 35 nautical miles from the winter quarters. Either location was vastly preferable to the brutally exposed Teplitz Bay, where the Italians saw their ship nipped by the ice and nearly sunk. Given the ridiculous miles expended during the Baldwin expedition to sledge supplies back and forth between West Camp Ziegler and East Camp Ziegler, a few miles spent running between either Coburg Island or De Long Bay and the winter quarters on Rudolf Island were a small price to pay to gain better odds in the vital protection of the ship.

With the tension on board the *America* at an uncomfortable pitch, Fiala began to feel the strain, as Seitz noted on September 6: "Fiala is sick today—from worry—and loss of sleep."[90] Fiala was also allowing Coffin's critics in the Field Department to influence his actions, very likely against his better judgment. Seitz recorded that "Shorkley had a plain talk with Fiala last night in which he voiced the feeling against the Capt. & the idea of going to Coburg I. & said that he would be perfectly frank to Mr. Ziegler on returning."[91]

That a medical officer like Shorkley would even be allowed to voice an opinion on such a critical matter of ship handling offers a revealing glimpse into what would become a chronic liability to the entire effort: Fiala's inability to control his men. There was doubtless a psychological comfort in keeping the ship nearby, but it was a fatal one. As Seitz recorded: "Fiala changed his mind 3 times in 1 hr. today about taking the ship to Coburg Is. The Capt. has him completely under his influence but Dr. Shorkley got him to change his mind & he says we will stay here & let the Capt. take the ship away."[92] Fiala's wavering on this critical issue sealed his fate as an expedition leader. He would never fully regain the trust and confidence of the men.

Porter agreed with Coffin but, in his usual generous way, gave Fiala a pass in his misjudgment. Teplitz Bay "was not much good as a harbor; it hardly indented the coastline. More sheltered places had been found among the islets further south, but at the first intimation of the ship's leaving us, such a protest arose from those who were to remain ashore that the commander decided, I am sure against his better judgment, to dock the *America* alongside the fast, old ice filling the bay."[93]

Porter's magnanimity was misplaced in this instance. Fiala had made a blunder that would be fatal to the expedition. If ever there were a time for a polar expedition leader to count his winnings and play with house money, that time was early September 1903. Instead, as the unloading of the ship commenced, Fiala panicked. Rather than agree with Coffin and remove the ship to the south for the winter, Fiala allowed himself to be worried by a nascent chorus of uninformed malcontents like Shorkley. The expedition leader made a sucker bet and threw the *America* into the pot.

THIRTY-NINE

Camp Abruzzi

Having settled the discussion of where the *America* would spend the winter, the crew went to work to unload its massive cargo. In his "General Order No. 15," Fiala decreed that the new camp, in tribute to the efforts of the Italians, would be called Camp Abruzzi. The tent where the Italians had endured the winters of 1899 and 1900 had been destroyed, but the heavy spars of the tent's framework were still standing.

Even better, Fiala found that the Italians had left behind their own mountain of surplus supplies: a cache of cases filled with food stores and, near the shore, a pile of coal embedded in the ice. And the Italians had also left behind their own odd exotics. "Not far from the coal pile was a great case containing a ruined balloon and near it a large military gas generator, and cases of sulphuric acid and barrels of iron filings were scattered around."[94] Seitz wrote that Fiala even issued a new "regular order," No. 12, "not to touch Abruzzi's supplies except on permission."[95]

Within a few days, the men had also used the *America* to retrieve most of the thirty thousand pounds of pemmican cache from the Boulder Depot at Cape Auk. The heavy work must nonetheless have seemed like child's play compared to the herculean effort that had been required to drag the tons of pemmican all the way from Alger Island in the spring of 1902. As if to add a small injury to this final insult to the leadership of Evelyn Briggs Baldwin, the following summer the cliff at Boulder Depot gave way, and

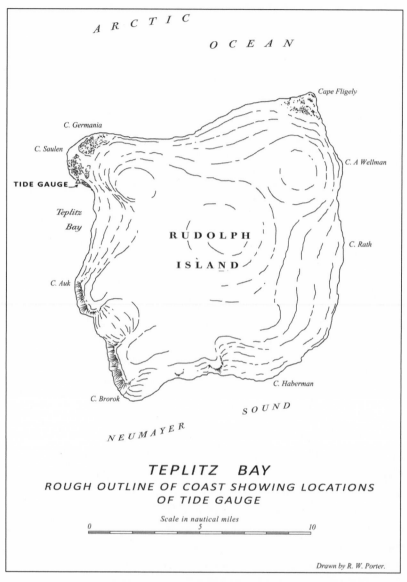

TEPLITZ BAY

ROUGH OUTLINE OF COAST SHOWING LOCATIONS
OF TIDE GAUGE

Scale in nautical miles

Redrawn version of Porter's map of Rudolf Island. Known previously as "Crown Prince Rudolph Land," the small ice dome was not a land route to the North Pole, and "Teplitz Bay" was hardly worth the name, being a mere indentation in the glaciated western coast of the island. *Copyright © 2016 The University of Oklahoma Press. All rights reserved.*

"an avalanche of water and rocks descended from the high face of Cape Auk and washed what remained of the cache into the sea, burying the site under a mass of rocks."[96]

The salvage of both the Teplitz Bay supplies of the Italians and Baldwin's Boulder Depot cache at Cape Auk was a tremendous boon to the expedition's hopes. Unfortunately, the discharge of the cargo from the *America* itself turned into a protracted nightmare. The dogs that managed to survive the sixty-seven day voyage from Tromsø were removed in good order on the morning of August 31 and allowed to run free across the island. Vaughan recorded that two had died of disease on board the ship, while two others had been killed in fights. "About half the pups died being too young to stand the trip, and five dogs were drowned, being under size."[97]

After the dogs were offloaded, it was the ponies' turn. Starved for freedom after two months of close confinement on the rolling, pitching deck of the ship, the animals stampeded as soon as they reached the ice that separated the ship from the shore. Fiala watched as the unchained animals began "jumping hummocks and rocks like kangaroos and finally disappear[ed] out of sight across the high glacier."[98] It was an unforgiveable lapse in procedure and led to several days when the men were forced to undertake hazardous trips tracking the newly wild ponies across the Rudolf Island ice dome. First three men, then six, then nine, set out across the ice to find the ponies. Seven of the animals were retrieved early the next morning, while one was found to have fallen into a crevasse. Unable to extricate the animal, one of the men shot it through the head.

Colin Vaughan was out all night tracking the two ponies that had run from him. He eventually found them at Cape Fligely, the northernmost point on land in the European Arctic and a place that combined utter desolation with an occasional glimpse of loose soil and even some plant life. "Vaughan saw horses on top of Cape Fligley [*sic*]—where it is bare of snow and lots of lichens & moss & some grass. Horses have been following the shore on top of the cliffs & glacier—very weary but scary. They have spent a great deal of their time on top of Cape Fligley."[99]

A search party with four men was sent out on September 2 and another with two men the next day. They eventually corralled all but five of the ponies. Of the five still missing, four were eventually found dead in deep crevasses in the ice, and one was never seen again. The men of the search parties returned to the base camp exhausted and depressed at being forced to shoot the helpless animals as they lay writhing in the ice. Seitz recorded that one of the animals found in a crevasse and shot was Isaac, a pony he described as the best draught animal they had.

While the horrifying sideshow with the ponies played out, the crew continued to unload the *America*'s remaining cargo. This had to be shifted first onto the ice and then dragged to the camp by the few ponies that had not run away. During this operation, high winds cracked the ice to which the ship was moored, and Coffin had to make several adjustments in its position to keep the vessel alongside the ice and prevent the cargo from slipping into Teplitz Bay before it even reached shore.

On September 2, the winds increased from forty to sixty knots and carried a large section of ice away from the shore. Teplitz Bay soon became a scene of chaos. Along with the ice went ten puppies and a single older dog, together with a large supply of lumber for the expedition hut and the ship's dingy. By the end of the day, fourteen dogs were lost at sea. Captain Coffin had to raise steam to keep the ship in place in the bay and prevent the mooring lines from snapping. As Anton Vedoe wrote: "Floe after floe floated off and we had hard times saving what stuff already lowered down on the ice.

> Some of the lumber and the gangway drifted off, but luckily we managed to drag all the valuable hay and sledge material out of reach of the furious waves so that it was saved for awhile, although the ice was cracking inside the place where we stacked them up for the time being, not having time to haul them through the exceedingly rough stretch of about 1000 ft. that separated us from the beach where they would be safe. The big hawser snapped off and we were forced to get up steam while the broken ones were replaced by new ones fore and aft to keep us from drifting away. . . . All the men were engaged in moving the supplies further in on the ice as it threatened to break off and go to sea any moment.[100]

Vedoe himself was climbing a rope up to the ship when it gave way, and he was plunged over his head into the icy waters of the bay. He was fished out and immediately changed into a fresh set of clothes. The stress and strain of the day's events were relieved by the issue of wine, whiskey, and cigars at dinner, but the continued absence of one of the men sent after the ponies, a scientist from Philadelphia named Robert R. Tafel, was causing some alarm.

Reusing the Duke of the Abruzzi's hydrogen gas generator to provide heat to Fiala's camp. Men of the engineering department: *(from left)* Assistant Engineer Charles Hudgins, Electrician and Assistant Engineer Anton Vedoe *(in rear)*, Fireman Augustinsen Hovlick, Seaman Elijah Perry, and Chief Engineer Henry P. Hartt. From Anthony Fiala, *Fighting the Polar Ice* (New York: Doubleday, Page & Company, 1906).

"He has not had anything to eat since this morning and went out poorly dressed," Vedoe wrote, "and the wind has increased so he must not have it very pleasant up on the glacier where the wind will go right through him."[101]

Tafel straggled back into camp later that evening, having tracked down two of the ponies at Cape Fligely. Trying to catch a brief nap on his return, he woke instantly when one of the ponies kicked him in the head. A few days later, it was Dr. Vaughan's turn to vanish while searching for the lost ponies and, again, search parties were sent out.

The unloading operation took a great toll not only on the ponies that remained but on the sledges as well. Several of the sledges were ground to pieces after being harnessed to the ponies and used to haul heavy loads across the hummocky ice near shore. The sledge loads ranged from eight hundred to over twelve hundred pounds, and one of the ponies, a survivor of the Baldwin fiasco, died from exhaustion during the overwork.

A large tent put up on shore to stable the ponies was also used by the men for shelter as they laid the foundations of the expedition hut. The original plan called for three tents, 50 × 20 feet—one each for the ponies, the dogs, and the supplies. Fiala now changed this to one massive tent, through the expedient of cutting out the two ends of one tent and a single end of each of the other two and sewing them together over a large timber framework. The order to leave Abruzzi's supplies alone did not extend to the Italian infrastructure: the framework for the new tent was created from lumber scavenged from the ruins of the former Italian tent.

A device to melt snow for water for the animals also owed its existence to Abruzzi's expedition. Seitz recorded that "Vaughan has been making during the last few days a little house outside the tent to melt ice & is now making a stove from Duke's balloon inflator."[102] Anton Vedoe worked closely with Vaughan on this scavenger project and was pleased with the results:

> I wonder what Abruzzi would say if he could see us how we handle his nice gas generator. The dome on the purifying tank is taken down, a hole cut in the side, and two grates put inside and furnished with a smoke stack. It makes an excellent stove. The upper part of the tank is cut down and all the rivet holes in the bottom are plugged up and several big patches are riveted and soldered onto the sides. It will be a large pot on top of the stove for melting ice in the dog tent and if it works the way it is expected to work it will furnish all the animals with water which is far better than snow, especially for the horses.[103]

Conditions dictated other changes to the expedition hut itself. The vicious winds caused Fiala to cut down the hut from two stories to one, and by the afternoon of September 3 the foundation timbers and joists were in place. A small magnetic observatory for Peters to conduct scientific research was built on the north side of the camp. To Vedoe, the area now resembled a small village. "All our stores together with Abruzzi's big stack of provisions together with all the dogs and horses and men hustling around makes things look very lively."[104]

By September 9 most of the stores that were coming off the ship had been unloaded and dragged to shore, and the *America* departed the following day to retrieve the pemmican cache at the Boulder Depot at Cape Auk. The crew found that the site was shielded by enormous masses of pressure ice near the shore, so they retreated back to Teplitz Bay, gathered up a large body of men, and returned to Cape Auk and the intensive work of recovering Baldwin's northernmost cache of supplies. Seitz wrote, "We worked very hard all day & about 2 hrs. after supper—the hardest day yet on the trip. Tossed the cans from one to another, forming a chain with 8–10 men. Required 3 such chains to reach the ship. Sledges scattered around 50–100 ft. by the wind & broken. Left several hundred tins of pemmican, all the army bread, dog cakes, butter & other things behind. Took along bacon, bacon fat, sausage, malted milk, L.J. [lime juice] nodules, 2 kayaks & several sledges."[105]

The surviving ponies were installed in the large tent by September 14, while the majority of the dogs—those without the desire to fight constantly—were allowed the run of the camp. Anton Vedoe took a break from his work on board the ship and walked up to see the camp. There he found that the "horse tent is a grand sight with all its sturdy ponies side by side in a long row, 27', with a long tin lined trough in front of them to eat hay oats."[106]

Vedoe noted that the men of the Field Department had now been forbidden to drink alcohol, but the rule apparently did not make its way back to the ship, where as often as not the chief engineer was in his cups, as Seitz observed when he next saw Henry Hartt: "Mr. Hartt since noon has had a merry jag on some booze he found on shore (port wine). Jimmy [James Dean, the cabin boy], this afternoon, bored a hole in the keg of gin in the cabin & this evening Mr. Hartt [and] Seargt. [Moulton] have been sampling it."[107]

Other personnel problems were beginning to crop up. As Vedoe wrote on the 17th, the ship's fireman, George Duncan Butland of Brooklyn, refused to do any work at all. "He is very lazy and it is almost impossible to make him do even the lighter work."[108] Another expedition member from Brooklyn, the assistant commissary, Spencer W. Stewart, "went to sleep during the night at Camp and let the fire go out & the pipes freeze & consequently lost his job and is now a sailor working in the mate's watch. Butland who is fired from the engine room took his place as nightwatchman."[109]

On September 16, Vedoe recorded the temperature as +13°F, the lowest on the expedition yet, followed by +8°F the next day. Teplitz Bay was rapidly filling with lightly packed ice, and soon the ship was completely hemmed in. The fore and main gallant yards were taken down, and Coffin went to the expedient of having large collections stashed on deck in case of emergency. Given the ice conditions in the bay, it seemed he had little doubt that one was coming, and soon.

Anton Vedoe could see trouble on the horizon as well. On September 19, he watched as the pack moved in. "Larger floes are coming in and a couple of tremendous icebergs are hovering a few miles off."[110] He tried to take his mind off the ship's obvious predicament by going ashore to find a hill where he could practice his ski jumping. "I made several jumps but my landing below the leap and sliding down the rest of the hill reminded more of a snowplow than a skier's beautiful attitude."[111]

On September 20 the scientific staff moved its belongings ashore as the ship was locked firmly into the ice of the bay. Vedoe estimated the distance from the ship to the shore was about six thousand feet, with another two thousand feet of ice beyond the ship. The remaining crew, led by Vedoe, rushed to blow the boiler down and begin to clean the overworked engine. They then worked to rig a line for electric power from the ship's generator to the expedition hut on shore. Only a handful of men remained on board: the captain, two mates, three engineers, and the cook and the mess boy.

On shore, the men arranged their individual rooms in the hut, "with the shelves and tables and seats each one to suit himself.

> Mr. Peters is setting up his instruments in the magnetic observatory and has great trouble keeping the place free from iron. There is not a single nail or iron object in the whole house. It is wholly put together with brass screws and copper nails and tacks and has been quite a difficult job. Even the dog collars may have to be taken off as the iron buckles cause the magnetic needle to vibrate when they happen to run around there. Mr. Porter is setting the great circle [loaned from the university observatory in Kristiania] in [the] astronomical observatory where he is to take the astronomical observations.[112]

On September 24 the expedition hut was completed and the fifteen men of the Field Department, along with Bernard E. Spencer, the ship's steward who had fled ashore, moved in. "The interior of the house had been divided into one large living room and a number of small rooms just large enough for two or four bunks. . . . In the living room a long table was erected over which was hung an arc light connected by wire with the ship more than six thousand feet away, the *America*'s dynamo supplying the current for lights aship and ashore."[113]

Hartt and Vedoe had also created a lighted pathway from the ship to the shore by mounting incandescent lights on three bamboo poles stuck in the snow at regular intervals. On September 25, Seitz and Shorkley used the new pathway to get to the ship and retrieve more medical supplies, as well as a generous ration of alcohol. "In the evening we had a little celebration (Fiala was over on the ship) & the keg of rum tapped. It was vile stuff—and with Rhine wine & later some blackberry brandy everybody was feeling happy when Fiala returned & found [Elijah] Perry, the night watch, out of business, Newcomb dead [drunk], and Pierre, Long, Tafel & one or two others enjoying the effects of the booze. Fiala was sore at first but soon calmed down."[114] Two days later, Seitz commemorated the anniversary of perhaps the most bizarre event in the bizarre history of the Baldwin expedition: "Two years ago this very day the '*America*' left W. Camp Ziegler for Norway—leaving a party of eight of which I was one behind."[115]

By early October, a routine of sorts had fallen on the camp. Digging out old sails left behind from the Abruzzi cache, Seitz and Shorkley worked on building an alleyway, putting the sails in position and banking the walls with snow, in order to separate the latrine area as far as practicable from the living areas. As the daylight continued to fade on October 8, other men worked on sledges or harnesses for the horses, still others continued to chase down errant animals, and the scientists began their recordings. Seitz recorded:

Did a little work helping Seargt. [Moulton] with horse-halters. My back is a great deal better and I hope to be able to work in a day or two. The horses were exercised again at 2 P.M. After breakfast J. & A. Vedoe went with a team of 5 dogs to Cape Auk after the bears (the 2nd cub was killed yesterday evening by A. Vedoe) and returned in the middle of the afternoon. Four dogs fell 20 ft. in a crevasse & Vaughan, Seargt. & Stewart went after them just before supper—about 6 miles from Camp. Moonlight and temp. -14 F. Several of the fellows have gone down to the magnetic observatory with Peters to watch the movements of the needle. Peters, Tafel & Porter take observations in turn—standing 4 hr. watches—4 hrs. each day—and 24 hrs. on Wed. when the recording instruments at Washington are run double speed. Rilliet went over to the ship today where he will stay and work on the sledges.[116]

The dogs trapped in the crevasse had been found by Anton Vedoe and his brother John as they sledged with a team of dogs to Cape Auk for more supplies. A mile and a half from Camp Abruzzi, as Anton Vedoe was running ahead of the sledge to lead the dogs, he suddenly felt the snow give way under his feet. "In the same instant I threw myself backward and escaped by a hair falling down into a 40–50 feet deep crevasse."[117] John Vedoe immediately stopped the dog team, and the two men followed the crack in the ice, which was covered with fresh snow and almost invisible. About a hundred feet from where they stopped, they found a deep hole, from which "came weak sound as of a *shrieking* dog. We drew the sledge to the edge and by creeping out on the ice we were able to see down the crack and about 30 feet down we could make out 3 dogs who had fallen down and been imprisoned how long is hard to tell."[118]

The sun fell below the horizon on October 15, not to return for nearly six months. By then, nearly twenty dogs had been either lost at sea or torn to pieces by other dogs, in addition to the five ponies lost in the mad rush away from the ship on September 1 and the one pony worked to death during the chaos of unloading the ship. With their collection of odd jobs to keep them occupied and their secreted stores of booze at the ready, the men began to settle in for what promised to be a very long winter.

FORTY

The Knowing Ones

On the day the sun disappeared for the winter, Fiala decided that it was time to travel across the island to Cape Fligely, which lay about ten miles to the northeast, in order to make a test-run on the sledges and cooking gear for the polar dash. As for the attempt on the North Pole itself, Fiala had scheduled it to begin in less than four months, on February 8, 1904. The trial journey would be done by Fiala, Vaughan, and LeRoyer, along with two dog teams of seven dogs each. Dr. Seitz and John Vedoe helped them along for the first mile or so, until the three men had made their way onto the Rudolf Island ice dome.

While Fiala was away, Peters began the science program. He rigged a tide gauge along the side of the ship, in the hole of open water created by the continuous discharge of warm water from the condenser in the boiler room. At the expedition hut, the alleyway to the water closet had been completed and the latrine itself was finished on October 20 after empty supply boxes were stacked into an outhouse.

In the fading dusk on October 17, Seitz recorded a similar milestone from the Baldwin expedition: "Two years ago today Leffingwell & I saw the sun for the last time at W. Camp Ziegler and DeBruler has promised to drink to my health today. I shall endeavor to join with him if possible, but the wherewithal is rather scarce around here."[119]

Meanwhile, Fiala, Vaughan, and LeRoyer continued their journey to Cape Fligely, an icy, barren, and impossibly remote cliff. Beyond the cape lay nearly 500 nautical miles of twisted and shifting ice that rotated around the geographic North Pole. Bears could often be seen ranging along the ice-covered northern shore. In the brief moments when the Arctic Ocean beneath the cliff was free of ice, one could occasionally observe whales powering their way through the cold waters.

The men reached the cape in two days, with LeRoyer leading the way on his Canadian snowshoes and Fiala and Vaughan following, each with a dog team and loaded sledge. On the 17th, a brief storm blew up from the southeast that pinned the men in their tent for a day, after which they shaped a course around the island and then back to Camp Abruzzi. "After the storm, the twilight revealed to us that we were on the summit of the glacier. Over a thousand feet below us stretched the panorama of Teplitz Bay with the ship frozen in, a thin column of smoke rising from her funnel; the desolate shore enlivened by the houses and tents of the camp."[120]

The men of the trial run raced down the glacier and back to Camp Abruzzi, arriving on the morning of October 21. Not counting the day that the storm had pinned them down, they had managed barely 4 nautical miles per day across the ice. It was a shockingly poor performance. While Fiala wrote that the trip was "a valuable experience, proving the sledges and equipment satisfactory,"[121] Seitz examined the men and found all three had been severely frostbitten: "Vaughan had his fingers quite badly frozen and the others were also frozen in various places."[122]

The equipment might have fared well on the brief trip across the Rudolf Island ice dome, but the humans had not. Fiala joined the men in a game of whist that night (he and John Truden lost to Seitz and Vaughan), but his mind had to be distracted by the men's poor performance, both in terms of nautical miles per day and their inability to survive without frostbite, even in the few days of relatively mild weather they had encountered. Even more remarkably, it remained the only trial trip of the entire fall, and it must have shaken Fiala's confidence that he could successfully accomplish a round trip to the North Pole of nearly 1,000 nautical miles.

There were soon other worries for the expedition commander. The grumbling that had accompanied the voyage from Norway, and temporarily abated during the off-loading of the ship, had returned. Captain Coffin protested that his ship's crew was not the servants of the scientific staff—with his usual sarcasm, he dubbed them "the knowing ones"—but with the ship now firmly locked into and at the mercy of the ice, Coffin's authority over his own crew had vanished. On the day after his first mate, Edward Haven, was ordered to create wire harnesses for the dogs, Coffin wrote that, on this day at least, "no *Orders* coming in from the knowing ones. Mr. Haven had a quantity of wire halters spliced in a neat manner. This morning one of the *Dog Doctors* (who never saw a wire spliced) found fault, that the work was not done right. *Hard to satisfy.* . . . Too many bosses."[123]

Such seeming trivialities were abruptly overshadowed the day after Fiala returned from his trial run across the island. On the evening of October 22, a light breeze across the icy shoreline suddenly freshened, and then almost immediately backed from the east and strengthened to gale force. Within an hour, a dagger wind was blowing over 60 knots. Anton Vedoe had just sat down in his room after a long day of work and was about to light a cigar "when the ship gave a jerk and heeled over to port.

> In a minute I was on deck and in the roaring storm. I could make out that a crack about 2 ft. wide had opened between the ship's side and the gangway, and as I went over to the other side I saw the ice move away from the ship's side rapidly opening up to about 50 ft. in a few instants. We had three lines out forward and one aft. The engine was gotten ready in a hurry in case the lines should break. At 9 o'clock we were all ready in the engine room.[124]

An hour later, the cable supporting the arc lights strung between the ship and the shore snapped. The bow cables parted at the same time, but by throwing the engine into reverse, the strain on the remaining stern line eased. Then the stern line became entangled with the propeller and killed the engine. The stern line snapped instantly, leaving the ship adrift in the sudden chaos of the bay.

If matters were not grave enough, Vedoe went to see Coffin and found both the captain and his first mate in their cups. The second mate, Vedoe observed, "kept his head and had got the anchor ready and [at 1 A.M.] dropped it with 85 fathoms of chain. It was a horrible situation. Every one was discouraged seeing their commander in such a state not knowing what to do."[125]

The anchor finally held and the ship was stabilized against the ice. The wind blew all night while the captain and first mate slept off their jags. In the morning, the men got to work freeing the propeller. "One man was lowered down on a rope and with an axe attached to a long pole kept chopping and cutting on the rope. A very tough work, the waves splashing up in the well drenching [him]."[126]

The prop was not cleared until early afternoon, and soon after the steam engine turned over. At that moment, the men realized that the anchor had lost its hold and the ship was adrift once again. They could see nothing in the dark except the waves that smashed against the sides of the ship. By keeping on full speed, the crew was able to hold their own against the wind, and by 7:30 on October 23, twenty-four hours after the gale began, the winds began to calm. Coffin thought they had drifted somewhere to the south of Teplitz Bay, but in the dark, with the ship's compass swinging wildly on account of local magnetic attraction, they were lost.

Vedoe was thoroughly exhausted after having been up for nearly two days straight. He still had to stand watch until midnight on the 23rd. At 11:00 P.M. he went on deck and from the corner of his eye saw a sharp flash. He told Hartt about it and the Chief Engineer brought two flares for the captain to fire off just in case the light Vedoe had seen was a signal from Camp Abruzzi. It was, and it showed the men that they were not south or southwest of Teplitz Bay, but north of it, somewhere between capes Säulen and Germania.

As the anchor continued to drag along the bottom, Coffin allowed the ice to come in against the ship, in an attempt to lift the anchor so that the men could try to haul it in. "When the floe did bring up against the ship's bow it dragged the anchor off as if it had been a straw," wrote Coffin.[127] In the end, the men were unable to raise the anchor, so Coffin ordered it cut from the ship with hacksaws. Steaming south past Cape Säulen, the *America* regained Teplitz Bay at noon on October 24. Miraculously, the *America*'s small boats, placed near the ship on the ice along with a large cache of provisions, were still sitting on the fast ice along the shore.

A year later, when he was sober and had plenty of time to turn over the events of the fall of 1903, Captain Coffin returned to these two difficult nights as justification for his earlier warnings about the danger of wintering the ship in Teplitz Bay: "With all, we were very fortunate to arrive back at the old berth without doing any damage. . . . This was the first proof that this bay was not a safe harbor, or any harbor at all. Also gave the crew an idea that they were unsafe, which was afterwards proved very clearly by most of them deserting the ship and going on shore to the Expidition [*sic*] house. Even the cook left his Galley, so demoralized had they got."[128] In this Coffin was wrong. The crew had not lost faith with the ship. Rather, after witnessing the drunken inability of the captain and the first mate to cope with the near-catastrophe, they had lost their trust in both of the top officers. As Vedoe wrote: "They all feel very bitterly towards the captain and mate for their actings [*sic*] in the storm."[129]

When the men started to come ashore from the ship, Dr. Seitz quickly learned what had happened and why:

> It seems that the Capt. & the first Mate started to tank up when the wind started and by time the ship was adrift, they were well tanked up. Hartt & [Second Mate James] Nichols refused to join them & Hartt fired some hot words to the Capt. Hartt & Nichols had really to manage the ship. The other two had to turn in. When the propeller was freed the ship steamed full speed with 60 fathoms of chain out. They struck a bank & finally Hartt persuaded the Capt. to let him cut (saw) the chain & let it slip. The forward part of the ship was much strained and the beams, etc. sprung several inches. The crew & Nichols say if there is another strong wind, they will come ashore and they are all ready to do so. Mac [D. S. Mackiernan, a member of the crew] says the Capt. has 6–8 doz. bottles of whiskey on board—although he has acted as if he had nothing, and tries to get what little liquor is left for medicinal purposes. Dr. Shorkley says the Capt. shows the effects of his boozing in his blood-shot eyes, tremor, etc.[130]

Fiala himself sensed that the men had lost faith in the leadership on board the ship, so he tried to turn the situation around by moving on board himself. "I had been living in the house on shore. . . . But, after the experience of the last storm, with the drifting away of the ship, and the uncertain feeling of safety aboard, I felt it my duty to take up my abode there, and moved my little store of personal belongings to my old cabin on the *America*."[131] Fiala directed Peters to take charge of things ashore, with Seitz and John Vedoe to act as quartermasters and Shorkley to oversee the camp's sanitation but, despite Fiala's constant recourse to military language, no one was given command authority over Camp Abruzzi.

Seitz, as usual, was far more direct in his account: "It is said [the *America*] drifted 40 hrs. & Fiala says there is considerable kicking on board & that some say they will come ashore to live. Fiala says he is going to live on the ship to look after things and take the responsibility of the ship upon himself. Peters will have charge over here."[132] Seitz was also trying his best to keep the chief engineer functioning, as Hartt had developed a painful and chronic anal fissure. The causes ranged from the restricted diet, the more or less constant drinking, or from the homosexual activity Hartt would later hint at in his correspondence.

The days after the storm were occupied in anchoring the ship, with several new mooring lines, to the fast ice along shore. By October 28 Vedoe and Hartt had reconnected the line that ran electricity from the ship to the expedition house. For a brief moment, it seemed as if the October ordeal would be the *America*'s great misadventure for the winter. It was not to be. November was on its way, and with it the beginning of the complete destruction of the ship.

FORTY-ONE

Shaking like a Young Tree in a Storm

On the first of November 1903, the temperature dropped to −22°F and the roof of the expedition house was gradually covered over with ice. During the days when a fire was kept lit, the ice on the roof melted and dripped over everything. The men could lie in their bunks and hear the creation and the cracking of new ice, a sound like glass breaking in the distance. Vedoe, recalling his Scandinavian boyhood, noted the fine strip of new ice just off the ship and thought that it would make for "excellent skating if skates had been at hand, but to the worse there is not a pair on board."[133]

Fiala had taken Vedoe aside to praise his performance during the storm. "Mr. Fiala called me up this evening and said he had heard that I had behaved very well during the storm and would like to congratulate me and said that he would not forget it and that he was glad to find me so interested in the expedition." The compliments were certainly deserved, even if the comment of Vedoe being "so interested" was a bit odd, given that Vedoe had signed on to the expedition even after his experiences with the Baldwin fiasco. "[Fiala] said a few words about the coming sledge journey and that he would see that I would get sufficient outdoor exercise so as to be prepared for the coming hardship. He is going to take 24 men in the field. The men with the horses will have two each to take care of and every dog team will be composed of 11 dogs."[134]

The performance of the ship's officer's during the storm left no room for praise. As Seitz recorded, feelings were running high against Captain Coffin and First Mate Haven. Hartt—who for all his drunkenness and profanity was a highly capable chief engineer and by all accounts beloved by the men and by Fiala himself—was furious at the inebriated incompetence of Coffin and Haven during the storm. He went so far as to have several members of the black gang, or engineering crew, as well as other members of the crew sign a damning report on the officers' actions during the storm. In response, Coffin and Haven tried to mollify the chief engineer: "Hartt says the Capt. & 1st Mate are making love to him now & that he has his report already made out & signed by 13 men. He told Fiala that he would let no one from the engine room go on the ice under the 1st Mate & the crew would not do so."[135]

Tempers were fraying ashore as well. Seitz, helping with the dog and horse harnesses for the planned polar dash, got into a shouting match with Moulton over the pace of the work. "In the A.M. Seargt. & I had a hot scrap about helping him make horse harness & who has done the most work, etc., but by noon we had made it all up."[136] Jefferson F. Moulton, in charge of the ponies, and Vaughan, in the same position with the dogs, engaged in running arguments, "swearing and cursing each other as usual" as Vedoe wrote when he visited the expedition house on November 7.[137]

When two bears approached the ship on November 4, the dogs chased them away, but when one ran directly toward the expedition house on shore, it was shot. One of the men who chased the bears had his ears frozen in the −20°F cold; Vedoe recorded that the man's ears were so badly frostbitten that large blisters had been raised on them.

Vedoe tried to lift his sights above all the turmoil, to the miracle that now began to appear above their heads on clear nights. Roused onto the deck of the ship by the alarm over the bears, Vedoe looked up to see "a faint aurora . . . stretching from horizon to horizon east and west through zenith. It forms three different lines running parallel to each other very much resembling colored ribbons shook by a strong wind."[138]

The scientific work proceeded despite the chaos on both ship and shore. Though he possessed vast experience in leading scientific expeditions, William Peters, the expedition second-in-command and geodesist from the National Geographic Society, seems to have had precious little time for the constant distractions provided by Coffin on board the *America* and the carping of the men of the expedition house ashore. He spent every possible moment in the observatory, occupied by the much more interesting electric storms that undulated over their heads. On November 5 Vedoe wrote that "Mr. Peters has some doubts as to the locality of the observatory. Last Sunday we had a violent magnetic storm and at the same time a brilliant aurora lit up the heavens. The weaker auroras he thinks have no influence on the magnetic needle."[139]

The weather remained clear on most days but the temperatures steadily dropped. Seitz tried to walk to the rocks of Cape Säulen on November 8 but had to turn back halfway when the wind picked up and blew directly onto his face through his Jaeger cap, nipping his right ear. He returned to camp to play chess with Moulton and Shorkley and then to engage in a "very long argument with Vaughan about evolution, religion, etc."[140]

On November 9 the temperature fell to -42°F. Vedoe heard "a terrible noise in the ice around the ship . . . probably caused by the severe cold expanding the ice and contracting the bolts in the ship causing them to crack loudly."[141] The next day, even from the distance of the expedition house, Seitz could hear the ice "roaring" in the bay.[142]

All of the various threads of the first months in Franz Josef Land—Fiala's failure to move the *America* further south and out of the exposed bay, Coffin's alcoholic leadership on board the ship, the onrush of winter and with it the accumulation of ice, and the tenuous morale of thirty-nine men thrown together at the last minute and delivered into one of the harshest environments on the planet—all now drew together to create the first and most serious crisis of the expedition.

On November 11 the men had little notion that their fortunes were about to change so radically. A brilliant aurora appeared above their heads. The men ashore organized a chess tournament. Sigurd B. Myhre, a Norwegian from Trondheim, fell ill. The dogs were divided into the teams that the men would begin to train for the polar dash. Fiala announced that he would make his polar plans known within the week. And the temperature dropped even further, to -46°F.

If anyone had a right to a premonition of disaster, it should have been the steady Anton Vedoe, who spent the afternoon of November 11 reading *Robinson Crusoe.* He went to bed in his bunk near the engine room at about the same time as a wind freshened from the south-southwest. Ice began to press hard against the ship soon after, and between two and three o'clock on the morning of November 12, the pressure became severe. The assaults came in waves from the south-southwest, about every half-hour, and lasted between five and ten minutes.

Vedoe was shaken awake at 4 A.M. when his bunk started shivering. "I lay and wondered what it could be thinking it being the little engine running away from controls but I was soon taken out of those illusions by a loud cracking and hammering on the ship's side and in an instant was well aware of what was going on."[143] The ship was being crushed. In the engine room, Vedoe joined Hartt as they coupled the engine and made ready to raise steam. They quickly had power restored and the lights on throughout the ship.

What followed was chaos. Fiala was also shaken awake, and lay for a time in his bunk listening to the agonized sounds of the ship's timbers being squeezed. He did not rise until the captain's dog "pushed his way into my cabin and put his paws on me, looking into my face with his great black eyes."[144] Fiala put on a heavy coat and went out onto the deck. In the darkness, he could distinguish enormous pressure ridges of ice as they moved in waves toward the ship. He retreated to his cabin to get dressed before emerging to "a scene of wild activity with a nerve-wracking accompaniment of shrieks and groans from the protesting and resisting ship."[145]

Captain Coffin also felt the sudden jolts on the sides of the ship and woke to find "many pressures on the steamer. The last one was hard and listed the ship to starboard, jamming her against the solid ice."[146] Coffin went to Fiala's cabin to tell him that he had ordered everyone off the ship, which, Fiala noted, harkening back to his days in the Spanish-American War, "was shaking as if with the ague."[147] Vedoe wrote that the vessel was "shaking from fore to aft like a young tree in a storm. The ice could be seen by the pale light from the moon tossing around, crumbling up, raising on end, and falling down doubling and redoubling while a good S.S.W. breeze was blowing."[148]

The ice relented at 4:25 A.M., and a fog settled over the ship. The men jumped ship while they could, sea bags slung over their shoulders. They continued to unload the ship, and at 5:20 the ice pressure started again. The men on board hurried to get everything they could onto the ice before the ship sank. The sledges and other materials for the polar dash were saved first, and then Fiala hurried back to his cabin to retrieve some writings and furs he had left behind in the rush to leave the ship. Another twenty minutes of violence and then quiet again, until a new pressure ridge rose up at 7:00 A.M., when "for about 15 minutes everything was in the wildest tumult. All sledges were taken on the ice. The noise in the poor ship was something horrid and we fear the worst."[149]

At eight in the morning, the *America* was wracked by the worst pressure yet. Hartt "reported that the water was above the fire-room plates and that he had started to pump the ship."[150] The pumps worked—the water had flooded the stern bilges as the bow was raised by the pressure of the ice. Vedoe found no large leaks despite the pounding the ship had taken. Nevertheless, the ship was heeled over to starboard and the starboard side was bulging, the bow raised up onto the ice and the gangway laying almost vertically.

At 8:20 A.M. the men from the camp arrived with several ponies. Everything of value was loaded onto the sledges and pulled ashore. The provisions cache that had been arranged on the ice in the weeks previous was also moved further inshore. In the darkness and because the ship was down at the stern, Vedoe could not evaluate the area around the rudder and propeller but considered it likely that both had been destroyed. Ice was now piled up fifteen feet high around the ship.

The men of the camp did not escape the frightening episode unscathed. Seitz and Moulton worked with the ponies all day and then when the scene had calmed, Seitz walked back to the camp and directly into the wire leading to the observatory. "[I]t struck me in the right eye which was open & scratched along for some distance—producing some pretty bad scratches on my cornea & causing much pain & inability to use my eye. Have been dropping cocaine into it to relieve the irritation."[151]

Fiala even considered that the *America* "in her new cradle of ice blocks seemed to be safer than before," but this was wishful thinking on the part of someone who never admitted his leading role in the ship's destruction.[152] Coffin agreed with the expedition commander that the giant pressure ridges now shielded the ship from ice moving past the bay but, as he had warned Fiala the moment he laid eyes on Teplitz Bay, the ship would not survive "a heavy direct blow from SW to West."[153]

Seitz, who kept a close watch on the temper of the men, witnessed the crew coming off the ship and saw in several of them something approaching total panic:

Fiala was over about 5 P.M. & told us to say nothing about the conduct of some of the men. Many of the men were badly excited esp. [First Assistant Engineer Charles] Hudgins & [cook Clarence] Thwing. Thwing came all the way over to Camp this A.M. with his belongings & said the ship was splintered from stem to stern. At the ship, he had a bag of lamps & chimneys which he "saved" & dropped over the gangway on to the ice with a great clatter. Hudgins said the engine room was a mass of ruin & again admitted to have prayed to be saved from the wreck. The Capt. & Mate were drunk. The Capt. was carrying his chronometer box around on the ice & report has it that it contained 5 or 6 bottles of gin. The Mate was stepping high to say the least & his speech was uncertain & verged on the maudlin. He could not get out the words when he wanted to tell Fiala where he wanted the cache moved & Fiala walked off in disgust. [Second Officer James] Nichols told Fiala that he would take no orders from drunken men.[154]

The next morning, Coffin recorded that several men had deserted the ship, some never to return. "Six of the men & the cook left the ship this morning between 4 and 6 o'clock, also one fireman, without saying a word to any one."[155] Again, Seitz was perceptive in recording both the names and the reasons for the sudden appearance of so many of the ship's crew at the expedition house ashore. "About 6 A.M. Thwing appeared over here & shortly after 7 others—[Allen W.] Montrose, [John J.] Duffy, [D. S.] Mac[Kiernan], [Elijah] Perry, [William R.] Meyers [Myers], [Franklin] Cowing & [Gustave] Meyers [Meyer]—all having deserted the ship. They had breakfast at 7 A.M., dinner at noon & supper after us. They spent the morning in the tent—the afternoon in the house & slept in the stable on hay with one blanket apiece."[156]

The crew members who fled the ship in a panic gradually straggled back to their cabins, where on November 14 Fiala called them together, along with the officers, in the workshop between decks. As Anton Vedoe recorded, Fiala "gave a short speech warning the men to be loyal and stay with the ship."[157] But the spirits of the crew—already damaged after the night the ship was swept to sea—were now gone. They had lost faith first in the captain, then in the mate, and now in the ship itself.

For Coffin, the feelings of distrust the crew felt for him were now mutual: "The rest of the men came off [the shore to the ship] this AM. . . . Cook showed up and will go to work in the galley. All the boys are badly demoralized . . . the ice has piled up . . . Everything looks favorable for a series of squeezes. . . . There are two on the steamer who in time of need will be somewhere else."[158] What Coffin did not record—could not record—was that the demoralization of the men resulted as much from his and the first mate's drunkenness as from the frightening episodes of the ship in the ice.

With the *America* now seemingly locked into a jumble of ice, the panic temporarily subsided, and in the days that followed the men could begin to relax a bit—all except Hartt, who had now been consulted by Shorkley and was advised to have an operation on his painful anal fissure, an operation Hartt refused.

True to his word, Fiala offered a team of dogs to Anton Vedoe. Vedoe was delighted, especially as he observed the various ineffective ways of training the teams that were going on all around him. "They are very affectionate dogs and a little good treatment will make them work double willingly and keep their spirits up.

> It is a very wrong thing to mistreat a working dog. As soon as he is licked, he will lose all interest for you and his work and he will behave so frightened for you that instead of paying attention to things in front of him he will now and then keep turning his head looking after you and stop pulling which is the cause [of] so much aggravating work on your side. I will probably take my dogs over to the ship so that I can attend to them myself.[159]

In the event, Vedoe got only one day of training runs with his dogs, on November 19, before the final battle for the ship commenced. It began early on the morning of November 21, 1903, and did not last long.

FORTY-TWO

Peculiar Answers and Replies

Portents of the final disaster for the ship seemed everywhere in mid-November. On the 16th Seitz went outside after a successful run at blackjack and saw ice "piling up and making considerable noise about 1/4 to 1/2 mile from the ship."[160] Looking up, he watched as three meteors arced through the dark sky overhead. The next day, Fiala issued his "Regular Order No. 29," proclaiming November 23 to be an official day of Thanksgiving for the entire expedition.

Before the celebrations of thanks could be held, strong winds sprang up on the afternoon of the 20th and eventually hauled around from the southwest, the worst possible direction for the ship in its exposed anchorage. Captain Coffin went on deck around midnight and watched a large segment of ice break off from the fast ice along shore, then watched as the wind directed it right back at the ship. By early the next morning, it was obvious to Coffin what was about to happen. At 5:30 A.M., the wind "brought up against the ice off south of the stmr [*sic*] and pushed it up like an egg shell, although [the hull] was more than three feet thick. It piled up against the ship's side so it bursted [*sic*] in the gangway and bulwarks forward [and] shoving on the deck pieces [of ice] that would weigh three to four tons."[161]

Anton Vedoe was awakened at 5:30 by one of the engineering crew, who told him that ice was again pressing on the ship. "I got out and went up on deck where I could hear a rumbling and roar of the ice on our starboard bow only about a 100 ft. off. Through the darkness I could perceive the glistening of water a little ways out"[162] He raced to the engine room where Hartt had woken up and managed to get the ship's lighting on. At that moment, Vedoe heard the ice crack into the side of the ship with a "horribly enervating grinding noise."[163]

Fiala, whose every word seemed to offer double and triple meanings, wrote of the ship that "she shrieked like a living thing in pain; every timber seemed to be under a frightful pressure to the very limit of resistance."[164] By now, everyone was awake, whispering to each other and nervous. The ship was being squeezed up and out of its bed of ice. Vedoe braced himself as the ship "leaned over to starboard and began to shiver like a leaf.

> The engine room grating commenced to shake as I stood watching the boiler. I could see it move over to port about a foot, the ventilator just touching the gauge glass. A rumble of ice falling in on deck was heard and of crashing timber. I ran below to see whether she was gaining any water and found it streaming in through some leak in the shaft alley and filling rapidly under the plates in the fire room. It was evident that she was crushed in somewhere mid-ships. We started the donkey pump, but it did not run long, the whole frame was sprung out of position and the fly wheel soon struck against the grating. The fire room was now flooded reaching up to the middle fire which was soon put out. Throwing down the grindstone, anvil and ash bucket to stand on I crawled along to the port bunker door, the starboard bunker door being completely submerged on account of the list, and managed to throw a few shovels of coal on the fire so as to keep steam to run the dynamo. It was high time to leave the place.[165]

Vedoe escaped just in time, as two pipe joints sprung a leak and sprayed boiling water all over the spot where he had just been standing. The ship was lost. Coffin was direct and to the point: "Steamer a total wreck. . . . Have given her up."[166]

The forward keel of the ship was now raised well out of the ice. Six feet of water had flooded the engine room. The railing on the starboard side of the ship had been torn away. The men quickly gathered up their clothes and threw them overboard, where men from the camp had arrived with ponies and sledges to move the jettisoned materials to a safer place on the ice.

The pressure eased on the ship by 9:30 A.M., but the damage was done. The men spent all day sledging coal from the ship to the shore, along with anything else that could safely be recovered. When the fires in the engine room finally went out, "the electric light slowly faded until they merely glowed red and dull. . . . It was the passing of the ship's soul."[167]

It was far too dangerous to remain on board, so all thirty-nine men would now have to fit into an expedition house designed for fifteen. The storehouse was cleared out and remade into accommodations for the sailors, while the officers and engineers like Vedoe slept on the floor, on tables, or on benches in the house, wherever room could be found. After an uncomfortable night, Vedoe woke the next morning on a seat alongside the mess room table. "Every joint and muscle was aching and sore all over from the hard board."[168]

Seitz helped the men tear out a bunk for Chief Engineer Hartt, and then gave a quick look around the ship for a few souvenirs: a postcard of the ship and a few medical books and supplies. The rest of the men worked all morning to take off bunks, doors, and dozens of bags of coal and sledge them to the camp. On the ice, Seitz turned to study the *America*. "The ship stands very high, especially the bow which is out almost or quite to the keel. . . . Ribs broken and inner sheathing splintered on the port side of main hold just after the main hatch. The old ship is a mass of wreck and ruin."[169]

Ice had punched through the ship in several places and it continued to settle lower in the water. Several wanted to continue to retrieve materials from the ship as long as they could, but if ever men needed a stiffener, it was now. Since it was now Sunday, Fiala called the men together at 8 P.M. for a religious service, followed by a glass of gin and a cigar for each man. The alcohol had the desired effect. "Hartt and the Steward especially felt the effects and talked till after midnight. In the afternoon, Seargt. put up the bunk in his room for Mr. Hartt."[170]

On the morning of the 24th, the wind moderated and allowed the men to get off the stores of lumber that remained on the ship, as well as anything else that remained useful, portable, and above water. As Vedoe wrote, "It was not very safe on board and now and then, while we were working, someone would shout, 'She is sinking, come aft,' and I guess we forgot about all the nice things we had collected and rushed headlong for the ladder. But it was only [a] false alarm. She is settling slowly and this afternoon she was riding on the hawsers which are as tight as violin strings."[171]

Within hours, however, as the wind increased to more than 60 knots, the men nailed an American flag to the ship and abandoned it to its fate. As soon as a large enough crack opened in the ice, the ship would sink to the bottom of the bay. The crew retreated to the expedition house, where the ship's carpenter, the Norwegian Peter Tessem, along with several other sailors, used the salvaged galley stove—weighing nearly a ton—and several bunks from the ship, to create a new living quarters in the storehouse for the marooned crew.

A new machine shop had to be created, and in it Hartt rigged up a boiler from another piece of the Duke of the Abruzzi's erstwhile hydrogen gas generator. (The following summer, the irrepressible Hartt would jury-rig this same boiler to one of the whale boats, create his own steam launch, and venture through the islands in one of history's strangest expeditions within an expedition.)

The storm raged for several days, while the expedition, hunkered down in cramped quarters, faced the cold revelation that without the ship their very survival was now an open question. Thirty-nine men would be forced to live, adapt, and, if possible, cooperate, in spaces originally meant for less than half that number. The nominal privacy available to the men while the two groups lived generally separate lives on ship and on shore was permanently gone. While the sailors lived in temporary quarters in the storehouse, new accommodations for them took shape over several weeks. In the meantime, the existing tensions between the officers and men, between sailors and scientists, between Captain Coffin and "the knowing ones," all would now come into the open.

The distraught Edwin Coffin had lost his command and would now spend the remainder of the expedition reliving the days between the beginning of September and the night of November 21, 1903, in a vain search for answers that would not come. Only two ships had ever reached Teplitz Bay, Abruzzi's *Stella Polaris* and Coffin's *America*, and both had been either heavily damaged or destroyed. In the case of the wreck of the *America*, Coffin was in no doubt as to who was to blame. A year later, as the wreck still festered, he wrote that Fiala had insisted on retrieving his papers even after Coffin told him the ship was not safe, "he not realizing any consequences any more than he did when he by pressure made me winter against my decision there . . . & so ends the *America* (condemned that same day)."[172]

The closest Fiala came to an admission of responsibility was his comment, upon seeing the interior of the ship, that "it brought a lump into my throat, as we . . . picked our way across the disordered decks, to view the devastation wrought in that one awful night."[173] That devastation also gutted Fiala, whose leadership had been at issue ever since his tortured decision to leave the ship in the bay. Seitz, the keen observer, recorded the resulting tension in the expedition after the loss of the ship and especially its effect on Fiala: "Peculiar condition of affairs at Camp. Sailors crowding our living room; everybody kept indoors on account of the storm—numerous scraps and everybody more or less irritable and grouchy. Vaughan and I have nothing to say and the time drags with indescribable slowness. Fiala has a thousand worries and cares and is played out and groggy—making peculiar answers and replies."[174]

Coffin placed his finger on another reason for Fiala's distress. It was the basic problem caused by the loss of the ship: "And this means hiking to Cape Flora."[175] The entire expedition—even such less-than-fit men as Hartt—would somehow have to make the 100+-nautical-mile journey south back to Cape Flora. Amid the ruins of the huts of Leigh Smith and Frederick Jackson and the leftovers of the Duke of the Abruzzi's expedition, it was the best and perhaps only place in Franz Josef Land where their chances of survival were better than even.

For the "played out and groggy" Fiala, even this vexing problem of survival was secondary to the immediate requirement to make space for all the new occupants of Camp Abruzzi while keeping a demoralized group of men focused on the reason they were at Teplitz Bay in the first place: a dash to the North Pole. The loss of the ship meant that Fiala's every move would now be dissected and not in a kindly way, as with his curious decision to bunk together with both disgraced ship's officers, Coffin and First Mate Haven. This did not sit well with the prickly Dr. Shorkley, who took the first opportunity to voice his displeasure. As Seitz recorded, "Shorkley & Fiala had a heated and personal talk in our room—starting with the misuse of the W.C. sanitary precautions . . . and then the drunkenness of the Capt. & Mate and the Capt.'s antagonisms for the welfare of the expedition and Fiala's 'coupling up' with him."[176]

The argument with Shorkley even caused Fiala to make one final forlorn visit to the ship in hopes it might still be saved. As everyone knew, there was no such option. It was only a matter of time before the ship sank for good. In the meantime, they had to take every chance to board the wreck and strip it of anything that might be useful at Camp Abruzzi.

After leading a divine service on Thanksgiving Day on November 26, with the winds outside still blowing over forty knots, the battered Fiala published his "provisional plan" for reaching the pole in the spring of 1904. It was a vast improvement on the rambling nonsense offered by Evelyn Briggs Baldwin at a similar moment in the life of the Baldwin expedition but, given the hard new realities that confronted a shipwrecked crew, it carried all the same air of fantasy.

Fiala first requested volunteers for the dash to the North Pole, writing that any of the men "wishing to take part in the march North should apply to the Commanding Officer before the end of November, 1903."[177] That he was unsure of whom—if any—of the men might accompany him on the polar dash says everything about the state of the expedition at this critical juncture. In the event, his caution proved justified.

The plan, had Fiala ever implemented it, offered by far the best chance of any of the three American expeditions to Franz Josef Land to either reach the North Pole or get closer to it than Nansen or Abruzzi. Twenty-four men would be assisted by twenty ponies and a dozen dog teams. This large party would be subdivided into three teams. These were named "First Support," "Second Support," and "Final Advance."

The First Support team of ten men would carry its own rations for ten days, along with additional supplies to keep the other two teams going for a week. Once the First Support team dropped off, the Second Support team of eight men would go on for an additional twenty-seven days before dropping off. As these teams used up their supplies and their sledges became lighter, the ponies would be shot and fed to the dogs.

The Final Advance group of six men would carry rations for ninety-two days, plus the supplies handed off to them by the first and second support teams, allowing these final six—along with their surviving five pony sledges and six dog teams—to reach for the pole with enough supplies remaining to return. In another irony, the devout Christian Fiala would choose the final five to accompany him through the strict use of Darwinian processes: "In the choice of men for the different detachments the Commanding Officer reserves decision until in the field and all members of Field, Deck, Engine, and Steward Departments taking part in the Sledge Trip may feel that they have a chance for the highest honours, and that the choice will only be made after experience has proved each member of the Sledge Party."[178] The ponies would be worked to death, the dogs would eat the ponies, and then the men if necessary would eat the dogs. In the final selection for a chance at the

"the highest honours," the men, metaphorically at least, would eat the men, to see which proved himself fittest to survive and stand at the North Pole.

Fiala also announced the starting date: Monday, February 8, 1904. This was little more than ten weeks away. The prospect was daunting, all the more so since most of the men seemed to pay little attention to Fiala's "provisional plan." Diarists like Dr. Seitz and Anton Vedoe recorded it as one might jot down a minor footnote. Seitz wrote that he missed most of Fiala's announcement because he was eating at the time. Anton Vedoe was with Rilliet at the ship, to retrieve a tarpaulin frozen alongside it. Chancing an inspection, they climbed on board and "walked around in the remains of the before comfortable *America.*

> The ice is all over the starboard side where the ceiling is totally crushed in. Down in the engine room the water has risen to half ways up the staircase. We found an old American flag in the cabin which we took and spread it over the tops of the cylinders as a last act of appreciation of the old engine. . . . By the time we got up on deck again the wind had increased and we were not able to see any distance off. We threw a few things down on the ice and climbed down with difficulty. [Then] the lantern blew out and we could not even see the ship much less the camp or trail, but we knew about how the wind was and all the heaven eventually was pretty clear and setting the course by the two stars, Castor and Pollux, we started off.[179]

When Vedoe heard Fiala's "provisional plan," what caught his ear was not so much the trip to the pole as the other sledge trip that would be required at the same time—the one that would take those not in the polar party to Cape Flora and, once there, a chance to get home at some point in 1904.

One notable exception to the general focus of the men on Cape Flora was the artist and surveyor Russell Porter. With his chronic deafness, he was spared much of the back and forth of too many men confined in too small a space and, consequently, held his thoughts on the main chance of the expedition. He mistakenly thought the other men were thinking along the same lines, and wrote that "each one of us jealous of his rights and hoping to be in that last group to stand on the Pole."[180]

Porter—not for the first or last time—overestimated the extent to which his fellow expedition members were prepared for such an enormous challenge. With medical cases like Hartt and the Norwegian Myhre unfit for strenuous work on the ice—along with such obviously disqualified men as the alcoholics Coffin and Haven, the experienced but too old Long and the teenage cabin boy James Dean—Fiala would need more than two-thirds of the rest of the men not only to volunteer for a spectacularly dangerous trek across the ice but be prepared to start in less than seventy-five days.

By the end of November, after raging for nine consecutive days, the storm that had permanently damaged the *America* finally blew itself out. The men, too, were exhausted, having worked continuously since the 21st to make room for the entire expedition to live and work at Camp Abruzzi. As for any Final Advance, according to Seitz the number of applications Fiala had received from men who wanted a chance to share the "highest honours" was exactly two. Whether first or last, the group "jealous of their rights" was a very small one.

FORTY-THREE

Dead Bones of an Engulfed Continent

Anton Vedoe continued to make trips to the ship throughout December, salvaging bits and bobs wherever they could be found. The ponies were used to haul four whaleboats off the ice and onto solid ground near the expedition house. On December 7, Vedoe and the other engineers began to remove everything on the ship that might help to rig up electricity for the house ashore. "Everything inside bears witness of destruction. All the staterooms are torn down. All available lumber taken ashore. In the engine room the ice is 8 inches thick and about 6 ft. from the floor so that we have to crawl on hands and feet under the grating. We managed today to fish up the anvil which was down in the fireroom under 8 ft. of water and ice."[181]

In between these forays to the wreck, Vedoe, along with Second Mate Nichols and First Assistant Engineer Hudgins, moved into the room previously occupied by Rilliet and the expedition commissary John Truden. "Mr. Truden has built a room for himself and Rilliet in the S.E. corner of the house with a door leading to Mr. Fiala's room."[182] Being the only expedition members with direct access to the commander was certain to be noted. Dr. Seitz noticed, of course, and twice made a note of the new arrangements, remarking on Truden's "opening into Fiala's room."[183] Similar to Shorkley's complaint at Fiala bunking with the discredited Captain Coffin and his first mate, everyone was now alive to the political implications of the slightest action and reaction.

For Anton Vedoe, the steady hand who had been sleeping on a bench since the evacuation of the ship two weeks earlier, such considerations were irrelevant. He considered that his new accommodations bordered on the luxurious. When he wasn't working at the wreck, he rigged up a telephone line between the expedition house and the astronomical observatory.

In an attempt to limit the men's contact with each other and the potential friction that attended it, Fiala placed the expedition on day and night shifts, with the newly arrived sailors put to work on a night shift under Rilliet to work on the sledges for the polar party. During the day, the steward, Bernard Spencer, kept the stoves working continuously, baking six hundred pounds of pork and bean biscuits—a kind of enhanced hardtack for use on the trail—in addition to weighing out over a thousand other rations for the sledge expedition.

The weather held steady in the first week of December and allowed Vedoe and his team to salvage a grindstone from the fire room on December 7. They left the ship as the wind picked up from the south, "and the old lead [opened] again so it is hard to tell what might happen, and we don't like to drift away in a sinking ship."[184] All of the exertion had put Vedoe in fine trim, and he proudly recorded that Dr. Shorkley's measurements of each man's chest expansion had found that Vedoe's 7 inches was exceeded only by Porter's 7¾.

The storm that drove Vedoe from the ship on December 8 continued to blow for nearly ten days. Just when the men thought they could get outside, the wind would pick up again and blow steadily at more than forty knots. At one point on December 12, Vedoe recorded gusts of almost 80 knots. When he was able to go outside for a brief time the following day, he found the camp blanketed with more the eight feet of snow. "The top wavey and furrowed resembling the waves on sea and offers a very difficult walking. It is all through beaten so hard that it is hardly possible to dig with a shovel."[185]

December 13 was also Porter's thirty-second birthday, and they celebrated with "a jolly feast [with] a punchbowl and cake being served and a few songs were sung." The hit song sung by Porter himself being: "The man with the elephant on his hand."[186] Four days later a similar party was thrown for Vedoe's twenty-third birthday. "A toast for my health proposed by Mr. Fiala was drunk and when [Augustinsen] Hovlick, my fireman, had had enough of the punch he sang us a few songs in Norwegian."[187] Dr. Shorkley, with nominal control of all alcohol supplies, was also given responsibility for mixing the punch for the occasion.

Shorkley also took the opportunity during the celebrations to take Dr. Seitz aside to tell him that "Fiala has reduced the number of days for this sledge trip to 100. It was first 140, then 120 and now 100."[188] If true, Fiala was now counting on moving at an average of ten nautical miles per day across the ice, certainly not impossible, but given that the men had been pinned in their expedition house for nearly ten days by a single storm, it left precious little margin for error. It was also an indication that Fiala was nowhere near the twenty-four volunteers he needed to carry out his "provisional plan" for a dash to the North Pole.

On December 18 the storm finally blew itself out and the men could return to the work of salvaging materials off the ship. A vise was chopped out of the engine room from underneath two feet of ice, and the men continued to chop coal from the bunkers. The work in the engine room areas was supervised by Hartt and the work in the rest of the ship by the second mate, James Nichols. The captain and the first mate remained in their cabin, virtual recluses from the activity around them.

At the camp, preparation for the polar dash continued, as Seitz recorded: "[Dr.] Newcomb & Seargt. [Moulton] finished bagging the oats for sledge rations today for 51 days. On the 51st day the last horse will be killed."[189] Rilliet designed and oversaw the construction of a kayak built in three sections that could be loaded on one of the sledges and used for crossing open water. No less than fifty sledges had now been built. Materials had been brought on the ship for sixty sledges, but nine of these had been lost when pans of ice along shore had broken off and drifted away, and another sledge had been pressed into service to haul ice around the camp.

On the 21st, one month after the destruction of the *America,* the men retrieved more material from the ship to use in creating a new electrical plant for the camp. Vedoe recorded that only with great difficulty was an "engine, two dynamos, pump, and anvil [gotten] on deck and brought on shore."[190] Seitz pitched in to help the men at the ship, writing that they "Had a lot of trouble getting the large dynamo up on the banks and had to haul it up by hand."[191] Vedoe looked at the ship and marveled that it had survived the ten-day storm. He now thought it would remain locked in its place at least until the following summer.

Christmas was celebrated with a new edition of the *Arctic Eagle* and a vast banquet. Vedoe looked on in wonder: "The [news]paper came out in six pages illustrated and with an illustrated wrapper. The menu was very handsomely gotten up with Mr. Ziegler's picture on the front page. The banquet itself was a great success and seldom has in the Arctic been seen a happier assemblage than at our prettily decorated table full of the most delicious eatables and all kinds of wine."[192] Seitz, who dressed for the occasion in his "civilization clothes," even noted a temporary repair of the split between Captain Coffin and "the knowing ones" as a result of the freely flowing alcohol, "the drinks being gin, rum and sherry, casaba & muscatel wine."

> Most everybody felt happy and everything went off smoothly, especially the series of toasts. . . . At the end of this Porter, Hartt & myself furnished music while the crowd sang songs. Fiala took a flashlight photograph. Pierre [LeRoyer] was feeling very gay and made a dreadful noise with his drum. The sailors also had enough to drink, some of them too much. The party broke up about 2 A.M. but we stayed up still after 4 A.M. There was much apparent good feeling between the Capt. & our crowd, expressed in various toasts.[193]

The men awoke the next morning to thundering hangovers. One of the sailors, Charles Kunold of New York, was furious over a profile of his life written for the newspaper and complained directly to Fiala. And Seitz wrote that one of the assistant scientists, Robert Tafel, deliberately broke the magnetometer so as to avoid an eight-hour shift in the observatory.

For his part, Captain Coffin felt the goodwill and wrote that both the Christmas and New Year's celebrations "passed happily. . . . All hands are enjoying themselves according to their own ideas of the word.

> The Scientific crowd of four [are] out in all kinds of weather standing a regular watch night and day. Doing fine and correct work which will show for itself if it ever reaches civilization.
>
> So the cure is work. Work of *any* kind. Now we actually have the day commencing, we need not be afraid to arrive at the point the Duke's party did. Furthermore, we have an immense lot of work more to accomplish to get the sled party North started.
>
> Then comes the march South to Cape Flora, to equip and all hands to get away towards our own country. A small part of the way. Still not a picnic to make [the journey to Cape Flora] in May.[194]

The *America*, already pinched and held in place by the ice in Teplitz Bay, in a remarkable midwinter photograph taken by Fiala. The image was taken on January 2, 1904, with an exposure time of an hour and a half. Before the end of the month, the expedition ship would be at the bottom of the bay. From Anthony Fiala, *Fighting the Polar Ice* (New York: Doubleday, Page & Company, 1906).

Porter noted a sliver of reflected midday light on December 27, and it spurred him to write his first diary entries in nearly two months. The slight appearance of something other than total darkness meant that the "back of this night is broken and, thank God, the sun returns."[195] In actuality, what had returned was a kind of twilight, as the sun would not rise above the horizon for weeks yet. "At Alger Island two years ago I noticed a faint light in the south at noon throughout the darkest part of the winter but here we are too near the Pole to allow of such a change in that respect."[196] Compared to the almost ceaseless storms of Teplitz Bay, "which is fast making a coward of me in this dark and cold," Porter considered the area around the Baldwin headquarters at East Camp Ziegler a relative paradise.[197]

As an artist and something of a scientific dreamer, Porter was akin to Fiala in that he always tried to see the best parts of his mates. He thought that the loss of the ship might even be a good thing, to force the men to look at the object of the expedition "squarely in the face. . . .

> For myself it worries me but little, so long as Fiala can hold his men together as he has so beautifully up to the present time. The losing of the ship was met and overcome in a way that surprised me. There was no friction, quarters for twenty odd men appeared as if by magic around and against the house, and the camp adapted itself to the sudden wrench in its domestic life without the slightest trouble.[198]

But Porter was no fool. He understood the deep psychological crisis caused by the loss of the *America*. The same loneliness of the Arctic icescape that so attracted men like Porter was at the same time a window on human futility: "Days after [the crushing of the ship on November 21] I went to the abandoned and dismantled hulk, and was struck with the awful desolation of it all.

> Desolation stares one in the face here on every hand, the bare rocks protruding through the snow—dead bones of an engulfed continent; the very barrenness of the dome-shaped islands. But how much more so was this intensified on that ship, surrounded with memories of human life aboard her, of a past that ever intruded itself on me at every turn; for I had lived on her for over a year![199]

Porter entered the hulk and found more ghosts at work, "where only a few weeks before I had entered to the glow of an open fire grate and the brightness of electric lights, where books lined the walls, instruments and timepieces were ticking a welcome, and a strain from the 'Geisha' issued from the music box; where the hum and throbbing of a dynamo, and the aroma of hot chocolate arose from depths below. This was all gone."[200]

On December 28 the winds again accelerated, to nearly 80 knots. The sailors dug a large pit alongside the expedition house to hold Hartt's proposed engine room. The men also continued to saw apart the wreck of the *America,* hauling sails and spars to the house. In between preparing a New Year's exposition to the men on the planned polar trip, Fiala attempted to photograph the aurora. "I made attempts to photograph the aurora on the Baldwin-Ziegler Expedition, but always failed. By long exposure, I could get some small effect of the light with that of the stars on the sensitive plate, valueless however as a matter of record, for the swift moving aurora, to be correctly depicted, would have to be photographed instantaneously, and, for that purpose, it does not give enough light."[201]

Fiala contented himself with making sketches of the aurora, by standing outside on the few clear nights when the temperatures were from thirty to forty degrees below zero. Several of these were eventually reproduced when Peters published the scientific record of the expedition in 1907.

On New Year's Day, after another feast, Porter and Anton Vedoe tried out their polar furs on a walk to Cape Säulen and back. Vedoe found that they were "quite *warm* and sweat and in order to see how the furs would act we climbed the hill above the house and lay down for half an hour without being the least bothered by the cold."[202] Porter and Vedoe repeated the trip on January 10 and again on the 12th, seemingly the only members of the expedition actively preparing for the planned start for the North Pole on February 8.

Fiala went down to the wreck of the ship during a full moon on January 2, 1904. He set up his camera, opened the lens, and walked back to the house, leaving the camera to make an exposure for over an hour and half. The resulting image was brilliant and perhaps the best work Anthony Fiala accomplished in three years of work in Franz Josef Land. Two weeks later, he published his thirty-second general order, to compliment the men on the recovery of 222 bags of coal from the wreck of the ship. "The sun is on its way towards us and soon darkness will give way to light. Let us salute the return of the sun with a spirit of enthusiastic activity, ready for the task that is before us, rejoicing in the opportunity to attempt the discovery of that which had been sought for centuries."[203]

Any rejoicing was put on hold a week later, on January 22, when another storm blew up. Anton Vedoe could distinctly hear the sound of waves as he tried to sleep. When Coffin awoke the next morning and walked out of the expedition house for his morning constitutional, he looked out at the ship only to see that it had vanished.

Ice had broken up all over bay. Vedoe went out to see large blocks of ice pressed up against the shore, from a nearby glacier that had calved during the night. He saw tremendous bergs floating in the bay where previously there had been none. The *America,* still hanging on a single large anchor, likely went straight to the bottom of Teplitz Bay as soon as the pressure of the ice supporting it gave way.

Fiala, in a ridiculous special pleading that reflected his guilt over the disastrous decision to anchor the ship in Teplitz Bay, saw another possibility: "The America had disappeared in the darkness of the Arctic night, and shrouded her doom in mystery! Whether she went to the bottom under the blast of that awful gale or whether she was blown toward the northern axis of the earth, where now she floats in unheralded victory, no man knows."[204]

Anton Vedoe, both practical and prescient despite his spare twenty-three years, evaluated the loss much more soberly: "But most of all, the ship with our coal and the cache of provisions containing more than half of our provisions has disappeared. It is a hard blow. The cache was left there to serve us in training our dogs and horses. Our loss is great and God only knows what will become of us if we are obliged to stay another winter. All our work in the shop is done for nothing as now we will have to save coal in order to take us through the winter."[205]

More than two hundred bags of coal had been salvaged from the ship, but most of them had been left on the ice along the shore, and now two-thirds were gone. On January 24, less than six months after leading one of the most well-supplied expeditions in history to Teplitz Bay—and finding there even more coal left behind by the Italians—Fiala reported to Seitz that they were down to little more than sixty bags of coal. Economies would now be necessary if the men were to survive.

FORTY-FOUR

His Crowd of Children

The final loss of the *America* in late January 1904 was one more blow to an already overburdened expedition. The need to salvage everything possible from the wreck, the sudden requirement for the entire crew of the ship to be housed and fed on shore, and the vicious storms of December and January at Teplitz Bay that reduced the days available to train the dog teams: all had conspired against Fiala's provisional start for the North Pole of February 8, 1904. The "provisional plan" had changed as well. Where he originally wanted twenty-four men, twenty ponies, and a dozen dog teams, Fiala now decided to leave for the pole on February 20 with twenty-six men, sixteen ponies, and nine dog teams. The original three teams of men and animals were now four. Keeping to his army experiences, Fiala had all of the sledges "numbered and coloured according to the detachment in which they belonged, as were also the rations."[206]

Captain Coffin, too old to undertake sledge work, helped Seitz and Porter test one of the field tents. Coffin looked on the preparations for the polar dash and was not impressed. "Twill be a job to find a place level enough (when out on the ice) to pitch their tents near each other as . . . the steward is to do all the cooking in one tent with assistance of several men (I don't think the scheme will work at all). One man from each tent goes around for food coming to that tent."[207]

Good weather in which to train the dog teams remained scarce throughout the month of February, as Fiala noted that only three *hours* of calm were recorded on the meteorological instruments. A planned test run to either Cape Säulen or to Cape Germania further north were cancelled by the bad weather. On February 9 Anton Vedoe made brief trip with a team of dogs to Cape Säulen, accompanied by Dr. Shorkley and one of the ponies. "The ice as far as could be seen is broken up in big cakes with intervening young ice," wrote Vedoe.

> A streak of open water stretched past the Cape about a mile north west. An ascent would be possible but under difficulty. After dinner Porter and I went with our teams out over the ice as far as the young ice which is now about 8 in. thick. Not the slightest trace of ship or cache to be seen. This dog driving in good weather certainly sets new life into me. I know nothing more pleasant. The sledges show up fine in the very rough ice. The length of them especially will enable them to cross cracks to a width up to four feet without difficulty.[208]

Vedoe's enthusiasm for polar sledging was not widely shared. When he returned to the camp, he was put to work helping Hartt retrieve one of the whaleboats, for an attempt to modify it into a steam launch for the retreat south. Hartt cast the blades for a propeller for his whaleboat/steam launch by using some blue clay that cropped out behind of the tent where he worked. "The crucible was left here by the Duke."[209] Anton Vedoe was then asked to build a signal pillar out of old crates to be placed at Cape Auk to aid the southern escape.

In camp, Fiala had begun to receive unsolicited advice on the arrangement of the men who would go to Cape Flora. He had planned to place Captain Coffin in charge of this party, but on February 2 Dr. Newcomb made it clear he would not serve under the captain and Fiala had to scramble to reconfigure the party. The second mate, Nichols, was the next obvious choice, but he refused to take the job. The expedition's commissary, Truden, began to tell some of the men that he would be left in charge of the camp. Seitz wrote that either Porter or Tafel would lead the party—including the captain—to Cape Flora, while the Arctic veteran Francis Long, too old to attempt the pole, would be stationed with a boat at Cape Fligely to keep a lookout for the returning polar party.

If the whole enterprise was beginning to taste like a dog's breakfast, the worst was still to come. Seitz put his finger on the issue on February 9: "It is quite the general opinion that Fiala is delaying matters purposely as things are dragging along and little being accomplished."[210] Two days later, according to Seitz, the feelings against Fiala were running deeper still: "The dissatisfaction continues and increases and Fiala is called all kinds of names and is said to be afraid to start out—has lost confidence in the dogs and horses, etc. He is certainly depressed."[211]

On February 16, in response to the general anxiety of the men, Fiala reluctantly published his "Instructions for Sledge Party North." These offered nineteen curious orders for the polar trip, tips such as "repair any holes [in the sleeping bags] at first opportunity" and "hot utensils containing food should not be placed on sleeping bags."[212] There were no words of inspiration. Even Coffin, whom Fiala personally briefed on the plans, admitted: "As usual, all were not satisfied. I do not exactly understand them myself."[213] Like Evelyn Briggs Baldwin before him, Fiala possessed no innate ability to rally men to his banner.

Seitz wrote that, in the ordering of the officers of the expedition, he came in around eighth or ninth, just behind Shorkley. To everyone's surprise, including Coffin's, the captain was placed in charge of getting the southern party from Rudolf Island to Cape Flora in May.

The doctors duly went on another round of physical examinations, and Coffin—who again managed to avoid his—wrote that Fiala had dropped from 157 to 151 pounds. Shorkley was furious with Fiala for appointing Haven to a ranking position in the sledge party, as that now guaranteed that he would not be able to "preserve complete physical statistics of the entire party."[214] Everyone had lost weight over the winter. Seitz found that he had dropped eight pounds. It didn't help that Fiala had to remove the expedition's cook on account of incompetence. Coffin wrote that this was a shame, as there existed no obvious replacement. "Many people are troubled with swelled heads in this kind of climate. Seems to be no cure."[215]

Unlike the men, when Vaughan surveyed the dogs he found that they had steadily improved during the time on the island, gaining an average of nine pounds. Of the dogs that the expedition had started with, 155 survived. The dead were lost on account of being swept out to sea or being killed by polar bears, falls into crevasses, or fights between themselves. Of those that remained, Vaughan also noted that they had "lost a good deal of their currish disposition due to humane handling."[216]

Fiala now set his departure for the pole for March 1, 1904, after which the men celebrated with blackberry brandy. Soon after, on February 25 Fiala sent Vaughan, Moulton, and Bernard Spencer with two dog teams to Cape Fligely to lay in a cache of supplies. Other caches were planned for the capes at Germania and Säulen. The men going to Fligely were supplied with six days' worth of food, but they returned within hours, having forgotten to take a tent or the signal poles with which they were to mark the crevasses along the way.

The team set out again but returned three days later, having gotten within two miles of Cape Fligely on the first day before their tent was ripped apart and they slept out in a snowstorm. The only positive to come from the trip was a sighting of the sun from the elevation of the cape. Seitz wrote that the ice around the island, while rough, was now strong enough to support the sledge teams if only they were ready. On February 28 Seitz wrote that "Newcomb says Fiala & Peters are going tomorrow to Cape Fligley and will be gone about 2 days. There seems to be no intention of starting soon and the amount of dissatisfaction is enormous."[217]

The protest against another pointless scouting trip to Cape Fligely canceled the trip, but March 1 came and went and still Fiala continued to dither. He sent Peters and Bernard Spencer to Cape Fligely ostensibly to test the sledge odometers, but it seemed as if he was desperate to find a way out of leading the men onto the polar pack. He announced that he wanted to take the entire polar party on a trial trip. But then he relented, saying that the tents might get wet and there would be no time to dry them before the actual start for the north.

So, too, the loss of the ship continued to stalk Fiala's conscience. He tried to confiscate the ship's logbooks before he started for the pole, but Coffin and Hartt both refused to turn them over. As Seitz recorded, "Fiala & Hartt had a big scrap this afternoon because Hartt refused to turn over his log. The Mate turned his over to Fiala which made the Capt. & Nichols very hot. Fiala and Hartt made up and the Capt. asked Fiala for the Mate's log and got it."[218]

Finally, on Saturday, March 5, 1904, Fiala could delay no longer and ordered the men to load the polar sledges, preparatory to a start for the North Pole the next morning. Seitz got sledge No. 16, weighing about seventy-five pounds. He and Porter loaded it with their tent and sleeping bags and were also assigned to load it with one of the kayaks. Anton Vedoe, along with every other man in the party, received six pounds of senne grass to be used as insulation underneath the sleeping bags in the tents. He also received a seven-day ration of bread and butter and sugar and was issued a new skin shirt, skin pants, two pairs of stockings, a small parka and some underwear, total weight, about ten pounds. He was itching to start, especially as the weather all morning was brilliant.

But the weather turned for the worse in the afternoon, and when the snow continued in the morning Fiala delayed the start until the 7th. At dinner on the 6th, Fiala read an inspirational letter that he had written to William Ziegler. Reveille would be sounded at 6 a.m., breakfast at 7, followed by departure. The men had heard it all before.

In the event, it was 10 a.m. before the massive party—Vedoe counted twenty-seven men, eleven dog teams, and seventeen ponies—departed Camp Abruzzi in a snowstorm. The long pack train crawled, as Porter saw it, like a worm up the Rudolf Island ice dome. Three hours later, they reached Cape Germania at an elevation of 700 feet, where Fiala ordered the men into camp for the night. Vedoe, for one, was thrilled to be off: "It makes a nice sight to see the 11 tents spread out on the snow."[219]

The men reached Cape Fligely the next day, where Rilliet was invalided back to Camp Abruzzi after suffering a hernia. The pack train descended from the exposed cape, down a rocky slope, to the shore of the Arctic Ocean. In the process, one sledge was destroyed as well as an odometer. The men went into camp at the base of Cape Fligely as the wind from the west increased to a gale. From this exposed shore, Fiala looked out on broken ice and some open water, and nearly 500 nautical miles to the North Pole.

It was the moment for which the expedition had been sent to Franz Josef Land. They had the men, the animals, and the equipment, and they were early enough to think that they could reach the pole and return before the Arctic summer made travel across the polar pack impossible. And it was this moment, of all others, when Fiala went numb with indecision. As the storm blew around them, he kept the party pinned at Cape Fligely. On the evening of March 8, less than two days after leaving Camp Abruzzi, Fiala abruptly announced that they would all return immediately to the expedition house.

As Seitz recorded: "Were surprised to learn that Fiala has decided to go back to Camp. He says 5 or 6 men are disabled. Rilliet, Vaughn [sic] spitting blood, Hudgins sprained back, Myhre ran a knife through his hand and Long too fat to walk much. The Mate is also not showing up very well. 2 cookers are out of order and it takes 3 or 4 hrs. to cook a small meal."[220]

Fiala announced on March 9 that he would scale back the expedition and try again with a much smaller party in a week or two. He did nothing to raise his standing with the men when he began to patronize them all. "Fiala said he may stay another year or may leave with a very small party if there is time this year after he has taken the rest South. He calls us his crowd of children."[221]

Porter, along with Seitz and Vedoe, was mystified. It seemed as if the labor of the entire winter had been completely for naught. "Sleds broken down, stoves out of order, six of the men unfit for the work. It was more or less a shock, but back we went."[222]

The "polar party" arrived back at Teplitz Bay on the afternoon of March 12, having traveled, in total, little more than a dozen miles. Along with the rest of men, Seitz was dying of thirst when they returned, the cookers having been largely inoperative on the trail and the men unable to get drinking water. "Everybody was exceedingly thirsty on the march and when we returned proceeded to fill up on water. I drank 2 glasses of water, 3 cups of coffee, a plate of soup, 3–1/2 glasses of lemonade and a cup of chocolate."[223]

After a winter's planning for detachments and support parties and advance parties, Fiala returned to Camp Abruzzi and chucked the lot of it. On March 13 he told several of the men that the new effort would include only ten men, along with six ponies, six dog teams, and provisions for seventy-three days—a number that would require Fiala to travel at least fourteen nautical miles per day, with no margin for error, if he wanted to reach the pole and return to Rudolf Island.

It was not a realistic notion, and the men saw right through it. Fiala "said to Vaughn [sic] that he wanted desperate men, men who had no ties. The general feeling is very bitter against Fiala, his late start and lack of executive ability and good leadership and it is felt that there is no chance to accomplish anything in the next trial because of the late start and with horses along."[224]

Even Fiala himself, in his published account, admits that when he ordered the expedition back, the men turned against him. "On the return to camp and after the cold experience on the glacier there was much disappointment expressed, some of the men criticising the dogs, the equipment, and the ponies. . . . Many a revelation of character was made during our sojourn in the land of ice."[225]

Coffin, who watched in amazement as the men straggled so quickly back to camp, wrote that Fiala "will [now] have to hustle to make a record as the travelling time will be short, April and May. Many of the expedition [sic] are unsuited for hardships. . . . This was the shortest journey by a party ever made."[226]

Fiala attempted to buck the men up with a tale of Civil War heroism, but few listened. Over the next several days, Fiala constantly changed the number and composition of his proposed second dash for the pole. The numbers of men, the names of the men, the number of ponies and dog and dog teams, all were revised and revised again. Seitz wrote that the expedition commander called "for volunteers, men who had no criticism to offer, who had no ties to hold them back, who were willing to go where he did and would be cheerful and not complain."[227] There simply were not many such men left.

On March 19 Seitz noted open water along the shore of Rudolf Island, all the way from Cape Auk to a distance north of the island. It had to be on everyone's mind that if the ship had been anchored somewhere just south, it could now be steaming the polar party north, avoiding the whole existential crisis that seemed to afflict Fiala every time he reached the point of no return at Cape Fligely.

It was not until March 24 that Fiala read yet another general order to the men and told them he would start the next day for the pole. There would be fourteen men, nine dog teams, and seven ponies. "The party left in camp will be in command of Mr. Truden until the 1st of May when Capt. Coffin takes charge of the party going south and Mr. Rilliet with a small party stays at camp awaiting the return of the last party and to continue the scientific work."[228]

The much-reduced but still too-large party was back at Cape Fligely on the afternoon on March 25, 1904, and descended to the ice the following morning. Anton Vedoe recorded that they took their departure from solid ground a little west of the cape, and then stepped out onto the ice. By noon, the men had managed to travel about a quarter of a mile out from shore. Seitz wrote that the condition of the ice was "indescribably rough and chaotic with almost no level spots to be seen. Pressure ridges 15+ ft. high. We waited for the horses and made camp. Fiala almost exhausted."[229]

Even Anton Vedoe found the going terrible. By 2 P.M. the men were less than a mile from shore. Most of the sledges had already broken down and needed repair. To Fiala, the ice was "a mass of jagged, broken pieces on end, covered with salt crystals and almost bare of snow. . . . [The] sledges were in a deplorable condition."[230]

Fiala was as broken as his sledges. Calling Peters and Porter into his tent, he sought to gain their assent for turning back once again. Peters, the

Russell Porter in his element, by himself and staring at the stars. At the Repsold Circle in the astronomical observatory at Camp Abruzzi, he timed the passage of stars across the meridian at Teplitz Bay in order to gain the precise local time. From Anthony Fiala, *Fighting the Polar Ice* (New York: Doubleday, Page & Company, 1906).

diffident scientist who never properly filled the role of second-in-command of the expedition, remarked that he was, as Porter remembered, "unqualified to give an opinion."[231] Porter, to his credit, was appalled. The thought of turning back before they were even out of sight of Cape Fligely was absurd. "I came out flatly against going back, didn't believe that Mr. Ziegler or the world at large would consider that we had made an honest effort."[232]

Porter convinced Fiala that he and Anton Vedoe should be allowed to go onward, to at least test the conditions north, before retreating through the eastern part of Franz Josef Land to explore and live off the supply caches laid out during the Baldwin expedition. Anxious to show something for what was now an abject disaster, Fiala agreed.

As for the rest of his expedition, he now announced that it was his sworn mission to see them safely through to Cape Flora, after which he would return to Rudolf Island, for a third attempt on the North Pole in 1905. "It was the test through which all who had the real fibre of the explorer would pass triumphant."[233] But no one was listening to Fiala anymore, and Porter and Vedoe were thrilled to be able to take several weeks' worth of supplies and as quickly as possible remove themselves from the poisonous atmosphere of the failed expedition.

As Vedoe and Porter watched the men retreat, some with perhaps a bit too much haste than was tasteful, Vedoe spat out: "A good riddance."[234]

FORTY-FIVE

Joy

When the second attempt to reach the North Pole barely managed to reach more than a single nautical mile onto the sea ice north of Cape Fligely and Fiala retreated back to Camp Abruzzi, the prevailing dissension broke into open revolt. Coffin wrote as he once again watched Fiala return after a pitiful performance on the ice: "This [makes] the expidition [*sic*] North this year a failure. . . . [The] plans for the future I do not know."[235]

The two men who were spared another demoralized return to Camp Abruzzi were Porter and Anton Vedoe. To Porter, Vedoe was perhaps the only reliable mate in the whole of the Ziegler Polar Expedition. "He stood head and shoulders above any other man in the party for the work at hand. . . . Vedoe had always made clean-cut work of any job entrusted to him. He was a good dog driver, kept his equipment in efficient working order, and above all had an even, buoyant temperament."[236] As the other men hastily beat a retreat "for warm bunks and hot meals," Porter and Vedoe prepared to make a real test of the ice conditions north of Rudolf Island.[237]

They had with them two sledges, sixteen dogs, and enough provisions to feed the small party for nearly a month. Their object was to try to reach the "Hvidtland Islands," a small collection of ice-covered islets in the extreme northeast of Franz Josef Land first seen by Fridtjof Nansen and Hjalmar Johansen. Fiala thought that there might be a chance to locate traces there of Francesco Querini, Felice Ollier, and Henrik Alfred Støkken, the three men lost during the polar attempt of the Duke of the Abruzzi.

The Hvidtland Islands were about 30 nautical miles east of the position where Porter and Vedoe slept on the night of March 26. Vedoe woke the next morning to Porter's snoring and their dogs "rest[ing] peacefully in the hay we had strewn out for them."[238] After breakfast, they hitched up the dogs and began traveling north. They were on the march for less than two hours when they came, as Vedoe wrote, "to some ice so badly pressed up that we saw no way out of it. . . . No sledges could make their way here. As far as we could see the same horrible case with not even as big a space as to give room for a decent camping ground."[239]

The two men and their dogs had gone barely a single mile north. Porter stopped to take some photographs and was astounded at the desolation. Thirty years later, working as an optics expert on the construction and installation of California Institute of Technology's Hale telescope at Mount Palomar, Porter had a chance to look through the lens and draw the craters of the moon. "The similarity of this moonscape to the snowscapes of the North was enough to transport me back again to the tip end of the eastern hemisphere, looking out over the frozen polar sea."[240]

As their mates had done the day before, Porter and Vedoe turned around and made their way back to Rudolf Island. The Hvidtland Islands were out of the question. The Americans never came close to the mark set by Captain Coffin the previous summer with the ship. If Fiala had not blundered in keeping the *America* at Teplitz Bay, the ship might have survived the winter and brought the expedition to 82° North in the spring of 1904. That would have placed them away from the torn and twisted coastal ice along Rudolf Island's northern shore and given the expedition a fighting chance to reach the pole.

By the end of the day, Porter and Vedoe were back on Rudolf Island. They found the remains of the camp of the main party at Cape Fligely, a forlorn place littered with a large pile of provisions, a broken sledge, and the abandoned and useless cooking sledge. They returned to the dogs and began to ascend the ice dome that covered the island. Halfway up, a storm began that kept the two pinned in their tent for nearly three days. Back at Camp Abruzzi, Fiala watched the storm intensify and, fearing that Porter and Vedoe were still on the ice, began to think that he would never see them alive again.

Trapped in their tent by several feet of snow, Porter and Vedoe nevertheless relaxed, cooking some pemmican and drinking coffee. They ate
chocolate and smoked their pipes, enjoying the rise in temperature inside
the tent to +37°F. They only needed to go outside when they required ice for
the cooker. "The dogs are all snowed under so it is no use to disturb them.
They will not eat in this sort of weather although they might be hungry not
having had any food for two days."[241]

The storm did not settle itself until the afternoon of March 30, when
the men hurriedly uncovered the sledges, fed the dogs, and set a course for
the sea ice on the south side of Rudolf Island. They descended from the ice
dome at a spot about four miles east of Cape Brorok. Once on the smooth
ice that lay fast between the small islands south of Rudolf, the men and
dogs raced along. They reached Hohenlohe Island that same evening, where
Vedoe watched "the sun set in beautiful colors and right opposite in the
heavens was the full moon smiling."[242]

The next morning, March 31, 1904, the men and dogs again raced between
the islands and reached the Baldwin cache at Coburg Island. It was here that
Coffin had sought to anchor the *America* over the winter, so it is interesting
to note that Vedoe found the "ice perfect [with] none of the rough screw
ice of two years ago."[243] If Coffin had had his way, the *America* would very
likely have survived the winter. Porter and Vedoe made a meal of some of
the pemmican, coffee, and a can of tomatoes they found at the site.

Porter was likewise thrilled with the sudden rapid progress, for "when
the going is good, sledge travel in the North is a joy. Smooth, fast ice joined
one islet to another, and over this royal highway we made fast time."[244]
Everywhere they traveled, the writings of the two men were filled with the
words "enjoyed," "beautiful," "glorious," and "perfect." They raced from the
site of one Baldwin cache to another, to record the contents and evaluate
what had been lost to marauding polar bears. They would push the surviving boxes of supplies further up onto the stony shores and mark the spots
with one of the expedition's flags.

The two men also stopped at every spot where a convenient elevation
could be reached so that Porter could continue the plane table mapping
of the islands he had begun under Baldwin. His resulting maps—glorious
in detail and beautiful in simplicity—would comprise perhaps the main
scientific results of the Ziegler Polar Expedition.

A few days later, as they picked their way south through the line of

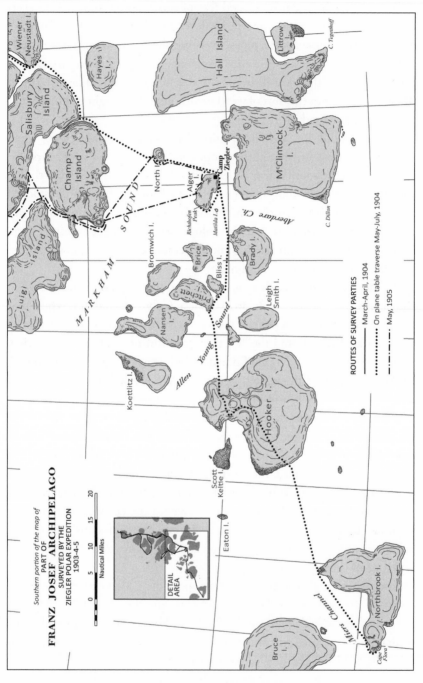

Redrawn detail from Porter's chart of Franz Josef Land, showing the newly demarcated Luigi and Champ islands separated by Cook Channel. This was the major area of operations of all three American expeditions to Franz Josef Land. *Copyright © 2016 The University of Oklahoma Press. All rights reserved.*

Baldwin's cache sites, one of the sledges broke down and was abandoned with a small flag swaying from it. With the dogs hitched to the one remaining sledge, the men continued on ski through slushy ice to Greely Island and the holy grail of the Baldwin expedition, Kane Lodge. As they rounded the island, the space available to maneuver the sledge on the ice shrank to little more than a yard. The dogs were further distracted by the sudden appearance of a few bears, and for a time it seemed the whole sledge would go into the water hole west of Greely Island. "In the water lots of little Auks were swimming around. After exciting and strenuous work we crept along foot by foot ready to see the sledge roll down into the water any minute. . . . At last we were past the most dangerous place and got down on the ice again utterly played out and weary stepping down knee deep in the water, and stumbling over scattered blocks dragging the dogs and lifting the sledge we at last got out on smooth going again."[245]

They thought they might miss the lodge, built as it was on a floor of ice. Tired and dispirited, for a time they thought they went past it. Then they spied the smokestack and parts of the roof. "We actually came to life again and shook hands, well knowing that our troubles had come to an end for some time to come."[246] They chained up the dogs and, after resting, began to take stock of the hut and its cache of supplies.

At Cape Flora, Porter had sensed that the men's survival might come down to such extra provisions as these. Now, with the ship gone and no relief ship in sight, he was certain of it. "Kane Lodge was found almost completely buried under snow, with only the peak of the roof and chimney protruding above it," he wrote. "Everything was taken outside, a fire built in the stove and the house thoroughly dried out. Everything here was found in good condition with the exception of several horse blankets and bags of cast off and worn out clothes. These were in such a decayed and rotting condition as to make them absolutely worthless."[247]

They also found bags and bags of clothing and other gear in fine condition, including "22 pair of deer skin pants, 48 pair of finnesko, 20 pair of komager, 9 heavy underdrawers, and 5 shirts, 5 silk tents, 2 canvas tents, 3 sledge sails, a lot of Icelanders goat hair stockings, heavy woolen stockings, lots of mittens and 20 big felt hats."[248]

It was every bit the treasure trove they remembered from the massive hauling operation of the spring of 1902, and the two men celebrated with a dinner worthy of William Ziegler's grant of an unlimited budget to Evelyn

Briggs Baldwin: "turkey, sugar, corn, tomatoes, 'Borden's' condensed coffee, and 'Palmer's' biscuits. Quite a good change from pemmican stew four times a day."[249] They also found nearly three quarters of a ton of coal stacked inside the hut. They cleared the hut of ice and snow and prepared to stay in the snug quarters for a week or more.

Over the days that followed, Porter and Vedoe uncovered three kayaks, two of which had been destroyed in a rock fall from the cliff above the hut. They also found two sledges, one of which Vedoe repaired to replace the one that they had been forced to abandon on the soft ice north of Greely Island. A sealed envelope, found nailed to the wall of the hut, was stowed away to be given later to Fiala. The men built a box outside the hut in which to stow the coal, then built a table of empty pemmican boxes under which they stowed broken cases of food. They had, in short, made the hut into a relief station ready to accommodate any party that sought shelter at the site.

On Saturday, April 9, the men took to their sledges again and raced south to Wiener Neustadt Island, making the 10 nautical miles in less than three hours. There, at the southern tip of the island, they located the boat left at the spot by Baldwin, still sitting on its sledge as it had been left two years before. To the cache of four boxes of emergency supplies also left at the site, they added more than fifty pounds of pemmican for the dogs. They stayed only twenty minutes, and were back at Kane Lodge the same evening.

The next day, Vedoe fried a bear's heart for dinner, and the men tucked into a box of baker's chocolate retrieved from the cache at Wiener Neustadt. They ate turkey again on Tuesday, and then finished their work at the hut. They departed that same day, April 12, but only made it as far as a small island west of Greely Island, where they went into camp. The following morning, Porter ascended about 600 feet on the tiny island, and Vedoe soon heard him shouting. Vedoe climbed after him, and "found him standing high on the rocks acting like a Wildman."[250] In a gully between a high mountain glacier and a mountain top, Porter had discovered a seam of coal fully ten feet wide.

All that day and the next, the two men dug coal from the island, filling a fifty-pound bag to take back to Chief Engineer Hartt for testing. Porter named the place Coal Mine Island and was thrilled with the find, especially given the loss of coal from the disappearance of the ship.

The two men had a celebration of sorts by making their way back to Rudolf Island by way of the ruins of Nansen's hut on Jackson Island, "so that Anton could see with his own eyes where Nansen, his fellow countryman, had hibernated like a bear through a long night."251 Vedoe was over the moon. After shooting a bear near the site, he gave the dogs a big feed, and then he and Porter settled themselves to a dinner of canned turkey "and a hot toddy to the two greatest of polar explorers' memory [*sic*], and were comparing our commodious life to what they had to suffer. It has been a glorious day all through."252 To mark the day, Vedoe took a bear skull from the sacred site.

In the days that followed, the two men followed the line of the *America*'s advance the previous summer. Porter's careful observations of the coastline as the ship steamed along the shore now returned to aid their progress. They regained the cache on Coburg Island by April 23 and the following morning, taking their sights for Cape Brorok on Rudolf Island, Vedoe spotted "a light object" on one of the nearby islands. Studying it through his telescope, he came to the conclusion that it was one of the expedition's tents. As they approached, they found a small camp, two tents, a sledge, and a dog team. "Going to the tent flap we opened and were welcomed by our Commander and the Steward in their bag."253

Fiala and Bernard Spencer had left Camp Abruzzi a day earlier, intent on finding some trace of Porter and Vedoe, whom most at the expedition house had given up for lost. While the two men had been away on their trip to Kane Lodge, Fiala at Camp Abruzzi had taken to arranging and rearranging the men who would go south to Cape Flora, since the number of men he could count on to remain for another year and another try at the North Pole dwindled by the day. Despite the lack of enthusiasm around him, "Fiala told Hartt . . . that he intends to devote the rest of his life to the quest for the Pole."254 Seitz, for one, doubted the practicality of this devotion, as he recorded several instances in the month of April when Fiala experienced sudden fainting episodes.

Since it was Sunday, Fiala led a service for the four men on Coburg Island, after which they packed up the temporary camp and began the return to Teplitz Bay. As they regained Rudolf Island on April 26, the men were pinned by a storm between capes Brorok and Auk and so sat out the weather "in the Commander's tent with hot toddy and smoking cigarettes."255

Ascending the glacier at Cape Auk, Spencer became snow blind and Fiala fell to his waist into a crevasse and had to be rescued. The men finally reached Camp Abruzzi on the morning of April 26, to be greeted by a main expedition party now desperate to reach Cape Flora and their expected salvation.

FORTY-SIX

The Death of Sigurd Myhre

At Camp Abruzzi, the expedition had broken down into a variety of cliques with no real central authority. Several of the ponies had been infected with glanders and had to be shot. By April 28 only seventeen remained. Several more dogs had died from overwork on the ice, fighting amongst themselves, and in encounters with polar bears. The men themselves had returned from the brief excursion onto the ice north of Cape Fligely "filled with the pain of a second failure."[256]

Fiala's pain was more than psychic. Seitz had treated him several times in April for sudden fainting spells. Chief Engineer Hartt spent the month of April hard at work on converting a whaleboat into a steam launch, and for a brief time Fiala encouraged the belief that he would use it to make a dramatic summer expedition north to the permanent polar ice pack. The men knew that there was nothing behind this talk, any more than when Fiala told Hartt on April 15 that he would devote the rest of his life to the search for the North Pole.

On April 22 Seitz wrote that the expedition commander "still gives evidence of his poor physical condition by staggering at various times."[257] It was not a sight to inspire confidence in the men. Seitz turned twenty-seven years old on April 26, and when Fiala asked him to remain at Camp Abruzzi for another year, he gave the idea a few hours' thought and then declined. When Fiala called for other men to remain on Rudolf Island for another try at the pole in 1905, there were precious few volunteers. As Fiala himself admitted, "the men lost interest in the northern campaign and openly expressed their deep felt desire to go home."[258]

Faced with rapidly disintegrating morale, Fiala went to pieces. He needed to plan a retreat to Cape Flora on Northbrook Island but was paralyzed with indecision. He told Colin Vaughan "to go ahead with packing the sledges as he had lots of things to think about during the coming week."[259]

On April 28 Fiala asked Porter and Vedoe to make another exploratory trip into the eastern part of the archipelago, and to take Rilliet with them. Porter, who somehow managed to escape the vast majority of the dissension and infighting that accompanied both the Baldwin and Fiala expeditions to Franz Josef Land, was thrilled with yet another chance to travel through the islands, mapping and sketching as he went. Peters, the nominal second-in-command and leader of "the knowing ones," was to remain at Camp Abruzzi to gather up the scientific records and instruments and close the astronomical observatory.

Besides the Porter party and Peters, the number of expedition members who would remain behind at Camp Abruzzi had shrunk to a skeleton crew that included assistant scientist Robert Tafel; Spencer W. Stewart, the assistant commissary; the steward, Bernard E. Spencer: three sailors from Massachusetts, William R. Myers, D. S. Mackiernan, and Elijah Perry; Anton Vedoe's brother John; two other Norwegians, the fireman Sigurd Myhre and the carpenter Peter Tessem; and the Chief Engineer Henry Hartt, who was still planning a Bogart-style escape by steam launch.[260]

Fiala's eventual decision to lead the group retreating to Cape Flora meant that fully twenty-five of the thirty-nine members of the expedition were abandoning Camp Abruzzi. Fiala admitted that by joining the Cape Flora group—where he expected a relief ship to arrive that summer and take this disheartened cadre home—he had probably inadvertently swelled their ranks even more. Even so, Fiala was unusually bitter in his denunciations of these men, describing them as "the homeseekers," "politicians," and "the weak and undecided."[261]

In a significant failure to manage his personnel, Fiala allowed the group that left Rudolf Island to include all of the expedition's medical personnel: the doctors Shorkley and Seitz, the medical student Colin Vaughan, and the veterinarian Newcomb. Because of the glanders epidemic, all of the ponies would be taken from Rudolf Island. The animals would be shot as the supplies they dragged were depleted. Vaughan and LeRoyer spent the days before departure shooting any dog that was ill and unlikely to survive the journey to Cape Flora.

The retreat got underway at 8 P.M. on Sunday night, May 1, 1904. Almost as soon as the Cape Flora party had left, Anton Vedoe wrote in his journal that both Tessem, the carpenter, and Sigurd Myhre, the fireman from Trondheim, had fallen ill. Vedoe spent the rest of the week packing a sledge for his own journey with Porter and Rilliet. Porter's group, enlarged at the last moment by the additions of Spencer and Mackiernan—both of whom now decided that they wanted to return home—set off on the morning of May 9.

Only nine men remained at Camp Abruzzi. Tessem soon recovered from his illness, but Myhre grew sicker. What happened next can only be glimpsed indirectly, as none of the men who remained at Camp Abruzzi kept a journal that survives. Dr. Shorkley's medical journal, largely compiled after he arrived at Cape Flora with the "homeseekers," contains several minatory hints that Myhre may have died from other than natural causes.

Shorkley's journal mentions Myhre in several places. On the initial journey from Norway to Franz Josef Land, Shorkley had examined each member of the crew save for Coffin and first officer Edward Haven, both of whom refused to submit to physical examination. Myhre's examination elicited the following details: he was twenty-nine years old, stood 5 feet 6 inches tall, and weighed 155 pounds. He had been born in Trondheim, Norway, and had a tattoo of an "Indian girl" on his right forearm and the initials "S. M." on his left hand. His teeth were in very poor condition, with two upper and two lower molars missing on each side of his mouth. When Shorkley weighed the crew later in the fall, Myhre had put on seven pounds, weighing in at 162 pounds.

On November 10, 1903, Shorkley wrote that he had gone from the base camp out to the ship to see Hartt, who was ill with his incapacitating rectal fissure, as well as Myhre. "[Myhre]" wrote Shorkley, "is a case of malingery [*sic*]."[262] Since the summer, Shorkley took note of several crew members he believed were shirking, and from this note it is clear that he felt Myhre was one of them. On March 8 Shorkley recorded the injury suffered by Myhre during the first attempt on the North Pole as the expedition marched to Cape Fligely. The Norwegian had stabbed his own hand while trying to cut a piece of pemmican.

When Shorkley and the rest of his medical staff left Camp Abruzzi on May 1, 1904, Anton Vedoe wrote in his diary that "Tessem and Myhre have been sick.

Most likely a bad touch of cold. They have been in bed most of the time and feel quite feeble. I have had a slight cold but not to interfere with my work."[263]

Four days later, Anton Vedoe left the camp on Porter's survey journey south via Austria Sound with Rilliet, Mackiernan, and Spencer. Peters, Tafel, and John Vedoe would journey south to Cape Flora via British Channel later in the summer. Porter and his party reached Cape Flora in mid-July, while Peters and his team did not reach Cape Flora until August 31. When they did, they brought with them the news that Sigurd Myhre had died on May 16.[264]

In his published account of the expedition, Fiala writes briefly that Myhre "died at Camp Abruzzi on May 16 after an illness of several weeks."[265] The surviving men at Camp Abruzzi buried Myhre four days later, on May 20, under a pile of rocks at Cape Säulen, just north of Teplitz Bay. Fiala describes the gravesit as "the most northern tomb, I believe, in the world."[266] He published a photograph of a carefully crafted and erected cross that marked Myhre's grave overlooking the Arctic Sea.[267]

Russell Porter, who by the end of the summer of 1904 had begun to entertain doubts over whether any of the men would survive the expedition, mentions Myhre's death in his diary. He wrote that the "person was one Murray [sic], a Norwegian fireman, who passed away at Camp Abruzzi, on 16 May, with no medical aid at hand (all the physicians had come south to go home). Score one against this expedition for the evil spirit hovering forever over the Arctic waste. May it be the last although I doubt it. This man was ill when I was there the first of May and I understand he never recovered, was unconscious a good deal of the time and would not answer when spoken to. He leaves a wife in Bergen."[268]

Shorkley, in overall charge of the health of the expedition, questioned the Peters group closely about what had happened to Myhre. Written beneath his notes on Myhre's physical examination, Shorkley added the following: "Party arriving at Cape Flora from Camp Abruzzi report the death of Myhre, at the latter place, on the 16th of May 1904. Cause of death unknown. The only significant symptoms available are that, during the last few days of his life, deceased was in a state of extreme cyanosis & of stupor amounting almost to complete coma. Buried in a cairn of rocks on the hill just NW of the camp, the cairn being marked by a wooden cross about 6 ft. in height, upon which is carved a suitable inscription."[269]

When ice prevented the expected relief ship from reaching Franz Josef Land in 1904, the expedition, already riven by dissension, crippled by short rations, and scattered in several groups around Franz Josef Land, descended into depression. Shorkley's medical journal soon diminished to barely a single line each day, and then ceased altogether on September 7, 1904.

As we will see, Fiala attempted his third, final, and equally brief attempt on the pole on March 16, 1905. The following day, Porter arrived at Camp Abruzzi from Cape Flora, bringing with him a letter to Hartt from Shorkley. Shorkley must have heard or been told by someone in the Peters party at Cape Flora that Charles Rilliet had given some medications to Myhre before he died, and Shorkley wanted to know just what those medicines had been.

In reply, Hartt wrote a long, tortuous letter describing his own rectal surgery at the hands of Seitz, who had returned to Camp Abruzzi the previous fall. Hartt additionally suffered from a sprained ankle, a sprained knee, and a broken rib. He had all but given up hope of seeing civilization again. Then, in answer to Shorkley's query about Myhre, Hartt wrote, "You were asking me to try and remember the kind of medicine that Rilliet gave Murry [Myhre]. I could not say what he gave him, I only heard him make the remark before he left here that he had given him enough medicine to kill two men. I suppose though he was fooling at the time he made the remark, because he thought as every one else did I suppose, Murry, was playing another one of his tricks to get out of work."[270] From this note, it is impossible to identify what substances Rilliet might have given to Myhre, or to know whether he received any more medications after Rilliet left Camp Abruzzi on May 9 with Porter's exploring party. At that time Porter and his group left, nine men, including Myhre, were left at Camp Abruzzi. These included Hartt; the Peters party of Peters, Tafel, and John Vedoe (which would leave after Myhre died and bring the news of his death to Cape Flora); and sailors Gustave Meyer and Elijah Perry, assistant commissary Spencer Stewart, and the carpenter Tessem.

Anton Vedoe, as noted earlier, merely thought both Myhre and Tessem were suffering from bad colds. He certainly gives no hint that he thought Myhre was near death. Tessem soon recovered from his "bad cold" but Myhre worsened and soon died. If the two "colds" were connected, did Rilliet give a bigger, punitive dose of medicine to Myhre than to Tessem because he thought—as did Hartt and Shorkley—that Myhre was a shirker?

Shorkley's list of medical supplies left behind at Camp Abruzzi—when the larger part of the expedition retreated in May 1904—includes enough drugs to supply a hospital pharmacy, including over thirty thousand pills of various types. A sense of what would have been included comes from Shorkley's medical journal entry of July 13, 1903, when Fiala asked Shorkley to prepare a package of medical supplies that would be left in a box at Cape Flora in case of emergency. These include morphine, laxatives, diarrhea tablets, and various other medicines for cough and headache.

The comments by both Shorkley and Rilliet about Myhre's avoidance of work cast an interesting light on his hand injury at Cape Fligely. Was the stab wound in fact accidental or had Myhre—like Fiala himself, for that matter—looked out over the implacable polar sea from the heights of Cape Fligely and searched for a way out of what was fast becoming a doomed expedition? By the time they reached Cape Fligely, Shorkley—who rarely saw anything but the worst in his fellows—was convinced that Fiala was incompetent, if not an outright loon. If Myhre had come to the same conclusion, then perhaps a cut on the hand was preferable to being led across a thousand miles of polar ice by a well-meaning commander whose grip on the expedition was at best uncertain.

Such an action would suggest a strong impulse to self-preservation, which would seem to rule out any suggestion that Myhre might have killed himself through an overdose once he was back at Camp Abruzzi. Shorkley's long-distance diagnosis from Cape Flora of extreme cyanosis could have been the result of hypothermia but also of any number of other causes including myocardial infarction or heart attack. The addition of the condition of stupor further suggests hypothermia. During a winter when the temperatures at Camp Abruzzi fell to more the 40 degrees below zero Fahrenheit, it is possible that Myhre was literally freezing to death. The possibility that he was suffering from the end stages of some other undiagnosed terminal illness cannot be discounted, but this seems unlikely to have escaped the notice of Shorkley.

Rilliet would have made his comment about giving Myhre enough medicine to kill two men both before he left Camp Abruzzi and before Myhre died. When the Peters party arrived at Cape Flora just after midnight on September 1, 1904, we have a sense of how he reacted to the news of Myhre's death. Most of the camp was asleep, except for Rilliet and Anton Vedoe, who were puttering about in their own small hut. John Vedoe, whose diary of the Peters trip south to Cape Flora is embedded in his brother's account of the expedition, writes that "the sad news of Myhre's death brought seriousness to the otherwise happy faces."[271] If Rilliet had indeed made light to Hartt that he had overmedicated Myhre, the sudden realization that Myhre was now dead and that he, Rilliet, might be the cause and could be held accountable, must have come as a tremendous shock.

Anton Vedoe, Tessem, and Rilliet all returned to Camp Abruzzi at the end of June 1905 to make one last visit to the site before their final retreat south. They stayed in the otherwise empty camp for a week. Vedoe spent the time taking photographs and cleaning the expedition hut. He makes no mention of what Rilliet did during this time, and there is no indication that any of them hiked to Cape Säulen to visit Myhre's grave.

What can be said for certain in this strange tale is that Sigurd Myhre died on May 16, 1904, after more than a week of suffering an extreme form of cyanosis accompanied by a near-coma, while his fellow countryman, Tessem, recovered from his illness. If, as Hartt suggests, Rilliet really thought Myhre was shirking and proceeded to medicate him to the point of overdose, his actions would amount to murder. Such an event would mark a new low for an expedition already replete with examples of human weakness. Added to the death by exposure of Bernt Bentsen at Fort McKinley in 1899, the Americans were now responsible for the deaths of two Norwegians in Franz Josef Land in less than six years.

FORTY-SEVEN

The More Kicking There Will Be

Fiala led the retreat party into camp at Cape Brorok on the southwest corner of Rudolf Island on the night of May 1, 1904. He remained close to Captain Coffin but clearly did not trust him, since he had placed Coffin in command of the retreat to Cape Flora but then insisted on leading the march himself. But Fiala's own lack of navigational skills soon became an issue. The following day, he led the men onto the ice toward the cache at Coburg Island but had trouble finding the cache in the thick weather.

Seitz recorded a heated discussion between Fiala and Francis Long from the previous evening, when "Fiala & Long were talking about the situation of Coburg Island. Fiala made a statement entirely wrong and Long told him if he couldn't find Coburg Island he couldn't find the Pole."[272] When they found the Coburg Island cache the next day, "Rabbit," an old pony and veteran of the Baldwin expedition, was shot and fed to the dogs.

The men were not in much better condition. Seitz wrote that Nichols was already "played out" and riding on a sledge, while Moulton and Long were both limping along. After all of the inactivity of the winter, all of the men, Seitz included, were feeling the effects. The expedition commander continued to have trouble finding the route south to Cape Flora. "Fiala was apparently lost from his numerous zigzag curves. Said he was going between Alexander Land & Jackson Island but switched off at Rainer Island and stopped for coffee and hard tack."[273]

Somewhat surprisingly, Coffin and the sailors fared better on this trip than the men of the Field Department. After a few days on the march, Coffin, in what was likely his first extended period of sobriety in years, even found time to enjoy himself. "We are doing much better than we figured on. Instead of 26 days to Flora we will probably make it in sixteen sure. Fine weather. I am feeling better every day and not at all tired. The first day out, I wrenched my back sliding down a glacier (playing boy) and it bothers me to get in the right position to sleep."[274]

By May 7 Fiala's detours were leading the men to either harass or ignore him. As Seitz observed: "Much kicking and men at times did not follow him. Fiala & Shorkley had some hot words." Shorkley soon began to argue with Seitz, even as the latter began to suffer from snow blindness. "My ankle & my right knee are very sore and stiff after going through the rough ice. My eyes still ache."[275]

The increasingly bitter retreat continued all the way to Cape Flora, as the men shot the ponies and dogs as they went lame, arguing openly with Fiala when they weren't arguing amongst themselves. All in all, it amounted to another pitiful performance by the Americans. Any semblance of discipline was gone. As Seitz wrote on May 9, "The kicking still continued and all kinds of remarks are made in Fiala's hearing. Truden had a scrap with him & Shorkley told him not to talk to him socially."[276]

The quibbling turned violent on May 11, as Truden got into a fight with Fiala "and said he would fight any man on the expedition when he got back."[277] Disgusted, Fiala took his sledge further onto the ice and went his own way toward Cape Flora, while his men hugged the ice along shore.

A miniature mutiny broke out on Friday, May 13, as the party reached Eaton Island. Fiala ordered the men to come on ahead and put up the tents, but they sat where they were. Coffin wrote: "While Mr. Fiala and myself were ahead on the lead, all the party went into camp without any orders.

> When we started to go back, the distance was about 1¾ miles, we supposed there had been some serious accident, but it only proved that the ponies were tired, ditto some of the Field party. So they stopped and camped for the night. The orders and intention [had been] to make Eaton Island. . . . When I got to the camp everybody was settled down and some eating lunch of hard bread, taking the world easy.[278]

Finally, on the morning of Monday, May 16, the retreat party straggled to Cape Flora. Once there, all but two of the ponies were shot, along with another dog. To the south, from which direction the men hoped to see their salvation, there was no open water to be seen. Seitz recorded that the men began to take stock of the supplies left behind at the camp of Frederick Jackson, and to settle into the surviving huts until their expected relief ship arrived.

Helped Truden unload the sledges and pile the supplies in the stable. The sectional house was cleared out and Fiala decided to let the Field Party occupy it while the rest live in the hut. Duke's letter and list of supplies found. Stable storehouse also cleared out. Coffee at 1 p.m. Cleared snow out of our house in the afternoon. Turned dogs loose and they at once began to eat the horses, 2 of which had glanders well developed. "Happy & Windy," [the two surviving ponies] turned loose to graze. Hung my sleeping bag and some clothing out in the sun to dry. [Francis] Long & Seargt. [Moulton] making a tide gauge below Leigh Smith's hut.[279]

The next day, when Captain Coffin found two bottles of Jamaican rum in the supplies and Fiala immediately confiscated them, there was another fight. "Fiala was jumped hard by Shorkley, Vaughn [sic] & Truden. He is going to keep it for medical purposes. He told Truden he was going back to Camp Abruzzi soon but on account of the kicking would stay here longer. (The longer he stays the more kicking there will be)."[280]

The amount of supplies the men had to fight over was considerable. Coffin and Haven inventoried the variety of goods stashed at Cape Flora by several separate expeditions and found more than two tons of biscuits, nearly fifteen hundred pounds of butter, to go with nearly a ton of canned meats. Fiala wrote, "In addition to the supplies we had brought with us, were the great cache placed there by the Duke of the Abruzzi and the food supplies left by Jackson and the Andrée Relief Expedition."[281] These extra rations would prove to be an astoundingly fortunate legacy of those previous expeditions.

The buildings at Cape Flora were cleared of snow, and the men began to settle in to await the relief ship they fully expected to appear within no more than a few weeks. The scientists and men of the erstwhile Field Department housed themselves in one of the octagonal storage huts left behind by Jackson, while Captain Coffin, First Mate Haven, Fiala, and most of the sailors of the lost *America* bunked in Elmwood, the hut that once served as Jackson's expedition base. Jackson had designed the structure to house eight men; it would now have to shelter twice that number.

Truden soon got into another fight with Fiala, even writing out his resignation as the expedition's commissary when Fiala refused to give him the Duke of the Abruzzi's list of supplies and gave it to Coffin instead. Seitz recorded the outcome: "Fiala backed down and Truden got the list."[282] Francis Long, a man who had lived through a similar collapse of order during the Greely expedition, quickly removed himself from the chaos. He began to monitor the tide gauge on Saturday, May 21, and collected data every hour and then every ten minutes at the high and low tides, scientific recording that allowed the Arctic veteran a measure of peace amid the open dissension.

By now, Fiala had also had more than enough. He had lost nearly all the ponies, and none would be available for any renewed attempt on the North Pole in the spring of 1905. At best, such an attempt would of necessity be made with only a few surviving dog teams. As for the number of reliable men he could count on, these, too, had dwindled to virtually none. Fiala himself wrote of this double burden—the vast majority of his men having retreated to Cape Flora, in an almost mad rush for a relief ship home, and the accompanying notion that "when the men left Teplitz Bay it was for good and meant the loss of service to the expedition of nearly all of them."[283]

That Fiala had only himself to blame for this state of affairs was a notion that he never acknowledged. He held "the homeseekers" in contempt but could not stop worrying about them, since "they could not be considered in any other light than as a care and source of anxiety to the leader until they were aboard the Relief Ship."[284]

The men at Cape Flora quickly divided into two cliques, with the 'knowing ones' in the storage hut and the sailors occupying Elmwood. Fiala made a hasty decision to divide the supplies between the two groups in an attempt to prevent anarchy. It was a huge mistake. Long recognized immediately that any such division was a de facto recognition that the expedition itself had been divided, and one side would be seen as holding the losing hand. Seitz recorded on May 25: "Truden looked after our interests & had quite a scrap with Fiala over the division, the Capt.'s share & so forth. Pierre & Newcomb walked over to Cape Gertrude this morning & saw no traces of game but found numbers of whale skeletons high above sea level. Fiala is living in the sailors' home now. He, Capt. & Haven have a little table to themselves. Our house has been christened 'Little Italy.'"[285]

Coffin, nominal leader of the sailors at Elmwood, looked on the "knowing ones" a bit differently. As he saw it, the rift between the two groups had begun even before the expedition had left Norway. Now, the desperation of men with little to do but wait on a relief ship that might or might not break through to Cape Flora had forced the split wide open. "Mr. Haven lent the only shovel he had to the folks at [Little Italy], to be returned in a few minutes.

> Sent one of the men after it after a lapse of half an hour. Doctor N. [Newcomb] replied to the man, at his request for the shovel, "Oh, let the sons of Bitches wait. They want everything." Fine gentleman talk.
> If the North Pole had been two miles North of Cape Fligely these men would never [have] reached it unless there had been another party ahead [that] might reach it before they did.[286]

Truden continued to berate Fiala over the division of supplies, first over the alcohol and then over the discovery of an unexpected cache of soap. Coffin, who for all his problems with Fiala was now sympathetic to the constant harassment suffered by the expedition commander, began to record his observations in the event he was called to testify against the men of the Field Department. "Truden was over here this afternoon on purpose to insult Mr. Fiala. . . . After Mr. F. told him to resign, he replied he would not and did not recognize him as the commander of this expidition [*sic*]. Mr. F. then said turn over all your books and . . . said, I relieve you from duty. Truden said he did not recognize his authority. . . . I record this as I think I may be called to witness the gross treatment of his Commander."[287]

The situation was now critical. Fiala had lost any semblance of control over the expedition and flailed about without a friend or ally on any side. As Seitz recorded when a new division of supplies came up on June 1, "Of course we were all a little excited as it practically amounts to cutting us off from the expedition.

> Long told Fiala it would result in his disgrace. Shorkley asked Fiala about the liquor (Duke's). Fiala told him he would take it North, that it was no business of Shorkley's, that the expedition was at Teplitz Bay & this was no part of the expedition. Fiala told Pierre today there was no one fit to be in charge of any liquor. Various ones have talked to Fiala today and he is sorry now, it seems. He had the division of food

& said he did not mean the expedition was divided. He has decided not to go North on account of the new trouble. Last night Capt. told him he was a g.d. figurehead and that he (Capt.) was in charge of their house.[288]

In his published account, Fiala devoted no less than twenty-five pages to the retreat to Cape Flora, five times the space he allowed for the half-hearted polar attempts of March. The trauma of the retreat, along with his obvious distress and his treatment by the men, combined to test even his considerable faith. As it did so often in the Arctic, it was nature itself that came to his rescue. "The sun circled above our horizon day and night, melting the great snow drifts and exposing the rocks. Beautiful little Arctic poppies lifted their white and gold cups to the King of the Sky, and green mosses and coloured lichens gave relief to the eye after the constant glare of snow and ice."[289]

Fiala vacillated between returning immediately to Teplitz Bay or remaining with the malcontents at Cape Flora. He finally decided he must stay with the Cape Flora group until they could all be shoved on board a relief ship. On June 2, as Seitz recorded, Fiala read out letters from William Ziegler that conferred authority upon him over the entire expedition. The reading was staged at great length and "was apparently intended for the Capt. & a few others. The Capt. recently said that he did not come up here for the Ziegler Polar Expedition, he didn't depend on his salary from the expedition & that we were robbing the storehouse of supplies."[290]

If Fiala intended to send a message that it was time for the men to line up behind him, it had the opposite effect. Coffin, for one, didn't understand what he talking about. "At 8:30 P.M., Mr. F talked to all the party at quite a length. I could not quite see the point of his address. He read the papers given him by Mr. Ziegler which gave him possession of the property owned by him. . . . They gave him power over all private contracts. Although of course not over a Government Commissioned officer and Master on the high seas or on land where there was no law."[291]

For Coffin, as for most of the shipwrecked men, it was now every man for himself, and he and the men acted accordingly. To avoid anarchy over the remaining supplies, Fiala was now reduced to making out menus for the separate groups in the different huts. The different groups had to establish ground rules for who was able to chase after any polar bears—and then over the division between the huts of the resulting meat. Fried bear was now served at two of the three meals each day.

Seitz recorded every meal in great detail and did his best to keep his head down by playing chess with Shorkley or wandering the surrounding talus slopes in search of fossils. Other men scoured the hills for birds and their eggs. Otherwise there was very little that did not immediately ignite a fight. Shorkley was "cussed out" on June 21 when he removed a sign placed at Cape Flora by the crew of the Russian icebreaker *Ermak* and Fiala ordered him to put it back.[292]

On June 27, the inevitable betting pool was started over when the relief ship would arrive. Seitz optimistically laid $1.25 that the expected event would occur just two days later, at 11 A.M. No one thought to place good money on a bet that absolutely no ship would arrive at Cape Flora in the year 1904.

FORTY-EIGHT

Joy, Part Two

When Fiala left Teplitz Bay at the head of "the homeseekers," he charged Russell Porter with a general exploration of both the Graham Bell Island discovered by Evelyn Briggs Baldwin in 1899 and the rapidly fragmenting "Zichy Land," which was now seen as a collection of islands rather than one large landmass. Along with Anton Vedoe, Porter was perhaps the last remaining member of the Ziegler Polar Expedition whom Fiala not only trusted but genuinely liked and admired. He complimented Porter "on the excellent work done [during the recent trip to Kane Lodge] and on the conscientious and able manner in which you have carried out my instructions."[293] These were words that Fiala could write of no other member of the expedition, with the exception of Porter's sledging partner Anton Vedoe.

When Porter and Vedoe left Teplitz Bay on the morning of May 9, their party had been enlarged by the addition first of Charles Rilliet, then by the additions of Bernard Spencer and D. S. Mackiernan, both of whom decided at the last moment to find their way to Cape Flora and return home. The men raced southward, arriving at the southern tip of Rainer Island on May 11. There, in temperatures rising to 20°F on May 12, Porter and Vedoe ascended to the highest point of the Rainer Island ice dome and took a series of survey angles. "The weather was brilliant and we could see the headlands of the surrounding islands very plainly."[294]

The following day, the men sledged in temperatures above freezing to

Porter's discovery at Coal Mine Island. While Vedoe watched over the dogs and made coffee, Porter with the other men climbed to the coal seam and dragged down a hundred pounds of coal. On May 14 the men reached Kane Lodge. There Porter gave the men the day off and Bernard Spencer took advantage of the cache of supplies to make the most of their meals: "For breakfast we had oatmeal with pancakes with maple sugar and coffee. For dinner we had croquettes made out of a composition of emerg. rations and chipped beef, corn fritters and gravy, tomatoes and coffee and H. and O. biscuits."[295]

With full stomachs, Porter and Rilliet took more survey angles while the other men climbed to the top of Greely Island and found more bits of coal, but could not locate any seam. By Saturday, May 21, the men had almost reached Cape Trieste on the island that would be eventually named for William Champ. Containers of oil had leaked in Porter's kayak, spoiling some sugar, pemmican, and tobacco. Vedoe had strained his back twice, yet wrote that he was "feeling a great deal better of late than I have for the last month."[296]

The men established a camp at Cape Trieste on the 23rd, where the next day they ascended to the highest point of what they still believed to be Zichy Land, at more than 1,500 feet. After a rest, they sledged to North Island and then on to Alger Island, where they arrived at East Camp Ziegler, the old winter quarters of the Baldwin expedition, in the evening. "The houses and stables were buried beneath the snow and through holes in the roof we could see that the whole inside of the stable was filled up by snow and would require lots of digging to get into the house."[297]

On Wednesday, May 25, Rilliet and Vedoe spent the day digging through the stable and into the main expedition huts. "The east house was almost empty while the west house was piled full of provisions. Everything smelled musty and after scraping and cleaning out we made a fire and washed up dishes and got things in order for the steward to cook breakfast."[298]

Vedoe and Mackiernan sledged to the site of West Camp Ziegler on May 28, where they went in search of more useful materials left behind by the Baldwin-Ziegler Polar Expedition. The temperatures were now in the mid-40s, and the two men even slept outside without sleeping bags. The vast amount of supplies deposited around Franz Josef Land by Baldwin had turned the archipelago into a gigantic treasure hunt, with no telling what might be found at each cache. They returned to East Camp Ziegler the following day loaded down with over a thousand pounds of coal, charcoal, half a barrel of flour, a box of turkey, and some ship's biscuits.

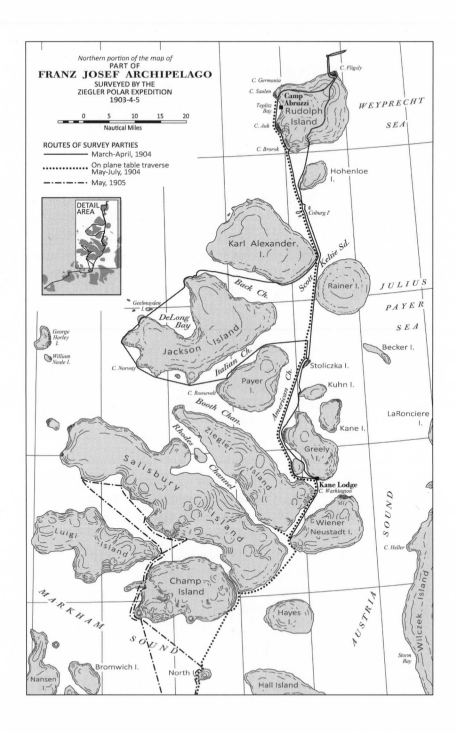

Northern portion of the map of
PART OF
FRANZ JOSEF ARCHIPELAGO
SURVEYED BY THE
ZIEGLER POLAR EXPEDITION
1903-4-5

0   5   10   15   20
Nautical Miles

ROUTES OF SURVEY PARTIES
—————— March-April, 1904
••••••••••• On plane table traverse
             May-July, 1904
—·—·—·— May, 1905

DETAIL
AREA

C. Germania
C. Saulen
Teplitz Bay
C. Auk
C. Brorok
C. Fligely
Camp Abruzzi
Rudolph Island
WEYPRECHT SEA

Hohenloe I.

Coburg I'

Karl Alexander I.

Keltie Sd.
Scott
Rainer I.
JULIUS PAYER SEA

Back Ch.

Geelmuyden I.

George Harley I.
William Neale I.

DeLong Bay
Jackson Island
C. Norway
Italian Ch.
C. Roosevelt

Payer I.

Becker I.

Stoliczka I.
Kuhn I.
Kane I.
LaRonciere I.

American Ch.

Booth Chan.
Rhodes
Ziegler Island
Channel
Salisbury Island

Greely I.

Kane Lodge
C. Washington

Luigi Island

Wiener Neustadt I.
C. Heller

AUSTRIA SOUND

Champ Island

MARKHAM

SOUND

Hayes I.

Wilczek Island

Storm Bay

Nansen I.
Bromwich I.
North I.
Hall Island

The scavenger hunt continued in a different way after the men returned, as they picked over the surrounding hills for fossils and Rilliet was rewarded with a fossil starfish. As "the homeseekers" at Cape Flora fought over every scrap of food, Porter's party at Camp Ziegler together created an oven in which to bake bread, then together shot guillemots and auks to fry up with bacon and Johnny cakes. Porter and Rilliet measured off the surveying baseline on Alger Island—over which Baldwin had given Porter such a hard time in 1901—and then enjoyed a dinner of sugar corn and stewed loons.

On Sunday, June 5, Vedoe and Mackiernan "were out sailing in the kayaks this afternoon and had a splendid time."[299] The next day, Porter asked the two men to take one of the kayaks and a heavily loaded sledge "to an unnamed isl. about 20 miles from here."[300] By the end of the day, they made camp on Brady Island, before proceeding on to Bliss Island in the fog the next day. Along the way, they found that their maps were wrong, that the large island on which Porter had asked them to cache the supplies turned out to be much smaller than previously recorded. "Our clothes bags we carried way up in good shelter place out of sight for bears and where it can not be spoiled by rain. The pemmican and kerosene we piled up on the rocks on the low beach. The clothes bags are about 100 feet high."[301]

The two returned in a blinding storm on June 9, covering the twenty-three miles in less than eight hours. The whole party packed and left East Camp Ziegler in the evening of June 13. The party traveled west, retracing the steps of Vedoe and MccKiernan, first to Brady Island and then to Bliss Island before stopping at Vedoe's unnamed island where the cache had been laid. Once there, the force of the wind and a driving snow tore at the men's tent.

When the weather cleared the next day, Rilliet patched the tent while Vedoe and Mackiernan found and dug out a cache that had been left at the island by Baldwin. They found five cases of emergency rations and a tin of coffee and, after shooting some birds along the shore, retreated to the tent to make a hot dinner. Heavy weather kept the men pinned on the stony shoreline all day on June 17, and Vedoe lay in his sleeping bag planning a trip through Norway with his brother John "to see our relatives which have not seen before."[302]

Opposite: Redrawn detail from Porter's chart of northern Franz Josef Land, from Greely Island to Rudolf Island—the end of the road of American polar ambitions in Franz Josef Land. *Copyright © 2016 The University of Oklahoma Press. All rights reserved.*

The men finally escaped the temporary encampment on Sunday, June 19. They lashed the sledges across the three kayaks to create a trimaran and then paddled furiously for three hours. High winds forced them to disassemble the raft for a second trip, and it was not until a third trip, and twenty hours of very hard work, until all the dogs and gear were ferried across, "taking dogs on the two small kayaks lashed together and towed by the big kayak."[303]

On June 22 the men reached the area near Rubini Rock on Hooker Island. There they made camp on bare ground, surrounded by "thousands of birds . . . and amongst them several wild geese which we have been chasing all day."[304] Vedoe needed to rest, having become snow blind while crossing the strait between the Baldwin cache site and Hooker Island. Porter had surveyed the route from Alger Island, and now used his plane table to survey Rubini Rock, 587 feet high. Vedoe climbed the rock with Mackiernan on June 29 and found the "whole top of the rock . . . flat [and] covered with big boulders and a lot of dry moss. On the west side there is a valley about 100 feet deep with running fresh water. Here we built a fire of moss, shot a few auks, and roasted them on the cleaning rod of Mac's gun. They went fine although we had neither salt or pepper."[305]

The party left Rubini Rock on July 2 after a week of surveying. Porter believed they had found "a fine winter harbor for a ship" in the area around the rock.[306] From the highest elevation on Hooker Island, they could see all the way from McClintock Island in the east to Camp Point, the northern point of Northbrook Island, to the southwest. To the south, the Barents Sea was free of ice as far as the eye could see. The men crossed to Camp Point the following day, the last stretch favored when they encountered a lead but also "a cake of ice waiting like a ferryboat for us on which we successfully landed the whole outfit on the other side, taking one sledge at a time."[307]

Anxious to regain their comrades at Cape Flora, both Mackiernan and Spencer left Camp Point on July 5 and made their way south. Seitz recorded their arrival: "They crossed over from Old Depot (on Hooker Island) in 1 day, & took 23 dogs in coming from Camp Ziegler. They left Camp Abruzzi on May 9th with 3 dog teams, 1 double kayak & 2 single kayaks. Spent about 15 days at Camp Ziegler then in open water at Abruzzi shot a she-bear & captured a young cub which is being kept up there."[308] Fiala, too, noted the men's arrival, writing that the men "made no secret of the fact that they had grown discouraged with the outlook."[309]

Porter, Vedoe, and Rilliet managed to delay their arrival with the retreat party at Cape Flora for two more days. Porter immediately noted the division between the men of the Field Department housed at Little Italy and the sailors of Elmwood. As he had so often during the expedition, he also diagnosed the problem in the men's anticipation of the imminent arrival of a relief ship: "One day we tried a ball game under the cliffs. Above the screech of the birds in the rookery overhead, someone cried, 'Ship,' and the diamond was deserted. It was a false alarm, and before long serious attention was given to the possibility that relief would not arrive and, caught like rats in a trap, some provision must be made for the winter."[310]

FORTY-NINE

How I Discovered H. P. Hartt Land

As Porter's party arrived amongst "the homeseekers" of Cape Flora, the expedition's chief scientist and nominal second-in-command, William J. Peters, departed from the northern base on Rudolf Island. He was accompanied by assistant scientist Robert Tafel and Anton Vedoe's brother John. They assembled the canoe that had been built in three sections and packed it with all of the expedition's scientific instruments and the record of continuous observations carried out during the previous ten months at the astronomical observatory above Teplitz Bay.

The three men paddled south from Teplitz Bay on Friday, July 8. "The canoe," John Vedoe wrote, "though heavy loaded proved a good sea boat, except when the waves struck us from the side when we felt that she was not as rigid as a one-piece boat."[311] By clinging to the shorelines to keep the winds from blowing the overloaded canoe out to sea, the men reached Cape Norvegia one week later, where they eventually crossed over to one of the expedition's caches that had been left on an islet in British Channel.

While paddling the three miles out to the islet, Vedoe noticed that the thumb screws holding together the first and second sections of the canoe had broken off, "causing [them] to give some every time a swell struck her; not so much, however, as to cause alarm, but it would not be very agreeable if any of the sections would part company with us at any time."[312]

At the cache, the men reinforced the bolts that held the canoe together, and then had to act quickly to keep their tent from being destroyed when the cooking stove caught fire. Keeping an eye out for Hartt and his expected appearance in his makeshift steam launch, the trio carefully made their way down the eastern side of British Channel, doubling back on the route that the *America* had taken to reach Teplitz Bay nearly a year earlier. On July 21, they came across a small cache of ruined supplies near Cape Alice Armitage, one that Vedoe hoped might be a remnant of the Andrée expedition but which proved to be leftovers from Frederick Jackson.

Taking two of Jackson's paddles to replace their own worn sticks, the men followed open water as much as possible before coming into an area clogged with ice. Like his brother Anton, John Vedoe possessed an enthusiasm for the occasional joy embedded within the hard work in the cold and wet:

> Where we passed open stretches we paddled for all we were worth and made the spray fly around the bow, and how contented we were when we thus sped along without interruption and watched the ghostly icebergs as they loomed up ahead and disappeared behind us; to me it seemed even a bit fascinating, this race with fog and ice, and good it felt to feel the warm blood travel down the legs, diffuse itself into the feet and out into the very toe-tips, which members had been tired out over the floe and soaked in the icy pools through the hours.[313]

The men arrived at Eaton Island on August 4, 1904, after paddling through icy waters past walrus and narwhals and, when necessary, dragging the canoe over fields of ice. At Eaton Island, they found the cache of supplies Fiala had laid down on the island as the expedition advanced up British Channel in 1903 and set up a camp of their own.

Looking out over the mass of moving ice in DeBruyne Sound, Peters wisely decided that it was too dangerous to risk the nearly twenty-nautical-mile crossing to Camp Point on Northbrook Island, especially with the canoe loaded with the expedition's instruments for recording magnetic anomalies.[314] Peters had the men cache the instruments at the southern point of the island and waited for DeBruyne Sound to be clear of ice.

They waited nearly three weeks. Finally, in despair, the men reloaded the canoe and pushed it into DeBruyne Sound. It was a daring crossing and took Peters and his companions five full days. John Vedoe, for once, was not enthusiastic at their prospects, both because they understood that there was now little likelihood of a relief ship in 1904, and that the supplies at Cape Flora, shared out among perhaps thirty men, would be a poor substitute for the relative luxuries of Camp Abruzzi at Teplitz Bay, "where there is plenty to eat and a good library."[315]

At Camp Point, the men cached the canoe and their field gear and walked over the intervening glacier to the men at Cape Flora. There they delivered the news of the death of Sigurd Myhre at Camp Abruzzi on May 16.

With the death of Myhre and the retreat of the Peters and Porter parties, the number of men who remained at the northern base at Camp Abruzzi at Teplitz Bay had shrunk to just five: the Chief Engineer Henry Hartt, the Norwegian carpenter Peter Tessem, the assistant commissary Spencer Stewart, and two sailors from the *America,* William Myers and Elijah Perry.

Throughout the winter and spring of 1904, Hartt had been busy transforming one of the expedition's whaleboats into a steam launch. As soon as the *America* was blown to the bottom of Teplitz Bay, the resulting shortage of coal meant Hartt's jury-rigged boiler could not be used to electrify the expedition house. Hartt immediately took the engine apart and began reassembling it for another purpose.

As Seitz wrote just four days after the loss of the ship: "Hartt took his engine apart today. He says he is going to arrange to burn kerosene when he puts the engine in one of the whaleboats."[316] By mid-February, as Seitz had observed, Hartt had cast the blades for the launch's propeller using some blue clay that cropped out in back of the supply tent and a crucible left behind at the site by the Italian expedition.[317]

A month later, after the failure of the two attempts on the North Pole and the sudden rush to retreat to Cape Flora, the chief engineer redoubled his efforts to build the launch. Hartt realized that his survival during a sledge trip back to Cape Flora was an uncertain proposition. He also began to recruit someone to go with him. As Seitz wrote in early April, "Hartt says Hovlick [a fireman from Trondheim] is going with him in the launch during the summer. Hartt is now working on the boiler for the launch. He says Fiala has given up the summer trip North in the steam launch."[318]

Hartt finished the boiler for the steam launch and had the engine ready to burn kerosene by mid-April. He was so pleased with his handiwork that he began to entertain delusions of grandeur himself, although these were likely given off as taunts to Coffin as much as anything else. As Seitz

"How I Discovered H. P. Hartt Land, by H. P. Hartt, C.E., Z.P.E., etc."
A cartoon from Fiala's *Arctic Eagle* newspaper. The chief engineer is seen
sleeping happily in the steam launch he created from leftovers from the Duke
of the Abruzzi's expedition, tied up at the Baldwin cache at Cape Auk, while
one of dogs tries to warn of approaching polar bears. Hartt did take his steam
launch on a remarkable foray around the archipelago in the summer of 1904.
Fiala claimed that Hartt threw the boiler overboard somewhere in British
Channel. From Anthony Fiala, *Fighting the Polar Ice* (New York: Doubleday,
Page & Company, 1906).

recorded, "[Hartt] says he intends to leave here for Cape Flora in early Aug.
with Hovlick & Peters. He also says he intends to beat the ship's record."[319]

At first, Seitz observed, Fiala himself was taken with the idea of using a
steam launch to explore the archipelago or even to stage a mid-summer dash
in the direction of the North Pole. Such intrepid ideas had preoccupied the
American exploration of Franz Josef Land ever since Walter Wellman failed
to bring such a craft into the islands in the summer of 1898. Evelyn Briggs
Baldwin, who bitterly criticized Wellman for this failure, did purchase a

steam launch for his expedition, but Hartt had found it to be worthless when he tried to get it to work in the spring of 1902.

Fiala himself soon soured on any plan to use the steam launch for polar exploration. Like Baldwin, he had little knowledge of engineering or water-craft, so he would be completely dependent for any such voyage on the expertise of Hartt to keep the machine running. And the idea of Hartt, the jovial, profane, hard-drinking banjo player, using a jury-rigged steam launch to beat the *America*'s farthest north—to say nothing of Fiala's own pitiful efforts by sledge—was too much.

When Hovlick left with "the homeseekers" and Peters decided to journey south with Tafel and John Vedoe in the sectional canoe, Hartt was left at Teplitz Bay with his steam launch. With no expedition commander or even a second-in-command, Hartt was suddenly the senior expedition member at Camp Abruzzi. As he later wrote to Shorkley, he also morosely realized that he would "have to take my blankets on my back [to Cape Flora] as I am one of the outcasts."[320]

Before that eventuality, Hartt decided to test his steam launch. He left Teplitz Bay on July 19, 1904, accompanied by Elijah Perry. The two men returned one month later, on August 18. Hartt wrote to Shorkely that he had managed to drive the steam launch all the way to Camp Ziegler, some 100 nautical miles to the south, and even another seven miles south of it, most likely in the direction of Cape Dillon, from which point any prudent expedition to Franz Josef Land would be on the lookout for a relief ship. Hartt promised Shorkley a copy of his chronicle of the trip, one that he called *The Voyage of the Steam Launch America*.

An edition of the *Arctic Eagle* printed on December 26, 1904, made light of Hartt's journey. It featured a tongue-in-cheek notice of publication of the account of the voyage (in two volumes, price: five dollars). An illustra-tion showed Hartt and Perry asleep on the steam launch, the launch tied by a painter to the "EBB cache" at Cape Auk. One of the dogs was also on board, tugging on the launch's steam whistle. The expedition history was entitled *How I Discovered H. P. Hartt Land,* by H. P. Hartt, C.E., Z.P.E., M.A.C.W.D.W.A.U. The civil engineer (C.E.) of the Ziegler Polar Expedition (Z.P.E.) was straightforward enough. But the meaning of the remainder of the letters, playing off the pomposity of author titles from weighty two-volume expedition accounts of nineteenth-century expeditions, is lost, along with the original tale itself. Other illustrations showed Hartt first in line at a still (labeled "XXX") that he had constructed, while another showed him retrieving a box of tobacco from the seemingly bottomless pile of supplies left behind at Teplitz Bay by the Duke of the Abruzzi.

No copy of Hartt's narrative survives in Shorkley's papers, or in any of the several surviving diaries of the expedition. In his published account of the expedition, Fiala devoted a single paragraph to Hartt's exploit, one that allowed a few more sparing details on the voyage. According to Fiala, Hartt was "in the British Channel [when] he almost lost the boat and had to throw the boiler overboard to save the launch."[321]

Like much of the American exploration of Franz Josef Land, the Ziegler Polar Expedition was sadly bereft of any humor. This makes the loss of Hartt's account of his remarkable journey all the more to be regretted. The story of the *ad hoc* jaunt through the islands in a makeshift steam launch in the summer of 1904, written with all of Hartt's endearing and self-deprecating sarcasm, would be worth its weight in gold.

FIFTY

A Profound Feeling of Gratitude
for My Dogs

On July 10 Seitz climbed the talus slope behind Cape Flora and saw open, ice-free water as far as the eye could see. Expecting to see William Champ at the bow of their relief ship at any moment, the men anxiously awaited the moment when they would gain some relief from a diet of the fried polar bear now served at each and every meal.

Porter and his party of Rilliet and Anton Vedoe lasted only a few days in Elmwood before the constant bickering drove them to set up their tent at the base of the talus. Always the aloof artist, Porter wrote that he "found no occasion to join in this antagonism, finding sufficient occupation in carrying on my work and obeying my commander. . . . [I] obtained permission to live in my own tent, where I could be quiet and work up my field notes."[322]

When a rockslide from the talus slope nearly killed them all on the morning of July 12, Vedoe and Rilliet claimed the observatory hut from Frederick Jackson's expedition. As Seitz recorded: "Jackson's old observatory (our tool shop & near where Pierre cleans hides) was moved farther back nearer the cliffs near the *Ermak* sign. Rilliet & Anton are putting in bunks for themselves."[323]

When a storm destroyed Porter's tent on July 16, he clung to its shreds until the last moment, "hoping I might be able to avail myself of the fresh air and independence that living under canvas gives," but when the rains came and soaked his entire kit, he was reluctantly forced to move back into Elmwood.[324] He did not stay long. The constant arguments there nearly drove him insane. But the last straw was when one of the men tried to harm Bismark, the leader of Porter's dogs.

> For whatever contemptible and ungrateful actions one encounters with human beings above the Arctic Circle, a person never leaves this region, who has had any experience with them, without a profound feeling of gratitude for his dogs. The life of suffering they must lead, their constant willingness to slave in their harness for you, together with the almost human affection and faithfulness they show to their master—all these traits endear them to a man up here far beyond what one might realize in civilization. And when I saw a fellow the other night pick up a rock as big as his fist with the apparent intention of killing or maiming Bismark, my leader, and who slunk away when he discovered that I was watching his cowardly action, surreptitiously parting from the stone at an opportune moment, do you wonder I feel like stamping brute on the man instead of the dogs?[325]

Porter asked for and received Fiala's permission to create a new camp, on the other side of Northbrook Island, where he could sketch and shoot walrus and, for all intents and purposes, be left alone with his dogs.

The view of Elmwood from Little Italy was much the same, as Seitz recorded on July 21:

> After breakfast Fiala came over & said they needed to burn our coal at the Sailors' Home [Elmwood]. The talk drifted to the general management of Camp & Vaughn [sic] gave Fiala some plain truths about his weakness of character. The Capt. is running him, the boats & so forth. Porter, Butland & Mackiernan have camped out at the open water with a dog team. Porter has had several scraps with Nichols, the Capt. & so forth & has enough of the daily scrapping in the Sailors' Home. From reports, the sailors cursed the ship's officers to their faces & they are continually growling at us & everybody else.[326]

Butland and Mackiernan joined Porter, and Seitz dubbed the new, third subdivision of the expedition "Camp Pacific," in contrast to the bifurcated chaos at Cape Flora. Porter himself affectionately referred to it as "Peace Point." No doubt to Porter's dismay, several other men seeking to escape from the nightmare of collapsed leadership at Cape Flora soon followed him to Camp Pacific/Peace Point. Coffin was disgusted at his abandonment by so many of his sailors, and soon wandered over to the new camp to see what the fuss was all about. "I went down to the point yesterday. They are situated all right with tents raised on rocks with a board bottom to each of the two. Mr. Porter seems to be King and his subjects seem to like him. I fancy he does not care for company as Mr. Haven & I, as he was barely civil to us in the way of talk. . . . This was a good sample of how big we are in our own minds."[327]

For his part, Porter, before he left Elmwood, recorded a telling anecdote of how the men felt about Coffin. "This morning when [the captain] took down his ham tin, which he hangs up by the stove pipe, and which he uses for a wash basin, he found something very bad in it which I cannot describe, for I did not see it. But as he told me at the top of his voice, 'As big as my fist, and I would give twenty-five dollars to know who did it.'"[328]

Whichever man thought to put a lump of feces in the captain's washing tin, the episode encapsulated life at Cape Flora in the summer of 1904. Fiala, a man of titanic faith but equally large inadequacies when it came to leading men, had by the end of the summer thrown up his hands: "The unlettered and uncultured man is coarse in his selfishness, while the man of education has learned to conceal his baser instincts under a mask of seeming modesty and virtue; but in the end it is a toss up as to which is the worse."[329]

The division of food and the use of the boats to hunt walrus were the sources of a series of blazing rows, as Fiala now accused the scientists of Little Italy of turning against him even before the expedition had reached Teplitz Bay. For their part, the men of Little Italy demanded that Fiala explicitly write out each and every one of his instructions, as his verbal orders could be understood by no one. When Fiala did so, the men of the Field Department promptly sent the order back, via Truden, and informed Fiala they would not accept it. Anton Vedoe, patiently working on an improved stove to heat the hut that he shared with Rilliet, was flabbergasted at the situation: "Whoever heard of men saying they would not accept an order by their commander!"[330]

As the days passed without any sign of a relief ship, the constant tension pushed the men to the verge of madness. Truden, the source of so much hostility during the march from Teplitz Bay, now made a sudden and bizarre about-face and made up with Fiala, to general disapprobation, as Seitz recorded. "Truden at present spends almost all of his spare time at the Sailors' Home making love to Fiala, to the disgust of both parties."[331]

On July 29, it was Seitz's day to collect on his bet if the relief ship arrived. It did not, and so he did not. He had a brief moment of excited hope at the appointed hour when Francis Long called out that a ship was coming from the east, but it was another false alarm. The men began to count the number of weeks left that they could rely on the canned food from the cache left behind by the Duke of the Abruzzi. Seitz figured that they had about eleven weeks remaining.

As July came and went, it was increasingly clear that no ship was coming for them in 1904. On July 31 Vedoe sat in the sun and enjoyed a cigarette "while my dogs were playing around me. No ship in sight yet."[332] And Seitz wrote on August 1: "We all have about given up for the relief ship getting here this year."[333]

Still, on every day when the weather allowed it, Seitz climbed the talus slope, to scan the southern horizon and gauge the nature of the shifting ice around Cape Flora. Otherwise, he played cards, hunted for fossils, and scavenged through the ruins of Leigh Smith's stone hut for souvenirs. "This afternoon hunted around Leigh Smith's hut—found a lot of water-soaked tour charts & part of a book on surgery."[334] The following day, another man found Leigh Smith's chart of Spitsbergen, one that marked out the routes of the Victorian explorer's daring cruises there in the 1870s.

Like Porter, Anton Vedoe tried his best to avoid the lassitude and poison of "the homeseekers." He worked with Rilliet as they fashioned a new stove for their hut and then, at the request of Fiala, took over tidal observations from Moulton when the sergeant simply stopped making them. He captured an Arctic fox alive and intended to take it home with him. To protect it from the dogs, he made a cage on top of his hut and would climb into the talus each day in search of fledgling birds to feed it, since it refused to eat walrus or bear meat.

On July 19, a day Vedoe described with his typical enthusiasm as "glorious," the temperature rose to 54°F and Vedoe and Rilliet took the chance to climb to the top of the talus slope behind Cape Flora: "A very hard and dangerous climb. We had to cut our way in the nearly perpendicular ice wall for long distance. From the top we had a good view in all directions. Miers

Anton Vedoe's discovery of coal high above Cape Flora, while he was out in search of young birds to feed to his pet fox, changed the fortunes of the "homeseekers." From Anthony Fiala, *Fighting the Polar Ice* (New York: Doubleday, Page & Company, 1906).

Channel is clear of ice up to Camp Point and Gunter [Günther] Bay is cleared out. The ice is closed in as far as we could see in all directions south."[335]

Vedoe continued to climb into the slopes behind Cape Flora when the weather allowed, and these trips to find food for his infant fox gave him the chance to study the behaviors of the auks, loons, and guillemots that nested in the rocks. They also led to one of the most significant discoveries of the expedition, when Vedoe redeemed an increasingly demoralized situation on August 14. As Porter had done on Coal Mine Island, Vedoe now spotted a seam of coal in the talus above Cape Flora. Not even Frederick Jackson in his three years at the site had made this discovery.

The fuel situation, increasingly dire in the days and weeks previous, was now solved for the winter. Here, at least, the entire camp was in agreement. Porter called the find a "godsend,"[336] and Coffin himself went to inspect

the "fine vein of coal. . . . So the great question of coal has been settled."[337] The men began to mine over a ton of coal a day from the seam, rolling it down the talus slope in large bags made from sealskins.

The weather had been turning against the men throughout early August, with heavy snows and winds. On August 7 Long had climbed the slope behind the cape and saw the ice packed tight on the southern horizon. Fiala and one of the sailors, Duffy, left on August 10 to construct a signal cairn at Cape Barents on the eastern end of Northbrook Island. They returned four days later, having seen not a trace of any relief ship.

Coffin scoffed at the men in the talus, and at Fiala and his signal beacon. "Simply because water is in sight they all think that the relief ship ought to come in. . . . Tis rather tiring to be in the same room and hear so much nonsense." On August 20 Coffin gave up any hope that Champ would get through to them in 1904. "I think [the rescuers believe] that the *America* is lost. That the crew [has survived] at Cape Flora, I do not think has entered any of their heads."[338]

Coffin was wrong. What he should have known—and what the other men could not know—was that the Norwegian vessel *Frithjof* had made every effort to find Fiala and his men in the summer of 1904. William Ziegler, after investing his money and his name in two massive expeditions, was not about to be held responsible for the loss of so many lives. He had sent William Champ to Norway, where Champ had chartered the *Frithjof* in mid-summer and was desperately trying to reach the expedition.

The *Frithjof* made two attempts to bash through the ice in 1904, at one point being stopped only 40 nautical miles south of Cape Flora. It is entirely likely that the smoke some of the men claimed to have seen on the southern horizon was arising from *Frithjof*'s stack. But, in the end, the ship was forced to return to Norway. As Champ wrote, "owing to the almost unprecedented heaviness of the ice . . . we were unable to connect with [Fiala] or reach land. A most careful watch was kept aboard *Frithjof* both night and day for any sign of the expedition, but nothing whatever was found during the entire period which we spent in the ice."[339]

Still, Champ, as Ziegler's representative, was convinced that the expedition was fine, "thoroughly equipped and [with] an abundance of food. In addition to what they carried last year, they have additional large stores to fall back on in case of necessity in several camps or depots in Franz Josef Archipelago. In addition to the food, they are thoroughly equipped to kill game."[340] What neither Champ nor Ziegler foresaw—but should have, given their experience with the Baldwin expedition—was that the expedition had been split by poor leadership and was at that moment dividing and sub-dividing into multiple factions.

As the summer of 1904 ended and it became clear that the expedition would have to endure another winter in Franz Josef Land, the resentments of the men turned to deep depression and bitter despair. Individuals in one group refused to speak with individuals in another group—and at times even with others within their own group—and precious few listened any longer to the expedition commander. Whether literally or figuratively, men of all ranks and stripes began to find lumps in their wash tins.

A prolonged fight broke out between Fiala and Shorkley over control of the remaining liquor. Shorkley threatened to resign as expedition surgeon if anyone except himself had control over the stock, as he had no desire to witness the captain go off on a winter-long bender. Fiala announced that the liquor would be under the control of his representative, subject to Shorkley's prescriptions. Shorkley again resigned, and once more Fiala refused to accept. Shorkley wrote out a longer bill of particulars and again submitted it to Fiala. Fiala said he would think about it, then, as was typical for Fiala when faced with a stubborn malcontent, he relented. Shorkley immediately took possession of the alcohol and retained his position as expedition surgeon.

Even the rock-steady Anton Vedoe began to question the expedition commander. When it still appeared that a ship might appear, Fiala began to expound on the orders he had given to Peters with regard to where Peters should situate himself when the relief ship arrived. Vedoe was stupefied. "It is absolutely impossible for me to understand how he can make such statements not knowing what time the ship would reach here. . . . Nor can I understand why he does not look for the ship at other points, seeing [that it is] impossible for a ship to get up here [to Cape Flora]. It might possibly have gotten through to the eastward to Cape Dillon or that neighborhood and might possibly have reached Camp Ziegler."[341]

Francis Long, who had seen it all before with Adolphus Greely, had no desire to live through the same torture again. "Long has given up hope of the ship & has spoken to Fiala about starting to Nova Zembla with 2 men & a canoe to take out news."[342]

The supplies of sugar and milk were gone by the end of August, at about the same time that the sailors of Elmwood announced that they had enough coal from the talus slope for themselves and promptly stopped working. Even so, Anton Vedoe's discovery of coal, while he was out in search of young birds to feed to his pet fox, changed the fortunes of the men at Cape Flora. Likewise, Porter and his men at "Peace Point" had killed more than a dozen walrus and a like number of polar bears, along with several hundred birds. Coffin estimated the total weight of meat that could now be shared out over the winter among the men and dogs at over ten tons.

When added to the great quantity of supplies left behind by the Duke of the Abruzzi, the men at Cape Flora would be warm and fed over the winter of 1904–1905. The problem now was that few men wished to remain at Cape Flora for one minute longer.

FIFTY-ONE

The Memory of a Satiated Desire

When it became clear that no relief ship was coming in 1904, the Ziegler Polar Expedition split into a bewildering number of small parties with no clear leadership. Between September 1904 and July 1905, these groups—all as anxious to be away from the chaos of Cape Flora as they were to be rescued and often working at cross-purposes to one another—tracked and backtracked almost the entire length and breadth of the Franz Josef Land archipelago.

By the end of the summer of 1904, Fiala himself wanted to get away from Cape Flora as quickly as he could. He told the men that he intended to make another attempt on the North Pole in the spring of 1905 and, sadly, would be able to bring only a select few men back with him to Teplitz Bay. Peters, the nominal second-in-command, used the excuse that he wanted to return to his astronomical observations at Camp Abruzzi. With Mackiernan and Anton Vedoe, Peters made his escape on September 19, saying good-bye to no one.

Russell Porter, desperate to get back in the field and away from "the home-seekers," was mortified when Fiala asked him to take charge of the men at Cape Flora. Porter was suffering from a painful bout of neuralgia in his jaw and "protest[ed] at this plan on the grounds that I did not feel myself competent to deal with the situation here (a very grave one); that there were older and wiser heads who could do it better, and that I deemed it my privilege to be at his side if he made another attempt over the Polar Sea next spring."343

Fiala relented, and then split the leadership of the expedition even further. He first placed Charles Rilliet in overall charge of the affairs of the expedition at Cape Flora. When the men of the two houses complained, he asked Francis Long to take charge of the men of Little Italy and Captain Coffin of the men of Elmwood. Fiala, along with Porter, Seitz, Rilliet, and three men from the *America,* the steward Bernard Spencer, a sailor, John Duffy, and the cabin boy, James Dean, then left Cape Flora on the morning of September 27. They left behind twenty-three of "the homeseekers," split into their two implacable camps at Little Italy and Elmwood.

Fiala's party reached Camp Point that same evening, where they found a note from Peters that informed them that Peters' party had only gotten away across DeBruyne Sound that very morning. If Fiala was perturbed that Peters had sat at Camp Point for nine days without sending a runner to so inform Fiala at Cape Flora, he never let on. Now, the same late summer conditions in the sound—too warm for the ice to freeze solid to allow sledge travel and too cold for the waterway to be free of moving ice to allow for a boat crossing—conspired to keep Fiala pinned at Camp Point until mid-October, as he refused to return to the festering mess at Cape Flora. Like Peters before him, he had no intention of turning around, "for I did not intend to return to Cape Flora no matter what came."[344]

On October 17, as daylight rapidly diminished, Fiala knew that he had to risk the crossing. It meant that at least one night would be spent sleeping on the shifting, twisting ice, and it also meant reducing the size of his party if the lone canoe was to hold them all. Realizing the predicament that his commander was in, Russell Porter selflessly albeit highly reluctantly volunteered to return to Cape Flora for the winter—but only if he could come north to Camp Abruzzi the moment that the sun reappeared after the winter, in order to accompany Fiala on the planned attempt on the North Pole in the spring of 1905.

Fiala, massively relieved that he did not have to face "the homeseekers" again, responded by dividing authority yet again, and created Porter as "third in command" of the expedition behind Fiala and Peters—both of whom had now abandoned the men at Cape Flora to their aggressive misery. With five dogs and a single kayak, Porter would be joined by the former cabinboy of the *America,* James Dean, along with two other men who would gather more supplies for Fiala and immediately return to the northern party.

Sixteen nautical miles of moving ice separated Fiala on Northbrook Island from his objective on Hooker Island. The two men who had gone with Porter to Cape Flora did not return until October 20. The next day—the start of six months of darkness in the archipelago—Fiala finally started his crossing of DeBruyne Sound, along with four men, three sledges pulled by twenty-seven dogs, the canoe, and a kayak. One of the dogs wandered off and could not be caught, so it was left behind. Scouting the way ahead, the ice gave way beneath Fiala and he fell into the sound up to his shoulders. When Duffy and Seitz finally pulled him out, he "had the rather unpleasant experience of disrobing on an ice cake to put on a complete change of dry clothing."[345] For Fiala, it was a small price to pay to get away from the men at Cape Flora.

The party made camp on the ice and found their way to Hooker Island the next day. There they settled on the rocks above a cache of supplies called "Old Depot." The next morning, after one of the dogs cut the pad of its paw and was released to its fate, the men struggled across the island. On the morning of October 26, Seitz woke up too early, and made breakfast for himself at 3 A.M. When he awoke again around seven, he made coffee and went out to harness the dogs for the day's march across the glaciers of Hooker Island: "Very cold work harnessing the dogs as the harness is frozen hard & stiff the result of all the rain & wet snow at Camp Point. Broke camp at 9 A.M. & made several miles through deep snow drifts."[346]

Rilliet was leading the way, breaking a trail through the snow, but at noon Fiala grew impatient and tried to take a short cut across the island. He promptly stepped onto a crevasse covered with fresh snow and plunged to his armpits. Bernard Spencer rushed to Fiala's aid and, as he grabbed him by the wrist at the edge of the crevasse, felt the snow give way. Both men fell into the crevasse and disappeared.

Seitz ran to the edge and shouted that he would get a line down to them as quickly as possible. Fiala, who devoted an entire chapter to the incident—without mentioning that he broke protocol and went ahead of Rilliet—wrote that he "began a frightful descent and knew no more. . . . I was entombed in ice. I found myself wedged between two curves in the walls of the crevasse. . . . Beneath me was a great black void in which I could move my legs without touching the walls."[347]

Both Fiala and Spencer were in shock:

Spencer was making a great deal of noise crying & lamenting & appeared to be completely unmanned. We tied together 3 lengths of rope & proceeded to get them out. We lost considerable time before

Fiala could or would be drawn up for he would shout all kinds of things for us to do & we would shout back for one of them to fasten themselves & be drawn up. . . . Finally we got Fiala to start up. It was very hard work to lift him as the rope cut deeply into the side of the crevasse. When he arrived . . . his pulse was very weak, face pale, hands cool, & he was barely able to stand & to talk. We then hauled up Spencer with little trouble & dragged him out, helpless but making much noise.[348]

Fiala attributed their salvation to nothing less than divine intervention, suspended as they had been between the sun above and the dark icy abyss below. They were dragged back to their self-created purgatory, where the temperatures had dropped to −27°F. Seitz stripped each man and examined their injuries. Spencer, having suffered a nasty gash in his head that required stitches, was "continually crying, & sobbing, whining & moaning, & had lost complete control over himself—apparently more from fear than from the shock of the injury. Fiala . . . would occasionally faint partly away—being in a drowsy, stuperous condition, replying to questions in a slow mumbling manner. He was injured much less than Spencer but suffered more from shock while Spencer was suffering more from the mental effects of the accident & was completely unnerved."[349]

The next morning, the men strapped Spencer to a sledge and descended the glacier back to the edges of British Channel. The ice conditions were horrific, but at least offered relief from the crevasses of the interior glaciers. By October 29, five weeks after their first departure from Cape Flora, the men struggled into West Camp Ziegler on Alger Island.

An hour and a half later they had covered the six miles to Baldwin's old main camp at East Camp Ziegler. There they were greeted by the Peters party, which itself had managed to reach the site only four days ahead of Fiala. With one of his men, Seaman Mackiernan, suffering from frostbite, Peters was planning to winter on Alger Island. Fiala's arrival was met by a storm that blew for five days and kept all the men pinned inside the old base camp.

Fiala now had three completely disparate groups of men scattered throughout the archipelago: Hartt and his four companions at the northern outpost at Teplitz Bay on Rudolf Island, the eight men of the Peters and Fiala parties at Camp Ziegler on Alger Island, and the twenty-five miserable men at Cape Flora on Northbrook Island. With the death of Sigurd Myhre and the near-catastrophe on the glacier of Hooker Island, the expedition as it headed into the winter of 1904–1905 had every possibility to tip over into a disaster of massive proportions.

The difficulties of Peters's and Fiala's parties in reaching Alger Island were those of men against nature. At Cape Flora, Russell Porter arrived to find the struggles of man on fellow man that he had tried so hard to avoid. Delivering the letter from Fiala that named him third-in-command of the expedition and officer in charge of Cape Flora during Fiala's absence, Porter wrote that he was immediately confronted by Colin Vaughan: "'Third in command, eh? [Expletive], I don't recognize you as third in command and I don't recognize Long in charge of us [in Little Italy]; for that matter I don't recognize Fiala himself' and a lot more disagreeable language I do not care to set down.'"[350] Captain Coffin, still jealously guarding his prerogatives within Elmwood and over the crew of the *America,* was hardly less equivocal: "I informed Mr. Porter he could give no orders to any of my men and I could in no way consider him as having any sort of command over any of my officers or crew. Told him I never was under Mr. Fiala. He replied that he wished . . . to do astronomical work and did not consider himself as being here to give orders. . . . He is staying here in this house with the steamer's crew (and he is welcome) as a guest, but with no power to govern, as Fiala wanted. . . . Mr. Fiala needs to be taught a lesson in many things."[351]

The paranoid captain was convinced that Fiala had sent Porter to spy on him throughout the winter. Porter, for the life of him, wanted nothing so much as to be left alone to observe nature and continue with his sketching. But the mood in the camp, one that continued throughout the winter, was hostile and dark. Even the noxious crank Shorkley, without Fiala around to criticize, had ceased his medical diary in early autumn and sank into a prolonged depression.

On the eve of his thirty-third birthday in mid-December, Porter himself wrote that he had been "getting rather morose, and ruminating over the effect of this Arctic business upon my life, blasting all my prospects for a successful business career, aging me beyond all natural bounds and bringing nothing but the memory of a satiated desire. My hair is rapidly falling out, my eyesight becoming defective more and more and my teeth fast going to pieces."[352] To add to his misery, just as Evelyn Briggs Baldwin had peered through a hole in his tent at the actions of the Norwegians of the Wellman expedition in the fall of 1898, so did Porter now catch the captain stealing glimpses of him at work during the winter:

Across from my corner lies the Captain's [berth]. He is in an upper bunk, the curtain drawn nearly closed, but near his [head] he has hung a towel which he can drop in connection with the sliding curtain that an admirable peephole may be constructed through which he can see, unobserved, everything going on. . . . [Often at night I would think] myself able to open or close an eyelid without the whole house knowing it, when a slight movement of the curtain opposite would attract my attention, the peep hole would change its shape slowly in the dim light and a faint sound of mutterings or hoarse whispers would reach my ears. This would last some ten minutes or so, then the peep hole would close with a violent agitation of the towel, the mutterings would reach their climax and suddenly cease; and I would find myself thinking, "For God's sake, when will this end?"[353]

Even the scientific work—the dogged recording of geographic angles or astronomical tracks in the sky—largely ceased as the sad winter dragged on. When he had first arrived at Cape Flora in the summer, after the long trip with Anton Vedoe and Rilliet, Porter had felt a great sense of satisfaction at the summer's research. They had continued the mapping required to sort the confusion over Zichy Land, a geographic puzzle that had confounded the explorers of Franz Josef Land ever since the area was first misidentified by Payer and Weyprecht.

Porter and his team had also identified and mapped the great new harbor on Hooker Island on the north side of the peninsula of Rubini Rock, a feature that had been misidentified as an island by Frederick Jackson. It was not the complete mapping of the archipelago that Porter had dreamed of since he first saw the islands during the Baldwin expedition, but he was realistic enough to know that such an effort was vastly beyond his resources, if not his abilities. "The yield of geographical knowledge may be small, but original research is usually small compared to the amount of effort and time necessary to obtain it."[354]

Upon his return to Cape Flora in late October, Porter had set about to distance himself from the noise at the camp by building a new astronomical observatory out of snow, and then sitting by himself at a table in the corner of Elmwood to write up his field notes from the joyful journeys of the previous spring and summer. But the science, though it distracted him from the chaos of the men, was in the end a very cold comfort. At the observatory, "the Berger theodolite [was] set up as a transit instrument for strengthening the meridian already located last summer. But when a man is poorly clothed, and on short rations, work in low temperatures up here is very fatiguing and arduous, and one must have considerable enthusiasm to prosecute, with any successful results, scientific work."[355]

Even this effort was destroyed in December, at the same time Porter began a long-term fight with Colin Vaughan over his dogs. As he had written previously, his dogs—proven hard workers—had been under jealous attack ever since he returned to Cape Flora. In December, when his dogs began to fight over a female at Little Italy, Porter was forced to chain his dogs in the observatory, which now became a kennel.

> Tibus clawed his way through the snow walls the first night, bringing down one section of the light wooden shutters I had spent so much time to construct. Patching this up again, on another night he worked through the north wall bringing down the whole frame, shutters and all, in one hopeless wreck. This damage to the astronomical observatory could not be remedied, at least this winter, with the means at hand, but I arranged to use the lower section on the north side. Last night he ripped that out, after first pulling through his collar, and tore through again.[356]

In a space of little more than two hundred square feet, Porter and John Vedoe were surrounded with fifteen disgruntled officers and men of the lost steamship. A few yards away was the Little Italy hut with the problematic malcontents Truden, Vaughan, and Shorkley. With even his cold scientific solitude taken from him, Porter survived the winter largely through the benefit of his deafness—which shut out most of the poisonous chatter in both Elmwood and Little Italy—and by laboriously creating an illustrated deck of playing cards and an inlaid-ivory box in which to hold them. When the sailors expressed their fascination with Porter's carving and his watercolors and asked for his help with their own work, Coffin wasted little time in ridiculing both Porter's work and his own men.

Porter was also helped in his survival through a newly formed friendship with Francis Long, a man Coffin also continuously belittled throughout his journal. The veteran of the Greely catastrophe was a kindred spirit for Porter, as Long was perhaps the most experienced Arctic hand—with the possible exception of the singular Charles Francis Hall—in all of American polar exploration history. Porter and Long would take extended and satisfying walks across the frozen surface of an ice-covered pond near Cape Flora. "He has been through it before, at Cape Sabine with Greely," Porter wrote, "and he never seemed to worry [and] were it not for his steadfastness, I would feel quite at sea at this place."[357]

FIFTY-TWO

The Breaking of Winter's Back

Fiala remained stormbound at East Camp Ziegler until early November. On November 5, as he traveled across one of the most challenging landscapes on the planet in the perpetual dark of an Arctic winter, Fiala and five others—Peters, Seitz, Vedoe, Duffy, and the recovered Spencer—made their way via Kane Lodge toward Camp Abruzzi on the shore of Teplitz Bay. They camped on the first night under a brilliant aurora at Cape Trieste, a place of gigantic and mysterious rounded rock formations with a place-name derived from the Adriatic origin of so much of the crew of Weyprecht and Payer's *Tegetthoff.*

The next day, the men reached the treacherous area they referred to as "the Waterhole." It was this mad rush of waters that came together to form a vortex between Zichy Land and Wiener Neustadt Island that had been one of the first clues that Zichy Land was in fact a series of several islands. It was Evelyn Briggs Baldwin who had realized that the waterway named Cecil Rhodes Fjord during the Jackson-Harmsworth expedition was in fact a channel (Baldwin had tried, unsuccessfully, to rename it "Baldwin-Ziegler Polar Expedition Channel") that separated Salisbury and Ziegler islands. The channel's rushing waters crashed into the waters of Collinson Channel at a narrow neck between Salisbury and Wiener Neustadt islands, thus creating the Waterhole, a place Fiala likened to the Inferno.

Even in the dead of winter, the Waterhole refused to ice over, and the men—as they had done so many times during the Baldwin expedition—carefully made their way around it, and on to the glaciers of Wiener Neustadt. There they located their "Rookery Camp," where a blue Norwegian boat had been cached atop one of the horse sledges, now rendered immobile by the loss of all the ponies.

As they crossed to Greely Island and reached Kane Lodge on November 7, the men were relieved to find pemmican for the dogs and, even better, a bag of tobacco to relieve their nicotine withdrawals. The lodge was soon scraped clear of ice and a fire started in the stove. Fiala, for one, wanted to hunker down in the cozy hut for a while, but the men were having none of it. They wanted to get to Camp Abruzzi as rapidly as possible. As Seitz noted: "Fiala had intended to stay at Kane Lodge for some time giving as reasons: insufficient lights, open water to N. & that a S.E. gale was coming! But this day was so bright & clear, & Fiala was not supported by Peters as he expected, that he decided to leave tomorrow. Anton & I chopped up 6 cans of pemmican into 96 pieces for the trail."[358]

Throughout the journey in darkness to Camp Abruzzi, the men repeatedly overruled Fiala, who more often than not wanted to wait in camp for better conditions while the men wanted to "go ahead and take chances."[359] This theme—Fiala's enthusiasm to get on the trail and then his reluctance to move once on it—was repeated time and again throughout the expedition, and was only exacerbated by his narrow escape from the bottomless pit of ice at the crevasse on Hooker Island. With no allies left, Fiala turned to his faith. The winter voyage to Camp Abruzzi was "like a passage through the regions of torment" and "a wild, bad dream."[360]

For the men, like Seitz, Fiala had lost his way in more ways than one. He would continually lead the party off the trail to the north and have to be brought back upon it by Peters. Traveling in the dark along ice surfaces of uncertain thickness or stability would have tried anyone's nerves, and the men began to snap at one another. It is another indication of how badly the men wished to be away from the even worse conditions prevailing at Cape Flora that this unbelievably risky journey was undertaken at all.

The men and dogs reached Coburg Island on November 13, and Hohenlohe Island two days later. There, just a few miles south of Rudolf Island, a storm pinned them down for the better part of five days. Once again, during lulls in the storm, the men wanted to press on but Fiala held them back. As Anton Vedoe wrote: "It is very hideous to lay still like this for so long a time."[361]

The temperature hovered at −24°F and the warmth of the expedition house at Camp Abruzzi—to say nothing of Chief Engineer Hartt's alcohol still—beckoned. "The bags were very wet & sleeping in them was simply misery. We had about 5 meals daily & had flapjacks several times. On the evening of the 18th, likewise, the weather was good & the moon about but we did not start."[362]

The storm finally ceased on November 19, and the men raced across to Cape Brorok on Rudolf Island. They ascended the steep glacier above Cape Auk around midnight, where Seitz looked up to see a shooting star "bursting like a rocket" overhead. As they gained the heights of the Rudolf Island ice dome just after three in the morning on November 20, 1904, they saw a ship's light on the roof of the expedition house about a mile away. Hartt had rigged up the lantern to guide any party that might try to reach the northern base as they descended down into the camp from the glacier above Cape Auk.

The dogs, hearing their pack coming for them in the distance, began tearing at their harnesses. As Anton Vedoe wrote, the dogs "dash[ed] off in wild disorder. We had to jump [the sledges] for fear they might go over the side of the glacier."[363] The men of the northern journey in the dark were welcomed by the five men at the camp, whom Seitz found to be "fat & in good health." Unlike the men of dispirited "homeseekers" of Cape Flora, the small party that remained at Camp Abruzzi under the genial light touch of Henry Hartt had been busy, and had located more of the Duke of the Abruzzi's goodies.

> Camp in good order showing the result of lots of work. Bulkhead across living room; canvas stretched over ceiling; cook-stove in living room; entrance at S.W. straight out; old galley & adjacent space made a store-room for our provisions, mostly Duke's; other side (forecastle) a work-shop communicating with machine shop; then a storehouse (inner); an outer large storehouse with a large pile of coal, kerosene & provisions; & a good passageway leading to the water closet & stable. . . . Everything to be used is under cover & at hand. . . . In the Duke's tent [was] found a large quantity of provisions & other stores: as, candles, lamps, lamp chimneys, butter, cheese, sugar, jams, brandied cherries, puddings.[364]

At Camp Abruzzi, Fiala wrote that it "was good to sit at the table with my united band of happy men," one that was less than a third of the men he arrived to Teplitz Bay with fourteen months earlier.[365] Fiala learned that

Meyer and Perry had camped at Hohenlohe Island for nearly a month, from October 5 to November 1, in hopes of seeing a party coming in from the south and aiding them on their way to Rudolf Island.

The men celebrated another Thanksgiving on the shore above the bay, and Seitz took full advantage of the camp's library and a renewal of cribbage with Hartt. Anton Vedoe took some of the balloon cloth left behind by the Duke of the Abruzzi and pinned it above his bunk to keep out the moisture. When Fiala asked Hartt if he would mind taking the former room of Rilliet and Truden, Hartt objected, "telling him that the room in question went by the name of the C—k suckers room. It seemed to surprise him very much, said he had never heard it before, so of course I had to go and now I supposed I am classed as a sucker, but God knows I am far from it."[366] Hartt was no less favorably inclined toward Captain Coffin—he referred to him as "Windy" in his correspondence with Shorkley—and thought the verbose skipper would make a fine overseer of "a Peg House," a homosexual brothel.

If there was a bright spot, it was the camaraderie of the men who now found themselves a much-reduced band at Camp Abruzzi. For the first time in the entire expedition, the feelings seemed genuine. Vedoe celebrated his twenty-fourth birthday on December 17 and, as Seitz recorded, the practical jokes the men played on each other were creative and gentle and a far cry from the lumps of excrement being left in the men's wash basins at Cape Flora. "[Hartt] told Fiala he had the record left here by Abruzzi. I copied a lot of Italian on a sheet of paper & Hartt showed it to Fiala who really believed it & wants a typewritten copy of it. Hartt has promised to give it to him on Christmas."[367]

The cartoons illustrating Hartt's *How I Discovered H. P. Hartt Land* were published in a special Christmas edition of the *Arctic Eagle*. The chief engineer, who had earlier used part of the Italian balloon apparatus for a boiler for his steam yacht, used another piece as the main component of his still. He now brewed up a special Christmas ale in his jury-rigged steam-launch balloon still, and it was served with polar bear steak on the appointed day, as the temperature dropped to −53°F. The low record for the expedition was recorded a week later, on January 5, 1905: −60.2°F.

Fiala set the men to work on a renewed attempt on the North Pole in 1905. Vedoe began to rebuild the stoves that had failed badly on the attempts from the spring of 1904, while Meyer strengthened the sectional canoe and the sledges. But the attempt was not destined to be a serious one, as Fiala himself soon realized. "The smallness of my party, the lack of ponies, and the few dogs at my command, together with the necessity of providing a number of dogs to be used by my Camp Abruzzi party in transporting food supplies to Camp Ziegler, rendered it impossible for me to arrange for supporting parties to accompany me except for a short distance from land."[368]

Occupied by the continuous work of preparing for another polar dash, as well as the inevitable depressions of a second winter in such a place, the men's journals trickled down to just a few words each day. Seitz's diary, normally full of camp gossip, shrank to a daily list of the books he had read—he worked through a novel a day, along with histories of other polar expeditions—as well as the outside temperature and his cribbage scores with Hartt. Anton Vedoe's typically effusive entries were reduced to the temperatures, and his chore of the day, viz. "Repaired a hammer for a gun" (January 24); "Made a drill for drilling rock for Mr. Peters" (January 26); "Working on my fur pants" (February 3).

The diaries picked up a bit after the first hints of the return of the sun in late January. On January 27 Vedoe made his first substantial comments in over a month: "The noon sank down like a bloodied half-round disc in the direction of Cape Auk this morning."[369] Seitz treated Hartt's lumbago in January, and then applied silver nitrate to the chief engineer's painful anal fissure in February. In a letter to Shorkley in March, Hartt wrote that Seitz had "cut and burnt hell out of those parts."[370]

On Sunday, February 19, Fiala held a religious service and then announced the plan for the upcoming dash for the North Pole. It was hardly a serious plan to cover more than a thousand miles of polar pack ice. By February 1905, Fiala had lost 100 percent of his ponies, 73 percent of his dogs, and 75 percent of his men were at each other's throats at Cape Flora. He told the men at Camp Abruzzi that a party of seven men would depart across Rudolf Island in mid-March. Two of these men would return to Camp Abruzzi after just two days, and then another three would return after five days. Fiala would then continue on with only John Duffy and three teams of dogs. If Porter arrived before the party departed, he would be allowed to continue on with another man. On February 27 Vedoe rigged a lantern atop the expedition house and kept it burning continuously, as a beacon to guide in Russell Porter.

As for Porter himself, his interminable winter at Cape Flora could not come to an end fast enough. Porter had planned to link with Fiala at Teplitz Bay on March 10, and to do so he would proceed via the old Baldwin base on Alger Island, a journey of some 200 nautical miles in extreme conditions.

Porter could not wait to leave. The "homeseekers" had just about driven him mad. "With the breaking of winter's back my thoughts centered on the trip I must prepare for [and it] didn't look any too good [as] I was scarcely fit for severe exposure after so long a diet on short rations."[371]

Four of his five dogs had come through the winter, but only Bismark had survived without any injuries. With only four healthy dogs and with the men of Little Italy denying him any surplus food for the dogs or rations for himself, Porter would be able to take only one man with him. With his preferred sledging partner Anton Vedoe already at Teplitz Bay, Porter chose George Duncan Butland, one of the firemen from the crew of the *America*. Butland "was a native of Newfoundland [and] had spent a winter with the Esquimaux of Northern Greenland, and could take care of himself in a tight place."[372]

While they would take along a tent, Porter had grown tired of the flimsy silk tents that were easily torn apart by high winds, so before the trip he and Butland experimented with building Inuit-style igloos. They got to the point where they could put up an igloo in forty minutes. The lack of dogs and extra rations meant they would have to leave the kayak behind. They would be able to cross no open water.

They got away from Cape Flora at the first possible moment, sledging away into the darkness on February 20. For the first four days, the changeable weather made for uneven progress as they traveled by way of Camp Point to DeBruyne Sound. They tried to cross the sound in one go but a storm pinned them on the ice for several days. When they finally reached solid ground on Hooker Island, they had put 40 nautical miles between themselves and Cape Flora but had only a few days' worth of food rations remaining.

Each night they slept in an igloo, which both men found a vast improvement over the expedition's tents. At their first camp on Hooker Island, they brought the dogs into the igloo and watched as drifting snow poured down on top of them. Finally they had to break out of the top of the igloo and build a new one closer to the shore ice. At the last moment, Porter stuck a ski in the top of the first igloo as a marker.

The next day, the two men returned to the first igloo to dig out their sledge, but could find it nowhere. Not even the ski could be seen, as no less than *fifteen feet* of snow had drifted on top of their sledge and former abode, burying both. Worse, their only shovel was on the sledge. They went back to their camp along the shore to make tea and think the situation over. They had barely enough food to reach the nearest Baldwin cache, one that Porter remembered being placed on an island nearby some four years earlier and that he estimated to be about twenty nautical miles distant. The dogs were nearly out of food and the men themselves were barely in condition to survive such a trip, emerging as they were from a winter on half rations at Elmwood.

Their course was decided for them by a consideration of the first alternative: a retreat to Cape Flora. Both men shared Butland's feelings: "If you're thinking of turning back to that hell at Cape Flora, I'll take chances and go on alone."[373] Then, suddenly, their fortunes changed. A mother polar bear with a cub wandered into their camp and both were shot, providing food for the men and the dogs. With no sledge, they bundled their gear into the tent and turned up the frozen tip of the tent to improvise a toboggan, and moved on.

For a week, the two men struggled only a few miles per day across Allan Young Sound, to a rocky islet named Jeaffreson Island. When they finally reached it on March 2, the men and dogs were exhausted, moving forward only on the strength of a four-year-old memory of Porter's that he had seen food landed in the area in 1901. He told Butland to look for yellow boxes and, miraculously, within a few minutes they had found them, signaled by three inches of an emergency ration box sticking out of the snow. They immediately built an igloo on the spot, one they had to rebuild twice when the roof collapsed. But they were saved, and so named the spot "Thank God Camp." The men cooked two batches of stew and savored both the food and their salvation.

> Before leaving "Thank God Camp" we carried three emergency ration cases, all we could find, back from the beach on to higher ground among some wind swept rocks. One of the cases had been opened and in an empty tin inside was a note from Mr. Peters dated October of the fall before, stating that his party at that time were all right but were having a pretty hard fight with the young treacherous ice floes. I took up this note, leaving a copy and left a message to whom it might concern, telling of our mishap and that we were trying to push through to Camp Ziegler; that my hands and Duncan's face were badly frozen and that we were pretty well pulled down.[374]

Alger Island was now 14 nautical miles away, but the storm that had kept them pinned down in Allan Young Sound also swept the snow from the ice, so the men now flew across to West Camp Ziegler and then careened the 6 farther nautical miles to East Camp Ziegler. They were prepared to break

Russell Porter *(behind sledge)* and Seaman D. S. Mackiernan raced to Rudolf Island in mid-winter in order to join Fiala's last attempt to reach the North Pole, but they arrived at the island a day late. In the end, Fiala never advanced out of sight of Rudolf Island and was back within days of starting out. From Anthony Fiala, *Fighting the Polar Ice* (New York: Doubleday, Page & Company, 1906).

in the roof of the old Baldwin base when Porter found the door to the hut and opened it. "Never shall I forget what I then saw as long as I live."[375] They had expected the camp to be deserted and all the men now at Teplitz Bay but, when they entered the hut, two soot-covered faces stared back at them: Rilliet and Mackiernan.

The four men exchanged news, all mutually surprised that no deaths had attended the expedition over the winter. Porter and Butland scoured the camp for food, and then slept for an entire day. It was now March 7, and Porter had promised Fiala that he would reach Teplitz Bay by the 10th. Duncan was frostbitten, so he stayed with Rilliet while Porter pressed on with Mackiernan.

With a sledge recovered from East Camp Ziegler, Porter and Mackiernan raced north to Rudolf Island, covering the 100 nautical miles in just five days. They were too late. They reached Camp Abruzzi just hours after Fiala had departed on his final dash for the North Pole.

FIFTY-THREE

The Same Old Tale

A s the time approached for final American attempt to reach the North Pole from Franz Josef Land, the tension at Camp Abruzzi increased accordingly. Seitz recorded that the assistant commissary Spencer Stewart was scrapping with both Hartt and Seitz himself. On March 5 the antagonism between Stewart and Hartt threatened to get out of hand: "Hartt & Stewart had another row. Stewart escorted him outside to settle the matter & Hartt made a bluff of getting a revolver & when he came out said the men didn't want him to kill Stewart, so he didn't. He then proceeded to get drunk & has been so all day."[376]

Bernard Spencer, who had broken down after the near-death experience in the crevasse at Hooker Island, was likewise feeling the strain. As the trip north grew near, Seitz began to administer the increasingly nervous Spencer a combination of sedatives and anti-epileptics.

Fiala, as one might expect, was also on edge. He had announced that the final dash would start on March 10, but the appointed day came and went with no action. It is possible that he was waiting until the last possible moment for an appearance by Porter. More likely—as it had been for Wellman and Baldwin before him—the enormity of the difference between the warm calculations of an expedition to the North Pole with its imminent reality again conspired to hold him back.

By March 14 the men were both agitated and frustrated. "Fiala shows not the least inclination to start on the sledge trip although the weather during the last 2 days has been good enough for traveling, especially today. No preparations are being made & nobody is ready to leave at once on a favorable opportunity. It is the same story over again of last year."[377]

The men finally prevailed upon Fiala to make a start, and the small party along with fifty-nine dogs left Camp Abruzzi on Thursday, March 17. Only Hartt and his variety of physical ailments remained behind. The polar party crossed the Rudolf Island ice dome, placing signal flags as they went, and neared the southeastern coast of the island at Cape Habermann. There, on Friday morning, Seitz and Perry turned back, as planned, while the remainder of the polar party descended to the ice. As Seitz arrived back at Camp Abruzzi, Porter and Mackiernan were just arriving from the south and too late and in no condition to join Fiala.

Fiala and his men on the ice traveled about ten nautical miles north of Cape Habermann on Saturday, March 18, at which point Fiala sent Spencer and Meyers back to Camp Abruzzi. The next day, Anton Vedoe recorded that the going across the ice northeast of Rudolf Island "was horrible. . . . We had to cut our way foot by foot for 4 hours over the most disgustingly pressed up ice."[378] Fiala led the men northeast, stopping continuously to get his bearings.

After four days on the march, Vedoe could still see the north coast of Rudolf Island, with Capes Germania and Fligely plainly in sight. The ice was "horribly broken up in small cakes slowly moving about."[379] By Wednesday, March 22, as Vedoe and the remaining men prepared to turn back and leave Fiala and Duffy alone on the ice, Vedoe wrote that "Mr. Fiala is considering whether to turn back, as at the rate we are travelling now we will not be able to accomplish anything. As far as we can see the ice is the same if not worse ahead."[380] Fiala himself was searching for justification to bring the final dash to an early conclusion: "At noon on March 21st I took an altitude of the sun and was disappointed to find that, after all our hard work, our latitude was only 81 degrees and fifty-five minutes North. On March 21, 1895, Nansen was at 85 degrees, nine minutes North and on March 23, 1900, Captain Cagni [of the Abruzzi expedition] sent back his ill fated First Detachment from 82 degrees, thirty-two minutes North."[381]

After comparing his progress to two professional explorers, Fiala then "wonder[ed] what Job would have done under similar circumstances."[382] Whether or not one could contemplate a biblical figure finding himself on an ice floe a few miles northeast of Rudolf Island, Fiala's predicament was soon compounded by a wide lead of open water that blocked his path north.

In his published account, Fiala shifted the blame onto Peters, writing that he reluctantly agreed with Peters's strong recommendation that the party turn back at this point. Anton Vedoe, on the other hand, writes that Fiala came into his tent on the morning of Thursday, March 23 and announced that they were all turning around, "that he had decided to turn back and take his medicine as he explained himself."[383]

Somewhat late in the day, it dawned on Fiala that his men's lives were at risk: "if it was right to go back it was not right to go any further north and thus chance the loss of men, dogs, or equipment."[384] Nor was it terribly becoming to compare his performance to Nansen or Cagni. Fiala in the end would not come close to beating the northing made by the steamship *America* in the late summer of 1903. As Vedoe noted, the final American attempt to reach the North Pole from Franz Josef Land turned back while the north coast of Rudolf Island was still plainly in sight.

They were back at Cape Habermann on March 31 and, appropriately or not, regained Camp Abruzzi on April 1, 1905. They had been on the march north for only seven days, and used another ten days on the retreat to Teplitz Bay. Porter laconically summed up the final efforts: "The polar party was back in a week with the same old tale of impossible going—storms, open water, failure."[385]

At Camp Abruzzi, Chief Engineer Hartt's physical maladies reflected the final state of the expedition, as he wrote to Shorkley: "Have now got sprained ankle, sprained knee, and a broken rib, how I am ever going to get home, God only knows . . ."[386]

FIFTY-FOUR

Joy, Part Three

With the collapse of the final, half-hearted attempt on the North Pole, Fiala's Ziegler Polar Expedition became a scramble to reshuffle all the various caches of food and other supplies south to Baldwin's old base at East Camp Ziegler. From that well-worn spot on Alger Island, Fiala would dispatch scout teams to Cape Dillon on McClintock Island to scan the southern horizon for a relief ship.

Porter's arrival at Teplitz Bay brought correspondence to Fiala from Rilliet at Camp Ziegler and Captain Coffin at Cape Flora. Both reported surviving the winter and begged for tobacco from the supplies at Camp Abruzzi. Accordingly, in one of the more incongruous thoughts of a strange expedition, Fiala's first priority after losing the North Pole was to send Anton Vedoe racing to Cape Flora via Alger Island with two sledge-loads of smokes for "the homeseekers."

Once Vedoe had satisfied these nicotine cravings, he was to go to Eaton Island to retrieve the magnetic observation instruments that Peters had cached the previous August and deliver them to East Camp Ziegler so that Peters could record observations there while awaiting the relief ship. Vedoe would then begin a continuous shuttle of supplies from Kane Lodge to Alger Island.

Vedoe accordingly left Camp Abruzzi with Stewart and Tessem on April 11. At the same time, a second group, led by Seitz and including Duffy and Mackiernan, began a secondary shuttle of supplies from the Coburg Island cache south to Kane Lodge. Vedoe and his team reached East Camp Ziegler on April 16, where Rilliet told him that a group from Cape Flora led by Colin Vaughan had already been to Alger Island, plundering the base for various and sundries for the divided men of Elmwood and Little Italy.

Vedoe dutifully continued on to Cape Flora with his cargo of tobacco, but without adding to his sledge loads any of the food at East Camp Ziegler. He arrived on April 22 at Cape Flora, where he made the promised delivery and recorded that three men were "over on Bell Isl. for the sake of taking an inventory of the house of Leigh Smith."[387] The men of the two houses insisted on receipts for all supplies received, with Truden acting as commissary for Little Italy and Haven for Elmwood. Each group was convinced that the one was trying to cheat the other out of its rightful share of supplies.

Vedoe stayed only two days, just long enough to give his dogs a rest, and when he left he brought his brother John with him, to rescue him from the demoralization at Cape Flora. The Vedoe brothers, along with Tessem and George Butland, arrived under Rubini Rock on Hooker Island on April 27, but for two days the conditions were not right for a crossing to Eaton Island.

They eventually left for East Camp Ziegler, where they arrived on May 1 by travelling in "miserable" conditions.[388] Porter and Peters were already at Alger Island, having arrived four days earlier. As at Cape Flora, Vedoe found the suddenly overcrowded base camp oppressive and quickly had his dogs ready to begin his shuttle to and from Kane Lodge.

The final scientific work of the Ziegler Polar Expedition was accomplished in the months of May through July 1905. Peters left Camp Abruzzi with the Repsold Circle and the other scientific instruments on April 17. He established a new magnetic and astronomical observatory behind East Camp Ziegler as soon as he arrived, while Porter prepared for a month-long mapping expedition into the interior of Zichy Land. Fiala had directed Porter to undertake this task, and Porter was only too happy to oblige. Fiala himself, still waiting at Camp Abruzzi for an opportune moment to bring the disabled Hartt south, promised to map the islands of Zichy Land from the north and west as Porter did the same from the south and east.

With Vedoe occupied shuttling supplies between Kane Lodge and East Camp Ziegler, Porter chose George Butland to accompany him into the interior of Zichy Land. Porter described this mini-expedition as perhaps "the most satisfying of all my experiences in the North."[389] A natural loner and dreamer, Porter wrote that it had "none of the cross-purposes and bickerings that go with a crowd."[390] The two men set off with five good dogs and enough food to remain in the field for a month.

Once again, Porter was able to revel in the joy of directing his own course in a little-known sector of Franz Josef Land. "[Amid] the thrill of being the first humans to enter this land. . . . Zichy Land proved to be one big nest of bears . . . [and] when we were not stormbound we were fighting bears.

> Later at Cape Farman six bears were in sight at one time, most of them too near for comfort. I had an uncomfortable moment snarled up with the dogs who had gone crazy, trying to stop a wounded mother bear who, badly wounded, was finally dropped among the dogs themselves.
>
> Almost as vivid as this fight was the catastrophe of falling into a tide crack an hour later. It is no joke to fall into ice water up to one's middle at 20 below zero without a change of underwear. Streaking to camp I disrobed completely and crawled into my sleeping bag while Butland hung up the soaked garments to freeze, the ice later to be pounded out of them. Fortunately I had been wearing pants of bear skin, from a bear shot at Flora the winter before. Bear fur has the property of releasing frost, snow, and moisture when it is vigorously shaken.
>
> Outside of all the excitement this trip afforded, nearly a thousand miles of unknown channels, bays, capes, island and glaciers were charted, the last part of the archipelago to give up its secrets.[391]

While Porter and the shuttle teams were in the field, Fiala remained at Camp Abruzzi with Henry Hartt. They passed the time puttering around the largely abandoned base, moving "a rifle, tools, ammunition, and pieces of equipment that could not be taken south to the observatory on the hill, reasoning that under its shelter they could not be injured by streams of glacier water [running] through the camp in the summer time."[392] A kayak, a sledge, fur clothing, and a tent: all were added to the observatory on the hill, in the event a polar party arrived at Rudolf Island in the future and found both the Duke's and Fiala's camps buried under snow.

The two men finally took their leave of Teplitz Bay on May 26. Fiala expected to be able to feed their dogs on pemmican stores at various caches along the way, but when they arrived at these sites, they found them destroyed by bears. This ended any hopes of travelling to Alger Island via the interior of Zichy Land and linking any resultant survey with that of Porter. When Fiala and Hartt finally reached East Camp Ziegler three weeks later, Seitz recorded an astounding tale of the departure from Teplitz Bay. Hartt was having trouble ascending the glacier above Cape Auk, but when at last he had, he proceeded to challenge Fiala to a race to the North Pole! "On the last of these attempts over the glacier Hartt found out he could travel, & dared Fiala to return & make a dash North with him. So they returned & loaded up with 2 months' supplies & left towards the W. When they were not far from shore they came upon moving ice & a little water, & then decided they had better return."[393]

It seems more than likely that this was the last of Henry Hartt's practical jokes, played on the ever-trusting Fiala. The men also listened to Fiala's description of sledging south. The expedition commander had tried and failed to get around or through the Waterhole. He then retraced his steps and came south along the shores of British Channel. As Seitz recorded, the men were still looking crosswise at each other at Fiala's efforts to make something from nothing:

Fiala said they had loads of 800 lbs. (I think). At any rate it was a great exaggeration—& they brought every dog along, even one with a leg shot off. Some of the dogs which nobody could ever get to work Fiala said worked fine, e.g., Thor, Niddie, & so forth, thus implying that he could make them work when no one else could (it is to laugh!). They followed our old route quite closely to the Coal Mine Island where they met open water, of course [at the Waterhole]. Fiala then went ahead some distance & said they could not get past (lost his nerve)—when it would have been quite easy to cover the mile or 2 necessary with their canvas boat. They tried both sides of Coal Mine Island, & then went up to Sternek Fjord where they also met water. They then went up to Gore Booth Fjord & down the British Channel. . . . They kept on down to Markham Sound, Fiala taking angles of Zichy Land & making some "wonderful discoveries" (?), & then struck for Alger Island & East Camp. . . . This was Fiala's first real experience with driving dogs & he couldn't stop talking of his wonderful experiences with them. He brought the odometer all the way—took a lot of angles, etc. & had lots of fun playing scientist.[394]

Fiala received a report on the supplies taken away by the men from Cape Flora, and watched as Peters and Porter kept the two observatories at East

Cape Flora as it appeared when the relief ship arrived to gather up the "homeseekers." "Elmwood" is on the left and "Little Italy" on the right, with a chasm between them. From Anthony Fiala, *Fighting the Polar Ice* (New York: Doubleday, Page & Company, 1906).

Camp Ziegler in continuous operation. The magnetic observatory had been slapped together with some old oars and rolls of ruberoid for walls and a roof. "The astronomical observatory was built of cases (still full of emergency rations), wire netting, and roofing material by Mr. Porter on his return from his trip of exploration."[395]

Before the arrival of Fiala and Hartt, Peters had dispatched Anton Vedoe along with Charles Rilliet and Peter Tessem to Camp Abruzzi via Kane Lodge to make a search for the expedition leader. They left Alger Island on June 18, just one day before Fiala made his appearance. Racing to Kane Lodge, which they reached the next day, they continued in drizzling weather until they arrived at Camp Abruzzi on June 26. The base was abandoned, and Fiala had left no note as to when he had left or where he was going. "The house seems to have been empty for quite a while," Vedoe wrote. "Things are

Wellman's old camp at Cape Tegetthoff on Hall Island as it appeared to the men of Fiala's expedition who visited it in the early summer of 1905. Within weeks, Fiala's expedition was rescued and the American exploration of Franz Josef Land was over. From Anthony Fiala, *Fighting the Polar Ice* (New York: Doubleday, Page & Company, 1906).

molding [*sic*]. . . . Found a camera in the observatory amongst other instruments packed away there and have been busy all day taking pictures."[396]

The three men stayed at the base on Rudolf Island until July 2. Then, nailing up the windows and doors, they left behind a note to the next person who might arrive. Then the last three representatives of this "American" expedition—a Norwegian, a Swede of Norwegian origin, and an American—left Rudolf Island for the final time. They arrived back at East Camp Ziegler on Alger Island in the evening of July 11.

The men spent their last weeks at East Camp Ziegler feasting on the supplies that had been stored at the base following Evelyn Briggs Baldwin's journey through Scandinavia in the winter of 1900–1901: Swedish conserves, oatmeal, rice, and flour, all to go with bird eggs from the surrounding hills, and the ever-present fried polar bear steaks that had kept the men alive for nearly two years. Hunting trips to add to the food supplies in the event no relief ship appeared in 1905 were made, and the men stationed at Cape Dillon killed no less than sixteen walrus. A trip to Wellman's old base at Cape Tegetthoff recovered a small stove but found no useable food supplies.

On July 30 Porter and Peters were working in one of the observatories at East Camp Ziegler when the Norwegian carpenter, Tessem, appeared, incongruously holding a bottle of beer from Mack's Ølbryggerie in Tromsø. The half-empty bottle was slowly and ceremonially placed on a table between the two scientists. Porter assumed it had been discovered in one of the old Baldwin caches. Tessem bade the men to drink.

As Porter later wrote: "I looked at [Tessem]. The perspiration was standing out in big drops over his forehead, and he seemed to find difficulty in breathing. Surely, I thought, this fellow has been hitting it rather heavily."[397] It took Porter some time to make the connection, but when he did, it hit him like a flash. The relief ship had come.

Fiala and Meyer had just launched the canvas canoe on the pond behind East Camp Ziegler that morning when a bugle sounded, recalling them to the base. They soon learned the news as well: the *Terra Nova,* with the doughty Johan Kjeldsen in command, was at Cape Dillon. Seitz, who had met the ship at Cape Dillon, handed Fiala a letter from William Champ, who was on board the *Terra Nova,* which informed him of the death in May of William Ziegler. It was the end of everything, and Fiala knew it. Never again would there exist a millionaire so free with his money as to equip such an expedition. Any hopes Fiala had of returning to the mysteriously seductive islands north of Russia were finished. Within twenty-four hours, East Camp Ziegler was closed and abandoned.

The American exploration of Franz Josef Land was over.

FIFTY-FIVE

Retreat

The men on Alger Island quickly gathered the scattered boxes and bags of two years in the field and stuffed them inside the buildings at East Camp Ziegler. The Field Department, which for all intents had been reduced to just Peters, Porter, and Anton Vedoe, packed the Repsold Circle and the magnetic instruments and the records of data collected during the expedition.

The men departed Alger Island just after noon on July 31, 1905. A few hours later, "wet over our knees, wading through big pools deep enough to float the boats on the sledges in many places,"[398] they came upon William Champ. After sending Seitz ahead with his letter for Fiala, Champ had asked the *Terra Nova* to wait at Cape Dillon while he wandered up Aberdare Channel to see Fiala personally.

Assured once he had rescued the expedition commander, Champ then directed the *Terra Nova* to Cape Flora. They arrived at noon on August 1 and, in less than three hours, "the homeseekers" were finally embarked for home. The ship left Franz Josef Land at full speed.

The initial good feelings, shared all around at the expedition's rescue, quickly gave way to the inevitable moment of reckoning. In Fiala's eyes, the men at Cape Flora had distinguished themselves through their constant efforts to undermine his leadership and the course of the expedition itself. To men like Shorkley, it was Fiala himself who was to blame, a naïve incompetent who never should have been given command of a major Arctic expedition upon which the prestige of the United States itself had been pegged.

The many streams of these stories soon flowed freely into Champ's cabin. Then Champ discovered that a parallel newspaper had been produced by the malcontents of Little Italy. It was called the *Polar Pirate* and had kept up a venomous drumbeat against Fiala and the organizers of the expedition, Champ included. At this, as Seitz recorded, Champ exploded: "Mr. Champ & all the members of 'Little Italy' & several others who had copies of the *Polar Pirate* held a long conference today which resulted in the turning in of all the copies & the retraction of statements in the paper derogatory to Mr. Champ or Mr. Ziegler, & an apology for the same. Shorkley & Fiala, & Fiala & Seargt. [Moulton] have agreed to let their troubles rest—not to bring them up for settlement."[399]

When William Ziegler died of a stroke at the age of sixty-two on May 24, 1905, he left behind an estate of thirty million dollars, a massive fortune that today would amount to a billion dollars or more. His decision, just before death, to leave most of it to an adopted fourteen-year-old son had set tongues wagging, as did his widow's threat to have the will declared null on account of insanity. The *New York Times* reported: "Until this statement was made none of Ziegler's friends had ever heard he was not of sound mind, although some of his friends believed that his mind was growing weak at the time he began sending out polar expeditions, which he equipped at great expense."[400]

Champ was in Tromsø, preparing to leave for Franz Josef Land on board the *Terra Nova* when it appeared that Ziegler's will—set to split a million dollars amongst three executors, one of whom was William Champ—would become regular public gossip, and Ziegler's very sanity questioned on account of his spending on polar expeditions. So as soon as Champ learned of the expedition's discord and dissension—especially the cuts directed at Ziegler, and Champ himself, in the *Polar Pirate*—Champ moved quickly to cauterize any hint of scandal. He had made a small fortune by closely aligning himself to William Ziegler and his money. Now that Ziegler was dead, Champ's only course to continued prosperity was as a zealous guardian of Ziegler's legacy and reputation, and in the public's mind that legacy centered on Ziegler's fabulously extravagant sponsorship of two polar expeditions.

A codicil in Ziegler's will had even set aside money for continued polar work, but with the will in contention, Champ knew that that would never happen. The best way to ensure his position was to keep the members of the expedition quiet, avoid any possible repeat of the disastrous return of the Baldwin-Ziegler expediton, and then publish a handsome bound volume of the expedition narrative written by Fiala and a second volume of scientific results edited by Peters and his staff.

This is just what Champ did. A note in the *New York Times* from later in October 1905 expressed the frustration of reporters at not getting at the dirt of what everyone suspected was a massive failure. "Just what the trouble was—whether occasioned by petty jealousies, disaffection, or refusal of some of the heads of the expedition to venture further—these tardy stragglers refuse to divulge on the plea that they are bound to secrecy, though they are willing to talk freely of the perils and adventures of the voyage."[401]

In the end, Champ handed over to Fiala a large sum of Ziegler's money, with orders to distribute it to one and all in exchange for what amounted to a non-disclosure agreement on the part of all hands. Ziegler himself had left instructions that the money was to be used to reward the men in proportion to their efforts. This allowed Fiala to provide extra consideration to truly excellent men like Vedoe and Porter, much to the infuriation of lesser men like Coffin and Shorkley, the petty ringleaders of the Elmwood and Little Italy factions.

But the money did its work. The men all kept silent. In the end, the cash allowed the public to instead read accounts of the loss of the *America* and how the shipwrecked men had gathered on the ice in praise of "Mr. Fiala, in whom all the crew had confidence."[402]

The veil would drop at times, sometimes inadvertently, as at the next annual dinner of the National Geographic Society, which had sent Peters on the expedition as second-in-command. Responding to the toast "The Arctic," Fiala began his response awkwardly: "A returned explorer has generally to face three questions—I know they have come to me. One is, 'How far did you get?' That one is a hard one to answer: it makes the explorer feel badly."[403]

Despite these occasional hints that all had certainly not been well, Champ's efforts on behalf of his late sponsor paid off. The Ziegler Polar Expedition under the direction of Anthony Fiala produced perhaps the finest unified publications of its efforts of any American polar expedition. Certainly they dwarfed the half-hearted efforts of either Wellman or Baldwin to properly record and publish their scientific observations in Franz Josef Land in anything like a systematic fashion.

John Edwards Caswell, the only historian to ever attempt a comprehensive history of the scientific research undertaken by all American Arctic exploration, wrote of the "two splendid volumes [that] record the achievements of the Fiala-Ziegler Expedition . . . [with] physical observations . . . carefully made on the basis of a systematic plan. Publication of the scientific results was unified, rather than fragmentary."[404]

Caswell was wrong, however, to attribute the splendidness of these results only to Peters's astronomical recordings, while dismissing the geographical results as "practically *nil*."[405] In fact, it was Russell Porter's mapping of the interior of the Franz Josef Land archipelago, combined with his sorting of the geographic naming problems and the surveying mysteries that had been created by both Wellman and Baldwin, that was perhaps the greatest scientific contribution of the Ziegler Polar Expedition.

Perhaps the most remarkable element of Porter's descriptions of his surveys of the interior of the archipelago is what is missing from it: his complete lack of reference to the fact that he and Fiala had already explored the area with Evelyn Briggs Baldwin during the spring sledge expedition of 1902. In this, it seems entirely likely that the obsessively secretive Baldwin never shared with Porter the 20,000-word report he wrote about the spring 1902 discoveries. Baldwin jealously guarded all of his Arctic papers, believing for much of the remainder of his life that a return to the north was only a matter of time.

Even without apparent access to this critical report, Porter was able to clear up many of the geographic problems that had stymied the exploration of the archipelago for decades. Perhaps the most important of these was the elimination of the word "land" from so many places like "Graham Bell Land," or "Zichy Land," or "Crown Prince Rudolf Land." As Porter later wrote: "The word 'land' has been dropped entirely as being misguiding, now that the Archipelago is known to consist only of several comparatively small islands."[406]

No other American contribution to the exploration of Franz Josef Land was so great as this: the certain knowledge that the once-supposed land-bridge to the North Pole was instead only a breathtakingly beautiful collection of ice-domed rocks that led precisely nowhere.

An American Tractor at the North Pole

The American exploration of Franz Josef Land resulted in the deaths of two Norwegians, one buried at Cape Säulen on Rudolf Island—the island itself the graveyard of American ambitions in the islands—and the other buried at Cape Heller, at an appropriately ironic spot called Fort McKinley, a place-name derived from the godfather of American intervention around the globe. Odd bits of this triptych of explorations began to turn up even before the expeditions themselves had finally left the islands.

On Saturday morning, May 9, 1903, a shepherd living on an arm of the Vopnafjord in northeastern Iceland found Baldwin's fifty-second buoy, sent from Alger Island early in the morning of June 13, 1902.[1] The note inside the buoy eventually found its way to the American consulate in Bergen, Norway, with a request for a "small gratuity" for its impoverished finder.

On October 16, 1903, Buoy No. 146—which had been attached to the twelfth balloon and launched on June 23, 1902—was picked up along the shores of Siglufjordur, the northernmost port in Iceland.[2] It, too, was sent to the consulate in Bergen with a request for a reward. On November 12, 1903, a third buoy, No. 160, launched with the thirteenth balloon on June 24, 1902, was picked up at sea off the northern tip of Norway in Finnmark.[3]

This was enough for the U.S. Department of State. In January 1904 the American consul in Bergen, E. S. Cunningham, wrote to Francis B. Loomis, the assistant secretary of state, that it was incumbent upon the United States to begin to offer rewards for the finding of the buoys. This "would prevent the impression getting abroad that the finders of buoys thrown out by American Polar Expeditions must not, not only not be rewarded, but must bear the expenses of the transmission of the message."[4] The State Department accordingly tracked down Evelyn Briggs Baldwin, then living in Edna, Kansas, and he quickly responded with fifteen dollars in cash, with instructions that the money be divided equally between the three people who had found the buoys.[5] Two more unrecorded messages washed up in northern Norway in January 1904 and were forwarded to Baldwin by the American consulate in Trondheim.[6]

An Arctic sealing vessel did finally retrieve one of the buoys, but not until July 10, 1906. A Captain Stenerson of the *Gottfred* found Buoy No. 229 "badly crushed" and bobbing in the tiny lagoon at Moffen Island off the north coast of Spitsbergen.[7] Stenerson did not believe that the buoy had been there the previous season, as he or one of the other vessels of the Spitsbergen sealing/walrus fleet would have noticed it and retrieved it. Two more buoys, Nos. 128 and 176, were found off the coast of Finnmark in the fall of 1907,[8] and another in Van Mijenfjord in Spitsbergen on August 18, 1910, by a Swedish geological expedition led by Bertil Högbom.[9] After the Swedish find, no more buoys were found for another twenty years.

The use of the balloon buoy in Arctic exploration lasted five years, from the launch of Salomon Andrée's *Örnen* from Danskøya on July 11, 1897, to Baldwin's last balloon buoy sent from Alger Island on June 30, 1902. Their success as means of communication was mixed. Over the two years from 1898 to 1900, five of the eleven buoys dropped by Andrée were eventually found (there were apparently more than a dozen buoys on board the balloon, one of which was never dropped).[10] The last one was not found until 1937.[11] On the other hand, between 1903 and 1910, a total of only twelve of Baldwin's 422 buoy messages were eventually found, a success rate of only 2.8 percent.

Baldwin's buoys were found in a triangle enclosed by Moffen Island in the north, Siglufjorden in Iceland in the west, and Finnmark in the south (one of Andrée's buoys also washed up in Finnmark).[12] If we add the 1930 Baldwin buoy find on Novaya Zemlya—discovered just a few weeks before the discovery of the body of Andrée himself—we get a diamond-shaped area where some of the remaining 410 messages may yet be found.

One recent artifact of likely Wellman-Baldwin-Fiala origin is a broken ski, found by my Swedish colleague Magnus Forsberg in the summer of 2006 at Cape Trieste on Champ Island, and just north of Alger Island.[13] If any of the remaining balloon buoys are ever found, they would be worth much more than the $5 Baldwin gave as a reward in 1903. One of the large Swedish buoys from Baldwin's expedition was recently auctioned in New York for $7,500![14]

Since 1930 Baldwin's East Camp Ziegler on Alger Island has been steadily eroded by the harsh environment, by visiting bears, by Norwegian sealers, probably by Soviet military and scientific personnel and, more recently, by groups of Arctic tourists carried on Russian icebreakers. Little if anything has been done to preserve the area. Recent photographs show that some of the walls of the main expedition buildings survive, but they remain exposed to the elements. Remains of the hydrogen generating process—iron turnings in their barrels—can be plainly seen.

The experienced Arctic guide Andreas Umbreit located a sizeable collection of large artifacts on the southwestern shore of Greely Island in late August 2012. These included boats and sledges and could very well be the surviving remains of Baldwin's Kane Lodge.[15] An expedition to survey the wildlife of Franz Josef Land in the summer of 2013 revisited the apparent site of Kane Lodge on Greely Island and reported seeing kayaks, sledges, and many boxes that once held food for humans and dogs.[16] All of these archaeological remains are the product of William Ziegler's fortune, and one of the few sites of the American exploration of Franz Josef Land that remains largely undisturbed by human contact. Unfortunately, as Andreas Umbreit noted, the remains survive on a very narrow stretch of shoreline that is being constantly eroded, so this site will not survive much longer before it is completely washed into the sea.[17]

Other sites, like the wreck of the *America* in Teplitz Bay or the West Camp Ziegler site on Alger Island, have never been located. The area around Teplitz Bay eventually became a substantial Soviet weather station and, in the 1930s, a staging point for Soviet research flights to the North Pole. Working on the island during this time, Yevgeny Fedorov described the remains of Fiala's Camp Abruzzi and the Italian base camp of the Duke of the Abruzzi as "a museum telling about the race to the Pole at the turn of the century" and added that this was a museum in great need of being put in order.[18] Fedorov, like the visitors from the *Sedov* mentioned later, realized that such sites as Camp Abruzzi, Camp Ziegler, and the scatter of remains at Cape Flora had all been pillaged for reusable materials by visitors from other scientific and military expeditions since their abandonment, to the detriment of the stories they could have told.

The ruins of East Camp Ziegler in 2006.
The steady encroachment of the sea around the site will
soon destroy the remnants of the base. *Courtesy of Robert Headland.*

If Fedorov marveled at the extent of the material Fiala had left behind on Rudolf Island, Mikhail Vodopyanov, who flew from the island toward the North Pole in the 1930s, was stupefied. Vodopyanov visited Fiala's base after some of his colleagues had cleared it of snow, and noted the large amount of expedition gear along with "wine, alcohol and books, including eighteen Bibles," and then follows these with a list that includes "top-hats, tail-coats, patent-leather shoes, shirt-fronts, neckties, combs and even gold-plated skis."[19] Vodopyanov's list is likely only slightly exaggerated by Soviet-era conceits regarding the wealth of Americans. Fiala's expedition went north with a store of supplies and extraneous paraphernalia that would have impressed Sir John Franklin.

Cape Flora today serves as the entry point of most tourist cruises to the islands and for those tourist-laden Russian icebreakers that transit the islands on their way to and from the North Pole. As such, the archaeological remains at the site have been steadily reduced in character and content by both cultural and natural formation processes.[20] The original Jackson-Harmsworth expedition huts have been reduced to outlines in the soil, while the overwintering hut of Benjamin Leigh Smith that was located near the steep seaside cliff has been washed into the ocean.

Given the almost complete obscurity of the American exploration of Franz Josef Land, it seems unlikely that tourist cruises to the islands in the near term will go out of their way to disturb the archaeological remains of this era in the history of polar exploration—as opposed to earlier Soviet expeditions that were on the lookout for both supplies and souvenirs. However, as tourist itineraries inevitably become stale, such cruises will invariably venture more deeply into those parts of the archipelago that hold the remains of the American presence. Sooner or later, such tours will stumble into the cluster of sites that we can refer to as the "American Supply Trail," the hundred-mile-long trail of cache sites deposited by Baldwin and picked over by Fiala. Here, sites like Kane Lodge hold the potential to reveal, in the words of Mikhail Vodopyanov, that "the wealthy American [Ziegler] had spared no expense to gratify his vanity."[21]

In contrast to the heavily visited or re-used sites like Cape Flora and Cape Tegetthoff, the chain of sites that comprise the American Supply Trail, with Kane Lodge as its fulcrum, has never been recorded or explored as the unified set of archaeological sites fitted to a landscape of Arctic exploration that it is. When speaking of this American Supply Trail, we need to separate out the northern terminus at Camp Abruzzi and the southern terminus at East Camp Ziegler. As noted, these two sites have seen heavy visitation by scientists and military personnel (Camp Abruzzi) and scientists and tourists (East Camp Ziegler).

Russian archaeologists have expended great efforts to record these sites, as well as those of Wellman's base camp on Hall Island and Fort McKinley at Cape Heller, work recently published in a brilliant catalog of historical archaeology in the islands.[22] The portable artifacts recovered by the Russians testify to the tonnage of supplies carried by the Americans, and include boats, clothing, tents, sledges, ammunition, matches, stoves, case after case of Diamond Condensed Soups, Cadbury Cocoa, Bovril, and Quaker Rolled White Oats, even the still-surviving base of the Repsold Circle above Teplitz Bay.[23] Not surprisingly, given the extreme difficulty in piecing together the story of the American exploration of Franz Josef Land, the excellent work by the Russians nevertheless missed many of the obscure locations where Wellman, Baldwin, and Fiala all left behind traces of the American attempt to reach the pole from the islands between 1898 and 1905.

Of the remaining sites in the American Supply Trail, with the exception of the recently rediscovered site of Kane Lodge, there is no recorded history of use during either the post-Ziegler Polar Expedition period (1906–28) or in fact any Soviet-era (1929–91) or post-Soviet-era (1991–present) scientific or military re-use or tourism visitations.[24] They are therefore potentially unique in the historical archaeology of polar exploration.

When Fiala's expedition retreated from Rudolf Island in 1905, it cannibalized much of the trail as it had been laid down by Baldwin's expedition in 1901–1902.[25] This supply route from Camp Abruzzi to Camp Ziegler offers the greatest potential for significant future archaeological finds related to the American exploration of Franz Josef Land between 1898 and 1905. The level of detail in surviving cache lists suggests a comprehensive material culture of polar exploration at the turn of the twentieth century. This includes technologies related to both overland and maritime travel, food supplies and processing, clothing, animal feed, communications, shelter, and weaponry with nearly seven hundred rounds of unused ammunition.

This trail, if studied as a unified archaeological site and afforded a level of cultural resource protection consistent with its unique character, could set an important precedent in the study, preservation and management of sites of exploration in the Russian Arctic. Other undiscovered sites, such as the "Temporary Camp" on Payer Island used by Fiala as a brief encampment for his entire party during his first retreat from Camp Abruzzi on May 4, 1904, would also be worth searching for any traces of a temporary encampment by a large polar party.

Given that any new archaeological research in the islands must originate, coordinate, or cooperate with Russian cultural resource management authorities, such a conception and plan will be fraught with challenges both local and international. Surviving cache lists from the Ziegler expeditions can provide guidance to such expeditions, as well as to local cultural resource authorities, to both the location of comparative archaeological data and to such practical concerns as the potentially lethal ammunition that might remain in the cache sites.

The lists serve both to narrow potentially enormous survey areas for archaeological field research and to alert archaeologists to known quantities of hazardous materials. If this research could lead to both survey and preservation, as well as actual demarcation of the trail with historical particulars and brief historical publications, it will have accomplished the kinds of necessary precautions against mass disturbance that are now a commonplace in similar heavy Arctic tourist areas such as the historical sites of Svalbard, where the site of Walter Wellman's airship base camp has been under strict conservation regulations for more than twenty years.

Actual cooperation with Russia—especially in the unique instance of the specifically American archaeology and geographic place-names—is another issue altogether. The steady decline in relations between the two countries since the rise of Vladimir Putin—a rise conspicuously focused on Russian prerogatives in both geography and history—has served to place Franz Josef Land once again largely beyond the direct study of Westerners. The triple irony of a Russian (and former Soviet) archipelago filled with geographic place-names associated with Gilded Age American capitalists amid a second Gilded Age is not a subject that lends itself to intensive examination on either side of the former Iron Curtain.

Walter Wellman's obeisance to these Hamiltonian captains of profit began in his journalism and continued into his polar exploration. His writings on the general unhappiness of new millionaires amid their millions underscored how men born into the American culture of work for work's sake could never easily relax—nor cease from the continuous acquisition of more money. Men like John R. Walsh and William Champ were determined to continue their accumulation of money by hook or by crook. For most of his final months of life, Walsh found himself in a prison cell on account of it. As for Champ, through his slavish devotion to William Ziegler, he worked his way into hundreds of thousands of dollars in estate-management fees, which he then parlayed into millions more in questionable land deals.

These men typified the secondary and tertiary layers of wealth created by the Gilded Age. They were born and raised in a nation that had long since elevated the continual acquisition of money above all other values. The very fact of their success in sticking money to themselves all but guaranteed that explorers like Wellman, Baldwin, and Fiala—each of whom was brought up to equate capital with freedom—would permanently affix their names to the capes and islands of Franz Josef Land.

That the geographic North Pole was a thing to be acquired, like a company or real estate or a yacht, was a concept implicitly understood and heartily endorsed with generous handouts of American capital. That such names—redolent with the aroma of *laissez faire*—somehow avoided a thorough scrubbing by Soviet geographers and indeed survive into the age of Putin, is a testament to the durability of a reputation constructed upon the acquisition of money.

Upon his return to the United States, Wellman told the press that he was "giving the islands, straits, and points [of Franz Josef Land] good American names."[26] In an article published soon after in *National Geographic*, Wellman wrote that "Upon these new lands, their capes and straits, we had the pleasure of placing the names of well-known American scientific and public men who had befriended the expedition."[27] "Public men" was a euphemism not only for politicians but for those generous capitalists who viewed the American acquisition of the North Pole as they understood the acquisition of any other property: all but ordained by cultural writ and enabled by a government dedicated to the fetish of *laissez faire;* in other words, an event merely in the natural order of things as they conceived such order.

John Edwards Caswell, the first historian to attempt a synthesis of the scientific results of all American Arctic expeditions between 1850 and 1909, finally threw up his hands when it came to the American experience in Franz Josef Land. The manuscripts available to Caswell in 1950 were a fraction of those available today, but even those that he could find were in a fairly hopeless state. Baldwin's papers at the Library of Congress Caswell found "quite miscellaneous."[28] Caswell stuck to his conclusions that the Baldwin-Ziegler expedition had broken down on account of the split between "the Swedish ship captain and his crew on one hand, and the Norwegian ice pilot, Baldwin, and the American personnel on the other."[29] Still, even then, Caswell was bothered by hints that "the whole truth had not been told."[30]

Indeed it had not. What Caswell, who passed away in 2001, would never know was that each of the three Americans who attempted to reach the North Pole from the Franz Josef Land archipelago in the years 1898–1905 carried a cargo of obsessions. Perversely, for none of the three was it a particularly burning desire to be first at the pole. They would take it if it came, of course. But each had other, more pressing obsessions to sort. Wellman was preoccupied by an affair and an illegitimate child, Baldwin was mad as a box of frogs, and Fiala wandered through the Arctic like a medieval monk in search of Christ beyond the snow-clad mountains.

More to the point, Walter Wellman, celebrity interviewer of the rich and

Cape Heller in the summer of 2005. Anders Larsson of the University of Gothenburg took this photo during a break in the fog to reveal Baldwin's "Observatory Ridge" in the background, with the ruins of "Fort McKinley" in the center amid a patch of snow, and the grave of Bernt Bentsen off to the left of the fort. *Courtesy of Anders Larsson.*

powerful, was obsessed with his own place in history—and how to sort his mistress and his wife. Evelyn Briggs Baldwin, strangest of these strange men, was preoccupied with his place in his own self-created Arctic fantasy—and thereafter spent a lifetime imagining himself in the basket of Salomon Andrée's balloon. And Anthony Fiala, the pious naïf, was focused almost exclusively upon his place in a kind of Boy's Own version of the kingdom of heaven—and whether he would be able to properly photograph it once he got there.

None of these obsessions prepared these explorers to lead men onto the arcane disturbances of pack ice north of Rudolf Island. Rather, they are large elements in understanding why Wellman foundered just off its eastern capes; why Baldwin barely reached Rudolf Island; and why Fiala turned tail while still in sight of its northern glacial escarpments. If the ruined huts of Cape Flora on Northbrook Island are the beginning and end of the British exploration of the archipelago, then Rudolf Island—an ice-domed bit of scree with a royalist name that survived even seventy years of Soviet communism—was the common graveyard of the bewilderingly inept American experience in Franz Josef Land.

The manifest void of competent leadership can be only partially blamed on the near-complete absence of official U.S. support for the expeditions. What Wallace Stegner wrote of John Wesley Powell's famous descent of the Colorado in 1869 could also be said of the American exploration of Franz Josef Land: "The Powell expedition was as barren of official backing as it was of official intentions. Congress had not authorized it. . . . All [Powell] had in the way of government aid was a few instruments and some good advice from the Smithsonian."[31]

That the Americans accomplished anything at all in Franz Josef Land is due to a historical and biographical accident: the blind luck of stumbling—thanks to Robert Peary's appropriation of northern Greenland and the enticing possibility that the riddle of the Andrée expedition might be solved in Franz Josef Land—into largely virgin Arctic territory. This luck was combined with the surveying, sketching, and photographic skills of just three of the Americans: Ernest de Koven Leffingwell, Russell Porter, and Fiala himself. Beyond these three, the remainder of the Americans who accompanied Wellman, Baldwin, and Fiala to Franz Josef Land was largely of a piece with the marginal knockabouts who explored the Grand Canyon with Powell.

Of the three men who made up the bulk of the American scientific effort in Franz Josef Land, only Russell Porter sought to explain in more emotional terms his connection to the landscape of the Arctic. The exploration of the north was a kind of neurological derangement for Porter, as it was for both Peary and Frederick Cook. As Michael Robinson so perceptively wrote, "It was a condition that afflicted the heart against the better judgment of the mind, operating beyond conscious control.

> Kane's passion was of different stuff than Peary's. It was a Romantic sensibility that led Kane to write about the polar regions with the self-conscious wonder of Walden. By contrast, Cook and Peary expressed passions that were torn from the pages of Call of the Wild, as if Arctic exploration were an impulse rooted deep within the primate brain.[32]

Porter returned to New York in 1905 with the rest of the Fiala expedition, his head feeling "like a block of wood,"[33] his deafness nearly complete. And who should be one of the first people to greet him at the docks? None other than the good doctor himself, Frederick Cook. "He took me to his home in Brooklyn and unfolded a plan for conquering the highest mountain on the North American continent, Mount McKinley."[34]

Unable to restrain himself, Porter followed Cook to Alaska. Though he did not participate in Cook's infamous claim to the summit of Mount McKinley, he found—as had Roald Amundsen—that the doctor possessed "sterling qualities as a companion in such pioneer work. Always in good spirits and ready for more than his share of drudgery, resourceful, and considerate of the others."[35] All in all, it is a description of a man who was the very polar opposite of Evelyn Briggs Baldwin, and one is left to wonder, once again, on the alternate future of polar exploration had William Ziegler chosen the affable, intriguing Dr. Cook, over the unstable fantasist Baldwin. A Cook triumph at the North Pole in the spring of 1902 would have short-circuited the entire Cook-Peary feud of the fall of 1909, and Robert Falcon Scott and his men would likely have survived their Antarctic expedition, since Roald Amundsen would not have had to publicly fake a North Pole expedition in 1910 and instead would have looked south much sooner than he actually did. Or else the race to the South Pole would have ended even before Norwegian independence from Sweden in 1905, since with the North Pole under the Star and Stripes, the great Fridtjof Nansen might have been roused to take up the challenge and beat the British to the South Pole a decade before his countryman Amundsen.

After his experiences in Alaska with Frederick Cook, Russell Porter retreated to Maine, where he failed to found an artist's colony. He did succeed in marrying the local postmistress and then building an observatory into an addition of his home so that he could look at the stars overhead from the comfort of a warm study—a welcome modification to the bitterly cold hours spent at the Repsold Circle station above Teplitz Bay. Thirty years after his experiences with Baldwin, Fiala, and Cook, Porter wrote a memoir, *Arctic Fever*, but, in the middle of the Great Depression, it never found a publisher.

Porter's growing expertise in optics and telescopes eventually gained him the notice of George Ellery Hale, who recruited Porter west to Pasadena, California, to work on the telescope at the Mount Palomar Observatory. The telescope was finally finished in 1948, one year before Porter's death from a heart attack at the age of seventy-seven. He was affectionately remembered as the "artist of Palomar," a man who made ornamental optical sundials for his friends' lawns and whose "detailed sketches of the 200-inch telescope have guided the builders of the instrument since the inception of the project in 1928."[36] A heavily edited version of his Arctic journal was finally published a quarter century after his death.

Baldwin's main nemesis among his Americans, Ernest de Koven Leffingwell, also returned to the United States intent on continuing his relationship with the north, and also in Alaska. He found a partner in another of the men who had turned so bitterly against Baldwin in Franz Josef Land, the Dane Ejnar Mikkelsen. Together they formed an expedition to return to the Arctic on the strength of a rumor of land north of Alaska's North Slope.

Mikkelsen dutifully beat the fund-raising bushes, and even created a minor scene when he stole into the Baltimore townhome of Alexander Graham Bell to importune the old man for cash. Since Leffingwell and Mikkelsen were not in competition with Robert Peary for the North Pole, Peary even went so far as to help Mikkelsen secure a profitable interview with Theodore Roosevelt himself. After granting the expedition the assistance of the Revenue Cutter Service and a few other governmental favors, Mikkelsen wrote that Roosevelt was really only interested in one thing: the president of the United States craved some juicy gossip and "asked my opinion about the fiasco of the Baldwin Expedition in 1902."[37]

Leffingwell went on to make important explorations of the North Slope and lay the groundwork for the subsequent discovery of oil in the region. Highly regarded for his work, Leffingwell was awarded the Patron's Medal of the Royal Geographical Society in 1922, the only veteran of the American exploration of Franz Josef Land to receive such a high honor. Still racing hot rods well into his 80s, Leffingwell survived all of the comrades he went north with. He lived in Carmel, California, where he often met with Porter to chew over old times. Leffingwell finally passed away in 1971 at the age of ninety-six, still waiting—like Theodore Roosevelt during his visit with Ejnar Mikkelsen sixty-five years earlier—for the "real story" of the Baldwin expedition to be told.

Mikkelsen likewise continued a brilliant exploring career, and carried out important geographic surveys of northeast Greenland. With appropriate irony, his desperate retreat from Greenland in 1912 was saved at the last moment by his knowledge of where Baldwin had ordered Johan Bryde to lay in large caches of supplies on Shannon Island and on Bass Rock in the spring of 1901. In 1909 Mikkelsen organized an expedition to northeast Greenland to search for the bodies and journals of the 1906–1908 *Danmark* expedition under Ludvig Mylius-Erichsen. Mikkelsen found Mylius-Erichsen's journals, but was himself trapped with a companion in northeast Greenland for three winters. Taking refuge finally at the Baldwin hut on the southeastern point of Shannon Island in the winter of 1911–12, Mikkelsen and a companion were rescued by the Norwegian sealer *Sjøblomsten* the following July.[38]

Baldwin himself wrote about the use of these huts for the relief of expeditions after the initial news arrived about the *Danmark* tragedy: "It is interesting to note that at the Baldwin-Ziegler station are ten of the balloons manufactured by Captain Thomas Scott Baldwin and his brother Samuel Yates Baldwin for the transmission of messages concerning the progress or welfare of an expedition."[39] It is not certain which station—Shannon Island or Bass Rock—holds the remains of the balloon buoy system. But Mikkelsen found the Shannon Island depot "in comparatively good order" when he first looked in on it during the fall of 1909, and the contents helped save the lives of himself and his companion for the next three summers.[40] A windowpane had been broken and snow had blown in, making it a winter den for foxes. On Bass Rock he found "ample provisions and coal in the two houses" when he reached them in November 1911.[41] During his last visit to the Shannon Island site in April 1912, Mikkelsen found that animals had broken in "and foxes had dragged books out through the window and left them scattered all over the snow."[42] Like Leffingwell, Mikkelsen lived a long and productive life, passing away in his nineties in Copenhagen in 1971. In 2009 the Danish navy named a Knud Rasmussen–class patrol vessel for him, the HDMS *Ejnar Mikkelsen*. Appropriately, the ship routinely cruises the waters around Greenland.

Others, like the execrable Dr. Shorkley, unrepentantly traded on their experiences in Franz Josef Land for the rest of their lives. In January 1910 Shorkley was quoted in the *Daily Picayune* in New Orleans in support of the claim to the North Pole of Robert Peary. The newspaper described the decidedly unheroic doctor as "one of the heroes of the quest for the North Pole" and "one of the most noted arctic explorers in the world, and a member of the National Geographic Society."[43] As if this wasn't enough to stuff a goat, Shorkley allowed the newspaper to print without correction the following calumny: "He also refused to state what part he took in preserving the lives of the men on the Ziegler expedition, but it is well known that it was through the skill and care of Dr. Shorkley that the whole party was saved from perishing between 81 and 83 degrees of latitude."[44] Shorkley served as an army officer in the First World War, promoted, as was his despised expedition commander Fiala, to the rank of major.

Thirty years after his rescue at Cape Flora, Shorkley unsuccessfully ran for Congress from a district in the Pacific Northwest. During his campaign, he gilded the lily of his year at Cape Flora, telling a reporter that in the summer of 1905, "all our ammunition was gone and we lived on what birds we could kill with clubs. The men who ate their own rawhide shoelaces, with the result that many froze their feet, refused to eat the dogs, which had saved our lives so often."[45] A tried and true Mason, Shorkely died of a heart attack at his home in Mount Vernon, Washington, on November 30, 1945, at the age of seventy-four. His body was returned to Pennsylvania for burial in a family plot in Lewisburg cemetery.[46]

Of the Norwegians who accompanied Wellman to Franz Josef Land, Paul Bjørvig lived into his seventies and, in a nation of polar heroes, became something of a minor polar legend himself. After the Wellman expedition, Bjørvig was a member of the German expedition to Antarctica on board the *Gauss* and led by Erich von Drygalski. He returned to the Arctic with Wellman as a member of Wellman's airship expeditions to Spitsbergen, overwintering on Danskøya in 1906–1907 and 1908–1909. During the latter period, he experienced the death of another Norwegian companion, Knut Johnsen, who fell through the ice and drowned.

Peter Tessem joined Roald Amundsen's *Maud* expedition in 1918, but when he and another man sought to leave the expedition a year later and walk out to Dickson Island, eight hundred kilometers away, both were lost. Three years later, Tessem's body was found just three kilometers from the Dickson Island telegraph station, and he "would have been able to see the lights there before he died. A gold watch engraved with Tessem's name and a gold ring engraved with the name of his wife were found on the corpse. It was presumed that Tessem in that case had almost reached his goal when he slipped on the way down the slope, knocked himself out and froze to death."[47]

The brothers Emil and Olaf Ellefsen continued their exploring ways after the Wellman expedition. Emil traveled abroad on sailing ships and later as an officer on the express route along the coast of Norway. In 1906 he became harbormaster in Hammerfest and settled down there, fathered five children, and passed away in 1943. Olaf, too, sailed the world for some years before he also returned to Hammerfest and settled down with a family.

He became the captain of a local passenger ship stationed in Hammerfest and died there in the mid-1940s.[48]

Of the Americans with Wellman, Dr. Edward Hofma became a banker and was later elected a senator in the Michigan state legislature. He served the Twenty-third District, comprising the counties of Ottawa and Muskegon, from 1912 to 1916. At the age of seventy-five, and two years before his death in 1936, he donated forty acres of land to the city of Grand Haven for the creation of Hofma Park and Nature Preserve.

The Coast and Geodetic Survey physicist and photographer Quirof Harlan returned from the Wellman expedition and was married soon afterward. He and his wife had a son in 1911, and Harlan passed away at the age of fifty-two in 1926.

Baldwin's problematic skipper/master/sailing master Carl Johan Johanson was connected with a large shipping company in Stockholm called Rederi AB after 1910. He was employed as mate and captain on a succession of Swedish merchant vessels.[49] He dropped from sight around 1927, having perhaps retired from the sea. It is believed that he died in Stockholm in 1942.

The bellicose American chief engineer of the *America*, Henry P. Hartt, completely vanishes from history after his remarkable times in Franz Josef Land.

The other Swedish officers of the *America* had careers of some note. Svante Rudolf (Ralph) Bergendahl went to Antarctica in 1903 onboard the *Frithjof*, in relief of Otto Nordenskjöld and the Swedish Antarctic expedition. In 1905 and again in 1907 he served under the Duke of Orleans as first officer on the *Belgica* during expeditions to Spitsbergen, northeast Greenland, and Novaya Zemlya. After his polar voyages he worked as a master mariner on both sailing ships and motor ships until he retired in 1939. During his polar expeditions he kept diaries, the Baldwin-Ziegler diary being the most extensive at 276 written pages. He settled in Göteborg and later in Ugglarp, County Halland, after his retirement, and died at the age of eighty-one in Malmö, Sweden, in January 1957.[50]

Johan Menander also went to Antarctica with the Nordenskjöld relief expedition. Afterward, he settled in Göteborg and became commander on the ship *Skagerak*, a research vessel belonging to the Swedish oceanographic commission that was used for oceanographic research in the Swedish west coastal waters and the North Sea. Some problems and controversies evolved during his time on the *Skagerak* and in October 1909 Menander escaped from his command in Hamburg. He turned up in the United States in 1910 and settled in New York, where he made contact with Anthony Fiala and was elected a member of the Explorers Club. He became a naval officer in the U.S. Navy during the First World War and later engaged himself in the oil industry in Texas—together with the Zelig-like Frederick Cook. After a few years, Menander moved to Detroit, where he became connected with the Chrysler Company. He died in Detroit in 1935, aged fifty-eight. He body was cremated and returned by post to his still-living mother in Sweden. There he was buried in Burlöv in Skåne County.[51]

As for the expedition leaders themselves, Wellman, Baldwin, and Fiala had possessed precious little of the scientific curiosity, writing genius, physical courage, and unquestioned leadership skills demonstrated by a John Wesley Powell, even as they explored a region of the planet in many ways as new and mysterious and beautiful as the Grand Canyon at the time when Powell began his explorations. Unlike Powell, who had to be dragged into writing a popular account of his scientific expedition, the three American explorers of Franz Josef Land had to be pushed to produce scientific accounts of their largely popular expeditions. Two of them, Wellman and Baldwin, never made proper scientific reports of their results, although Baldwin did pen a meteorological study of his year in Franz Josef Land with Wellman. Fiala, the only one of the three to arrange for a proper scientific account, left the job to his second-in-command, William Peters. Peters was a U.S. government surveyor—a kind of Powell-lite, if you will—and he hastily cobbled together lists of observations into a thick and well-produced volume. But even this rudimentary job Peters could not see through. He quickly tired of the task and departed Washington, D.C., for a study of magnetic phenomena in the tropics. He left his assistants to finish the job.

It was perhaps too much to ask of any American—much less men with such debilitating limitations as Wellman, Baldwin, and Fiala—to compete on the Arctic stage with a giant like Fridtjof Nansen. Wellman was only fractionally correct in his 1897 estimation: "Nansen is getting rich." Nansen was unique among polar explorers in the titanic range of his intellect, the strength of his physique, the magnitude of his physical preparations, and the power of his writing and credibility of his scientific reports.

Even the popular reports of the American exploration of Franz Josef Land, submitted in newspapers and monthly magazines, never achieved the literary heights of a Nansen or a Powell, to say nothing of the first great American hero of the Arctic, Elisha Kent Kane. Describing the Rio de la

Virgen, Powell wrote, "At ordinary stages it is very wide but very shallow, rippling over the quicksands in tawny waves. On its way it cuts through the Beaver Mountains by a weird canyon. On either side greasewood plains stretch far away, interrupted here and there by bad-land hills."[52] On board *Fram,* Nansen had filled his diaries with similar such descriptions of the Arctic landscape, and then added to them the recurring nightmares of failure that haunted him: "I had a strange dream last night. I had got home. I can still feel something of the trembling joy, mixed with fear, with which I neared land and the first telegraph station. I had carried out my plan; we had reached the North Pole on sledges, and then got down to Franz Josef Land. I had seen nothing but drift-ice; and when people asked what it was like up there, and how we knew we had been to the Pole, I had no answer to give; I had forgotten to take accurate observations, and now began to feel that this had been stupid of me. It is very curious that I had an exactly similar dream when we were drifting on the ice-floes along the east coast of Greenland, and thought that we were being carried farther and farther from our destination."[53] Walter Wellman, a professional writer one might have expected to raise his pedestrian journalism to new heights once stimulated by the magnificent scenery of the Arctic, never elevated his craft to meet the challenge of the Franz Josef Land wilderness. Certainly Wellman never produced the kinds of brilliant constructions Powell could employ to describe the American West or Nansen the torments of a professional explorer of the Arctic. His description of the death of Bernt Bentsen was more exploitation than elegiac.

Even so, his Norwegian comrades always spoke well of him, and that counted for something. Paul Bjørvig, the Ellefsen brothers, Daniel Johansen—none of these rugged men ever had a bad word to say about the remarkable journalist-explorer. Bjørvig returned to work for Wellman again and again, even enduring another overwintering and the death of his lone companion that winter—this time in 1906–1907 at Wellman's fantastical aeronautical base camp on Danskøya in Spitsbergen.

For it was on Danskøya, the same place where the lonely Professor Øyen had denounced him in 1894 and where Salomon Andrée had lifted off toward the pole in 1897, where Wellman continued his pursuit of the North Pole after Franz Josef Land. He not only abandoned Franz Josef Land as a base, he abandoned the use of sledges as a method of polar travel, and abandoned completely his relationship with E. B. Baldwin.

In 1906, a year after the final American retreat from Franz Josef Land, Wellman's newspaper, now renamed the *Chicago Record-Herald,* fronted him an enormous sum for yet another polar expedition. These funds allowed Wellman to attempt an unprecedented, privately funded, real-life Vernian expedition that demolished the existing limits of polar exploration technology. In Paris, Wellman had a dirigible balloon constructed and, at Virgo Harbor on Danskøya in Spitsbergen, erected a large airship hangar and expedition base camp.

In a somewhat ghoulish homage, Wellman built his base at Virgo Harbor in plain view of the ruins of the hangar used by Salomon Andrée in 1896–97. Wellman's airship hangar was not completed until August 1906, and when he tested the airship's engines, the machines promptly self-destructed.

Wellman returned to Virgo Harbor in the summer of 1907, in possession of a new airship, one configured by an extremely clever American mechanic, wanderer, and photographer by the name of Melvin Vaniman. Vaniman scrapped the original French car created a year earlier by Louis Godard in Paris and designed one of his own. This car could carry enough fuel to power the airship all the way to the North Pole and back. The expedition was pinned on Danskøya by strong winds that did not abate until early September 1907. By then, an impatient Wellman ordered an ill-advised trial flight that covered only fifteen miles. Still, the brief excursion marked the first time a motorized airship had flown in the Arctic.

In the summer of 1909, after a year away from the Arctic to cover the American presidential election of 1908—the third and final attempt by William Jennings Bryan to turn the tide of the American business elite— Wellman tried for the North Pole one last time. About sixty miles north of the hangar at Virgo Harbor, a trailing ballast line that Wellman called an "equilabrator," fell off. The loss of so much ballast caused Wellman to turn the airship around and receive a rescue tow from a Norwegian survey ship that had been cruising nearby. As he returned to Norway, Wellman learned of the competing claims to the North Pole by Robert Peary and Frederick Cook. Just as the Americans had abandoned Franz Josef Land as a path to the pole in 1905, Wellman abandoned Spitsbergen in September 1909. His final retreat from the north also marked the end of American exploration of the polar basin from the European side of the globe.

In search of a new sensation, Wellman the following year turned his attention to the Atlantic Ocean. In another dirigible designed by Vaniman,

Wellman, along with Vaniman and a few other men, lifted off from Atlantic City, New Jersey, in October 1910. They flew for over a thousand miles— far more than the distance from Virgo Harbor to the North Pole—before engine trouble forced the crew to abandon ship not far from Bermuda. The airship came down within a mile of a passing steamer, which delivered the journalist and his crew to shore. His Atlantic adventure set a record for the longest airship flight to that moment in aviation history.

After the Atlantic flight in 1910, Wellman never again left the surface of the earth. His rocky marriage to Laura finally fell apart, with his wife for years afterward writing bitter denunciations over his lack of support for her. She ended her life dividing her time as a boarder with her five daughters. For his part, Wellman fulfilled at least a part of his Scandinavian dream when he married Bergljot Bergersen, a Norwegian woman twenty-four years younger than himself, and had three children with her. To the last, Wellman continued to borrow heavily from his ever-tolerant brother Arthur, as well as others who were far less tolerant. In 1926 he spent a brief time behind bars after he left a $250 loan unpaid for a year and a half.[54]

Wellman's reputation recovered after his passing. When he died, Wellman received generous if somewhat bemused obituaries in national newspapers and magazines. The *Wall Street Journal* wrote that American journalism had "germinated no personality more picturesque than Walter Wellman. . . . He was aviation's earliest writing enthusiast . . . and into strenuous practicality from strenuous writing went Wellman. 'Vividest of my dreams,' he wrote, 'is visioning myself from my plane saluting the North Pole.'

> One day last summer he sent this note to an old Wall Street journalist friend:
>
> "Let's spend an evening together—ruminating on half a century of close-ups to newspapers, and the hundred varieties of folks that newspapering brings into acquaintance. Gee! But don't humans fluctuate."[55]

During the Second World War, the United States Maritime Commission mass produced more than twenty-seven hundred cargo ships, dubbed "Liberty Ships." The ships were named after prominent deceased Americans, beginning with Patrick Henry and the signers of the Declaration of Independence and continuing through the presidents of the United States, including William McKinley. Robert Peary had a Liberty Ship named for him, as did other famous American explorers like Meriwether Lewis and Zebulon Pike, as well as even famous showmen, such as P. T. Barnum. So it was entirely appropriate that on September 29, 1944, the Todd Houston Shipbuilding Corporation in Houston, Texas, launched the SS *Walter Wellman*.[56]

Walter Wellman died of liver cancer in New York City in January 1934. In his will, he recognized his first wife and his five daughters with the sum of one dollar each. Unlike Fiala, who is interred at Arlington National Cemetery, or Baldwin, lying under his self-created "Arctic Explorer" monolith in Kansas, Wellman's family recalls only that he requested that his body be cremated.[57] The final disposition of the ashes of this man who lived a full life right to the end has been lost to time.

Like Wellman, Anthony Fiala had several more adventures to live after Franz Josef Land. He completed and published his history of the Ziegler Polar Expedition in 1906, a well-produced volume that is primarily valuable today for Fiala's own fine photographic record and the inclusion of Russell Porter's excellent sketches and maps. The text consists largely of Fiala's uninspired religious wanderings amongst the heathens who accompanied him to Franz Josef Land.

While he occasionally ventured onto the lecture circuit to retell his dramatic escape from the crevasse on the Hooker Island glacier, Fiala also continued to build a career as a serious explorer. Ten years after the start of the Ziegler Polar Expedition, Fiala and his film camera accompanied part of Theodore Roosevelt's 1914 descent of a tributary of the Amazon, a disastrous expedition beset by disease and murder. Fiala, as the veteran expedition naturalist George Cherrie wrote, was removed as "utterly incompetent for the work he has to do without previous experience in the tropics without any knowledge of the character of the people with whom he must treat and the almost insurmountable handicap of not having any knowledge of the language."[58] Somewhere, George Shorkley no doubt enjoyed a snort of recognition.

Fiala then served on the home front during the First World War, and eventually received a commission as a major in the U.S. Army. He also continued his "chalk talks" into the 1920s, lecturing on quasi-biblical subjects—such as speculations that mammoths were still alive and roaming the tundra of Russia, and proposing an expedition to go and find them (later American polar myths would have Richard Byrd spotting a living wooly mammoth from the air as he flew over the North Pole. As luck would have it, neither event ever happened, not the mammoth nor Byrd flying over the pole). Fiala opened a sporting goods store at 25 Warren Street in Brooklyn, in what is now the Columbia Street Waterfront District, "where explorers [could] assemble supplies and equipment for expeditions."[59]

In 1928, at the age of fifty-eight, Fiala proposed a new North Pole expedition. Such was his standing that, even a quarter-century after the Ziegler expedition, Fiala could still command attention in the *New York Times.* "According to his present plans, which are tentative, Mr. Fiala would lead a small expedition of three or four men across the polar regions from Franz Josef Land to Grant Land, whence he can return to the American mainland. The trip will be made in two American tractors and one of the tractors will be left at the North Pole as a landmark and as proof that the spot has been crossed by his expedition."[60] Still settling scores all those years later, Fiala could not restrain himself from taking another jab at his erstwhile "homeseekers." Describing the aftermath of the half-hearted attempt on the pole in 1904, Fiala related how the expedition subsequently split into two groups, one determined to try again for the pole and the other, the "homesick group," equally determined to retreat. Given Fiala's experience with both Scandinavians and Americans in Franz Josef Land, as well as the new Norwegian primacy in polar exploration created by Fridtjof Nansen and Roald Amundsen, Fiala's proposed $150,000 expedition would sail from Norway—and employ only Norwegian explorers. The expedition never came off, but its plan showed how the Americans had come full circle from Wellman's Norwegian-dependent foray to Franz Josef Land in 1898.

In 1930, after the discovery of Andrée on Kvitøya, Fiala was back in the news. Fiala told a fabulous tale implicating Captain Coffin in the failure to find Andrée in Franz Josef Land in 1903. "I have not mentioned this before," Fiala told a reporter, "but now that Captain Edward Coffin, the navigator of the *America,* is dead, I feel that I am free to do so."[61] While cruising northward "almost due east of White Island [Kvitøya]," a lookout on board *America* had seen "the body of a man, dressed in furs" near Rudolf Island but, according to Fiala, the superstitious Coffin refused to stop and retrieve the dead man. This was, of course, impossible, as the route of the *America* in 1903 was hundreds of nautical miles to the east of the location where Andrée and his two companions were eventually found. Fiala certainly knew this, yet still compounded his fiction with the claim that he had sent Porter and Vedoe to "White Island," all the while knowing that the White Islands of Franz Josef Land were not in any way the same as the White Island (Kvitøya) of Svalbard.

A radically different version of this macabre story turned up in the Norwegian newspaper *Nordland Avis* of October 7, 1930. In this version, Fiala is said to have met the wife of a North Dakota doctor by the name of Engstad during a cruise in the Baltic in 1903. In the wife's diary of June 8, 1903, she writes that Fiala said to her that the Baldwin-Ziegler Expedition, while en route to Franz Josef Land, passed so close to White Island that they could see the bodies of the Andrée and his men, dressed in fur clothes. The observation was forwarded to the captain but due to his superstitious nature he refused to take the bodies onboard.[62] Since the captain of the ship in this instance would have been Andrée's fellow countryman Carl Johan Johanson—who would have become a national hero in Sweden as well as famous internationally had he returned with the bodies of the balloonists—this version is simply not credible. However, both stories worked, albeit briefly, to place Fiala back in the news.

Anthony Fiala was the last of the three Americans to command an expedition in Franz Josef Land to pass. He died in April 1950 at the age of eighty. By then, the details of his experiences in the Arctic had become a bit garbled, and Franz Josef Land itself—by then long hidden behind the curtain of Soviet communism—was not even mentioned in his obituaries. A funeral service was held at the Christ Protestant Episcopal Church in Brooklyn, where Fiala, the "Christian fatalist," had been a vestryman. Along with his two sons, U.S. Navy veteran Reid Fiala, who earned a Silver Star as commander of the destroyer USS *Remey* during the Battle of Leyte Gulf during the Second World War and retired as a rear admiral, and Anthony Fiala, Jr., a U.S. Army veteran, Fiala is buried in Arlington National Cemetery.

Fiala's fibs in the wake of the discovery of Salomon Andrée in the far northeast of Svalbard were nothing compared to the whoppers let loose by Evelyn Briggs Baldwin both before and after his expedition leadership in Franz Josef Land. From the moment he was fired by William Ziegler, Baldwin was destined to spend the rest of his days reliving and reimagining his place in the aeronautical exploration of the Arctic. He seems never to have become discouraged by his repeated failure to advance his polar ambitions beyond Cape Auk. Instead, he spent much of the rest of his life agitating for support for a polar drift similar to Nansen's 1893–96 *Fram* expedition.

Soon after his return from Franz Josef Land, Baldwin proposed, on the basis of his auroral research in both Greenland and Franz Josef Land, that there existed "great electrical currents passing through the earth from the North to the South Pole" and that these currents would supply the electricity needs of the entire planet.[63]

Baldwin's proposed four-year drift expedition, first announced ten years later in the summer of 1909, sought to combine many of his ideas for polar exploration. He proposed to deposit a group of scientists on an island of ice near the Bering Strait, and then gradually cross the Arctic Basin on board this floating island. Balloons and dirigibles would allow the scientists to explore the area around their ice island—and provide a means of escape if necessary. A hothouse cut into the ice itself would allow the explorers to grow fresh vegetables to supplement their diet of whale, walrus, and bear meat. There was no mention of Swedish conserves.

Within months of this announcement, however, both Peary and Cook had staked their claims to the North Pole, and Baldwin's ice island expedition stalled. Baldwin proposed a similar expedition in 1912, this time with a ship specially designed and strengthened for the drift across the Polar Sea. The 150-foot vessel would be equipped with wireless telegraphy for communication with the outside world and a windmill—similar to that employed by Nansen on *Fram*—to generate electricity. Before these plans could proceed anywhere, they were interrupted by the First World War.

By the war's conclusion, Baldwin was approaching sixty years of age and his active field exploration career was over. From 1926 to 1930 he worked as an historian in the Office of Naval Records and Library of the Navy Department in Washington, D.C., where odd bits of his past career occasionally returned him to the spotlight. In early August 1930 one of Baldwin's 1902 balloon messages was found on Novaya Zemlya.

The Russian expedition on board the Soviet icebreaker *Sedov* that found the buoy had just come from a visit to Baldwin's base camp on Alger Island. When the *Sedov* expedition searched the Alger Island site, they found that it had been heavily disturbed. A number of buildings were explored, and inside was a confusion of expedition gear, medical supplies, and cans of spoiled food. The Russians decried the looting apparent at Baldwin's old base camp, and implored the Soviet government to protect these artifacts which were "of great historical interest."[64]

The renewed interest in the balloon messages and the explorations of the base camp allowed the aging Baldwin a few more seconds of public glory. The *New York Times* immediately sent a reporter to interview the long-forgotten explorer in Washington. "On my return I offered a prize of $5 for the return of any of these," Baldwin noted, without mentioning that he had been requested to pay out these rewards by the U.S. government.[65] But Baldwin's brief return to polar glory was soon overwhelmed by the innervating discovery of the remains of the Andrée expedition on Kvitøya.

The very next day, visited by an Associated Press reporter, the other advocate of balloon buoy messages in the Arctic repeated, for one last time, his autobiographical mythology. Now sixty-eight-years old and "a white-haired veteran of the frozen North," Baldwin explained that only "a delay of forty-eight hours prevented his going on the ill-fated North Pole expedition of Salomon-August Andrée, whose body has been found in the Arctic after a lapse of thirty-three years."[66]

Seeking to extend his sudden return to fame and capitalize on the great public fascination with the return of the artifacts of Andrée's expedition to Sweden, Baldwin in December 1930 presented to the Norwegian legation in Washington, D.C., the message he had retrieved after burrowing through the snow and into Nansen's hut in 1902. It was the last remaining trinket from an expedition that had begun three decades earlier with more men, money, and promise than any other American polar expedition before it. With his return of the Nansen message to Norway, the circle of Baldwin's ambitions in the Arctic was finally complete.

The inattention shown by Baldwin to actual operational details was a common theme during all three American expeditions to Franz Josef Land. Each took their respective successes in financing and publicity as substitutes for operational expertise. Baldwin took the opportunity afforded by Ziegler's money to order literally tons of equipment for the expedition from friends as well as relatives, like the balloon-making Baldwin Brothers, but seems not to have taken much of their advice on how to make the best use of it in the field. Instead, as in his almost desperate pursuit of the Nansen message, he went off in search of "discoveries."

Baldwin's cousin Thomas Scott Baldwin, an accomplished aeronaut, had not in 1901 pushed beyond the fairground amusement stage in his ballooning. He had encountered innumerable delays in his search for an internal combustion engine both light and powerful enough to drive a small dirigible. It was not until 1904 that he could add the construction of dirigibles to his existing balloon-construction business and go on to greater fame with his dirigible, the *California Arrow*.[67] In the hands of a skilled aeronaut like

Thomas Scott Baldwin, even Walter Wellman's polar dirigible might have stood a far better chance of success.

Three years after his brief return to public notice in August 1930, Baldwin was dead. As he tried to cross a busy street in Washington, D.C., on the evening of October 25, 1933, he was struck by a passing car.[68] His skull was fractured and he died en route to the hospital, aged seventy-one.

Today, more than a century after his Franz Josef Land adventures, the memory of his polar ambitions has been kept alive, perhaps fittingly, in obscure and rather bizarre ways. On one Internet site called "Women in History: A List of Names," the re-gendered "Evelyn Briggs Baldwin— U.S. meteorologist, arctic explorer" occupies a spot between Emily Greene Balch, an American economist and 1946 Nobel Peace Prize winner, and Maria Baldwin, the first African-American woman principal in the state of Massachusetts.

Then there is a work of fiction entitled *Indiana Jones and the Hollow Earth*. In this adventure novel, Indiana Jones and a character named Ulla Tornaes, "a beautiful Danish scientist," use data uncovered by Arctic explorer Evelyn Briggs Baldwin to race Nazi explorers to an Arctic portal where they find "the key to Hitler's mad plan for world domination." Writes novelist Max McCoy: "the story was inspired by a real-life Arctic explorer from Kansas by the name of Evelyn Briggs Baldwin."[69] His failed associations with the self-styled dashing journalist Walter Wellman now long forgotten—along with his even greater failure to lead William Ziegler's capital to the North Pole—Baldwin might be heartened to learn that a modern generation of pulp fiction readers now link his name and career with the even more dashing—albeit fictional—archaeologist named Indiana Jones, and with the salvation of civilization itself.

It was reported that Baldwin was nearly destitute at the time of his death. It is tempting to believe that, as he stepped into the road on the night he was killed, his mind was distracted, floating somewhere above the Arctic landscape, maybe in the Swedish balloon that had finally found a place for him. He lies in Oswego Cemetery in Labette County, Kansas, under a monolith he made certain was incised with the only two words he ever wanted attached to his name: "Arctic Explorer."

A Note on Sources

The reader will note, especially in the chapters concerning Walter Wellman, a wide variety of citations from newspapers both national and regional. The inclusion of such a wide geographic dispersal of representative articles—testifying to the national syndication of Wellman's work—was made possible only by access to the searchable database of "America's Historical Newspapers," a collection managed by the Archive of America, published by Readex, a division of Newsbank, Inc., and one of several invaluable databases available to the faculty of the Pennsylvania State University through an excellent system of libraries.

Original materials related to the 1898–99 Wellman expedition are contained in the Walter and Arthur Wellman Collection at the National Air and Space Museum Archives at the Udvar-Hazy Center in Chantilly, Virginia, and in the papers of Evelyn Briggs Baldwin at the Library of Congress in Washington, D.C. Additional materials can be found in the Evelyn B. Baldwin scrapbook collection in the Western Historical Manuscript Collection of the University of Missouri at Columbia. Emil Ellefsen's diary is in the possession of his grandson, Eivind Klykken, in Hammerfest, Norway. Materials related to Eivind Astrup were kindly made available by Tom Bloch-Nakkerud in Oslo.

For the Baldwin-Ziegler Polar Expedition, one begins with Baldwin's papers at the Library of Congress, where some of the papers of Leon Barnard

A NOTE ON SOURCES

are also housed. Additional Barnard papers are held at the Scott Polar Research Institute at the University of Cambridge in Cambridge, United Kingdom (MS 1514). Major collections of papers from Ernest Leffingwell, Russell Porter, Charles Seitz, George Shorkley, and Anton Vedoe are all archived within the excellent Stefánsson collections at the Rauner Library at Dartmouth College. Mikkelsen's brief journals from 1901 reside in Det Kongelige Bibliotek (the Royal Library of Denmark and Copenhagen University Library).

The author is particularly grateful to Mary Louise Crocker and Helen Frykman for permission to use material from the papers of Anthony Fiala, their grandfather and great-grandfather, respectively. Translations from Swedish sources were provided by my excellent colleagues in Gothenburg, Magnus Forsberg and Anders Larsson.

For the Ziegler Polar Expedition under Fiala, the above-mentioned papers of Porter, Seitz, Shorkley, and Vedoe are essential. Additional materials can be found in the papers of Francis Long, stored at the archives of the Explorers Club in New York. The diary of Edwin Coffin, Jr., as well as Arthur Railton's series of articles based upon them and published in the Dukes County *Intelligencer,* can be found at the Martha's Vineyard Historical Society on Martha's Vineyard, Massachusetts.

Notes

Baldwin journal | "Journal of the Wellman Polar Expedition" (unpublished typescript), 1899. Baldwin Papers. Manuscript Division, Library of Congress, Washington, D.C.

Baldwin Papers | Anonymous. "Biographical Sketches of the Members and Crew of the Baldwin-Ziegler Polar Expedition. S.S. *America*." [1901.] E. B. Baldwin Papers. Folder "Biographies— Baldwin-Ziegler Expedition." Box 8. Manuscript Division. Library of Congress. Washington, D.C.

Barnard Papers, LC | Alice Barnard Thomsen, "History of the Baldwin-Ziegler Expedition." Papers of Leon F. Barnard, 1901–1993. Library of Congress, Manuscript Division, Washington, D.C.

Barnard Papers, SPRI | Leon F. Barnard Papers, Scott Polar Research Institute Archives.

Fiala Papers | Anthony Fiala Papers, privately held.

MVHS | Martha's Vineyard Historical Society.

SPRI   Scott Polar Research Institure Archives.
STEF   Stefansson Collection, Rauner Special
                    Collections Library, Darmouth College.
WAWC/NASM   Walter and Arthur Wellman Collection,
                    National Air and Space Museum.

Preface

1. Leffingwell, "My Polar Explorations, 1901–14," 2.

Introduction: Off the American Route

1. New York *Herald,* June 3, 1845, p. 1. For an introduction to Arctic exploration generally, a very high standard is still set by Berton, *The Arctic Grail.*

For an excellent introduction to American exploration in the Arctic, see Robinson, *The Coldest Crucible.* Caswell's *Arctic Frontiers* remains the only synthesis of the scientific results of the American exploration of the Arctic, and was based on his 1951 dissertation at Stanford, "The Utilization of the Scientific Reports of United States Arctic Expeditions, 1850–1909."

2. See, for example, Simmonds, *The Arctic Regions,* 325–27.

3. Quoted in Simmonds, *The Arctic Regions,* 328.

4. Caswell, *Arctic Frontiers,* 15. De Haven died in Philadelphia in 1865 and was buried a few feet from Benjamin Franklin in Old Christ Church Burial Ground in the city. Two U.S. Navy destroyers were named for him during the Second World War.

5. Kane became famous with the publication of *The U.S. Grinnell Expedition in Search of Sir John Franklin* and an international icon with *Arctic Explorations.* George Corner's *Doctor Kane of the Arctic Seas* was the first modern attempt at a life of Kane and there has been an upsurge of interest in Kane in the twenty-first century, with Ken McGoogan's *Race to the Polar Sea* and Mark Sawin's *Raising Kane.* Kane's extravagent funeral cortège, one that extended from Havana, Cuba, where he died, to Laurel Hill Cemetery in Philadelphia, where he was interred in an almost pharaonic tomb above the Schuylkill River, remains one of the most elaborate ceremonial spectacles in American history. Elder's 1858 biography of Kane devotes more than a hundred pages to the funeral obsequies alone.

6. Kane, *Arctic Exploration,* 305.

7. Hayes, *The Open Polar Sea,* 315.

8. The life and explorations of Hall are described in the still-unrivaled biography by Chauncey Loomis, *Weird and Tragic Shores.*

9. See, for example, Beau Riffenburgh's excellent account of this era in *The Myth of the Explorer.*

10. For a comprehensive overview of the *Jeannette* disaster, see Leonard Guttridge, *Icebound.*

11. For more on Greely, see Greely et al., *Report on the Proceedings of the United*

States expedition to Lady Franklin Bay, Grinnell Land; as well as the modern accounts contained in Leonard Guttridge's *Ghosts of Cape Sabine* and Alden Todd's *Abandoned*.

12. The best account of Peary and his obsessive quest for the North Pole is contained in Sir Wally Herbert's immense *The Noose of Laurels*. The struggles of the mystical Frederick Cook are chronicled in minute detail in Robert Bryce's *Cook and Peary*. Eivind Astrup's brief, brilliant life has been comprehensively covered in Tom Bloch-Nakkerud's excellent *Polarforskeren Eivind Astrup*.

13. The Western discovery and exploration of Franz Josef Land is covered in Susan Barr's seminal edited volume *Franz Josef Land* and in her own contribution to that volume, "The History of Western Activity in Franz Josef Land." Gunnar Horn's *Franz Josef Land: Natural History, Discovery, Exploration, and Hunting* (Oslo: J. Dybward, 1930) remains invaluable. A stunning historical archaeology of the islands has just been published in Russian by I. B. Baryshev, *Zemlya Frantsa-Iosfia*.

14. For Payer's own account of the discovery, see *New Lands Within the Arctic Circle*.

15. Leigh Smith's life and expeditions are covered in Capelotti, *Shipwreck at Cape Flora*.

16. See, in particular, Nansen's own account in *Farthest North*, as well as Roland Huntford's *Nansen: The Explorer as Hero*.

17. Jackson's own account of his extended exploration of Franz Josef Land is contained in *A Thousand Days in the Arctic*.

18. For excerpts from the diaries and journals of Salomon Andrée and his companions, see *Andrée's Story*. Several editions were published, including one under the name of the Swedish Society for Anthropology and Geography: *Andrée's Story: The Complete Record of His Polar Flight, 1897*.

19. On the first of January 1925, the name of the capital of Norway was changed from Kristiania—as well as its earlier Danish spelling, Christiania—to Oslo.

20. The Duke of the Abruzzi's account of his polar expedition is found in Luigi Amedeo of Savoy, *On the "Polar Star" in the Arctic Sea*.

EXPEDITION ONE: THE GREAT AMERICAN ACT OF HUSTLING

1. Joshua Wyman Wellman, *Descendants of Thomas Wellman of Lynn, Massachusetts*, 69–72, 407, 500–502.

2. Cohen, "The Emancipation of Boyhood."

3. *Cincinnati Post*, http://en.wikipedia.org/wiki/The_Cincinnati_Post, accessed September 29, 2008.

4. "Insolent Clerks," *Cleveland Plain Dealer*, February 25, 1885: 42 (46): 1.

5. "Purveyors of News," *Jackson (Miss.) Citizen*, April 19, 1892, p. 6.

6. Emmet Pierce, "George Pullman's company town a social experiment that derailed," *San Diego Union Tribune*, May 15, 2005, http://www.utsandiego.com/uniontrib/20050515/news_1h15pullman.html, accessed June 2, 2013.

7. "Pullman a Success," *Aberdeen (S.Dak.) Daily News*, 1 (117): 2, December 8, 1886

8. Ibid.

9. Ibid.

10. Ibid.

11. "Rich Men of Chicago," *Augusta (Ga.) Chronicle*, July 22, 1888, p. 12.

12. "Money Has No Charm," *Wheeling (W.V.) Register,* 28 (66): 9, September 18, 1892.

13. "Celestial Scenery," *Knoxville (Tenn.) Journal,* October 26, 1892, 8 (244): 6.

14. See Capelotti and Forsberg, "The Place Names of Zemlya Frantsa-Iosifa."

15. "Dignity of the Senate," *Aberdeen (S.Dak.) Daily News* 4 (201): 4, April 1, 1890.

16. "Swell Tea Parties," *Columbus (Ga.) Daily Enquirer* 34 (13): 11, January 15, 1893.

17. "Interviewing Big Men," *(Columbia, S.C.) State* 1 (70): 2, April 27, 1891.

18. Ibid.

19. "Girls at the Capital," *Augusta (Ga.) Chronicle* 1484: 2, January 11, 1891.

20. "Chief Justice Fuller," *Aberdeen (S.Dak.) Daily News* 4 (124): 2, December 31, 1889.

21. "Under the Ground," *Duluth (Minn.) Daily News* 2 (108): 3, September 10, 1887.

22. "Passenger Elevators," *Augusta (Ga.) Chronicle* 1214: 6, August 24, 1889.

23. "Advertising as Art," *Duluth (Minn.) News-Tribune* 22 (102): 11, April 12, 1891.

24. "Memorable Names," *Knoxville (Tenn.) Journal* 8 (145): 6, July 19, 1892.

25. "Cape May Musings," *Duluth (Minn.) News-Tribune* 22 (230): 6, August 30, 1891.

26. "Old Naval Heroes," *Idaho Statesman* 28: 3, January 28, 1892.

27. "Electrical Power," *Columbus (Ga.) Daily Enquirer* 32 (226): 10, September 11, 1892.

28. "Aerial Destroyers," *Idaho Statesman* 30: 5, March 1, 1894.

29. "Columbus's first landing place," *New York Times,* June 5, 1891, p. 2.

30. "On Watlings Island," *Idaho Statesman* 29: 6, October 1, 1892.

31. Ibid.

32. "The Herald's Expedition," *Chicago Herald,* June 16, 1891, p. 2.

33. "On Watlings Island," *Idaho Statesman* 29: 6, October 1, 1892.

34. Ibid.

35. Ibid.

36. Ibid.

37. Ibid. The precise Bahamian island where Columbus made first landfall on October 12, 1492, remains unsolved. But, by the 1920s, the accumulating weight of opinion agreed with Wellman, and Watling Island was renamed as the San Salvador of Columbus.

38. "World's Fair talk," *Idaho Statesman* 28: 3, March 26, 1892.

39. "The woes of office," *Idaho Statesman* 29: 6, February 26, 1893.

40. "A glorious spot," *Idaho Statesman* 29: 7, May 2, 1893.

41. "Railway train exhibit," *Idaho Statesman* 29: 6, May 23, 1893.

42. "Some big words," *Jackson (Miss.) Citizen,* May 23, 1893, p. 11.

43. "Walter Wellman on Future Modes of Travel," *Duluth (Minn.) News-Tribune,* 13: 12, May 7, 1893.

44. Bolotin and Laing, *The World's Columbian Exposition,* 41.

45. "Fish at the fair," *Worcester (Mass.) Daily Spy,* June 15, 1893, p. 6.

46. Ibid. Wellman was no doubt also drawn to Norway by the other exhibits at the fair, including an "exact replica of the 1,000-year-old vessel commanded by Leif Ericson" (Bolotin and Laing, *The World's Columbian Exposition,* 111) and an entire reconstruction of a Norse stave church. The church is one of the few buildings constructed for the 1893 fair that survives to the present day, at the living museum site of Little Norway in Blue Mounds, Wisconsin.

47. See Kjell-Gudmund Kjær, "Serial slaughter," 1–20. As Kjær writes: "The fleet increased almost eightfold, from 6 vessels in 1859 to 46 in 1909 while the harvest of seals increased from less than 1500 to over 30000 animals annually. The geographical range of the hunting grounds expanded correspondingly from a limited area around Jan Mayen and the west coast of Spitsbergen to a huge area which included the western ice (north and south of Jan Mayen), the northern ice (Svalbard), the eastern ice (Kola Peninsula to Novaya Zemlya, the White Sea), Zemlya Frantsa-Isoifa [Franz Joseph Land], the Denmark Strait and northeast Greenland."

48. "A great work of art," *Idaho Statesman* 29: 6, June 24, 1893.

49. Huntford, *Nansen,* 179.

50. "Greatest of Them All," *Idaho Statesman* 29: 6, August 5, 1893.

51. Wellman, *The Aerial Age,* 17.

52. Kjær, "Serial Slaughter," 1–20.

53. See, for example, Parry, *Narrative of an attempt to reach the North Pole;* and Capelotti, *Shipwreck at Cape Flora,* 13–18.

54. Wellman, *The Aerial Age,* 17.

55. "Lost in the Arctic," *Chicago Herald,* October 28, 1893.

56. Wellman, *The Aerial Age,* 17.

57. "The Gridiron roast," *Trenton (N.J.) Evening Times,* February 7, 1894, p. 6.

58. Kjell-G. Kjær, personal communication, August 31, 2013. The spelling of Ålesund in Wellman's time would have been Aalesund, and Tromsø would be spelled Tromsoe. These contemporary spellings have been retained in quotations from original documents, but the modern spelling used everywhere else.

59. Wellman, *The Aerial Age,* 17; Carlheim-Gyllensköld, *På Åttionde Breddgraden,* 107.

60. "Will try to reach the North Pole," *Philadelphia Inquirer* 130 (56): 1, February 25, 1894.

61. Ibid.

62. Ibid.

63. Alme, *Om Spitsbergen og den Wellmanske polarekspedisjon,* 2; and Alme, "Om Spitsbergen og den Wellmanske polarekspedition."

64. Kjell-G. Kjær, personal communication, August 31, 2013.

65. "Will Try to Reach the North Pole," *Philadelphia Inquirer* 130 (56): 1, February 25, 1894.

66. "Arctic Explorers Talk," *Trenton (N.J.) Evening Times,* March 8, 1894, p. 6.

67. "A Flag for the North Pole," *Trenton (N.J.) Evening Times,* March 12, 1894, p. 2.

68. Wellman to family, letter, April 12, 1894, Walter and Arthur Wellman Collection, National Air and Space Museum (hereafter referred to as WAWC/NASM; see complete crew list in Alme, *Om Spitsbergen og den Wellmanske polarekspedisjon,* 2; and Alme, "Om Spitsbergen og den Wellmanske polarekspedition").

69. See Alme, *Om Spitsbergen og den Wellmanske polarekspedisjon,* 2. Paul Bjørvig's name appears in many different forms in as many publications. Wellman usually spelled it "Bjoervig," while Baldwin used "Bjorvik" and, occasionally, "Bjorvig," sometimes using these variant spellings within the same paragraph. I have retained the spellings that Wellman and Baldwin used in their original accounts, but have substituted the current Norwegian spelling of "Bjørvig," as well as "Bentsen" for Bernt Bentsen, in my text.

70. Wellman to family, letter, April 26, 1894, WAWC/NASM.

71. "Honors to Wellman in Norway," *New York Times,* May 20, 1894.

72. Wellman to family, letter, April 26, 1894, WAWC/NASM.

73. Ibid.

74. Ibid.

75. Ibid.

76. Kjell-G. Kjær, personal communication, August 31, 2013.

77. "Lost in the Arctic Floes," *New York Times,* July 25, 1894.

78. Wellman, *The Aerial Age,* 21.

79. Ibid., 21–22.

80. Ibid.

81. Ibid., 18.

82. "The Wellman Polar Expedition," *The Times,* September 3, 1894.

83. "The Wellman Polar Expedition," *The Times,* September 10, 1894.

84. Kjell-G. Kjær, personal communication, August 31, 2013; see also Pearson, *Beyond Petsora Eastward.* Feilden's ice pilot was none other than Captain Johan Kjeldsen (1840–1909), who would join Feilden on Henry Pearson's expedition to Novaya Zemlya in 1897 and would figure so prominently in the later American expeditions to Franz Josef Land and Wellman's airship expeditions in Spitsbergen. Kjeldsen was already in 1894 a Norwegian Arctic legend, with expedition experience that traced as far back as Weyprecht and Payer's *Isbjørn* voyage in 1871.

85. "The Wellman Arctic Expedition," *The Times,* July 25, 1894.

86. Ibid.

87. Wellman, letter to H. W. Leman, May 15, 1894, Chicago Historical Society.

88. Ibid.

89. Wellman, *The Aerial Age,* 23.

90. Ibid.

91. Wellman, *The Aerial Age,* 24; see also "Explorer Wellman Alive," *New York Times,* August 3, 1894, p. 3.

92. H. W. Leman to Edward G. Mason, letter, February 8, 1898, Chicago Historical Society.

93. Wellman, *The Aerial Age,* 24.

94. Kjell-G. Kjær, personal communication, August 31, 2013; see also Bottolfsen, *Dagbok.*

95. Wellman, *The Aerial Age,* 25.

96. See Capelotti, "Benjamin Leigh Smith's First Arctic Expedition," 8, for a discussion of the search for the elusive Giles Land.

97. "Explorer Wellman Alive," *New York Times,* August 3, 1894, p. 3.

98. Wellman, *The Aerial Age,* 26.

99. Ibid., 29.

100. "Driven Back by Cold," *New York Times,* August 17, 1894, p. 3. Cape Gresham was located on the eastern coast of Kapp Platen (see Alme, *Om Spitsbergen og den Wellmanske polarekspedisjon,* 5). As for the derivation of Armour, Wellman had shipped two and a half tons of Armour brand processed meats for the expedition (see letter from Wellman to family, April 26, 1894, WAWC/NASM). Walsh was John R. Walsh, the owner of Wellman's paper, the *Chicago Herald;* Gresham derived from Secretary of State Walter Q. Gresham; and Whitney is most likely to have referred to William

Collins Whitney, secretary of the navy from 1885 to 1889. He, like Gresham, would have been one of Wellman's many contacts in Washington, D.C., society.

101. Heyerdahl, "*Kanes reise langs Spitsbergens vestkyst.*"

102. "The Wellman Arctic Expedition," *The Times,* August 9, 1894, p. 5.

103. Wellman, *The Aerial Age,* 31.

104. "The Wellman Arctic Expedition," *The Times,* August 4, 1894, p. 5.

105. "Relief for Wellman," *New York Times,* August 4, 1894, p. 5.

106. Wellman to family, letter, August 20, 1894, WAWC/NASM. Remarkably, as of 2013, the *Berntine,* built in 1890, still operates, sailing from the southern Norway port of Tønsberg (Kjell-G. Kjær, personal communication, August 31, 2013).

107. Wellman to family, letter, August 20, 1894, WAWC/NASM.

108. Ibid.

109. Ibid.

110. "The Wellman expedition," *The Times,* September 11, 1894, p. 4.

111. Ibid.

112. Wellman to family, letter, August 20, 1894, WAWC/NASM.

113. "Baffled by the Ice Packs," *New York Times,* September 27, 1894, p. 4.

114. "Explorer Wellman Alive," *New York Times,* August 3, 1894, p. 3.

115. "Advertisement," *Boston Journal,* September 8, 1894, Volume 61, Issue 20082, p. 1.

116. *New York Herald,* September 2, 1894, Issue 21195, p. 4.

117. Wellman, *The Aerial Age,* 35.

118. Wellman, *The Aerial Age,* 37.

119. See Capelotti and Forsberg, "The Place Names of Zemlya Frantsa-Iosifa."

120. "To the Pole by balloon," *Omaha (Neb.) World Herald,* September 18, 1894, vol. 29, p. 5.

121. Wellman, *The Aerial Age,* 36.

122. Ibid., 38.

123. Ibid., 39.

124. Ibid., 38.

125. "Peary's Crisis," *Boston Daily Advertiser,* September 27, 1894, vol. 164, p. 4.

126. "Astrup Will Try to Reach the Pole," *Philadelphia Inquirer,* September 29, 1894, vol. 131, issue 91, p. 1.

127. "A Talk with Astrup," *Philadelphia Inquirer,* October 11, 1894, vol. 131, issue 103, p. 1.

128. Bryce, *Cook and Peary,* 133.

129. "On a Spree," *Cleveland Plain Dealer,* September 17, 1894, p. 2.

130. "Wellman at Home," *Kansas City (Mo.) Times,* September 30, 1894, p. 20.

131. "For another trip," *Boston Daily Journal,* October 9, 1894, vol. 61, issue 20113, p. 7.

132. Wellman to Baldwin, letter, November 12, 1894, Baldwin Papers.

133. "To Find the North Pole," *Kansas City (Mo.) Star,* December 9, 1894, vol. 15, issue 83, p. 2.

134. "Told by Famous Men," *Wheeling (W.Va.) Register,* July 15, 1895, vol. 30, issue 334, p. 2.

135. "Diplomatist Olney," *Duluth (Minn.) News-Tribune,* December 29, 1895, vol. 15, p. 2.

136. "Aluminum Boats," *Aberdeen (S.Dak.) Daily News,* October 19, 1895, vol. 10, issue 69, p. 2.

137. "Walter Wellman in Iowa," *Sioux City (Ia.) Journal*, October 9, 1896, p. 7.

138. Huntford, *Nansen*, 349.

139. Ibid., 272.

140. Bryce, *Cook and Peary*, 138.

141. "Will Use Balloons," *Philadelphia Inquirer*, December 15, 1896, vol. 135, issue 168, p. 3.

142. "These to Go North," *New York Herald*, January 3, 1897, p. 16.

143. Walter Wellman to Arthur Wellman, letter, February 1899, WAWC/NASM.

144. "A Glorious Climate," *Idaho Statesman*, July 7, 1897, p. 5.

145. "Uncle Sam Will Annex Cuba," *Kansas City (Kans.) Semi-Weekly Capital*, May 21, 1897, vol. 19, issue 41, p. 3.

146. "Statement of All Aid to the Wellman Expedition," WAWC/NASM; see also Capelotti and Forsberg, "The Place Names of Zemlya Frantsa-Iosifa."

147. Walter Wellman to Arthur Wellman, letter, July 10, 1897, WAWC/NASM. Wellman also demonstrated his political connections in obtaining a pension for their father "of eight dollars a month, with a year's back pay. I have advised him of it. Mr. [H. Clay] Evans, the commissioner of pensions, is a warm friend of mine, and I did not have much difficulty in getting it pushed through."

148. "A correspondent abroad," *Columbus (Ga.) Daily Enquirer*, August 22, 1897, vol. 38, issue 250, p. 12. It also appears likely that Wellman met Frederick Jackson during this trip through England. In *The Lure of Unknown Lands*, 249–50, Jackson writes of the aftermath of Wellman's expedition to Franz Josef Land: "Wellman (American) had the misfortune seriously to injure a leg, which stopped further sledging, and was still very lame when I met him again in London on his return. He extended my discoveries in the neighbourhood of Brady Island, and, but for ill luck, might have done other useful work. He did me the honour giving my name to a new island 'Jackson Island.'" "I met him *again* [emphasis added]" suggests that the two met in London after Jackson returned from Franz Josef Land and before Wellman left on his own expedition, and the moment seems to have been in August 1897.

149. Ibid.

150. "Nansen Is Getting Rich," *Idaho Statesman*, December 23, 1897, p. 6.

151. "Walter Wellman's Polar Trip," *New York Times*, August 25, 1897, p. 5; see also "To the pole," *Broad Ax (Salt Lake City)*, January 1, 1898, p. 2.

152. "Ny Nordpolsexpedition," *Aftenposten*, August 25, 1897.

153. Huntford, *Nansen*, 375.

154. Ibid.

155. "Nansen Is Getting Rich," *Idaho Statesman*, December 23, 1897, p. 6. Wellman, no doubt thinking back with extreme guilt on his treatment of his own dogs in 1894, also expounded sympathetically on Nansen's story of killing his last two dogs. "No one familiar with the circumstances will place any blame upon the explorer," Wellman wrote, in words he no doubt wished could be applied to himself. "At his beautiful home in Norway, overlooking that matchless sheet of water, the Kristiania fiord, Dr. Nansen keeps several dogs as pets, and no one that has seen him caressing them would ever suspect him of cruelty to these dumb servants."

156. "Wellman's Next Venture," *New Haven (Conn.) Register*, vol. 34, issue 304, p. 12.

157. "To the Pole," *Broad Ax (Salt Lake City)*, January 1, 1898, p. 2.

158. Ibid.

159. "His next venture," *Columbus (Ga.) Daily Enquirer,* January 14, 1898, vol. 39, issue 12, p. 7.

160. "An Andree Searching Party," *New York Times,* March 14, 1898, p. 5. See also Wellman's detailed exposition in his article "Where Is Andrée?" *McClure's Magazine,* March 1898.

161. Phillips, *William McKinley,* 87.

162. For a discussion of these contributions and the naming of geographic places in Franz Josef Land, see Capelotti and Forsberg, "The Place Names of Zemlya Frantsa-Iosifa."

163. Walter Wellman to Arthur Wellman, letter, July 1, 1898, WAWC/NASM.

164. Ibid.

165. Baldwin, Journal of the Wellman Polar Expedition, 30, italics in original journal (hereafter referred to as Baldwin journal).

166. "Cyclone Cellars in Demand," *New York Tribune,* May 2, 1898, p. 11.

167. Walter Wellman to Arthur Wellman, letter, July 1, 1898, WAWC/NASM. As soon as he arrived in Scandinavia, Baldwin was further dispatched to Göteborg, Sweden, to meet with Salomon Andrée's brother Ernst, to offer the expedition's assistance in searching for the missing aeronaut, and no doubt also in an attempt to tap into any potential Swedish funding (see "Wellmans Nordpolsexpedition," *Tidningen Kalmar,* no. 89, June 13, 1898). This was no doubt a much sought-after assignment for Baldwin, desperate as he was to prove his bona fide associations with the Swedish balloon expedition.

168. See *Conditions for engaging the men to the Wellman polar expedition, 1894/1898,* Baldwin Papers.

169. Walter Wellman to Arthur Wellman, letter, July 1, 1898, WAWC/NASM.

170. Baldwin journal, 119.

171. "Off for the Pole," *Minneapolis (Minn.) Journal,* May 6, 1898, p. 8.

172. Wellman, *The Aerial Age,* 42–43.

173. Walter Wellman to Arthur Wellman, letter, July 1, 1898, WAWC/NASM. The careers of the *Laura* and the *Frithjof* would be entwined again a decade later. "*Frithjof* participated in several North Pole expeditions between 1898 and 1907 and was also involved in several relief expeditions. Her most frequent commander was Captain Johan Kjeldsen, who was an internationally famous ice pilot. *Frithjof* was built in 1884 at Stokke on Oslo fjord, Norway. After . . . Wellman's North Pole expedition . . . she was the expedition ship for the Kolthoff expedition to Greenland, Spitsbergen and Jan Mayen. Between 1901 and 1904 she was engaged in Ziegler's North Pole expeditions both as expedition ship and as relief vessel. In 1903 the Swedish government chartered *Frithjof* in order to search for the Nordenskjöld expedition in the Antarctic. In 1906–1907 the ship was again chartered for Wellman's North Pole airship expeditions. In late September 1907, *Frithjof* sailed from Tromsø on a relief expedition to search for *Laura,* an expedition vessel to Greenland that had not been heard of for three months. On 5 October 1907 she was lost in a storm off Iceland and only one man survived from her crew of 17." Kjell-G. Kjær, "The Polar Ship *Frithjof,*" 281–89.

174. Walter Wellman to Arthur Wellman, letter, July 1, 1898, WAWC/NASM.

175. Ibid.

176. The results of the expedition—Coats's addition to a long British tradition of

yacht explorations of the far north—were delivered by Bruce to the Scottish Geo-graphical Society and later written up for *The Scottish Geographical Magazine* 15, no. 3, 113–26. In the event, the state of the ice in the summer of 1898 prevented *Blencathra* from reaching Franz Josef Land, but the cruise did sail along the northern coast of Russia to explore the island of Kolguev and then northward to the coast of Novaya Zemlya. A second cruise north of Norway reached Bjørnøya (Bear Island), Hopen (Hope Island), and again to Novaya Zemlya.

177. Walter Wellman to Arthur Wellman, letter, July 1, 1898, WAWC/NASM.

178. Ibid.

179. E. B. Baldwin to Arthur Wellman, letter, July 3, 1898, WAWC/NASM.

180. Walter Wellman to Arthur Wellman, letter, July 1, 1898, WAWC/NASM.

181. "Prof. Gore Leaves Wellman," *Wisconsin Weekly Advocate,* September 29, 1898, p. 2.

182. Baldwin journal, July 15, 1898.

183. Ibid., July 16, 1898.

184. Wellman, *The Aerial Age,* 42.

185. Walter Wellman to Arthur Wellman, letter, July 16, 1898, WAWC/NASM.

186. Ibid.

187. Baldwin, *The Franz Josef Land Archipelago,* 28.

188. Bjørvig, *Norwegian Bravado,* 3.

189. Baldwin journal, 122.

190. Baldwin, *The Franz Josef Land Archipelago,* 28.

191. Ibid., 29.

192. Ibid., 29–30.

193. Ibid., 30.

194. Ibid., 31.

195. Ibid., 32.

196. Ibid., 33.

197. Ibid., 34.

198. Ibid.

199. Wellman, *The Aerial Age,* 42–43. Wellman was correct to assume that any knowledge of the fate of Andrée would create enormous interest in the press. When the remains of Andrée and his companions were finally located in the summer of 1930 on Kvitøya (White Island), an ice-covered island between the rest of Spitsbergen and Franz Josef Land, the discovery created an international sensation. The tragedy led to the publication of innumerable books and articles that were raced into print during the autumn after the discovery. A documentary novel about the expedition published by Swedish writer Per Olof Sundman in 1967 was translated in 1981 into a movie star-ring Max von Sydow as Andrée. Scholarly interest in the expedition and speculations as to why it failed and the crew perished continue to the present; see, for example, Wråkberg, "Andrée's Folly," 200. Bjørvig, *Norwegian Bravado,* 3.

201. Bjørvig, *Norwegian Bravado,* 3.

202. Baldwin, *The Franz Josef Land Archipelago,* 36–37.

203. Ibid., 37.

204. See Capelotti and Forsberg, "The Place Names of Zemlya Frantsa-Iosifa." According to Wellman's "statement of all aid" in his papers at the National Air and Space Museum Archives, Lambert Tree (1832–1910) donated $150 to the expedition.

Also listed on the statement is "Comp. Dawes," a reference to the then-Comptroller of the Currency Charles G. Dawes (1865–1951), who donated $100 to the expedition.

205. Baldwin, *The Franz Josef Land Archipelago*, 38. Bjørvig's journal identified it as the *Herta* [*Hertha*], out of Drammen; Baldwin's as the *Hekla,* from Tønsberg.

206. Ibid.

207. Walter Wellman to Arthur Wellman, letter, August 2, 1898, WAWC/NASM.

208. Ibid.

209. Ibid.

210. Walter Wellman to his daughters, August 2, 1898, WAWC/NASM.

211. Ibid.

212. Baldwin, *The Franz Josef Land Archipelago,* 39.

213. Walter Wellman to his daughters, August 2, 1898, WAWC/NASM.

214. Baldwin, *The Franz Josef Land Archipelago,* 39–40.

215. Ibid., 41.

216. Wellman, *The Aerial Age,* 43.

217. Baldwin, *The Franz Josef Land Archipelago,* 42.

218. Walter Wellman to Arthur Wellman, letter, August 2, 1898, WAWC/NASM.

219. Wellman, *The Aerial Age,* 49.

220. Ibid., 49–50.

221. Ibid., 50–52.

222. Walter Wellman to his daughters, August 2, 1898, WAWC/NASM.

223. Baldwin, *The Franz Josef Land Archipelago,* 42.

224. Wellman, *The Aerial Age,* 51.

225. Ibid., 51–52.

226. Ibid., 53.

227. Going ashore at Cape Tegetthoff in August 2006, more than a century after Wellman's camp was built, the author found that the floorboards, the tiny stove, and a few of the walls of this hut still remained.

228. Baldwin, *The Franz Josef Land Archipelago,* 42.

229. Wellman to Baldwin, quoted in Baldwin, *The Franz Josef Land Archipelago,* 127–29.

230. Ibid., 129.

231. Kjell-G. Kjær, personal communication, August 31, 2013.

232. Bjørvig, *Norwegian Bravado,* 4.

233. Baldwin, "Meterological Observations of the Second Wellman Expedition," 351.

234. Bjørvig, *Norwegian Bravado,* 4.

235. Baldwin, *The Franz Josef Land Archipelago,* 42–44.

236. Ibid., 44.

237. Ibid., 45.

238. Ibid., 130.

239. Emil Ellefsen *dagbok,* August 7, 1898, privately held.

240. Baldwin, *The Franz Josef Land Archipelago,* 45.

241. Ibid.

242. Ibid.

243. Ibid., 46.

244. Ibid., 47.

245. Ibid., 47–48.

246. Ibid.

247. Emil Ellefsen *dagbok,* August 12, 1898.

248. Baldwin, *The Franz Josef Land Archipelago,* 130–31.

249. Bjørvig, *Norwegian Bravado,* 4.

250. Baldwin, *The Franz Josef Land Archipelago,* 130.

251. Ibid., 140.

252. Ibid., 49.

253. Ibid. For a discussion of the raised beaches found by historic expeditions to the Arctic, see Capelotti, "Benjamin Leigh Smith's Third Arctic Expedition."

254. Baldwin, *The Franz Josef Land Archipelago,* 50.

255. Ibid., 50–51.

256. Ibid., 52.

257. Ibid., 52.

258. Baldwin, "Meterological Observations of the Second Wellman Expedition," 349–436. Later, as he cast about for places he could name in order to justify the expedition, Wellman appropriately named the small island after Julius Payer, perhaps recalling his experience at the Chicago fair and Payer's painting of his own struggles in Franz Josef Land. Baldwin, who makes no mention of a name for the new island in his journal, later wrote a report for the U.S. Weather Bureau in which he claimed that he had immediately named the island after the incumbent chief of the Weather Bureau, Willis L. Moore. But this was almost certainly special pleading after the fact. By the time Baldwin wrote his Weather Bureau report, he had long since fallen out with Wellman and sprinkled his weather bureau report with subtle critical remarks about the expedition's logistics. In the event, both names were discarded, and Berghaus became the name of the new island.

259. Baldwin, *The Franz Josef Land Archipelago,* 53.

260. Ibid., 54.

261. Bjørvig, *Norwegian Bravado,* 4.

262. Baldwin, *The Franz Josef Land Archipelago,* 131–32.

263. Ibid., 55.

264. Ibid.

265. Ibid., 56.

266. Bjørvig, *Norwegian Bravado,* 5.

267. Baldwin, *The Franz Josef Land Archipelago,* 56.

268. Ibid., 57.

269. Bjørvig, *Norwegian Bravado,* 5.

270. Baldwin, *The Franz Josef Land Archipelago,* 132–33.

271. Ibid., 134.

272. Ibid.

273. Ibid.

274. Ibid., 136–37.

275. Ibid., 137.

276. Ibid., 139.

277. Ibid.

278. Ibid., 140.

279. Ibid., first italics mine.

280. Ibid., italics in original.

281. Bjørvig, *Norwegian Bravado*, 5.
282. Baldwin, *The Franz Josef Land Archipelago*, 57, italics in original.
283. Ibid., 57.
284. Ibid.
285. Ibid.
286. Ibid.
287. Ibid., 58–59.
288. Ibid., 59.
289. Ibid.
290. Ibid.
291. Ibid., 60.
292. Ibid.
293. Emil Ellefsen *dagbok*, August 20, 1898.
294. Baldwin, *The Franz Josef Land Archipelago*, 61.
295. Ibid.
296. Ibid., 62.
297. Ibid., 63.
298. Ibid., 64.
299. Emil Ellefsen *dagbok*, August 25, 1898.
300. Baldwin, *The Franz Josef Land Archipelago*, 141.
301. Ibid., 144.
302. Ibid., 142.
303. Ibid., 142–43.
304. Ibid., 144.
305. Ibid.
306. Ibid., 145.
307. Ibid., 149.
308. Ibid., 149.
309. Ibid., 145–46.
310. Ibid., 146.
311. Ibid., 147–48.
312. Ibid., 148.
313. Ibid., 150.
314. "Wellman's Brave Attempt to Find the North Pole," *Chicago Times-Herald*, May 15, 1898.
315. Baldwin journal, 42.
316. Baldwin, *The Franz Josef Land Archipelago*, 68.
317. Ibid., 69–70.
318. Ibid., 70.
319. Ibid.
320. Ibid., 76.
321. Ibid.
322. Ibid., 71–72.
323. The Soviets later named them the Komsomol'skie Islands after the All-Union Leninist Young Communist League (Komsomol), but it is probable that a re-examination of the history of the area would produce a solid case to rename the larger island for Norway, after the Norwegians of Wellman's expedition, and the small island after

Bernt Bentsen, who died during the Wellman expedition and is buried a few miles north at Cape Heller.

324. Bjørvig, *Norwegian Bravado*, 6.

325. Ibid.

326. Ibid.

327. Baldwin, *The Franz Josef Land Archipelago*, 71.

328. Ibid.

329. Ibid., 72.

330. Ibid., 72–73.

331. Ibid., 74.

332. Ibid., 74–75.

333. Ibid., 74.

334. Ibid., 76.

335. Ibid., 75.

336. Ibid., 77.

337. Ibid., 81.

338. Ibid.

339. Ibid., 77.

340. Ibid., 79.

341. Ibid., 81.

342. Ibid., 85–86.

343. Ibid., 85.

344. Ibid.

345. Bjørvig, *Norwegian Bravado*, 6.

346. Ibid., 7.

347. Ibid., 7.

348. Ibid., 7–8.

349. Baldwin, *The Franz Josef Land Archipelago*, 88.

350. Ibid., 89–90.

351. Ibid., 90, italics in original.

352. Ibid.

353. Bjørvig, *Norwegian Bravado*, 8.

354. Baldwin, *The Franz Josef Land Archipelago*, 90–91.

355. Ibid., 91.

356. Bjørvig, *Norwegian Bravado*, 8.

357. Ibid.

358. Ibid., 8–9.

359. Emil Ellefsen *dagbok,* September 28, 1898.

360. Kjell-G. Kjær, personal communication, August 15, 2013.

361. Magnus Forsberg, personal communication, October 17, 2013.

362. Baldwin, *The Franz Josef Land Archipelago*, 93.

363. Ibid., 150.

364. Baldwin, "Meterological Observations of the Second Wellman Expedition," 353.

365. The Italian-born Albert Operti (1852–1927) was an artist who painted dozens of Arctic scenes including those from Peary's 1896 expedition to Greenland. Rudolf Kersting (1856–1931) was a photographer who had been on Cook's disastrous *Miranda* expedition to Greenland in 1894.

366. Baldwin, *The Franz Josef Land Archipelago,* 150.

367. Ibid., 94.

368. Ibid., 95.

369. Ibid., 97.

370. Bjørvig, *Norwegian Bravado,* 9.

371. Baldwin, *The Franz Josef Land Archipelago,* 98.

372. Ibid., 99.

373. Ibid., 100.

374. Ibid.

375. Emil Ellefsen *dagbok,* October 3, 1898.

376. Baldwin, *The Franz Josef Land Archipelago,* 101.

377. Ibid.

378. Emil Ellefsen *dagbok,* October 5, 1898.

379. Baldwin, *The Franz Josef Land Archipelago,* 103.

380. Ibid.

381. Ibid., 104.

382. Ibid., 105.

383. Ibid., 105.

384. Ibid., 151.

385. Ibid., 154.

386. Ibid., 152.

387. Emil Ellefsen *dagbok,* October 9, 1898.

388. Baldwin, *The Franz Josef Land Archipelago,* 105.

389. Ibid., 106.

390. Ibid., 108.

391. Ibid., 107.

392. Ibid., 97.

393. Ibid., 98, italics in original.

394. Ibid., 108.

395. Ibid.

396. Ibid.

397. Ibid.

398. Ibid., 109.

399. Ibid.

400. Ibid., 111.

401. Ibid.

402. Ibid.

403. Wellman's attempt to name the larger island Whitney Island did not survive; Payer's earlier La Ronciere survived but as the name of the new island.

404. Wellman to Baldwin, August 27, 1898, Baldwin Papers.

405. Wellman, *The Aerial Age,* 48.

406. Wellman to Baldwin, August 27, 1898, Baldwin Papers.

407. Wellman, *The Aerial Age,* 48.

408. Ibid.

409. It was during this march southward that Baldwin first used the name Quereau Glacier in his journal, to indicate the ice barrier that separated Cape Heller from Storm Bay on the west coast of Wilczek Land (Baldwin, *The Franz Josef Land*

Archipelago, 117). In his later report to the U.S. Weather Bureau, Baldwin first uses this name for his entry for August 29, writing that he "ascended slope of Quereau Glacier, overlooking Storm Bay," although his journal indicates this ascent was actually made the following day (Baldwin, "Meterological Observations of the Second Wellman Expedition," 416). There is no certain origin for the name Quereau, though the likeliest is perhaps an American geologist/glaciologist E. C. Quereau.

410. Baldwin, *The Franz Josef Land Archipelago,* 120.

411. Ibid., 125.

412. Ibid.

413. Ibid.

414. Wellman to Baldwin, August 15, 1898, Baldwin Papers.

415. Wellman to Baldwin, August 27, 1898, Baldwin Papers.

416. Wellman, *The Aerial Age,* 49.

417. Ibid., 54.

418. Wellman, "The Wellman Polar Expedition," 495.

419. Baldwin, "Meterological Observations of the Second Wellman Expedition"; Baldwin, "Report on Auroras."

420. Baldwin, "Report on Auroras," 36.

421. Wellman, "The Wellman Polar Expedition," 492.

422. Ibid.

423. Walter Wellman to Arthur Wellman, December 31, 1898, WAWC/NASM.

424. Ibid.

425. Ibid.

426. Ibid.

427. Ibid.

428. Ibid.

429. Walter Wellman to Arthur Wellman, February 15, 1899, WAWC/NASM, italics in original.

430. Ibid.

431. Ibid.

432. Andreas Aagaard to Eckels, January 20, 1899, WAWC/NASM.

433. Ibid.

434. Ibid.

435. Andreas Aagaard to Arthur Wellman, January 20, 1899, WAWC/NASM.

436. Fridtjof Nansen to Andreas Aagaard, January 2, 1899, WAWC/NASM.

437. Henry S. Pritchett to Arthur Wellman, March 22, 1899, WAWC/NASM. It is interesting to note that a check on the annual reports of the Coast and Geodetic Survey for the five years following the return of the Wellman expedition show no contribution either from Harlan himself or on Franz Josef Land generally.

438. Arthur Wellman to Andreas Aagaard, February 9, 1899, WAWC/NASM.

439. Andreas Aagaard to Arthur Wellman, April 17, 1899, WAWC/NASM.

440. Walter Wellman to Arthur Wellman, February 15, 1899, WAWC/NASM.

441. Ibid.

442. Ibid.

443. Ibid.

444. Wellman, "The Wellman Polar Expedition," 491.

445. Bjørvig, *Norwegian Bravado,* 9.

446. Ibid.
447. Ibid., 10.
448. Ibid.
449. Ibid.
450. Ibid., 12.
451. Ibid.
452. Ibid., 13.
453. Ibid., 14.
454. Ibid.
455. Ibid., 15.
456. Ibid., 16.
457. Ibid., 17.
458. Ibid., 18.
459. Wellman, "The Wellman Polar Expedition," 498.
460. Wellman, *The Aerial Age*, 71.
461. Ibid., 72.
462. Ibid., 73.
463. Ibid., 75.
464. Ibid.
465. Bjørvig, *Norwegian Bravado*, 19.
466. Ibid.
467. Ibid.
468. Wellman, *The Aerial Age*, 79–80.
469. Ibid., 80.
470. Wellman, "The Wellman Polar Expedition," 498–99.
471. Wellman, *The Aerial Age*, 83.
472. It is certainly possible Wellman waited until March 17, as he later wrote that March 20 was the day when the sun would return to the North Pole and mark the unofficial start of a six-month period in which to reach the pole in daylight. However, Wellman's dallying does not square with his private correspondence to his brother that he intended to start for the pole early in February as well as his actual start date of February 18.
473. Bjørvig, *Norwegian Bravado*, 21.
474. Ibid.
475. Ibid.
476. Wellman, *The Aerial Age*, 105, 108.
477. Bjørvig, *Norwegian Bravado*, 22.
478. Ibid.
479. Wellman, *The Aerial Age*, 113.
480. Ibid., 114.
481. Bjørvig, *Norwegian Bravado*, 23.
482. Wellman, *The Aerial Age*, 116.
483. Baldwin, "Discovery of Graham Bell Land," 1.
484. Payer, *New Lands Within the Arctic Circle*, 2: xvi–xvii.
485. Baldwin, "Journal of the Wellman Polar Expedition," 2.
486. Bjørvig, *Norwegian Bravado*, 24.
487. Paul Bjørvig was by no means past his bitter feelings over Baldwin, and wrote

that "Baldwin says there are three small islands that we can see about two English miles from the spit. I think they are three large bergs we can see" (Bjørvig, *Norwegian Bravado*, 24).

488. Bjørvig, *Norwegian Bravado*, 24.

489. Baldwin, "Meterological Observations of the Second Wellman Expedition," 355.

490. Ibid.

491. Bjørvig, *Norwegian Bravado*, 25.

492. Ibid., 24.

493. Ibid., 25.

494. Baldwin, "Meterological Observations of the Second Wellman Expedition," 355.

495. Baldwin, "Discovery of Graham Bell Land," 6.

496. Ibid.

497. Baldwin, "Journal of the Wellman Polar Expedition," 8.

498. Ibid., 8–9.

499. Ibid., 9.

500. Ibid., 10.

501. Ibid.

502. Ibid., 12.

503. Ibid.

504. The name does not survive on modern charts but in 1955 was attached by Soviet geographers to the south side of Payer Island.

505. Bjørvig, *Norwegian Bravado*, 25.

506. Ibid., 26.

507. Baldwin, "Journal of the Wellman Polar Expedition," 20.

508. Bjørvig, *Norwegian Bravado*, 27.

509. Ibid.

510. Wellman, "The Wellman Polar Expedition," 503.

511. Wellman, *The Aerial Age*, 117.

512. Wellman, "The Wellman Polar Expedition," 500.

513. Wellman, "The Wellman Polar Expedition," 503. Brief notes had on the presumed progress of the expedition had appeared in *National Geographic Magazine* in 1899, including one authored by J. Howard Gore ("The Wellman Polar Expedition"). The final results, such as they were, appeared in the magazine later in 1899 under Wellman's name and were followed by a brief recapitulation of the meteorological results by Baldwin. These Baldwin later expanded in a report to the U.S. Weather Service.

514. Fawcett, "By Balloon to the North Pole," 481–87.

515. Wellman, *The Aerial Age*, 118.

516. Bjørvig, *Norwegian Bravado*, 28.

517. Quoted in "Geographical Notes," American Geographical Society *Journal* 26 (1894): 391–93.

518. *New York Times*, August 18, 1899, p. 7.

519. *New York Times*, August 29, 1899, p. 7.

520. *New York Times*, September 14, 1899, p. 7.

521. *New York Times*, November 19, 1899, p. 2.

522. *New York Times*, August 21, 1900, p. 7.

523. "Walter Wellman home," *Boston Globe*, October 9, 1899.

EXPEDITION TWO: CIGARETTE-SMOKING DUDES

1. Baldwin, "Short Autobiographical Sketch," 1.

2. Ibid.

3. Ibid.

4. Baldwin, "Some Gleamings of the Twi-light days of Aviation."

5. See, for example, *New York World,* 1896.

6. Scamehorn, *Balloons to Jets,* 10–12.

7. Renamed North Central College in 1926 and no relation to Northwestern University in Evanston, Illinois, forty miles to the northeast on the shores of Lake Michigan.

8. Baldwin, "Short Autobiographical Sketch," 2.

9. Ibid., 2–3.

10. Ibid., 3.

11. See, for example, Bryce, *Cook and Peary,* 86–87. Verhoeff's family was hardly comforted by Peary's evasive answers as to the circumstances and his evident lack of enthusiasm for mounting a proper search for the lost man.

12. Baldwin, *The Search for the North Pole,* 446.

13. Ibid., 449.

14. Bryce, *Cook and Peary,* 132.

15. Baldwin, *The Search for the North Pole,* 449, 450. Baldwin lists the source for this superlative quotation as "a recent college publication." It is more than likely that the author was Baldwin himself.

16. Baldwin, "Short Autobiographical Sketch," 4.

17. Bryce, *Cook and Peary,* 133.

18. Eivind Astrup to Baldwin, October 18, 1894, Baldwin Papers.

19. Wellman, *The Aerial Age,* 17–34; Alme, *Om Spitsbergen og den Wellmanske polarekspedisjon.*

20. Walter Wellman to Baldwin, November 12, 1894, Baldwin Papers.

21. Baldwin, *The Search for the North Pole,* 463.

22. Eivind Astrup to Baldwin, December 1, 1894, Baldwin Papers.

23. Baldwin to Eivind Astrup, July 22, 1895, letter in possession of Astrup archives via Astrup biographer Tom Bloch-Nakkerud.

24. Ibid.

25. Anders Larsson, personal communication, January 13, 2014.

26. "Resolution adopted by the under-signed members of the North Greenland Expedition, 1893–4," document in possession of Astrup archives via Astrup biographer Tom Bloch-Nakkerud.

27. Article transcribed by E. B. Baldwin and enclosed in a letter to Astrup, September 5, 1895. The article—as well as the resolution—is in the possession of Astrup archives and made available via Astrup biographer Tom Bloch-Nakkerud.

28. Baldwin to Eivind Astrup, September 9, 1895, letter in possession of Astrup archives via Astrup biographer Tom Bloch-Nakkerud.

29. "Peary's Terrible Trip," *Philadelphia Inquirer,* September 22, 1895.

30. Bloch-Nakkerud, *Polarforskeren Eivind Astrup,* 186. Also Tom Bloch-Nakkerud, personal communication, December 12, 2014.

31. Helgesen, apparently to Baldwin, n.d., transcript, Baldwin Papers.

32. "He knew Astrup," *Duluth News-Tribune,* January 23, 1896; see also "Astrup Found Dead," *Chicago Daily Inter Ocean,* January 22, 1896.

33. "Quickly Disproved," *Philadelphia Inquirer,* May 8, 1896.

34. Anonymous, "Disputing over Nansen."

35. Baldwin, *The Search for the North Pole,* 507.

36. Baldwin Papers.

37. Andrée et al., *Andrée's Story,* 6.

38. Ibid., 8.

39. Ibid., 10; Anders Larsson, personal communication, January 13, 2014. Additional details on Andrée's early ballooning experiences courtesy of Tom Bloch-Nakkerud, personal communication, December 12, 2014.

40. Tucker, "Voyages of Discovery on Oceans of Air," 146.

41. Swedish Society for Anthropology and Geography, *Andrée's Story,* 38.

42. Wråkberg, "Andrée's Folly," 67.

43. See *"En Reise der Westküste Spitzbergen's bis zur Eiskante," Spitsbergen Gazette,* August 24, 1897. The many later versions that Baldwin told of his arrival at the site of Andrée launch site were all designed to make it seem as if he had arrived only days, if not hours, after the balloon lifted off. By examining articles from *Aftenposten* in the summer of 1897, and cross-referencing these with the firsthand accounts of visits to Spitsbergen that summer by the mountaineer Sir Martin Conway and the German Max Wiskott, Magnus Forsberg and Anders Larsson have quite brilliantly set this story straight. Baldwin did not arrive in Spitsbergen until late July, on board the *Lofoten,* a regular summer tourist and mail steamer out of Hammerfest. At Advent Bay, Baldwin transferred to a small coastal steamer, the *Kvik,* for a brief excursion around the northwestern coast of Spitsbergen and a visit to the Andrée launch site. Baldwin ("who was in Greenland with Lieut. Peary") was noticed and even noted by Conway in his book *With Ski and Sledge over Arctic Glaciers,* 67–68. Conway and his party were deposited on July 25 at the head of Kings Bay in order to do several weeks of mountaineering, while Baldwin continued on to visit the Andrée launch site. Baldwin arrived on Danskøya in the evening of July 27, 1897, more than two weeks after the lift-off of Andrée and his crew (Wiskott, *Nach Spitzbergen bis zum ewigen Eise*). The coastal steamer *Kvik* was back at Advent Bay on July 30, where Baldwin would have taken the *Lotoften* back to Norway. Max Wiskott published a small edition book about his travels in the area, and it includes a photograph that purports to show Baldwin at the Andrée launch site.

44. Anders Larsson, personal communication, January 13, 2014, letter in the archives of the Grenna Museum in Gränna, Sweden.

45. *Los Angeles Times,* March 24, 1912, Baldwin Papers.

46. *San Francisco Examiner,* March 10, 1911, Baldwin Papers.

47. *Masonic Standard,* March 3, 1906, Baldwin Papers.

48. *Grit,* July 7, 1901, Baldwin Papers.

49. *New Orleans Daily Picayune,* January 31, 1900, Baldwin Papers.

50. S. A. Andrée to Baldwin, December 20, 1896, Baldwin Papers.

51. S. A. Andrée to Baldwin, April 13, 1897, Baldwin Papers.

52. See note 43 above.

53. Receipt, Worm-Petersen Fotograf, July 15, 1897, Baldwin Papers.

54. Receipt, Grand Hotel, July 14, 1897, Baldwin Papers.

55. Pond to Baldwin, February 9, 1898, Baldwin Papers, italics mine.

56. Wellman, *The Aerial Age*, 117–18.

57. *New York Times*, May 28, 1899.

58. *New York Times*, July 8, 1900; see also Ernst Andrée to Baldwin, December 14, 1899, Baldwin Papers.

59. Amedeo of Savoy, *On the "Polar Star" in the Arctic Sea*, 491–92.

60. *Chicago Times*, July 4, 1900.

61. "Explorer Baldwin Now in New Orleans," *Daily Picayune*, January 28, 1900.

62. See Baldwin, "Meteorological Observations of the Second Wellman Expedition."

63. "The Great Race for the North Pole," *Daily Picayune*, January 31, 1900.

64. Ibid.

65. See Charles Haller, *German-American Business Biographies* (Asheville, N.C.: Money Tree Imprints, 2001), 483–84.

66. "He Wants the Pole," *Minneapolis Journal*, October 29, 1900, p. 8.

67. *Philadelphia Inquirer*, October 15, 1900, p. 16.

68. Ibid.

69. Ibid.

70. Ibid.

71. Ibid., italics mine.

72. Baldwin, "Short Autobiographical Sketch."

73. Ibid.

74. Ibid.

75. See Federal Judicial Center, http://www.fjc.gov/servlet/nGetInfo?jid=621&cid =999&ctype=na&instate=na, accessed September 9, 2013.

76. Baldwin, "Short Autobiographical Sketch."

77. See, for example, several articles from October 13, 1900: "To Spend a Million in Search for North Pole," *New York Journal*; "$1,000,000 Cruise to Find the Pole," *New York Press;* "Bound to Reach the Pole," *New York World*.

78. Baldwin, "Meterological Observations of the Second Wellman Expedition," 59.

79. "To find the North Pole," *The (London) King*, December 22, 1900.

80. "North Pole Fever," *Washington Bee*, November 3, 1900, p. 2.

81. Ibid., italics mine.

82. *Chicago Times-Herald*, November 1, 1900.

83. Riffenburgh, *The Myth of the Explorer*, 196.

84. *Chicago Times-Herald*, November 1, 1900.

85. Anders Larsson, personal communication, January 13, 2014. This possibility was first broached in an article in the Swedish annual research journal *Ymer* as early as 1891. See Hamberg, "Slutligen framlade fil. kand."

86. "Arctic Trip," *Grand Forks Daily Herald*, April 26, 1901, p. 1.

87. "To Find the North Pole," *The (London) King*, December 22, 1900.

88. "North Pole Expeditions," *New York Times*, December 11, 1900, p. 9.

89. Ibid.

90. "To Search for Andree," *The (Elizabeth, N.J.) Journal*, January 8, 1901. Baldwin had first met Ernst Andrée prior to the Wellman expedition to Franz Josef Land, when Baldwin visited Göteborg in June 1898 and promised Wellman's help in the search for Salomon Andrée (see "Wellmans nordpolsexpedition," *Tidningen Kalmar*, June 13, 1898).

91. "Baldwin Will Seek Andree," *New York Times,* May 17, 1901. In fact, the "number" of Swedish sailors was precisely one. "Of the crewmembers of the *America* only Johan Menander had served on expeditions sent out in search for Andrée, namely the two expeditions organized by A. G. Nathorst to Spitsbergen 1898 and northeast Greenland in 1899" (Anders Larsson, personal communication, January 30, 2014).

92. *Chicago Times-Herald,* November 1, 1900.

93. "Arctic Explorer Baldwin Here," *New York Times,* February 4, 1901, p. 7.

94. Ibid., italics mine. Baldwin did not live up to this cryptic reference to the experiences of the Norwegians in 1898. During their first sledging efforts in Franz Josef Land, the Swedes on the Baldwin-Ziegler expedition would complain—just as had the Norwegians—that Baldwin refused the men either tents or sleeping bags (Magnus Forsberg, personal communication, June 16, 2014).

95. "To Plant Our Flag on the North Pole," *Philadelphia Inquirer,* February 4, 1901, p. 2.

96. Ibid.

97. "New York Daily Letter," *Cleveland Plain Dealer,* April 15, 1901, p. 4.

98. The confusion lies in the newspaper record, with some sources referring to "thirty truck-loads," totaling 170 tons, with each truck hauled by four horses to the docks, while other articles refer to 300 tons. These sources all say that the supplies were shipped on the *Pretoria,* while the only bill of lading preserved in Baldwin's papers is for a shipment of 9,585 pounds of supplies to be shipped on the *Phoenicia* from New York to Hamburg, for further shipment onward to Johan Bryde of Sandefjord, Norway.

99. Claude Sintz to Baldwin, June 3, 1901, Baldwin Papers.

100. *Troy (New York) Semi-Weekly Times,* April 16, 1901, p. 1.

101. See "Biographical Sketches of the Members and Crew of the Baldwin-Ziegler Polar Expedition, S.S. *America,*" Baldwin Papers.

102. Barnard polar diary, p. 5, Barnard Papers, LC.

103. Milton Crampton to Leon Barnard, Leon F. Barnard Papers, Scott Polar Research Institute Archives (hereafter SPRI), MS 1514/2/8.

104. "Copy of crew agreement," June 13, 1901, Leon F. Barnard Papers, SPRI, MS 1514/2/12.

105. "Artist Turns Trooper to Fight Spaniards," *Brooklyn Eagle,* August 28, 1898, p. 7.

106. "Four of Baldwin's Party Sail on the St. Paul," *Brooklyn Eagle,* May 29, 1901, p. 22.

107. "Arctic Diary of Anton Vedoe," p. 16, Stefansson Collection, Rauner Special Collections Library, Dartmouth College (hereafter STEF), MSS 233(2).

108. Larsson, ". . . *skönt att än en gang vara bland isen,*" 153–54.

109. See Mikkelsen, *Mirage in the Arctic* and *Conquering the Arctic Ice.*

110. "To Frozen North," *Fort Worth Morning Register,* June 4, 1901, p. 4.

111. "Baldwin Will Seek Andree," *New York Times,* May 17, 1901.

112. "Arctic Trip," *Grand Forks Daily Herald,* April 26, 1901, p. 1.

113. "Explorer Talks plainly," *St. Albans (Vt.) Daily Messenger,* May 25, 1901, p. 1.

114. Ibid.

115. "Fear of an Arctic Pirate," *Kansas City Star,* June 1, 1901, p. 1.

116. "To the Frozen North," *Kansas City Journal* article quoted in *Fort Worth Morning Register,* June 4, 1901, p. 4.

117. Fawcett, "By Balloon to the North Pole."

118. Rilliet, "Detailed Report of the Aeronautical Section," 16.

119. See, for example, "Messages in the air," *St. Albans (Vt.) Daily Messenger,* June 11, 1901, p. 1.

120. Ibid.

121. "To Frozen North," *Fort Worth Morning Register,* June 4, 1901, p. 4.

122. Porter, *The Arctic Diary of Russell Williams Porter,* 78.

123. Barnard polar diary, p. 1, Barnard Papers, LC.

124. "Addendum to contracts, signed at Dundee, Scotland, on June 28, 1901," Barnard Papers, SPRI, MS 1514/2/12.

125. Barnard polar diary, p. 1, Barnard Papers, LC.

126. See "Hedrande försvensk industry."

127. Baldwin to Johan Bryde, July 6, 1901, Baldwin Papers.

128. Cross and Bevan to Baldwin, June 24, 1901, Baldwin Papers.

129. Seitz diary, p. 20, STEF, Mss 244.

130. "*America*'s Crew Arraign Baldwin," *Brooklyn Daily Eagle,* December 27, 1903.

131. Barnard polar diary, p. 3, Barnard Papers, LC.

132. "Polar Dash Perils Described by Baldwin Ziegler Explorer," *San Francisco Chronicle,* June 6, 1932, transcription in "Arctic Diary of Anton Vedoe," p. 18, STEF, MSS 233(2).

133. "Reference notes," August 18, 1901, Baldwin Papers. It is not clear which of the medical personnel wrote this account, whether Verner, Seitz, or DeBruler.

134. "Reference notes," August 18, 1901, Baldwin Papers.

135. Baldwin to Champ, July 16, 1901, Baldwin Papers.

136. Baldwin letters, September 1, 1901, Baldwin Papers. The only Matilda who can be connected to Baldwin was the wife of Ernst Andrée (Magnus Forsberg, personal communication, April 23, 2014). If this is so, it further indicates the depth of Baldwin's desire to tie himself as closely as possible to the Swedish balloon expedition.

137. "Arctic Diary of Anton Vedoe," p. 13, STEF, MSS 233(2).

138. Ibid.

139. Ibid., 14.

140. Anders Larsson, personal communication, January 30, 2014.

141. Larsson, "*. . . skönt att än en gang vara bland isen,*" 155. See also Palle Koch's biography of Mikkelsen, *Kaptajnen. Logbog over polarforskeren Ejnar Mikkelsens togt gennem tilværelsen* (København: Gyldendal, 1980), 48–49.

142. "May Clash in the Arctic," The Biloxi *Daily Herald,* October 23, 1901, p. 7.

143. Barnard polar diary, p. 4, Barnard Papers, LC.

144. Ibid.

145. "*America*'s Crew Arraign Baldwin," *Brooklyn Daily Eagle,* December 27, 1903.

146. Ibid.

147. Anders Larsson, personal communication, January 30, 2014. See also Larsson, "*. . . skönt att än en gang vara bland isen,*" 41.

148. Ibid.

149. Baldwin, "The Baldwin-Ziegler Polar Expedition," Part 1, 398.

150. "Reference Notes," September 9, 1901, Baldwin Papers.

151. "Arctic Diary of Anton Vedoe," p. 14, STEF, MSS 233(2).

152. Barnard polar diary, p. 7, Barnard Papers, LC.

153. From anonymous journal in Baldwin's "Journal" folder, Baldwin Papers.

154. Barnard polar diary, p. 12, Barnard Papers, LC.

155. Ibid., 12–13.

156. Ibid., 16.

157. Ibid., 17.

158. McKinley was killed by a young mill worker–turned–anarchist, unemployed and adrift since the Panic of 1893, who walked to the head of a receiving line at the Pan-American Exposition in Buffalo, New York, and with a small pistol, fired two bullets into the president's belly.

159. Barnard polar diary, p. 13, Barnard Papers, LC.

160. Anders Larsson, personal communication, February 12, 2014.

161. Barnard polar diary, p. 19, Barnard Papers, LC.

162. *"America's* Crew Arraign Baldwin," *Brooklyn Daily Eagle,* December 27, 1903. There was also a curious side note to all of Baldwin's contractual maneuvering. Mikkelsen began keeping a journal, in Danish, on July 26. On August 6 Baldwin ordered him to keep his journal in English, ostensibly so that the paranoid Baldwin could peek at what was being written about him. Mikkelsen gave it a try, and then gave up both Danish and English entries on September 19, 1901, at about the time when Baldwin began to lose control of the expedition completely. The brief journals reside in Det Kongelige Bibliotek (the Royal Library of Denmark and Copenhagen University Library) in Copenhagen and have been digitized at http://www.kb.dk/da/nb/materialer/haandskrifter/HA/e-mss/ejnar_mikkelsen/index.html.

163. Barnard polar diary, p. 21, Barnard Papers, LC.

164. *"America's* Crew Arraign Baldwin," *Brooklyn Daily Eagle,* December 27, 1903.

165. Barnard polar diary, p. 23, Barnard Papers, LC.

166. Ibid., 23.

167. Ibid.

168. Ibid.

169. Baldwin, "The Baldwin-Ziegler Polar Expedition," Part I: 398.

170. Ibid.

171. Baldwin letter of September 26, 1901, Baldwin Papers.

172. Anders Larsson, personal communication, February 12, 2014. See also Larsson, *". . . skönt att än en gang vara bland isen,"* 44.

173. "Autopsies," October 27, 1901, Baldwin Papers.

174. "Polar Dash Perils Described by Baldwin Ziegler Explorer," *San Francisco Chronicle,* June 6, 1932, transcription in "Arctic Diary of Anton Vedoe," p. 20, STEF, MSS 233(2).

175. Barnard polar diary, p. 54, Barnard Papers, LC.

176. "Polar Dash Perils Described by Baldwin Ziegler Explorer," *San Francisco Chronicle,* June 6, 1932, transcription in "Arctic Diary of Anton Vedoe," p. 21, STEF, MSS 233(2).

177. *"America's* Crew Arraign Baldwin," *Brooklyn Daily Eagle,* December 27, 1903.

178. Ibid.

179. Porter, *The Arctic Diary of Russell Williams Porter,* 84.

180. "Reference Notes," February 5, 1902, Baldwin Papers.

181. Ibid., September 8, 1901.

182. Barr, ed., *Franz Josef Land*, 86–87.

183. Barnard polar diary, p. 64, Barnard Papers, LC.

184. Porter, *The Arctic Diary of Russell Williams Porter*, 92.

185. Mikkelsen, *Conquering the Arctic Ice*, 1.

186. Porter, *The Arctic Diary of Russell Williams Porter*, 84.

187. Barnard polar diary, p. 51, Barnard Papers, LC.

188. Porter journal, September 8, 1901–January 27, 1902, Baldwin Papers.

189. Barnard polar diary, p. 49, Barnard Papers, LC.

190. Leon F. Barnard Papers, SPRI, MS 1514/3/6. Also quoted in part in Larsson, "*. . . skönt att än en gang vara bland isen*," 47.

191. Porter Journal, September 8, 1901–January 27, 1902, Baldwin Papers.

192. Speech by Baldwin to members of expedition in aft mess-room, New Year's, 1902, from Fiala Papers.

193. Barnard polar diary, p. 55, Barnard Papers, LC. Bergendahl also recorded the speech, noting that the pay of the Swedes would be increased from 65 to 100 kroner, and this figure doubled during sledge trips (see Larsson, "*. . . skönt att än en gang vara bland isen*," 50).

194. Ibid.

195. Fiala diary, January 5, 1902, Fiala Papers.

196. Ibid.

197. Ibid.

198. Ibid., January 7, 1902.

199. Barnard polar diary, p. 64, Barnard Papers, LC.

200. "*America*'s Crew Arraign Baldwin," *Brooklyn Daily Eagle*, December 27, 1903.

201. Ibid.

202. Barnard polar diary, p. 67, Barnard Papers, LC.

203. See, for example, "Baldwin-Zieglerexpeditionen."

204. Barnard polar diary, p. 72, Barnard Papers, LC.

205. Anders Larsson, personal communication, February 12, 2014. See also Larsson, "*. . . skönt att än en gang vara bland isen*," 51.

206. Baldwin, "The Baldwin-Ziegler Polar Expedition," Part 2: 436; Capelotti, "The 'American Supply Trail.'"

207. Barnard polar diary, January 22, 1902, Barnard Papers, LC.

208. "Historic Banners: Masonic Flags Carried by Arctic Explorer Baldwin," *Masonic Standard* 11, no. 9 (March 3, 1906), from Evelyn B. Baldwin Scrapbooks, 1898–1929, Western Historical Manuscript Collection-Columbia, Ellis Library, University of Missouri.

209. "Polar Dash Perils Described by Baldwin Ziegler explorer," *San Francisco Chronicle*, June 6, 1932, transcription in "Arctic Diary of Anton Vedoe," p. 21, STEF, MSS 233(2).

210. Barnard supplementary diary, p. 5, Barnard Papers, LC.

211. Ibid.

212. Ibid., 14.

213. Porter, *The Arctic Diary of Russell Williams Porter*, 86.

214. Porter to Baldwin, March 2, 1902, Box #3, General correspondence, January–June 1902, Baldwin Papers.

215. Barnard supplementary diary, p. 20, Barnard Papers, LC.

216. Ibid., 29–30.

217. Ibid., 22.

218. Ibid., 30.

219. Speech by Baldwin to expedition crew, March 5, 1902, transcribed by Fiala, Fiala Papers.

220. Barnard supplementary diary, p. 22, Barnard Papers, LC.

221. Ibid., 25–26.

222. "Baldwin-Peary Polar Race Starts April 1," *St. Louis Post-Dispatch,* March 23, 1902.

223. Ibid.

224. "Polar Dash Perils Described by Baldwin Ziegler explorer," *San Francisco Chronicle,* June 6, 1932, transcription in "Arctic Diary of Anton Vedoe," p. 22, STEF, MSS 233(2).

225. "Spring Sledge Work," April and May 1902, p. 1, Baldwin Papers.

226. Ibid.

227. Ibid.

228. Ibid., 1–2.

229. Ibid., 2.

230. Ibid.

231. *"America's* Crew Arraign Baldwin," *Brooklyn Daily Eagle,* December 27, 1903.

232. See "Baldwin-Zieglerexpeditionen."

233. "Spring Sledge Work," April and May 1902, p. 2–3, Baldwin Papers.

234. Ibid., 3.

235. Ibid.

236. Ibid., 4.

237. Porter, *The Arctic Diary of Russell Williams Porter,* 86.

238. "Spring Sledge Work," April and May 1902, p. 4, Baldwin Papers.

239. Ibid., 5.

240. Ibid., 6–7.

241. Ibid., 7.

242. Ibid., 8.

243. Ibid., 9.

244. Ibid.

245. Ibid.

246. Ibid., 9–10.

247. Ibid., 10.

248. Ibid., 11.

249. Anders Larsson, personal communication, February 26, 2014. See also Larsson, *". . . skönt att än en gang vara bland isen,"* 156n39.

250. These are today known as the Lesgaft Reefs, after the Russian anatomist Peter Lesgaft (1837–1909).

251. "Spring Sledge Work," April and May 1902, p. 16, Baldwin Papers.

252. Ibid., 17–18.

253. Ibid., 18.

254. Ibid.

255. Ibid., 20.

256. Ibid., 23–24.

257. Ibid., 24.

258. Ibid.

259. Porter, *The Arctic Diary of Russell Williams Porter,* 86.

260. "Spring Sledge Work," April and May 1902, p. 24, Baldwin Papers.

261. *"America's* Crew Arraign Baldwin," *Brooklyn Daily Eagle,* December 27, 1903.

262. "Spring Sledge Work," April and May 1902, p. 25, Baldwin Papers.

263. Ibid., 24.

264. Ibid., 26.

265. Ibid., 29.

266. Ibid., 30.

267. Ibid., 31.

268. Ibid., 32. The name did not stick, and in fact Baldwin's "Verner Channel" is now labeled "American Channel" on modern charts of the archipelago.

269. Ibid.

270. Baldwin named it after Leffingwell, but today it survives as Italian Channel.

271. "Spring Sledge Work," April and May 1902, p. 34, Baldwin Papers, LC. "Querini" refers to Francesco Querini, and "Ollier" is Felice Ollier.

272. Ibid., 33.

273. Ibid., 36.

274. Ibid.

275. Ibid.

276. Ibid., 37.

277. Ibid.

278. Ibid.

279. Ibid., 38.

280. Ibid.

281. Barr, "The History of Western Activity in Franz Josef Land," 88.

282. Baldwin, "The Baldwin-Ziegler Polar Expedition," part 3: 591.

283. "Spring Sledge Work," April and May 1902, p. 38, Baldwin Papers.

284. Ibid.

285. Ibid., 39.

286. The name does not survive: the waterway is today known as Rhodes Channel.

287. "Spring Sledge Work," April and May 1902, p. 39, Baldwin Papers.

288. Ibid., 40.

289. Ibid., 41.

290. Ibid.

291. Ibid., 44.

292. Ibid. Baldwin's name survives today in modified form as "Luigi Island." The waterway previously seen as Brown Fjord on the west coast of Salisbury Island now became Brown Channel and separated Salisbury Island on the north from Abruzzi/ Luigi and Scott/Champ islands on the south.

293. "Spring Sledge Work," April and May 1902, pp. 45–46, Baldwin Papers.

294. "Polar Dash Perils Described by Baldwin Ziegler Explorer," *San Francisco Chronicle,* June 6, 1932, transcription in "Arctic Diary of Anton Vedoe," p. 23, STEF, MSS 233(2).

295. Ibid.

296. Baldwin, "The Baldwin-Ziegler Polar Expedition," part 3: 589.

297. "Spring Sledge Work," April and May 1902, p. 12, Baldwin Papers.

298. Barnard supplementary diary, p. 12, Barnard Papers, LC.

299. Leon Barnard to Baldwin, May 23, 1902, SPRI, MS 1514/3/6.

300. Larsson, ". . . skönt att än en gang vara bland isen," 61.

301. "Polar Dash Perils Described by Baldwin Ziegler Explorer," *San Francisco Chronicle*, June 6, 1932, transcription in "Arctic Diary of Anton Vedoe," p. 24, STEF, MSS 233(2).

302. Baldwin, "The Baldwin-Ziegler Polar Expedition," Part 3: 592; see also "Reference Sheet, Aeronautical Section, June, 1902. Baldwin-Ziegler Polar Expedition, Franz Josef Land," Evelyn B. Baldwin, Scrapbooks, 1898–1929, Western Historical Manuscript Collection-Columbia, Ellis Library, University of Missouri. According to Bergendahl's diary, work had begun as early as January to build a snow wall to shield the balloons during ascents discussed for February(!) (Anders Larsson, personal communication, February 9, 2015).

303. Berson, "The Use of Balloons in Geographical Work."

304. Capelotti, *By Airship to the North Pole*, 145–61; Capelotti, "Virgohamna and the Archaeology of Failure."

305. Lundström, *Andrée's Polarexpedition,* 62.

306. See, for example, Wråkberg, "Andrée's Folly: Time for Reappraisal?"

307. Amedeo of Savoy, *On the "Polar Star" in the Arctic Sea,* 36.

308. Baldwin, "Meterological Observations of the Second Wellman Expedition," 62.

309. Rilliet, "Detailed Report of the Aeronautical Section," 17.

310. When *Stella Polare* was almost wrecked in Teplitz Bay, Amadeo's steel hydrogen-generating apparatus was dragged ashore and the balloon experiment abandoned. Given that Baldwin's later inflation of his slightly larger balloons on Alger Island only produced an average net ascension force of 46.93 pounds (see Rilliet, "Detailed Report of the Aeronautical Section," Reference Sheet), the Duke's balloons would not have made much difference in lightening the load of his thirteen sledges, each of which carried over five hundred pounds of food and equipment (Tenderini and Shandrick, *The Duke of the Abruzzi,* 59).

311. Fiala, *Fighting the Polar Ice,* photograph facing page 75.

312. Baldwin, Letter to Johann Bryde.

313. Baldwin, "How I Hope to Reach the North Pole," 67–68.

314. Fawcett, "By Balloon to the North Pole," 481–87.

315. Berson, "The Use of Balloons in Geographical Work," 541.

316. Scott, *The Voyage of the Discovery,* 1: 145–48. See also Fiennes, *Captain Scott,* 57–59.

317. Baldwin, "How I Hope to Reach the North Pole."

318. Ibid.

319. Fawcett, "By Balloon to the North Pole."

320. Rilliet, "Detailed Report of the Aeronautical Section," 15.

321. Fawcett, "By Balloon to the North Pole."

322. Fawcett, "By Balloon to the North Pole," 486.

323. Ibid., 485–86.

324. Baldwin, "How I Hope to Reach the North Pole."

325. Ibid., italics in original.

326. Rilliet, "Detailed Report of the Aeronautical Section," 1.

327. Ibid., 2.

328. Ibid.

329. Ibid., 18.

330. Ibid., 3.

331. Ibid., 15.

332. Baldwin, Balloon Buoy Messages.

333. Rilliet, "Detailed Report of the Aeronautical Section," 4.

334. Ibid.

335. Ibid., 5.

336. Ibid.

337. Ibid.

338. Ibid., 6.

339. Ibid., 7.

340. Ibid.

341. These compact iron residues became the most visible archaeological remains from these attempts to use hydrogen in the Arctic (see Capelotti, *The Wellman Polar Airship Expeditions*, 71–84).

342. Rilliet, "Detailed Report of the Aeronautical Section," 8.

343. Ibid., 18. Baldwin had been warned by his British acid supplier that they could not vouch for the quality or the electrolytic action of the iron because the metal supplier would not make any practical trial of the process (Cross to Baldwin, May 24, 1901, Baldwin Papers). Like the letter from the supplier of his gas-powered small boat, this letter supports the notion that Baldwin left fundamental operational questions to such a late date that he was left with no choice but to improvise after the expedition was in the field.

344. Rilliet, "Detailed Report of the Aeronautical Section," 18.

345. Rilliet, "Extracts from Personal Notes of Chas. E. Rilliet, June 1902."

346. Rilliet, "Detailed Report of the Aeronautical Section," 9.

347. Ibid., 11.

348. Ibid., Reference Sheet. The higher success rate of the later balloons was perhaps due to the different ascensional power of the two groups of balloons. The average ascensional force of balloons one through nine was 134.55 pounds. Starting with balloon ten, the remainder of the balloons launched from Alger Island had an average ascensional force of 172.5 pounds, nearly 30 percent more than the first group. On average, the balloons disappeared from sight less than twelve minutes after launch, at an average altitude of 2,000 feet. Throughout the operations, the launch-time temperature averaged just below the freezing point.

349. Rilliet, "Detailed Report of the Aeronautical Section," 14.

350. Ibid., 15. In all, some 398 pounds of zinc, 2,961 pounds of iron, and 3,546 pounds of acid were left at the base camp on Alger Island.

351. Ibid., 18.

352. Ibid., 19.

353. Baldwin, "Spring Sledge Work of the Baldwin-Ziegler Polar Expedition."

354. Anders Larsson, personal communication and translation, February 27, 2014; see also Larsson, ". . . *skönt att än en gang vara bland isen*," 66.

355. Fiala diary, July 15, 1902, Fiala Papers.

356. Ibid.

357. "*America*'s Crew Arraign Baldwin," *Brooklyn Daily Eagle,* December 27, 1903.

358. Remarks by Baldwin, transcribed by Fiala, Fiala Papers.

359. Ibid.

360. Fiala diary, August 1, 1902, Fiala Papers.

361. Porter, *The Arctic Diary of Russell Williams Porter,* 96.

362. "*America*'s Crew Arraign Baldwin," *Brooklyn Eagle,* December 27, 1903.

363. *New York Times,* August, 2, 1902, p. 3.

364. "Sensational Rumors about E. B. Baldwin's Expedition," *New York Times,* August 4, 1902, p. 1.

365. See Larsson, "*. . . skönt att än en gang vara bland isen,*" 68–82.

366. "Statement," signed by Barnard and Rilliet, August 1, 1902, Barnard Papers, LC.

367. "On Board the *America,* Harbor at Tromsoe, Norway, August 3, 1902," Barnard Papers, LC.

368. Barnard's daughter would find the diary in her father's papers fifty years later, and eventually it found its way to the Library of Congress. It resides there still, with appropriate irony, in the same room as Baldwin's papers. Baldwin apparently found nothing to offend him in the diaries of Anton Vedoe, Seitz, or Fiala, as these have also survived, as have at least two diaries kept by members of the Swedish crew of the *America.*

369. Transcription from Fiala Papers.

370. A not inconsiderable conflict of interest, as Giæver was also the owner of the *Frithjof* (Kjell-G Kjær, personal communication, July 4, 2014; see also Giæver, *Turister og jegere i Ishavet*) and undoubtedly anxious to preserve his shipping contracts with whomever was responsible for paying the expedition's bills.

371. Transcription from Fiala Papers.

372. Anders Larsson, personal communication, February 27, 2014. See also Larsson, "*. . . skönt att än en gang vara bland isen,*" 82.

373. Porter, *The Arctic Diary of Russell Williams Porter,* 96. Porter is mistaken here. The person he met was the Astronomer Royal for Scotland, Ralph Copeland (1837–1905). While Copeland conducted astronomical observations from Greenland, there is no evidence he ever visited Franz Josef Land.

374. *Brooklyn Standard-Union,* August 3, 1902, Baldwin Papers.

375. "Arctic Exploration," *New York Times,* August 7, 1902, p. 8.

376. *Kansas City Star,* September 17, 1902, Baldwin Papers.

377. "Almost Reach Pole," *Chicago Record-Herald,* August 2, 1902, Baldwin Papers, italics mine. Baldwin was not completely without allies. Carl Christensen, a Norwegian acquaintance from Baldwin's 1897 trip to Spitsbergen, tried defending him in the Stavanger *Aftenblad* in late August, but the effect was to make Baldwin seem as out of touch as ever (see "Mr. Baldwin, En Karakteristik," *Stavanger Aftenblad,* August 21, 1902, with thanks to Magnus Forsberg for the translation).

378. "Statement by E. B. Baldwin," *New York Times,* September 5, 1902, p. 9.

379. See "Baldwin-Zieglerexpeditionen."

380. Ibid.

381. *New York Herald,* October 3, 1902, Baldwin Papers.

382. "Norwegian and Swede Are Bad When Together," *Philadelphia Inquirer,* October 3, 1902, p. 1.

383. "Summary of Work Done by Mr. Evelyn Briggs Baldwin in the Arctic Regions," Baldwin Papers.

384. *"America's* Crew Arraign Baldwin," *Brooklyn Daily Eagle,* December 27, 1903.

385. Fiala to Barnard, October 27, 1902, SPRI, MS 1514/5/11.

386. Porter to Barnard, November 4, 1902, SPRI, MS 1514/5/13.

387. J. K. Hare to Barnard, November 9, 1902, SPRI, MS 1514/5/13.

388. See, for example, David A. March, *The History of Missouri* (New York and West Palm Beach: Lewis Historical Publishing Co., 1967), 2: 1229–30.

389. *"America's* Crew Arraign Baldwin," *Brooklyn Daily Eagle,* December 27, 1903.

390. Ibid. Bergendahl managed to sneak a pair of walrus tusks back to Sweden, where they remain in the possession of his daughter, who was eighty-seven years young in 2014 (Anders Larsson, personal communication, February 27, 2014).

391. *"America's* Crew Arraign Baldwin," *Brooklyn Daily Eagle,* December 27, 1903.

392. Porter, *The Arctic Diary of Russell Williams Porter,* 92.

393. Leffingwell, "My Polar Explorations, 1901–14," 2.

Expedition Three: Onward, Christian Soldier

1. Fiala, *Fighting the Polar Ice,* ix.

2. Ibid.

3. Ibid.

4. Roald Amundsen, "Diary of First Sledging Journey on the Antarctic Pack," quoted in Huntford, *Scott and Amundsen,* 66.

5. "A Pole Hunt Without Frills," *Brooklyn Eagle,* December 22, 1902, p. 9.

6. Ibid.

7. Porter, *The Arctic Diary of Russell Williams Porter,* 100.

8. "The Ziegler Polar Expedition," *Geographical Record* 35, 1903 (2): 192–93.

9. Fiala, *Fighting the Polar Ice,* 4.

10. Ibid.

11. "Rescue Due to W. S. Champ," *New York Times,* August 11, 1905, p. 7.

12. Fiala, *Fighting the Polar Ice,* 4–5.

13. Ibid., 5.

14. "Arctic Diary of Anton Vedoe," pp. 32–33, STEF Mss 233(2).

15. Ibid., 33.

16. Ibid.

17. Ibid., 37.

18. Ibid., 39.

19. Fiala, *Fighting the Polar Ice,* 16.

20. "Arctic Diary of Anton Vedoe," p. 39, STEF Mss 233(2).

21. Fiala, *Fighting the Polar Ice,* 16.

22. Seitz polar diary, Ziegler Expedition, June 1, 1903, p. ii, STEF Mss 244.

23. Ibid., iii–iv.

24. Ibid., 92.

25. Fiala, *Fighting the Polar Ice*, 19.

26. "Arctic Diary of Anton Vedoe," p. 40, STEF Mss 233(2).

27. Fiala, *Fighting the Polar Ice,* 10.

28. Ibid., 15.

29. Seitz polar diary, Ziegler expedition, June 12, 1903, p. vi, STEF Mss 244.

30. Report to Fiala, February 24, 1904, Shorkey papers, I-9, STEF Mss 207.

31. Fiala, *Fighting the Polar Ice,* 20.

32. "Arctic Diary of Anton Vedoe," p. 42, STEF Mss 233(2).

33. Seitz polar diary, Ziegler expedition, July 4, 1903, p. 107, STEF Mss 244.

34. Pinegin, *Georgiy Sedov,* 67–68, translation courtesy of William Barr.

35. Ibid., 69–70.

36. Ibid., 70.

37. Fiala, *Fighting the Polar Ice,* 22.

38. Ibid., 23.

39. Ibid., 24.

40. Ibid., 26.

41. Seitz polar diary, Ziegler expedition, July 12, 1903, p. 112, STEF Mss 244.

42. Ibid., 120.

43. Ibid., 122.

44. Railton, "Shipwrecked," Martha's Vineyard Historical Society (hereafter MVHS), *Dukes County Intelligencer* 40 (1): 8.

45. Shorkley, "Medical Records," August 15, 1903.

46. Shorkley papers, STEF Mss 207, 1, I-4.

47. Shorkley, "Medical Records," August 23, 1903.

48. Porter, *The Arctic Diary of Russell Williams Porter,* 136.

49. Ibid.

50. Vedoe papers, STEF Mss 233, Box 2, folder 11.

51. Vedoe papers, STEF Mss 233(2): 4: 3.

52. Ibid.

53. Ibid.

54. Porter journal, July 27, 1903, STEF Mss 118(1): 10.

55. Railton, "Shipwrecked," MVHS, *Dukes County Intelligencer* 40(1): 26.

56. Ibid., 27.

57. Seitz polar diary, Ziegler expedition, August 8, 1903, p. 128, STEF Mss 244.

58. Fiala, *Fighting the Polar Ice,* 31.

59. William Mouat had been a seaman on board Frederick Jackson's *Windward.* He died at Franz Josef Land in June 1895.

60. Seitz polar diary, Ziegler expedition, August 12, 1903, p. 131, STEF Mss 244.

61. Porter diary, August 13, 1903, I-10, STEF Mss 118(1): 14.

62. Ibid.

63. Ibid., 15.

64. Fiala, *Fighting the Polar Ice,* 33.

65. Ibid., 34.

66. Seitz polar diary, Ziegler expedition, August 20, 1903, p. 137, STEF Mss 244.

67. Ibid., 139.

68. Ibid., 137.

69. Ibid., 140.

70. Ibid., 141.

71. Porter diary, August 13, 1903, I-10, STEF Mss 118(1): 19.

72. Ibid., 20.

73. Fiala, *Fighting the Polar Ice,* 35. It is difficult to know just where Fiala thought he was at this point, as there are three small islands opposite this cape, and all of them were charted by Frederick Jackson during his expedition. Fortunately, Seitz placed the spot as Geelmuyden Island, one of a small collection of islets northwest of the northwestern corner of Jackson Island and loosely named by Fridtjof Nansen in 1895 (Nansen, *Farthest North,* 360) after the Norwegian astronomer at the University of Oslo's observatory, Hans Geelmuyden. But even Nansen had not quite been certain where he was, writing: "They are only indicated approximately (as Geelmuyden Island and Alexander's Island), as I am not certain of either their number or their exact situation."

74. Railton, "Shipwrecked," MVHS, *Dukes County Intelligencer,* 40(1): 34.

75. Seitz polar diary, Ziegler expedition, August 29, 1903, p. 144, STEF Mss 244.

76. Fiala, *Fighting the Polar Ice,* 36. Nansen's Geelmuyden Island was located near the western entrance of the newly defined De Long Bay.

77. Fiala, *Fighting the Polar Ice,* 36.

78. Seitz polar diary, Ziegler expedition, August 31, 1903, p. 146, STEF Mss 244.

79. Fiala, *Fighting the Polar Ice,* 37.

80. Railton, "Shipwrecked," MVHS, *Dukes County Intelligencer* 40(1): 36.

81. Ibid.

82. Fiala, *Fighting the Polar Ice,* 37.

83. Railton, "Shipwrecked," MVHS, *Dukes County Intelligencer* 40(1): 38.

84. Ibid., 39.

85. Ibid.

86. Ibid., 40–41.

87. Vedoe papers, STEF Mss 233(2): 4: 11–12.

88. Ibid., 4.

89. Fiala, *Fighting the Polar Ice,* 42–43.

90. Seitz polar diary, Ziegler expedition, September 6, 1903, p. 151, STEF Mss 244.

91. Ibid., 150.

92. Seitz polar diary, Ziegler expedition, September 3, 1903, p. 149, STEF Mss 244.

93. Porter, *The Arctic Diary of Russell Williams Porter,* 102.

94. Fiala, *Fighting the Polar Ice,* 38.

95. Seitz polar diary, Ziegler expedition, August 31, 1903, p. 146, STEF Mss 244.

96. Fiala, *Fighting the Polar Ice,* 43.

97. Report to Fiala, February 24, 1904, Shorkley papers, I-9, STEF Mss 207.

98. Fiala, *Fighting the Polar Ice,* 41.

99. Seitz polar diary, Ziegler expedition, August 31, 1903, p. 146, STEF Mss 244.

100. "Arctic Diary of Anton Vedoe," p. 51, STEF Mss 233(2).

101. Ibid., 52.

102. Seitz polar diary, Ziegler expedition, September 26, 1903, p. 163, STEF Mss 244.

103. "Arctic Diary of Anton Vedoe," p. 51, STEF Mss 233(2).

104. Ibid., 53.

105. Seitz polar diary, Ziegler expedition, September 10, 1903, p. 153, STEF Mss 244.

106. "Arctic Diary of Anton Vedoe," p. 54, STEF Mss 233(2).

107. Seitz polar diary, Ziegler expedition, September 13, 1903, p. 155, STEF Mss 244.

108. "Arctic Diary of Anton Vedoe," p. 56, STEF Mss 233(2).
109. Seitz polar diary, Ziegler expedition, September 19, 1903, p. 159, STEF Mss 244.
110. "Arctic Diary of Anton Vedoe," p. 56, STEF Mss 233(2).
111. Ibid.
112. Ibid., 57.
113. Fiala, *Fighting the Polar Ice,* 45.
114. Seitz polar diary, Ziegler expedition, September 25, 1903, p. 162, STEF Mss 244.
115. Ibid., 164.
116. Ibid., 170–71.
117. "Arctic Diary of Anton Vedoe," p. 63, STEF Mss 233(2).
118. Ibid.
119. Seitz polar diary, Ziegler expedition, October 17, 1903, p. 175, STEF Mss 244.
120. Fiala, *Fighting the Polar Ice,* 46–47.
121. Ibid., 47.
122. Seitz polar diary, Ziegler expedition, October 21, 1903, p. 177–78, STEF Mss 244.
123. Railton, "Shipwrecked," MVHS, *Dukes County Intelligencer* 40(2): 56.
124. "Arctic Diary of Anton Vedoe," p. 65, STEF Mss 233(2).
125. Ibid.
126. Ibid.
127. Railton, "Shipwrecked," MVHS, *Dukes County Intelligencer* 40(2): 60.
128. Ibid., 61.
129. "Arctic Diary of Anton Vedoe," p. 67, STEF Mss 233(2).
130. Seitz polar diary, Ziegler expedition, October 24, 1903, p. 179, STEF Mss 244.
131. Fiala, *Fighting the Polar Ice,* 50.
132. Seitz polar diary, Ziegler expedition, October 24, 1903, p. 180, STEF Mss 244.
133. "Arctic Diary of Anton Vedoe," p. 68, STEF Mss 233(2).
134. Ibid.
135. Seitz polar diary, Ziegler expedition, October 31, 1903, p. 184, STEF Mss 244.
136. Ibid., 184.
137. "Arctic Diary of Anton Vedoe," p. 69, STEF Mss 233(2).
138. Ibid.
139. Ibid.
140. Seitz polar diary, Ziegler expedition, November 9, 1903, p. 189, STEF Mss 244.
141. "Arctic Diary of Anton Vedoe," p. 69, STEF Mss 233(2).
142. Seitz polar diary, Ziegler expedition, November 10, 1903, p. 189, STEF Mss 244.
143. "Arctic Diary of Anton Vedoe," p. 70, STEF Mss 233(2).
144. Fiala, *Fighting the Polar Ice,* 52.
145. Ibid., 53.
146. Railton, "Shipwrecked," MVHS, *Dukes County Intelligencer* 40(2): 62.
147. Fiala, *Fighting the Polar Ice,* 53.
148. "Arctic Diary of Anton Vedoe," p. 70, STEF Mss 233(2).
149. Ibid.
150. Fiala, *Fighting the Polar Ice,* 53.
151. Seitz polar diary, Ziegler expedition, November 12, 1903, p. 191, STEF Mss 244.
152. Fiala, *Fighting the Polar Ice,* 54.
153. Railton, "Shipwrecked," MVHS, *Dukes County Intelligencer* 40(2): 64.
154. Seitz polar diary, Ziegler expedition, November 12, 1903, p. 192, STEF Mss 244.

155. Railton, "Shipwrecked," MVHS, *Dukes County Intelligencer* 40(2): 63.
156. Seitz polar diary, Ziegler expedition, November 13, 1903, p. 193, STEF Mss 244.
157. "Arctic Diary of Anton Vedoe," p. 72, STEF Mss 233(2).
158. Railton, "Shipwrecked," MVHS, *Dukes County Intelligencer* 40(2): 64.
159. "Arctic Diary of Anton Vedoe," p. 72, STEF Mss 233(2).
160. Seitz polar diary, Ziegler expedition, November 16, 1903, p. 195, STEF Mss 244.
161. Railton, "Shipwrecked," MVHS, *Dukes County Intelligencer* 40(2): 65.
162. "Arctic Diary of Anton Vedoe," p. 73, STEF Mss 233(2).
163. Ibid.
164. Fiala, *Fighting the Polar Ice,* 55.
165. "Arctic Diary of Anton Vedoe," p. 73, STEF Mss 233(2).
166. Railton, "Shipwrecked," MVHS, *Dukes County Intelligencer* 40(2): 65.
167. Fiala, *Fighting the Polar Ice,* 56.
168. "Arctic Diary of Anton Vedoe," p. 74, STEF Mss 233(2).
169. Seitz polar diary, Ziegler expedition, November 22, 1903, p. 200, STEF Mss 244.
170. Ibid.
171. "Arctic Diary of Anton Vedoe," p. 74, STEF Mss 233(2).
172. Railton, "Shipwrecked," MVHS, *Dukes County Intelligencer* 40(2): 66.
173. Fiala, *Fighting the Polar Ice,* 57.
174. Seitz polar diary, Ziegler expedition, November 24, 1903, p. 201, STEF Mss 244.
175. Railton, "Shipwrecked," MVHS, *Dukes County Intelligencer* 40(2): 68.
176. Seitz polar diary, Ziegler expedition, November 25, 1903, p. 202, STEF Mss 244.
177. Fiala, *Fighting the Polar Ice,* 59.
178. Ibid., 60.
179. "Arctic Diary of Anton Vedoe," p. 76, STEF Mss 233(2).
180. Porter, *The Arctic Diary of Russell Williams Porter,* 106.
181. "Arctic Diary of Anton Vedoe," p. 78, STEF Mss 233(2).
182. Ibid., 77.
183. Seitz polar diary, Ziegler expedition, December 2, 1903, p. 206, STEF Mss 244.
184. "Arctic Diary of Anton Vedoe," p. 78, STEF Mss 233(2).
185. Ibid., 79.
186. Ibid.
187. Ibid., 80.
188. Seitz polar diary, Ziegler expedition, December 17, 1903, p. 215, STEF Mss 244.
189. Ibid., 216.
190. "Arctic Diary of Anton Vedoe," p. 80, STEF Mss 233(2).
191. Seitz polar diary, Ziegler expedition, December 21, 1903, p. 217, STEF Mss 244.
192. "Arctic Diary of Anton Vedoe," p. 81, STEF Mss 233(2).
193. Seitz polar diary, Ziegler expedition, December 25, 1903, p. 219–20, STEF Mss 244.
194. Railton, "Shipwrecked," MVHS, *Dukes County Intelligencer* 40(2): 71–72.
195. Porter diary, December 27, 1903, I-10, STEF Mss 118(1): 23.
196. Ibid.
197. Ibid.
198. Ibid., 24.
199. Ibid., 27.
200. Ibid., 28.

201. Fiala, *Fighting the Polar Ice,* 65.
202. "Arctic Diary of Anton Vedoe," p. 82, STEF Mss 233(2).
203. Fiala, *Fighting the Polar Ice,* 67–68.
204. Ibid., 66.
205. "Arctic Diary of Anton Vedoe," p. 85, STEF Mss 233(2).
206. Fiala, *Fighting the Polar Ice,* 70.
207. Railton, "Shipwrecked," MVHS, *Dukes County Intelligencer* 40(2): 80.
208. "Arctic Diary of Anton Vedoe," p. 87, STEF Mss 233(2).
209. Seitz polar diary, Ziegler expedition, February 10, 1904, p. 247, STEF Mss 244.
210. Ibid., 246.
211. Ibid., 248.
212. Fiala, *Fighting the Polar Ice,* 76.
213. Railton, "Shipwrecked," MVHS, *Dukes County Intelligencer* 40(2): 81.
214. Shorkley to Fiala, February 20, 1904, Shorkley papers, I-9, STEF Mss 207.
215. Railton, "Shipwrecked," MVHS, *Dukes County Intelligencer* 40(2): 83.
216. Vaughan to Fiala, February 24, 1904, Shorkley papers, I-9, STEF Mss 207.
217. Seitz polar diary, Ziegler expedition, February 28, 1904, p. 258, STEF Mss 244.
218. Ibid., 261.
219. "Arctic Diary of Anton Vedoe," p. 92, STEF Mss 233(2).
220. Seitz polar diary, Ziegler expedition, March 9, 1904, p. 264, STEF Mss 244.
221. Ibid., 264.
222. Porter, *The Arctic Diary of Russell Williams Porter,* 116.
223. Seitz polar diary, Ziegler expedition, March 12, 1904, p. 266, STEF Mss 244.
224. Ibid., 267–68.
225. Fiala, *Fighting the Polar Ice,* 81.
226. Railton, "Shipwrecked," MVHS, *Dukes County Intelligencer* 40(2): 86.
227. Seitz polar diary, Ziegler expedition, March 14, 1904, p. 269, STEF Mss 244.
228. "Arctic Diary of Anton Vedoe," p. 95, STEF Mss 233(2).
229. Seitz polar diary, Ziegler expedition, March 26, 1904, p. 275, STEF Mss 244.
230. Fiala, *Fighting the Polar Ice,* 85–86.
231. Porter, *The Arctic Diary of Russell Williams Porter,* 116.
232. Ibid.
233. Fiala, *Fighting the Polar Ice,* 86.
234. Porter, *The Arctic Diary of Russell Williams Porter,* 118.
235. Railton, "Shipwrecked," MVHS, *Dukes County Intelligencer* 40(3): 139.
236. Porter, *The Arctic Diary of Russell Williams Porter,* 118.
237. Ibid.
238. "Arctic Diary of Anton Vedoe," p. 97, STEF Mss 233(2).
239. Ibid.
240. Porter, *The Arctic Diary of Russell Williams Porter,* 120.
241. "Arctic Diary of Anton Vedoe," p. 98, STEF Mss 233(2).
242. Ibid.
243. Ibid.
244. Porter, *The Arctic Diary of Russell Williams Porter,* 124.
245. "Arctic Diary of Anton Vedoe," p. 101, STEF Mss 233(2).
246. Ibid., 98.
247. Porter to Fiala, April 27, 1904, Vedoe papers, 2:6 STEF Mss 233(2): 2.

248. "Arctic Diary of Anton Vedoe," p. 101, STEF Mss 233(2).

249. Ibid., 98.

250. Ibid., 104.

251. Porter, *The Arctic Diary of Russell Williams Porter*, 126.

252. "Arctic Diary of Anton Vedoe," p. 105, STEF Mss 233(2).

253. Ibid., 108.

254. Seitz polar diary, Ziegler expedition, April 15, 1904, p. 287, STEF Mss 244.

255. "Arctic Diary of Anton Vedoe," p. 109, STEF Mss 233(2).

256. Fiala, *Fighting the Polar Ice*, 88.

257. Seitz polar diary, Ziegler expedition, April 22, 1904, p. 291, STEF Mss 244.

258. Fiala, *Fighting the Polar Ice*, 88.

259. Seitz polar diary, Ziegler expedition, April 22, 1904, p. 294, STEF Mss 244.

260. Fiala, *Fighting the Polar Ice*, 12–14; Vedoe, *The Arctic Diary of Anton M. Vedoe*, 115–16.

261. Fiala, *Fighting the Polar Ice*, 93.

262. Shorkley, "Medical Records."

263. Vedoe, *The Arctic Diary of Anton M. Vedoe*, 116.

264. Ibid., 137.

265. Fiala, *Fighting the Polar Ice*, 121.

266. Ibid.

267. Susan Barr was shown the remnants of this cross when she visited the Soviet meteorological station at Teplitz Bay in 1990 (Barr, "Soviet-Norwegian Historical Expedition to Zemlya Frantsa-Iosifa").

268. Porter, *Arctic Fever*, 50. Fiala writes that when the expedition was rescued by the ship *Terra Nova* in mid-summer 1905, "great bags of mail" arrived with the ship, including a single letter addressed to Myhre, by then already dead for over a year. It related the news that Myhre's wife in Norway had also died (Fiala, *Fighting the Polar Ice*, 195).

269. Shorkley, "Medical Records."

270. Hartt, "Letter to George Shorkley."

271. Vedoe, *The Arctic Diary of Anton M. Vedoe*, 212.

272. Seitz polar diary, Ziegler expedition, May 2, 1904, p. 297, STEF Mss 244.

273. Ibid.

274. Railton, "Shipwrecked," MVHS, *Dukes County Intelligencer* 40(3): 143.

275. Seitz polar diary, Ziegler expedition, May 7 and 8, 1904, pp. 300, 301, STEF Mss 244.

276. Ibid., 302.

277. Ibid., 303.

278. Railton, "Shipwrecked," MVHS, *Dukes County Intelligencer* 40(3): 145.

279. Seitz polar diary, Ziegler expedition, May 17, 1904, p. 307, STEF Mss 244.

280. Ibid., 308.

281. Fiala, *Fighting the Polar Ice*, 111.

282. Seitz polar diary, Ziegler expedition, May 21, 1904, p. 309, STEF Mss 244.

283. Fiala, *Fighting the Polar Ice*, 95.

284. Ibid.

285. Seitz polar diary, Ziegler expedition, May 25, 1904, p. 312, STEF Mss 244.

286. Railton, "Shipwrecked," MVHS, *Dukes County Intelligencer* 40(3): 150.

287. Ibid., 152.

288. Seitz polar diary, Ziegler expedition, June 1, 1904, p. 315–16, STEF Mss 244.

289. Fiala, *Fighting the Polar Ice,* 112.

290. Seitz polar diary, Ziegler expedition, June 2, 1904, p. 317, STEF Mss 244.

291. Railton, "Shipwrecked," MVHS, *Dukes County Intelligencer* 40(3): 153.

292. Seitz polar diary, Ziegler expedition, June 21, 1904, p. 329, STEF Mss 244.

293. Fiala, *Fighting the Polar Ice,* 97.

294. "Arctic Diary of Anton Vedoe," p. 117, STEF Mss 233(2).

295. Ibid.

296. Ibid., 119.

297. Ibid., 120.

298. Ibid.

299. Ibid., 122.

300. Ibid.

301. Ibid.

302. Ibid., 124.

303. Ibid.

304. Ibid., 125.

305. Ibid., 126.

306. Porter, *The Arctic Diary of Russell Williams Porter,* 130. Porter was correct. Sedov wintered at the site in 1912–13, and in 1929 the Soviets established a major base on the shores of the harbor that was used as a meteorological station until 1963. The fossil of a plesiosaur was discovered on the island in the 1930s.

307. "Arctic Diary of Anton Vedoe," p. 128, STEF Mss 233(2).

308. Seitz polar diary, Ziegler expedition, July 5, 1904, p. 338, STEF Mss 244.

309. Fiala, *Fighting the Polar Ice,* 115.

310. Porter, *The Arctic Diary of Russell Williams Porter,* 132.

311. "Account of a Canoe Trip," by John Vedoe, in Vedoe diary, STEF Mss (233) 2: 194.

312. Ibid., 199.

313. Ibid., 202.

314. One notable exception to this cache of instruments was the meridian or Repsold Circle loaned by Professor Geelmuyden of the observatory at Kristiania, which remained at Teplitz Bay until it was moved to Alger Island in April 1905. In May 2015 Susan Barr tracked the circle down to the Museum for Universitets-og Vitenskapshistorie (MUV) in Oslo (Barr, personal communication, June 2, 2015).

315. "Account of a Canoe Trip," by John Vedoe, in Vedoe diary, Stef Mss (233) 2: 208.

316. Seitz polar diary, Ziegler expedition, January 25, 1904, p. 237, STEF Mss 244.

317. Ibid., 247.

318. Ibid., 282.

319. Ibid., 284.

320. Hartt to Shorkley, March 21, 1905, I-8, Shorkley papers, STEF Mss 207.

321. Fiala, *Fighting the Polar Ice,* 154.

322. Porter diary, I-11, STEF Mss 118(1): 41.

323. Seitz polar diary, Ziegler expedition, July 13, 1904, p. 344, STEF Mss 244.

324. Porter diary, I-11, STEF Mss 118(1): 41.

325. Ibid., 42–43.

326. Seitz polar diary, Ziegler expedition, July 21, 1904, p. 348–49, STEF Mss 244.

327. Railton, "Shipwrecked," MVHS, *Dukes County Intelligencer* 40(3): 159.

328. Porter diary, I-11, STEF Mss 118(1): 63.

329. Fiala, *Fighting the Polar Ice,* 124.

330. "Arctic Diary of Anton Vedoe," p. 131, STEF Mss 233(2).

331. Seitz polar diary, Ziegler expedition, July 24, 1904, p. 352, STEF Mss 244.

332. "Arctic Diary of Anton Vedoe," p. 132, STEF Mss 233(2).

333. Seitz polar diary, Ziegler expedition, August 1, 1904, p. 357, STEF Mss 244.

334. Ibid., 359.

335. "Arctic Diary of Anton Vedoe," p. 130, STEF Mss 233(2).

336. Porter diary, I-11, STEF Mss 118(1): 44.

337. Railton, "Shipwrecked," MVHS, *Dukes County Intelligencer* 40(3): 165.

338. Ibid.

339. "The Ziegler Polar Expedition," *National Geographic,* 427–28.

340. Ibid., 428. Champ, no doubt seeking to defuse another potential media nightmare similar to what had occurred with Baldwin's return, also noted that all of the mail sent to the members of the expedition that he carried with him "has been placed in hermetically sealed tins and deposited in the Tromsoe Private Bank." Ibid.

341. "Arctic Diary of Anton Vedoe," p. 136, STEF Mss 233(2).

342. Seitz polar diary, Ziegler expedition, August 15, 1904, p. 364, STEF Mss 244.

343. Porter diary, I-11, STEF Mss 118(1): 49.

344. Fiala, *Fighting the Polar Ice,* 129.

345. Ibid., 131.

346. Seitz polar diary, Ziegler expedition, October 26, 1904, p. 395, STEF Mss 244.

347. Fiala, *Fighting the Polar Ice,* 136.

348. Seitz polar diary, Ziegler expedition, October 26, 1904, p. 396, STEF Mss 244.

349. Ibid., 397.

350. Porter diary I-11, STEF Mss 118 (1): 59.

351. Railton, "Shipwrecked," MVHS, *Dukes County Intelligencer* 40(3): 170.

352. Porter diary I-11, STEF Mss 118 (1): 65.

353. Ibid., 81.

354. Ibid., 43.

355. Ibid., 61.

356. Ibid., 65–66.

357. Ibid., 75.

358. Seitz polar diary, Ziegler expedition, November 8, 1904, p. 404, STEF Mss 244.

359. Fiala, *Fighting the Polar Ice,* 147.

360. Ibid., 148.

361. "Arctic Diary of Anton Vedoe," p. 144, STEF Mss 233(2).

362. Seitz polar diary, Ziegler expedition, November 15–19, 1904, p. 408, STEF Mss 244.

363. "Arctic Diary of Anton Vedoe," p. 144, STEF Mss 233(2).

364. Seitz polar diary, Ziegler expedition, November 19, 1904, p. 409–10, STEF Mss 244.

365. Fiala, *Fighting the Polar Ice,* 153.

366. Hartt to Shorkey, March 21, 1905, Shorkley papers, I-8 Stef mss 207.

367. Seitz polar diary, Ziegler expedition, December 19, 1904, p. 415–16, STEF Mss 244.

368. Fiala, *Fighting the Polar Ice*, 154–55.

369. "Arctic Diary of Anton Vedoe," p. 147, STEF Mss 233(2).

370. Hartt to Shorkley, March 21, 1905, Shorkley papers, STEF Mss, I-8. Hartt also wrote, "Since he did the cutting I have been getting better." The detailed diary of Seitz only mentions the silver nitrate treatment, and so it seems unlikely that he performed surgery, although the silver nitrate no doubt created the burning sensation experienced by Hartt.

371. Porter diary, I-3, STEF Mss 118(1): 75.

372. Porter, in Fiala, *Fighting the Polar Ice*, 258–59.

373. Quoted in ibid., 266.

374. Porter, in ibid., 273.

375. Porter, in ibid., 278.

376. Seitz polar diary, Ziegler expedition, March 6, 1905, p. 434–35, STEF Mss 244.

377. Ibid., 437.

378. "Arctic Diary of Anton Vedoe," p. 152, STEF Mss 233(2).

379. Ibid., 153.

380. Ibid.

381. Fiala, *Fighting the Polar Ice*, 170.

382. Ibid., 171.

383. "Arctic Diary of Anton Vedoe," p. 154, STEF Mss 233(2).

384. Fiala, *Fighting the Polar Ice*, 174.

385. Porter, *The Arctic Diary of Russell Williams Porter*, 146.

386. Hartt to Shorkley, March 21, 1905, Shorkley papers, I-8, Stef mss 207.

387. "Arctic Diary of Anton Vedoe," p. 161, STEF Mss 233(2).

388. Ibid., 164.

389. Porter, *The Arctic Diary of Russell Williams Porter*, 147–48.

390. Ibid., 148.

391. Papers of Russell W. Porter, STEF Mss 118, I-3: 80–81.

392. Fiala, *Fighting the Polar Ice*, 182–83.

393. Seitz polar diary, Ziegler expedition, June 19, 1905, p. 487, STEF Mss 244.

394. Ibid., 488.

395. Fiala, *Fighting the Polar Ice*, 185.

396. "Arctic Diary of Anton Vedoe," p. 173, STEF Mss 233(2).

397. Porter, *The Arctic Diary of Russell Williams Porter*, 150–52.

398. "Arctic Diary of Anton Vedoe," p. 177, STEF Mss 233(2).

399. Seitz polar diary, Ziegler expedition, August 3, 1905, p. 508, STEF Mss 244.

400. "Compromise Ends Suit to Test Ziegler will," *New York Times*, August 2, 1905, p. 7.

401. "The Call of the Ice-Locked North," *New York Times*, October 29, 1905, p. SM2.

402. Ibid.

403. "Annual Dinner of the National Geographic Society," *National Geographic*, January 1906.

404. Caswell, *The Utilization of the Scientific Reports of United States Arctic Expeditions*, 151, 155.

405. Ibid., 155, italics in original.

406. Porter, in Peters, et al., *The Ziegler Polar Expedition*, 628.

AFTERMATH: AN AMERICAN TRACTOR AT THE NORTH POLE

1. S. Johansen, Letter to E. S. Cunningham, American Consul in Bergen, May 20, 1903, Folder "Correspondence re: Balloon Buoys, 1902–1925," Box 12, Baldwin Papers.

2. B. Knudtzon, Letter to the American Consul in Bergen, November 11, 1903, Folder "Correspondence re: Balloon Buoys, 1902–1925," Box 12, Baldwin Papers.

3. Henry Bordewich, Letter to Francis B. Loomis, Assistant Secretary of State, December 2, 1903, Folder "Correspondence re: Balloon Buoys, 1902–1925," Box 12, Baldwin Papers.

4. E. S. Cunningham, Letter to Francis B. Loomis, Assistant Secretary of State, January 7, 1904, Folder "Correspondence re: Balloon Buoys, 1902–1925," Box 12, Baldwin Papers.

5. E. B. Baldwin, Letter to Herbert H. D. Peirce, Third Assistant Secretary of State, February 16, 1904, Folder "Correspondence re: Balloon Buoys, 1902–1925," Box 12, Baldwin Papers.

6. Claud Berg, Letter to Hydrographic Office, Washington, D.C., January 26, 1904, Folder "Correspondence re: Balloon Buoys, 1902–1925," Box 12, Baldwin Papers.

7. E. S. Cunningham, Letter to Assistant Secretary of State, September 29, 1906, Folder "Correspondence re: Balloon Buoys, 1902–1925," Box 12, Baldwin Papers.

8. Henry Bordewich, Letter to Assistant Secretary of State, October 2, 1907. See also Letter to Francis B. Loomis, Assistant Secretary of State, December 2, 1903, Folder "Correspondence re: Balloon Buoys, 1902–1925," Box 12, Baldwin Papers.

9. Ernest L. Harris, Letter to Secretary of State, April 18, 1911, Folder "Correspondence re: Balloon Buoys, 1902–1925," Box 12, Baldwin Papers.

10. Swedish Society, *Andrée's Story*, 258.

11. Anders Larsson, personal communication, February 17, 2014.

12. Swedish Society, *Andrée's Story*, 64–65.

13. Capelotti, "Century-Old Ski Found."

14. Anders Larsson, personal communication, May 18, 2007.

15. Umbreit, "Franz Josef Land."

16. Maria Gavrilo, personal communication, January 29, 2014.

17. Umbreit, "Franz Josef Land," 11.

18. Fedorov, *Polar Diaries*, 106.

19. Vodopyanov, *Wings over the Arctic*, 189.

20. See, for example, Hansson and Norris, "Human Impact and Environmental Management," 155.

21. Vodopyanov, *Wings over the Arctic*, 188–89.

22. Baryshev, *Zemlya Frantsa-Iosfia*.

23. Ibid., 244–77.

24. Krenke, "Russian Research in Franz Josef Land," 129–47.

25. See Capelotti, "The 'American Supply Trail.'"

26. Anonymous, "Walter Wellman Home."

27. Wellman, "The Wellman Polar Expedition," 503.

28. Caswell, *The Utilization of the Scientific Reports*, 5.

29. Ibid.

30. Ibid.

31. Stegner, "Introduction," vii–viii.

32. Robinson, *The Coldest Crucible,* 162–63.

33. Porter, *The Arctic Diary of Russell Williams Porter,* 156.

34. Ibid.

35. Ibid.: 159.

36. *New York Times,* February 24, 1949, p. 24.

37. Mikkelsen, *Mirage in the Arctic,* 27.

38. Mikkelsen, *Alabama-Expeditionen til Grønlands Nordøstkyst,* 136–39; Schledermann, "Einar Mikkelsen (1880–1971)," 352–54.

39. Baldwin, "Drifting Across the Pole."

40. Mikkelsen, *Alabama-Expeditionen til Grønlands Nordøstkyst,* 13.

41. Ibid., 136.

42. Ibid., 139.

43. "News and Notables at the New Orleans Hotels," *Daily Picayune,* January 18, 1910, Shorkley papers, STEF.

44. Ibid.

45. "Seattle *Times* Story Tells of Shorkley's Experiences," *Seattle Times,* August 15, 1936.

46. "Dr. George Shorkley," *Mifflinburg (Penn.) Telegraph,* December 13, 1945; Shorkley papers.

47. Susan Barr, "Peter Lorents Tessem (1875–1919)," http://www.frammuseum.no/Polar-Heroes/Crew-Heroes/Tessem.aspx. See also William Barr, "The Last Journey of Peter Tessem and Paul Knutsen, 1919," 311–27. For details of the life of Paul Bjørvig, see "Paul Bjørvig, 1857–1932, Fangstmann, deltok på mange ekspedisjoner i Arktis og Antarktis, blant annet Wellmanns ekspedisjoner," http://www.polarhistorie.no/personer/Bjorvig,%20Paul. See also Lawrence Millman's tribute, "An Unsung Hero," at http://lawrencemillman.com/an-unsung-hero/.

48. Eivind Klykken, personal communication, February 10, 2014.

49. Anders Larsson, personal communication, February 12, 2014.

50. Anders Larsson, personal communication, February 17, 2014

51. Ibid.

52. Powell, *The Exploration of the Colorado River and its Canyons,* 20.

53. Nansen, *Farthest North,* 152.

54. "Wellman Pursued by His Old Ill Luck," *New York Times,* July 20, 1926, p. 6. On May 10, 2015, the author located Bergersen's grave in Vestre Gravlund near Majorstua in Oslo. Wellman died in New York in 1934, and though his Norwegian wife was a quarter century younger, she herself passed away just a few years later, in 1938, so the possibility existed that she might have taken his ashes to Norway with her and that Wellman's name might be recorded on her grave marker. But there was no evidence of his presence besides the name of his Norwegian widow: Bergljot Wellman.

55. "By-the-Bye in Wall Street," *Wall Street Journal,* February 5, 1934, p. 8.

56. The ship was scrapped in 1972. See "Todd Houston Shipbuilding, Houston, TX," http://www.shipbuildinghistory.com/history/shipyards/4emergencylarge/wwtwo/toddhouston.htm

57. Robert Wellman Chamberlain, personal communication, January 31, 2014.

58. Millard, *The River of Doubt,* 110–11. Millard's account of Fiala's leadership of the Ziegler Polar Expedition is brief and flawed, but its conclusion—that Fiala has failed so badly that no one wanted him anywhere near another expedition—was not

far from the mark. She even quotes (p. 32) Wellman's old nemesis, Henry Feilden, who seems to have never missed a chance to criticize American leadership in the Arctic.

59. "Fiala Plans Trip to Pole by Tractor," *New York Times,* May 6, 1928, p. 28.

60. Ibid.

61. "Sailor's Superstition about Dead Men on Ship May Have Prevented Finding Andree in 1903," *New York Times,* August 23, 1930, p. 3.

62. Anders Larsson, personal communication, February 17, 2014.

63. "Aurora Borealis Will Furnish World's Light and Power," *New York Herald,* October 1, 1899.

64. "Find Arctic Cairn Left By American," *New York Times,* August 5, 1930, p. 18. Many thanks to historian Dmitry Kiselyov for alerting me to a photograph of Vladimir Vize and writer Ivan Sokolov-Mikitov examining the Baldwin buoy found at Russian Harbour.

65. "Red Explorers Find Air Message of 1902," *New York Times,* August 10, 1930, p. 5.

66. "American Just Missed Joining Andree Trip," *New York Times,* August 24, 1930, p. 2.

67. Scamehorn, *Balloons to Jets,* 16.

68. "E. B. Baldwin Dies When Hit By Auto," *New York Times,* October 26, 1933, p. 12.

69. McCoy, *Indiana Jones and the Hollow Earth.*

Works Cited

Aftenposten. 1897. "Ny Nordpolsexpedition." August 25, 1897.

Alme, Helge H. 1998. *Om Spitsbergen og den Wellmanske polarekspedisjon.* Skien, Norway: Vågemot miniforlag.

———. 1894–1895. "Om Spitsbergen og den Wellmanske polarekspedition." *Det Norske Geografiske Selskabs Aarbog,* 6, 1894–1895.

Amedeo of Savoy, Luigi. 1903. *On the "Polar Star" in the Arctic Sea,* 2 vols. London: Hutchinson.

———. 1901. "The Italian Arctic Expedition, 1899–1900." *The Geographical Journal* 18 (3): 282–84.

"Amerikansk undsättningsexpedition för Nansen?" 1896. *Tidningen Kalmar,* no. 40, March 13, 1896.

Andrée, Salomon A., et al. 1930. *Andrée's Story: The Complete Record of His Polar Flight, 1897. From the Diaries and Journals of S. A. Andrée, Nils Strindberg, and K. Frænkel, Found on White Island in the Summer of 1930.* Translated from the Swedish by Edward Adams-Ray. New York: Blue Ribbon.

Anonymous. 1903. "Rules and Regulations: Ziegler Polar Expedition." Trondhjem: A/S Adresseavisens Bogtrykkeri.

Anonymous. 1902. "The Arctic Expeditions: Return of Sverdrup, Peary, and Baldwin." *The Geographical Journal* (20) 4: 434–38.

Anonymous. [1901.] "Biographical Sketches of the Members and Crew of the Baldwin-Ziegler Polar Expedition. S.S. *America.*" E. B. Baldwin Papers. Folder "Biographies—Baldwin-Ziegler Expedition." Box 8. Manuscript Division. Library of Congress. Washington, D.C.

Anonymous. "Walter Wellman Home." *Boston Globe.* October 9, 1899.

Anonymous. "Disputing over Nansen." *New Haven Register.* March 20, 1896.

Baldwin, Evelyn Briggs. 2004. *The Franz Josef Land Archipelago: E. B. Baldwin's*

Journal of the Wellman Polar Expedition, 1898–1899, edited by P. J. Capelotti. Jefferson, NC: McFarland.

———. n.d. "Summary of Work Done by Evelyn Briggs Baldwin in the Arctic Regions." E. B. Baldwin Papers. Folder "EBB—Typescripts—Polar Subjects." Box 13. Manuscript Division. Library of Congress. Washington, D.C.

———. "Some Gleamings of the Twi-light days of Aviation." Unpublished lecture notes, dated September 17, 1930. E. B. Baldwin Papers. Folder "EBB—Typescripts—Polar Subjects." Box 13. Manuscript Division. Library of Congress. Washington, D.C.

———. 1908. "Drifting Across the Pole." *New York Herald.* September 6, 1908. Magazine Section.

———. 1903. "The Baldwin-Ziegler Polar Expedition, Parts I, II, and III." *Wide World Magazine* 10 (58):396–402; 10 (59): 432–36; 10 (60): 587–93.

———. 1902b. Balloon Buoy Messages. E. B. Baldwin Papers. Folder "Correspondence re: Balloon Buoys, 1902–1925." Box 12. Manuscript Division. Library of Congress. Washington, D.C.

———. 1902a. Letter left behind at Camp Ziegler, June 30, 1902. E. B. Baldwin Papers. Folder "Correspondence re: Balloon Buoys, 1902–1925." Box 9. Letter Binder. Manuscript Division. Library of Congress. Washington, D.C.

———. 1902. "Spring Sledge Work of the Baldwin-Ziegler Polar Expedition, April and May, 1902." E. B. Baldwin Papers. Folder "Notes & Journals." Box 9. Manuscript Division. Library of Congress. Washington, D.C.

———. 1901b. "How I Hope to Reach the North Pole." *The Windsor Magazine* 15 (1): 59–69. London: Ward, Lock. December.

———. 1901a. Letter to Johann Bryde. July 5, 1901. E. B. Baldwin Papers. Folder "Supplies, 1901." Box 13. Manuscript Division. Library of Congress. Washington, D.C.

———. 1901. "Meteorological Observations of the Second Wellman Expedition," *Report of the Chief of the Weather Bureau, 1899–1900,* Part 7. Washington, D.C.: Government Printing Office.

———. n.d. [1900]. "Short Autobiographical Sketch—Evelyn Briggs Baldwin, for William Ziegler, Esq." Seven pp. E. B. Baldwin Papers. Manuscript Division. Library of Congress. Washington, D.C.

———. 1899. "Journal of the Wellman Polar Expedition." Unpublished typescript. E. B. Baldwin Papers. Manuscript Division. Library of Congress. Washington, D.C.

———. 1899a. "The Meteorological Observations of the Second Wellman Expedition." *National Geographic* 10 (12): 512–16.

———. n.d. [1899a]. "Report on Auroras." Thirty-six pp. E. B. Baldwin Papers. Manuscript Division. Library of Congress. Washington, D.C.

———. n.d. [1899b]. "Discovery of Graham Bell Land." Fifty-six pp. E. B. Baldwin Papers. Manuscript Division. Library of Congress. Washington, D.C.

———. 1896. *The Search for the North Pole.* Chicago: Privately printed.

"Baldwinexpeditionen." 1902. *Tidningen Kalmar.* No. 135, September 5, 1902.

"Baldwin-Zieglerexpeditionen." 1902. *Aftonbladet.* October 4, 1902.

Barr, Susan, editor. 1995. *Franz Josef Land.* Oslo: Norsk Polarinstitutt.

Barr, Susan. 1995. "The History of Western Activity in Franz Josef Land." In Susan Barr, ed., *Franz Josef Land.* Oslo: Norsk Polarinstitutt.

————. 1991. "Soviet-Norwegian Historical Expedition to Zemlya Frantsa-Iosifa." *Polar Record* 27 (163).

Barr, William. 1983. "The Last Journey of Peter Tessem and Paul Knutsen, 1919." *Arctic* (36) 4: 311–27.

Baryshev, I. B. 2013. *Zemlya Frantsa-Iosfia*. Moscow: Paulsen.

Berson, Arthur. 1896. "The Use of Balloons in Geographical Work." *Geographical Journal* 7 (5): 541–44.

Berton, Pierre. 1988. *The Arctic Grail: The Quest for the North West Passage and the North Pole, 1818–1909*. New York: Viking.

Bjørvig, Paul. 2004. *Norwegian Bravado: Diaries from Franz Josef's Land and Danes Island*. Skien, Norway: Vågemot Miniforlag.

Bloch-Nakkerud, Tom. 2011. *Polarforskeren Eivind Astrup: En pioner blandt Nordpolens naboer*. Oslo: Bastion forlag.

Bolotin, Norman, and Christine Laing. 1992. *The World's Columbian Exposition*. Washington, D.C.: Preservation Press.

Bottolfsen, Johannes. 1894. *Dagbok*. Tromsø: Norsk polarinstitutt archive.

Brooklyn Standard-Union. 1902. "Mr. Ziegler's Expensive Picture." August 3, 1902. E. B. Baldwin Papers. Scrapbooks. Box 10. Manuscript Division. Library of Congress. Washington, D.C.

Bryce, Robert M. 1997. *Cook and Peary: The Polar Controversy, Resolved*. Mechanicsburg, Penn.: Stackpole Books.

Capelotti, P. J. 2013. *Shipwreck at Cape Flora: The Expeditions of Benjamin Leigh Smith, England's Forgotten Arctic Explorer*. Northern Lights Series. Calgary: University of Calgary Press.

————. 2012. "Extreme Archaeological Sites and Their Tourism: A Conceptual Model from Historic American Polar Expeditions in Svalbard, Franz Josef Land and Northeast Greenland." *Polar Journal* 2 (2): 236–55.

————. 2011. "The 'American Supply Trail': Archaeological Notes on the Remains of the Ziegler Polar Expedition in Zemlya-Frantsa Iosifa, 1903–05." *Polar Record* 47 (3): 193–201. On-line at doi: 10.1017/S003224741000046X.

————. 2010. "Benjamin Leigh Smith's Third Arctic Expedition: Svalbard, 1873." *Polar Record* 46 (4): 359-371.

————. 2009. "Further to the Death of Sigurd B. Myhre at Camp Abruzzi, Rudolf Island, Franz Josef Land, May 16, 1904, during the Ziegler Polar Expedition." *Polar Research* 28 (3): 463–67.

————. 2008. "A 'radically new method': Balloon Buoy Communications of the Baldwin-Ziegler Polar Expedition, Franz Josef Land, June 1902." *Polar Research* 27 (1): 52–72.

————. 2007. "Century-Old Ski Found at Mys Triest, Ostrov Champa, Zemlya Frantsa-Iosifa, Russia." *Polar Record* 43 (3): 272–75.

————. 2006. "E. B. Baldwin and the American-Norwegian Discovery and Exploration of Graham Bell Island, 1899." *Polar Research* 25 (2): 155–71.

————. 2005. "Benjamin Leigh Smith's First Arctic Expedition: Svalbard, 1871." *Polar Record* 42 (1): 1–14.

————. 1999a. *By Airship to the North Pole: An Archaeology of Human Exploration*. New Brunswick: Rutgers University Press.

————. 1999b. "Virgohamna and the Archaeology of Failure," in Urban Wråkberg, editor. *Centennial of S.A. Andrée's North Pole Expedition Proceedings of a Conference on S.A. Andrée and the Agenda for Social Science Research of the Polar Regions.* Bidrag till Kungl. Svenska Vetenskapsakademiens Historia, (Contributions to the History of the Royal Swedish Academy of Sciences), No. 28 (Stockholm): 37–52.

———. 1997. *The Wellman Polar Airship Expeditions at Virgohamna, Danskøya, Svalbard: A Study in Aerospace Archaeology.* Oslo: Norwegian Polar Institute, Meddelelser Nr. 145.

Capelotti, P. J., and Magnus Forsberg. 2015b. "The Place Names of Zemlya Frantsa-Iosifa: Wellman polar expedition, 1898–1899." *Polar Record* 51 (6): 624–36.

Capelotti, P. J., and Magnus Forsberg. 2015a. "The Place Names of Franz Josef Land: *Eira* Expeditions, 1880 and 1881–82." *Polar Record* 51 (1): 16–23.

Carlheim-Gyllensköld, Vilhelm. 1900. *På Åttionde Breddgraden (At the 80th Degree).* Stockholm: Albert Bonnier.

Caswell, John Edwards. 1956. *Arctic Frontiers: United States Explorations in the Far North.* Norman: University of Oklahoma Press.

———. 1951. *The Utilization of the Scientific Reports of United States Arctic Expeditions, 1850–1909.* Stanford University, Department of History Thesis, and Technical Report II, Contract N6onr 25122, Office of Naval Research.

Chicago *Times*. 1900. "Revived interest in the fate of Andree." July 4, 1900. E. B. Baldwin Papers. Scrapbooks. Box 10. Manuscript Division. Library of Congress. Washington, D.C.

Chicago Times-Herald. 1900. "Two Americans planning a great polar expedition." November 1, 1900.

Cohen, Lara Langer. 2013. "The Emancipation of Boyhood." *Common-Place* 14: 1 (Fall 2013).

"Conditions for engaging the men to the Wellman polar expedition." 1894/1898. 4 pp. E. B. Baldwin Papers. Manuscript Division. Library of Congress. Washington, D.C.

Conway, Sir Martin. 1898. *With Ski and Sledge over Arctic Glaciers.* London: J. M. Dent.

Corner, George W. 1972. *Doctor Kane of the Arctic Seas.* Philadelphia: Temple University Press.

Cross, C. F. 1901. Letter to Evelyn Briggs Baldwin. May 24, 1901. E. B. Baldwin Papers. Folder "May 15–May 31, 1901 (Baldwin-Ziegler Expedition)." General Correspondence. Box 3. Manuscript Division. Library of Congress. Washington, D.C.

Elder, William. 1858. *Biography of Elisha Kent Kane.* Philadelphia: Childs and Peterson.

(Elizabeth, N.J.) Journal. 1901. "To Search for Andree." January 8, 1901. E. B. Baldwin Papers. Scrapbooks. Box 10. Manuscript Division. Library of Congress. Washington, D.C.

Fawcett, Waldon. 1901. "By Balloon to the North Pole." *Metropolitan Magazine* 14 (4): October 1901.

Fedorov, Yevgeny. 1983. *Polar Diaries.* Moscow: Progress Publishers.

Fiala, Anthony. 1906. *Fighting the Polar Ice.* New York: Doubleday, Page and Company.

Fiala, Anthony. 1906a. "Two Years in the Arctic: I: Shipwrecked above the 81°," *McClure's Magazine* 26 (4): 341–57, February 1906.

Fiala, Anthony. 1906b. "Two Years in the Arctic: II: The Advance North in the Darkness," *McClure's Magazine* 26 (5): 471–84, March 1906.

Fiennes, Ranulph. 2003. *Captain Scott.* London: Hodder and Stoughton.

Fleming, J. A., editor. 1907. *The Ziegler Polar Expedition, 1903–1905: Scientific Results.* Washington, D.C.: National Geographic Society.

Giäver, Magnus K. 1944. *Turister og jegere i Ishavet.* Oslo: Johan Grundt Tanum.

Gore, Howard. 1899. "The Wellman Polar Expedition." *National Geographic* 10 (7): 267–68.

Greely, A. W., et al. 1888. *Report on the Proceedings of the United States Expedition to Lady Franklin Bay, Grinnell Land.* Washington, D.C.: Government Printing Office.

Guttridge, Leonard. 2000. *Ghosts of Cape Sabine: The Harrowing True Story of the Greely Expedition.* New York: Putnam.

———. 1986. *Icebound: The Jeannette Expedition's Quest for the North Pole.* Annapolis: Naval Institute Press.

Hamberg, Axel. 1891. "Slutligen framlade fil. kand. A. Hamberg några betraktelser öfver möjligheten af Nordpolsfrågans lösning" ("A. Hamberg offers some reflections and solutions on the possibility to reach the North Pole"). *Svenska Sällskapet för Antropologi och Geografi, Ymer* (11): 75–77.

Hansson, R., and S. Norris. 1995. "Human impact and environmental management." In S. Barr, editor. *Franz Josef Land.* Oslo: Norsk Polarinstitutt (Polarhåndbok 8).

Hartt, Henry. 1905. "Letter to George Shorkley." The Papers of George Shorkley (1871–1945), Rauner Special Collections Library, Stefánsson Manuscripts No. 207, Dartmouth College, Hanover, N.H.

Hayes, Isaac Israel. 1867. *The Open Polar Sea.* London: S. Low, Son, and Marston.

"Hedrande försvensk industry." 1901. *Tidningen Kalmar* No. 70, May 8, 1901.

Herbert, Wally. 1989. *The Noose of Laurels: Robert E. Peary and the Race to the North Pole.* London: Hodder and Stoughton.

Heyerdahl, Trygve. 1894–1895. "*Kanes* reise langs Spitsbergens vestkyst." *Det Norske Geografiske Selskabs Aarbog,* VI, 1894–1895.

Huntford, Roland. 1997. *Nansen: The Explorer as Hero.* London: Duckworth.

———. 1979. *Scott and Amundsen.* London: Hodder and Stoughton.

Jackson, Frederick G. 1935. *The Lure of Unknown Lands.* London: G. Bell and Sons.

———. 1899. *A Thousand Days in the Arctic.* London: Harper and Brothers.

———. 1895. *The Great Frozen Land.* London: MacMillan and Co.

Kansas City Star. 1902. "Cigarette Smoking Dudes." September 17, 1902. E. B. Baldwin Papers. Scrapbooks. Box 10. Manuscript Division. Library of Congress. Washington, D.C.

Kane, Elisha Kent. 1856. *Arctic Exploration: The Second Grinnel Expedition in Search of Sir John Franklin, 1853, '54, '55.* Philadelphia: Childs and Peterson.

———. 1854. *The U.S. Grinnell Expedition in Search of Sir John Franklin: A Personal Narrative.* New York: Harper and Brothers.

Kjær, Kjell-G. 2011. "Serial slaughter: the development of the north Norwegian sealing fleet: 1859–1909." *Polar Record* 47 (1): 1–20.

———. 2006. "The Polar Ship *Frithjof*." *Polar Record* 42 (4): 281–89.

Krenke, A. N. 1995. "Russian research in Franz Josef Land." In S. Barr, ed., *Franz Josef Land.* Oslo: Norsk Polarinstitutt (Polarhåndbok 8).

Larsson, Anders. 2011. "*. . . skönt att än en gang vara bland isen. Ralph Bergendahl och Johan Menander, svenska sjöbefäl i polarforskningens tjänst.*" Göteborg: B4 Press.

Leffingwell, Ernest de Koven. 1961. "My Polar Explorations, 1901–14." *Explorers Journal,* October 1961.

———. 1915. "A Communication from Leffingwell." *University of Chicago Magazine* (January 1915): 76–79.

Loomis, Chauncey. 1971. *Weird and Tragic Shores: The Story of Charles Francis Hall, Explorer.* New York: Knopf.

Lundström, Sven. 1988. *Andrée's Polarexpedition.* Gränna: Wiken.

McCoy, Max. 1997. *Indiana Jones and the Hollow Earth.* New York: Bantam.

McGoogan, Ken. 2009. *Race to the Polar Sea: The Heroic Adventures of Elisha Kent Kane.* Berkeley: Counterpoint.

Mikkelsen, Ejnar. 2005. *Mirage in the Arctic.* Introduction by Lawrence Millman. Guilford, Conn.: The Lyons Press.

———. 1922. *Alabama-Expeditionen til Grønlands Nordøstkyst 1909–1912.* København: *Meddelelser om Grønland* BLII.

———. 1909. *Conquering the Arctic Ice.* London: W. Heinemann.

Millard, Candice. 2005. *The River of Doubt: Theodore Roosevelt's Darkest Journey.* New York: Doubleday.

Nansen, Fridtjof. 1999. *Farthest North.* New York: The Modern Library.

New York Herald. 1902. "Baldwin Denies He Led a Fiasco." October 3, 1902. E. B. Baldwin Papers. Scrapbooks. Box 10. Manuscript Division. Library of Congress. Washington, D.C.

New York Herald. 1899. "Aurora Borealis Will Furnish World's Light." October 1, 1899.

New York Times. 1933. "E. B. Baldwin Dies When Hit By Auto." October 26, 1933, p. 12.

New York Times. 1930a. "Find Arctic Cairn Left By American." August 5, 1930, p. 18.

New York Times. 1930b. "Red Explorers Find Air Message of 1902." August 10, 1930, p. 5.

New York Times. 1930c. "Bodies of Airmen Lost 33 Years Found Near Where Balloon Fell in Arctic; Andree and Comrades Frozen at Camp." August 23, 1930, p. 1.

New York Times. 1930d. "American Just Missed Joining Andree Trip." August 24, 1930, p. 2.

New York Times. 1902. "Baldwin-Ziegler Expedition Fails." August 2, 1902, p. 3.

New York Times. 1901. "Baldwin Will Seek Andree." May 17, 1901. E. B. Baldwin Papers. Scrapbooks. Box 10. Manuscript Division. Library of Congress. Washington, D.C.

New York Times. 1900. "To Seek for Andre [*sic*]." July 8, 1900, p. 8.

New York Times. 1899. "In Search of the Pole." May 28, 1899, p. 19.

New York Times. 1894. "Driven back by cold." August 17, 1894, p. 3.

New York Tribune. 1909. "E. B. Baldwin's Plan to Drift Across the Arctic Ocean." June 27, 1909, pp. 4–5.

New York World. 1901. "Andree Divined His Awful Fate." January 10, 1901. E. B. Baldwin Papers. Scrapbooks. Box 10. Manuscript Division. Library of Congress. Washington, D.C.

New York World. 1896. "Is the North Pole a Yawning Hole?" March 1, 1896.

Parry, William Edward. 1828. *Narrative of an Attempt to Reach the North Pole.* London: John Murray.

Payer, Julius. 1876. *New Lands Within the Arctic Circle: Narrative of the Discoveries of the Austrian Ship Tegetthoff in the Years 1872–1874.* 2 vols. London: MacMillan and Co.

Pearson, Henry J. 1899. *Beyond Petsora Eastward.* London: R. H. Porter.

Peters, William J., et al. 1907. *The Ziegler Polar Expedition, 1903-1905: Scientific Results.* Washington, D.C.: National Geographic Society.

Phillips, Kevin. 2003. *William McKinley.* New York: Henry Holt.

Pierce, Emmet. 2005. "George Pullman's Company Town a Social Experiment That Derailed," *San Diego Union Tribune,* May 15, 2005. Online at http://www.utsandiego.com/uniontrib/20050515/news_1h15pullman.html, accessed June 2, 2013.

Pinegin, N. V. 1948. *Georgiy Sedov.* Moscow-Leningrad: Izdatel'stvo Glavsevmorputi.

Porter, Russell. 1976. *The Arctic Diary of Russell Williams Porter.* Charlottesville: University Press of Virginia.

———. n.d. *Arctic Fever* (unpublished manuscript). The Papers of Russell W. Porter (1871–1949), Rauner Special Collections Library, Stefánsson Manuscripts No. 118, Dartmouth College, Hanover, New Hampshire.

Powell, John Wesley. 1895 (1995). *The Exploration of the Colorado River and its Canyons.* Introduction by Wallace Stegner. New York: Penguin.

Princeton (Ill.) Republican. 1901. "Baldwin and Dogs." June 13, 1901. E. B. Baldwin Papers. Scrapbooks. Box 10. Manuscript Division. Library of Congress. Washington, D.C.

Railton, Arthur R. 1998. "Shipwrecked 525 Miles from North Pole with Captain Coffin of Edgartown, Part One." *Dukes County Intelligencer* 40 (1): 3–41.

———. 1998. "Shipwrecked 525 Miles from North Pole with Captain Coffin of Edgartown, Part Two." *Dukes County Intelligencer* 40 (2): 51–87.

———. 1999. "Shipwrecked 525 Miles from North Pole with Captain Coffin of Edgartown, Part Three." *Dukes County Intelligencer* 40 (3): 136–71.

———. 1999. "Shipwrecked 525 Miles from North Pole with Captain Coffin of Edgartown, Part Four." *Dukes County Intelligencer* 40 (4): 189–226.

Riffenburgh, Beau. 1993. *The Myth of the Explorer.* London: Belhaven Press.

Rilliet, Charles E. 1902. "Detailed Report of the Aeronautical Section." E. B. Baldwin Papers. Letter to E. B. Baldwin, July 1, 1902. Folder "Notes & Journals." Box 9. Manuscript Division. Library of Congress. Washington, D.C. (This report includes an unsigned "Reference Sheet, Aeronautical Section, Baldwin-Ziegler Polar Expedition, Franz Josef Land, June, 1902.")

———. 1902a. "Extracts from Personal Notes of Chas. E. Rilliet, June 1902." Baldwin-Ziegler Polar Expedition Papers. Scott Polar Research Institute Archives, MS 1514/3/9.

Robinson, Michael F. 2006. *The Coldest Crucible: Arctic Exploration and American Culture.* Chicago: University of Chicago Press.

Sawin, Mark. 2008. *Raising Kane: Elisha Kent Kane and the Culture of Fame in Antebellum America.* Philadelphia: American Philosophical Society.

Scamehorn, Howard L. 1957. *Balloons to Jets: A Century of Aeronautics in Illinois, 1855–1955.* Chicago: Henry Regnery.

Schlederman, Peter. 1991. "Einar Mikkelsen (1880–1971)." *Arctic* 44 (4): 351–55, December 1991.

Scott, Robert Falcon. 1907. *The Voyage of the Discovery,* vol. 1. London: Smith, Elder.

Shorkley, George. 1903/04. "Medical Records—Ziegler Polar Expedition, June 22, 1903–September 7, 1904." The Papers of George Shorkley (1871–1945), Rauner Special Collections Library, Stefánsson Manuscripts No. 207, Dartmouth College, Hanover, New Hampshire.

Simmonds, Peter Lund. 1854. The Arctic Regions. Auburn and Buffalo, N.Y.: Miller, Orton and Mulligan.

Sintz, Claude. 1901. "Letter to Baldwin-Ziegler Expedition, 3 June 1901." E. B. Baldwin Papers. Folder June, 1901 (Baldwin-Ziegler). General Correspondence. Box 3. Manuscript Division. Library of Congress. Washington, D.C.

Stegner, Wallace. 1987. "Introduction." The Exploration of the Colorado River and its Canyons, by John Wesley Powell. New York: Penguin.

Swedish Society for Anthropology and Geography. 1930. Andrée's Story: The Complete Record of His Polar Flight, 1897. New York: The Viking Press.

Tarr, Joel A. 1966. "J. R. Walsh of Chicago: A Case Study in Banking and Politics, 1881–1905." Business History Review 40, no. 4: 451–66.

Tenderini, Mirella, and Michael Shandrick. 1997. The Duke of the Abruzzi: An Explorer's Life. London: Bâton Wicks.

Tessem, Peder. 2007. Peter Lorents Tessem: hans liv, virke og tragiske død. Privately published.

Thomsen, Alice Barnard. 1993. "History of the Baldwin-Ziegler Expedition." Papers of Leon F. Barnard, 1901–1993. Manuscript Division, Library of Congress, Washington, D.C.

Todd, Alden. 2001. Abandoned: The Story of the Greely Arctic Expedition, 1881–1884, 2nd ed. Fairbanks: University of Alaska Press.

Tucker, Jennifer. 1996. "Voyages of Discovery on Oceans of Air: Scientific Observation and the Image of Science in an Age of 'Balloonacy.'" Osiris, 2nd Series, Vol. 11, Science in the Field: 144–76.

Umbreit, Andreas. 2012. "Franz Josef Land: Possible Discovery of the Kane Lodge Depot of the Baldwin-Ziegler Expedition (1901/02)." Report to the Russian Arctic National Park. Online at http://www.franz-josef-land.info.

Vedoe, Anton. 1992. The Arctic Diary of Anton M. Vedoe (unpublished, revised February 1992). The Papers of Anton M. Vedoe (1880–1942), Rauner Special Collections Library, Stefánsson Manuscripts No. 233, Dartmouth College, Hanover, New Hampshire.

———. [1902]. "Journal of Anton M. Vedoe," January 1, 1900. E. B. Baldwin Papers. Folder "Journals, June, 1901–March, 1902." Box 8. Manuscript Division. Library of Congress. Washington, D.C.

Vodopyanov, Mikhail. 2001. Wings over the Arctic. Amsterdam: Fredonia.

Wellman, Joshua Wyman. 1918. Descendants of Thomas Wellman of Lynn, Massachusetts. Boston: Arthur Holbrook Wellman.

Wellman, Walter. 1911. The Aerial Age. New York: A. R. Keller.

———. 1907. "By Airship to the North Pole." McClure's Magazine 29 (2): 189–200.

———. 1907b. "Will the America Fly to the Pole?" McClure's Magazine 29 (3): 229–45.

———. 1906. "The Polar Airship." National Geographic 17 (4): 205–207.

———. 1902. "A Tragedy in the Far North." In R. Kersting, ed., The White World: Life and Adventures within the Arctic Circle Portrayed by Famous Living Explorers, pp. 174–88. New York: Lewis, Scribner and Co.

————. 1901. "Long-Distance Balloon Racing: From France to Russia in Thirty-Six Hours." *McClure's Magazine* 17 (3): 203–14.

————. 1901b. "Faster Than the Express Train: the Automobile Race from Paris to Berlin." *McClure's Magazine* 18 (1): 21–32.

————. 1900. "The Race for the North Pole." *McClure's Magazine* 14 (4): 318–28.

————. 1900b. "Sledging Toward the Pole." *McClure's Magazine* 14 (5): 405–13.

————. 1899. "The Wellman Polar Expedition." *National Geographic* 10 (12): 481–505.

————. 1899b. "On the Way to the North Pole: The Wellman Polar Expedition." *The Century Magazine*, February 1899: 531–37.

————. 1898. "Where Is Andrée?" *McClure's Magazine* 10 (5): 422–26.

————. 1897. "Mr. Kohlsaat of Chicago and His Part in the Political History Making of 1896." *Review of Reviews* 15: 41.

"Wellmans nordpolsexpedition." 1898. *Tidningen Kalmar* No. 89, June 13, 1898.

Willard, Berton C. 1976. *Russell W. Porter: Arctic Explorer, Artist, Telescope Maker.* Freeport, Maine: Bond Wheelwright Co.

Wiskott, Max. 1897. *Nach Spitzbergen bis zum ewigen Eise.* Als Manuscript gedruckt. Breslau, C. T. Wiskott.

Wråkberg, Urban. 1999. "Andrée's Folly: Time for Reappraisal?" In *Centennial of S.A. Andrée's North Pole Expedition Proceedings of a Conference on S.A. Andrée and the Agenda for Social Science Research of the Polar Regions.* Stockholm: Bidrag till Kungl. Svenska Vetenskapsakademiens Historia (Contributions to the History of the Royal Swedish Academy of Sciences), No. 28: 56–99.

Wråkberg, Urban, editor. 1999. *Centennial of S.A. Andrée's North Pole Expedition Proceedings of a Conference on S.A. Andrée and the Agenda for Social Science Research of the Polar Regions.* Stockholm: Bidrag till Kungl. Svenska Vetenskapsakademiens Historia (Contributions to the History of the Royal Swedish Academy of Sciences), No. 28.

"Ziegler Polar Expedition." 1903. *Geographical Record* 35 (2): 192–93.

"The Ziegler Polar Expedition." 1904. *National Geographic Magazine* 25 (10): 427–28.

Acknowledgments

This research was generously supported by the Anthropology Fund, by the Associate Dean's Research and Development Fund, by two Faculty Development Grants, and by two Summer Faculty Fellowships at Penn State University Abington College. The author is grateful to several excellent associate deans of academic affairs at Penn State, most especially Drs. Leonard Mustazza, Peter Pincemin Johnstone, and Norah Schultz, and to continually supportive division heads Jim Smith, Gary Calore, David Ruth, and Manohar Singh. Other colleagues at Abington have contributed in special ways: Mikhail Kagan provided translations from Russian and Ella Adams from German. Especially grateful thanks go to Yvonne Love, whose artistic exhibit "The Naming of Islands" brought whole new ways to imagine and think about geography and place-names.

My Swedish colleagues Magnus Forsberg and Anders Larsson in Gothenburg both provided extensive commentary through several drafts of the manuscript, as well as insights from their own research and travels in and around Svalbard and Franz Josef Land. So, too, did my colleagues in Norway, beginning as always with Susan Barr in Oslo, who provided constant advice, encouragement, and knowledge, and the great Kjell-G. Kjær in Tromsø.

Others who provided support and insights include Helle Goldman of the Norsk Polarinstitutt in Tromsø (especially for insights into her husband's great-grandfather, Peter Lorents Tessem), Michael Suever (for discussions of

Arthur Berson's work in particular and aeronautics in the Arctic generally), Robert Chamberlin (for discussions of his grandfather Walter Wellman), as well as Heddi Vaughan Siebel in Boston, Tom Bloch-Nakkerud in Oslo, Urban Wråkberg in Tromsø, Eivind Klykken in Hammerfest, William Barr in Calgary, Maria Gavrilo in Archangel, and Dmitry Kiselyov in Moscow. Mary Lu Crocker and Helen Frykman kindly gave access to the papers of Anthony Fiala—their grandfather and great-grandfather respectively—and in the process we learned of another irony that connected us: their late father and grandfather, Rear Admiral Reid P. Fiala, earned a Silver Star for his command of the destroyer USS *Remey* during the battle of Leyte Gulf, while my son serves as a junior officer on board the Ticonderoga-class cruiser named for that famous naval engagement of the Second World War.

Victor Boyarsky and the captain and crew of the mightly Russian icebreaker *Yamal* made it possible for me to visit Franz Josef Land four times in the summer of 2006. The Arctic guide Andreas Umbreit has led tours into Franz Josef Land for a decade, and maintains an extensive web-based archive related to the history and archaeology of Franz Josef Land at http://www.franz-josef-land.info. His long-term interest and contributions to the documentation of the islands is both impressive and appreciated.

Across several visits to the Scott Polar Research Institute, very great thanks go to Drs. Julian Dowdeswell, Huw Lewis-Jones, and Beau Riffenburgh, as well as Ms. Naomi Boneham and Ms. Heather Lane. Additional and pro-found thanks go to Nathanial Janick of the Martha's Vineyard Museum for his help with Captain Coffin's papers; as well as to the patient staff of the Manuscript Reading Room of the Library of Congress; to Chris Brackley of As the Crow Flies Cartography of Ontario; and to the Chicago Historical Society; the Western Historical Manuscript Collection of the University of Missouri at Columbia; the National Air and Space Museum archives (espe-cially Brian Nicklas); the archive of the Explorers Club in New York; the Rauner Special Collections Library, Stefánsson Manuscripts, at Dartmouth College; and the library and archives of the Royal Geographical Society at Kensington Gore, the Gothenburg University Library, and the Norsk Polar-institutt in Tromsø. Thanks as well to the Housman Society for help with the stanza from "The Defeated" from *A Shropshire Lad and Other Poems*.

Chapter 19 in Expedition 1, "The Discovery of Graham Bell Land," appeared originally in different form in 2006 as "E. B. Baldwin and the American-Norwegian Discovery and Exploration of Graham Bell Island,

1899," in *Polar Research* 25 (2): 155–71. Chapters 32 and 33 in Expedition 2, "Louisiana Cypress on Alger Island" and "The Launch of the Balloons," appeared originally in slightly different form in 2008 as "A 'Radically New Method': Balloon Buoy Communications of the Baldwin-Ziegler Polar Expedition, Franz Josef Land, June 1902," in *Polar Research* 27 (1): 52–72. Chapter 46 in Expedition 3, "The Death of Sigurd Myhre," appeared originally in different form in 2009 as "Further to the Death of Sigurd B. Myhre at Camp Abruzzi, Rudolf Island, Franz Josef Land, May 16, 1904, during the Ziegler Polar Expedition" in *Polar Research* 28 (3): 463–67.

As always, I am indebted to several close friends and colleagues who provided support and encouragement throughout the work, especially Anne Millbrook, Brendan McNally, and Bill Thomas, and to my small and loving clan: C. L., Jeremy, and Jenny.

Any errors in the work are solely my own.

Index

References to illustrations appear in italic type; references to maps appear in bold type.